Y0-BDF-136

272-2775

GLOBAL
MACROECONOMICS

GLOBAL MACROECONOMICS

Thomas F. Dernburg

The American University

Harper & Row, Publishers, New York
Cambridge   Philadelphia   St. Louis   San Francisco
1817   London   Singapore   Sydney   Tokyo

Sponsoring Editor: John Greenman
Text Design Adaptation: Barbara Bert/North 7 Atelier Ltd.
Cover Design: Grafica
Text Art: RDL Artset Ltd.
Production Manager: Jeanie Berke
Production Assistant: Beth Maglione
Compositor: TAPSCO, Inc.
Printer and Binder: R. R. Donnelley & Sons Company
Cover Printer: Lynn Art Offset Corporation

GLOBAL MACROECONOMICS

Copyright © 1989 by Harper & Row, Publishers, Inc.

All rights reserved. Printed in the United States of America. No part of this book may be used or reproduced in any manner whatsoever without written permission, except in the case of brief quotations embodied in critical articles and reviews. For information address Harper & Row, Publishers, Inc., 10 East 53rd Street, New York, NY 10022.

Library of Congress Cataloging-in-Publication Data

Dernburg, Thomas Frederick.
    Global macroeconomics / Thomas F. Dernburg.
        p.   cm.
    Includes index.
    ISBN 0-06-041674-2
    1. International economic relations. 2. Macroeconomics.
    I. Title.
HF1359.D47 1989
339—dc19   88-21284
                                                CIP

    89 90 91 9 8 7 6 5 4 3 2

For Carol
and the support group

Contents

Preface   xi

Part One   Issues and Concepts   1

Chapter 1   Introduction to Global Macroeconomics   3

    1.1 Macroeconomics and Open-Economy Macroeconomics   3
    1.2 The International Monetary System   13
    1.3 Gains from Trade and Investment   21

Chapter 2   Introduction to International Monetary Issues: The Foreign Exchange
               Market, Exchange Rates, External and Internal Balance   28

    2.1 The Foreign Exchange Market   28
    2.2 Exchange Rates and Government Intervention   36
    2.3 External and Internal Balance: Criteria for Balance-of-Payments
        Equilibrium   39
    2.4 Arbitrage, Forward Exchange, and Speculation   42

Chapter 3   International Transactions: The Balance of Payments   49

    3.1 The Balance-of-Payments Equation   49
    3.2 The U.S. Balance of Payments   59
    3.3 Behind the Balance-of-Payments Equation   62

Part Two   Macroeconomic Variables in the Open Economy   65

Chapter 4   Income Transmission and Foreign Trade Multipliers   67

    4.1 The Closed Economy: A Review   67
    4.2 Income Determination in the Open Economy with Autonomous
        Exports   75
    4.3 Endogenous Exports: A Two-Country Analysis   81
    4.4 Many Countries: The Foreign Trade Matrix   86

Chapter 5   Interest Rates, Capital Mobility, and Income Determination   92

   5.1 Income Determination in a Closed Monetary Economy   92
   5.2 The Foreign Balance Function and the IS-LM Model   104
   5.3 Income and Balance-of-Payments Adjustments Under Fixed
          Exchange Rates   112
   5.4 Adjustment Under Flexible Exchange Rates   117

Chapter 6   The Impact of Stabilization Policies Under Fixed and Flexible
                  Exchange Rates   122

   6.1 Stabilization Policy in the Financially Insular Economy   122
   6.2 Stabilization Policy in the Financially Open Economy with Perfect
          Capital Mobility   130
   6.3 Stabilization Policy in the Financially Open Economy with Imperfect
          Capital Mobility   134
   6.4 Coordinating Monetary-Fiscal Policies to Reduce Shock
          Transmission   143
   6.5 Some Econometric Evidence on Policy Effects   147

Chapter 7   Aggregate Demand, Aggregate Supply, Employment, and
                  Inflation   151

   7.1 The Aggregate Demand and Supply Functions   151
   7.2 Aggregate Supply and the Behavior of Wages   157
   7.3 Wage Policy and Employment   165
   7.4 Aggregate Supply and International Adjustment   177

Appendixes to Part Two   183

**Part Three   Balance of Payments and Exchange Rate
                  Economics   213**

Chapter 8   The Current Account (I): Price Elasticities and the Trade
                  Balance   217

   8.1 Elasticity Pessimism   217
   8.2 Elasticities Analysis of Devaluation: A General Approach   222
   8.3 Elasticity Estimates and the *J*-Curve   233
   8.4 Exchange Rate Stability and Macroeconomic Stability   236

Chapter 9   The Current Account (II): Income-Expenditure Effects of
                  Devaluation   239

   9.1 The Absorptionist Attack on Elasticities Analysis   239
   9.2 Devaluation, the Price Level, and Absorption   244
   9.3 Synthesizing Elasticities and Absorption Analysis as a Guide to
          Policy   250
   9.4 International Cooperation to Achieve External and Internal
          Balance   255

Chapter 10   The Monetary Theory of the Balance of Payments   260

   10.1 Introduction to Monetary and Asset-Market Theories   260
   10.2 Monetarism   264

10.3 The Monetary Theory Under Fixed Exchange Rates   267
10.4 The Monetary Approach: IMF Variety   283
10.5 Flexible Exchange Rates and the Monetary Approach   288

Chapter 11   Asset Markets and Flexible Exchange Rates   295

11.1 Introduction   295
11.2 Portfolio Choice and Foreign Investment   296
11.3 Short-Run Asset-Market Equilibrium   304
11.4 The Current Account and Long-Run Exchange Rate
      Adjustment   314

Chapter 12   External and Internal Balance and the Theory of Economic
             Policy   320

12.1 The Static Theory of Economic Policy   320
12.2 Mundell's Analysis of Fixed Exchange Rates and the Monetary-Fiscal
      Mix   326
12.3 Discrete Policy Adjustment and the Problem of Overshooting   331
12.4 Continuous Adjustment, Stability, and Exclusive Assignment   337
12.5 Correct Assignment: A Simulation for the U.S. Economy   340
12.6 Summary   342

Appendixes to Part Three   346

Part Four   The International Monetary System   369

Chapter 13   The International Monetary System to 1973   371

13.1 The Nineteenth-Century Gold Standard   371
13.2 Between the World Wars: 1918–1940   381
13.3 Bretton Woods: 1944–1973   390
13.4 Postmortem: The SDR and the Reform Debate   400

Chapter 14   The Flexible Exchange-Rate System and the Global Debt
             Problem   409

14.1 International Monetary Arrangements in the Post–Bretton Woods
      Period   409
14.2 The Behavior of Real Exchange Rates   416
14.3 The Flexible Exchange-Rate System: Promises versus Realities   423
14.4 The Global Debt Problem   438

Chapter 15   Improving the International Monetary System   454

15.1 Stabilizing the Flow of Capital   454
15.2 Government Intervention as a Source of Exchange Rate
      Instability   472
15.3 Criteria for Government Exchange Market Intervention   477
15.4 Geographic Intervention: The Optimum Currency Area   487
15.5 An International Monetary System for the Future?   492

Index   499

Preface

A welcome reflection of the times is the fact that many colleges and universities are expanding their international economics offerings to two-semester sequences, one of which is devoted to open-economy macro-economic issues. This book attempts to supply appropriate teaching material for the macroeconomics portion of such an undergraduate sequence. However, to broaden its utility, the open-economy material is developed against the closed-economy backdrop. This permits the book to dovetail the open-economy perspective with the materials students are most likely to have studied in their standard introductory macro courses, and it permits them to see the enormous effects of international trade, capital mobility, and exchange rate variations.

Unquestionably the 1980s have been the decade of the international economy. Inward-looking perspective is out, and outward-looking perspective is in. In the realm of macroeconomics, countries are discovering that their attempts to slow or stimulate their economies bring about effects profoundly different from those predicted by a closed-economy perspective. After being led to believe that the adoption of flexible exchange rates would insulate economies from foreign shocks, we have discovered that shock transmission is greater than ever. One country's monetary and budget policies are, therefore, everyone else's vital business. Diseases such as unemployment, inflation, and inadequate economic growth can no longer be tackled effectively without international cooperation. The explosion of global debt of the past 15 years is everyone's problem. When debtor countries are forced to reduce their imports because of their debt, this slows the growth of their economies; and since this threatens the export markets of creditor countries, it spreads stagnation to those economies as well.

When proposing curriculum change, an author quickly lands on controversial ground. It was therefore gratifying to find that Harper & Row and its Senior Economics Editor, John Greenman, were willing to encourage this project. I owe a major vote of thanks to them for their willingness to sail in somewhat uncharted waters.

I am also very grateful to these reviewers, who read all or part of the manuscript during various stages of its preparation: Dennis Boland, University of the District of Columbia; Gerald Epstein, University of Massachusetts at Amherst; Jon T. Innes, Lehigh University; Jeorg Martinez, Georgia State University; J. Carter Murphy, Southern Methodist University; and Darrel A. Young, University of Texas at Austin. I owe a special debt to Alfred Reifman and William Cox, who permitted me to pick their brains on a daily basis when I served as a consultant to the Economics Division of the Congressional Research Service of the Library of Congress during a university sabbatical. Dr. Lucy Malan read a number of chapters in early drafts and contributed to shaping the project during its infancy. A special vote of thanks is due to Dr. Elinor Yudin Sachse, who not only read the manuscript with the critical eye of a trained economist but contributed editorial improvements as well.

I do, of course, have no one to blame but myself for the outcome.

THOMAS F. DERNBURG

GLOBAL
MACROECONOMICS

PART ONE

ISSUES AND CONCEPTS

Open economies differ in many important ways from the imaginary closed economies of macroeconomics textbooks. A closed economy cannot borrow goods and services from itself, nor can it consume more than it produces. An open economy can borrow from foreign economies, and it can consume more than it produces by importing more than it exports. The closed economy must deal with such problems as unemployment and inflation at home. Open economies have been known, all too often, to try to export these problems to other countries. A closed economy does not have to worry about the effects of external shocks to its economy. The open economy is very prone to such shocks, a problem that appears to be getting worse as financial interdependence increases. The central bank of a closed economy can control the supply of money and credit as it wishes, and it has a powerful effect on interest rates. In the open economy a central bank has far less influence over interest rates, and, under some conditions, it may have very little control over its domestic money supply.

If the analysis of how the macroeconomy behaves were not substantially affected when an economy is opened to international trade and finance, the procedure of most textbooks, wherein international considerations are brought in as an afterthought, would be adequate. But that is not the case. The effects of governments' monetary and fiscal policies, for example, are far different in an open economy than they are in a closed economy. Since there is no such thing as a closed economy— except perhaps behind the Iron Curtain—it follows that much of macroeconomic analysis is not only incomplete, but it is also incorrect.

Chapter 1 introduces our subject by showing how recent policy measures had quite unexpected consequences because the expectations were based on closed-economy analysis. The chapter also highlights the relationship between budget deficits, trade deficits, and Third World debt. Section 1.2 briefly describes the characteristics of international monetary systems, aimed at establishing the basic criteria needed for the successful operation of such a system.

Chapter 2 provides some basic tools of analysis. The foreign exchange market, exchange rates, and government intervention in the foreign exchange market are described and discussed. Criteria for policy action are then developed by way of introducing the internal and external balance criteria. The chapter closes with a description of such concepts as arbitrage, forward exchange, speculation, and purchasing-power and interest-rate parity.

Chapter 3 describes the balance of payments and the monetary accounts. The relationships among money supply, domestic credit, and the balance of payments outcome are traced. The chapter develops the notion that the balance of payments can be analyzed either by determination of the various components of international payments or as the product of changes in the demand for money relative to changes in domestically generated money supply.

Chapter 1

Introduction to Global Macroeconomics

1.1 MACROECONOMICS AND OPEN-ECONOMY MACROECONOMICS

In 1979 the federal budget deficit of the United States was about $20 billion, and consumer prices rose at a rate of 13.8 percent. Six years later, in 1985, the budget deficit had increased tenfold to $200 billion, yet inflation, as measured by the consumer price index (CPI), had decelerated to 3.8 percent. How does one explain such an astonishing paradox? If one tries to do it with conventional macroeconomic analysis of the kind that abstracts from international trade and finance—"closed-economy" macroeconomics—the task is all but impossible. A monetarist might make a valiant effort at an explanation by pointing out that after President Jimmy Carter appointed Paul Volcker as chairman of the Federal Reserve, the Fed sharply and abruptly shifted its policies to restrict the supply of money and credit so as to contain the inflation that had gotten steadily worse since 1976. This monetary restriction had the predictable effect of raising interest rates. This reduced borrowing by consumers and businesses, thereby reducing total spending in the economy, and that broke the back of the inflation. The monetarist might add that only misguided Keynesians would have expected the increase in the budget deficit to be inflationary. Monetarists, if not others, are privy to the fact that a rise in the deficit forces up interest rates and that "crowds out" private expenditures, thereby leaving total spending unaffected.

Plausible? Perhaps. But hardly convincing. Consider the following facts:

1. The effects of the monetary restriction were unexpectedly devastating. The recession of 1982–83 was the worst economic ca-

lamity to befall the U.S. economy since the Great Depression of the 1930s. Had the Federal Reserve correctly anticipated the consequences of its actions, it would surely have thought twice about embarking on its monetary misadvendure of 1979–81. Everyone was surprised—forecasters, government officials, and most economists. How could monetary policy suddenly have such enormous bite?

2. The fall in the inflation rate by 10 full percentage points was also completely unexpected. The unemployment rate rose from 5.8 percent in 1979 to 9.5 percent in 1982. Standard "Phillips curve" calculations predicted that this would reduce the inflation rate by no more than 3 or 4 percentage points. Yet inflation fell 10 percentage points. Whatever happened to the Phillips curve that looks so impressive in textbooks?

3. Foreign countries were complaining loudly that the restrictive monetary policies of the United States were causing inflation in their economies. How can that be, when standard theory teaches that the effects of tight money in one country tend to spill over to other countries because the demand for imports drops in the country undergoing deflation? Since this reduces the exports of other countries, it tends to slow their economies. How, then, can a deflationary monetary policy in one country cause inflation in others?

4. As a percentage of real gross national product (GNP), consumption rose from 62.8 percent in 1979 to 64.8 percent in 1985. The share of government purchases also increased from 19.1 to 20.1 percent. That had to mean that investment must have been crowded out. Or did it? Investment actually increased from 18.0 to 19.1 percent of GNP. So much for the "crowd out" argument that monetarists like to invoke as a reason for not running budget deficits.

5. If consumption, investment, and government purchases together added up to 104 percent of GNP in 1985 as compared with 99.9 percent in 1979, this had to mean that the U.S. economy was getting a lot of extra output from somewhere else. And, sure enough, by 1985 we had developed a mammoth trade deficit that came to 4 percent of GNP. One might guess that this could only have happened if the United States had a lot more inflation than our trading partners, since inflation makes lower-cost imports attractive and makes it tougher for exports to compete abroad. But that was not the case. Although Germany and Japan had less inflation than the United States, that was not true for other

major trading partners such as Canada, France, Italy, and the United Kingdom. How then do we account for the deluge of imports that virtually wiped out the steel industry, produced severe hardship and retrenchment in the automobile industry, and virtually took over the domestic market for electronic equipment? Why did our exports stagnate so badly that American agriculture, our most important export industry, suffered an eclipse reminiscent of the 1930s? Its primacy in the world market has been extinguished, and there were some months in 1986 during which the United States imported as much food as it exported.

These facts, based on recent events, demonstrate beyond any doubt that macroeconomic relationships do not behave either the way they used to, or the way policymakers think they ought to, or the way most macroeconomics textbooks have led us to expect. Actually there is no great mystery about these seeming paradoxes. But to get at the truth, we have to abandon our habit of pretending that ours is a closed economy and must, instead, think in terms of the open economy—not just as an afterthought or as an appendage, but front and center.

Several fundamental facts explain why macroeconomic interactions are a lot different than they used to be. The list could probably be extended by careful thought and analysis, but for the moment, three stand out.

1. The degree of openess of an economy has usually been framed in terms of the size of an economy's foreign trade sector relative to its GNP. Thus, the United States, with imports in 1985 representing 13 percent of real GNP is generally regarded as a relatively closed economy compared, for example, with Belgium, which imports fully 60 percent of its GNP. But trade dependence is only one factor making for openess, and it may be of limited significance. Of far greater importance is the fact that countries' financial markets have become so closely integrated during the last several years that they are inseparable. Funds flow so swiftly and smoothly from one financial center to another that interest rates tend to be speedily equalized throughout the world. Consequently, policy-making institutions such as the Federal Reserve or the Bank of England would be kidding themselves if they thought they could pursue interest-rate policies separate from the policies of other countries without creating major disruptions. The foreign exchange market, which is where national currencies are traded for each other, has become the world's largest financial market, vastly eclipsing such markets as the New York Stock

market. On a typical trading day, it is not at all unusual for more than $100 billion in national currencies to be traded, one for the other. This is far more than is needed to finance international trade. Most of it represents financial transactions—Americans buying British bonds, Japanese investors acquiring dollars to invest in the U.S. stock market, and the like. Economists call such transactions capital movements, and when such movements flow as easily between New York and London as between New York and Los Angeles, we say that the degree of international capital mobility is high, or perfect, or relatively perfect, or we use some other adjective that describes the ease with which international moneys flow.

2. Much of the world's experience with international finance was gathered during periods of so-called fixed exchange rates. Exchange rates are the prices at which currencies are converted into each other. If one British pound (£1) can be purchased for $2, we say that the exchange rate equals 2; that is, the dollar price of £1 is $2. Historically, governments have not been willing to permit market forces to determine exchange rates. They have, rather, fixed or pegged them by the device of offering to buy and sell their own currency in exchange for foreign currencies at a fixed price. Under such a guarantee of "convertibility" no one has to buy a pound for more than $2 or sell it for less than $2 since he or she can always convert for that price at the government's fiscal agent, whether it be its central bank, its treasury, or an exchange-stabilization fund created for the purpose.

   The international gold standard, which prevailed from 1870 until the outbreak of World War I in 1914, was a fixed exchange-rate system. Countries defined the "par value" of their currencies in terms of gold, and they maintained the parity by buying and selling gold to and from all comers at a fixed price. This system was suspended during World War I, but was resurrected in modified form during the mid-1920s, only to be abandoned again in 1931. In 1944, countries agreed once again to restore a fixed exchange-rate system, which, however, collapsed in the 1971–73 period. Since that time, many major trading countries, such as the United States, Japan, Canada, and the European Economic Community, have permitted market forces to determine exchange rates. This development has radically altered the behavior of macroeconomic variables and, as we will see later, the way in which monetary and fiscal policies impact on economies. It is a major additional source of instability in countries' export and import levels. If the exchange rate is fixed, our import demand is likely to change only because domestic inflation makes imports more attractive, or because we have enjoyed a rise in national income that enables consumers to purchase additional imports. But if our currency appreciates, we can get more foreign currency per dollar, and that also makes foreign goods more attractive. Similarly, with fixed exchange rates, exports are likely to rise in response to foreign inflation and increases in foreign income levels. But if our currency depreciates, foreigners have to give up fewer units of their currency to acquire a dollar, and that lowers the cost of our goods as seen by them. Consequently, when exchange rates bounce around, countries' exports and imports will also tend to bounce around, and that will transmit severe shocks to entire economies.

3. Taken together, the combination of flexible exchange rates and a high degree of international capital mobility have created a climate in which macroeconomic shock transmission from one country to another is enormous, and in which monetary and fiscal policies may have unexpected and far-reaching consequences both at home and abroad. To see this, it is helpful to return to the effects of the monetary and fiscal policies of the United States between 1979 and 1985. That will also help to clean up some of the waters that were deliberately muddied at the outset.

When the Federal Reserve put the economy on its stringent monetary diet in late 1979, this had the predictable effect of raising interest rates in the United States. Foreign investors, on seeing attractive yields in the United States, responded by moving capital to our shores. For example, upon seeing that interest rates in the United States had risen to 10 percent, a British investor holding a British bond paying 5 percent would naturally wish to swap the lower-yielding security for the higher-yielding one. To make this portfolio shift, the investor sells the local bonds for British pounds, then sells the pounds in exchange for dollars in the foreign exchange market, and finally uses the dollars to buy the U.S. bonds. When investors are doing this on a large scale, the foreign exchange market develops an excess supply of pounds and an excess demand for dollars. This results in an appreciation of the dollar relative to the pound. Consequently, the initial effect of the Fed's tight money policy was to launch the dollar on an appreciation that was to reach about 50 percent by 1985.

The rise in the dollar meant that imports became much cheaper. Consequently, Hondas and Sonys flooded into the United States, and American tourists spent happy vacations enjoying the bargains they could pick up in foreign countries. Since a dollar spent on foreign goods and services comes largely at the expense of expenditures on domestic production, the rise in imports had a sharply restrictive effect on the U.S. economy. At the same time, the rise in the dollar increased the cost of American goods to foreigners, so they curtailed purchases from us and our exports stagnated, adding to the restrictive forces. The enormous swing in our balance of trade had the effect of pushing the economy into the worst recession since the 1930s. Because of its effect on the exchange rate, the tight money policy had a far greater deflationary impact on the economy than anyone had anticipated.

The appreciation of the dollar also helps to explain why inflation declined so sharply. Since foreign goods enter the cost of living, a decline in the prices of foreign goods lowers the CPI. This means that even if you don't stem domestic inflation, you can nevertheless show good inflation numbers simply by appreciating your currency. Indeed, some estimates indicated that fully one-half of the decline in the inflation rate was due to the appreciation of the dollar.

A major trouble with this change in our foreign trade position is that our exports are someone else's imports and our imports are other countries' exports. Consequently, when our trade deficit rises and has a restrictive effect on our economy, some other country will have a rising trade surplus that stimulates its economy. Consequently, our deflationary monetary policy had an expansionary effect on most other countries. Furthermore, just as the appreciation of the dollar reduced inflation in the United States, the depreciation of other currencies that went with it caused more inflation in foreign countries as the cost of U.S. goods increased. It seems fair to say, under the circumstances, that rather than controlling inflation in the United States, the Federal Reserve's actions simply shipped inflation abroad.

Foreign countries were not prepared to stand idly by as their currencies depreciated and their inflation rates increased. They therefore reacted to the restrictive monetary policy of the United States with monetary restrictions of their own. These restrictions were designed to raise interest rates, thereby reversing the flow of capital, so as to appreciate their currencies. Unfortunately, competitive appreciation between countries is a dangerous game. Since it is not possible for all countries to appreciate their currencies simultaneously, competition to do so caused a degree of all-around monetary restriction that greatly reduced the world's money stock, thereby throwing the entire world economy into a severe and senseless recession. The U.S. recession spread like a plague throughout the world thanks to a set of misguided and uncoordinated monetary policies on the parts of most of the world's major countries. Not only was this recession senseless and costly, but it left the world economy with a legacy of chronic problems that, as we will see, have not been solved and may not be solvable.

The administration of President Ronald Reagan next proceeded to compound the felony with a set of reckless fiscal policies. In 1981 the President asked for, and received, legislation that sharply slashed federal income taxes. At the same time, he began a series of large annual increases in defense expenditures. In combination, these fiscal policies produced a flood of federal red ink that reached $200 billion in 1985. The reason such an enormous amount of fiscal stimulus did not cause runaway inflation is that the stimulus was largely exported to other countries. Consumers spent their tax cuts mostly on foreign goods, so the domestic economy did not get the stimulus it needed to recover from the recession. Fiscal policy worked the way it is supposed to, but in the wrong place.

When the government's tax receipts fall short of its expenditures, it has to make up the difference by selling government bonds. When the deficit increases and the Treasury's bond sales increase, this has a depressing effect on the bond market, so interest rates will rise. Consequently, the expansionary fiscal policies acted to further push up interest rates in the United States. This helped to maintain the interest-rate differential between the United States and other countries, thereby continuing the capital inflows and further appreciating the dollar. As a consequence, exports fell, imports rose, and the fiscal stimulus had its main expansionary impact elsewhere.

Economists have spent a great deal of valuable time and effort at the task of forecasting exchange rates. Although the competing theories are quite elegant, forecasting has proved elusive. But if exchange rates cannot be forecasted with any degree of precision, it has to follow that the effects of macroeconomic policies cannot also be assessed with any degree of confidence. We know that restrictive monetary policy will appreciate the currency, but we do not know by how much. Therefore, we cannot tell what will happen to exports, imports, and GNP. Furthermore, since our policies will severely shock foreign economies, we can expect retaliatory measures from others that, in turn, will affect our exports, imports, and GNP. Thus, in making policy, we also have to be able to predict the policy responses of a myriad of other countries, as well as the likely effects of the policies. Furthermore, since each country's policy responses are not apt to be of the other's liking, there is the constant danger of economic warfare and a deterioration of the world economic climate. This happened in the 1930s; it happened again in 1981–83, so apparently very little was learned in between. It seems obvious from all this that countries can no longer effectively go it alone in attempting to steer their economies and that the only solution to ensure effective policy is through a cooperative multilateral effort to coordinate and harmonize interest-rate and other policies. Although much lip service has been paid to harmonizing fiscal and monetary policies internationally, hardly anything constructive has as yet emerged.

Economic diseases have a way of occupying attention in ten-year cycles. The 1930s was the decade of depression and unemployment. The war years of the 1940s renewed interest in inflation control. The postwar period brought on an enormous preoccupation with issues of reconstruction, economic growth, and the problems of developing nations. The 1970s ushered in the era of supply-side restrictions marked by increasing oil and food prices and the scourge of stagflation that went with these developments. The 1980s has most surely been the decade of the international economy. Countries have had to confront the problems created by sharp fluctuations in exchange rates, huge swings in their exports and imports, and an enormous accumulation of foreign debt that represents an ever-present threat to the stability and growth of the world economy.

All around us there are enormous and growing debt problems, each of which is a threat to economic stability and economic growth in the entire world economy. Indeed, Gerald Epstein of the New School for Social Research has talked of a "triple debt crisis"—the U.S. budget deficit, the U.S. trade deficit, and the massive accumulation of debt by Third World countries. He writes:

> These three crises . . . have the world economy in a serious bind. World economic growth is necessary to solve these problems, but world economic growth seems to be out of reach—largely because of the troublesome and paralyzing ways in which these debts interact with the dollar problem. [1]

He then goes on to suggest that the combination of the Federal Reserve's tight money policies and the fiscal policies of the Reagan administration were, in large measure, responsible for this triple debt crisis. Although President Reagan did not invent Latin American debt, it is probably fair to say that U.S. fiscal policies have aggravated the problems of debtor countries.

The first thing we need to understand is that the trade deficit is, to a large extent, the consequence and mirror image of the federal budget deficit. When the government raises spending so that it exceeds its receipts, this government deficit requires some other sector to make room by running a surplus of receipts in excess of expenditures. Such an adjustment is necessary to bring total expenditures into line with total national income.

[1] Epstein, Gerald, "The Triple Debt Crisis," *World Policy,* Fall 1985, p. 626.

We can examine these relationships as follows. In a closed economy the level of production, which equals national income, Y, must equal the sum of expenditures on consumption, C, investment, I, and government purchases, G. Therefore we can write

$$Y = C + I + G \qquad (1.1)$$

as a condition for macroeconomic equilibrium. In the open economy, exports, X, are an addition to expenditures, whereas imports, V, add to the supply of goods and services available for use. Therefore, in the open economy, (1.1) becomes

$$Y + V = C + I + G + X$$

It is customary to place imports on the right-hand side. The expression is therefore usually written

$$Y = C + I + G + (X - V) \qquad (1.2)$$

On the income side, national income can either be spent on consumption, be saved, S, or be taken by the government in the form of taxes net of government transfer payments, T. Therefore,

$$Y = C + S + T \qquad (1.3)$$

When (1.1) is equated with (1.3), we can see that C appears on both sides of the equation and can therefore be canceled. We then have

$$I + G + (X - V) = S + T$$

Simply rearrange this as

$$G - T = (S - I) + (V - X) \qquad (1.4)$$

where $G - T$ is the government deficit. As (1.4) makes clear, the government deficit must equal the sum of the surplus of income over expenditure in the private sector—that is, $C + S - C - I$, or $S - I$—plus the surplus of the foreign sector. If $V - X$ is positive, we have a trade deficit, but the foreign sector has a surplus because its expenditures on our exports are less than its earnings from the sale of imports to us.

A rise in the budget deficit affects $S - I$ through its effects on national income and the rate of interest. A rise in government purchases, for example, raises national income, which raises saving, and interest rates, which reduces investment. Therefore, as $G - T$ widens, so does $S - I$. Similarly, a rise in the budget deficit tends to widen $V - X$. The rise in income raises imports, and the rise in the rate of interest appreciates the currency, thereby increasing imports and reducing exports.

The distribution of the changes between the private- and foreign-sector surpluses depends in large measure on the degree to which higher interest rates attract foreign capital and appreciate the exchange rate. If domestic assets are highly coveted by foreign investors, only a small rise in interest rates will be needed to attract a large inflow of capital. This means that interest rates will rise by less than if the response of foreign investors had been less enthusiastic. Consequently, domestic investment need not decline significantly. Also, because of the enthusiastic response of foreign investors, there will be a large appreciation of the currency, which raises imports and lowers exports. Since, finally, this means the rise in national income is less, there will be a smaller rise in savings. Consequently, it is the foreign-sector surplus that does the bulk of the adjusting when capital is highly mobile and therefore sharply responsive to small changes in interest rates. This, clearly, was the kind of reaction that the United States economy evoked in response to its expansionary fiscal policies. It meant that $S - I$ changes were small relative to the changes in $V - X$. And, under these conditions, it is appropriate to say that the trade deficit mirrors the budget deficit, and that crowd out is largely foreign rather than domestic.

The Third World debt problem enters the picture in the following way. The restrictive monetary policies of the United States and other industrial countries were the factors most heavily responsible for causing the deep recession of 1982–83. As a consequence of recession in the industrial countries, their import demand for the products of Third World suppliers declined. Much of this supply is in the form of agricultural products and raw materials. Such activities tend to be characterized by a low responsiveness of supply to changes in price. As a consequence, the decline in demand caused very sharp price declines, and this greatly reduced the receipts earned from exports by the Third World countries. In order to maintain their imports from industrial countries—imports badly needed to sustain the growth of their economies—the developing countries resorted to heavy borrowing, thereby increasing their foreign debt, already greatly bloated by the need to finance oil imports after two rounds of oil price increases during the 1970s. In addition, the fiscal and monetary policies of the United States had appreciated the dollar, and since much of what these countries import, including oil, is invoiced in dollars, the cost of their import bills rose sharply as the dollar appreciated. Finally, the high interest rates caused by the policies led to worldwide interest-rate escalation that greatly increased the burden of servicing the debt.

Many developing countries now have to earn huge trade surpluses in order to pay the interest and amortization on their debt. That means that poor countries are transferring resources to the rich creditor countries, so per capita income rises in rich countries as it falls in poor countries. If the debtor countries cannot generate trade surpluses, possibly because the industrial countries make that impossible, they have no choice left but to engage in further borrowing to pay their current interest and amortization charges, thereby making their future problems seem all the more difficult and hopeless. Small wonder that countries are tempted simply to default on their debt. If that happened, it could well bring the entire banking structure of the industrial world into a state of panic and collapse. The credit needed to finance developing country imports would vanish. Exports of industrial countries would, therefore, dwindle, and the entire world economy would again sink into a monstrous depression. Not a happy scenario to contemplate.

Getting out of this "vicious cycle of economic sabotage," as Epstein calls it, will not be easy. The United States could ease the problem by reversing its mixture of monetary and fiscal policies, that is, by reducing its budget deficit and simultaneously moving to a more expansionary monetary policy. This combination of policies would lower interest rates, which would directly ease the debt service burden of the debtor countries. At the same time, the lower interest rates would stimulate growth in the industrial countries, thereby increasing the export markets of the developing countries. But this avenue of relief has been blocked by the difficulty of raising taxes in the face of presidential opposition as well as President Reagan's determination to prevent cuts in defense spending. Meanwhile, the United States has had little more to contribute than to coax other countries into imitating the atrocious fiscal policies of the United States. The idea is that this would stimulate their economies and reduce the U.S. trade deficit by increasing the demand for U.S. goods. But this would also mean even higher world interest rates and a stronger dollar, and therefore do nothing to ease the problems of the debt-burdened developing countries.

Sharp fluctuations in exchange rates, huge swings in export and import levels, interactions between economic variables that are sharply at variance with traditional concepts of causality, and an enormous accumulation of international debt are some of the major issues that we will attempt to analyze in this book. We certainly don't pretend to have all the answers, but it is a lot of fun trying. Certainly no one can characterize these subjects as irrelevant, dull, or impractical.

1.2 THE INTERNATIONAL MONETARY SYSTEM

In Part Four we discuss the history of the international monetary system in some detail. There is considerable terrain to be traversed before we arrive there. The theory behind that choice of organizing our work is that the assessment of the international monetary system goes more smoothly and effectively if we have the analytical tools at our disposal that permit us to understand the weaknesses and advantages of different forms of international monetary organization. Why the systems have encountered periodic crises and why reform efforts took particular directions are matters that can be far more readily understood and digested if we have the tools of open-economy macroeconomics to work with. In the meantime, however, we have to get a feeling for the subject, so a very short description of some essential elements of international monetary systems is essential.

Modern economies cannot function or develop without money. They also need a mechanism that provides enough new money to accommodate economic growth, but not so much as to cause inflation. Such statements are so obvious that they require no elaboration. The conduct of trade and investment across national boundaries is complicated by the fact that different countries have different currencies and that their governments pursue different monetary policies. An international monetary system has to come to grips with these problems if it is to function. Four elements must be there in one way or another.

1. The international monetary system must have a way of determining the value of one national currency in terms of another. *Exchange rates* have to be determined in a suitable manner.

2. If a country exports more than it imports while another country imports more than it exports, there has to be some way to settle the difference. In the domestic economy, if you sell more than you buy during a year, this will be reflected in an increase in your cash balance. In the international economy such a cash balance residual has to be in a form that is generally acceptable. This role of a generally acceptable financial asset is played by the *reserve* asset of the system. Changes in reserves enable surpluses and deficits to be financed when the value of international transactions does not balance. Such a reserve currency could be gold or silver, dollars or deutsche marks, or an international currency created for the purpose of serving as a reserve asset such as the Special Drawing Rights (SDRs) issued to countries by the International Monetary Fund.

3. In the long run a country would be foolish to export more than it imports, thereby being a perpetual lender. Perpetual borrowing is also not generally tolerated, although there are exceptions. Consequently, the international monetary system must provide a mechanism for *adjustment* that evens out deficits and surpluses in the longer run.

 4. Finally, just as the domestic money supply should be made to grow at a rate that accommodates economic growth without inflation, an effective form of international monetary organization requires the growth of international reserve money so as to accommodate growing international trade and investment. This growth of reserves is often called the growth of international liquidity.

The name given to an international monetary system is usually determined by its principal reserve asset. Under the gold standard, the operative reserve assets were the gold holdings of countries' treasuries and central banks. In the nineteenth century in the United States, Populists campaigned to add silver to gold as an additional reserve asset in order to increase the money supply. Such a standard was referred to as bimetallism. After World War I both gold and certain national currencies were used as reserve assets. That system was called the gold exchange standard. After World War II, gold and the dollar become the principle reserve assets under the so-called Bretton Woods system. However, in 1967 a two-tier gold price system was adopted; gold was no longer sold in private markets by monetary authorities; and the United States discouraged other countries from cashing in their dollars for U.S. gold. This meant that gold lost its function as a reserve asset, and the Bretton Woods system then became a dollar standard for all practical purposes.

Exchange rates can be market determined, in which case it is said that exchange rates are *flexible,* or *fluctuating,* or *freely floating.* Governments have not generally been willing to permit their currency prices to be determined by what they call the "vagaries" of the market, and they have attempted to fix or "peg" exchange rates. Pegging is accomplished by a *convertibility* commitment. This usually means that a country's central bank stands ready to purchase and sell its own currency in exchange for the reserve asset of the system. Under the gold standard central banks bought and sold gold at a fixed price to all comers and permitted the unrestricted exportation and importation of gold. Under the Bretton Woods system, countries pegged their currency prices to the dollar, and they maintained the parity of their currencies with the dollar by buying and selling dollars in exchange for their own currencies. Such action by central banks causes the free-market prices of the currencies to equal the "official" prices. The reason is that if the official price of a pound is $2, a British importer who needs dollars to pay for U.S. goods never has to pay more than half a pound to acquire a dollar since the importer can get that price at the central bank, and a British exporter who earns dollars never has to take less than half a pound for each dollar earned from export sales because the Bank of England will buy the dollars from the exporter at the guaranteed price.

Fixed exchange-rate systems have tended to break down periodically and then are automatically replaced by flexible exchange rates. Governments have permitted their currencies to float usually only after they are no longer able to honor their convertibility commitment, that is, when they have run out of reserves. Having run out of options, they permit their currencies to float in sheer desperation. Consequently, flexible exchange-rate periods have usually coincided with severe economic turmoil, and this has given flexible exchange rates a black eye that they probably do not deserve. Usually, the turmoil had its antecedents in attempts to maintain unworkable fixed exchange-rate systems, so the subsequent arrival of flexible exchange rates can hardly be blamed for the prevailing chaos. As an example, during the 1960s and early 1970s the United States ran increasingly large balance-of-payments deficits. This meant that the amount of dollars earned by foreigners was in excess of their need for them. Had exchange rates been free to fluctuate, the excess supply of dollars would have caused the dollar to depreciate substantially. This fact meant that official exchange rates were greatly overvaluing the dollar. But under the system then in operation, foreign central banks had to maintain the overvalued dollar price, which they did by purchasing the surplus dollars. However, when a foreign central bank buys dollars, it does so with its own currency, which means that its domestic money supply increases. In the early 1970s countries that were having to support the dollar were finding that their domestic money supplies were exploding with severely inflationary consequences. When there seemed to be no end to the dollar deluge, countries simply had no choice but to suspend official dollar purchases, and such suspension automatically turned the determination of currency prices over to free markets.

Past failures of fixed exchange-rate systems have generally been caused by the failure of the systems to provide for adequate and systematic reserve growth, and by the failure of the systems to provide adequate balance-of-payments adjustment mechanisms consistent with countries' desires to maintain high employment and sustained economic growth. Reserves are essential, because without them a country cannot sustain its convertibility commitment. A deficit in the balance of payments caused either by excessive imports relative to exports or by capital outflows means that other countries are earning an excessive amount of the deficit country's currency. The deficit country must be able to repatriate its own currency to maintain its par value, and it can do this only by paying for its own currency out of its stock of reserves. When the reserves dwindle due to a continuing deficit, the country will have to adjust in some way. One way is to *devalue* its currency, which means it lowers the par value of its currency so that the official price of foreign exchange increases. Another way is to let its currency float freely. A final, and often very painful way, is to reduce its import demand and take steps to make its exports more competitive.

A critical flaw of the gold standard was its inability to increase gold reserves in an adequate or systematic manner to accommodate the growth of international trade. This problem became especially acute after World War I because many countries had experienced severe inflation as a consequence of the war. This meant that the nominal value of trade increased enormously, so the monetary gold stock, valued at prewar parities, became grossly inadequate as a reserve asset. The problem could have been eased if countries had been willing to raise the official price of gold. But this step was foreclosed when the United States announced its intention to resume gold sales at the prewar price. The British, too, wanted to restore the prewar gold–pound parity. To raise the price of gold would throw a windfall gain in the direction of those who had hoarded gold at the expense of those who held other assets, trusting that they could be converted into gold at a safe, predetermined price. Changing the price of gold was therefore considered to be a betrayal of trust by the upright British.

The post–World War II system suffered from the same problem. There was no provision in the charter negotiated at Bretton Woods in 1944 for reserve creation. After 1955, when the United States began to run deficits so that the dollars flowed to foreign central banks, the growth of these dollar balances provided much needed reserve growth. But later, as the outstanding dollar balances began to exceed the value of the U.S. gold stock, the U.S. commitment to redeem dollars for gold lost its credibility. This created a serious dilemma for the international monetary system. It needed the U.S. deficits to supply reserves. But the continuation of the deficit meant that the system was building up to a "crisis of confidence." When central banks got nervous enough about the U.S. ability to redeem dollars for gold, they would begin to demand gold from the United States. And when one central bank did this, all the others would panic and come clamoring for gold. Such a gold rush engulfed Great Britain in 1931, forcing her to abandon the gold standard. Had it happened under the Bretton Woods system, dollar reserve balances would have been destroyed, and the resulting destruction of liquidity might have had severe deflationary effects.

The strength of a country's competitive position in international trade is determined by its *real exchange rate*. The real exchange rate r can be written as

$$r = \frac{ep^*}{p}$$

$$\frac{\left(\$\!/\yen\right)\left(\yen\right)}{\left(\$\right)}$$

where p measures domestic prices, p^* measures foreign prices, and e is the *nominal* exchange rate, that is, the dollar price of foreign currency (exchange). A rise in the real exchange rate improves a country's competitiveness. As can easily be seen, this could happen if foreign price levels rise, if the domestic price level falls, or if the price of foreign exchange is raised, that is, if the currency is devalued or permitted to depreciate. Foreign inflation makes domestic goods more attractive than foreign goods, so imports decline while exports increase. A fall in the domestic price level has equivalent effects. A rise in the price of foreign exchange makes imports more expensive, whereas exports tend to rise because they become cheaper to foreigners.

To simplify the following discussion, suppose that a country's balance-of-payments surplus or deficit is determined entirely by the value of its exports and imports. Therefore, we can write

$$S = X\left(\frac{ep^*}{p}, Y^*\right) - V\left(\frac{ep^*}{p}, Y\right)$$

where S is the balance-of-payments surplus, X stands for exports, and V stands for imports. Exports and imports both depend on the real exchange rate. But there are two additional arguments in these functions. It is known that when national income rises at home, this increases the demand for imports, and when national income rises abroad, this increases export demand. Consequently, domestic national income Y is entered as an argument in the import function, and foreign national income Y^* is an added variable in the export function.

An appropriate balance-of-payments adjustment mechanism means that in the long run S has to average out to a value of zero. Otherwise the country would either have a perpetual surplus or a perpetual deficit in its balance of payments. If it runs a deficit, the country will run out of reserves, and if it runs a perpetual surplus it is continually exporting more than it is importing, thereby transferring domestic production to foreign countries as a steady diet. It is extending unlimited credit to deficit countries and reducing its own standard of living unecessarily.

A glance at the expression for S suggests that there are three ways in which a country can adjust its balance of payments. It can alter its exchange rate; it can change its price level; or it can change its real income level. If it is running a deficit, it can devalue. In doing this, it raises the price of foreign exchange, making imports more expensive to domestic residents and exports less expensive to foreign residents. Under a rigidly fixed exchange-rate system such as the gold standard, this option is not available. The second option is a fall in its price level or, perhaps more appropriately, a reduction in its inflation rate relative to foreign inflation.

Indeed, under the gold standard it was expected that adjustments would come about through changes in price levels. If the United States had a deficit vis-à-vis Great Britain, the United States would lose gold to Britain. As the U.S. Treasury sells gold, it buys back dollars, reducing the U.S. money supply, and as the Bank of England buys the gold, it pays in pounds, thereby increasing the British money supply. These money supply changes would exercise a deflationary effect on the U.S. economy and an inflationary effect on the British economy, so the U.S. price level p would fall, and the British price level p^* would rise. The real exchange rate would therefore adjust to eliminate the U.S. deficit and, possibly, convert it into a surplus. In addition, it was expected that countries would supplement the automatic adjustment mechanism by having the central banks of deficit countries raise their discount rates—the interest rate charged by the central bank on its loans to commercial banks—while surplus countries were to do the opposite. When these rates are changed by the central banks, other interest rates in the country will tend to follow.

Such a system can work satisfactorily if wages and prices in countries are flexible. But if they are not, the deflationary monetary changes will cause reductions in real income and employment rather than in the price level. If, for example, there is excess supply in labor markets, the excess supply can be eliminated by a reduction in wages. But if wages refuse to budge, perhaps because strong labor unions can prevent wage cuts or because the government has a minimum-wage law on the books that makes it illegal to pay lower wages, the excess supply persists and the country suffers unemployment. Real income changes also adjust the balance of payments because a decline in income reduces the demand for imports. But it is a very costly and inefficient way to adjust the balance of payments, because it inflicts unemployment and output losses on an economy. Prior to World War I, wages and prices were reasonably flexible, but after the war they proved to be downwardly rigid. The deflationary route to balance-of-payments adjustment came to be an exceedingly painful one. To make matters worse for deficit countries, some surplus countries refused to share in the adjustment burden. The United States enjoyed a balance-of-payments surplus and a gold inflow during the 1920s. But rather than permitting the gold inflows to increase the money supply, the Federal Reserve *sterilized* the gold inflows, thereby preventing them from causing inflation. When the gold purchases increased the money supply, the Fed neutralized this by selling government securities.

It is now easy to see that the case for flexible exchange rates is fairly simple and straightforward. It recognizes that wages and prices in most industrial countries tend to be downwardly sticky, so adjustments through changes in internal demand are likely to cause painful fluctuations in real income and employment. It therefore concludes that the only sane avenue to balance-of-payments adjustment is to bring about the necessary changes in the real exchange rates by permitting movements in nominal exchange rates to do the adjusting. The growth of unions and oligopolistic industries, the proliferation of minimum-wage legislation, and widespread indexing of wages to the cost of living have produced such rigidities in wage-price structures that it is best to recognize these facts of life and permit the exchange rate to fluctuate. At least that way the balance-of-payments tail will not be permitted to wag the economic dog.

Governments have generally been reluctant to draw the same conclusion and have attempted to maintain control over exchange rates. Recognizing that fixed rates are too rigid while believing that freely floating rates are also disadvantageous, governments have tried to steer a middle course between the extremes. At the outset it was the intention of the Bretton Woods charter to have an *adjustable peg* system. This meant that exchange rates would be fixed, but since they would tend to get out of line if, for example, countries had different inflation rates, periodic adjustment of official parities would be needed in order to bring exchange rates to more appropriate levels.

One plan for controlled flexibility is called the *crawling peg*. Under this system the government permits the market to determine the equilibrium exchange rate, but government intervention in the foreign exchange market is such that the adjustment to an appropriate exchange rate is slow and smooth rather than quick, abrupt, and disruptive. The crawling peg is especially useful when a country suffers very rapid inflation. The annual rate of the crawl is then simply calculated as the difference between the domestic and foreign inflation rates. For example, if the annual inflation rate is 100 percent in Mexico while annual inflation in the United States is 6 percent, a crawling devaluation of the peso of 94 percent $(100 - 6)$ in one year would keep the dollar–peso real exchange rate constant.

The present system is essentially a flexible exchange-rate regime. But that has not prevented governments from periodic intervention in foreign exchange markets when they think something can be gained by intervention. This is sometimes called a managed float. In popular jargon it is known as a dirty float, and when the intervention becomes heavy and persistent, it is a filthy float. The meanings of the terms "intervention" and "nonintervention" are not completely clear. Normally, *nonintervention* means that central banks are not buying or selling foreign currencies, which means that their foreign exchange reserves remain unchanged. By that standard, the United States has practiced a fairly clean float. But the Federal Reserve does regularly conduct monetary policy, which it does by buying and selling government securities, thereby adding to, or subtracting from, the money supply. The purchase of government bonds will force down interest rates and depreciate the currency almost as surely as the purchase of foreign exchange. Consequently, it is not at all clear what a clean float is supposed to mean or whether it is possible to have one.

The advantage that economists have most often found in fixed exchange-rate systems is that fixed exchange rates simulate the conditions of a uniform currency throughout the world in much the same way as a domestic currency does this inside a country. One can imagine how chaotic and inefficient the U.S. economy would be if each of the 50 states had its own currency that fluctuates daily in relation to the other 49 currencies. This would add confusion, increase the riskiness of interstate commerce, and probably reduce interstate trade. That would mean less efficient resource allocation and real income losses. There is, obviously, much to be said for a uniform currency. But fixed exchange-rate systems have tended to run into trouble. The biggest difficulty has been that the requirements of balance-of-payments adjustment were frequently incompatible with countries' desires to manage their economies so as to maintain high employment and stable, noninflationary growth. There are many reasons for this, but one already stands out: when countries peg their exchange rates, they lose control over monetary policy. Thus, balance-of-payments adjustments have tended to come about by painful and costly fluctuations in income and employment levels. And when surplus countries refused to permit inflation, the entire burden of adjustment landed in the laps of the deficit countries. Since these countries then had to sustain additional deflation and unemployment in order to adjust, the failure of the surplus countries to play by the rules of the game gave the fixed exchange-rate system an overall deflationary bias. The world economy therefore had less output and less employment than it was possible and desirable to have.

1.3 GAINS FROM TRADE AND INVESTMENT

The free flow of goods, services, and factors of production to the places in which resources achieve the highest returns is fundamental to the maximization of the real income of nations. Broadly speaking, we are prepared to accept this proposition when it applies to the internal conduct of our own economy, but we often do not apply it to our economic relations with the rest of the world. Most countries have their own monetary units and insist on autonomous monetary and fiscal policies without much

care or concern for the well-being of others. There are also barriers to
the free flow of productive factors between countries in the nature of
immovable natural endowments, such as soil and sunshine, and there
are language and legal barriers that obstruct the free flow of labor services.
Trade theorists have argued that factor immobility need not be an impediment to efficient production if goods and services are free to be exchanged internationally, and they have argued that such free exchange
will equalize factor prices throughout the world, ensuring the optimal
use of labor and capital.

Obviously it is essential to trade. We need oil, coffee, minerals, raw
materials, and countless other products that we either do not have ourselves or that we could produce only at a very high cost. It also pays to
trade because that provides competitive pressure that forces domestic
industries to use the latest technology and cut costs wherever possible.
Just imagine what kind of cars we might be riding around in today had
there been no German or Japanese competition in the last 15 years.
Among other benefits, import competition helps to hold the line on inflationary wage increases and moderate oligopolistic price behavior and
therefore makes it far easier to control inflation.

The fact that we can't produce everything ourselves creates an obvious need for trade. A more subtle notion is that it pays to trade even
if we can produce everything ourselves, because trade permits us to realize
the gains from specialization. This is the famous law of comparative
advantage, first enunciated by the English economist David Ricardo.
Ricardo's celebrated example involved a comparison of the labor hours
needed to produce wine and cloth in Portugal and England. In the accompanying table, the first two columns show the number of labor hours
needed to produce 1 unit of wine and 1 unit of cloth in the respective
countries. In the absence of trade England can produce 1 unit of each
commodity with a labor cost of 210 hours. Portugal can produce 1 unit
of each with a labor input of 150 hours. Portugal is clearly more efficient
in producing both commodities. She is therefore said to enjoy an *absolute
advantage* in producing both wine and cloth. England, on the other hand,
is less efficient in producing both goods, but her inefficiency is least in
the production of cloth. She is therefore said to enjoy a *comparative
advantage* in the production of cloth. For example, if England specializes
in cloth, producing 2 units, her total labor input is 180 hours. Portugal
then specializes in wine and her 2 units cost 140 hours of labor input.
Total labor input is then 320 hours. Thus if England and Portugal specialize in cloth and wine, respectively, and if England exchanges 1 unit
of cloth for 1 unit of Portuguese wine, the two countries can enjoy the

same consumption level as when they each produced 1 unit of each good, and they can save 40 hours of labor input, which can then be used to produce additional output.

	Wine	Cloth	No trade	Trade
England	120	90	210	180
Portugal	70	80	<u>150</u>	<u>140</u>
			360	320

One doesn't need heavy analytical artillery to understand the law of comparative advantage. It rests on the fact that one person can't do everything at the same time. Thus, even though my wife may be both a better driver and baby nurse than I, she can't drive and tend the baby simultaneously, so it pays for me to drive while she minds the baby, even though her vision and reaction speed are better than mine. Although she is a better driver, it would be disastrous to have me tend the baby.

Good analogy

If you will, then, think of the law of comparative advantage as the explanation for the fact that there is an economic role even for incompetents. That goes for countries as well as people. One country can't do everything simultaneously. Therefore, it should specialize in the activities in which its absolute advantage is the greatest while leaving the land of the incompetents to do what the country is *least inefficient* at doing.

Next consider international investment. When society saves and invests, it forgoes a certain amount of current consumption in order to increase future consumption. This saving and investment amounts to the trading of current goods in exchange for future goods. The additional future output that results from the trade, relative to the current sacrifice, is called the real rate of interest. Suppose then that country A has a shortage of capital reflected in a high real rate of interest of 15 percent. Country B, a more economically mature economy, has plenty of capital, so the law of diminishing marginal productivity suggests that its rate of return on new capital is less, say 5 percent. It pays for B's citizens to invest in country A. That way 15 percent more future output is realized rather than the 5 percent that would be realized if B's citizens had to invest at home. This capital transfer is in the interest of both countries. Country B's citizens receive a return in excess of 5 percent on their saving, whereas citizens of country A, by using B's capital, are thereby enabled to save less and enjoy a higher current level of consumption.

This process of capital transfer will tend eventually to equalize real interest rates between the two countries, because as the supply of capital in A increases the marginal product of capital declines. The capital flow stops, and the optimal pattern of production is reached when the real rates of return are equal in both countries. No country then has a capital shortage relative to other countries.

The mechanism through which the transfer of resources takes place under a system of flexible exchange rates would probably work as follows. When B's citizens purchase financial assets in A, this creates added demand for A's currency, which therefore appreciates relative to B's. This encourages imports from B and discourages exports to B. Thus country A will have a trade deficit while B will have a surplus, and in this way real resources are transferred from B to A. Deficits and surpluses in the *current account,* where goods and services are exchanged, are offset by corresponding surpluses and deficits in the *capital account,* where financial assets change hands.

Freer trade and freer access to international capital markets are among the major objectives to which countries have subscribed by their participation in the International Monetary Fund (IMF), the General Agreements on Tariffs and Trade (GATT), and the Organization for Economic Cooperation and Development (OECD), whose memberships include most industrial countries in the free world. Although all of these organizations attempt to promote free trade and free movement of capital, the post–World War II effort to liberalize trade and payments has encountered continuing snags and obstacles. Protectionism grew even after the adoption of flexible exchange rates by the major industrial countries in 1973, surprising the many influential economists who expected flexible exchange rates to promote trade liberalization.

Countries impose tariffs and quotas on imports, subsidize exports, and obstruct the flow of capital for a variety of reasons. Usually the case for protecting a domestic industry is couched in noble terms. The industry is said to be vital to national defense and therefore deserves protection and subsidization even when it is hopelessly backward and inefficient. Or it is essential to preserve the industrial base, a reason given to justify protection of the U.S. steel industry. Or, it is necessary to protect *infant industries* until they develop sufficiently to realize the economies of mass production. In the old days tariffs were raised to increase government revenue. That is no longer advocated in the United States, but it might be a relevant objective in a poor country with an inadequate tax system.

Many of the justifications for obstructing trade are macroeconomic in nature. In recent years the U.S. auto and steel industries have demanded that foreign countries accept "voluntary" quotas on the number of autos and the amount of steel they send to the United States on the grounds, it is said, that domestic employment in these industries requires protection. Labor unions have joined in the drive for protection. Auto unions have been pushing for "domestic content" legislation that would require a large fraction of the parts that enter an automobile to be produced domestically. The domestic employment argument is nothing new. During the 1930s, countries embarked on competitive devaluation of their currencies and import restriction so as to raise exports, reduce imports, and in this manner stimulate their depressed economies. Such use of tariffs, quotas, and exchange rate policies is generally characterized by the unflattering appellation *beggar-my-neighbor* policy, because such measures attempt to raise domestic employment at the expense of employment in other countries rather than by generating the added employment through domestic aggregate expenditure expansion.

In the post–World War II world many countries attempted to maintain undervalued exchange rates in order to gain a competitive advantage vis-à-vis their neighbors, thereby promoting the *export-led* growth that so dramatically produced the reconstruction, growth, and prosperity of countries such as West Germany and Japan. This is sometimes called *exchange rate protection.*

In the 1970s, when inflation rather than unemployment came to be widely viewed as the most pressing macroeconomic problem, many countries reversed their policies, striving to attain overvalued exchange rates in order to obtain cheap imports to dampen inflation. The good inflation performance of the United States after 1982 was largely attributable to the fact that the overvalued dollar permitted the United States to import low-cost foreign goods and productive inputs. On the other hand, foreign countries had to pay dearly for the goods they purchased from the United States and the goods, such as oil, that are invoiced and traded in dollars.

Another major reason for obstructing trade and payments has been the desire to prevent a loss of foreign exchange or to build up foreign exchange *reserves.* Under the Bretton Woods system, exchange rates were fixed by government intervention. If the British pound showed a tendency to decline vis-à-vis the dollar, this indicated an excess supply of pounds in currency markets. The Bank of England was responsible, in such a situation, for removing the surplus pounds by purchasing pounds in exchange for dollars. These dollars, held by the Bank of England (as well as her gold holdings), constituted her official international reserves. But the Bank of England could only intervene in this manner if she had a supply of dollars and gold on hand. Therefore, countries were concerned with their reserve position. A country with an overvalued exchange rate would lose reserves because of her adverse trade balance. But rather than *devalue,* that is, lower, the official price of the currency, the country might be tempted to restrict imports and impose barriers to the exportation of capital. Therefore, a balance-of-payments motive can be added to the list of reasons for interfering with trade and investment.

In conclusion: Intelligent macroeconomic policy and effective organization of the international monetary system are two vital ingredients in the success of the global economy. The world needs the free flow of trade and capital in order to utilize its scarce resources effectively today and to build for tomorrow. Macroeconomics has an important role to play in this quest.

QUESTIONS FOR REVIEW

1. Why did the restrictive monetary policies of the Federal Reserve during 1979–82 have an unexpectedly powerful restrictive effect on the U.S. economy?
2. Why did foreign economies feel an inflationary shock from the deflationary policies of the United States?
3. Why did the U.S. inflation rate drop more sharply than expected?
4. Why did other countries respond to the shock with restrictive monetary policies? Why was world monetary contraction excessive?
5. In what sense is the trade deficit the mirror image of the budget deficit? Suppose international capital is immobile; that is, suppose a rise in U.S. interest rates does not lead to an inflow of foreign capital. Under these conditions:
   (a) Would interest rates have risen more or less than they did in response to U.S. expansionary fiscal policies?
   (b) Would national income have responded differently?
   (c) What would have happened to exchange rates? to exports? to imports?
   (d) What would have happened to the proposition that the trade deficit is the mirror image of the budget deficit?
6. What is the importance of international reserves? Why does an international monetary system need reserves?
7. How are currencies "pegged" by governments under a fixed exchange-rate system?
8. Why is wage-price flexibility an important requirement for a fixed exchange-rate system?
9. How can a surplus country insulate its money supply from the balance of payments? What are the effects of this on deficit countries? on the world economy?

SUGGESTIONS FOR FURTHER READING

Dornbusch, Rudiger, *Dollars, Debts, and Deficits,* MIT Press, 1986, part II.

Epstein, Gerald, "The Triple Debt Crisis," *World Policy,* Fall 1985.

Maris, Stephen, "Deficits and the Dollar: The World Economy at Risk," *Institute for International Economics,* No. 14, 1985.

Wachtel, Howard, *The Money Mandarins,* Pantheon Books, 1958.

Chapter 2

Introduction to International Monetary Issues: The Foreign Exchange Market, Exchange Rates, External and Internal Balance

2.1 THE FOREIGN EXCHANGE MARKET

This chapter attempts to set the analytical stage for the study of open-economy macroeconomics (Chapter 3 is designed to set the empirical stage.) Discussion usefully begins with the foreign exchange market, noting the relationship between the demand for one currency and the supply of another, and illustrating stable and unstable equilibria in the foreign exchange market. Section 2.2 discusses the foreign exchange market under fixed exchange rates. Section 2.3 introduces normative criteria for policy action by defining the *internal* and *external balance* criteria. The chapter ends with an introduction to the concepts of forward exchange, interest-rate parity, and the difference between arbitrage and currency speculation.

"Foreign exchange" is the general term applied to foreign money. Foreign exchange held by the central bank or a national treasury is known as *official reserves*. Importers wishing to purchase foreign goods create a demand for foreign exchange, as do tourists and investors wishing to purchase foreign assets. Exporters who sell goods abroad earn foreign exchange, thereby adding to the supply of foreign exchange, as do domestic residents who sell stocks, bonds, and other earning assets to foreign investors. A country's reserves consist of the financial assets that permit it to settle international claims. Such reserves consist of the holdings of gold, convertible foreign currencies, and credit with the IMF. The total of such reserves is often called a country's international liquidity position. For the world as a whole, the total reserves of all countries is usually described as *international liquidity*. The orderly provision of international liquidity so as to provide for the expansion of world trade and finance without generating inflation has been an important ongoing concern in international monetary reform discussions and negotiations.

Currencies are converted into each other in foreign exchange markets. The prices at which currencies trade for each other are the *exchange rates*. The current price of pounds is the *spot* rate, whereas the rate at which pounds can be currently purchased for future delivery is the *forward* rate. The price of a specific currency in terms of another currency is a *bilateral* exchange rate. The price of a currency defined in terms of an average of other currencies is a *multilateral* exchange rate. A certain amount of confusion sometimes results from the fact that economists and financial writers sometimes talk about the exchange rate as if it were the price of foreign money in terms of the domestic monetary unit, and sometimes they talk about it as if it were the foreign price of the domestic currency. The choice is a matter of taste and convenience although it is important to be consistent. In this book we adopt the convention that the exchange rate is the price of foreign exchange. Consequently, from our point of view it is like any other commodity price in terms of dollars, where the commodity, in this case, is the foreign currency.

By the preceding convention, it can be seen that *depreciation* of the dollar means a rise in the price of foreign exchange and, therefore, an *appreciation* of the foreign currency. Under such forms of international monetary organization as the gold standard of the nineteenth century and the Bretton Woods system, which prevailed from 1944 to 1973, exchange rates are fixed by government intervention. These fixed exchange rates are called *official* exchange rates, and a change in the official exchange rate is called a *devaluation* if the official price of foreign currency is raised, and a *revaluation* if the official price of foreign exchange is reduced.

The exchange rate is the number of dollars needed to purchase a unit of foreign currency. Therefore, we can write

$$\text{dollars} = e \times \text{francs}$$

where e is the price of francs (Fr). Rearranging this, we see that

$$\text{francs} = \frac{1}{e} \times \text{dollars}$$

so that the reciprocal of the exchange rate is the price of dollars in terms of francs. If $e = 0.1$, Fr 1 costs \$0.10, and \$1 costs Fr 10. If the exchange rate rises to 0.2, that would mean that francs cost \$0.20. Therefore, the dollar has depreciated while the franc has appreciated.

In the very long run there is the expectation that trade will be balanced so that the value of exports equals the value of imports. When the dollars and francs spent on these goods are split into price and quantity components, we can write

$$pq = ep^*q^*$$

where q and q^* are U.S. and French exports, respectively, and p and p^* are the prices of the respective exports. This expression can be rearranged to

$$\frac{q}{q^*} = \frac{ep^*}{p}$$

which shows that q units of U.S. exports will purchase q^* units of French goods. This ratio is called the *real terms of trade*. A deterioration in the terms of trade is generally taken to mean that the ratio q/q^* has increased, implying that a greater volume of domestically produced goods must be sacrificed to obtain a given quantity of foreign goods.

Observe that the real terms of trade can also be measured by looking at the right-hand side of the preceding equation, where it can be seen that the real terms of trade equals the product of the exchange rate and the ratio of foreign to domestic prices. This is called the *real exchange rate*. The price of foreign currency in terms of domestic currency e is usually termed the *nominal exchange rate*. The real exchange rate measures the competitiveness of a country in international trade. A rise in the price of foreign exchange makes domestic goods more attractive to foreign buyers. But the same thing happens if there is inflation abroad relative to the movement of prices at home, that is, if p^*/p rises.

Using the definition of the real exchange rate to calculate percentage changes, we get

$$\frac{\Delta q}{q} - \frac{\Delta q^*}{q^*} = \frac{\Delta e}{e} + \frac{\Delta p^*}{p^*} - \frac{\Delta p}{p}$$

An important theory of exchange rate determination, known as the purchasing-power-parity theory, holds that competitive forces will prevent the real exchange rate from changing in the longer run. Therefore, there is no change on the left-hand side of the expression, so

$$\frac{\Delta e}{e} = \frac{\Delta p}{p} - \frac{\Delta p^*}{p}$$

Therefore the theory of purchasing-power parity implies that the nominal exchange rate must reflect relative domestic-foreign inflation rates. Specifically, the nominal exchange rate will rise at a rate equal to the difference between the domestic and foreign rates of inflation. Thus a major deter-

minant of the nominal exchange rate—certainly in the longer run—is
the rate of domestic inflation relative to foreign inflation.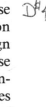

We next turn our attention to the foreign exchange market. We first
consider the market for dollars, and then we consider the market for
francs. These markets can usefully be studied in conventional supply and
demand terms. Therefore, consider Figure 2.1, which shows the market
for dollars. We assume that francs and dollars are the only two currencies
entering this market and that the demand and supply curves are both
linear. The franc price of dollars is the reciprocal of the exchange rate,
as we have defined it, and is measured on the vertical axis. The quantity
of dollars demanded and supplied at different prices is measured on the
horizontal axis. Thus the dollar is the commodity being traded in this
market.

The demand for dollars arises because French nationals wish to
spend dollars to import merchandise from the United States, because
French tourists wish to visit Washington, D.C., and because transportation
and shipping charges have to be paid when imports arrive in foreign
aircraft and foreign bottoms. French investors also may wish to purchase
financial assets in the United States, thereby engaging in portfolio investment, and French business concerns may wish to build subsidiaries
in the United States, thereby engaging in direct investment. The slope of
the demand curve is negative. As the price of dollars increases, more
francs have to be expended to gain the dollars needed to conduct business
in the United States. Appreciation of the dollar therefore means that U.S.

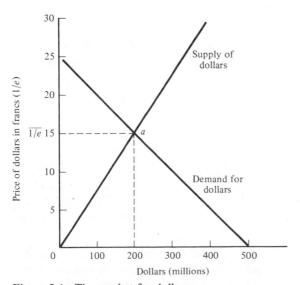

Figure 2.1 The market for dollars.

goods and services become more expensive to French nationals, who therefore reduce their purchases of U.S. goods.

The supply of dollars to the foreign exchange market represents French earnings of dollars from export sales, U.S. tourist expenditure in France, and U.S. investments in France, both direct and portfolio. For the moment we assume that the supply curve is positively sloped, much like most other supply curves. Accordingly, a rise in the price of dollars means that U.S. importers have to give up fewer dollars to purchase French goods; thus, imports increase, thereby presumably adding to the supply of dollars.

Figure 2.1 shows that the demand for dollars and the supply of dollars are equal when the franc price of dollars is 15. The quantity of dollars bought and sold is $200 million. Thus $1/e = $ Fr 15 and $e = \$0.15$. Looking at Figure 2.1, we can see that if the dollar equals Fr 10, a supply of $133.3 million is offered to the foreign exchange market. It must therefore also be the case that Fr 1333.3 million (10×133.3) is demanded. If the price of the dollar rises to Fr 15, the supply of dollars is $200 million, so Fr 3000 million (15×200) must be demanded. If the price of the dollar rises to Fr 20, the supply of dollars is $226.7 million, so Fr 5333 million is demanded. Consequently, it can be seen that if we know the dollar supply curve, the franc demand curve can be easily derived as a mirror image.

The demand for francs is drawn in Figure 2.2, which shows the market for francs. In this case the commodity being traded is francs, and the price is the dollar price of francs, that is, the nominal exchange rate e. For convenience the vertical axis is drawn as a logarithmic scale.

If the demand for dollars at different prices is known, the supply of francs follows directly as its mirror image. Figure 2.1 shows that at a price of Fr 10, the demand for dollars is $300 million. Consequently, the number of francs supplied is $10 \times 300 = $ Fr 3000 million. If the dollar rises to Fr 15, $200 million is demanded, which must mean that 15 $\times 200 = $ Fr 3000 million are supplied. Finally, if the dollar rises to Fr 20, $100 million is demanded, so that 20×100 million becomes the supply of francs.

It can be seen in Figure 2.2 that the demand for francs equals its supply at a price of $\frac{1}{15}$ dollar per franc. This is consistent with the equilibrium dollar price of francs of 15. Similarly, at the equilibrium exchange rate Fr 3000 million is traded in exchange for the equilibrium dollar volume of $200 million.

An important property of the hypothetical franc supply curve is that it is backward-bending. The supply of francs initially increases as the price of francs rises, but then declines as the price continues to rise. The

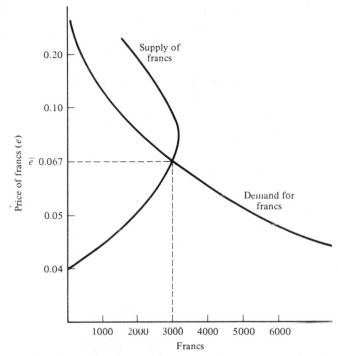

Figure 2.2 Demand and supply for foreign exchange (francs).

reason for this lies in the price elasticity of the demand for dollars. At dollar prices above 12.5, the demand for dollars is price elastic, that is, when the dollar falls, the percentage increase in the quantity of dollars demanded exceeds the percentage decline in the price of dollars. This means that at the new exchange rate the total dollar outlay purchases more francs than previously, so the supply of francs increases as the price of francs increases. On the other hand, when the dollar reaches Fr 12.5, a further drop in the dollar causes the percentage increase in the quantity of dollars demanded to be less than the percentage decline in the price of dollars. Consequently, the total dollar outlay purchases fewer francs. The supply of francs therefore declines when the price of francs rises as the dollar declines.

In general, we could write

$$Q = eQ*$$

where Q is the total number of dollars demanded and $Q*$ is the total number of francs supplied. Taking percentage changes of the above expression gives approximately

$$\frac{\Delta Q}{Q} = \frac{\Delta e}{e} + \frac{\Delta Q}{Q*}$$

or

$$\frac{\Delta Q}{Q} - \frac{\Delta e}{e} = \frac{\Delta Q^*}{Q^*}$$

where $\Delta e/e$ is the rise in the price of francs as the dollar declines, and $\Delta Q/Q$ is the increase in the quantity of dollars demanded. The change in the supply of francs, $\Delta Q^*/Q^*$, will be positive if the proportionate increase in quantity exceeds the proportionate fall in price, that is, if the demand for the dollar is price elastic.

Figure 2.3 is an exaggerated replica of Figure 2.2. The demand and supply curves for francs intersect at points a and b. These points of intersection are equilibrium points. For point a the equilibrium is said to be *stable*. If the initial price of francs is e_0, there is excess demand for francs. Consequently, competition to acquire francs in exchange for dollars will raise the price of francs toward the equilibrium price e_a, thereby eliminating the excess demand as the higher price attracts added supply and rations potential buyers out of the market. Similarly, if the initial price of francs is e_1, there is an excess supply of francs. Competition among sellers to unload francs for dollars will lower the price of francs and raise the price of dollars. As this happens, potential buyers of francs come into the market while potential sellers withdraw.

Point b, however, is an *unstable* equilibrium point. Suppose the

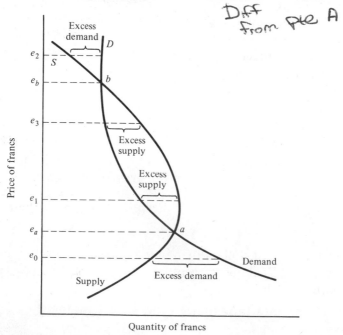

Figure 2.3 Stability of the foreign exchange market.

initial price of francs is e_2. This situation implies excess demand for francs, since the quantity of francs demanded at that price exceeds the quantity supplied. Consequently, competition among potential buyers of francs will raise the price of francs to a still higher value. That increases the excess demand, causing price to rise still farther away from equilibrium. Similarly, if the initial price is e_3, there is excess supply in the market for francs. The price of francs therefore falls, and the movement is once again away from point b. Point b is still an equilibrium point, in the sense that the curves intersect there, but it is an *unstable* equilibrium point because any slight movement away from b produces progressive divergence from b.

The possibility that equilibrium in the foreign exchange market may be unstable has been much discussed in balance-of-payments literature, and is a subject that we take up in detail in Chapter 8. It is important, also, to test our equilibrium solutions to make sure that the equilibria are stable, since otherwise they would not be reached. If we look only at points of intersection of functions to indicate where we are headed, we are very likely going to make mistakes. Such testing for stability of equilibrium is called *stability analysis,* and the procedure for conducting such an analysis is developed in detail in the appendix to Chapter 5.

Now that we have some acquaintance with the foreign exchange market, we can usefully discuss some of the related issues that will occupy us throughout this book.

First, we have seen that the possibility of an unstable foreign exchange market arises from the backward-bending supply curve. We need therefore to go behind the scenes to study the underlying factors that influence the shapes of the demand and supply functions. This is done in Chapter 8.

Second, it is important to study the factors that cause *shifts* in the demand and supply functions. The most important sources of such shifts are changes in income levels, price levels, and interest rates. A rise in real income in the United States increases the demand for imports and therefore affects the demand for foreign exchange. A rise in the U.S. price level reduces U.S. international competitiveness. Consumers switch to cheaper foreign goods, thereby increasing the demand for foreign exchange while producers find it more difficult to export, which is reflected in a reduced supply of foreign exchange. A rise in interest rates in the United States increases the attractiveness of U.S. financial assets to foreign investors. This causes a *capital inflow* that increases the supply of foreign exchange.

In view of the enormous importance of these factors, the study of the balance of payments necessitates a careful study of how income, prices, and interest rates are determined. We do this in Part Two.

Third, the demand and supply functions for foreign exchange give the impression of being an arm of microeconomic analysis. In microeconomics it is often acceptable to assume that factors outside the individual market under study remain unchanged in response to changes in the individual market. This is the *ceteris paribus* assumption. However, the luxury of such an assumption cannot be afforded in the study of the foreign exchange market. For example, a rise in the price of foreign exchange tends to stimulate exports. This, in turn, raises national income and prices and may also raise interest rates. These changes are then likely to cause the demand and supply curves of foreign exchange to shift. Consequently, movements *along* the demand and supply functions are apt to interact powerfully with *shifts* in the functions.[1] Therefore the study of the balance of payments and the foreign exchange market cannot proceed adequately by assuming constant income, prices, and interest rates. These various variables have to be determined jointly, along with the exchange rate. Chapter 9 takes up these issues.

2.2 EXCHANGE RATES AND GOVERNMENT INTERVENTION

The rules governing the post–World War II international payments system were established at Bretton Woods, New Hampshire, in 1944. The Bretton Woods conference restored a system of fixed exchange rates, sometimes referred to as the par-value system. The system represented an attempt to establish a modified form of the pre–World War I gold standard. The keystone of the system was the acceptance by participating countries of the obligation to purchase excess supplies of their own currencies at predetermined minimum prices. The specific obligation required member governments, other than the United States, to redeem their currencies at a fixed price in U.S. dollars. The United States, in turn, undertook to buy and sell dollars from foreign monetary authorities in exchange for gold at an official price of $35 per ounce. In this manner all currency prices were anchored to gold, to the dollar, and to each other at officially fixed exchange rates.

Figure 2.4 shows the entire market for foreign exchange as it might be viewed by the United States. The demand and supply curves intersect at point a at an exchange rate of $\bar{e}$. If the predetermined official price of

---

[1] A movement along a demand curve implies that *quantity* demanded changes because price changes. However, an *increase in demand* implies a shift to the right of the entire demand curve. In this event a greater quantity is demanded at any price than was the case prior to the increase in demand.

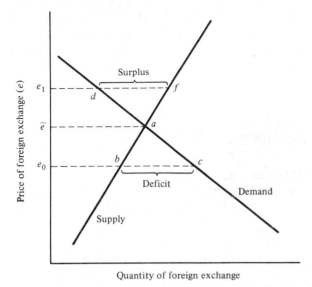

Figure 2.4 The foreign exchange market under fixed exchange rates.

foreign exchange is e_1, the supply of foreign exchange is at point f and the demand for foreign exchange is at d. There is therefore an excess supply of foreign exchange—U.S. receipts exceed payments—and the United States is said to have a *balance-of-payments surplus* equal to the distance df in terms of foreign exchange. Other countries have an equivalent deficit in their balances of payments.

The reverse is the case if the official exchange rate values foreign exchange at a price of e_0. In this event there is an excess demand for foreign exchange and a deficit in the U.S. balance of payments equal to bc measured in terms of foreign exchange. In Figure 2.4 exchange rate e_0 implies that the dollar is overvalued while foreign exchange is undervalued.

In a free market the price of foreign exchange would rise and the dollar would depreciate. However, under the par-value system foreign exporters could take their dollar earnings and deposit them at their commercial banks in exchange for domestic deposit credit. The banks could then convert the dollars into domestic reserves at their central banks. The central bank could then either hold the added dollars as part of their official reserves, or they could demand that the U.S. Treasury repatriate its dollars in exchange for gold. Such guaranteed *convertibility* ensures that the price of dollars and foreign currencies remain at their official values. Since earners of dollars can always sell their earnings to the central bank at the official price, there is never a need to sell dollars at a lower price in the foreign exchange market. Similarly, anyone who wants dollars can always get them at the official price through the central bank.

The Bretton Woods rules recognized that official exchange rates might get permanently out of line, usually because of different rates of inflation in different countries, and therefore recognized the need for periodic realignment of exchange rates in the event of "fundamental disequilibrium." If there is a persistent U.S. surplus, foreign countries would eventually lose the ability to redeem their own currencies because their reserves of dollars and gold would become exhausted. To prevent this, the foreign countries could *devalue* their currencies, as a decline in the official value of local currency is called. In the process dollars would automatically be *revalued* (raised), as a rise in the official price of a currency is called.

If the official price of foreign exchange is e_0, it is the United States that has the deficit. Gold and foreign exchange flow out, and foreign monetary authorities accumulate dollars. To restore equilibrium, one option is to devalue the dollar, which would have meant a rise in the official price of gold had the United States taken the initiative. However, this would not have guaranteed a revaluation of exchange rates since, under the rules of the system, the United States had control only of the dollar price of gold, not the dollar price of foreign currencies.

During the 1960s and early 1970s the United States ran persistent deficits in its balance of payments. Through a variety of devices and agreements the United States was able to persuade foreign governments to hold onto the bulk of the dollars they were accumulating. A major drawback of this is that as foreign monetary authorities accumulate the dollars earned by their citizens, they do this in exchange for domestic money balances. Therefore, when a monetary authority accumulates foreign exchange, it automatically increases its domestic money supply with potentially inflationary consequences. It appears to have been this fact more than any other that led to the abandonment of the par-value system by the major industrial countries in 1973.

The lack of monetary control is one of the most important and potentially destructive characteristics of a fixed exchange-rate system. Deficits in the balance of payments require monetary authorities to purchase their own currencies, thereby reducing their money supplies, whereas surpluses imply the sale of local currency, thereby increasing the money supply. Therefore, surpluses imply automatically inflationary monetary policies, whereas deficits imply automatically deflationary monetary changes. One key difference between a fixed exchange-rate system and a market-determined exchange-rate system is that under the fixed-rate system the exchange rate is controlled at the expense of loss of control of the money supply. Under flexible exchange rates the opposite is true. The exchange rate fluctuates, but the money supply can normally be controlled.

Throughout this book we take pains to distinguish how changes, especially stabilization policy changes, affect the economy under fixed exchange rates, as opposed to flexible exchange rates. Although the fixed exchange-rate system is something of a relic, it is important to understand its drawbacks, and not just for reasons of nostalgia. Many countries still maintain official parities, almost all countries intervene periodically in foreign exchange markets, and there is continuing sentiment for the modification or abandonment of the flexible exchange-rate system.

2.3 EXTERNAL AND INTERNAL BALANCE: CRITERIA FOR BALANCE-OF-PAYMENTS EQUILIBRIUM

When is the balance of payments in equilibrium? What value of the exchange rate is appropriate? A quick look at this issue is important here. Refinements can wait until later.

Under fixed exchange rates, equilibrium in the balance of payments is generally considered to imply equality of international payments with receipts, and the implied absence of either accumulation or "decumulation" in the foreign exchange reserves of the monetary authority.

Some economists have expressed a preference for a concept of equilibrium called *basic balance.* The basic balance excludes short-term capital movements that often fluctuate sharply in response to changes in interest-rate differentials, political upheavals and their anticipated arrival, and other presumably temporary forces that do not reflect basic underlying trends.

Under flexible exchange rates, receipts and payments balance automatically as the exchange rate adjusts to eliminate excess demand or supply of foreign exchange. Although some economists, such as Beryl W. Sprinkel, chairman of the Council of Economic Advisers and former undersecretary of the treasury for monetary affairs, appear satisfied that any market-determined exchange rate is an equilibrium rate, others object to such a definition. Objectors might point out that the dollar was severely overvalued between 1980 and 1985, as was clearly indicated by the enormous deterioration that took place in the U.S. trade balance after 1980. They might argue that an appropriate exchange rate is one that balances the *current account* of the balance of payments. Roughly, current-account balance occurs when receipts from export sales plus net income from overseas investment equal payments made for imports. When the current account is in balance, the country is paying for its imports out of current overseas earnings, capital inflows equal outflows, and the country's net international debt position is not changing.

Even this modification may not supply an appropriate definition of balance-of-payments equilibrium. Suppose the current account is in balance at the existing exchange rate but that the economy suffers from excessive unemployment. An appropriate policy response would be to use expansionary fiscal and monetary policies to raise employment. This would raise national income and probably also the price level. The rise in income increases the demand for imports, as does the rise in the price level, in addition to which exports are placed at a competitive disadvantage in foreign markets. Therefore, a policy designed to restore full employment, that is, *internal balance,* in the economy has the effect of disrupting *external balance.* The reason is that, under fixed exchange rates, the policy would most likely cause a current-account deficit, and under flexible exchange rates it would cause the currency to depreciate. Therefore, the fact that the current account might have been in balance in the initial situation does not imply that the exchange rate prevailing at that time was the appropriate exchange rate. In order to be considered appropriate, the exchange rate must not only *secure external balance, but it must be consistent with internal balance as well.*

The relationship between the exchange rate and external and internal balance can be usefully studied with the aid of Figure 2.5. The exchange rate is measured on the vertical axis. The level of internal aggregate expenditure, which equals consumption, C, investment, I, and government purchases, G, and is sometimes called absorption, A, is measured on the horizontal axis. Assume that point a is a point of internal balance, in the sense that the economy enjoys noninflationary full employment. It is therefore a point on the internal balance (IB) curve.[2]

Suppose the price of foreign exchange rises so as to place the economy at point b. The rise in the exchange rate causes the country's international competitive position to improve so that net exports rise. This normally has an expansionary effect on the economy as activity in export industries increases and as consumers replace imports with cheaper domestically produced goods. To offset the adverse inflationary effects of the rise in the exchange rate, total spending in the economy must be reduced. Therefore absorption must be reduced to reach a point such as

[2] The external-internal balance model can be found in Swan, Trevor, "Longer Run Problems of the Balance of Payments," in Arndt, H. W., and M. W. Corden, eds., *The Australian Economy: A Book of Readings,* Melbourne, Cheshire Press, 1963.

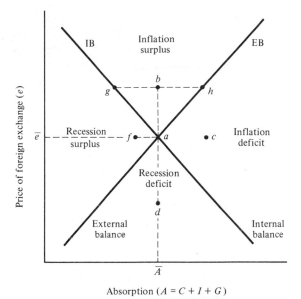

Figure 2.5 Internal and external balance.

g, so point g is also a point of internal balance. Consequently, it can be seen that the internal balance function is normally negatively sloped: the lower the exchange rate, the lower the level of net exports, and the higher the level of domestic absorption needed to maintain full employment without inflation.

Observe that the IB curve partitions the diagram into two zones. To the left of IB, absorption is too low and the exchange rate is too low to prevent recession. Points such as d and f therefore imply recession and excessive unemployment. Conversely, to the right of IB, points such as b and c imply inflation. Absorption and the exchange rate are too high to prevent inflation.

Next, go back to point a and assume that current-account equilibrium prevails at that point. Let the exchange rate rise again to move the economy from point a to point b. The rise in the price of foreign exchange causes exports to rise and imports to decline so that net exports rise and the current account moves into surplus. To remove the surplus, national income could be raised by a rise in absorption. Since this raises the demand for imports, point h could also be a point of external balance. It follows that the EB curve has a positive slope. As the exchange rate rises, the country becomes more competitive, net exports rise, and the current account moves into surplus. But that can be offset by a rise in absorption that increases imports.

The EB curve partitions the diagram into two zones. To the left of EB there is a current-account surplus, and to the right there is a current-account deficit. In combination, the IB and EB curves partition the diagram into four zones: recession combined with a surplus, as at point f; inflation combined with a surplus, as at point b; recession combined with a deficit, as at point d; and inflation combined with a deficit, as at point c.

Clearly, the only place that achieves internal and external balance simultaneously is at point a with exchange rate $\bar{e}$, at an absorption level equal to $\bar{A}$. Therefore, a desirable exchange rate can be determined only if done in conjunction with a desirable level of absorption. Absorption depends primarily on fiscal and monetary policies, so discussion of appropriate exchange rate policy cannot avoid simultaneous consideration of monetary and fiscal policies, nor can discussion of monetary and fiscal policies long ignore exchange rate considerations.

This discussion illustrates an important principle of the theory of economic policy, which we study in detail in Chapters 9 and 12. The principle is that if there are two targets of policy, internal and external balance for example, then achieving both targets simultaneously requires the adjustment of at least two policy instruments. Moving to point a from point g and point h cannot be accomplished by changing the exchange rate alone, nor can it be accomplished by changing absorption alone.

2.4 ARBITRAGE, FORWARD EXCHANGE, AND SPECULATION

Communications between foreign exchange centers are now so swift that the value of each currency in terms of other currencies quickly becomes the same in all major financial centers. If the franc is worth $0.10 in New York and $0.11 in London, a dealer can purchase francs for $0.10 in New York and sell them for $0.11 in London. This drives up the New York price and lowers it in London until such transactions, known as *arbitrage,* equalize the dollar price of francs in all markets.

Arbitrage ensures that *cross rates* will be "orderly," that is, consistent.[3] If the franc is worth $0.10 and the deutsche mark (D-mark or DM) is worth $0.25, then the D-mark must be worth Fr 2.5. Like simple ar-

---

[3] The nuts and bolts can be found in many competent international finance texts aimed at business administration students. Maurice Levi's *International Finance,* McGraw-Hill, 1983, is excellent in this and other respects.

bitrage, *triangular arbitrage* involving three currencies will ensure that the exchange rates are consistent with each other in all markets. If Fr 1 = $0.10 and DM 1 = $0.25 in New York, and DM 1 = Fr 3 in London, a New York arbitrager could spend $10 to buy DM 40 in New York. He could then use the DM 40 to buy Fr 120 in London, and he could then sell the francs for $12 in New York, thereby making a profit of $2. This arbitrage will continue until francs can no longer be bought more cheaply in one market than the price at which they are sold in another market.

Suppose an American wine importer contracts for the delivery of several hundred cases of the current vintage of burgundy wine with a French negotiant at a price of Fr 600 per case to be paid at the time of delivery. It is understood that the wine will not be ready for delivery until a year later. Along with other risks, the importer has to assume exchange risk, that is, the risk that the exchange rate will be different in a year. If the franc appreciates, the dollar cost of the wine will increase; if the franc depreciates, the opposite will occur. Even if there is no firm expectation that the franc will move one way or the other, the importer nevertheless cannot be sure of this. The resulting uncertainty represents a real cost to the importer, a cost that he or she might be willing to pay someone else to bear. It is the demand for such an insurance policy that creates the *forward* exchange market, which permits the importer to *hedge* against exchange risk.

The current exchange rate is called the *spot* rate. The current value placed on the exchange rate at some time in the future is the *forward* rate. There are, of course, many different forward rates, depending on the time period involved. If he or she so wishes, the wine importer can contract for future delivery of the Fr 600 at the forward rate. By doing this, the importer knows exactly how much the wine is going to cost in dollars. He or she is guaranteed future delivery of the Fr 600 at the current forward rate so that he or she can pay for the wine when it is delivered in a year.

The relationship between the spot and forward rates depends on interest rates in the United States and France. If the present value of a sum of francs is F_p, then the value of this sum one year from now will be F_p plus the interest that can be earned on francs. Therefore,

$$F_f = F_p(1 + i^*)$$

where F_f is the future value of the francs and i^* is the interest rate that can be obtained by lending francs. Similarly, for the dollar we must have

$$D_f = D_p(1 + i)$$

where D_p is the current value of a sum of dollars, D_f is the future value, and i is the interest rate that can be earned by lending dollars. If the future value of the francs is to equal the future value of the dollars, their ratio must be the forward exchange rate. Therefore, divide D_f by F_f to get

$$\frac{D_f}{F_f} = \frac{D_p(1 + i)}{F_p(1 + i^*)}$$

where D_f/F_f is the forward dollar price of francs, and D_p/F_p is the spot dollar price of francs. Consequently,

$$e_f = e_p \frac{1 + i}{1 + i^*}$$

If $i > i^*$, the forward price of francs exceeds the spot price, because by purchasing francs for future delivery, the selling bank sacrifices a higher return on the dollars it would otherwise have kept (i) in favor of the lower-yielding francs that earn i^*. The bank therefore charges a forward premium to the wine importer. If $i < i^*$, the bank purchases higher-yielding francs in exchange for the lower-yielding dollars. Competitive pressure then forces the forward price of the franc below the spot price, so the importer gains a premium.   *should be appreciate*

Speculators differ from arbitragers in that the latter take *covered* positions to eliminate risk, whereas speculators accept exchange risk and buy and sell currencies forward because they expect the future spot rate to be different from the forward rate. If the forward price is Fr 10 per dollar, and speculators expect the dollar to depreciate to Fr 5 per dollar, they can sell $1 worth of francs forward for Fr 10. They then deliver the francs at a future date and get $20 in return, thereby doubling their money. Or, if they expect the franc to depreciate to 20 per dollar, they can sell Fr 10 for $1 on the forward market, and then buy back Fr 20 for $1 if their expectation is realized.   *I think should be #2*

Speculators differ from other users of foreign exchange in that they purchase and sell currencies for their own sake, currency demands being attributable to expected changes in currency prices rather than to finance trade and investment. Speculation in foreign exchange may be beneficial, helping markets avoid wide price swings and speeding the process of adjustment if expectations are *inelastic* Inelastic expectations imply that speculators have some "normal" or "equilibrium" price in mind to which they believe the exchange rate will gravitate. Under the circumstances a rise in the franc causes speculators to believe that the rise is temporary and that the franc will subsequently fall. They therefore sell francs, thereby pushing down the franc when it is on the rise, and they buy francs when the franc is declining, thereby moderating exchange rate movements and accelerating the return to equilibrium.

But if speculators as a group have *elastic* or *extrapolative* expectations, a rise in the franc leads to the expectation that further increases are imminent, and a fall in the franc leads to the expectation that the fall is the beginning of a declining trend. This causes speculators to buy francs when the franc is rising and to sell francs when it is falling. In both cases the action of the speculators reenforces the swings of the exchange rate and delay or forestall a return to equilibrium. It has been pointed out that speculators with elastic expectations tend eventually to bankrupt themselves, since consistent market participation based on elastic expectations means that speculators generally buy dear and sell cheap. That fact has not, however, prevented periodic destabilizing speculative raids and disruptive flights of hot money.

The adjustable peg system, which allowed for occasional changes in official exchange rates, was particularly vulnerable to speculative attacks. Speculators needed only to observe the depletion of a country's foreign exchange reserves in order safely to predict devaluation. As reserves continue to shrink, speculators reason that the currency is overvalued and that government action to devalue is likely. Speculators therefore sell the beleagured currency on the expectation that they will be able to buy it back more cheaply after the devaluation. If the devaluation takes place, windfall profits are earned; if it does not, the speculators lose only their brokerage costs. Meanwhile, the fact that they were selling the currency in anticipation of devaluation accelerated the foreign exchange drain from the monetary authority and may have been instrumental in forcing a devaluation that might otherwise have been avoided.[4]

In Chapters 5 and 6 we will study the importance of capital movements in response to interest-rate differentials and how this affects balance of payments and national income adjustment and the effectiveness of fiscal and monetary policies. Here we should recognize the importance of the relationship between interest-rate differentials and the exchange rate. In today's financially open economies, financial capital is highly *mobile.* When interest rates rise in the United States, wealth holders in other countries sell domestic earning assets to purchase dollars, which they then use to buy the higher-yielding U.S. financial assets. Since such a short-term capital movement raises the demand for dollars, it tends to appreciate the dollar vis-à-vis foreign currencies. The extreme form of capital mobility occurs when any interest-rate differential provokes capital

[4] This problem was pointed out many years ago by the late Frank D. Graham of Princeton University, one of the earliest American advocates of flexible exchange rates. See his classic paper, "Achilles Heels in Monetary Standards," *American Economic Review,* March 1940.

movements that persist until the interest-rate differential is eliminated. Foreign investors, by purchasing U.S. securities and selling their own, drive up the price of the U.S. securities and drive down the prices of foreign securities. This lowers interest rates in the United States, raises them in foreign countries, and brings the rates back into equality.

Under these circumstances of *perfect capital mobility,* the only way in which a domestic–foreign interest-rate differential could persist is if the exchange rate is expected to change by a percentage equal to the interest-rate differential. The condition for *uncovered interest parity* is

$$i - i^* = E\left(\frac{\Delta e}{e}\right)$$

where i is the domestic rate of interest, i^* is the foreign rate of interest, and $E(\Delta e/e)$ is the expected percentage rate of depreciation of the local currency.[5] If i^* exceeds i by 2 percentage points, investors would tend to move funds to the higher-yielding foreign assets. However, if the dollar appreciates by 2 percent in one year, the principal plus the interest on the foreign investment leaves investors with a foreign asset whose dollar value is exactly the same as if they had invested at home despite the higher foreign interest rate. We can see therefore that if the foreign rate of interest exceeds the domestic rate by 2 percentage points, an annual appreciation of the domestic currency by 2 percent would equalize the yields on foreign and domestic bonds. Conversely, if the home rate of interest exceeds the foreign rate of interest by 2 percent, the choice between domestic and foreign assets would be a matter of indifference if the local currency were expected to depreciate 2 percent. Consequently, a rise in the domestic rate of interest will attract foreign capital, but this could be offset by an anticipated depreciation equal to the interest-rate differential. Similarly, a rise in the foreign rate of interest tends to induce a capital outflow, but that can be neutralized by an anticipated appreciation equal to the interest-rate differential.

In this chapter we have familiarized ourselves with a significant number of issues even before we have much in the way of analytical tools to work with. The external-internal balance model, for which we have Trevor Swan to thank, provides insights into the determination of an appropriate exchange rate, and it points to the need to combine exchange rate policy with macroeconomic policy in general. Parts Two and Three elaborate on many of the issues discussed here and provide the analytical

---

[5] The notation $E(x)$ is a standard way to describe the concept of the expected value of x. Mathematical expectation becomes important in the discussion of the asset-market theory of exchange rate determination, which is discussed in Chapter 11. See the appendix to that chapter for an explanation of expected value concepts.

tools needed for effective thinking and analysis. Meanwhile, we move to Chapter 3, which supplies some essentials of balance-of-payments measurement and traces the monetary effects of international transactions.

QUESTIONS FOR REVIEW

1. Define the following concepts:
   (a) spot exchange rate
   (b) forward exchange rate
   (c) bilateral exchange rate
   (d) multilateral exchange rate
   (e) real exchange rate
   (f) nominal exchange rate
   (g) real terms of trade
   (h) arbitrage
   (i) speculation
   (j) purchasing-power parity
   (k) uncovered interest parity

2. According to the theory of purchasing-power parity, a country's exchange rate should depreciate at a rate equal to the difference between the domestic and foreign inflation rates. Explain the rationale for this view. If a country operated a crawling peg system conforming to purchasing-power parity, would this necessarily produce equilibrium in its balance of payments?

3. What factors give rise to a demand for foreign exchange? What factors produce a supply of foreign exchange? Why is the demand for foreign exchange the mirror image of the supply of the local currency? Why is the supply of foreign exchange the mirror image of the demand for the local currency? How can supply curves in foreign exchange markets be backward bending? What are the implications of backward-bending foreign exchange supply curves?

4. What is an appropriate exchange rate? What is an equilibrium exchange rate? Are the two the same?

5. What is the importance of equilibrium in the current account of the balance of payments as opposed to equilibrium in the overall balance of payments?

6. A country suffering a combination of inflation and deficit in its current account should reduce domestic absorption as a first step in the adjustment process. Why is this preferable to reducing the deficit by devaluation?

7. A country suffering recession and a deficit in its current account should probably devalue its currency. Why is this preferable to eliminating its deficit by reducing absorption? Why is it important for this country to make sure that other countries approve of its action?

8. If all countries are suffering recession, what is the appropriate policy response for a deficit country? for a surplus country? Who should take the lead in achieving adjustment?

9. What is the appropriate policy response for a country that suffers from inflation but enjoys a current-account surplus?

10. What is the relationship between the forward exchange rate, the spot exchange rate, and the rate of interest?

11. How can there be a domestic-foreign interest-rate differential if capital mobility is perfect? under fixed exchange rates? under flexible exchange rates?

SUGGESTIONS FOR FURTHER READING

Graham, Frank D., "Achilles Heels in Monetary Standards," *American Economic Review,* March 1940.

Ingram, James C., *International Economics,* Wiley, 1983, chaps. 2 and 4.

Swan, Trevor, "Longer Run Problems of the Balance of Payments," in Arndt, H. W., and M. W. Corden, Eds., *The Australian Economy: A Book of Readings,* Cheshire Press, 1963.

Williamson, John, *The Open Economy and the World Economy,* Basic Books, 1983, chap. 1.

Chapter 3

International Transactions:
The Balance of Payments

3.1 THE BALANCE-OF-PAYMENTS EQUATION

A balance-of-payments account records the receipts and expenditures of the nation that resulted from international transactions during the year. In general, items that involve an inpayment are recorded as credit items, and a plus (+) sign is attached. Items that involve payments to foreigners are debit items, and a minus (−) sign is attached. It is useful to think of credit items as earning foreign exchange, whereas debit items represent expenditures of foreign exchange. The currency in which transactions are made is immaterial. A credit item can just as well be thought of as causing an inflow of dollars, whereas a debit implies an outflow.

Credit items include exports of merchandise, income from services such as shipping, insurance, and foreign tourist expenditures, income from overseas investments, and purchases by foreigners of investment properties in the United States. The latter could include direct investments in the form of real property (land, buildings, equipment) or portfolio investments in stocks and bonds, or even a transfer of a foreign bank account to a U.S. bank.

Debit items include U.S. purchases of foreign goods, services such as tourist expenditures abroad, and payments of interest and dividends to foreign owners of U.S. assets, government transfer payments (economic aid and military assistance), and unilateral transfers to foreign residents in the form of gifts, pensions, reparations, and the like.

For analytical purposes the balance of payments is most usefully subdivided into two major segments plus a residual or balancing item. The first major segment is the *current account*, which includes items that generate current income, either at home or abroad. Included are merchandise exports and imports, services such as travel and transportation, interest and dividends on investments, military transactions, and unilateral transfers.

The second major segment is the *capital account*. Dollars flow in when foreigners purchase U.S. earning assets, and dollars flow out when U.S. citizens purchase foreign earning assets. These transactions represent transfers of existing assets that do not generate current income. They do, however, involve international payments and receipts and must be included in the balance of payments so that the overall deficit can be measured and analyzed and so that all factors that contribute to the determination of the exchange rate can be considered. Foreign purchases of U.S. assets are called capital inflows. Since such transactions either earn foreign exchange or reduce U.S. liabilities abroad, they are credit items, to which a plus sign is attached. Conversely, U.S. purchases of foreign earning assets (real or financial) are capital outflows. Either dollars or foreign exchange flow out, or U.S. liabilities to foreigners decline. Capital outflows are debit items, to which a negative sign is attached.

If current-account payments equal current-account receipts, we say the current account is in equilibrium. If there is a deficit in the current account, and if this is exactly matched by a surplus in the capital account, overall payments equal receipts, so the balance of payments is said to be in equilibrium. Under flexible exchange rates the overall balance of payments automatically equilibrates so that any surplus or deficit in the current account is matched by an equal deficit or surplus in the capital account. If there is an incipient overall deficit, with payments tending to exceed receipts, this implies excess demand for foreign exchange and excess supply of dollars. The dollar therefore depreciates, thereby eliminating the incipient deficit so that payments equal receipts.

Under fixed exchange rates the excess of payments over receipts results in a reduction in U.S. official reserves or in an increase in foreign official reserves. The reason is that the fixed exchange-rate commitment permits earners of dollars (foreign exporters, for example) to convert their earnings into domestic currency at the central bank at a fixed price. The foreign central bank either holds the dollars so that its official reserves increase, or it sells the dollars to the Federal Reserve in return for gold or its own currency, in which case U.S. official reserves decline. Consequently, there is a residual item in the balance of payments in the form of a change in official reserve assets that reflects the difference between receipts and payments in the current and capital accounts. To the extent that central banks intervene in currency markets to stabilize exchange rates, official reserve balances will change even under flexible exchange rates.

For analytical purposes we write the current account surplus, CS, as

$$CS = X - V + i^* F$$

where X represents exports of goods and services (not counting investment income), V represents imports of goods and services, $i^* F$ represents net investment income, F is the net value of domestically owned foreign earning assets, and i^* is the average rate of return on such assets. Unilateral transfers are autonomous and may therefore be ignored. The term $X - V$ is sometimes called net exports, the trade balance, or net foreign investment. Consequently, we could write

$$NX = X - V$$

where NX is net exports, and

$$CS = NX + i^* F$$

which states that the current-account surplus equals net exports plus net income from foreign investment.

If the capital inflow exceeds the outflow, there is a surplus on capital account. Denote this surplus by K. The overall balance of payments surplus therefore equals $CS + K$. If this is positive, it implies that receipts exceed payments, so the foreign exchange reserves of the central bank increase as the central bank sells dollars in exchange for foreign currency. Let this reserve change be ΔR. We then have

$$\Delta R = CS + K = (X - V + i^* F) + K \qquad (3.1)$$

This is the fundamental balance-of-payments equation that we use throughout this book. Clearly, one way to analyze the balance of payments is to study the factors that influence the levels of the various current- and capital-account aggregates as defined in (3.1).

Another productive way to analyze the balance of payments is to study international money flows. Indeed, changes in national monetary accounts play a major role in most discussions of the balance of payments. To simplify the study of international money flows, we consolidate the balance sheets of all domestic banks, both private and public, into a single balance sheet. In the aggregation process intrabank assets and liabilities are netted out. For example, the domestic reserve assets of commercial banks appear as liabilities on the balance sheet of the Federal Reserve. When the balance sheets are consolidated, these and other such intrabank items cancel out. What is left is the *consolidated balance sheet of the domestic banking system,* sometimes called the monetary survey. Such a balance sheet contains three major components. On the left-hand side as assets the banking system holds IOUs of the government and the

T-bills

loans

private sector. These domestic assets are usually referred to as *domestic credit,* which we denote by D. The other major asset of the banking system is its holdings of foreign exchange reserves, R. These assets are balanced by liabilities equal to the country's money stock, M. Therefore the assets and liabilities of the domestic banking system may be represented by the following consolidated balance sheet of the domestic banking system. To use a shorter term, we call this the *monetary survey.*

Monetary Survey

Assets	Liabilities
D, domestic credit R, foreign exchange	M, money stock

The monetary survey suggests that the money stock can be increased either by an increase in domestic credit or by a balance-of-payments surplus that increases foreign exchange reserves. When the Federal Reserve purchases foreign exchange, it pays in domestic money, so the *domestic money supply rises* while the *foreign money supply declines.* It is essential always to remember that, when exchange rates are fixed, balance-of-payments surpluses imply that the money supply is increasing, whereas deficits imply the opposite.

Remember

Now consider some of the major ways in which the monetary survey is affected.

1. *Domestic Open-Market Operations.* To stimulate the economy, the Federal Reserve purchases $100 of government securities from the nonbank private sector. Private wealth holders give up bonds, which then appear as an additional asset in the balance sheet of the Federal Reserve. When the checks are deposited in commercial banks, demand deposit liabilities (ΔM) increase, for which the banks acquire the checks. When the checks are deposited with the Fed, the Fed grants deposit credit to the member banks, whose reserve assets increase. The balance sheet changes for the three affected sectors are as follows:

Federal Reserve

U.S. bonds +100	Member bank deposits +100

Commercial Banks

Reserves +100	Deposits +100

Nonbank Private
Sector

Deposits +100 U.S. bonds -100	

When the balance sheets of the Fed and the commercial banks are consolidated into the monetary survey, we see that the balance sheet changes are as follows:

Monetary Survey

U.S. bonds +100	Deposits +100

or

$\Delta D = +100$	$\Delta M = +100$

Accordingly, we can see that the open-market purchase represents an extension of domestic credit, which results in an increase in the money stock.

2. *Commercial Bank Credit Expansion.* Next suppose that commercial banks have excess reserves that are used to make loans to the nonbank private sector. The lending bank accepts an IOU from the borrower and grants deposit credit. Therefore,

Commercial Banks

Loans and investments +100	Deposits +100

The borrower then uses the $100 to pay suppliers. This reduces deposits of the borrower but increases the deposits of the suppliers. Therefore, the monetary survey will show

ΔD, Change in domestic credit = +100	ΔM, Change in money supply = +100

and we therefore see that it does not matter whether it is the Fed or the commercial banks that extend domestic credit. In either case the money supply increases by the amount of the increase in domestic credit.

3. *Government Deficit Financing.* If the government increases expenditures without raising taxes, it must finance the expenditure

by a bond (ΔB) sale. If it sells the bonds to the nonbank private sector, bond holdings rise by ΔB and deposits fall by the same amount. However, when the government spends the proceeds of the loan, the deposit loss is exactly offset. Therefore, the balance sheet of the nonbank private sector shows an increase in assets (ΔB) matched by an increase in net worth (financial wealth, ΔW); thus

Nonbank Private Sector	
U.S. bonds + 100	
Deposits +100	Net worth +100
−100	

or

$\Delta B = +100$	$\Delta W = +100$

The balance sheet of the banking system is not affected. A deficit financed by a bond sale to the nonbank private sector has no effect on domestic credit or the money supply.

But if the government is unable to find private lenders, which may happen if deficits are large or the country is poor with little savings and a poorly developed capital market, it may turn to the central bank for credit. The central bank receives the bonds as an asset and creates a line of credit for the government. Therefore,

Central Bank	
Government bonds +100	Government deposits +100

But when the government spends the proceeds, it draws down its account, so its deposits are shifted to individuals in the nonbank private sector. The commercial banks add to their deposit liabilities and reserves. Therefore,

Commercial Banks	
Reserves +100	Deposits +100

and in the central bank the government deposits are replaced by commercial bank deposits. Consolidating the bank balance sheets after all these transactions gives

Monetary Survey

Government bonds	Deposits
+100	+100

or $\Delta D = \Delta M$.

Apparently a government deficit financed by bond sales to the central bank represents domestic credit expansion that increases the money supply. This does not happen when the deficit is financed by bond sales to the nonbank private sector.

4. *Balance-of-Payments Surplus.* Suppose the balance of payments is initially in equilibrium and that exports then increase by $\Delta X = \$100$. Exporters receive payment in foreign currency which they deposit in their commercial banks, receiving dollar-denominated deposits. Therefore,

Commercial Banks

Foreign exchange	Domestic deposits
+100	+100

Exporter

Deposits +100	
Foreign exchange −100	

The commercial bank then sells the foreign exchange to the central bank in return for an increase in its domestic currency reserve account. This means that

Central Bank

Foreign exchange	Member bank deposits
+100	+100

Commercial Banks

Foreign exchange −100	
Reserves +100	

When we consolidate these balance sheet changes, we see that

Monetary Survey
| $\Delta R = +100$ | $\Delta M = +100$ |

The result shows that a balance-of-payments surplus raises the money supply if the foreign exchange proceeds are deposited in the domestic banking system. This would not happen if exporters used their *But* foreign exchange earnings to purchase imports or foreign assets. If they buy foreign earning assets, the balance-of-payments account would show that the export surplus is balanced by an equal capital outflow, so there is no change in reserves or money supply.

In general, we can see that the balance sheet identity implied by the monetary survey is

$$\Delta D + \Delta R = \Delta M$$

so the change in reserves must be

$$\Delta R = \Delta M - \Delta D$$

and it therefore equals the increase in the total money supply minus that component of the money stock attributable to expansion of domestic credit.

The balance sheet identity is the jumping-off point for the monetary theory of the balance of payments, which we will study in Chapter 10. Its essential message is that a balance-of-payments deficit with negative ΔR implies that domestic credit is expanding too rapidly relative to the demand for money. A surplus implies the opposite. Thus the monetary theory suggests that chronic deficits are generally associated with excessively rapid domestic credit expansion, such as might be caused by government budget deficits, and that the solution to a balance-of-payments problem lies in more effective control of domestic credit expansion, including that component due to bank-financed budget deficits.

For 1984 the monetary survey of the United States appeared as in Table 3.1. Over 80 percent of the domestic credit was extended to the private sector and was split fairly evenly between business and consumer credit. Government claimed the rest, with the federal government receiving over twice the credit extended to state and local governments. The narrowly defined money supply, M_1, consists of coin, Federal Reserve notes, and checking deposits. Quasi money consists of repurchase agreements, Eurodollars, money market mutual funds, and saving and time deposits.

TABLE 3.1   MONETARY SURVEY: UNITED STATES, 1984
(billions of dollars)

Assets		Liabilities	
Net foreign assets	37.7	Money (M_1)	570.4
Domestic credit	2,917.3	Quasi money	1,690.4
federal govt.	388.3	Other liabilities	694.2
state + local	170.9		
private	2,358.9		
Total assets	2,955.0	Total liabilities	2,955.0

Source: IMF, International Financial Statistics, 1985.

Export demand is a component of overall expenditure. Imports are an addition to domestic output as a source of supply. Consequently, the balance of payments is intimately linked to the national income and product accounts of the nation. Aggregate expenditure, E, may be written

$$E = C + I + G + X \qquad (3.2)$$

where C is aggregate consumption, including import consumption, I is net planned or intended investment, G is government purchases of goods and services, and X is the level of exports. We stipulate that these aggregates are presently defined in real (constant purchasing power) terms, so they would have to be multiplied by an index of the price level, p, to convert them into nominal or current dollar terms.

The total supply of available resources equals the nation's production, Y, plus imports, V. When the economy is in equilibrium, expenditures must equal the value of production plus import supplies. Therefore, using (3.2), we have

$$Y + V = C + I + G + X$$

which is usually written as

$$Y = C + I + G + (X - V) \qquad (3.3)$$

Consequently, when national income is in equilibrium, national income equals domestic absorption, $C + I + G$, plus net exports. Therefore, (3.3) can be written

$$Y = A + (X - V) \qquad (3.4)$$

as discussed in Chapter 2. It can readily be seen from (3.4) that to increase net exports to eliminate a current-account deficit, either domestic absorption must be reduced or national production must be raised without raising absorption. Thus (3.4) suggests an alternative to the monetary approach to the balance of payments, which emphasizes the importance of containing aggregate domestic expenditure.

When national income is in equilibrium, total expenditures must equal total income receipts. This implies that if there is an individual sector of the economy that spends more than its income, the resultant sectoral deficit must be matched by a corresponding surplus in some other sector. In Chapter 1 we saw that this fact is crucial for understanding how the trade deficit is related to the government budget deficit. To repeat briefly, note that national income can be divided into consumption, saving, and taxes:

$$Y = C + S_p + T \qquad (3.5)$$

where S_p is private saving, and T stands for all taxes minus government transfer payments. Combining this with (3.4) to make expenditure equal income gives

$$C + I + G + (X - V) = C + S_p + T$$

On rearranging this slightly, we get

$$G - T = [(C + S_p) - (C + I)] + (V - X) \qquad (3.6)$$

The term $C + S_p$ is the income of the private sector, and $C + I$ is the sector's expenditure. The difference between the two therefore is the private-sector surplus of income over spending and equals $S_p - I$. The term $G - T$ is the government budget deficit, and $V - X$ is the surplus of the foreign sector. The value of imports, V, represents the foreign sector's receipts, and exports represent its expenditures in the domestic economy. A trade deficit therefore implies a foreign-sector surplus.

Notice from (3.6) that, since consumption can be canceled from the expression, it may be written in the usual way as

$$(G - T) = (S_p - I) + (V - X) \qquad (3.7)$$

so the private-sector surplus may be viewed as the excess of private saving over planned investment.

From (3.7) it can be seen that an increase in the government's budget deficit due to either a fall in T or a rise in G must be offset either by a reduction in investment relative to private saving or by an increase in the trade deficit. Either the private sector must reduce its expenditures relative to its income, or the foreign sector must do so. If there is an overall domestic deficit, absorption exceeds income, so there must be a trade deficit (a foreign-sector surplus) that supplies the additional goods needed to balance aggregate expenditure with income. In 1985 the sectoral deficits and surpluses, calculated as percentages of GNP, were as follows for the U.S. economy. The deficit of the government sector was 4.3 percent of GNP. This was compensated by a surplus of saving relative to investment of 1.2 percent of GNP and a trade deficit of 3.2 percent of GNP. Thus the bulk of the budget deficit was compensated by a huge surplus of receipts over expenditure by the foreign sector. Had there been no increase in the trade deficit, the rise in the government's deficit would have had to have been offset by an increase in the private-sector surplus. Investment would have had to be driven down by higher interest rates, or saving would have had to rise as the result of income expansion.

3.2 THE U.S. BALANCE OF PAYMENTS

Table 3.2 shows the U.S. balance of payments for 1984. Beginning at the top, it can be seen that merchandise exports of $219.9 billion (line 1) were swamped by imports of $334.0 billion (line 2), implying a merchandise deficit of $114.1 billion (line 3). This deficit is popularly known as the trade deficit. It is reported monthly and never fails to make the news or evoke adverse commentary.

The U.S. earned $87.6 billion in interest and dividends from its foreign investments (line 4). However, foreigners earned $68.5 billion from their investments in the U.S. (line 5), giving net investment income of $19.1 billion (line 6). Net investment income reached its maximum value of $34.1 billion in 1981. However, since that time huge current-account deficits have greatly increased U.S. IOUs owned by foreigners, with the result that outpayments have increased sharply. In 1980, outpayments of interest and dividends were $42.1 billion, but this increased to $68.5 billion in 1984.

Lines 8 and 9 report service income. The outpayments include U.S. payments for insurance, transportation, tourism, and miscellaneous services purchased from foreigners.

The sum of the items from lines 1 to 9 gives the balance on goods and services of $95.9 billion (line 10). This total comes very close to the net exports total of the national income and product accounts. However, note that this differs from the way the term "net exports" was earlier defined for the purposes of the analysis of this book. Our concept of net exports includes all current-account items other than investment income. The reason for doing this is that investment income needs to be singled out for separate treatment from the other current-account items, because *Why?* the factors that determine investment income are different from the factors that underlie the other current-account items.

TABLE 3.2   U.S. INTERNATIONAL TRANSACTIONS, 1984
[billions of dollars, credits (+), debits (−)]

	Credits	Debits	Net
Current transactions			
Merchandise			
1. Exports	+219.9		
2. Imports		−334.0	
3. Merchandise balance			−114.1
Investment income			
4. Receipts	+87.6		
5. Payments		−68.5	
6. Net investment income			+19.1
7. Net military transactions		−1.8	
8. Net travel and transportation		−9.0	
9. Other services	+9.8		
10. Balance on goods and services			−95.9
11. Unilateral transfers			−11.4
12. Balance on current account			−107.4
Capital transactions			
Private			
13. Increase in U.S. private assets abroad (outflow)			−11.8
14. Increase in foreign assets in U.S. (inflow)	+93.9		
Government			
15. U.S. official reserves		−3.1	
16. Other U.S. government		−5.5	
17. Foreign reserves	+3.4		
18. Statistical discrepancy	+30.5		
Balance	+445.1	−445.1	0

Source: Department of Commerce, Bureau of Economic Analysis, reproduced as Table B-98 in the *Economic Report of the President*, 1986.

In 1984, unilateral transfers represented a debit item of $11.4 billion (line 11). Such transfers consist of gifts, remittances, and pensions by U.S. citizens and firms to foreign residents. The addition of this item to the balance on goods and services gives the current-account deficit of $107.4 billion.

The current-account deficit represents the excess of outpayments over current receipts. A negative total implies that foreigners were extending credit to the United States, so U.S. net indebtedness to foreigners must have increased by this amount. This fact should be reflected in the capital account, which is shown in lines (13–17). In 1984, U.S. residents acquired foreign earning assets of $11.8 billion (line 13). However, the massive current-account deficit caused foreign private claims against the U.S. to increase by $93.9 billion (line 14). Thus there was a net private capital inflow of $82.1 billion. Total U.S. reserves declined $8.6 billion (lines 15 and 16) while foreign reserves increased $3.4 billion. This leaves a discrepancy of $30.5 billion between the current-account deficit and the surplus in the capital account. Since, in theory, inpayments equal outpayments, the balance of payments must balance, so it is necessary to add a statistical discrepancy (line 18) of $30.5 billion. This discrepancy has been quite large since about 1979 and is a cause for concern because it could mean that either exports have been underestimated or imports have been overestimated and that the current account may not have been as weak as it appears. The Commerce Department attempts to measure each international transaction twice. For example, information about export transactions is obtained directly from the exporter who shipped the merchandise and from the bank through which payment was made. In theory the value of the transactions should equal the value of payments. But in fact there are errors in reporting and measurement, so the statistical discrepancy must be entered.

Table 3.3 presents a capsule summary of the developments of the U.S. balance of payments since 1955. Current-account surpluses were regularly run between 1955 and 1970 as merchandise exports exceeded imports and positive net investment income was earned. However, these current-account surpluses were to a large extent offset by continuing cap-

TABLE 3.3 DEVELOPMENT OF THE U.S. BALANCE OF PAYMENTS, 1955–1984

	1955	1960	1965	1970	1972	1980	1984
1. Current surplus	+0.4	+2.8	+5.4	+2.3	−5.8	+1.9	−107.4
2. Merchandise	+2.9	+4.9	+5.0	+2.6	−6.4	−25.5	−114.1
3. Investment income	+2.7	+3.4	+5.3	+6.2	+8.2	+30.4	+19.1
			Capital account				
4. Net inflow (+)	NA	−3.9	−6.2	−5.4	+7.0	−19.9	+80.0
5. U.S. official reserves	NA	+2.1	+1.2	+2.4	0	−8.2	−3.1

Source: Department of Commerce, Bureau of Economic Analysis, reproduced as Table B-98 in the *Economic Report of the President,* 1986.

ital outflows (line 4), as U.S. investors acquired foreign earning assets and established overseas subsidiaries. The balance of payments deteriorated sharply between 1970 and 1972. A merchandise trade deficit appeared for the first time in 1971, which then rose to $6.4 billion in 1972, and the capital outflow experienced since World War II shifted dramatically to an inflow of $7.0 billion. This was the period of crisis for the Bretton Woods system, which led to the dollar devaluations of 1971 and 1973 and culminated in the abandonment of the fixed exchange-rate commitment by the European Economic Community in early 1973.

During the 1970s U.S. trade performance remained weak, as deficits were run in all years except 1973 and 1975. For the most part these deficits were offset by rapidly rising investment income, although current-account deficits of $14.5 billion and $15.5 billion were run in 1977 and 1978. By 1980 the merchandise trade deficit had reached $25.5 billion but was offset by investment income of $30.4 billion. There then followed the massive deterioration of the current account discussed in Chapter 1. As interest rates rose in the United States and foreign capital flooded in ($80 billion in 1984), the dollar appreciated, thereby causing imports to rise sharply while exports decreased, bringing the merchandise trade deficit to $114.1 billion in 1984. Notice that net investment income dropped between 1980 and 1984. This fact reflects the large increase in foreign holdings of the U.S. IOUs that are accumulated as the result of the current-account deficit. Continuation of such a deficit implies even less investment income available to finance trade deficits in the future.

3.3 BEHIND THE BALANCE-OF-PAYMENTS EQUATION

In Section 3.1 we saw that there are several ways to approach a balance-of-payments problem. One way is the *absorption* approach, which emphasizes the need to contain absorption to eliminate a balance-of-payments deficit. An alternative way is the *monetary* approach, which emphasizes the need to contain domestic credit expansion. It is hardly surprising that much effort has gone into exploring the relative superiority of the various approaches and in attempts to reconcile them. That is why we need Part III. Chapter 9 explores the absorption approach, Chapter 10 discusses the monetary approach, and Chapter 11 discusses the modern *asset-market* approach, which does a fair job of reconciling the other approaches.

Meanwhile, let us return to the balance-of-payments equation to see where Part II fits in. Combining (3.1) with the balance sheet identity, we get

$$(X - V + i^*F) + K = \Delta R = \Delta M - \Delta D \qquad (3.8)$$

In thinking about export demand, we might expect exports to depend largely on foreign business activity and on the competitiveness of exports as measured by the real exchange rate ep^*/p. Imports will tend to rise if domestic national income, Y, rises and if domestic goods become less competitive relative to imports, as indicated by a decline in the real exchange rate. A first approximation to a hypothesis about capital inflows suggests that capital movements respond to domestic-foreign interest rate differentials, $i - i^*$. Similarly, on the right-hand side of the equation it is clear that changes in the demand for money are crucial in explaining a deficit or a surplus. These changes probably depend on changes in interest rates, income, and prices. Consequently, linking up the balance of payments to the domestic economy is essential. We have to know how income, interest rates, and price levels are determined if we are to study the balance of payments effectively. Conversely, the balance of payments will affect variables such as p, Y, and i. Studying these interrelationships is taken up in Part II. Note, finally, that Y, i, and p will be affected by domestic monetary and fiscal policies, so these policies will also have important effects on the balance of payments.

QUESTIONS FOR REVIEW

1. What is the essential distinction between the current account of the balance of payments and the capital account?

2. In what sense must the balance of payments balance?

3. The U.S. dollar appreciated sharply over the period 1980–85, causing a current-account deficit. Many economists believe that restoration of current-account equilibrium will necessitate a depreciation of the dollar that exceeds the amount of the appreciation. What are the reasons for this?

4. What is the significance of a current-account deficit? What does it have to do with foreign debt?

5. The monetary approach to the balance of payments emphasizes that elimination of a balance-of-payments deficit requires a reduction in the rate of monetary growth. The absorption approach emphasizes the need to reduce absorption relative to national income. What are the intuitive reasons for these views? As we will learn later, both approaches cast doubts about the

efficacy of exchange rate devaluation in curing a deficit. Can you develop the reasons for such doubt?

SUGGESTIONS FOR FURTHER READING

Principal Data Sources

U.S. Council of Economic Advisers, *Economic Report of the President,* statistical appendices, published annually.

U.S. Department of Commerce, *Survey of Current Business,* published monthly.

Organization for Economic Cooperation and Development, *Economic Outlook.*

United Nations, *Monthly Bulletin of Statistics.*

Other References

Ingram, James C., *International Economics,* Wiley, 1983, chaps. 2, 3.

Williamson, John, *The Open Economy and the World Economy,* Basic Books, 1983, chap. 7.

MACROECONOMIC VARIABLES IN THE OPEN ECONOMY

Part Two integrates closed-economy macroeconomics with the realities of the modern financially open economy. Chapters 4 and 5 both begin with the closed economy for purposes of reference and review, and then open the economy to trade in Chapter 4 and to finance in Chapter 5.

Chapter 4 expands conventional multiplier analysis, beginning with the closed economy, then moving to an open economy with induced imports and autonomous exports, proceeding then to make exports depend on foreign income so that a two-country analysis is needed, and finally finishing with a multicountry foreign trade multiplier table.

Chapter 5 begins by reviewing the familiar closed-economy IS-LM model for purposes of review and reference. It then incorporates exports and imports into the IS function and international money flows into the LM function, and it introduces the foreign balance function. Then balance-of-payments adjustment is studied in a way that incorporates the interactions between fluctuating national income and interest rates with the balance of payments.

Chapter 6 provides a taxonomy of the effects of monetary and fiscal policies on income levels, interest rates, and the balance of payments in domestic and foreign economies under both fixed and flexible exchange rates with alternative capital mobility assumptions. That analysis lays the groundwork for a discussion of policy coordination designed to minimize disruptions to foreign economies and macroeconomic retaliation by these economies. An attempt is therefore made to spell out the appropriate ingredients for good-neighbor macroeconomics in a way that might be termed the golden rule of macroeconomic behavior—that is, conduct your monetary-fiscal policies in consideration of others, as you would have others conduct their policies in consideration of you.

The first three chapters of Part Two analyze various aspects of the demand side of economies. Chapter 7 adds the supply side. Aggregate demand and supply curves are derived, thereby permitting explicit determination of price levels along with real income levels. The effects of countries' wage policies are examined, and it is shown how supply-side factors affect balance-of-payments adjustment.

Appendixes to Chapters 4, 5, and 6 may be found at the end of Part Two. These appendixes have been designed to demonstrate the validity of, or prove, the propositions developed in the text. They also provide instruction in the techniques of comparative static and dynamic analysis. Students with little background in mathematics can nevertheless study these appendixes, since instruction in the necessary mathematical techniques is provided, or they can omit the appendixes with the confidence that the bulk of the analytical material is also provided in the text. However, we encourage students to try them out. If they intend to go on to higher levels of difficulty in macroeconomics, either because they wish to study the technical literature or to conduct their own research, they will have little choice but to develop some skill in the rudimentary techniques of analysis. The mathematical topics are not difficult; they require only some rudimentary knowledge of differential calculus, linear algebra, and differential and difference equations.

Income Transmission and Foreign Trade Multipliers

4.1 THE CLOSED ECONOMY: A REVIEW

The famous English philosopher-economist David Hume is credited with developing the first systematic theory of the adjustment of the balance of payments. Hume reasoned that a deficit country under the gold standard would suffer a loss of gold to surplus countries. The gold outflow reduces the supply of money, and this acts to reduce the deficit country's price level. The opposite happens in surplus countries. As a consequence, the deficit country would become more competitive in international trade, the surplus countries would become less competitive, and the deficit would turn into a surplus, at which point the gold flow would be reversed. Thus, argued Hume, balance-of-payments deficits and surpluses tend to be automatically self-correcting. This theory is known as the classical *price-specie flow theory.*

During the 1920s a number of studies, under the direction of Professor Frank Taussig of Harvard, investigated the balance-of-payments behavior of different countries. These studies all found that current-account adjustment takes place far more rapidly than could be explained by the rather slow adjustment of national price levels. The paradox was not fully resolved until the publication, in 1936, of John Maynard Keynes's famous book, *The General Theory of Employment, Interest, and Money.*[1] Although dealing with a closed economy, Keynes introduced the important idea that national income could not always be expected

[1] Keynes, John Maynard, *The General Theory of Employment, Interest, and Money,* Harcourt, Brace, London, 1936.

to equilibrate at full employment and that many variables, such as consumption, are primarily determined by the level of income.

From there it was but a short step for Joan Robinson, Fritz Machlup, and Lloyd Metzler, among others to recognize that imports tended to fluctuate in response to income changes, and from there it was possible to deduce a more rapid and powerful source of balance-of-payments adjustment. If country 1's exports increase due to a change in foreign tastes, argued the new view, its balance of payments would move into surplus. However, the rise in exports would stimulate activity in export industries and then spread throughout the economy via the Keynesian multiplier process. But the resulting increase in national income would also stimulate imports, thereby quickly eliminating a part of the initial surplus even without price-level changes.

This chapter studies this process of income adjustment and its effect on the balance of payments. It abstracts from relative price changes and therefore assumes that neither national price levels nor exchange rates are permitted to vary. It further assumes that investment and international capital movements are autonomous and that interest rates are constant. Finally, it assumes that economies are operating below full employment so that real income levels are free to fluctuate in response to changes in aggregate expenditure.

We begin with a review of income determination and multiplier analysis in a closed economy. The discussion moves rapidly and does not cover all the fine points. Those who are unfamiliar with this turf should consult the relevant portions of a collateral macroeconomics text.[2]

In a closed economy, aggregate expenditure, E, consists of consumption, C, planned or intended investment, I, and government purchases of goods and services, G. Therefore aggregate expenditure may be written as

$$E = C + I + G \qquad (4.1)$$

where, by virtue of the fixed price-level assumption, these are all real magnitudes.

For macroeconomic equilibrium to be achieved in this economy, aggregate expenditure must equal national income, Y. If $E > Y$ there is not enough production to meet demand. Goods must therefore be withdrawn from inventory. Since that cannot persist for long, there is an incentive to raise production until Y catches up with E. The opposite happens when $E < Y$. In that case unwanted inventories pile up, providing an incentive to cut back production until income and output are sufficient

---

[2] For example, see Dernburg, *Macroeconomics,* 7th ed., chaps. 4, 5.

to meet demand. Consequently, we can state the equilibrium condition as

$$E = Y \tag{4.2}$$

or, on using (4.1) and (4.2),

$$Y = C + I + G \tag{4.3}$$

The situation is illustrated in Figure 4.1, which measures expenditures on the vertical axis and income (or output) on the horizontal axis. The 45° line is a guideline along which aggregate expenditure equals income. The curve C measures aggregate consumption expenditure, and its upward slope reflects the Keynesian hypothesis that consumption is an increasing function of income. Expressed in the form of a linear equation, we can write the *consumption function* as

$$C = C_a + b(Y - T) \qquad 0 < b < 1 \tag{4.4}$$

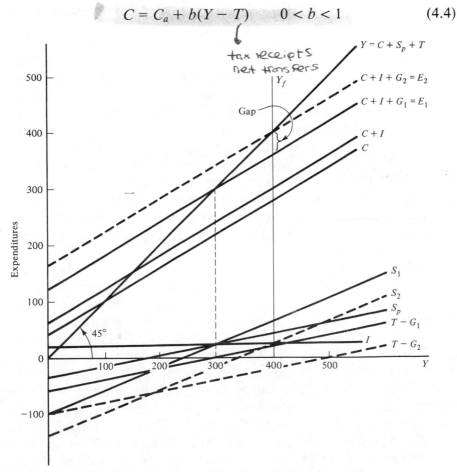

Figure 4.1 Income determination in a closed economy.

where C_a is called autonomous consumption. It is the vertical intercept of the C function and has a value of 40 in the example shown in Figure 4.1. The symbol T represents taxes net of government transfer payments. Then, $Y - T$ equals personal disposable income (i.e., income after taxes). The parameter b is called the marginal propensity to consume. It measures the increase in consumption that accompanies a $1 increase in disposable income.

We assume in this example that all taxes are income taxes and that the yield from taxes is proportional to income. Therefore, the tax function may be written

$$T = tY \qquad 0 < t < 1 \tag{4.5}$$

where t is the marginal tax rate. When the tax function is substituted into the consumption function (4.4), the consumption function becomes

$$C = C_a + b(1 - t)Y \qquad \tag{4.6}$$

Thus the slope of the consumption function is $b(1 - t)$. In the example shown in Figure 4.1 it is assumed that the tax rate is 20 percent and that the marginal propensity to consume is 0.75. Under these assumptions a rise in national income of $1 increases tax collections by $0.20. Therefore disposable income rises by $0.80 $(1 - t)$, and of this increase 0.75, or $0.60 $[b(1 - t)]$, is spent on consumption while the remainder is the increase in private saving. Clearly, the increase in consumption is $b(1 - t)$, and the increase in private saving is $(1 - b)(1 - t)$. The quantity $(1 - b)$ is the marginal propensity to save disposable income.

Planned investment, I, and government purchases are assumed to be autonomous, as reflected in the $C + I$ and $C + I + G_1$ functions parallel to C. In the numerical example in Figure 4.1, $I = 20$ and $G_1 = 60$.

The aggregate expenditure function is $E_1 = C + I + G_1$. It cuts the 45° line at an income level of 300, which is the equilibrium level, since that is where aggregate expenditures equal income. If producers were excessively optimistic and produced at 400, the consumption level associated with $Y = 400$ would be 280. Adding I of 20 and G of 60 to 280 gives aggregate expenditure of 360. Since production of 400 exceeds aggregate expenditure of 360, there would be unintended investment (accumulation) in inventories of 40, which would then lead to a reduction in output and income to reduce surplus stocks. Conversely, if producers are excessively pessimistic and produce only 200, consumption would be 160 and aggregate expenditure would be 240, so inventories would be unintentionally reduced by 40. To rebuild stocks and meet demand, producers must raise output and income. Clearly, then, 300 is the income level toward which the economy will gravitate. That is the only level where expenditures equal output, and there is no unintentional accumulation or decumulation of inventories.

It is easy enough to find the equilibrium level of income using (4.3) and (4.6). Substitute (4.6) into (4.3) to get

$$Y = C_a + b(1 - t)Y + I + G$$

Solving for Y gives

$$Y = \frac{1}{1 - b(1 - t)} (C_a + I + G) \tag{4.7}$$

or, numerically,

Alternative approach

$$Y = \frac{1}{1 - 0.75(1 - 0.2)} (40 + 20 + 60) = \frac{120}{0.4} = 300$$

The equilibrium condition can be stated in an alternative way that we will find useful throughout this book. The receipt of income can either be spent on consumption, saved in the private sector, S_p, or used to pay taxes, T. Therefore

$$Y = C + S_p + T \tag{4.8}$$

Equating this with $C + I + G$ and subtracting consumption from both sides gives

$$I + G = S_p + T \tag{4.9}$$

where $I + G$ are nonconsumption expenditures often called *injections.* Similarly, S_p and T are unspent income, and their sum is called *leakages.* Thus, in equilibrium the injections must equal the leakages.

Next subtract G from both sides of (4.9). This gives

$$I = S_p + (T - G) = S \tag{4.10}$$

where S_p is private saving, $T - G$ is the budget surplus, or government saving, so that S is total national saving, private and public. Planned investment therefore must equal total national saving as a condition of equilibrium in a closed economy.

These relationships are also shown in Figure 4.1. The I schedule is simply a line parallel to the horizontal axis having a value of 20 at all income levels. Since the tax function is $T = tY$, and G is autonomous, the budget surplus is

$$T - G = tY - G = 0.2Y - 60 \tag{4.11}$$

which is shown as the $T - G_1$ function in the diagram, where its slope equals the tax rate and the negative intercept measures the government purchases of 60. The budget surplus rises as income rises, because higher income generates additional tax receipts. Private saving is the difference between consumption and disposable income. Therefore, using (4.5) and (4.6), we obtain

$$S_p = Y - T - C = Y - tY - C_a - b(1 - t)Y$$

$$= -C_a + (1 - b)(1 - t)Y \tag{4.12}$$

and, numerically,

$$S_p = -40 + (0.25)(0.8)Y = -40 + 0.2Y$$

Finally, total national saving is

$$S = S_p + (T - G) = -C_a + (1 - b)(1 - t)Y + tY - G$$

$$= -C_a - G + [1 - b(1 - t)]Y$$

and, numerically,

$$S = -40 - 60 + [1 - 0.75(0.8)]Y = -100 + 0.4Y$$

which is the S_1 curve in Figure 4.1. Notice that $I = S$ at an income level of 300. Thus, the two ways of identifying the equilibrium level of income are identical.

Since investment must equal national saving in equilibrium,

$$I = -C_a - G + [1 - b(1 - t)]Y$$

it again follows that

$$Y = \frac{1}{1 - b(1 - t)} (C_a + I + G) = 300 \tag{4.13}$$

To summarize: At the equilibrium level of income of 300, taxes equal 60, so disposable income equals 240. Consumption is 220. Adding investment of 20 and government purchases of 60 gives $220 + 20 + 60 = 300$. Since $T = G = 60$, the government budget is balanced and government saving is zero. Private saving is the difference between disposable income and consumption, so $240 - 220 = 20$, which equals investment. In other words,

$$I = S_p + (T - G) \qquad 20 = 20 + (60 - 60)$$

Next suppose that its stock of capital and labor force would permit this economy to produce real income of 400. Thus the full-employment level of income, Y_f, is 400, as shown by the vertical line erected at $Y = 400$. At an income of 400, consumption would be 280, so on adding investment of 20 and government purchases of 60, we see that aggregate expenditure at $Y_f = 400$ is 360. In order to reach an income of 400, aggregate expenditure would also have to be 400. Consequently, there is an aggregate expenditure shortfall of 40, which is usually referred to as the *deflationary gap.*

To make up the shortfall, the government may wish to raise G by 40 to a new level of 100. This raises aggregate expenditure to E_2 and lowers the $T - G$ and S functions by 40. Therefore the new equilibrium level of income is 400. Thus, income rises by 100 in response to an increase in aggregate expenditure of 40. Apparently a rise in G raises national income by a multiplied value of 2.5, since the rise in Y is 2.5 times the rise in G.

We can see several ways why this happens. First consider (4.7). If we change G by ΔG and hold the other autonomous expenditures constant, we obtain

$$\Delta Y = \frac{1}{1 - b(1 - t)} \Delta G \qquad (4.14)$$

where ΔY is the change in income. The multiplier is the ratio of the change in income to the change in government purchases that brought the change in income about. It therefore is given by $\Delta Y / \Delta G$, which can be seen from (4.14) to be

$$\frac{\Delta Y}{\Delta G} = \frac{1}{1 - b(1 - t)} = \frac{1}{1 - 0.75(0.8)} = 2.5 \qquad (4.15)$$

Notice, in passing, that the equilibrium level of income equals the multiplier times the sum of the autonomous expenditure components, or, in the new equilibrium, $Y = 2.5(40 + 20 + 100) = 400$.

The reason we get a multiplier effect is that the added production of 40 needed to satisfy the higher level of government spending generates additional income equal to the rise in G. But that, in turn, raises disposable income, which, in turn, raises consumption. This means that production has to be raised again to satisfy the higher level of consumer demand. But this causes the process to repeat itself in successive rounds until the time arrives when production catches up to aggregate expenditure. The ability to catch up and reach a new equilibrium requires that successive expenditure increases be less than the income increases that brought them about. This will happen as long as the national marginal propensity to save, $1 - b(1 - t)$, is positive.

To see why the multiplier takes on the value given in (4.15), we can reason using the equilibrium conditions. We know that in equilibrium $Y = C + I + G$. Therefore, if I is held constant,

$$\Delta Y = \Delta C + \Delta G \qquad (4.16)$$

that is, the change in income must equal the change in consumption plus the change in government purchases. The change in disposable income must be $\Delta Y - \Delta T = (1 - t) \Delta Y$. The change in consumption is the marginal propensity to consume times the change in disposable income. Therefore $\Delta C = b(1 - t) \Delta Y$. Substituting this into (4.16), we get,

$$\Delta Y = b(1 - t) \Delta Y + \Delta G$$

from which it follows that

$$\frac{\Delta Y}{\Delta G} = \frac{1}{1 - b(1 - t)} = \frac{1}{1 - 0.75(0.8)} = 2.5$$

Another way to look at it

Similarly, since it must be true in equilibrium that investment equals national saving, that is,

$$I = S_p + (T - G)$$

it follows that if I is unchanged,

$$0 = \Delta S_p + \Delta T - \Delta G \qquad (4.17)$$

From the tax function we know that $\Delta T = t \Delta Y$. Since the change in disposable income is $(1 - t) \Delta Y$ and the change in consumption is $\Delta C = b(1 - t) \Delta Y$, the change in S_p must be

$$\Delta S_p = \Delta Y - \Delta T - \Delta C = (1 - t) \Delta Y - b(1 - t) \Delta Y$$

$$= (1 - b)(1 - t) \Delta Y$$

Using these results in (4.17), we get

$$0 = (1 - b)(1 - t) \Delta Y + t \Delta Y - \Delta G,$$

from which it again follows that

$$\frac{\Delta Y}{\Delta G} = \frac{1}{1 - b(1 - t)} = 2.5$$

In inspecting the expression for the multiplier, observe that the multiplier rises with a rise in the marginal propensity to consume. This occurs because a higher marginal propensity to consume implies that a larger fraction of any income increase is spent on consumption. Similarly, an increase in the tax rate lowers the multiplier, because a higher tax rate implies that a larger fraction of any income increase is siphoned off in taxes, leaving a smaller increase in disposable income and therefore consumption.

As can be seen in Figure 4.1, in the new equilibrium $Y = 400$. With a tax rate of 20 percent, taxes equal 80 and disposable income equals

320. Since government purchases have risen to $G = 100$, there is now a budget deficit of 20. The rise in G has thrown the budget into deficit, but not by as much as ΔG, because the rise in income raises additional tax revenue for the government. Since disposable income is 320, consumption equals 280. Adding I of 20 and G of 100, we find that aggregate expenditure of 400 equals income of 400. Private saving is the difference between disposable income and consumption, and it therefore equals 40. Total national saving, which equals private saving plus the budget deficit, is 20, which exactly equals planned investment. All of these results are corroborated in Figure 4.1.

In the next section we will consolidate private and government saving into a single national saving function, where

$$S = S_p + (T - G)$$

As we have already seen,

$$S = -C_a - G + [1 - b(1 - t)]Y$$

so the slope of the national saving function is $1 - b(1 - t)$. Henceforth, we will denote this parameter by s:

$$s = 1 - b(1 - t)$$

which measures the increase in national saving (private and public) that accompanies a $1 rise in national income. The symbols b and t are both positive fractions, so s will also be a positive fraction. Note that s could still be a positive fraction if the marginal propensity to consume is greater than 1, if the tax rate is sufficiently high.

Finally, note that a rise in government purchases shifts the national saving function down and therefore raises national income. On the other hand, a rise in the tax rate rotates the national saving function in a counterclockwise manner, raising its slope, and therefore lowering national income as well as the multiplier.

4.2 INCOME DETERMINATION IN THE OPEN ECONOMY WITH AUTONOMOUS EXPORTS

We now open the economy to foreign trade by including exports, X, and imports, V, in the model. Imports add to the supply of domestically produced goods, and exports are an addition to aggregate expenditure. Therefore, in the expression $Y = C + I + G$, we now add imports to Y and exports to $C + I + G$ to obtain

$$V + Y = C + I + G + X$$

as the new equilibrium condition. It is customary to move V to the right-hand side, so

$$Y = C + I + G + (X - V) \tag{4.18}$$

where $X - V$ is the level of net exports. Since it is still true that $Y = C + S_p + T$, we also have

$$I + G + X = S_p + T + V$$

where exports are now an additional injection while imports are an additional leakage. A dollar spent on exports has the equivalent income-generating effect as a dollar spent on investment or government purchases, and imports are a leakage from the domestic spending stream just as savings and taxes are.

Rearranging the preceding expression, we get

$$I = S_p + (T - G) + (V - X)$$

or

$$I = S + (V - X)$$

where $V - X$ is the trade deficit, sometimes called the surplus of the foreign sector, just as $T - G$ is the surplus of the government sector.

Imports, like consumption and taxes, are a function of income. When income rises, consumers increase their purchases of foreign finished goods and their tourist expenditures. Domestic businesses increase their use of foreign energy, raw materials, and semifinished goods, and they may also import more machine tools as part of their investment programs. Even government purchases may have some import content if the economy relies on foreign energy and raw material sources. For these reasons we may write the import function as

$$V = V_a + mY \qquad 0 < m < 1 \tag{4.19}$$

where V_a is the autonomous component of imports and m is the marginal propensity to import.

Since the country's exports are other countries' imports, exports will depend on foreign income levels. However, for the moment we assume that exports are autonomous. This is sometimes called the "small-country" assumption, because it implies that developments in the domestic economy are so insignificant relative to the rest of the world that a rise in the small country's imports will have so little effect on foreign income levels that any change in foreign imports will be insignificant.

Figure 4.2 shows the effect of the introduction of imports. At the

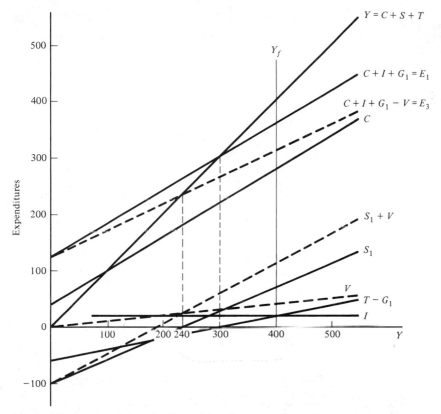

Figure 4.2 Income determination with endogenous imports.

outset there is no trade, and aggregate expenditure, E_1, cuts the 45° line at $Y = 300$. Similarly, investment equals national saving (S_1) at that income level, and the budget is balanced with $T = G = 60$.

Suppose that at each income level 10 percent of income is diverted toward imports. The import function is therefore

$$V = mY = 0.10Y \qquad (4.20)$$

as shown by the V line in Figure 4.2, where the slope of the line measures the marginal propensity to import, m. Since imports are a leakage, they should be added to the S schedule to get the total leakage schedule, $S_1 + V$. Using (4.13) from the last section, we get

$$S_1 + V = -C_a - G + sY + mY = -C_a - G + (s + m)Y \qquad (4.21)$$

and, numerically,

$$S_1 + V = -100 + (0.4 + 0.1)Y = -100 + 0.5Y$$

It is important to bear in mind that the slope of $S_1 + V$ is $s + m$, the national marginal propensity to save plus the marginal propensity to import.

The new $S_1 + V$ schedule cuts the I schedule at an income of 240. Thus the diversion of expenditures to the purchase of foreign goods lowers the level of income. Since

$$I = S + (V - X)$$

is the requirement for equilibrium, it follows from (4.3) and (4.20) that

$$I = -C_a - G + sY + mY - X$$

Hence,

$$Y = \frac{1}{s + m}(C_a + I + G + X) \qquad (4.22)$$

or, numerically,

$$Y = \frac{1}{0.4 + 0.1}(40 + 20 + 60 + 0) = \frac{120}{0.5} = 240$$

The result confirms Figure 4.2 in showing that the equilibrium level of income is 240.

The economy still spends according to the original aggregate expenditure function E_1. But now a fraction of this expenditure is no longer spent domestically. Therefore when we subtract imports from aggregate expenditure, we arrive at the new aggregate domestic expenditure function E_3. It measures expenditures on *domestic* goods. This curve cuts the 45° line at $Y = 240$, where domestic expenditure equals income.

The introduction of imports lowers the slope of the aggregate expenditure function in much the same way as an increase in the tax rate. Such a flattening of aggregate expenditure should be expected to lower the value of the multiplier. From (4.22) we can see that this has happened, since the multiplier now becomes

$$\frac{\Delta Y}{\Delta G} = \frac{\Delta Y}{\Delta I} = \frac{1}{s + m} \qquad (4.23)$$

The multiplier therefore becomes the reciprocal of the national marginal propensity to save plus the marginal propensity to import. Imports, like taxes, play a stabilizing role in the sense that they reduce the multipliers. As income rises and spending increases, some of the increased spending leaks abroad so that domestic expenditure expands by less than would otherwise have been the case.

At the new equilibrium of $Y = 240$, imports equal 24. Taxes equal 20 percent of income, or 48. With government purchases remaining at 60, the effect of the income shrinkage is to cause a budget deficit of 12. Disposable income, $Y - T$, is 192. The consumption function $C = 40 + 0.6Y$ establishes that $C = 184$. Add investment of 20, government purchases of 60, and subtract imports of 24 to see that aggregate expenditure is 240. That is,

$$E = Y = C + I + G + (X - V)$$
$$240 = 184 + 20 + 60 + (0 - 24)$$

Similarly, since

$$I = S + (V - X) \qquad S = S_p + (T - G)$$

we know that $T - G = 12$. Since disposable income is 192 and consumption is 184, private saving is 8. Consequently, $S = 8 - 12 = -4$, which when added to the excess of imports over exports of 24, just equals investment of 20. Everything is therefore consistent.

Adding exports to the problem is a simple matter, as shown in Figure 4.3, which reproduces the relevant parts of Figure 4.2. E_3 is reproduced in the upper part of the diagram. In the lower part the import function V and the $S_1 + V$ function are shown. Such functions as C, I, $T - G$, and S_1 are not shown, to prevent excessive clutter in the diagram.

Exports add to aggregate expenditure. If exports rise from 0 to 40, the aggregate expenditure function shifts up by 40, becoming E_4. Similarly, exports are shown as the X function in the lower part of the diagram. When investment is added, we obtain the $I + X$ schedule. Aggregate expenditure equals income at $Y = 320$, and $I + X$ also equals $S_1 + V$ at that income level.

The rise in income from 240 to 320 is 80, thereby implying a multiplier of 2. From (4.22) it is apparent that

$$\Delta Y = \frac{1}{s + m} \Delta X \qquad \Delta Y = \frac{1}{0.4 + 0.1}(40) = 2(40) = 80 \qquad (4.24)$$

In the new equilibrium $Y = 320$. Taxes equal 64, so disposable income equals 256 and consumption therefore equals 232. Adding investment of 20, government purchases of 60, exports of 40, and subtracting imports of 32 gives aggregate expenditure of 320. Similarly,

$$S = S_p + (T - G) = 24 + (64 - 60) = 28$$

and

$$I = S + (V + X) = 28 + (32 - 40) = 20$$

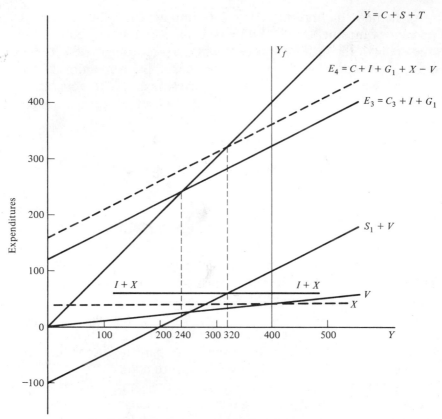

Figure 4.3 Effect on national income of a rise in exports.

Next consider the changes that took place from the old equilibrium ($Y = 240$) to the new equilibrium ($Y = 320$). The rise in income is 80, and the rise in taxes is 16. Therefore the rise in disposable income is 64, the rise in consumption is 48, and the rise in private saving is 16. The higher tax yield caused by the rise in income swings the budget from a deficit of 12 to a surplus of 4.

At the income level of 240, imports were 24 while exports were 0. The trade deficit was therefore 24. The rise in exports of 40 would produce a trade surplus of 16 ($40 - 24$) if income remains unchanged. However, because income rises in response to the rise in exports, imports increase by 8, so the trade surplus at $Y = 320$ is only 8 ($16 - 8$).

The key point to grasp is that a rise in autonomous exports will cause a trade surplus, but not by as much as the rise in exports, because income will increase and this automatically raises the level of imports. The extent to which induced imports offset the effect of the exogenous rise in exports depends on the value of the national marginal propensity to save. A lower marginal propensity to save implies a higher multiplier and therefore a greater level of induced imports. At the extreme, suppose the marginal propensity to save is zero. The export multiplier is

$$\Delta Y = \frac{1}{s + m} \Delta X$$

When $s = 0$, this becomes

$$\Delta Y = \frac{1}{m} \Delta X$$

so the multiplier becomes the reciprocal of the marginal propensity to import. In this event there are no domestic leakages, so income must rise by enough to raise imports to a level that equals the rise in exports. Since

$$\Delta V = m \, \Delta Y$$

it follows from the preceding expression that

$$\Delta V = \Delta X$$

This case is most unlikely to occur in practice, especially in the age of high marginal tax rates, because s can normally be expected to be positive. We therefore conclude that the adjustment of the trade balance to an autonomous change in exports will be only a partial adjustment.

4.3 ENDOGENOUS EXPORTS: A TWO-COUNTRY ANALYSIS

The next step is to drop the small-country assumption and treat exports as endogenous rather than autonomous. Since exports depend on foreign income levels, it is necessary also to account for the income levels of foreign countries. A convenient way to begin such an analysis is to split the world into two economies: the home country, country 1, and the rest of the world, country 2. The respective equilibrium conditions are

$$Y_1 = C_1 + I_1 + G_1 + (V_2 - V_1)$$

$$Y_2 = C_2 + I_2 + G_2 + (V_1 - V_2) \qquad (4.25)$$

where V_2 is country 2's imports and therefore country 1's exports. Similarly, V_1 is country 1's imports and country 2's exports.

Define the respective consumption and import functions as

$$C_1 = C_{a1} + (1 - s_1)Y_1 \qquad C_2 = C_{a2} + (1 - s_2)Y_2 \qquad (4.26.1)$$

$1 - s_1 = mpc$

$$V_1 = V_{a1} + m_1 Y_1 \qquad\qquad V_2 = V_{a2} + m_2 Y_2 \qquad (4.26.2)$$

Using these expressions to substitute in (4.25), we get the set of simultaneous linear equations

$$(s_1 + m_1)Y_1 - m_2 Y_2 \qquad\quad = E_1 \qquad (4.27.1)$$

$$-m_1 Y_1 + (s_2 + m_2)Y_2 = E_2 \qquad (4.27.2)$$

where E_1 and E_2 are the sums of all the autonomous expenditure components:

$$E_1 = I_1 + G_1 + C_{a1} + V_{a2} - V_{a1} \qquad (4.28.1)$$

$$E_2 = I_2 + G_2 + C_{a2} + V_{a1} - V_{a2} \qquad (4.28.2)$$

All symbols are as previously defined, with the subscripts 1 and 2 identifying the country.

The simultaneous equations (4.27) may be solved in a straightforward manner to yield equilibrium solutions for Y_1 and Y_2, namely,

$$Y_1 = \frac{s_2 + m_2}{D} E_1 + \frac{m_2}{D} E_2 \qquad (4.29.1)$$

$$Y_2 = \frac{m_1}{D} E_1 + \frac{s_1 + m_1}{D} E_2 \qquad (4.29.2)$$

where

$$D = (s_1 + m_1)(s_2 + m_2) - m_1 m_2 \qquad (4.30)$$

is positive for positive values of the parameters.

For a change in autonomous expenditure in country 1, the respective multipliers are

$$\frac{\Delta Y_1}{\Delta E_1} = \frac{s_2 + m_2}{D} \qquad \frac{\Delta Y_2}{\Delta E_1} = \frac{m_1}{D} \qquad (4.31.1)$$

Since D is positive, both countries enjoy an increase in income if $dE_1 > 0$. Notice that country 2's income rises, because a rise in Y_1 increases country 1's imports, thereby raising the exports and national income of country 2. Note also that the income change will be greatest in country 1 in the likely case that $s_2 + m_2 > m_1$. Therefore the rise in income will normally be greatest in the country in which the autonomous expenditure change occurs.

The multipliers with respect to a change in autonomous expenditure in country 2 are

$$\frac{\Delta Y_1}{\Delta E_2} = \frac{m_2}{D} \qquad \frac{\Delta Y_2}{\Delta E_2} = \frac{s_1 + m_1}{D} \qquad (4.32.1)$$

where again both income changes are positive, and the country in which the change in autonomous expenditures occurs enjoys the greater rise in income.

Now consider the effect of ΔE_1 on the net exports of the respective countries. Country 1's net exports are

$$NX_1 = V_2 - V_1$$

Assumes
$\Delta E_1 > 0$

so the change in net exports must be

$$\Delta NX_1 = \Delta V_2 - \Delta V_1$$

It follows from the import functions that $\Delta V_1 = m_1 \Delta Y_1$ and $\Delta V_2 = m_2 \Delta Y_2$, so on using (4.31.1), we obtain

$$\frac{\Delta NX_1}{\Delta E_1} = \frac{-m_1 s_2}{D} < 0 \qquad (4.33.1)$$

and

$$\frac{\Delta NX_2}{\Delta E_1} = \frac{m_1 s_2}{D} > 0 \qquad (4.33.2)$$

Country 1's net exports must decline, whereas country 2's must increase. Since there is no autonomous expenditure increase in country 2, its income level could not have risen without an increase in net exports.

Notice from (4.33) that there will be no change in net exports if s_2, country 2's marginal propensity to save, is zero. In this case the multipliers reduce to

$$\frac{\Delta Y_1}{\Delta E_1} = \frac{1}{s_1} \qquad \frac{\Delta Y_2}{\Delta E_1} = \frac{m_1}{s_1 m_2} \qquad (4.34)$$

Consequently, it appears that country 1's income rises by the reciprocal of her marginal propensity to save, as in the closed-economy case, and the adjustment of the trade balance is complete, since $\Delta NX_1 = 0$ in this case.

To understand this special case, we reason by use of the injections-leakages equilibrium condition. We know that for country 2, equilibrium requires

$$I_2 = S_2 + (V_2 - V_1)$$

so it must also be true that

$$\Delta I_2 = \Delta S_2 + \Delta V_2 - \Delta V_1$$

Since there were no autonomous changes in country 2, all changes must be induced. Therefore $\Delta I_2 = 0$, and

$$\Delta S_2 = \Delta V_1 - \Delta V_2$$

Explanation

But if country 2's marginal propensity to save is zero, $\Delta S_2 = 0$, so

$$\Delta V_1 = \Delta V_2$$

Evidently, then, as country 2 receives the stimulus caused by the rise in its exports, Y_2 expands; but since this induces no domestic savings, income must continue to rise until the increase in leakages, which in this case consists only of imports, matches the rise in injections.

In much the same way we can figure out what must have happened in country 1. The changes in its equilibrium magnitudes must be

$$\Delta I_1 = \Delta S_1 + \Delta V_1 - \Delta V_2$$

where we assume for convenience that $\Delta E_1 = \Delta I_1$. Since we already know that $\Delta V_1 = \Delta V_2$, it follows that

$$\Delta I_1 = \Delta S_1$$

as in the closed economy. Since $\Delta S_1 = s_1 \Delta Y_1$, it must be the case that

$$\frac{\Delta Y_1}{\Delta I_1} = \frac{1}{s_1}$$

which is the closed-economy multiplier for country 1, and is consistent with (4.34).

The next task is to consider the effects of an autonomous shift in exports or imports. Suppose there is a change in tastes that causes citizens of country 1 to switch from domestic goods to goods produced in country 2. Analytically, this implies $\Delta V_{a1} = -\Delta E_1$, and for country 2 it implies $\Delta V_{a1} = +\Delta E_2$. Therefore, in this case autonomous expenditures change in both countries, the change being negative for country 1 and positive for country 2. From (4.29) we see that

$$\Delta Y_1 = \frac{-s_2}{D} \Delta V_{a1} < 0 \qquad (4.35.1)$$

and

$$\Delta Y_2 = \frac{s_1}{D} \Delta V_{a1} > 0 \qquad (4.35.2)$$

Country 1's income declines because of the autonomous rise in imports, whereas country 2's income rises because of the autonomous rise in its exports. Notice from (4.35) that there would be no overall change in world income if the two countries had identical marginal propensities to save.

The change in country 1's net exports is

$$\Delta \text{NX}_1 = \Delta V_2 - \Delta V_1$$

From the import functions (4.26) we see that $\Delta V_2 = m_2 \Delta Y_2$, and $\Delta V_1 = \Delta V_{a1} + m_1 \Delta Y_1$. Therefore, using the solutions for the ΔY's (4.35), we get

$$\Delta NX_1 = \frac{m_2 s_1}{D} \Delta V_{a1} - \Delta V_{a1} + \frac{m_1 s_2}{D} \Delta V_{a1}$$

The term $(m_2 s_1/D) \Delta V_{a1}$ is the change in country 1's exports. This is positive because Y_2 rises; ΔV_{a1} is the positive autonomous change in imports; $(m_1 s_2/D) \Delta V_{a1}$ is the induced change in imports, which is negative because Y_1 drops. Gathering terms, we get

$$\Delta NX_1 = \left[\frac{m_2 s_1 + m_1 s_2}{D} - 1 \right] \Delta V_{a1} < 0$$

which is negative because $(m_2 s_1 + m_1 s_2)/D$ is a positive fraction.[3] Country 1's net exports decline even though both the induced effects on exports and imports work to offset the effect of the autonomous change.

If $s_2 = 0$, (4.35) shows that $\Delta Y_1 = 0$, $\Delta Y_2 = (1/m_2)\Delta V_{a1}$ and $\Delta NX_1 = 0$. The change in country 1's net exports is

$$\Delta NX_1 = \Delta V_2 - \Delta V_1$$

But $\Delta V_1 = \Delta V_{a1}$, since there is no induced reduction in imports because $\Delta Y_1 = 0$, and $\Delta V_2 = m_2 \Delta Y_2$, which also equals ΔV_{a1}. Therefore, when $s_2 = 0$, country 2's income rises by enough to raise its imports (country 1's exports) by enough to offset the autonomous increase in country 1's imports. Country 1 is therefore spared both income shrinkage and deterioration of its net export position.

If the situation is reversed and $s_1 = 0$, $\Delta Y_1 = (-1/m_1)\Delta V_a$, $\Delta Y_2 = 0$, and

$$\Delta NX_1 = \Delta V_2 - \Delta V_1 = 0 - \Delta V_{a1} - m_1 \Delta Y_1$$

But since $\Delta Y_1 = (-1/m_1) \Delta V_{a1}$, it follows that

$$\Delta NX_1 = -\Delta V_{a1} + \Delta V_{a1} = 0$$

---

[3] The term

$$\frac{m_2 s_1 + m_1 s_2}{D} = \frac{m_2 s_1 + m_1 s_2}{(s_1 + m_1)(s_2 + m_2) - m_1 m_2}$$

which, in turn, equals

$$\frac{m_2 s_1 + m_1 s_2}{s_1^2 + m_1 s_2 + m_2 s_1}$$

Since s_1^2 is positive, the denominator exceeds the numerator, and the entire expression is therefore a positive fraction.

so that once again there is no change in net exports. In this case income in country 1 falls by enough to induce a sufficient fall in imports to offset fully the autonomous increase.

We may summarize our results as follows.

1. If there is an increase in autonomous spending in country 1, this raises income in both countries and causes country 1's net exports to decline. However, if the marginal propensity to save in country 2 is zero, there will be no change in net exports because country 2's income and imports rise by enough to offset the increase in exports.

2. If there is a transfer of expenditures from country 1 to country 2, Y_1 will fall, Y_2 will rise, and country 1's net exports decline. If both countries have equal national marginal propensities to save, there will be no net change in world income. However, if $s_2 = 0$, $\Delta Y_1 = 0$, $\Delta Y_2 = (1/m_2) \Delta V_{a1}$ and $\Delta NX_1 = 0$. Country 2's income rises by enough to offset the autonomous increase in country 1's imports. If $s_1 = 0$, $\Delta Y_1 = (-1/m_1) \Delta V_{a1}$, and $\Delta NX_1 = 0$, but this time because Y_1 falls by enough to reduce country 1's imports by the amount of the autonomous increase in imports.

3. In general, we cannot expect national marginal saving propensities to be zero. This could be the case in very poor countries, but cannot be so in industrial countries with both private saving and high marginal income tax rates. Consequently, we may conclude that, as a rule, autonomous expenditure changes, including shifts in autonomous expenditure from one country to another, will not produce income changes sufficient to offset the effects of the autonomous changes on the balance of payments.

4.4 MANY COUNTRIES: THE FOREIGN TRADE MATRIX

The analysis can easily be extended to include as many countries as desired. Suppose there are three countries, 1, 2, and 3. The information needed to conduct multiplier analysis is the same as in the two-country case, namely, the consumption and import functions of the three countries. Now, however, each marginal propensity to import must be divided into separate marginal propensities to import from each of the other two countries. For example, $m_1 = m_{21} + m_{31}$, where m_1 is country 1's overall marginal propensity to import, m_{21} is its marginal propensity to import from country 2, and m_{31} is its marginal propensity to import from country 3. Using the equilibrium condition and the consumption and import functions, we can write for country 1,

$$Y_1 = (1 - s_1 - m_1)Y_1 + m_{12}Y_2 + m_{13}Y_3 + E_1$$

where $(1 - s_1 - m_1)Y_1$ is the induced component of country 1's consumption and imports, $m_{12}Y_2$ is the induced component of country 1's exports to country 2, $m_{13}Y_3$ is the induced component of country 1's exports to country 3, and E_1 is the sum of country 1's autonomous expenditure components. Note that the expression can be rewritten as

$$(s_1 + m_1)Y_1 - m_{12}Y_2 - m_{13}Y_3 = E_1$$

Symmetrical considerations apply to countries 2 and 3. We can therefore write the complete model as

$$(s_1 + m_1)Y_1 - m_{12}Y_2 - m_{13}Y_3 = E_1$$

$$-m_{21}Y_1 + (s_2 + m_2)Y_2 - m_{23}Y_3 = E_2$$

$$-m_{31}Y_1 - m_{32}Y_2 + (s_3 + m_3)Y_3 = E_3 \qquad (4.36)$$

This is a set of three simultaneous linear equations.[4] The equations can be solved for the equilibrium values of Y_1, Y_2, and Y_3 expressed as functions of the E's alone. Such a solution is called the reduced form of the equations and is written

$$Y_1 = k_{11}E_1 + k_{12}E_2 + k_{13}E_3$$

$$Y_2 = k_{21}E_1 + k_{22}E_2 + k_{23}E_3$$

$$Y_3 = k_{31}E_1 + k_{32}E_2 + k_{33}E_3$$

where the k's are the various multipliers. For example, k_{11} is the change in Y_1 caused by a $1 increase in E_1. This increase in E_1 changes Y_2 by

---

[4] The general case may be written

$$(s_1 + m_1)Y_1 - m_{12}Y_2 - \cdots - m_{1n}Y_n = E_1$$
$$-m_{21}Y_1 + (s_2 + m_2)Y_2 - \cdots - m_{2n}Y_n = E_2$$
$$\vdots$$
$$-m_{n1}Y_1 - m_{n2}Y_2 + \cdots + (s_n + m_n)Y_n = E_n$$

For an analysis of this case, see L. A. Metzler, "A Multiple-Region Theory of Income and Trade," *Econometrica*, 18:329–54, 1950. A similar analysis that splits a country into regions and examines interregional income flows is J. S. Chipman, "The Multi-Sector Multiplier," *Econometrica*, 18:355–73, 1950.

TABLE 4.1 FOREIGN TRADE MULTIPLIERS FOR OECD COUNTRIES

	U.S.	Germany	Japan	Canada	OECD
U.S.	1.47	0.05	0.04	0.06	1.81
Germany	0.23	1.25	0.05	0.03	2.38
Japan	0.25	0.60	1.26	0.03	1.84
Canada	0.68	0.60	0.06	1.27	2.32
OECD	0.74	0.23	0.21	0.10	2.04

Source: Organization for Economic Cooperation and Development.

k_{21} and Y_3 by k_{31}. Similarly, k_{12} measures the effect on Y_1 of a change in E_2, and k_{13} measures the effect on Y_1 of a change in E_3.

The chapter appendix shows how to compute an entire matrix of multipliers. Here it is instructive to report such a matrix as calculated by the OECD.[5]

Table 4.1 shows foreign trade multipliers for the United States, Germany, Japan, Canada, and all OECD countries combined. The multiplier values are stated as percentage changes in national income as caused by a 1 percent change in autonomous expenditures. Therefore, a 1 percent increase in autonomous spending in the U.S. raises U.S. national income 1.47 percent. The first (U.S.) column of the table also shows that German income rises 0.23 percent, Japanese income rises 0.25 percent, and Canadian income rises 0.68 percent. The last entry in the column shows that U.S. economic expansion raises the income of the OECD countries as a whole by 0.74 percent. It appears that economic expansion in the U.S. has the most pronounced effect on the Canadian economy, which is our most closely linked trading partner.

The entries in the first (U.S.) row of the table show the effect of autonomous expenditure increases in the other countries on national income in the United States. These multipliers are all very small because the U.S. economy is very large relative to the other countries, which also are characterized by the fact that their marginal propensities to import U.S. goods are fairly low.

The multipliers in the main diagonal (northwest to southeast) show the effects of the expansion of autonomous spending in the respective countries on their own income levels. Observe that these multipliers are

[5] OECD Occasional Papers, "The OECD International Linkage Model," January 1979. Organization for Economic Cooperation and Development. Paris, France.

very similar for Germany, Japan, and Canada, and that they are substantially less than the U.S. multiplier of 1.47. All three economies are more "open" than the U.S. economy, and have large marginal import propensities. In addition, Germany and Japan have high marginal propensities to save, and their marginal tax rates are also high.

As inspection of the table makes clear, there are three major factors that affect the magnitude of the multipliers.

1. The *size* of the country is important. Canada, which has a relatively small economy, has little effect on the other countries even though her own multiplier value is 1.27.
2. *Openness* to trade is another major determinant. As the table shows, U.S. economic expansion has a very powerful effect (0.68) on the Canadian economy.
3. The *pattern of trade* is important, as can be seen by the fact that U.S. national income rises relatively more due to Canadian economic expansion (0.06) than to German economic expansion (0.03), reflecting the fact that Canada has a higher marginal propensity to import with respect to the United States than it does with respect to Germany.

Finally, the celebrated "locomotive" theory of international economic recovery relies on the notion that income expansion in one country can serve as the locomotive that pulls up the national income of other countries. However, the small size of most of the multipliers suggests that the induced multiplier (sometimes called spillover) effects tend to be fairly low. Consequently it is fair to conclude that countries ought not to rely on other countries as a substitute for their own stabilization policies. Joint expansion is more promising. This is evident from the last column, which shows the multiplier values if *each* country raises its autonomous expenditures by 1 percent.

QUESTIONS FOR REVIEW

1. (a) In a closed economy, national income cannot be in equilibrium unless $I + G = S_p + T$. Explain why?
   (b) In the absence of income taxation, the closed-economy multiplier is the reciprocal of the marginal propensity to save. Why?
   (c) When proportional income taxation is introduced, the slope of the ag-

gregate expenditure function becomes $b(1 - t)$ instead of b. Why? The value of the multiplier becomes

$$\frac{1}{1 - b(1 - t)}$$

instead of the reciprocal of the marginal propensity to save. Why?

2. In an open economy in equilibrium, a deficit in the government budget must equal the sum of the surpluses in the private and foreign sectors. Why is this? If government purchases rise to increase the budget deficit, how do income changes act to generate offsetting increases in the surpluses of the other sectors?

3. What is the small-country multiplier? Why is it less than the closed-economy multiplier?

4. What is the effect on net exports of an autonomous increase in exports? Is it possible for income to rise by enough to generate an equivalent increase in imports?

5. What is the effect on net exports of an autonomous increase in investment or government purchases? Would it be possible for these changes to leave net exports unaffected?

6. How are the results in Questions 4 and 5 altered when exports are endogenous, that is, dependent on foreign income levels?

7. Why is the value of the foreign trade multiplier greater than the small-economy multiplier but lower than the closed-economy multiplier?

8. Suppose that in a two-country trade model, the value of the **A** matrix (see Appendix A4.4) is

$$\begin{array}{cc} & \begin{array}{cc} 1 & \quad 2 \end{array} \\ \mathbf{A} = & \begin{bmatrix} 0.6 & 0.2 \\ 0.3 & 0.5 \end{bmatrix} \begin{array}{c} 1 \\ 2 \end{array} \end{array}$$

Compute $(\mathbf{I} - \mathbf{A})$ and invert it to find the multipliers. You should get

$$\begin{array}{cc} & \begin{array}{cc} 1 & \quad 2 \end{array} \\ (\mathbf{I} - \mathbf{A})^{-1} = & \begin{bmatrix} 3.57 & 1.43 \\ 2.14 & 2.86 \end{bmatrix} \begin{array}{c} 1 \\ 2 \end{array} \end{array}$$

(a) Why does a rise in internal autonomous spending in country 1 raise Y_1 by more than an increase in internal autonomous spending in country 2 raises Y_2?

(b) Why does a rise in autonomous spending in country 1 raise Y_2 by more than an increase in autonomous spending in country 2 raises Y_1?

(c) What happens to the income levels of the two countries if there is an autonomous increase in country 1's exports?

SUGGESTIONS FOR FURTHER READING

Dernburg, Thomas F., *Macroeconomics,* McGraw-Hill, 1984, chaps. 4, 5.

Goodwin, Richard M., "The Multiplier as Matrix," *Economic Journal,* Dec. 1949.

Keynes, John Maynard, *The General Theory of Employment, Interest, and Money,* Harcourt, Brace, 1936.

Metzler, L. A., "A Multiple Region Theory of Economy and Trade," *Econometrica,* April 1942.

Organization for Economic Cooperation and Development, "The OECD International Linkage Model," OECD Occasional Papers, January 1979.

Chapter 5

Interest Rates, Capital Mobility, and Income Determination

5.1 INCOME DETERMINATION IN A CLOSED MONETARY ECONOMY

In this chapter we begin by relaxing the assumption of constant interest rates and autonomous investment. As before, we begin with the closed economy, but now we have to determine the equilibrium rate of interest along with the level of income. This necessitates the introduction of the demand for money, the supply of money, and the concept of monetary equilibrium. In Section 5.2 we introduce international trade and capital movements, and we complete the chapter by showing how balance-of-payments adjustment and adjustments of the level of income and the rate of interest interact to produce macroeconomic equilibrium.

We begin by treating investment as an endogenous variable. Students of investment behavior have focused on the importance of interest rates in determining planned investment. One approach calculates an expected rate of return on new investment projects and argues that if this *internal* rate of return exceeds the *external* rate of return—that is, the yield on existing assets such as bond interest or the cost of borrowing—it pays for a firm to undertake the investment either by borrowing or by using available resources to expand capacity.

Alternatively, the rental price of capital is identified as roughly equal to the rate of interest plus the rate of depreciation of capital, and it is argued that the rental price of capital relative to the real wage rate determines firms' optimal mixes of capital and labor. In either case it follows from analysis that a rise in the rate of interest will discourage investment, whereas a fall in the rate of interest encourages investment.[1]

---

[1] See Dernburg, *Macroeconomics,* chap. 6, for elaboration of the theory of investment.

These considerations suggest that the first step that needs to be taken in abandoning the autonomous investment assumption is to make investment a decreasing function of the rate of interest. Such an *investment function* is shown in the southeast quadrant of Figure 5.1. With an interest rate of i_0, planned net investment of I_0 is forthcoming. But if the interest rate rises to i_1, investment will decline to I_1.

The 45° line in the northeast quadrant of Figure 5.1 shows investment-saving equality. National income is in equilibrium when investment of I_0 is matched by total national saving of S_0. The northwest quadrant shows saving as a function of income. The $T - G$ curve shows government saving, and its slope is the marginal tax rate. The S curve shows total national saving. Therefore the difference between S and $T - G$ is private saving, S_p. The slope of the S function is $1 - b(1 - t) = s$, as shown in Chapter 4. The saving function shows that if total national saving is S_0, income is Y_0, since that is the income level at which S_0 of saving is generated.

In the southwest quadrant of Figure 5.1 the vertical axis measures the rate of interest, and the horizontal axis measures the level of income. If the rate of interest is i_0, this implies investment of I_0. If national income

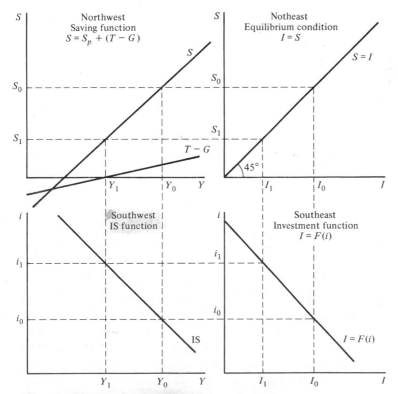

Figure 5.1 Derivation of the IS curve.

is to be in equilibrium, national saving must equal investment. But that level of saving is generated by income level Y_0. Consequently, the combination i_0 and Y_0 in the southwest quadrant shows one possible combination of i and Y that meets the requirement that planned investment equals saving.

Next pick any arbitrary income level, such as Y_1. In the northwest quadrant we can see that this generates saving of S_1. If this is to equal investment, investment (northeast) must be I_1. But I_1 is lower than I_0, so the rate of interest that brings forth I_1 is the higher interest rate i_1 (southeast). Therefore, (southwest) income level Y_1 and interest rate i_1 provide another combination of i and Y that make I and S equal. Clearly, there is an unlimited number of combinations of i and Y that make $I = S$. These combinations are shown by the negatively sloped curve in the southwest quadrant. It is customary to label it the IS curve.

In Chapter 4 we assumed that all functions were linear. Here we make no such assumption, but instead we write out the model in general (implicit) terms. We begin with the equilibrium condition

$$I = S \tag{5.1}$$

and the investment function

$$I = F(i) \qquad F_i < 0 \tag{5.2}$$

Total national saving is

$$S = S_p + (T - G)$$

where S_p is private saving and $T - G$ is the government budget surplus (government saving). Taxes are an increasing function of income. Therefore,

$$T = T(Y) \qquad 0 < T_y < 1 \qquad \xrightarrow{} dT/dY \tag{5.3}$$

where T_y is the marginal tax rate. Consequently,

$$T - G = T(Y) - G$$

gives government saving. Private saving, S_p, equals disposable income minus consumption. Therefore,

$$S_p = Y - T(Y) - C[Y - T(Y)] \qquad 0 < C_y < 1 \qquad dC/dY \tag{5.4}$$

where C_y is the marginal propensity to consume. Adding private and government saving together, we get total national saving

$$S = Y - C[Y - T(Y)] - G \qquad T(y) \text{ cancels out} \tag{5.5}$$

We can now use the investment function (5.2) and the national saving function (5.5) to substitute into the equilibrium condition (5.1).

The result is the equation for the IS curve

$$F(i) = Y - C[Y - T(Y)] - G$$ *equ*. (5.6)

Its slope can be easily calculated and is given by[2]

$$\left(\frac{di}{dY}\right)_{IS} = \frac{1 - C_y(1 - T_y)}{F_i} = \frac{S_y}{F_i} < 0$$ *Slope* (5.7)

which is negative because the numerator is positive while the denominator is negative. That is, a rise in the rate of interest reduces investment and, therefore, national income.

As the IS curve shows, we now face the problem that we cannot know the equilibrium level of income without first knowing the equilibrium rate of interest, and we cannot know that until we know the equilibrium level of income. A mathematician would say there is only one equation and two unknowns, so a solution is not possible unless a second equation with the same two unknowns is found. At the moment, all we have is an unlimited number of combinations of Y and i that satisfy the requirement that planned investment equal total national saving.   *need another equation*

The second relationship between Y and i is provided by the concept of monetary equilibrium, that is, the combination of interest rates and income levels that cause the demand for money to equal its supply. The supply of money can, for the time being, be treated as autonomous, being determined by the actions of the central bank, which in the United States is the Federal Reserve System. This assumption will have to be abandoned as soon as we introduce international considerations.   *M_c = autonomous*

The demand for money to hold can conveniently be divided into a transactions-precautionary motive and a liquidity-preference or portfolio motive. Transactions balances are held because receipts of income and outlays are generally not perfectly synchronized with respect to time for individuals and businesses. There is, therefore, some average idle bank deposit or currency holding, called the transactions demand for money. Since this average idle balance tends to rise as the volume of transactions increases, it is considered to be a function of income. In its simplest form the transactions demand may be written   *always → classify*

$$m_1 = \frac{M_1}{p} = kY \qquad k > 0$$

---

[2] To calculate the slope of IS, simply take the equation for the IS curve and differentiate it with respect to i and Y while holding G constant. This gives

$$F_i \, di = [1 - C_y(1 - T_y)] \, dY$$

so that when we solve for di/dY, we get (5.7).

where M_1 is the nominal quantity of transactions money, p is the price level, so m_1 is the *real* transactions demand for money; k is called the cash balance ratio, and it measures the length of time the average dollar is held between transactions, and Y is the level of real income.

A more satisfactory treatment of the transactions demand for money recognizes that determining the optimum level of cash balances is an inventory decision. Holding an inventory of idle cash is expensive because of forgone interest. Wealth holders may therefore be induced to convert transactions balances temporarily into short-term interest-bearing bonds and then to liquidate the bonds as transactions cash is needed. For example, a bond purchase using one-half of a beginning balance at the beginning of the period leaves the wealth holder with enough cash to last until one-half of the relevant time period expires. At that time he or she cashes in the bonds and spends the cash down to zero by the end of the period. The effect of this entry into and exit from the bond market is to reduce the wealth holder's average cash balance by one-half. If interest rates rise, he or she may be induced by the higher yield, relative to the brokerage (transactions) cost, to enter the bond market three times. He or she puts two-thirds of the initial income into bonds, selling them off in two equal installments when he or she needs cash, the first sale coming when one-third of the time period has expired and the remainder when two-thirds of the period has expired. By doing this, the wealth holder reduces the average cash balance to one-third of the average balance that would have been held had he or she not entered the bond market at all.

As can be seen, the transactions demand for cash is also a function of the rate of interest. A rise in the rate of interest raises the opportunity cost of holding cash and encourages wealth holders to economize their cash balance holdings. Therefore, we can write

$$m_1 = L_1(\overset{+}{Y}, \overset{-}{i}) \qquad L_{1y} > 0 \quad L_{1i} < 0$$

which states that the real transactions demand for money is an increasing function of the level of income and a decreasing function of the rate of interest.

2. The liquidity-preference or portfolio demand for money is a Keynesian concept. In the Keynesian interpretation a portfolio demand for money may arise if there is an expectation that interest rates will return to some higher "normal" level. Under such circumstances bondholders figure to incur a capital loss when interest rates rise, and there may therefore be a preference for liquidity. The modern interpretation, which is largely due to James Tobin,[3] derives from the common obser-

[3] Tobin, James, "Liquidity Preference as Behavior Towards Risk," *Review of Economic Studies,* 25(2):65–68, 1958.

vation that wealth holders generally attempt to hold balanced portfolios characterized by the presence of different types of assets that differ with respect to return and risk. Risk in this interpretation is the variance of the possible capital gains and losses.[4] Even without any interest-rate expectations, and therefore without the expectation of either a capital gain or a loss, the investor is not certain of the outcome. A risky asset is one that has a high probability of substantial capital gain or loss. The variance of such an asset is high. A riskless asset, such as money, has a zero variance, neither capital gains nor losses being possible.

A wealth holder who has two assets, bonds and money, will shift his or her portfolio in the direction of more bonds and less money if the interest rate rises. The reason is that the higher return on bonds now partially overcomes the wealth holder's aversion to risk. A lower rate of interest does the opposite. If the rate of interest falls the wealth holder will sacrifice some return in favor of a reduction in risk. His or her portfolio therefore will shift in the direction of greater liquidity—more money and fewer bonds.

The portfolio demand for money can therefore be seen to be a decreasing function of the rate of interest. In addition, an important implication of the risk-aversion theory for international finance is that the portfolio demand for money also depends on the level of wealth. If an investor is given more bonds or other assets, he or she will diversify the incremental holdings by spreading them among different assets, including money. A rise in wealth therefore increases liquidity preference.

These considerations suggest that the portfolio demand for money may be written

$$m_2 = L_2(\overset{-}{i}, \overset{+}{W}) \qquad L_{2i} < 0 \quad L_{2w} > 0$$

where W stands for wealth. When the transactions and portfolio demands for money are added together, we get

$$m_1 + m_2 = L_1(Y, i) + L_2(i, W)$$

---

[4] Let g be the capital gain or loss on an investment asset. If gains and losses are expected to cancel in the long run, we say that the *expected value* of the gain is zero. Therefore, $E(g) = 0$. To compute the variance, first take the gain and subtract its expected value. This gives $g - E(g)$. Then square this quantity to get $[g - E(g)]^2$. Finally, take the expected value of this quantity to get the variance. Therefore,

$$\text{Variance of } g = E[g - E(g)]^2$$

Since $E(g) = 0$, this becomes

$$\text{Variance of } g = E(g)^2$$

A riskless asset has a very small chance that g will differ from 0, and has a small variance. A risky asset is one for which g may differ substantially from 0, and therefore has a high variance.

which can be consolidated to

$$m_1 + m_2 = L(Y, i, W) \qquad L_y > 0 \quad L_i < 0 \quad L_w > 0 \qquad (5.8)$$

When the autonomous money supply is equated with the demand for money, we obtain the condition for monetary equilibrium

$$m_s = m_1 + m_2 \qquad Equ.$$

so

$$m_s = L(\overset{+}{Y}, \overset{-}{i}, \overset{+}{W}) \qquad L_y > 0 \quad L_i < 0 \quad L_w > 0 \qquad (5.9)$$

The monetary equilibrium relation is shown in Figure 5.2 for a fixed level of wealth. It is called the LM curve and is superimposed on the IS curve in the illustration. The slope of the LM curve is

$$\left(\frac{di}{dY}\right)_{LM} = \frac{-L_y}{L_i} > 0 \quad Slope$$

The LM curve is a positively sloped function because a rise in the rate of interest causes wealth holders to economize their money holdings, thereby permitting the existing money supply to support a higher level of income. Alternatively, a higher level of income requires additional transactions cash. In order to acquire the necessary cash with a given money supply, wealth holders sell bonds or take out loans, thereby, in either case, causing interest rates to rise. $b = \cancel{Bd} + \text{11}$

The intersection of the IS curve with the LM curve identifies the equilibrium level of income, Y_0, and the equilibrium rate of interest, i_0.

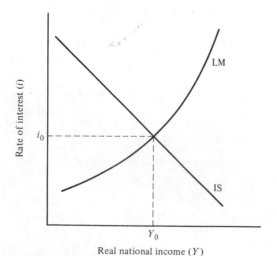

Figure 5.2 Joint saving-investment and monetary equilibrium.

This is the only combination that equates both investment with saving and the demand for money with the supply of money.

An increase in the money supply has the effect of shifting the LM curve to the right.[5] If, for example, the Federal Reserve conducts an open-market purchase of securities, wealth holders will temporarily find that they have an excess supply of money. This excess supply can be eliminated either by a rise in national income, which raises transactions requirements, or by a fall in the rate of interest, which causes wealth holders to desire additional transactions and portfolio cash.

The effect of the expansionary monetary policy is shown in Figure 5.3. The initial equilibrium is at the intersection of the IS curve with the LM_0 curve at Y_0 and i_0. The increase in the money supply shifts the LM curve to LM_1, and the new equilibrium is then at the higher income level Y_1 and lower interest rate i_1. By increasing the money supply through a purchase of bonds, the Federal Reserve drives up bond prices, lowers interest rates, and provides banks with additional loanable funds. The lower interest rate stimulates investment, which, via the multiplier process, raises the equilibrium level of income. Although the LM curve shifts horizontally by the distance $Y_2 - Y_0$, income rises only to Y_1. The new money is partially absorbed into increased transactions holdings, caused by the rise and income, and portfolio holdings, caused by the fall in the rate of interest.

The quantitative impact of monetary policy depends on the slopes of the various functions. The effect on the level of income will be magnified if the marginal propensity to save is lower, since that implies greater amounts of respending on consumption. Similarly, the money multiplier will rise if the responsiveness of investment to changes in the rate of interest increases. And, finally, the money multiplier will decline if the responsiveness of the demand for money to the rate of interest increases, since a larger fraction of any increase in the money supply would then be absorbed into idle balances.

There are two important extreme cases. First, the classical case in which the demand for money is independent of the rate of interest. In

---

[5] To calculate the magnitude of the shift, take the equation for the LM curve,

$$m_s = L(Y, i, W)$$

and differentiate with respect to m_s and Y while holding i and W constant. Therefore,

$$dm_s = L_y \, dY$$

so the increase in income that would occur if the rate of interest remains unchanged is

$$dY = \frac{1}{L_y} \, dm_s$$

which is the magnitude of the horizontal shift in the IS curve.

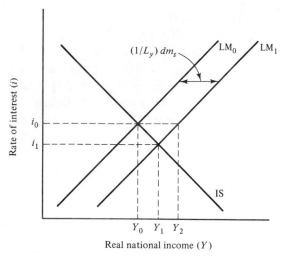

Figure 5.3 Expansionary monetary policy lowers the rate of interest and raises the level of income.

that case the LM curve is vertical, so a shift to the right caused by an increase in the money supply causes a directly proportional increase in income. The second extreme is the Keynesian liquidity trap in which the demand for money is infinitely elastic with respect to the rate of interest. This deep depression phenomenon implies a horizontal LM curve, so income cannot be changed by monetary policy. An increase in the money supply is entirely absorbed into portfolios; there is no reduction in the rate of interest and no change in income.

To analyze the effects of a fiscal policy, we reproduce the two western quadrants of Figure 5.1. Recall that the difference between the S and $T - G$ functions is private saving S_p. In the top panel of Figure 5.4 the initial saving and budget functions are S_0 and $T - G_0$. Investment I_0 equals saving of S_0 at an income level of Y_0. Then, let government purchases rise by $\Delta G = G_1 - G_0$. The new budget surplus function is $T - G_1$, having shifted down by ΔG. The total national saving function shifts down by an equal amount, becoming S_1. The S_1 function now cuts I_0 at an income level Y_1. In the lower panel this implies that the IS curve has shifted to the right, so the new IS function cuts interest rate i_0 at income level Y_1.

The relationship between the magnitude of the change in government purchases and the shift in the IS curve can be seen by focusing attention on the triangle abc in the upper panel. The vertical distance bc measures the increase in government purchases. The horizontal segment ab is the shift in the IS curve. This distance clearly depends on the tangent cb/ab of the angle at a. But that is the slope of the S function, which is

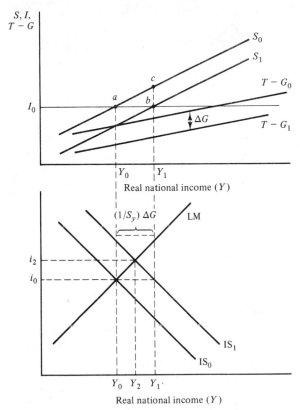

Figure 5.4 Expansionary fiscal policy raises income and the rate of interest.

the national marginal propensity to save, S_y. Therefore, we see that the shift in the IS curve equals the standard multiplier, $1/S_y$, multiplied by the change in government purchases.

However, in the lower part of the diagram, we see that income nor- *But* mally will not rise by that amount because of the positively sloped LM *✱* curve that intersects IS_1 at income level Y_2. The reason is that, as income expands, the transactions demand for money increases, thereby driving up the interest rate, which, in turn, crowds out some investment.

In the Keynesian extreme the LM curve is horizontal, so there is *magnitude* no rise in the rate of interest. The change in income therefore equals the *of* horizontal shift of the IS curve and is therefore given by the simple mul- *Crowd–* tiplier $1/S_y$ times the change in government purchases. In the classical *out* case the LM curve is vertical, so there is no income change. The new IS *of I* curve cuts the LM curve at the same income level, but at a higher rate *in the 2* of interest. There is dollar-for-dollar investment crowd out. *extremes*

Finally, it is important to understand the adjustment process when the economy is out of equilibrium. Consider Figure 5.5, and assume that

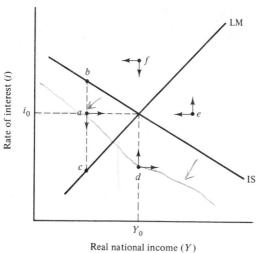

Figure 5.5 Dynamic adjustment to disequilibrium.

i and *Y* are at point *a*. At that income level the rate of interest would have to be at *b* to equalize saving and investment. Since the interest rate is below *b*, investment must exceed saving, so income expands toward the IS curve. Also, at point *a* the interest rate is higher than at *c*, which is the rate that would be required to equate the demand and supply for money. Since this implies excess supply of money, the interest rate tends to decline toward the LM curve.

Similar reasoning can be undertaken for disequilibrium states such as exist at *d, e,* and *f*. In all cases we find that the path of motion is such that income moves horizontally in the direction of the IS curve while the rate of interest moves vertically in the direction of the LM curve.

The equilibrium in Figure 5.5 is said to be *stable* because *Y* and *i* tend to gravitate to the point of intersection of the IS and LM curves. There may, however, be *unstable* equilibria. The point of intersection of the curves is still an equilibrium, but it is said to be unstable if the variables move away rather than toward the point of intersection. As an example, suppose investment depends on the level of income as well as the rate of interest. The increased investment induced by a rise in income is called the *marginal propensity to invest*. If the marginal propensity to invest exceeds the national marginal propensity to save, the IS curve will have a positive slope. This is true because as income rises investment rises by more than saving, so saving could never catch up with investment unless the growth of investment is contained by a rise in the rate of interest.

This possibility is illustrated in Figure 5.6, where the IS curve cuts the LM_0 curve at point *a*, implying income Y_0 and interest rate i_0. Let the LM curve be shifted to the right by an expansionary monetary policy.

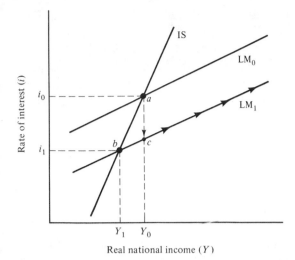

Figure 5.6 Dynamic instability in the IS–LM model.

The new equilibrium is at point b with income Y_1 and interest rate i_1. *Comparative static* analysis, which merely compares equilibrium points, predicts a *fall* in income from Y_0 to Y_1. However, that hardly seems reasonable. How can a rise in the money supply cause a fall in income?

To see where the trouble lies, we must examine the dynamics of adjustment. Suppose that the rate of interest adjusts very quickly to monetary disturbances, but that it takes time for income to change. The first thing that would happen in response to the monetary policy is that the rate of interest would drop until it reaches the new LM curve LM_1. This implies point c. At point c the lower rate of interest implies that planned investment exceeds saving. Therefore income will *rise,* following the arrows upward along the LM_1 curve.

In a case such as this, we say that a and b are unstable equilibria. Then the comparative static results are incorrect, since income never gets to point b. Thus, dynamic *stability analysis* is an important supplement to comparative statics, because it helps to verify or refute comparative static results. Furthermore, if we believe that the system is stable, we can rule out the comparative static results in unstable cases.

In the present case instability occurs because the slope of the IS curve is greater than the slope of the LM curve. The *stability condition* is that the opposite must be true. If the stability condition is met, it would then be seen that a rise in the money supply could not possibly lower the level of income.

Stability analysis is a very powerful and important tool. The techniques for conducting such an analysis and deriving stability conditions are explained at length in the chapter appendix. The reader is strongly urged to consult that appendix, since stability analysis is indispensible at many junctures throughout this book.

We are now ready to internationalize the IS-LM model. To do this efficiently, we must first thoroughly digest the material of this section. The reader who feels uneasy about such a short course in closed-economy IS-LM and the building blocks that underpin it may wish to consult a suitable macroeconomics text.[6]

5.2 THE FOREIGN BALANCE FUNCTION
AND THE IS-LM MODEL

For purposes of the present analysis it is important to distinguish between the current and the capital accounts in the manner of Chapter 3. As a reminder, current transactions in the balance of payments include merchandise exports and imports, service income (including interest and dividends from foreign investment), and unilateral transfers. The balance of receipts over outlays on these items is the surplus on current account.

The capital account records the value of foreign investment activity. Americans build plants in foreign countries, purchase shares in foreign companies, and buy foreign bonds. All these transactions result in an outflow of dollars (or an expenditure of foreign exchange) and are called *capital outflows*. Similarly, when foreigners invest in the United States, there is a *capital inflow*. But since none of these transactions reflect current income and product flows, they are not part of national income.

Under the Bretton Woods fixed exchange-rate system that prevailed between 1944 and 1973, a deficit in the U.S. balance of payments implied either that foreign central banks were building up their dollar holdings or that the United States was either losing gold or increasing its indebtedness to foreign central banks. When a foreign firm receives payments in dollars for its exports to the United States, the firm may convert the dollars into local currency at its bank. The bank may hold the dollars to lend to importers or to investors desiring to purchase financial assets in the United States. In this case the current-account deficit is offset by a surplus in the capital account, and there is therefore no overall deficit in the balance of payments. Notice also that there is no change in money supplies. Dollars flow out through the current account but flow back in through the capital account.

[6] For example, Dernburg, *Macroeconomics,* chap. 6, analyzes investment spending, chap. 7 discusses the demand for money, chap. 8 discusses the supply of money, chap. 9 constructs the IS-LM model, and chap. 10 supplies applications and extensions to the closed-economy environment.

But

If no private foreign citizen or firm wants the dollars earned by the sale of exports, they can get rid of them at their central banks because, under the Bretton Woods agreement, central banks were obliged to buy and sell their own currencies in exchange for dollars at a fixed official price. In this event there is a deficit in the U.S. balance of payments, because the current-account deficit is not matched by a capital inflow.

If the central banks accumulate the dollars, their foreign exchange reserves rise. In this event foreign money supplies are increasing while the U.S. money supply shrinks. Part of the U.S. money supply goes into foreign reserves, and foreign money supplies increase because central banks are selling their own currency in exchange for dollars. Therefore, in any reasonably realistic analysis of the open economy, it is necessary to abandon the assumption of an autonomously determined money supply.

Alternatively, foreign central banks may consider their dollar holdings excessive. In that event they could demand payment in gold at the U.S. Treasury's "gold window." The U.S. gold stock then dwindles as foreign central banks replace dollar reserves with gold reserves. Such an official transaction has no effect on money supplies, defined as currency and deposits in the nonbank private sectors of economies. The Treasury could forestall the gold loss by purchasing the surplus dollars from foreign central banks in exchange for U.S. government bonds. When this is done by mutual agreement, it is called a *swap* arrangement.

The stage is now set for the analysis of income determination and balance-of-payments adjustment within the context of an open economy. The IS-LM model is of great value here, provided we first amend the IS curve to include exports and imports, and the LM curve to incorporate endogenous changes in the money supply. However, before we do that it is important to introduce a new function into the IS-LM diagram. This is the balance of payments equilibrium function, denoted FB (for foreign balance).

If we ignore investment income, the balance-of-payments surplus equals the level of net exports plus the surplus on capital account. Equilibrium in the balance of payments occurs when these sums total zero. Therefore, we may write

$$FB = X - V + K = 0 \qquad (5.10)$$

where X and V stand for exports and imports, respectively, and K is the net inflow of capital. Equilibrium in the balance of payments occurs when FB = 0. Therefore if balance-of-payments equilibrium is to be attained, positive net exports must be offset by an equivalent net capital outflow, whereas if imports exceed exports, this current-account deficit must be offset by a capital-account surplus.

Consider the individual components of the FB function. In the small-country case we treated the real value of exports as autonomous, since exports depend on foreign developments. However, we should also recognize that if the domestic price level falls relative to foreign price levels, domestic goods will gain a competitive advantage in foreign markets, and exports will therefore increase. Thus domestic prices relative to international prices must be entered as an argument in the export function.

Similarly, if the exchange rate varies, this will vary the prices of exports as perceived by foreigners, and that will affect the volume of exports. Since we have defined the exchange rate as the price of a unit of foreign currency in terms of the domestic currency, a rise in the exchange rate lowers the price of U.S. goods to foreign importers, since they have to give up fewer units of their own currency to purchase the dollars needed to purchase U.S. goods. Similarly, the rise in the price of foreign exchange increases the number of dollars needed to buy foreign goods, and that will tend to reduce imports.

$\$ = domestic$
$\yen = foreign$

$e = \dfrac{\$}{\yen}$

On gathering these strands together, we see that both exports and imports depend on the real exchange rate ep^*/p. An increase in the nominal exchange rate or a reduction in domestic prices makes exports less expensive to foreigners. An increase in the foreign price level p^* makes exports more attractive to foreign buyers. Consequently, we define the export function as

$$X = X\left(\frac{ep^*}{p}\right) \qquad X_e > 0 \quad X_p < 0 \quad X_{p^*} > 0 \tag{5.11}$$

$X = X\left(\dfrac{\$ \cdot \yen}{\$}\right)$

$X_e = \dfrac{dx}{de}$ etc

where the positive sign attached to the parameter X_e indicates that a rise in the nominal price of foreign exchange raises the real exchange rate and increases the real value of exports. The opposite is true when the domestic price level rises so that the parameter X_p is negative. However, a rise in p^* increases the real exchange rate, so X_{p^*} is positive.

Explanation of variables

In addition to the real exchange rate, imports also depend on national income. Therefore we write the import function as

$$V = V\left(Y, \frac{ep^*}{p}\right) \qquad 0 < V_y < 1 \quad V_e < 0 \quad V_p > 0 \quad V_{p^*} < 0 \tag{5.12}$$

opposite of that for exports

The parameter V_y is the marginal propensity to import and is a positive fraction; V_e is the change in imports that accompanies a rise in the nominal exchange rate. We assume that V_e is negative, although this is a shaky assumption, as explained in Chapter 8. A higher nominal exchange rate means that more dollars have to be expended to acquire a particular quantity of foreign goods. Since the domestic price of imports rises when the price of foreign exchange increases, there will be a reduction in the physical quantity of imports. The value of imports denominated in the local currency will decline, provided the proportionate increase in the home price of imports is less than the proportionate decline in physical volume. Similarly, a rise in p makes imports more attractive, so V_p is assumed to be positive; conversely, a rise in p^* makes imports more expensive, so V_{p^*} is negative.

The movement of international capital depends on investment opportunities as reflected in interest rates and on anticipated changes in the exchange rate. A rise in the domestic rate of interest attracts foreign capital. A rise in foreign interest rates reverses the flow in the direction of other countries. The expectation that the local currency will appreciate attracts capital, whereas an anticipated depreciation makes for capital flight to other countries. The condition for uncovered interest parity discussed in Chapter 2 points the way to the treatment of capital flows. There will be a capital inflow if the differential between the domestic rate of interest and the foreign rate of interest exceeds the expected rate of appreciation of the local currency. Therefore, we use (2.3) to write

variables in capital mvmt

$$K = K\left[i - i^* - E\left(\frac{\Delta e}{e}\right) \right]$$

where i is the domestic rate of interest, i^* is the foreign rate of interest, and $-E(\Delta e/e)$ is the expected rate of appreciation of the local currency. For present purposes we will assume that foreign interest rates are autonomous and that there is no expectation that the exchange rate will vary one way or the other. Under these assumptions we can compress the expression for the capital inflow to

assume

$$K = K(i) \qquad K_i > 0 \tag{5.13}$$

We can now pull these strands together, using (5.11), (5.12), and (5.13) to make substitutions in (5.10). Accordingly, the FB function can be written as

e, P, P^*, i *fixed*

$$0 = X\left(\frac{ep^*}{p}\right) - V\left(Y, \frac{ep^*}{p}\right) + K(i) \tag{5.14}$$

Inspection of this expression shows that if the exchange rate and price levels are fixed, the real exchange rate will be constant, and the FB function then becomes a function of the level of income Y and the rate of interest i.

The FB function is illustrated in Figure 5.7(a). It is a positively sloped function that defines the combinations of income levels and interest rates that keep the balance of payments in equilibrium. Choose point a

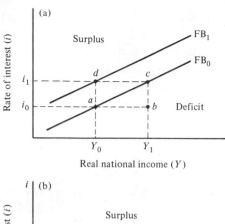

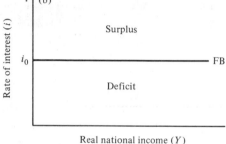

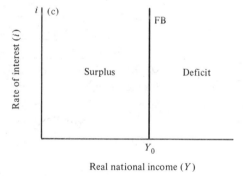

Figure 5.7 (a) Imperfect capital mobility; (b) perfect capital mobility; (c) zero capital mobility.

as the starting point, with both the current account and the capital account in equilibrium at interest rate i_0 and income level Y_0. A rise in income to Y_1 would put the economy at point b. The rise in income raises imports, thereby causing a deficit in the current account and in the overall balance of payments. Thus, point b is in the deficit zone. The deficit on current account can, however, be offset by a rise in the rate of interest to i_1. The rise in the rate of interest attracts foreign capital and produces a surplus in the capital account, thereby offsetting the deficit in the current account.

Alternatively, begin again at point a and let the rate of interest rise to i_1. The rise in the rate of interest attracts foreign capital and produces a surplus at point d. The surplus can, however, be eliminated by a rise in income to Y_1, since that raises imports and causes the current account of the balance of payments to deteriorate.

It is apparent that any point below and to the right of the FB function implies a deficit in the balance of payments, whereas any point above and to the left of the FB function implies a surplus. A rise in the price of foreign exchange shifts the FB function to the right. Exports rise because they become less expensive to foreigners, and imports decline because foreign goods become relatively less attractive to our own citizens. It would require a rise in income (to raise imports) or a fall in the rate of interest (to repel capital) to restore equilibrium in the balance of payments. Similarly, a rise in the price level makes home goods relatively less competitive internationally, so the FB curve would shift to the left, widening the deficit zone. A rise in the foreign price level has the opposite effect. [7]

A flattening of the FB curve implies that capital movements become increasingly responsive to changes in the rate of interest. Such a development is said to be an increase in the degree of capital mobility. The extreme form of this occurs when domestic and foreign financial assets are perfect substitutes. The FB curve becomes horizontal, as illustrated in Figure 5.7(b), and capital mobility is said to be perfect. The condition of the balance of payments is then completely dominated by the rate of interest and the capital account. If the domestic rate of interest exceeds i_0, unlimited quantities of capital flow in and there is a surplus in the balance of payments regardless of the condition of the current account. At domestic interest rates below i_0, foreign interest rates are high relative to the domestic interest rate, and the flight of capital then becomes so extreme that there is a deficit in the balance of payments regardless of the condition of the current account. This is a relevant case. The high

---

[7] With fixed price levels, the FB function is

$$FB = X(e) - V(Y, e) + K(i) = 0$$

We obtain its slope by differentiating with respect to Y and i, to get

$$\left(\frac{di}{dY}\right)_{FB} = \frac{V_y}{K_i} > 0$$

When capital mobility is perfect, $K_i \rightarrow \infty$ and the slope of FB is zero. When there is zero capital mobility, $K_i = 0$ and the FB curve is vertical. We obtain the shift in the FB curve that occurs in response to a rise in the exchange rate by differentiating with respect to e and Y while holding i fixed. This gives

$$\frac{dY}{de} = \frac{X_e - V_e}{V_y} > 0$$

since $X_e > 0$ and $V_e < 0$.

degree of capital mobility strengthened the dollar between 1979 and 1984 despite a sharply deteriorating current-account position.

The opposite extreme is zero capital mobility. In this case capital is unresponsive to changes in the rate of interest and the FB curve is vertical, as illustrated in Figure 5.7(c). It is now the current account that determines whether the overall balance of payments will be in deficit or in surplus. To the right of the FB function the level of income is high; imports are therefore also high and exceed the level of exports, so there is a deficit in the balance of payments. To the left of the FB function, income and imports are low; exports exceed imports, and there is a surplus in the current account and in the overall balance of payments.

This case is also relevant, as we shall see in detail later. If it is, it explains why many theories of the balance of payments have emphasized the current account to the exclusion of the capital account. After World War II most industrial countries imposed severe restrictions on the movement of capital, so that is one relevant case. Even today many developing countries lack sufficiently developed capital markets to enjoy either the benefits or the adverse consequences of the capital mobility that characterizes relations between industrial countries.

Now consider the IS curve. The income-expenditure equilibrium condition in the open economy is

$$I = S_p + (T - G) + (V - X)$$

or

$$I = S + (V - X) \tag{5.15}$$

where S is total national saving and $V - X$ is the trade deficit. By previous arguments we can rewrite the national saving function as

$$S = S(Y, t) - G \qquad 0 < S_y < 1 \qquad 0 < t < 1 \tag{5.16}$$

which states that total national saving depends on income, the tax rate, and the level of autonomous government purchases. The parameter S_y continues to be the national marginal propensity to save. Substituting (5.11), (5.12), and (5.16) into the equilibrium condition (5.15) gives the equation for the IS curve as

$$F(i) = S(Y, t) - G + V\left(Y, \frac{ep^*}{p}\right) - X\left(\frac{ep^*}{p}\right) \tag{5.17}$$

As long as the price level and the exchange rate remain fixed, (5.17) implies a straightforward negatively sloped IS curve. A rise in income raises the leakages from private saving, taxes, and imports; thus, in order to maintain equilibrium, the rate of interest must fall to generate additional investment. A rise in the price level or a decline in the price of foreign exchange will shift the IS curve to the left, because imports will rise while exports will fall, thereby simultaneously causing a given level of income to be associated with higher leakages (imports) and lower injections (exports). The same level of income can, however, be sustained if these changes are compensated by a greater level of investment, which implies a lower rate of interest.[8] Since the IS curve shifts to the left, appreciation (a decline in the price of foreign exchange) will have a deflationary effect on the economy.

Finally, consider the LM curve. As previously written, it is

$$m_s = L(Y, i, W)$$

where the money supply was considered autonomous. This assumption will still be usable under flexible exchange rates. However, under fixed exchange rates we must take into account the fact that the money supply will increase if there is a surplus in the balance of payments, and the supply will decrease if there is a deficit. From the monetary survey studied in Chapter 3, we know that the money supply is a liability of the banking system offset by the domestic assets held by the banking system plus its foreign exchange reserves. Therefore, we now write the LM function as

$$M_s = D + R = pL(Y, i, W) \qquad \text{LM curve} \atop \text{in open econ} \qquad (5.18)$$

where D stands for domestic assets and R for foreign exchange reserves. A rise in domestic assets unaccompanied by a decline in reserves increases the money supply, which would occur if the central bank purchases government securities. A rise in reserves also increases the money supply, which would occur if the central bank purchased foreign exchange in order to stabilize the exchange rate. Finally, if domestic assets rise and foreign exchange reserves decline an equal amount, nothing happens to

---

[8] We determine the slope of the IS curve by differentiating with respect to Y and i, holding t, G, and e constant. This gives

$$\left(\frac{di}{dY}\right)_{IS} = \frac{S_y + V_y}{F_i} < 0$$

which is negative because the numerator is positive while the denominator is negative. Notice that the numerator is the marginal propensity to save plus the marginal propensity to import. We can examine the effect of a rise in the exchange rate on the IS curve by differentiating the IS curve with respect to Y and e, holding i, G, and t constant. We have

$$\frac{dY}{de} = \frac{X_e - V_e}{S_y + V_y} > 0$$

which is positive because X_e is positive while V_e is negative. Thus the IS curve shifts to the left when the price of foreign exchange rises.

the money supply. This is a very important possibility, as we will soon see.

We are now armed with sufficient tools to examine the interaction of national income and the balance of payments. In the next section we undertake such an analysis, assuming fixed exchange rates. The final section of the chapter takes up adjustment under flexible exchange rates.

5.3 INCOME AND BALANCE-OF-PAYMENTS ADJUSTMENTS UNDER FIXED EXCHANGE RATES

LM will do the adjus in fixed

We begin our discussion of adjustment by assuming a commitment to fixed exchange rates. Initially we also assume that countries' internal price levels are rigid. We then drop this assumption and consider adjustment under flexible exchange rates.

How get to equil.

Consider the economy depicted in Figure 5.8. The IS curve cuts the initial LM curve (LM_0) at point a, implying income level Y_0 and interest rate i_0. Point a is below and to the right of the FB curve, and there is a deficit in the balance of payments. This implies that there is an excess supply of the local currency in foreign exchange markets and an excess demand for foreign currencies. If exchange rates were free to be market determined, the local currency would depreciate against foreign currencies. To prevent the depreciation of the local currency, the country's

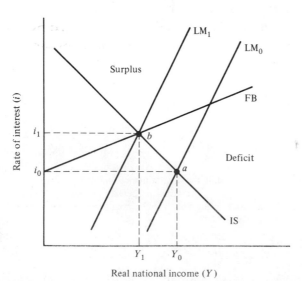

Figure 5.8 Balance-of-payments adjustment with fixed exchange rates.

monetary authority is obliged to intervene by supplying foreign currencies to the market from its own reserves of foreign exchange. But in selling foreign currencies, the monetary authority purchases local currency, thereby reducing the money supply. Thus, the monetary survey shows a loss of reserves matched by an equal reduction in the domestic money supply.

In Figure 5.8 this implies that the LM curve shifts automatically to the left if there is a balance-of-payments deficit, because as long as there is, the money supply will be declining. Since the deficit persists as long as Y and i lie below and to the right of the FB curve, it follows that the money supply will continue to fall until the LM curve shifts all the way to point b where the IS curve intersects the FB curve.

The balance-of-payments deficit is eliminated because income declines, reducing imports, and because the rate of interest rises, reducing the net outflow of capital. Thus the balance of payments adjusts automatically, but at a heavy cost because national income shrinks from Y_0 to Y_1, and because the rate of interest rises to i_1, reducing investment and thereby harming economic growth prospects. The price of the fixed exchange-rate system is loss of control of the domestic money supply and a very likely inability to maintain full employment or to avoid inflation. It is crucial to note that the fixed exchange-rate system implies that it is the LM curve that adjusts in such a way as to be consistent with the IS and FB curves.

[margin note: why LM shift left causes deficit to be eliminated]

If the country finds the income loss unacceptable, it can attempt to offset the decline in the money supply by domestic open-market operations. This is called sterilization, and it means that as the foreign exchange loss reduces the money supply, the money supply loss is restored by the central bank's purchases of domestic assets, usually government securities. The changes in the monetary survey are as follows:

$-\Delta R =$	$-\Delta M$
$+\Delta D =$	$+\Delta M$

The difficulty with conducting monetary policy so as to prevent the LM curve from shifting away from LM_0 is that continuous action is required that will ultimately force abandonment of the sterilization policy as reserves are depleted. Among the available options are borrowing from the IMF, borrowing from other countries through "swap" arrangements, or getting other countries to finance the deficit by getting them to accumulate the currency that is in excess supply. It was this latter option that largely held the Bretton Woods system together during the period of persistent U.S. deficits in the late 1960s and early 1970s. As the U.S. ran

[margin note: Problem w/ sterilization]

deficits, foreign central banks were initially happy to accumulate dollars as international reserves. The U.S. deficit, however, persisted, in part because the Federal Reserve system prevented the U.S. money supply from shrinking. Meanwhile, surplus countries that were accumulating dollars became increasingly nervous about the loss of control of their money supplies. It was the explosive money supply growth that largely undermined the Bretton Woods system, leading to its abandonment in 1973 and the adoption of flexible exchange rates by the European Economic Community (EEC). Robert Triffin notes that

> The overall deficits of the United States could not have totaled about SDR 66 billion over the five years 1970–74 if 93 percent of them had not been financed by other countries' acceptance of U.S. IOUs as international reserves. The adoption of floating rates was a desperate attempt by each surplus country acting independently to stem this inflationary flood.[9]

The situation confronted by a surplus country might be as in Figure 5.9. The IS_0 and LM_0 curves intersect at point a at income Y_0 and interest rate i_0. However, at point a there is a surplus in the balance of payments. This means there is excess demand for the local currency and excess supply of foreign currencies, so the exchange rate tends to appreciate. To preserve the fixed exchange-rate commitment, the monetary authority must accumulate foreign exchange, in the process adding to the domestic money supply. The monetary survey shows an increase in R and an equal rise in M. In Figure 5.9 this means the LM curve shifts to the right. The surplus is eliminated at Y_1 and i_1 when the LM curve reaches LM_1, where it intersects the IS_0 and FB_0 curves at point b.

But suppose Y_0 is the full-employment level of income. Then Y_1 is unattainable because real income cannot be expanded. The result is excessive aggregate expenditure and an inflationary gap that threatens to raise the domestic price level and bring on the many problems associated with inflation. Thus, the surplus country may be forced to import inflation by its importation of foreign reserves. The country has to choose between two unpleasant options. It can sterilize the money supply effects of the foreign exchange inflow by selling domestic assets, or it can tolerate the inflation. In the former case the surplus in the balance of payments will persist, which means the surplus country is extending unlimited credit to deficit countries. The surplus country finds itself persistently giving away more goods and services in the form of exports than it receives as imports.

[9] Triffin, Robert, "Jamaica: Major Revision or Fiasco?", in Bernstein, E. M., *Reflections on Jamaica*. Essays in International Finance, Princeton University, No. 115, April 1976, p. 46.

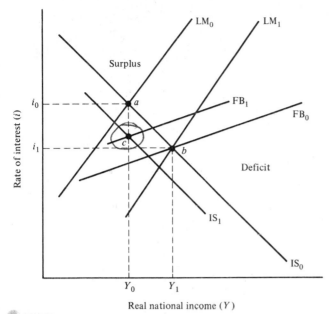

Figure 5.9 Elimination of a surplus in the balance of payments with fixed exchange rates.

If the country accepts the inflation, the surplus will eventually disappear because the rise in the country's price level reduces its international competitiveness, thus lowering exports and increasing imports. This shifts the IS curve to the left and the FB function to the left. Equilibrium is eventually reached when all three functions intersect at a point such as c, which implies full employment combined with the elimination of the balance-of-payments surplus as well as the inflationary gap. ⟨Problem w/

The classical theory of the balance of payments viewed price-level [classical model] changes rather than income changes as the primary avenue of adjustment, even in response to the deflationary effects of deficits and shrinking money supplies. Figure 5.10 returns to the deficit situation at point a of Figure 5.8. If wages and prices are downwardly flexible, the deflationary effects of the reduction in the money supply are felt in the form of a fall in the price level rather than in real income. The fall in the price level improves international competitiveness, causing the IS and FB curves to shift to the right, eventually reaching a point such as c where all three functions intersect at Y_0, the full-employment level of income. But cannot assume w+p

Unfortunately, experience shows that such a happy outcome cannot will be anticipated with confidence. Deflationary forces in industrial countries drop generally have their primary impact on output and employment rather than on wages and prices. It has been estimated, for example, that if

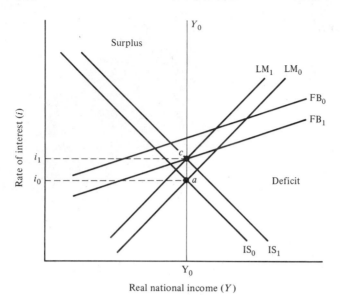

Figure 5.10 Price-level adjustment in response to a deficit.

aggregate expenditure in the United States is reduced by $1 the result in the short run is a reduction in real income of $0.90, whereas only a dime is saved in less inflation. Thus, the price level may eventually adjust to a balance-of-payments deficit, but until it does the deficit country is in for a long siege of subpar economic performance characterized by excess capacity, heavy unemployment, and a depressed level of real income.

The classical theory also assumed that full employment was the norm toward which economies would gravitate. Unemployment would be temporary and would be associated with a deficit in the balance of payments, and inflation would be temporary and would be associated with a surplus in the balance of payments. But it is entirely possible for deficit countries to be well below full employment, so the further deflation needed to eliminate the deficit conflicts sharply with the need to raise domestic employment. Similarly, surplus countries that need to permit inflation to eliminate their surpluses may already be suffering more inflation than is tolerable, so asking them to accept more inflation in the interest of reducing their surpluses is asking them to further destabilize their economies. Evidently, there frequently is a sharp conflict between the needs of the domestic economy and the need to attain external equilibrium. This is the conflict between external and internal balance that we met as early as Chapter 2.

Similarly, because of the income transmission mechanism discussed in our examination of foreign trade multipliers, it is hardly surprising that recessions and inflations tend to coincide internationally. When internal aggregate spending falls in one country, this reduces her demand for imports and transmits a deflationary shock, making for recession in other countries. These countries will find their net exports declining. They therefore suffer from both recession and an external deficit, neither of which were of their own making. Should such countries expand their economies to restore full employment, thereby widening the deficit by causing imports to rise, or should they eliminate their deficits by pursuing restrictive policies to reduce the demand for imports, thereby worsening the recession from which they are suffering? Neither alternative is pleasant. Fixed exchange rates clearly make the task of maintaining high employment without inflation difficult without, at the same time, creating large balance-of-payments deficits and surpluses.

5.4 ADJUSTMENT UNDER FLEXIBLE EXCHANGE RATES

IS & FB Shift in flex e's.

If the fixed exchange-rate system does not cause complete loss of control of money supplies, it at least severely compromises monetary policy. Adjustment in the balance of payments is often purchased at the price of fluctuations in output, employment, and rates of inflation. If prices and wages were readily flexible, downward as well as upward, the problem of fluctuating output and employment would be reduced, but that is a vain hope given the institutions of industrial countries in the modern world. These are among the reasons why many economists welcomed the transition to flexible exchange rates in 1973. Fluctuations in the exchange rate would replace fluctuations in national income and inflation rates as the mechanism for improving the international competitiveness of countries with declining, or depreciating, exchange rates, while worsening the competitive position of countries with appreciating exchange rates, thereby bringing receipts and payments into balance.

Why want flexible

Better still, flexible exchange rates eliminate the link between the balance of payments and domestic money supplies. Since there is no obligation to buy or sell foreign exchange, there are no fluctuations in internal money supplies other than those deliberately caused by monetary policies.

severs link between BOP & domestic ms

It is important to recognize that a fundamental difference between fixed and flexible exchange rates is that, whereas under fixed exchange rates the LM curve does the bulk of the adjusting, under flexible exchange rates it is the IS and the FB curves that do the adjusting.

Consider Figure 5.11. The zones are now identified as *incipient* surplus and *incipient* deficit rather than surplus and deficit, respectively. The

NOTE THE DIFF

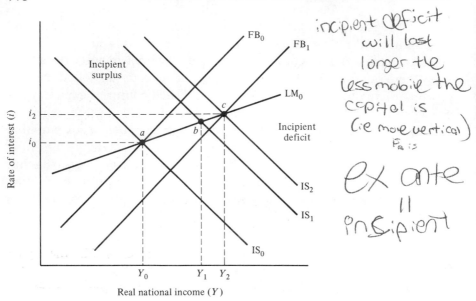

Handwritten annotations (right margin): incipient deficit will last longer the less mobile the capital is (ie more vertical) F_a is

ex ante = incipient

Figure 5.11 Adjustment under flexible exchange rates with relatively immobile capital.

reason is that movements in the exchange rate automatically produce foreign balance, so there can be no deficit or surplus in the balance of payments. However, if at the moment FB is at FB_1 and if Y and i are at point b, there will be a tendency for the exchange rate to appreciate. Economists sometimes describe this situation as an *ex ante* surplus to indicate a market condition prior to the adjustment. After adjustment the situation is described as *ex post,* at which time there can be no surplus or deficit. The international finance literature typically replaces the word "ex-ante" with the word "incipient," and there is no objection to that.

Handwritten annotation (left margin): ie will have surplus just before the adj occurs

Suppose the economy is initially in equilibrium at point a in Figure 5.11, with income at Y_0 and interest rate i_0. Then suppose the IS curve shifts to IS_1 because of an autonomous increase in consumption (which could be caused by a tax cut). The IS_1 and LM curves intersect at point b, implying an incipient deficit, because in this case the FB curve is fairly steep, implying a low degree of capital mobility. The rise in income causes net exports to decline, and the rise in the rate of interest attracts capital. But with a low degree of capital mobility the current-account effect overcomes the capital-account effect, with the consequence that an incipient deficit develops. As a result the local currency depreciates, and this raises exports and reduces imports, thereby shifting the FB curve to the right to FB_1. At the same time the IS curve also shifts to the right to IS_2, because of the effect of the depreciation on the trade deficit. Therefore, we find that the IS curve first shifts to the right because of the rise in internal aggregate expenditure, and then again because of the depreciation of the currency. In the final equilibrium there is a sizable trade deficit, but this is offset by the higher interest rate, i_2, which improves the capital account. National income rises because of the increase in aggregate expenditure and gets an added boost because of the depreciation which raises exports and reduces imports.

This result follows from the assumption of relatively immobile capital. The FB curve is steeper than the LM curve in this example. However, if capital is relatively mobile, by which we mean the slope of FB is less than the slope of LM, we get a result that differs in an important respect. This can be seen in Figure 5.12.

The rightward shift of the IS curve caused by the rise in autonomous consumption now causes an incipient surplus at point b. This occurs because the deterioration of the trade balance caused by income expansion is less than the improvement in the capital account caused by the higher interest rates. The local currency therefore appreciates, thereby shifting the FB curve to the left. The IS curve shifts to the left for the same reason. The final intersection may be at a point such as c, where income (Y_2) is higher than Y_0 but less than Y_1, which represents the income level that would have been attained had there been no change in the exchange rate. Because the interest rate is higher at c than at a, there is a greater capital inflow than initially, which finances a larger trade deficit than existed at a. National income rises, but this is to a large extent offset by an increase

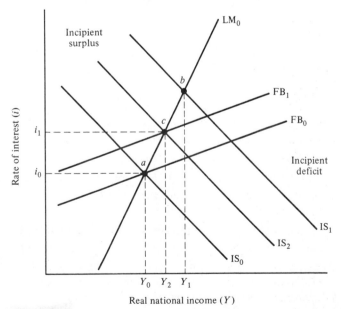

Figure 5.12 Adjustment under flexible exchange rates with relatively mobile capital.

in the trade deficit. This analysis makes it easier to understand why the expansionary fiscal policies pursued in the United States from 1981–85 have had only modest success in raising domestic income. The bulk of the fiscal stimulus was exported via the rising trade deficit in response to the rising dollar.

In conclusion, it is obvious from the foregoing examples that the outcome of a change in internal aggregate expenditure depends to a great extent on the degree of capital mobility. It is clear also that countries will not stand still in the face of inflationary and deflationary shocks that originate abroad. Therefore, it is important to examine the effects of government monetary and fiscal policies under fixed and flexible exchange rates with differing degrees of capital mobility. That is done in the next chapter.

QUESTIONS FOR REVIEW

1. Explain the meaning of the IS curve and why it has a negative slope? What factors determine the flatness or steepness of the IS curve?

2. Explain the meaning of the LM curve. Why does it have a positive slope? What factors determine the flatness or steepness of the LM curve?

3. What is the effect on the equilibrium level of income and the rate of interest of a rise in government purchases? Why do income and the rate of interest move in the same direction? Why is the income increase less than the value predicted by the multiplier?

4. What is the effect on the equilibrium level of income and the rate of interest of an increase in the money supply? Why do income and the rate of interest move in the opposite direction? Why is the rise in income not proportional to the increase in the money supply?

5. Explain the adjustment of income and the rate of interest if both are
   (a) above the intersection of the IS and LM curves
   (b) below the intersection of the IS and LM curves
   (c) to the left of the intersection of the IS and LM curves
   (d) to the right of the intersection of the IS and LM curves.

6. Why is it essential to study the dynamics of adjustment in order to verify the validity of comparative static results?

7. How is the IS curve altered by introducing international trade? What is the effect on the IS curve of a rise in the real exchange rate?

8. How is the LM curve altered by introducing international trade? How is it altered under fixed exchange rates? under flexible exchange rates? What is the effect of a loss of foreign exchange reserves on the LM curve?

9. Define the foreign balance function. Why is it normally positively sloped? What determines the flatness or steepness of the function?

10. If we have fixed exchange rates and rigid prices, we can have either equilibrium at full employment or equilibrium in the balance of payments. But we can't have both, except by accident. Why? What would happen if price levels became flexible? What would happen if the exchange rate were free to fluctuate?

11. Have you studied the appendixes to this chapter in order to learn how to conduct comparative static and stability analysis systematically?

SUGGESTIONS FOR FURTHER READING

Dernburg, Thomas F., *Macroeconomics,* McGraw-Hill, 1984, chaps. 6–10.

Ingram, James C., *International Economics,* Wiley, 1986, chaps. 6, 7.

Tobin, James, "Liquidity Preference as Behavior Towards Risk," *Review of Economic Studies,* 1958.

Triffin, Robert, "Jamaica: Major Revision or Fiasco?" in E. M. Bernstein, ed., *Reflections on Jamaica,* Essays in International Finance, No. 115, April 1976.

Chapter 6

The Impact of Stabilization Policies Under Fixed and Flexible Exchange Rates

6.1 STABILIZATION POLICY IN THE FINANCIALLY INSULAR ECONOMY

The study of the relationship between the balance of payments and the macroeconomy is enormously facilitated by separating that body of analysis that is appropriate to the so-called *financially insular* economy from analysis that deals with the *financially open* economy. The distinction has been suggested by Professor Ronald McKinnon of Stanford University. [1] Analysis of the financially insular economy ignores short-run capital movements and focuses on the determinants of the current account. The sequence of events in response to a monetary disturbance in such an economy might be depicted as follows:

Monetary disturbance → interest rate → prices output →

current account → deficit or exchange rate

The exchange rate under flexible exchange rates or the balance-of-payments deficit under fixed exchange rates are determined by national income, which affects import demand, and prices, which determine international competitiveness. Absent from this approach is the direct effect of interest rates on short-term capital movements and, thus, on the balance of payments.

[1] McKinnon, Ronald I., "An International Standard for Monetary Stabilization," Institute for International Economic Policy, vol. 8., 1984, p. 24.

In the financially open economy the sequence could be depicted as

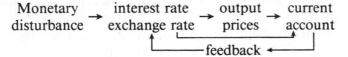

$$\begin{array}{cccc} \text{Monetary} & \text{interest rate} & \text{output} & \text{current} \\ \text{disturbance} & \text{exchange rate} & \text{prices} & \text{account} \end{array}$$
feedback

Therefore, in the financially open economy an important factor in determining exchange rates is the change in asset preferences, reflected in domestic-foreign interest-rate differentials. The exchange rate then becomes important as a determinant of output and prices and is only secondarily and indirectly influenced by output and prices.

We begin the analysis of the impact of monetary and fiscal policies with the financially insular economy, and proceed, in subsequent sections, to develop the contrast with today's financially open economy.

In the financially insular economy the term $K(i)$ in the foreign balance functions is constant, reflecting the fact that capital movements are assumed to be long-run in character and not susceptible to short-run variations in interest rates. Capital movements are therefore autonomous and the FB curve is vertical, as in Figure 6.1, where it can be seen that the presence of a deficit or surplus depends entirely on the level of income. An income level in excess of Y_0 implies a high import demand and a deficit in the balance of payments, whereas at income levels below Y_0 the demand for imports is low enough to ensure a surplus.

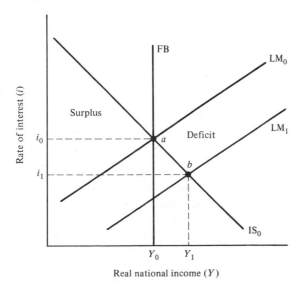

Figure 6.1 Expansionary monetary policy in the financially insular economy with fixed exchange rates.

Begin at point a with income at Y_0, interest rate i_0, and the balance of payments in equilibrium. Assume that Y_0 is below full employment, an assumption retained throughout this chapter, since there is no point in attempting to raise real income above the full-employment level. Suppose also that the exchange rate is fixed by a commitment on the part of the monetary authority to buy and sell foreign exchange. Then assume that the monetary authority attempts to expand the level of income by an increase in the money supply that shifts the LM curve to LM_1.

The intersection of the IS and LM_1 curves is at point b in the deficit zone. The expansionary monetary policy raises aggregate expenditure and, therefore, the demand for imports. As a consequence, the demand for foreign exchange exceeds its supply, and the local currency tends to depreciate. To prevent depreciation, the monetary authority must sell foreign exchange and in the process purchase back its own currency. Thus the money supply declines and the monetary survey shows

$$
\begin{array}{c|c}
+\Delta D = & +\Delta M \\
-\Delta R = & -\Delta M
\end{array}
$$

so that the LM curve shifts back to LM_0 because of the need to support the exchange rate.

Notice that in this situation it is not even possible to expand the money supply by a one-time open-market purchase. This will be the case as long as the fixed exchange-rate assumption is maintained and, as we will see, is independent of capital mobility and whether the economy is financially open.

It is clear that the monetary policy fails to attain its objective of reaching Y_1, and it could do this only by continuous monetary injections and corresponding reserve losses.

Fiscal policy fares no better in this environment. In Figure 6.2 we assume that government purchases are raised so as to shift the IS curve to IS_1 to attain income level Y_1 at point b. This policy also generates a balance-of-payments deficit because the rise in income increases imports. The local currency therefore tends to depreciate, so once again the monetary authority must intervene and sell foreign exchange from its reserves in exchange for domestic money balances. The monetary survey shows

$$
\begin{array}{c|c}
-\Delta R = & -\Delta M
\end{array}
$$

which means that the net effect of the rightward shift of the IS curve is to produce an offsetting leftward shift in the LM curve. The economy then comes to rest at point c, having nothing to show for the attempt to

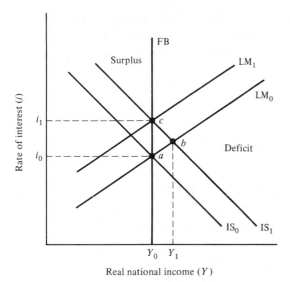

Figure 6.2 Expansionary fiscal policy in the financially insular economy with fixed exchange rates.

raise Y other than a higher rate of interest that reduces investment by the amount of the increase in government purchases. Therefore, we see that there is 100 percent investment crowd out because of the development of the balance of payments.

This situation provides the starkest picture of the extent to which stabilization policy is hamstrung under fixed exchange rates. The conflict between external and internal balance is insurmountable. But, as we will see, the picture is not as dark as this when capital becomes less immobile. However, it is this kind of scenario that many economists seem to have had in mind when they began to challenge the desirability of maintaining the fixed exchange-rate system. Let us see, therefore, how the flexible exchange-rate alternative improves the situation.

It is useful to recall the condition for balance-of-payments equilibrium by again writing the foreign balance function:

$$0 = X\left(\frac{ep^*}{p}\right) - V\left(Y, \frac{ep^*}{p}\right) + K(i)$$

In the financially insular economy, $K(i)$ is constant (call it K), and if the exchange rate is fixed at the official rate $\bar{e}$, we have

$$0 = X\left(\frac{\bar{e}p^*}{p}\right) - V\left(Y, \frac{\bar{e}p^*}{p}\right) + K$$

which can be satisfied by only one level of real income if price levels remain fixed. However, if the exchange rate is free to equilibrate in the market place, any number of real income levels are possible, depending on the value of the exchange rate, even if price levels are rigid. Alternatively, a target income level can be picked, and an exchange rate can be found that is consistent with that income level. This means the vertical FB function can be shifted, moving to the right when the currency depreciates and to the left when the currency appreciates.

Now consider Figure 6.3, where the actual level of income is Y_0 and the policy target income level is Y_1. Let monetary policy shift the LM curve to LM_1, where it intersects IS_0 at point b. The fall in the rate of interest raises investment and, via the multiplier, raises national income. The rise in income increases the demand for imports and produces an incipient balance-of-payments deficit. But, freed of the fixed exchange-rate commitment, the monetary authority does not respond with intervention. The excess demand for foreign currency now causes the price of foreign exchange to rise, thereby bringing the balance of payments back into equilibrium as the depreciation raises exports and reduces imports.

In the final equilibrium at Y_1 the FB function is

$$0 = X\left(\frac{e_1 p^*}{p}\right) - V\left(Y_1, \frac{e_1 p^*}{p}\right) + K$$

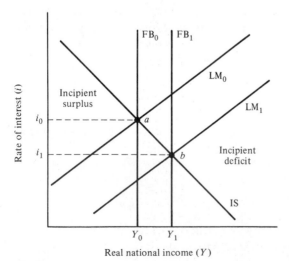

Figure 6.3 Expansionary monetary policy in the financially insular economy with flexible exchange rates.

which means that the FB curve has shifted to the right (to FB_1). Exports are higher because the price of foreign exchange is higher. Imports are also higher because of the rise in income, although the depreciation moves import demand in the opposite direction. Flexible exchange rates therefore appear to permit the conflict between internal and external balance to be resolved. National income of Y_1 is attained by monetary policy, and this is consistent with simultaneous equilibrium in the balance of payments without the need for flexible wages and prices. Professor Milton Friedman of the University of Chicago, an early and influential advocate of flexible exchange rates, wrote in 1953 that

> Governments . . . are no longer willing to submit themselves to the harsh discipline of the gold standard or any other standard involving rigid exchange rates. They will evade its discipline by direct controls over trade if that will suffice and will change exchange rates before they will surrender control over domestic monetary policy . . . we had best recognize the necessity of allowing exchange rates to adjust to internal policies rather than the reverse. [2]

It is important to note, in the transitions from point a to b in Figure 6.3, that exports and imports have both increased, but these are equal increases because no deficit exists either at Y_0 or Y_1. Recall that

$$Y = C + I + G + (X - V) = A + (X - V)$$

The sum $C + I + G$ is domestic absorption. Since net exports, $X - V$, remain unchanged, the relationship between income and absorption is unaffected by foreign leakages and injection. Therefore, because the monetary policy raised investment and that, in turn, raised consumption, it must be that

$$\Delta Y = \Delta C + \Delta I$$

so the change in income equals the change in absorption. As shown in the chapter appendix, the multiplier is

$$\frac{\Delta Y}{\Delta m} = \frac{F_i}{L_i S_y + F_i L_y} > 0$$

where the parameters are defined as in Chapter 5. The important point is that this multiplier equals the closed-economy multiplier.

Similarly, the fact that the home country's net exports have not

---

[2] Friedman, Milton, "The Case for Flexible Exchange Rates," in his *Essays in Positive Economics,* Chicago, 1953, pp. 179–80.

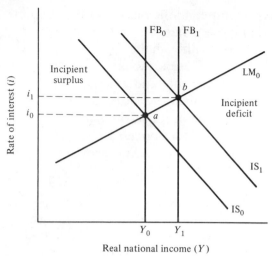

Figure 6.4 Expansionary fiscal policy in the financially insular economy with flexible exchange rates.

changed means that foreign countries' net exports also remain the same, so there is no income transmission to other countries. The economies are, for all practical purposes, *macroeconomically independent*. One country's policies do not spill over onto others.

This very important conclusion contributed powerfully to the case for flexible exchange rates. Indeed, it was claimed that countries with ambitious employment targets could pursue these goals even if others were less ambitious. This would be impossible under fixed exchange rates, since a country with an ambitious employment target would be likely to suffer more inflation than other countries and therefore would have a balance of payments that was permanently in deficit. Harry G. Johnson of the University of Chicago wrote as follows in 1969:

> Flexible rates would allow each country to pursue the mixture of unem-
> ployment and price trend objectives it prefers, consistent with international
> equilibrium being secured by appreciation of the currencies of "price sta-
> bility" countries relative to the currencies of "full employment" countries.[3]

To complete this discussion, we need to check out the effects of fiscal policy in the financially insular economy with flexible exchange rates. In Figure 6.4 we begin again at point *a*. Government purchases are now raised so as to cause the IS curve to intersect the LM curve at point *b*, to attain income level Y_1. The rise in government purchases

---

[3] Johnson, Harry G., "The Case for Flexible Exchange Rates," Federal Reserve Bank of St. Louis, *Review,* 51, June 1969, p. 18.

raises income and imports. This causes an incipient deficit in the balance of payments, so the local currency depreciates. This raises exports and lowers imports until the incipient deficit is eliminated.

It is again true that

$$0 = X\left(\frac{e_1 p^*}{p}\right) - V\left(Y, \frac{e_1 p^*}{p}\right) + K$$

because flexible exchange rates permit the FB curve to shift to FB_1, where it is consistent with the LM and IS_1 curves. Once again,

$$Y = C + I + G + (X - V) = A + (X - V)$$

and since $X - V$ remains unchanged, there is no change in net exports. It therefore follows that

$$\Delta Y = \Delta C + \Delta I + \Delta G = \Delta A$$

so the change in income equals the change in absorption and is given by the closed-economy multiplier, which, as shown in the chapter appendix, is

$$\frac{\Delta Y}{\Delta G} = \frac{L_i}{S_y L_i + F_i L_y} > 0$$

Macroeconomic independence is therefore again ensured, with no country sending its monetary-fiscal shocks to any other country.

To recap this discussion, consider developments in the foreign exchange market. Figure 6.5 shows the demand and supply for foreign

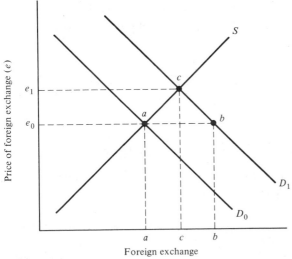

Figure 6.5 Effects of expansionary macroeconomic policy on the foreign exchange market.

currency. The market is initially in equilibrium at exchange rate e_0 with the demand for foreign exchange equal to its supply at point a. Expansionary monetary and/or fiscal policy initially raises national income and the demand for imports. It therefore increases the demand for foreign exchange, as shown by the rightward shift of the demand curve from D_0 to D_1. Under fixed exchange rates there would be a deficit of ab, which then forces monetary contraction so that income again declines and the demand curve shifts back to D_0. Under flexible exchange rates the rise in income tends to raise imports by ab. But since the price of foreign exchange rises to e_1, imports decline by bc and exports increase by ac. At point c exports again equal imports, and both have risen by ac relative to the initial position at point a. Economic activity increases in export industries and declines in import-competing industries, but there is no change in net exports.

A footnote should be added with respect to the issue of macroeconomic independence. In a well-known paper published in 1950, Sven Laursen and Lloyd A. Metzler disputed the argument that economies under flexible exchange rates would be insulated from macroeconomic shocks from abroad.[4] They noted that income expansion in country A would tend to appreciate the currencies of A's trading partners. These countries would therefore enjoy improved terms of trade and a rise in real income reflected in the lower domestic cost of imports from A. Inasmuch as the fraction of income saved increases as real income increases, the change in the terms of trade will shift down the consumption functions of A's trading partners. This reduces their domestic absorption levels and tends to contract their economies. Thus the Laursen-Metzler theorem argues that a boom in country A may, under flexible exchange rates and immobile capital, actually lower absorption in the economies of A's trading partners. It is hard to know how important this effect is likely to be in practice. However, even if it is of limited importance it is one consideration that enters into the analysis of the effects of devaluation, and we will, therefore, encounter it again when we discuss devaluation in Chapters 8 and 9.

6.2 STABILIZATION POLICY IN THE FINANCIALLY OPEN ECONOMY WITH PERFECT CAPITAL MOBILITY

To draw as sharp a contrast as possible between the financially insular and financially open economies, we now move to the opposite extreme

---

[4] Laursen, Sven, and Lloyd A. Metzler, "Flexible Exchange Rates and the Theory of Employment," *Review of Economics and Statistics,* November 1950.

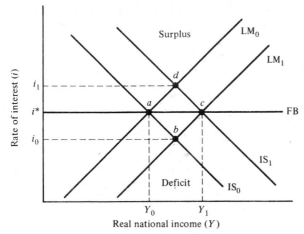

Figure 6.6 Effects of expansionary monetary and fiscal policies with perfect capital mobility.

and assume that capital mobility is perfect. As seen in Chapter 5, this implies that $K_i \rightarrow \infty$, so the FB curve is horizontal. In Figure 6.6 we draw such a horizontal FB curve at interest rate i^*.

The analysis of this important case was supplied at roughly the same time by Robert A. Mundell of Columbia University and J. Marcus Fleming of the IMF.[5] In addition to assuming perfect capital mobility, Mundell assumed that the home country is small enough so that its internal monetary developments are not sufficient to have a significant effect on the world money stock and interest rates. Consequently, the interest rate i^* is determined autonomously by world financial conditions.

In Figure 6.6 the economy is at income level Y_0 with the IS_0 and LM_0 curves intersecting at the autonomously given interest rate i^*. We assume a commitment to a fixed exchange rate and begin by examining the effects of an expansionary monetary policy. In replacing domestic assets with money balances in the private sector of the economy, the monetary authority shifts the LM curve to LM_1 so that it intersects the IS curve at point b.

At point b the domestic interest rate i_0 is below the world level i^*. Consequently, there is a capital outflow as investors seek higher returns elsewhere, and this creates excess demand for foreign exchange. To prevent the currency from depreciating, the monetary authority must supply the market with foreign exchange, buying back its own currency in the

[5] Mundell, Robert A., "Capital Mobility and Stabilization Policy Under Fixed and Flexible Exchange Rates," *Canadian Journal of Economics and Political Science,* 29, 1963. Fleming, J. Marcus, "Domestic Financial Policies Under Fixed and Floating Exchange Rates," International Monetary Fund, *Staff Papers,* November 1962.

process. Therefore the LM curve shifts back toward LM_0, and the monetary survey again shows

$+\Delta D =$	$+\Delta M$
$-\Delta R =$	$-\Delta M$

The capital outflow continues as long as the domestic interest rate is below i^*. Therefore pressure on the exchange rate is not eliminated until the two interest rates are the same. This means the LM curve must shift all the way back to LM_0. Consequently, the initiating monetary expansion has been ineffective in raising the level of income. The monetary authority is again unable to control the money supply because of its fixed exchange-rate commitment.

Fiscal policy is far more promising. Let the IS curve in Figure 6.6 shift to the right to IS_1, as the result of an increase in government purchases or a tax reduction. The IS_1 and LM_0 curves intersect at point d with interest rate i_1. The expansionary fiscal policy places the economy in the surplus zone because the higher domestic interest rate i_1 attracts foreign capital. The capital inflow creates excess demand for the local currency so the currency tends to appreciate. The appreciation forces the monetary authority to purchase the surplus foreign exchange and, in so doing, pays with domestic money. Therefore, the money supply increases, the LM curve shifts to the right, and the monetary survey shows

$+\Delta R =$	$+\Delta M$

As long as the domestic interest rate exceeds i^*, the capital inflow and pressure on the exchange rate persist. Therefore, the LM curve must shift all the way to LM_1, where it cuts the IS_1 curve at point c. The fiscal policy is therefore very effective, causing income to rise from Y_0 to Y_1.

From both of these results it appears that the environment of perfect capital mobility and fixed exchange rates creates a situation that provides essentially Keynesian results, but for different reasons. Recall from the discussion of the closed economy in the previous chapter that in the extreme Keynesian case of a liquidity trap, the LM curve is horizontal, so an increase in the money supply fails to lower the rate of interest, and it therefore does not stimulate investment and raise national income. Here we see that the effective LM curve is horizontal because of the automatic money supply adjustment that comes about as the result of domestic-foreign interest-rate differentials under fixed exchange rates.

Similarly, fiscal policy in the closed economy yields a full multiplier effect if the LM curve is horizontal as in the liquidity trap. Since the expansionary fiscal policy does not raise interest rates in such a case, there is no investment crowd out and income rises by the full amount of the horizontal shift in the IS curve. In the financially open economy with fixed exchange rates and perfect capital mobility, we get the same result, because the money supply automatically increases, thereby off-setting any tendency for the fiscal policy to raise the rate of interest.

Suppose next that the fixed exchange-rate commitment is abandoned, and reconsider the effect of expansionary monetary policy. Figure 6.6 is still useful. An expansionary open-market operation shifts the LM curve from LM_0 to LM_1. The intersection with IS_0 is at point b, implying a decline in the domestic interest rate to i_0. The reduced yield on domestic securities then prompts a portfolio shift in favor of higher-yield foreign assets, so there is a capital outflow. This creates excess demand for foreign exchange and raises the price of foreign exchange. This raises exports and reduces imports, which means the IS curve shifts to the right. As this continues, the domestic interest rate rises because of the need for added transactions money balances. However, pressure on the exchange rate will not stop until interest rate i^* is restored in the domestic financial market. Therefore, we may infer that the depreciation of the local currency is such that it shifts the IS curve all the way to IS_1, yielding an income gain of $Y_1 - Y_0$.

We can see that monetary policy suddenly acquires magic punch relative to its enfeebled condition under fixed exchange rates. The result is very "classical" in the sense that the change in income is directly proportional to the increase in the money supply. In the closed economy this happens if the demand for money is completely insensitive to changes in the rate of interest and the LM curve is vertical. Here it happens because the IS curve automatically shifts in response to monetary expansion. There is, however, an important difference. In the classical closed-economy case the rise in income comes about because of lower interest rates and a rise in investment and consumption. But in this open-economy case the rise in income is caused by a rise in net exports. Unfortunately, this means that other economies suffer a decline in net exports, and their income levels shrink. While economists of the monetarist persuasion seemed delighted that flexible exchange rates provided monetary policy with enormous power, others were less sanguine, pointing out that the monetary policy raised domestic employment at the expense of other countries. In some eyes monetary policy under flexible exchange rates was viewed as beggar-my-neighbor policy, since it merely exported unemployment to others, much as tariffs, quotas, and export subsidies are often intended to do.

Finally, consider the effect of expansionary fiscal policy with flexible exchange rates and perfect capital mobility. In Figure 6.6 let government purchases rise so as to shift the IS curve from IS_0 to IS_1. Whereas the expansionary monetary policy lowered the domestic interest rate, expansionary fiscal policy does the opposite. The intersection of IS_1 with LM_0 is at point d in the surplus zone. Foreign capital is attracted, and this appreciates the currency. As a result of the appreciation, exports decline and imports increase. Therefore, the induced rise in leakages and decline in injections shift the IS curve back in the direction of IS_0. Since the incipient surplus and pressure on the exchange rate are not eliminated until the rate of interest returns to i^*, we may infer that the IS curve shifts all the way back to IS_0. There is, therefore, no income gain because the rise in government purchases is offset by an equal decline in net exports. We know that

$$Y = C + I + G + (X - V)$$

but in this case

$$\Delta G = -(\Delta X - \Delta V)$$

so $\Delta Y = 0$.

    This is again a classical result. In the closed economy the rise in G failed to raise income because, the demand for money being unresponsive to interest-rate increases, additional transactions could not be financed without an increase in the money supply. The rate of interest therefore rose by enough to cause investment crowd out to equal the rise in government purchases. Therefore, $\Delta G = -(\Delta I)$, and $\Delta Y = 0$. But in the open economy with perfect capital mobility and flexible exchange rates, the crowd out is international rather than domestic. Investment remains unchanged because the equilibrium rate of interest remains unchanged, but activity in export- and import-competing industries is crowded out because of the appreciation of the currency, much the way this actually happened in the United States in response to the expansionary fiscal policies of 1981–85.

    It appears then that perfect capital mobility combined with flexible exchange rates greatly enfeeble fiscal policy, since there is no income change. However, foreign economies are stimulated because their net exports rise. Therefore, it is not correct to say that fiscal policy is ineffective; it should rather be said that it is effective in the wrong place, since it stimulates foreign economies rather than the domestic economy, much as the U.S. fiscal policies of 1981–85 had been doing.

6.3 STABILIZATION POLICY IN THE FINANCIALLY OPEN ECONOMY WITH IMPERFECT CAPITAL MOBILITY

In Sections 6.1 and 6.2 we studied the extremes in order to highlight differences in analytical results. It is now time to round out the discussion

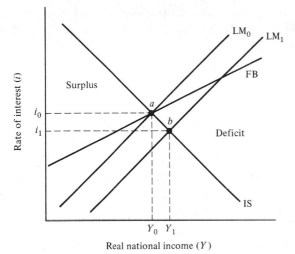

Figure 6.7 Effects of expansionary monetary policy under fixed exchange rates with relatively high capital mobility.

by considering the intermediate case characterized by imperfect capital mobility. That means the FB curve takes on a positive slope and that it is possible for domestic-foreign interest-rate differentials to be sustained. A further distinction is needed to subdivide the imperfect capital mobility case into a *relatively mobile* category versus a *relatively immobile* category. Figures 6.7 and 6.8 show the two cases. In the relatively mobile case of Figure 6.7 the FB curve has a lower slope than does the LM curve. In

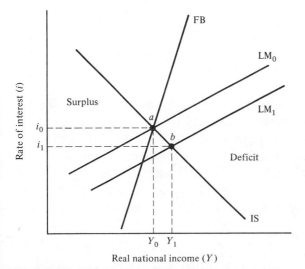

Figure 6.8 Effects of expansionary monetary policy under fixed exchange rates with relatively immobile capital.

the relatively immobile case of Figure 6.8 the opposite is true. There the LM curve is flatter than the FB curve. Recall that the slopes of the LM curve and the FB curve are, respectively,

$$\left(\frac{di}{dY}\right)_{LM} = \frac{-L_y}{L_i} > 0 \qquad \left(\frac{di}{dY}\right)_{FB} = \frac{V_y}{K_i} > 0$$

The slope of the LM curve depends on the cash balance ratio, L_y, and the responsiveness of the demand for money to changes in the rate of interest, L_i, which may be thought of as the rate at which domestic bonds are substituted for money in portfolios in response to a rise in the rate of interest. The slope of the FB curve depends on the marginal propensity to import, V_y, and the responsiveness of capital inflows to changes in interest rates. The parameter K_i may therefore be thought of as the rate at which domestic earning assets are substituted for foreign earning assets in investor portfolios as the domestic rate of interest rises. Relatively high capital mobility implies a high degree of substitution between domestic and foreign assets relative to the degree of substitutability of domestic assets for money.

Figure 6.7 shows the effect of monetary expansion under fixed exchange rates with relatively high capital mobility. An open-market purchase of domestic earning assets by the monetary authority increases the money supply and shifts the LM curve to LM_1, where it intersects the IS curve at point b. Since point b is in the deficit zone, the local currency tends to depreciate, thereby causing the monetary authority to sell foreign exchange, thereby reducing the money supply. The LM curve shifts back to LM_0, and there is again no gain in income. The monetary survey again shows the familiar pattern

$+\Delta D =$	$+\Delta M$
$-\Delta R =$	$-\Delta M$

If capital is relatively immobile, the LM curve is flatter than the FB curve, as in Figure 6.8. Expansionary monetary policy again attempts to raise national income by an open-market purchase that shifts the LM curve to LM_1, where it intersects the IS curve at point b. Point b is again in the deficit zone. Therefore, the monetary authority must again sell foreign exchange, thereby reducing the domestic money supply. Once again the LM curve shifts back to LM_0, and the monetary survey shows the familiar pattern

$+\Delta D =$	$+\Delta M$
$-\Delta R =$	$-\Delta M$

All of the examples considered show that monetary policy is hamstrung under fixed exchange rates. This result is independent of the degree of capital mobility. The reason is that expansionary monetary policy causes both the current and the capital accounts to deteriorate. A rise in income raises imports and deteriorates the current account, and the decline in the interest rate induces a capital outflow, thereby deteriorating the capital account. There is, therefore, no way of avoiding a balance-of-payments deficit in response to expansionary monetary policy. If we look at the monetary survey one more time, we see that in all the fixed exchange rate cases we get

$$
\begin{array}{c|c}
+\Delta D = & +\Delta M \\
-\Delta R = & -\Delta M
\end{array}
$$

It is not surprising that it has frequently been remarked that monetary policy under fixed exchange rates is an ineffective way to change national income but a highly effective way to control the foreign exchange reserves of the monetary authority. The net effect of expansionary monetary policy is to cause a substitution of domestic assets in place of foreign exchange reserves in the assets of the banking system. Restrictive monetary policy brings about the opposite.

Expansionary monetary policy causes current and capital accounts to deteriorate. However, expansionary fiscal policy raises the rate of interest as it raises the level of income. Therefore, the current account deteriorates because of the greater demand for imports, but the capital account improves because the higher interest rate attracts foreign capital. The effect that dominates is determined by the relative mobility of capital. With no capital mobility in the financially insular economy, fiscal policy affected only the current account and therefore caused a deficit that led to automatic contraction of the money supply, thereby rendering the fiscal policy ineffective. With perfect capital mobility, the capital-account effect caused by the higher interest rate was all important, leading to a surplus that caused automatic monetary expansion that made the fiscal policy highly effective.

Now consider Figure 6.9, which shows the effect of expansionary fiscal policy under fixed exchange rates with relatively mobile capital. Initially the IS_0 curve cuts LM_0 and FB at income level Y_0 and interest rate i_0. An expansionary fiscal policy shifts the IS curve to IS_1, which now intersects the LM_0 curve at point b at income level Y_1 and interest rate i_1. This is the income level that would be attained in the absence of monetary repercussions. However, point b is in the surplus zone. The rise in income has lowered net exports and deteriorated the current ac-

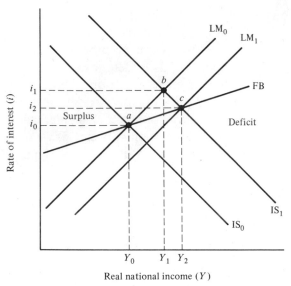

Real national income (Y)

Figure 6.9 Effects of expansionary fiscal policy under fixed exchange rates with relatively mobile capital.

count, but, because capital is relatively mobile, by less than the improvement in the capital account caused by the higher interest rate. The balance of payments is therefore in surplus, and the currency tends to appreciate. The monetary authority must now purchase foreign exchange, thereby increasing the money supply, which shifts the LM curve to the right. Equilibrium is restored when the monetary expansion moves the LM curve to LM_1, where it intersects the IS_1 curve at point c. Therefore, automatic monetary repercussions are such as to supplement the effects of the fiscal policy, with Y_2 exceeding Y_1.

Figure 6.10 shows the effects of the same fiscal policy with relatively immobile capital. In this case the outward shift of the IS curve to IS_1 produces an intersection with LM_0 at point b, implying income level Y_1 and interest rate i_1. Again, this is the income level that would be attained in the absence of monetary repercussions. But point b is now in the *deficit* zone because the capital inflow caused by the higher interest rate is small relative to the deterioration of the current account caused by the rise in income. To prevent the exchange rate from depreciating, the monetary authority must sell foreign exchange, thereby reducing the money supply. Therefore the LM curve now shifts to the left, causing the rate of interest to rise even more, thereby reducing investment and partially negating the expansionary effect of the fiscal policy. The final equilibrium is at point c with interest rate i_2 and income level Y_2. Thus, in this case the automatic monetary response caused by the fixed exchange-rate commitment reduces the magnitude of the income expansion.

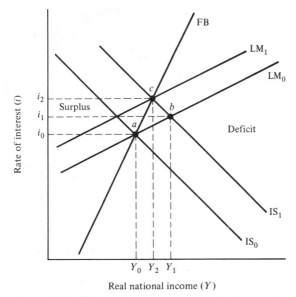

Figure 6.10 Effects of expansionary fiscal policy under fixed exchange rates with relatively immobile capital.

In summary, we see that the effectiveness of fiscal policy under fixed exchange rates is magnified by increases in the degree of capital mobility. Fiscal policy does not work at all in the financially insular economy; it is weakened by money supply shrinkage if capital is relatively immobile; strengthened by monetary expansion if capital is relatively mobile; and rendered fully effective without investment crowd out if capital mobility is perfect, because the fiscal expansion is fully accommodated by automatic monetary expansion that prevents the interest rate from rising.

Finally, we drop the fixed exchange-rate commitment and examine the effect of the respective policies under flexible exchange rates. Unlike fiscal policy, there is no need to distinguish between relatively mobile and relatively immobile capital when we consider the effects of expansionary monetary policy. The reason is that expansionary monetary policy inevitably causes an incipient deficit in the balance of payments. This depreciates the local currency, raises exports, lowers imports, and therefore adds stimulus to the economy beyond the purely domestic effect of higher investment. This can be seen in Figure 6.11. Beginning at point a with Y_0 and i_0, expansionary monetary policy shifts the LM curve to LM_1, where it cuts IS_0 at point b at income level Y_1 and interest rate i_1. These are the values that would be observed if there were no change in the exchange rate. However, point b is in the deficit zone, so the currency depreciates. The depreciation raises exports and lowers imports. It therefore shifts the IS curve to the right (to IS_1), and also shifts the FB curve

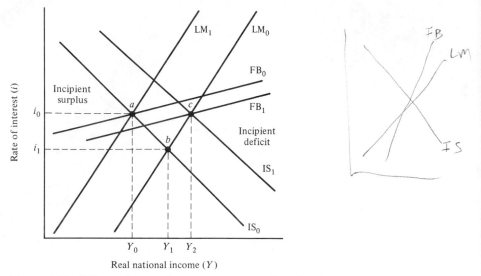

Figure 6.11 Effects of expansionary monetary policy with flexible exchange rates and imperfect capital mobility.

from FB_0 to FB_1. All three curves—IS_1, LM_1, and FB_1—intersect at income level Y_2, which exceeds Y_1. The drawbacks of this outcome are that the interest rate (i_2) is higher than i_1, implying less investment, and that a deflationary shock is inflicted on foreign economies that find their net exports declining.

The effects of expansionary fiscal policy with relatively mobile capital are shown in Figure 6.12. The fiscal expansion shifts the IS curve to IS_1, which intersects LM_0 at point b, implying an income gain to Y_1 in the absence of a change in the exchange rate. However, since capital is relatively mobile, point b is in the surplus zone. Therefore, the local currency appreciates, exports decline, and imports rise, so the IS and FB curves both shift to the left to IS_2 and FB_1, respectively. The economy comes to rest at point c, where IS_2, LM_0, and FB_1 intersect, thereby implying income level Y_2, which is below Y_1 because of the net export deterioration.

When capital is relatively immobile as in Figure 6.13, the outcome is different. The shift in the IS curve to IS_1 produces intersection with LM_0 at Y_1 and i_1. This, again, is the income change that would occur if there were no change in the exchange rate. However, because capital is relatively immobile, point b is in the deficit zone. The local currency therefore depreciates and this raises exports, lowers imports, and therefore shifts the IS curve out to IS_2 and the FB curve to FB_1, where they intersect the LM curve at point c, implying a further rise in income to Y_2. Although there is an advantage to having the fiscal stimulus augmented by a rise in net exports, the disadvantages are that the interest rate rises even more

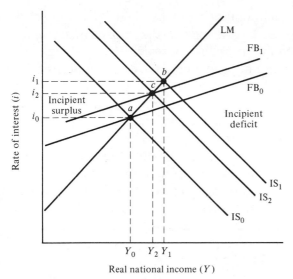

Figure 6.12 Effects of expansionary fiscal policy with flexible exchange rates and relatively high capital mobility.

than in the relatively mobile case, and the shock to foreign economies is also greater because of the greater deterioration of their net export positions.

To summarize: The effect of fiscal policy on the level of income under flexible exchange rates is magnified by a reduction in the degree

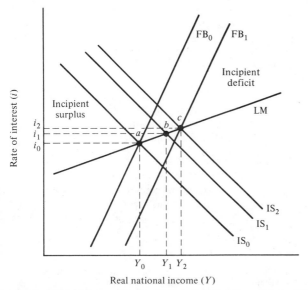

Figure 6.13 Effects of expansionary fiscal policy with flexible exchange rates and relatively low capital mobility.

of capital mobility. High capital mobility causes fiscal policy to appreciate the local currency, thereby tending to negate the expansionary effect of the fiscal stimulus. Low capital mobility causes fiscal policy to depreciate the currency, therefore tending to augment the expansionary effects of the fiscal stimulus.

Pause for a minute to study Table 6.1, which summarizes all the results obtained thus far. The entries are the national income multipliers with respect to a $1 rise in the money supply or a $1 rise in government purchases. The chapter appendix shows how the multipliers may be calculated. However, they are no different from the results deduced in the text. As the table makes clear, monetary policy under fixed exchange rates is completely ineffective regardless of capital mobility. Fiscal policy is powerless under fixed exchange rates with zero capital mobility, but the multiplier rises as the degree of capital mobility increases, reaching a maximum value equal to the closed-economy multiplier of the liquidity trap, when capital mobility is perfect. Under flexible exchange rates, expansionary monetary policy always raises income, the rise being greater as the degree of capital mobility increases, reaching a maximum value of $1/L_y$, which is identical to the closed-economy multiplier with the classical money demand assumption that $L_i = 0$. Fiscal policy is effective when capital mobility is low, but the multiplier declines as capital mobility increases, reaching a value of zero when capital mobility is perfect.

TABLE 6.1   CAPITAL MOBILITY[a]

	Zero mobility	Relatively immobile	Relatively mobile	Perfect mobility
		Fixed exchange rate		
Monetary policy ($\Delta m = 1$)	0	0	0	0
Fiscal policy ($\Delta G = 1$)	0	Multiplier increases as degree of capital mobility increases		$\dfrac{1}{S_y + V_y}$
		Flexible exchange rate		
Monetary policy ($\Delta m = 1$)	$\dfrac{F_i}{L_iS_y + F_iL_y}$	Multiplier increases as degree of capital mobility increases		$\dfrac{1}{L_y}$
Fiscal policy ($\Delta G = 1$)	$\dfrac{L_i}{L_iS_y + F_iL_y}$	Multiplier declines as degree of capital mobility increases		0

[a] S_y is the marginal propensity to save national income, V_y is the marginal propensity to import, L_i is the change in the demand for money with respect to the rate of interest, F_i is the change in investment with respect to the rate of interest, L_y is the change in the transactions demand for money with respect to a change in income.

6.4 COORDINATING MONETARY-FISCAL POLICIES TO REDUCE SHOCK TRANSMISSION

It is important to recognize that capital mobility destroys the proposition that flexible exchange rates provide economies with macroeconomic insulation from foreign shocks. Capital mobility means that net exports are apt to show large swings in response to the exchange-rate variations that are caused by capital movements, in a manner that destabilizes foreign economies, inflicting inflationary and deflationary shocks on the world economy as a whole. James Tobin of Yale, a member of President John F. Kennedy's Council of Economic Advisers, hit the nail on the head in noting:

> When the export–import balance becomes the strategic component of aggregate demand, one country's expansionary stimulus is another country's deflationary shock. [6]

How, then, should macroeconomic policy be conducted under the present regime of flexible exchange rates in financially open economies in order to achieve the desired domestic objective without harming foreign economies? We have seen that expansionary monetary policy under flexible exchange rates with a high degree of capital mobility raises income and employment by improving net exports, thereby shipping the unemployment abroad. Foreign countries are not apt to stand still for this and will probably attempt to neutralize the capital inflows and consequent appreciation of their currencies with expansionary monetary policies of their own. The result, then, would be a neutralization of the effect of the initiating country's monetary expansion on net exports. Consequently, the initiating country would find that its monetary policy is not nearly as effective as it would have been had foreign countries not responded with monetary expansion. As a result of such all-around expansion, the world money stock would rise and world interest rates might decline. If that happens, there is all-around expansion of investment in the world economy. The initiating country's income would then rise because the lower world interest rate would stimulate investment, but income would rise for no other reason. The idea that a system of flexible exchange rates provides monetary policy with magic potency is a dangerous illusion.

---

[6] Tobin, James, "A Proposal for International Monetary Reform," *Eastern Economic Journal,* 4, July/Oct. 1978, p. 156.

The restrictive monetary policies of the United States of the early 1980s produced effects that were entirely consistent with this analysis. The monetary restriction sent inflationary shocks to other countries, both because their economies were stimulated by rising net exports and because their import costs increased as their currencies depreciated. Attempting to stem the depreciation of their currencies, other countries reacted with restrictive monetary policies. The overall result was excessive monetary restriction throughout the world, all-around escalation of interest rates, and a major worldwide collapse of economic activity.

Now consider fiscal policy. As we have seen, expansionary fiscal policy is ineffective in raising domestic income under flexible exchange rates when the degree of capital mobility is high. But foreign countries receive an inflationary shock because of the rise in their net exports. To eliminate the interest-rate differential and the capital outflows that were caused by the initiating country's fiscal policy, foreign countries could undertake fiscal expansion of their own. That would drive up their own interest rates, neutralize their capital outflows, and eliminate the expansionary effects of a surplus in their trade balances. However, if inflation is a major fear and economic growth a major target, the other countries are not apt to engage in expansionary fiscal policies. In fact, they might instead go in the opposite direction, reasoning that expansionary fiscal policy would be inflationary and harm economic growth because higher interest rates will reduce investment. That, in fact, was the response of many industrial countries to the expansionary fiscal policies of the United States between 1981 and 1985. The consequence of such a response was to *widen* interest-rate differentials, accentuate the capital inflows to the United States, further appreciate the dollar, and perpetuate and widen the mammoth U.S. trade deficit, which reached $150 billion in 1985.

A constructive approach to macroeconomic policy would have recognized that it is the capital movements, responding to interest-rate differentials, that cause the bulk of the instability of net exports, thereby transmitting shocks to other countries. The obvious solution is to coordinate the two policy instruments. Expansionary fiscal policy raises interest rates and appreciates the currency. Expansionary monetary policy does the opposite. Therefore, appropriate stabilization policy suggests the use of both instruments in such a way as to prevent international interest-rate differentials and capital movements.

The effect of such coordinated expansion in the perfect capital mobility case can be seen by consulting Figure 6.6 one more time. Suppose that income is at Y_0 and that Y_1 is the target income level. The trick is to shift the IS curve to the right, and when that appears to be forcing up the domestic rate of interest, prevent the increase by expanding the money supply through open-market purchases of domestic assets. Therefore, coordinated monetary-fiscal policy would move both the IS and LM curves to the right, with the adjustment path along the segment *ac,* so as to reach intersection of the IS and LM curves at point *c* with income level Y_1. In this way short-run capital movements and large fluctuations in the exchange rate can be avoided. Income expands to the target level, and foreign economies are spared the discomfort of major inflationary and deflationary shocks. It can be shown, finally, that if such coordinated policy is pursued, the rise in income will be the same per dollar of monetary-fiscal stimulus regardless of whether the exchange rate is fixed or flexible.[7] Coordinated domestic policy is the way to go about expanding national income in either case.

If coordination is possible when capital is perfectly mobile, it should certainly be possible under other circumstances as well. This is shown in Figure 6.14, where the starting point is again point *a* with interest rate i_0 and income level Y_0. Let Y_1 be the target income level toward which policy aims. If the IS and LM curves are simultaneously shifted to the right to IS_1 and LM_1, respectively, income level Y_1 can be reached without disequilibrium in the foreign exchange market. There is no deficit under fixed exchange rates to cause monetary repercussions, nor is there any variation in exchange rates under flexible exchange rates to destabilize net exports and inflict shocks on foreign economies. The higher income level will imply higher imports and a decline in net exports in the initiating country, and a rise in foreign net exports, so there is some stimulus transmitted abroad. But this is limited to the effect on imports of higher income in the initiating country, while no country suffers a deficit or surplus in its overall balance of payments or pressure on its exchange rate. The initiating country's lower net export level is exactly balanced by a greater capital inflow caused by the rise in the rate of interest from i_0 to i_1.

It can be concluded that a coordinated application of domestic monetary and fiscal policies is needed if it is the intention of policy to minimize disturbances to other countries and, in the process, to avert foreign retaliatory responses. This is true regardless of whether the exchange rate is fixed or free to fluctuate. The notion, put forward by monetarist flexible exchange-rate advocates, that flexible exchange rates free monetary policy to pursue domestic goals is seen by the analysis of this chapter to be largely untrue in any relevant sense. Needed clearly is an international golden rule of macroeconomic policy: Do unto other countries as you would have other countries do unto you.

[7] This was demonstrated in the author's paper "Exchange Rates and Coordinated Stabilization Policy," *Canadian Journal of Economics,* vol. III, No. 1, 1970, 1–13.

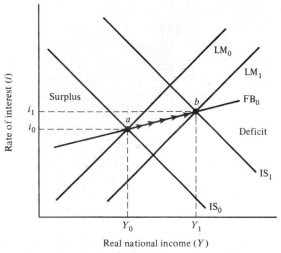

Figure 6.14 Effects of coordinated expansionary monetary-fiscal policy with imperfect capital mobility.

Attempts could also be profitably made to coordinate monetary policies internationally. Because domestic monetary expansion results in a deflationary shock and loss of employment abroad, an offsetting foreign monetary policy response is to be expected unless foreign countries are suffering from inflation caused by excessive demand. Consequently, it would appear essential to reach international understanding with respect to the desirability of joint monetary expansion in an effort to minimize interest-rate differentials, disruptive capital movements, wide exchange rate swings, and fluctuating trade balances.

As already noted, the failure to coordinate monetary policies is one of the principal reasons for the depth and severity of the 1980–82 world economic decline. This decline came in the wake of the oil shock of 1979, which saw international oil prices double through actions of the OPEC cartel. Except for Japan, all industrial countries responded with restrictive monetary policies designed to neutralize the inflationary effects of the oil shock. Countries appeared individually to have tightened their monetary policies not only to curtail domestic demand but also to appreciate their exchange rates to keep down the domestic cost of imports. Given the restrictive policies pursued elsewhere, however, countries wishing to appreciate their currencies had to embark on a greater degree of restriction than other countries, with the consequence that overall world monetary restriction was excessive. The result was a far more severe recession than was necessary. It is impossible for all countries simultaneously to appreciate their currencies. Uncoordinated competition to do so can therefore contribute to an economic collapse such as that of 1980–82, just as competitive devaluation added to the decline of 1929–33, which plunged the world economy into the Great Depression of the 1930s.

6.5 SOME ECONOMETRIC EVIDENCE ON POLICY EFFECTS

What does empirical research disclose about what is likely to happen in today's world economy in response to monetary and fiscal shocks? The Federal Reserve's Multi-Country Model (MCM) provides the following results for economies operating with flexible exchange rates.[8]

1. Monetary expansion causes a much larger depreciation of the currency than fiscal expansion per unit GNP or employment increase for all major industrial countries. This result conforms to expectations given the differential impact of monetary and fiscal policies on domestic interest rates.
2. The United States is the only large country that shows a systematic tendency toward currency appreciation in response to expansionary fiscal policy. This means that the effect of fiscal expansion on interest rates and capital inflows overpowers the effect of higher income and larger imports. The difference between the United States and countries where this is not so appears to stem from two circumstances. The first is that the demand for money is less sensitive to interest-rate changes in the United States, that is, the U.S. LM curve is steeper than elsewhere. The second factor is that U.S. securities are highly coveted as financial assets by foreign investors, so our FB curve is fairly flat. Despite the fact that the U.S. current account deteriorates because the fiscal policy raises income and imports and because the appreciation of the dollar reduces international competitiveness, this increase in the current-account deficit appears to produce little downward pressure on the dollar. A current-account deficit implies that foreign investors are accumulating wealth in the amount of the deficit. However, since a large fraction of this increase in wealth is then allocated by foreign investors into U.S. securities, the deficit is largely self-financed. The U.S., in other words, has tended to be in a favored position relative to other countries in being able to generate foreign financing for its current-account

[8] Oudiz, Gilles, and Jeffrey Sachs, "Macroeconomic Policy Coordination Among the Industrial Countries," *Brookings Papers on Economic Activity,* 1984.

deficit. The conclusions of the MCM model undoubtedly do not hold in the longer run. The continued accumulation of U.S. IOUs caused by the current-account deficit means that, ultimately, foreign portfolios will become overstocked with U.S. financial assets and their prices will then have to come down. That means the dollar must depreciate as, in fact, it did at the beginning of 1985.

3. Fiscal expansion has a smaller effect on inflation than monetary expansion per unit of real GNP or employment generated. This important result comes about because expansionary fiscal policy, even when it depreciates the currency, does so by less than a monetary policy that has the same employment-generating effect. Because of the higher value of the currency, import prices in local currency will be lower, so there is less inflation than with expansionary monetary policy.

The MCM model implies that the dollar tends to rise in response to expansionary fiscal policy in the United States because of the capital flows attracted by higher interest rates. The rise in national income increases the demand for imports, and the appreciation of the dollar accentuates the import increase and also lowers exports. Consequently, the expansionary domestic effect of the fiscal policy is far less than it would have been had the exchange value of the dollar remained constant or depreciated. At the same time the expansion causes less inflation than with fixed exchange rates, because aggregate expenditure rises by less and because the appreciation reduces the domestic cost of imports. It seems clear enough that the highly expansionary fiscal policies pursued in the United States between 1981 and 1984 resulted in little domestic inflation because of the ability of the United States to export much of the expansionary thrust of its fiscal policies to the rest of the world and because of the falling domestic price of imports caused by appreciation.

The inflationary effect of U.S. fiscal policies on foreign countries is greater than the effect that would have taken place had foreign currencies not depreciated, because depreciation raises the cost of imports from the United States. If other countries had been enjoying noninflationary full employment prior to the change in U.S. policy, the external stimulus would have generated substantial inflation and possibly a retaliatory response. That response could involve fiscal restriction, which, according to the MCM model, appreciates their currencies. Part of the original inflationary impulse is then shifted back toward the United States. Under the conditions prevailing in 1982–84 the stimulus to their exports was welcome, although the adverse effects of currency depreciation on inflation and on the burden of dollar-denominated debt was not.

An alternative for other countries would have been to counter U.S. expansionary fiscal policy with monetary restriction. But that implies all-around escalation of interest rates and a worldwide bias against economic growth. To avoid such interest-rate escalation, foreign countries should offset U.S. fiscal expansion with restrictive fiscal policy rather than with monetary contraction.

The MCM model suggests that foreign fiscal expansion depreciates foreign currencies, whereas U.S. fiscal expansion appreciates the dollar. This suggests an important asymmetry between the effects of fiscal policies conducted by the United States as opposed to other industrial countries. The asymmetry implies that foreign fiscal expansion produces a sharper localized employment effect and less of an impact on other countries. In the case of the United States, this conclusion is reversed. Thus the United States has a special responsibility to ensure that its fiscal policies are not inconsistent with the economic objectives of its allies and trading partners.

QUESTIONS FOR REVIEW

1. In the absence of capital mobility, monetary and fiscal policies cannot raise national income without causing a balance-of-payments deficit. Why? What would this imply about the effectiveness of the policies under fixed exchange rates? What would it imply under flexible exchange rates?

2. In the absence of capital mobility, flexible exchange rates ensure that domestic income equals absorption and that macroeconomic shocks are not transmitted abroad. Explain carefully why this is true.

3. Under fixed exchange rates the LM curve shifts automatically in response to the balance of payments. Under flexible exchange rates the IS and FB curves shift automatically. Explain why.

4. Assume that capital mobility is perfect. Then analyze
    (a) the effect of expansionary monetary policy on national income under fixed exchange rates.
    (b) the effect of expansionary fiscal policy on national income under fixed exchange rates.
    (c) the effect of expansionary monetary policy on national income under flexible exchange rates.
    (d) the effect of expansionary fiscal policy on national income under flexible exchange rates.

5. In the flexible exchange-rate cases, what are the effects of the respective policies on foreign economies?

6. How can a target level of income be attained in a way that minimizes shock transmission to other countries? Would the answer differ if exchange rates

were fixed? Does coordinated policy to stabilize capital movements imply exchange-rate pegging?

7. Why is the proposition that monetary policy cannot raise the level of income under fixed exchange rates independent of the degree of capital mobility?

8. When will expansionary fiscal policy tend to depreciate the currency, and when will it tend to cause appreciation? What are the implications for stabilization policy of these differences?

9. Interpret the following results of the Federal Reserve's MCM model:
   (a) Monetary expansion causes a larger depreciation of the currency than fiscal expansion for all major industrial countries.
   (b) Fiscal expansion has a smaller effect on inflation than monetary expansion per unit of real GNP increase.

SUGGESTIONS FOR FURTHER READING

Dernburg, Thomas F., "Exchange Rates and Coordinated Stabilization Policy," *Canadian Journal of Economics,* 3, 1970.

Fleming, J. Marcus, "Domestic Financial Policies Under Fixed and Floating Exchange Rates," International Monetary Fund, *Staff Papers,* November 1962.

Johnson, Harry G., "The Case for Flexible Exchange Rates," Federal Reserve Bank of St. Louis, *Review,* 51, June 1969.

Friedman, Milton, "The Case for Flexible Exchange Rates," *Essays in Positive Economics,* Chicago, 1953.

Laursen, Sven, and Lloyd A. Metzler, "Flexible Exchange Rates and the Theory of Employment," *Review of Economics and Statistics,* November 1950.

McKinnon, Ronald I., "An International Standard for Monetary Stabilization," *Institute for International Economic Policy,* 8, 1984.

Mundell, Robert A., "Capital Mobility and Stabilization Policy Under Fixed and Flexible Exchange Rates," *Canadian Journal of Economics and Political Science,* 29, 1963.

Oudiz, Gilles, and Jeffrey Sachs, "Macroeconomic Policy Coordination Among the Industrial Countries," *Brookings Papers on Economic Activity,* 1984.

Tobin, James, "A Proposal for International Monetary Reform," *Eastern Economic Journal,* 4, July/October 1978.

Chapter 7

Aggregate Demand, Aggregate Supply, Employment, and Inflation

7.1 THE AGGREGATE DEMAND AND SUPPLY FUNCTIONS

Determination of the price level, and therefore analysis of such problems as inflation and stagflation, necessitates introduction of the aggregate demand and supply functions. The aggregate expenditure function of previous chapters showed total spending in relation to the level of income. Aggregate demand, on the other hand, shows aggregate spending in relation to the domestic price level. Similarly, aggregate supply shows the supply of output that the economy will produce at different domestic price levels.

We will derive these relationships in a moment. But first, assume we already have them, and let us use them to show the issues and problems that these tools permit us to consider and investigate. In Figure 7.1 the aggregate demand function (AD_0) is a negatively sloped curve that indicates that a rise in the price level is associated with a decline in aggregate expenditure. It looks like an ordinary demand curve in an individual market, but there is much more to it than that. The illustrated aggregate supply curve (AS_0) is drawn as a positively sloped function between price levels p_d and p_f, indicating that within that range a rise in the price level causes the economy to supply additional output. However, at p_d the aggregate supply curve is assumed horizontal, and above p_f it is vertical. The functions intersect at point a, implying an equilibrium price level of p_a and equilibrium real income at Y_a. Nominal national income is the product of p_a and Y_a and is therefore measurable as the rectangle Op_daY_a.

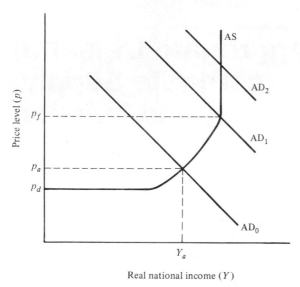

Real national income (Y)

Figure 7.1 The aggregate demand and aggregate supply functions.

Expansionary fiscal and monetary policies tend to shift AD to the right—to AD_1 for example—and they therefore tend to raise both real national income and the level of prices. As can easily be seen, the distribution of the increase in nominal total spending between higher output and higher prices depends on the slope of the AS curve. When AD intersects AS in the positively sloped portion of AS, a rightward shift in AD to AD_1 raises both p and Y. But a further increase (to AD_2) has no output effect and merely causes inflation. Such a situation is usually associated with full employment, although, as has been claimed, a vertical AS curve could come about at less than full employment for other reasons, such as the inflation indexing of money wages, which prohibits real wages from falling. Under such circumstances there is little value in expanding AD through monetary and fiscal policies. The added total spending is merely frittered away into higher prices without raising output and employment.

Conversely, if AD cuts AS at p_d—a situation that could occur during severe recession—expansion of AD raises real income and employment and has no adverse price-level effects. The first thing we have to keep in mind, then, is that the shape of AS is all important in determining the extent to which demand expansion raises output as opposed to prices. Clearly, aggregate supply repays careful study.

Next consider Figure 7.2 to study the appropriateness of policy responses to macroeconomic shocks. Assume initially that the economy is in equilibrium at point a with price level p_a and real income Y_a. Then

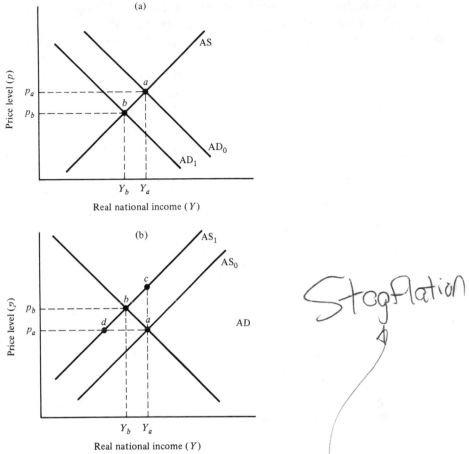

Figure 7.2 Policy response to shocks: (a) demand shock; (b) supply shock.

let AD decline to AD_1, perhaps because of a fall in investment or exports, so that the new equilibrium is at the lower income level Y_b and price level p_b. If policy wishes to restore income to its Y_a level, it should offset the AD shock by shifting AD back to AD_0 by using expansionary monetary and fiscal policies. The directive for policy seems fairly clear. Offset a demand shock with a demand-side policy response.

But suppose the decline in Y comes about because AS shifts to the left, which could happen if the cost of imported oil, food, or raw materials rose sharply. As can be seen in panel (b) of Figure 7.2, the decline in output is accompanied by a rise in the price level to p_b. Thus we can immediately see that the stagflation syndrome—that is, a situation in which output falls as inflation gets worse—must be intimately connected with restrictions in AS.

Stagflation

Easy to solve using F+M policies

Impossible to fix, since must go thr. S, not D, channels

Furthermore, when that happens, conventional monetary-fiscal policy tools encounter an impossible dilemma. For inflation to be prevented, AD would have to be lowered to cut AS_1 at point d, thereby causing income to fall even farther. And if policy attempted to raise Y back to Y_a, AD would have to be increased to cut AS_1 at point c, thereby worsening inflation. Small wonder that policymakers become schizophrenic in the face of stagflation and that economists begin to look for ways to improve the aggregate supply conditions of the economy. For example, had there been some way to replace higher-priced imported oil with stockpiled domestic supplies, the supply shock caused by the action of the OPEC cartel in 1973–74 might have been offset. But trying to do the job through demand management is obviously not going to work very well.

We move next to the derivation of the aggregate demand function. The top panel of Figure 7.3 shows IS_0 and LM_0 cutting at income level Y_0 and interest rate i_0. In the lower panel we assume that the price level

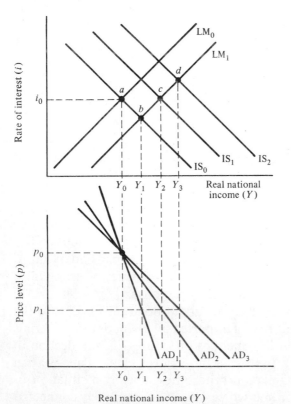

Figure 7.3 Deriving the aggregate demand function.

is initially at p_0. We then assume that the price level declines to p_1. This will have several effects on aggregate expenditure, as follows:

1. *The Keynes effect.* When the price level declines, the real quantity of money increases. Wealth holders find themselves with surplus money balances because the prices of the goods they buy have declined. They therefore purchase bonds and other financial assets with their surplus cash. This drives up the prices of bonds and lowers the rate of interest, which, in turn, raises investment and, via the multiplier, consumption. In Figure 7.3 this means that the LM curve shifts to the right (to LM_1) and intersects the IS_0 curve at point b at the higher income level, Y_1. In the lower panel we can see that this implies that Y_1 is the level of aggregate expenditure associated with the lower price level p_1. Therefore, if the Keynes effect were the only expenditure effect caused by the fall in the price level, the AD function would be AD_1.

2. *The real-balance effect.* Nearly all empirical evidence, as well as consumption theory, supports the hypothesis that consumption depends on wealth as well as income. For example, in the life-cycle theory of consumption, individuals are seen as attempting to equalize their consumption levels over the number of years they expect to live. Individuals whose wealth suddenly increases will obviously be able to raise their average annual future consumption levels.

   When the price level drops, that component of private wealth that consists of claims against the government will become more valuable. The relevant components of this form of wealth are the stock of privately held government bonds, the stock of currency, and the level of bank reserves. The sum of the latter two wealth components is usually referred to as "outside" or "high-powered" money. We could write the real value of such wealth as

$$W = \frac{M + B/i}{p}$$

   where M is outside nominal money, B/i is the value of the stock of privately held government bonds, and p is the price level. The function W is then entered as an argument in the aggregate consumption function along with Y. A fall in the price level then has the effect of raising W. This shifts the consumption function upward so that each income level is associated with a higher level of consumption than before, and this means that the IS curve shifts to the right. In Figure 7.3 we assume that the shift in the IS curve to IS_1 is caused by the real-balance effect. Line IS_1 intersects LM_1 at point c, which implies that aggregate demand at price level p_1 is Y_2. Thus the real balance effect adds further flattening to the AD function, which is now given by AD_2.

3. *The foreign trade effect.* The fall in the price level raises the real exchange rate ep^*/p, thereby making the economy more competitive in international trade. Exports increase and imports decline, so the IS curve again shifts to the right. Let the new IS curve be IS_2. It intersects LM_1 at point d, implying that aggregate expenditure is now Y_3; thus when all three spending effects are taken into account, the AD curve becomes AD_3.

These three effects do not exhaust the possible ways in which a change in the price level affects aggregate expenditure. However, discussion of such additional effects can conveniently be postponed to Chapter

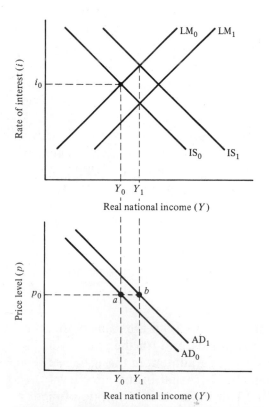

Figure 7.4 Shifts in aggregate demand caused by policy changes.

9 where the expenditure effects of devaluation are discussed. Meanwhile, we inquire into the various ways in which the AD curve can be shifted. The obvious answer to this question is that AD will shift when aggregate expenditure changes for any reason *other than* a change in the domestic price level.

Figure 7.4 shows the effects on AD of expansionary monetary and fiscal policies. We begin with IS_0 and LM_0, which intersect at income level Y_0 and interest rate i_0, and we assume the initial price level is p_0. The AD curve is AD_0. We then increase the nominal money supply by an open-market purchase of government securities, thereby shifting the LM curve to LM_1, which raises aggregate expenditure to Y_1. In the lower panel we can see that a new AD function must now intersect price level p_0 at point b. That is, AD will now be higher than before at *any* price level. The same effect occurs if the IS curve shifts due to expansionary fiscal policy. If such policy shifts the IS curve to IS_1, its intersection with LM_0 implies a rise in aggregate expenditure to Y_1, so Y_1 is the level of aggregate expenditure associated with price level p_0. Thus AD shifts to AD_1 as a result of either of these expansionary policies. Line AD will also shift to the right if the foreign price level p^* or the nominal exchange rate e rise, because either of these changes raises the real exchange rate ep^*/p and improves the economy's international competitiveness and, therefore, its net exports.

7.2 AGGREGATE SUPPLY AND THE BEHAVIOR OF WAGES

The aggregate supply function specifies the supply of output that the producers of goods and services in the economy will offer at different price levels. The study of aggregate supply conveniently begins with what economists call the aggregate production function. This function is a technological relationship that translates productive factor inputs into output levels. It could be written

$$Y = F(N, K) \qquad F_n > 0 \quad F_k > 0$$
$$F_{nn} < 0 \quad F_{kk} < 0$$
$$F_{nk} > 0 \quad F_{kn} > 0 \qquad (7.1)$$

where total output Y depends on the level of labor input (employment N) and the economy's stock of capital K—that is, its stock of machinery, equipment, factories, and other business establishments. The assumptions most commonly made about the production function are as follows:

1. *Constant returns to scale.* This assumption means that if both capital and labor are increased by a certain percentage, output will increase by the same percentage.

2. *Positive but diminishing marginal products.* The term F_n is the increase in output obtained by hiring one more unit of labor while holding the quantity of capital constant. This increase is called the marginal product of labor, whereas F_k is the marginal product of capital—that is, the additional output obtained from one more unit of capital while holding the quantity of labor constant. These marginal products are assumed to be positive. However, the famous law of diminishing marginal productivity holds that as more labor is added to a fixed stock of capital, the extra output produced by worker $n + 1$ will be less than the extra output produced by the nth worker. This does not mean the last worker hired is less skilled or energetic than other workers are; it simply means that all the workers have less capital to work with. The same is true for capital. The last machine installed yields less extra output than the preceding machine does, because, after the last machine is installed, each machine will have to make do with less cooperating labor. Positive marginal products mean that F_n and F_k are positive. The assumption of diminishing marginal productivity means that F_{nn} and F_{kk} are negative. The term F_{nn} is the change in the marginal product of labor as one more worker is hired. Since that worker's marginal product is less than that of the preceding worker, the change in the marginal product of labor is negative. The same goes for capital.

3. *The marginal product of one factor increases as more of the other factor is added.* This simply means that the extra output produced by each factor of production will increase if it has more of the other factor with which to cooperate. Thus the marginal product of labor rises when the quantity of capital is increased, and the marginal product of capital rises when the quantity of labor increases. These assumptions imply that F_{kn} and F_{nk} are both positive.

The marginal product of labor for an individual firm is illustrated in Figure 7.5. As employment increases, the extra output is positive but declining, so the marginal product of labor curve is negatively sloped. Initially we assume that there are k_0 units of capital, so $f_n(k_0)$ is the

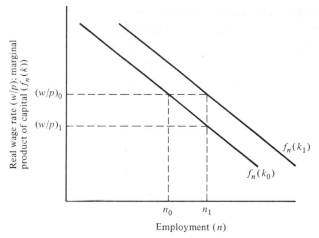

Figure 7.5 Employment determination for an individual competitive firm.

relevant marginal product of labor function. If we multiply the marginal product of labor by the price at which the firm sells its output, we get the value, to the firm, of the output produced by the last worker. This concept is called the value of the marginal product:

$$\text{Value of } f_n(k_0) = pf_n(k_0)$$

For example, if the last worker hired adds 10 units of output to daily production, and if each unit sells for $4.00, then the value of that production is $40.00 per day.

It clearly makes sense for the firm to hire the next worker if the value of the worker's marginal product exceeds the wage that must be paid. If the daily wage is $30.00, then the firm will increase its profits by $10.00 by hiring the next worker. In fact, it pays to keep expanding employment as long as the value of the marginal product exceeds the wage. Profits are then maximized when the value of the marginal product of labor just equals the wage rate. Therefore, the condition for profit maximization is that employment should be at the level which makes

$$w = pf_n(k_0)$$

If we divide both sides of this expression by price, we get

$$\frac{w}{p} = f_n(k_0) \tag{7.2}$$

where the term w/p is called the *real* wage. Thus profit maximization implies that firms hire workers up to the point where the marginal product of labor equals the real wage. The demand for labor is therefore a function of the real wage. In Figure 7.5 we assume that the existing real wage rate is $(w/p)_0$. Consequently, the firm maximizes profits when it hires n_0 workers.

It appears that there are two ways to expand employment to n_1. Either the real wage must be reduced to $(w/p)_1$ or the capital stock must be increased to k_1 so that the marginal product of labor curve shifts to $f_n(k_1)$. However, the assumption that is commonly made in short-run macroeconomic analysis is that the capital stock cannot be increased in the short run. Consequently, the firm is restricted to the $f_n(k_0)$ marginal productivity curve so that employment, in the short run, can be increased only by a reduction in the real wage. Either the money wage paid to workers must decline, or the price at which output is sold must increase. Otherwise there is no incentive for firms to hire more labor.

Reasoning by analogy from the micro to the macro level is usually not recommended as a suitable analytical procedure. However, in this case economists have not been reluctant to infer that the aggregate labor demand function depends on the real wage and the stock of capital. This is shown in Figure 7.6, where the demand for labor function, N_d, is shown as a decreasing function of the real wage. The labor demand curve is, in fact, the marginal product of labor curve derived from the aggregate production function. Clearly, in the short run, the expansion of employment implies that the economy's real wage rate must fall.

Different theories of labor supply abound. In traditional analysis it was customary to assume that workers were rational and would not be deceived into thinking that a wage increase made them better off if prices also rose in the same proportion. Consequently, it was assumed that labor supply was also a function of the real wage, and that additional labor effort would be forthcoming only if the real wage increases. This is the assumption under which the labor supply, N_s, function is drawn in the top panel of Figure 7.6. In that figure, the labor market is cleared at the intersection of the demand and supply functions at employment level, N_f, and real wage w_0/p_0. The bottom panel shows aggregate demand and supply. We assume that the output level associated with N_f is Y_f and that the price level initially is p_0.

To derive the aggregate supply function, we assume that the price level declines to p_1. In the top panel of Figure 7.6 we can see that this raises the real wage rate to w_0/p_1, assuming no change in the money wage w_0. As a result of this, employers cut back their hiring to N_d, and this reduces output to Y_d. Thus it is apparent that the fall in the price level has reduced aggregate supply to Y_d. Therefore the aggregate supply function must pass through points a and b, and the aggregate supply function is therefore the curve AS_0. We therefore see that aggregate supply is an increasing function of the price level.

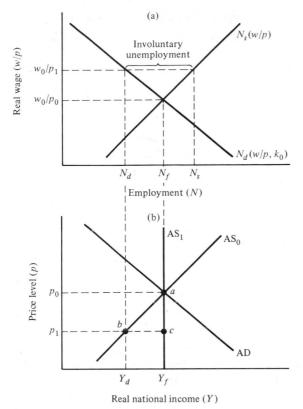

Figure 7.6 Deriving the aggregate supply curve: (a) labor market; (b) aggregate demand and supply.

Important Linkage

In the labor market it can be seen that the demand for labor is N_d, whereas the higher real wage has increased labor supply to N_s. There is therefore excess supply in the labor market equal to the difference between N_s and N_d. This excess supply measures *involuntary unemployment*, that is, the amount of labor willing to be employed at the existing real wage that cannot find work. In a competitive labor market the excess supply of labor would set off a process of wage cutting as workers compete with each other for available jobs. Presumably, such money-wage cutting would continue until the labor market is again cleared. This would happen if the money-wage fell to w_1, so w_1/p_1 would equal w_0/p_0—that is, if the real wage returned to its initial level. In that event employment would return to N_f and output would return to Y_f. Thus, in this event, the AS curve must cut points a and c, and it would therefore be the vertical curve AS_1. Competition in the labor market therefore ensures a return to full employment, and since this happens regardless of the position of the AD curve, output and employment would then be entirely determined by the supply-side conditions of the economy.

or else wont be vertical?

It appears that the positively sloped AS curve necessitates the important assumption of downward rigidity of the money-wage rate. There are several possible factors that might explain such wage stickiness. Strong unions might be able to prevent wage cutting even when there is involuntary unemployment. In some European countries, for example, unions tend to bargain more with the government than with private employers. The results of these bargains are usually called stabilization agreements, and they often find unions trading wage restraint in favor of a promise on the part of the government not to raise taxes. Minimum-wage legislation sets a floor to money-wages in many countries. A third hypothesis, originally due to John Maynard Keynes, is that labor is subject to money illusion. By that, Keynes meant that individual workers would not accept money-wage cuts because that would subject them to invidious comparisons with their more highly paid neighbors. They would, however, accept a reduction in real wages if that were brought about by a rise in prices, since that would affect all workers in a nondiscriminatory manner. Consequently, it makes a difference whether the real wage is lowered by a reduction in w as opposed to a rise in p, and that is why it is considered to reflect money illusion rather than strict rational behavior concerned only with w/p.

Finally, a frequent way to interpret wage stickiness is to distinguish between the short run and the long run. In the short run, money-wages tend to be fixed by existing labor contracts whose terms may run for from two to three more years. Money-wages remain fixed until the contracts expire. However, when wages are renegotiated, changes in the cost of living are taken into account and money-wages are adjusted accordingly. In this interpretation AS_0 in Figure 7.6 would represent the short-run aggregate supply curve, whereas AS_1 would be the long-run aggregate supply curve.

If this latter interpretation of aggregate supply is correct, it would follow that policy-induced changes in aggregate demand would affect output and employment only temporarily. The lasting effects would be price-level changes and possibly also changes in the composition of total spending. This can be seen in Figure 7.7. In the top panel let the IS curve shift to the right (to IS_1) due to an expansionary fiscal policy. The intersection with LM_0 implies income level Y_1. Therefore, the aggregate demand curve shifts to the right by the distance $Y_1 - Y_f$. The intersection of AD_1 with the short-run aggregate supply curve is at point c, implying short-run equilibrium output of Y_2 at price level p_2. In the top panel we note that the higher price level reduces the real quantity of money, therefore shifting the LM curve to LM_1. Consequently, the short-run effect with a positively sloped AS curve is to raise both real income (to Y_2) and

Good discussion

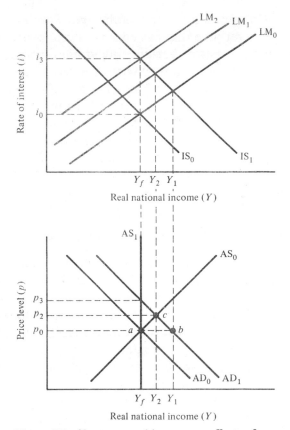

Figure 7.7 Short-run and longer-run effects of expansionary fiscal policy.

the price level (to p_2). Note also that in the labor market the real wage must have declined and that there must now be excess demand for labor.

As time passes, existing labor contracts expire, and when the time comes for renegotiation of wages the conditions for wage increases will be very favorable. The excess demand for labor implies shortages of workers, and the higher price level implies that workers are entitled to some wage catch-up adjustments to restore their real wages. As these wage increases are granted, AS begins to rotate in a counterclockwise manner, so aggregate supply declines. This creates excess demand for goods and services (that is, AD exceeds AS), so the price level continues to rise. However, since the excess demand for goods is not eliminated as long as wages keep rising, the process continues until AD intersects the long-run aggregate supply curve AS_1. Consequently, once all adjustments have been made, output returns to Y_f, the price level rises to p_3, and in the top panel the LM curve shifts to LM_2 because the rise in the price level reduces the real quantity of money.[1] If we inspect the final equilibrium, we can see that the only real variable that has been changed is the rate of interest, which has risen from i_0 to i_3; hence, investment must have declined. If the fiscal policy represented an increase in government purchases, its long-run effect is to crowd out investment through the higher rate of interest. If the fiscal policy was a cut in taxes, consumption rises but again at the expense of investment. Budget deficits are therefore often viewed as causing investment crowd out, which impairs an economy's long-run growth prospects because it is investment that brings about additions to the stock of productive capital.

Had the expansionary policy been a monetary policy, this would have had the initial effect of raising investment and therefore output and employment as well as the price level. Subsequent wage adjustments would then have rotated the AS curve, thereby creating excess demand for goods and services, which further raise the price level. These price-level changes reduce the real value of the money supply, so the LM curve, after an initial shift to the right, then shifts back to the left. In the final equilibrium we find that the price level has risen in direct proportion to the increase in the nominal stock of money. All real variables return to their original equilibrium levels. The only permanent changes are increases in the price level and the nominal wage in direct proportion to the increase in the nominal stock of money.

It may be helpful to summarize the discussion of this section by constructing some simple formal models of income determination for a closed economy. When wages and prices are flexible and labor market competition causes the labor market to be cleared, the level of employment and the real wage rate are supply-side determined in the labor market. That is, the equation

$$N_d\left(\frac{w}{p}, K_0\right) = N_s\left(\frac{w}{p}\right)$$

determines equilibrium employment N_f and the equilibrium real wage. The production function

$$Y = F(N, K_0)$$

translates N_f into equilibrium output Y_f. The IS curve requires aggregate expenditure to equal income. This may be written as

$$Y = E(Y, i, p) + A$$

---

[1] Notice that in this example we have ignored the fact that the rise in the price level will also affect the IS curve because of the real-balance and foreign trade effects.

where E is the induced component of aggregate expenditure and A is the autonomous component. If Y is predetermined as Y_f, the IS curve operates only to determine the rate of interest and the price level. The LM curve, finally, specifies monetary equilibrium:

$$\frac{M}{p} = L(Y, i)$$

but since the equilibrium level of income is predetermined, we can see that the IS and LM curves must intersect at Y_f, and they therefore jointly determine the equilibrium rate of interest and the price level.

An alternative to this so-called classical model is a Keynesian model in which the money-wage rate is assumed to be fixed. In this model the combination of the IS curve

$$Y = E(Y, i, p) + A$$

and the LM curve

$$\frac{M}{p} = L(Y, i)$$

together with the assumption that the price level is known determine real income and the rate of interest. The production function

$$Y = F(N, K_0)$$

translates the demand for output into a demand for labor. The labor demand curve

$$N_d = N_d\left(\frac{w_0}{p}, K_0\right)$$

together with the assumption of a predetermined money-wage w_0 then determines the equilibrium price level.

Although these are simultaneous equations in which all equilibrium values are jointly determined, it is helpful to think in terms of a sequence of events. Clearly, the classical model implies that the supply side is all important in determining the level of income, whereas in the Keynesian model the IS and LM curves, and therefore also the implied aggregate demand function, are important in determining real income.

7.3 WAGE POLICY AND EMPLOYMENT

The wage policies of governments, such as minimum-wage legislation and wage indexing to the cost of living, are usually well-intentioned measures that, however, are often believed to interfere with the objectives of full employment, price stability, rapid economic growth, and external balance. It is important to study these issues, since wage policies appear, on several occasions, to have caused governments to refrain from badly needed expansionary measures, and they have also prevented much needed global macroeconomic cooperation.

The recession of 1974–75 was a major debacle for nearly all oil-importing industrial countries. Industrial production fell in 1975 by 8.8 percent in the United States, 10.6 percent in Japan, and 6.7 percent in the European Economic Community. Subsequent recovery proceeded more rapidly in the United States than in the economies of its trading partners. This caused U.S. import demand to rise more rapidly than exports, led to a widening current-account deficit, and a severe depreciation of the dollar. Efforts by the United States to foster recovery thus clearly seemed to be impaired by the fact that expansionary measures would accentuate the external imbalance unless other countries undertook to stimulate their economies. Under the circumstances, that would have made very good sense since the United States could not act as the locomotive to recovery because of the condition of the balance of payments. Yet, despite urgent exhorations by the United States, most other industrial countries remained deaf to the plea to expand internal demand in their economies despite the presence of heavy unemployment.

The most frequently cited rationale for such reluctance lay in the claim that wages in many countries were indexed to the cost of living. This, it was claimed, makes it impossible to lower real wages even when unemployment is high, and without real wage reduction it is not possible to get employers to hire more workers. The expansionary policies then merely bring about inflation without raising employment.

In the 1985–87 period the mounting difficulties caused by a stagnant world economy were again causing the United States to attempt to prod such countries as Japan and West Germany into stimulating their economies. However, again we were being told that, because of real wage rigidity, demand expansion would be futile. It would raise money wages and prices, but it would not raise output and employment. Since what is at issue here is whether the entire world economy is going to grow or stagnate, it is a major problem that requires careful study.

The pessimistic argument is illustrated in Figure 7.8. Panel (a) shows the labor market. Because of diminishing marginal productivity of labor, the demand for labor is a decreasing function of the real wage, and it is also an increasing function of the capital stock K. Because of wage indexing, labor supply is perfectly elastic with respect to the real wage up to employment level N_f. The existing employment level is at the inter-

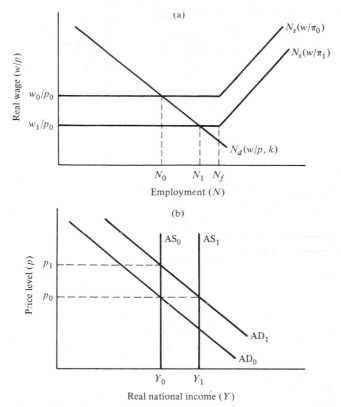

Figure 7.8 Effects of real wage rigidity: (a) labor market; (b) aggregate demand and supply.

section of the functions at N_0. The difference between N_f and N_0 measures involuntary unemployment. As long as the real wage cannot be lowered, employment cannot be raised. The aggregate supply function in panel (b) is therefore vertical, aggregate supply being, in this case, independent of the price level. Expansion of aggregate demand from AD_0 to AD_1 creates excess demand for goods and services so that the price level rises. However, since money-wages must also rise because of wage indexing, the real wage returns to its initial level and so also do employment and output. Demand expansion cannot raise employment above N_0, even though the existing employment level at N_0 is below the level, N_f, that would require a rise in the real wage to induce additional labor effort.

Before we get into a critical appraisal of this argument, we note that it contradicts the analysis of the effects of fiscal and monetary policy of Chapter 6. It can now be seen that that analysis is valid only if the aggregate supply curve is elastic with respect to the price level. That happens when money-wages are rigid, but not when real wages are fixed, because in that

only of AS is horizontal (ee
nominal wage only fixed) con + to M
policy work

event the AS curve is vertical. Indeed, Jeffrey Sachs[2] has gone so far as to claim that the results with respect to monetary and fiscal policy under flexible exchange rates are reversed. Recall that, with a high degree of capital mobility, expansionary monetary policy depreciates the currency and expands national income by raising net exports. On the other hand, expansionary fiscal policy appreciates the currency so that the fiscal stimulus is offset by a decline in net exports, and the fiscal stimulus is transferred to other countries. Sachs then tells us that these conclusions are not only wrong but, indeed, must be reversed when real wages are downwardly inflexible.

Sachs points out that the real wage relevant to hiring decisions differs from the real wage relevant to labor supply decisions. Employers are concerned with the wage in relation to the price of domestic output. Sachs calls this the product real wage. However, workers and consumers are concerned with the relationship between wages and the cost of living, which includes the cost of imports. Indeed, most wage indexing is conducted on the basis of what is happening to consumer prices, rather than domestic output prices. Therefore, let the consumer price index be denoted as π, and assume that it is a weighted average of domestic and import prices according to a simple function, such as

$$\pi = p^b(ep^*)^{1-b} \qquad 0 < b < 1$$

where p^* represents the price of imports in foreign currency, e is the nominal exchange rate, and ep^* therefore measures the domestic cost of imports.

Currency appreciation lowers ep^* and therefore also the consumer price index. Workers see this as an increase in the real wage rate, so the labor supply curve with respect to the product real wage shifts downward and to the right. The equilibrium product real wage is now lower, so employment and output rise. In Figure 7.8 the new labor supply function is N_{s1} so the equilibrium employment level rises to N_1. At the same time the aggregate supply curve shifts to the right, and equilibrium output rises to Y_1.

Such a result could be brought about by expansionary fiscal policy if the fiscal policy has the effect of appreciating the currency. Consequently, the Chapter 6 result that fiscal expansion is incapable of raising income and employment when capital mobility is perfect is regarded as incorrect.

Since monetary expansion depreciates the currency, the domestic cost of imports increases, so the consumer price index rises. Wage indexing

[2] Sachs, Jeffrey, "Wages, Flexible Exchange Rates, and Macroeconomic Policy," *Quarterly Journal of Economics,* June 1980.

then raises the nominal wage rate to restore w/π to its original level. Equilibrium cannot be restored until w/p and w/π both return to their original values. This necessitates a rise in the domestic price level equal to the proportionate depreciation if it is assumed that p^* remains unchanged. To see this, consider again the consumer price index

$$\pi = p^b (ep^*)^{1-b}$$

Using this to calculate the real wage as seen by suppliers of labor, we get

$$\frac{w}{\pi} = wp^{-b}(ep^*)^{b-1} = \left(\frac{w}{p}\right)p^{1-b}(ep^*)^{b-1} = \left(\frac{w}{p}\right)\left(\frac{ep^*}{p}\right)^{b-1}$$

The right-hand form of the expression shows that w/π depends on the product real wage and the real exchange rate. It follows that if there is to be no change in w/π and w/p, the real exchange rate ep^*/p cannot change. Consequently, $dp/p = de/e$, so the monetary policy cannot improve international competitiveness. Net exports therefore do not rise, national income remains the same, and the monetary expansion is purely inflationary.

This type of analysis suggests that expansionary fiscal policy under flexible exchange rates will raise national income, provided it causes currency appreciation. However, as noted in Chapter 6, expansionary fiscal policy tends to depreciate the currencies of most industrial countries, with the United States being the lone exception. Consequently, in the case of most industrial countries, downward real wage rigidity would tend to deter countries from attempting to raise employment by the use of both its monetary and its fiscal instruments.

This fact may explain the seemingly odd article of faith among European and Japanese officials that demand expansion, if it comes in the form of greater export orders, will have a beneficial effect on production and employment. But if the demand expansion is generated internally, it will only lead to inflation. A rise in export demand tends to appreciate the currency. Since this lowers consumer prices, domestic prices can rise without provoking a wage increase. Consequently, the product real wage falls, and output and employment expand. Internal demand expansion, whether monetary or fiscal, is likely to depreciate the currency, thereby raising consumer prices and provoking an upward money-wage adjustment. A government that subscribes to this theory will be very reluctant to assume any locomotive responsibilities. Indeed, one is tempted to infer that it is this theory that underwrites the disease of "Eurosclerosis" that has been much talked about.

The real wage is crucial in determining employment because of the assumption that the marginal product of labor declines as employment expands. This follows from the assumption of a neoclassical production function in which labor and capital are imperfect substitutes, that the capital stock is fully employed, and that only the intensity of utilization of the capital stock is variable in the short run. But these are strong assumptions that clearly do not describe many production processes and that may be inappropriate in macroeconomic modeling as well.

The most obvious case of alternative technology that could lead to different results is the case of fixed factor proportions. Output, capital, and labor are directly proportional, and labor and capital must be used in a fixed ratio. In such a case the marginal products of capital and labor are both zero, so the real wage is not relevant to determination of the factor mix. If exactly one person plus one broom are needed to sweep one room per hour, no extra output is obtained by adding a broom without adding another person, or adding another person without adding a broom. To get a second room swept requires both another person and another broom. Whether the person will be hired depends on whether it is profitable to sweep the second room and on whether the second broom is available. It therefore depends on the demand for output and has little to do with the cost of hiring. If the operation involves the sweeping of three rooms requiring three laborers and three brooms and it is subsequently decided to curtail activity to two rooms, this results in the unemployment of one laborer as well as one broom. The broom is not normally discarded or destroyed and is simply put in a closet pending the revival of demand. Thus, when demand revives, it is possible to activate the idle broom without any further addition to the stock of brooms (capital).

The example may be extreme, but it is hardly unrealistic. It calls attention to the fact that it is important to distinguish between the total stock of capital (three brooms) and the stock of capital in use (two brooms). When the stock of capital exceeds capital in use, as is the case during recession, expansion of output and employment can proceed without diminishing marginal labor productivity, because idle capacity is often readily at hand.

The same result would apply from so-called putty-clay-type technology. With such technology, labor and capital are imperfect substitutes at the planning stage, so the incremental capital-labor ratio is variable and therefore dependent on factor prices. However, once the capacity is installed and running, the soft putty turns to hard clay and it then takes a fixed amount of labor to operate the process. Subsequent changes in the relative prices of capital and labor have no influence on the factor mix for any vintage of capital in the clay stage. Output and employment can be reduced only by shutting down an entire unit of capital and laying off the labor that goes with it. Then, during revival, the labor and capital can be reactivated without any decline in average labor productivity.

Even when technology is putty-putty so that capital and labor are imperfect substitutes, there are likely to be limits to the extent to which factor substitution is possible. Figure 7.9 shows production isoquants for an individual firm. (A production isoquant, often called an equal-product curve, shows the different combinations of capital and labor that yield a fixed level of output.) It is assumed that the firm desires to produce y_f units of output and that the real wage and the rental price of capital are such that costs are minimized at point a, where k_f units of capital and n_f units of labor are employed. In the range between points b and c capital and labor are imperfect substitutes. But once the capital-labor ratio rises to its point b value, further increases in capital yield no extra output. Consequently, at point b there is so much capital relative to labor that the marginal product of capital becomes zero and the isoquant becomes vertical. Similarly, at point c the capital-labor ratio is so low that the marginal product of labor becomes zero and the isoquant becomes horizontal.

Firms minimize the cost of producing a given output level by selecting that factor mix (amount of labor and capital) at which the ratios of the marginal products of the factors to their respective factor prices are equal. This minimum-cost condition can be written

$$\frac{f_n}{w/p} = \frac{f_k}{\theta}$$

where f_n and f_k are the marginal products of labor and capital, respectively, w/p is the real wage rate, and θ is the rental price of capital, that is, the cost of employing one unit of capital stock for a given time. The condition simply states that the additional output that can be gained per dollar of expenditure on labor and capital must be the same. If another dollar

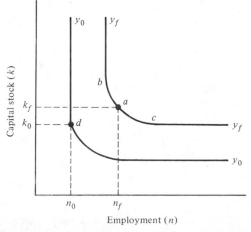

Figure 7.9 Determination of factor mix in deep recession.

spent on labor yields more extra output than a dollar spent on capital, it pays for the firm to hire more labor and to use less capital. Since a rise in the real wage reduces the output that can be gotten by spending one more dollar on labor, such a rise in the real wage would cause the firm to substitute capital in place of labor in the production process.

But this standard and well-known condition may not be applicable for firms during a severe recession. Consider Figure 7.9 again and suppose that the economy moves into a severe recession and that this firm's desired production level falls to y_0. If the firm's capital stock is divisible, the firm will elect to operate at point d with a ratio of capital in use to labor of k_0/n_0. The firm chooses this because the interest expense and the depreciation that enter into the rental price of capital are fixed charges that cannot be avoided by taking capital out of production. Therefore, the firm's cost-minimization objective is met by minimizing variable labor costs, thereby reducing employment to its lowest feasible level. This occurs when the factor mix is such that the marginal product of capital is zero. The real wage is now quite irrelevant to the determination of the factor mix. As far as the firm is concerned, labor costs are always minimized at point d regardless of the real wage.

At the recession point d the firm utilizes k_0 units of capital and puts $k_f - k_0$ units into mothballs. When the economy revives and it is desired to expand output to y_f, this can be accomplished by mobilizing its idle capacity and combining this with additional labor without running into diminishing marginal labor productivity. Thus revival from recession could easily be accompanied by a rising real wage, which often happens.

A simple macroeconomic model for a closed economy suffering from severe recession can now be constructed. As we study this model, the reader may wish to refer back to the models of the preceding section for purposes of comparison. We can write

$$Y = E(Y, i, p) + A \qquad (7.3)$$

$$\frac{M}{p} = L(Y, i) \qquad (7.4)$$

$$Y = F(K, N) \qquad K < K_f \qquad N < N_f \qquad (7.5)$$

$$F_k = 0 \qquad (7.6)$$

$$N_s = N_s\left(\frac{w}{p}\right) \qquad (7.7)$$

$$\frac{w}{p} = \left(\frac{w}{p}\right)^* \qquad (7.8)$$

Equations (7.3) and (7.4) are the IS and LM curves, respectively, where E is the induced component of aggregate expenditure, A is the exogenous component, M is the nominal stock of money, and i is the rate of interest. With a fixed price level these two equations would determine real national income and the rate of interest. Equation (7.5) is the production function. It is specified that capital in use, K, is less than available capacity, K_f. With output determined, the production function, combined with the minimum-cost condition (7.6) that the marginal product of capital, F_k, equal zero, determines the factor mix, thereby determining employment, N, and capital in use, K. Equation (7.7) is the labor supply function, and (7.8) specifies the downwardly rigid real wage hypothesis.

The model is illustrated in Figure 7.10. Panel (a) shows the intersection of IS and LM at real income level Y_0 and interest rate i_0. In panel (b) AD_0 is the associated aggregate demand function, which, at output Y_0, implies price level p_0. Panel (c) shows the labor market. Since the demand for labor is independent of the real wage rate, the labor demand function is vertical. Its intersection with N_s implies a real wage rate of $(w/p)^*$, the institutionally determined minimum real wage rate.

An expansionary monetary policy shifts the LM curve to the right (to LM_1), thereby reducing the rate of interest and raising aggregate expenditure to Y_1. This shifts the aggregate demand function to AD_1. The labor demand function then also shifts to the right to N_{d1} as firms move to higher production isoquants using both additional labor and existing ~~due to~~ idle capacity. Since N_1 is less than N_f, the rise in employment leaves the ~~recession~~ real wage undisturbed. Consequently, the price level remains at p_0, so the aggregate supply curve in the middle panel is perfectly elastic with respect to the price level in the recession range. The monetary policy is therefore fully effective in raising real output without generating inflation. It is, in fact, enough just to look at the IS and LM curves to analyze the effects of expansionary stabilization policies. Therefore, aggregate demand analysis, such as that of Chapter 6, appears quite valid, although the caveat must now be entered that it is valid in strictest terms only when AS is horizontal, and that is likely to happen only during severe recessions.

In summary: The present hypothesis is that a substantial number of firms undoubtedly operate under technological conditions characterized by divisible capital stock and limited capital-labor substitution possibilities. A large reduction in output causes such firms to minimize labor costs by moving to a ratio of capital in use to labor associated with zero marginal product of capital. Remaining capital stock is put on standby. The real wage therefore plays no role in determining the factor mix. The demand for labor then becomes a derived demand depending on the demand for output. Movements in real wages are not relevant to the factor mix and only incidentally to the determination of output and employment. These variables now respond positively to expansionary fiscal and monetary policies.

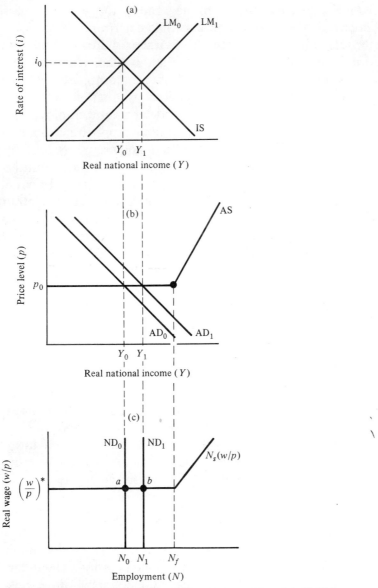

Figure 7.10   Aggregate supply with excess capacity: (a) IS-LM curves; (b) aggregate demand and supply; (c) labor market.

The recessions of 1974–75 and 1982–83 were very severe, far more, certainly, than the recessions of the 1950s and 1960s. Yet, this analysis suggests that the standard notion that employment depends on real wages is more applicable to the earlier period than the later period. A situation in which real wage rigidity stands as an impediment to higher employment is likely to be one in which economies are already approaching full-capacity utilization. Under such conditions it hardly seems relevant to analyze the impact of demand expansion since such policy is inappropriate to begin with. What needs analysis and consideration is the impact of monetary and fiscal policy in a global economy characterized by extensive international mobility of capital within the severe recession framework. That implies highly price-level elastic aggregate supply, and when that is the case it is entirely appropriate to focus attention on the demand (IS − LM) side of the economy. Under such conditions real wage rigidity is not an adequate reason for refraining from demand expansion.

Instead of indexing wages to the cost of living, some countries, such as the United States, legislate legal minimum money-wage rates. Such legislation represents a well-intentioned effort designed to provide adequate incomes for low-paid workers. Many economists, however, have misgivings about such legislation on the grounds that setting a floor to money-wages may interfere with the attainment of full employment, price stability, and external balance.

As in the case of wage indexing, it is advisable to distinguish the effect of the wage policy when the economy is near full employment from its effects during severe recession. We therefore take these cases up in order, beginning with an economy at full employment.

Figure 7.11 begins with the economy at full employment, N_f, with real income Y_f. Money-wages are assumed to be sticky in the short run, so the aggregate supply curve is the positively sloped function AS_0. The equilibrium price level is p_0, the prevailing money-wage rate is w_0, so the real wage rate is w_0/p_0. We then assume that the equilibrium is disrupted by the passage of a law that prevents employers from paying a money-wage below w_m, where w_m is in excess of w_0. Employers see this as a rise in the real wage, and they therefore reduce output and employment to the level at which the marginal product of labor equals the real wage. This is employment level N_0 in the top panel of Figure 7.11.

Since employers are no longer willing to supply output of Y_f at price level p_0, we can infer that the rise in the minimum-wage rate causes the aggregate supply curve to shift to the left. Thus, it can be seen that only Y_0 would be supplied if the price level stays at p_0. Consequently, we can see that minimum-wage legislation causes a restriction in aggregate supply very similar to any other supply shock that raises the cost of production.

The intersection of the new AS_1 curve with AD_0 is at income Y_1 and price level p_1, and the equilibrium level of employment is N_1, which is consistent with a real wage of w_m/p_1. Thus the overall effect of the minimum-wage law is to reduce output and employment and to raise the price level. The stagflation syndrome is thus clearly visible.

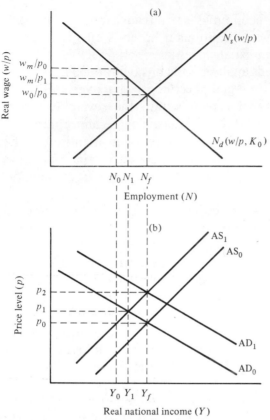

Figure 7.11 Effects of a rise in the legal minimum money-wage rate: (a) labor market; (b) aggregate demand and supply.

Let us review the argument to make sure we understand it. A rise in wages causes profit-maximizing firms to reduce employment and output. The decline in output reduces aggregate real income by an equal amount. However, because the marginal propensity to consume is less than unity, aggregate consumption falls by less than the decline in output. This means that excess demand arises in markets for goods and services, and this causes the price level to rise. The rise in the price level then adversely affects aggregate expenditure through all the factors that cause the AD curve to be negatively sloped. Specifically, the Keynes effect comes into play because the rise in the price level reduces the real quantity of money and raises interest rates. The real-balance effect is restrictive because the rise in the price level reduces the value of real balances, thereby adversely affecting consumption. And the foreign trade effect is restrictive because net exports decline as the price level rises.

The outcome is clearly unsatisfactory, so the government is likely to be called upon to restore full employment. It can do this by raising AD to AD_1. But now notice that if Y_f is to be restored, AD_1 has to cut AS_1 at that income level, so the price level must rise again up to p_2. With income restored to its full employment level Y_f, employment is restored to its original level of N_f. But this can happen only if the real wage drops to its initial level. Consequently, w_m/p_2 must equal w_0/p_0, and this means that workers are no better off in terms of real wages than they were prior to the well-intentioned effort to raise their incomes. The effect of the minimum-wage legislation has simply been inflated away by a rise in the price level.

Worse still, the economy's price level is higher than before, which implies that its net exports will have declined. If the government produced the increase in AD by cutting taxes, net exports will be lower, and this is offset by higher consumption. If the AD shift involved an increase in government purchases, the net export loss is offset by a larger government share in national expenditure. If AD was increased by an increase in the money supply, the net export loss will be offset by a rise in investment. In all cases, a rise in minimum wages that is inflated away by policy-induced demand expansion will cause a decline in net exports and a potential balance-of-payments problem.

Minimum-wage legislation is apt to have adverse employment effects even in the severe recession case. With available excess capacity, firms' marginal cost of production is constant and equal to the ratio of the money-wage rate to the average product of labor. A rise in the money-wage shifts these marginal cost curves up and causes profit-maximizing firms to reduce output. The resulting reduction in aggregate real income reduces consumption, but by less than the reduction in real income. Consequently, excess demand develops in commodity markets, which raises the price level. Since the rise in the price level reduces aggregate expenditure, the equilibrium levels of output and employment decline. Individual firms find themselves operating on still lower production isoquants. Both excess capacity and unemployment increase.

7.4 AGGREGATE SUPPLY AND INTERNATIONAL ADJUSTMENT

With aggregate supply in hand, we can study international adjustment in a more complete way than was possible in Chapters 5 and 6. We still lack an adequate way to explain capital movements, but that need not deter us here.

The theory of the gold standard applies to a regime of fixed exchange rates. Balance-of-payments adjustment comes about through the internal wage-price flexibility of competitive economies and the "rules of the game," according to which monetary authorities were expected to regulate the supply of money and credit so as to attain external balance.

Consider Figure 7.12, which reflects the gold standard assumptions. The top panel shows the IS and LM curves. To keep the example simple, we assume that capital mobility is absent, so the FB curve would be vertical had we bothered to draw it. The bottom panel shows aggregate demand and supply. The vertical aggregate supply curve reflects the assumption of wage-price flexibility. The panel also shows a new curve, NX, which specifies zero net exports. The NX curve is negatively sloped. A rise in income raises import demand and causes net exports to become negative. But this can be offset by a fall in the domestic price level, which improves international competitiveness.

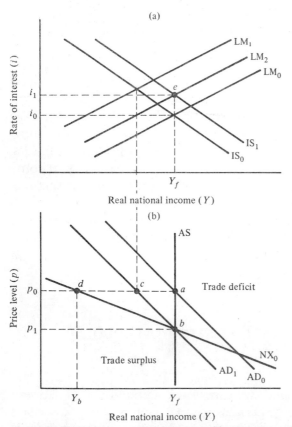

Figure 7.12 Balance-of-payments adjustment under fixed exchange rates with flexible wages and prices: (a) IS-LM; (b) AD, AS, and net exports (NX).

We assume that the economy is at full employment with income Y_f, interest rate i_0, and price level p_0. The only problem is that there is a deficit in the balance of payments, as reflected in the NX curve, which, at p_0 and Y_f, implies a trade deficit. At p_0 full employment implies income Y_f, but balanced trade necessitates income Y_b. Thus there is a potential clash between internal and external balances. This conflict can be resolved by a rise in the real exchange rate ep^*/p, but if the nominal exchange rate is fixed, then reconciliation between internal balance and external balance will necessitate a decline in the domestic price level.

The deficit in the balance of payments causes the nominal money supply to decline as the central bank sells foreign exchange to support the exchange rate. Consequently, assume that the LM curve shifts to LM_1. This also has the effect of shifting the AD curve to the left. The leftward shift of AD means that at price level p_0 there is excess supply of goods and services. Therefore if markets are competitive, the price level will decline. Since this raises the real wage, there must then be excess supply of labor, hence, money-wages also fall. Equilibrium is established at point b in the lower panel, where the AD_1 curve cuts the NX_0 and AS_0 curves at their point of intersection. The price-level changes do not shift any of the curves in the lower panel. However, the AD curve shifts until point b is reached because the money supply keeps declining for as long as the deficit persists. In the top panel we can see that the deficit reduces the real money stock, whereas the declining price level increases it. Similarly, the declining price level has expansionary expenditure effects reflected in a rightward shift of the IS curve. Consequently, overall equilibrium will be established at a point such as e. Since the rate of interest is higher, investment is lower, but this is offset by a rise in net exports.

Most analysts feel that the international gold standard worked fairly well during the period from 1870 to World War I. The conditions making for stable adjustment without major disruptions to economies, of which wage-price flexibility is the most important, were generally present. However, different countries suffered widely disparate rates of inflation during World War I and its aftermath, so the reestablishment of prewar currency parities (nominal exchange rates) provided real exchange rates that were at variance with purchasing-power parity and therefore implied either huge payments deficits or the necessity for substantial income or price-level shrinkage.

Figure 7.13 attempts to simulate the kind of situation that Great Britain faced in the 1920s when it attempted to restore gold convertibility at prewar parities. The aggregate supply curve (AS_0) is assumed to be horizontal for real income levels up to Y_f, reflecting the institutional fact of downward wage-price rigidity. Full employment would be established

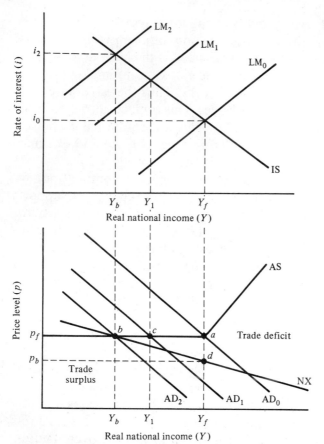

Figure 7.13 Balance-of-payments adjustment under fixed exchange rates with rigid prices.

if AD cuts AS at Y_f, as is the case for AD_0. This is also intended to be consistent with LM_0 and IS in the top panel.

However, the country's established price level is p_f. Since foreign countries suffered less inflation, the domestic price level needed to balance trade is the much lower price level p_b. Consequently, the country suffers a deficit in its balance of payments. The deficit forces the monetary authority to sell gold and foreign exchange, so the domestic money supply shrinks. The LM curve therefore shifts to LM_1, and the AD curve shifts to AD_1. This implies excess supply of goods and services at price level p_f of $Y_f - Y_1$. However, if the price level is downwardly rigid, the excess supply must be eliminated by a reduction in real income. Although this lowers imports, it does not do so by enough to remove the trade deficit. Therefore the deficit persists, the money supply keeps shrinking, and equilibrium is finally established at income level Y_b, where the income shrinkage is sufficient to eliminate the trade deficit, thereby preventing further shrinkages of the money supply.

In the final equilibrium the level of income is Y_b and the rate of interest is i_2. This economy is saddled with low income and high unemployment as the price of returning to the gold standard. Internal balance has been sacrificed to external balance. The country cannot raise employment by expansionary policies because that would restore the trade deficit and continue the loss of reserves. Indeed, the deflationary forces set in motion by the return to an unrealistic fixed exchange rate served to deny to Great Britain the prosperity that most countries enjoyed during the 1920s.

The only viable options for a country caught in such a dilemma would appear to be a major devaluation, and/or the imposition of import restrictions and the subsidization of exports. Nor is it difficult to see why flexible exchange rates are widely regarded as a logical necessity that follows from the fact of wage-price rigidity.

QUESTIONS FOR REVIEW

1. Assuming known IS and LM curves, derive the associated aggregate demand (AD) function. Why does it have a negative slope? What are the effects of an increase in G and/or m on AD?

2. What is the shape of the aggregate supply (AS) function if:
   a. Money-wages and prices are flexible and competitively determined?
   b. Money-wages are downwardly rigid?
   c. Real wages are downwardly rigid and the marginal productivity of labor is positive and diminishing? How does this differ from part a?

3. What is the importance of the slope of the AS curve from the standpoint of stabilization policy?

4. Is the AS curve apt to be more or less elastic with respect to the price level in the long run as opposed to the short run?

5. Explain the Sachs paradox that the results of the Mundell-Fleming model discussed in Chapter 6 are reversed by the presence of downward real wage rigidity. Does the Sachs paradox also help to explain why some countries seem to believe that increases in aggregate demand that come about by export expansion will raise output and employment, whereas internally generated increases in aggregate demand will not?

6. Using AD and AS analysis, compare adjustment under fixed exchange rates with
   a. downwardly inflexible wages and prices.
   b. competitively determined wages and prices.

7. What is the effect on aggregate supply of a shock such as a rise in the cost of oil imports? Use AD and AS analysis to analyze the effect, on industrial countries, of a large increase in the world price of oil or agricultural products.

8. What special policy problems are caused by a restriction of AS as opposed to a restriction in AD?

SUGGESTIONS FOR FURTHER READING

Branson, W. H., and J. J. Rotenberg, "International Adjustment with Wage Rigidity," *European Economic Review,* 13, 1980.

Dernburg, Thomas F., *Macroeconomics,* 7th ed., McGraw-Hill, 1985, chaps. 11, 12.

Sachs, Jeffrey, "Wages, Flexible Exchange Rates, and Macroeconomic Policy," *Quarterly Journal of Economics,* June 1980.

Appendixes to Part Two

APPENDIX TO CHAPTER 4

A.4.1 The Closed-Economy Model

Macroeconomic equilibrium requires aggregate expenditure to equal income. Therefore,

$$Y = C + I + G \tag{A.4.1}$$

or

$$I = S_p + (T - G) = S \tag{A.4.2}$$

where all symbols are the same as in the text. In this economy investment and government purchases are autonomous.

The consumption function is

$$C = C_a + b(Y - T) \tag{A.4.3}$$

where $Y - T$ is disposable income. Assume a proportional income tax so that the tax function is

$$T = tY \tag{A.4.4}$$

where t is the marginal (and average) tax rate. Disposable income may then be written as

$$Y - T = (1 - t)Y \tag{A.4.5}$$

and this permits the consumption function to be stated as

$$C = C_a + b(1 - t)Y \tag{A.4.6}$$

Private saving is the difference between disposable income and consumption. Therefore,

$$S_P = (1 - t)Y - C_a - b(1 - t)Y = -C_a + (1 - t)(1 - b)Y \quad \text{(A.4.7)}$$

Inspection of the consumption and saving functions as written in (A.4.6) and (A.4.7) discloses that the slope of the consumption function is

$$\frac{\Delta C}{\Delta Y} = b(1 - t)$$

while the slope of the private saving function is

$$\frac{\Delta S_p}{\Delta Y} = (1 - t)(1 - b)$$

National saving S is the sum of private saving plus the budget surplus. Therefore,

$$S = S_p + (T - G) \quad \text{(A.4.8)}$$

Substituting from (A.4.7) for S_p and the tax function (A.4.4) for T yields

$$S = S_p + (T - G) = -C_a + [1 - b(1 - t)]Y - G \quad \text{(A.4.9)}$$

It follows that the slope of the national saving function is

$$s = 1 - b(1 - t)$$

To solve for the equilibrium level of income, substitute the consumption function into (A.4.1) or the national saving function into (A.4.2). In either case the answer is

$$Y = \frac{1}{1 - b(1 - t)}(C_a + I + G) = \frac{1}{s}(C_a + I + G) \quad \text{(A.4.10)}$$

Using this expression, we see that the multiplier for a change in investment or government purchases is

$$\frac{\Delta Y}{\Delta I} = \frac{\Delta Y}{\Delta G} = \frac{1}{1 - b(1 - t)} = \frac{1}{s} \quad \text{(A.4.11)}$$

A.4.2 The Open Economy with Autonomous Exports

In the open economy the equilibrium conditions become

$$Y = C + I + G + (X - V) \quad \text{(A.4.12)}$$

or

$$I = S_p + (T - G) + (V - X) = S + (V - X) \quad \text{(A.4.13)}$$

where $V - X$ is the trade deficit. Imports depend upon national income. Therefore let the import function be

$$V = V_a + mY \qquad\qquad (A.4.14)$$

where m is the marginal propensity to import. Aggregate expenditure now equals

$$E = C_a + b(1 - t)Y + I + G + X - V_a - mY$$

so the change in aggregate expenditure caused by a change in income is

$$\Delta E = [b(1 - t) - m]\, \Delta Y$$

and it therefore follows that the slope of the aggregate expenditure function becomes

$$\frac{\Delta E}{\Delta Y} = b(1 - t) - m \qquad\qquad (A.4.15)$$

Similarly, the saving plus import function (total leakages) is

$$S + V = -C_a + sY + V_a + mY - G$$

so the slope of the total leakage function is

$$\frac{\Delta(S + V)}{\Delta Y} = s + m \qquad\qquad (A.4.16)$$

Next substitute the consumption function (A.4.6) and the import function into (A.4.1) and solve for Y. The result is

$$Y = \frac{1}{s + m}(C_a + I + G + X - V_a) \qquad\qquad (A.4.17)$$

Using this equation, we see that the multipliers for a change in G, I, and X are all given by

$$\frac{1}{s + m}$$

while a rise in autonomous imports lowers income by the same multiplier.

The change in net exports is

$$\Delta NX = \Delta X - \Delta V \qquad\qquad (A.4.18)$$

If national income rises because of a rise in investment or government purchases, $\Delta X = 0$, and the change in net exports is

$$\Delta NX = -m\, \Delta Y = \frac{-m}{s + m} \Delta G < 0 \qquad\qquad (A.4.19)$$

so there is a decline in net exports due to higher imports. If Y rises because of an autonomous increase in exports,

$$\Delta NX = \Delta X - m\, \Delta Y = \frac{s}{s + m} \Delta X > 0 \qquad\qquad (A.4.20)$$

Therefore, an autonomous rise in exports raises net exports, but not by as much as the rise in exports because of the induced increase in imports.

If the national marginal propensity to save is zero ($s = 0$), (A.4.17) becomes

$$Y = \frac{1}{m}(C_a + I + G + X - V_a)$$

and the multiplier in this case is the reciprocal of the marginal propensity to import. From (A.4.20) it follows that in this case

$$\Delta NX = 0$$

The effect of the autonomous rise in exports on net exports is therefore entirely offset by an induced rise in imports.

A.4.3 The Two-Country Model with Induced Exports and Imports

Consider two countries, 1 and 2, and let the respective equilibrium conditions be

$$Y_1 = C_1 + I_1 + G_1 + (V_2 - V_1)$$
$$Y_2 = C_2 + I_2 + G_2 + (V_1 - V_2) \qquad (A.4.21)$$

where V_1 and V_2 are the imports of the respective countries. Let the consumption and import functions be

$$C_1 = C_{a1} + (1 - s_1)Y_1 \qquad C_2 = C_{a2} + (1 - s_2)Y_2$$
$$V_1 = V_{a1} + m_1 Y_1 \qquad V_2 = V_{a2} + m_2 Y_2$$

When these expressions are substituted into (A.4.21), we obtain the simultaneous linear equations

$$(s_1 + m_1)Y_1 - \qquad m_2 Y_2 = E_1$$
$$-m_1 Y_1 + (s_2 + m_2)Y_2 = E_2 \qquad (A.4.22)$$

where E_1 and E_2 consolidate all the autonomous expenditure terms, namely,

$$E_1 = I_1 + G_1 + C_{a1} + V_{a2} - V_{a1}$$
$$E_2 = I_2 + G_2 + C_{a2} + V_{a1} - V_{a2}$$

A change in any autonomous term, such as dG_1, is reflected in an equivalent dE_1. Notice that if country 1's import function shifts upward, we have $dV_{a1} = -dE_1 = dE_2$, because in this event autonomous expenditure is affected in both countries.

Simultaneous solution of these equations gives

$$Y_1 = \frac{(s_2 + m_2)E_1 + m_2 E_2}{D}$$

$$Y_2 = \frac{m_1 E_1 + (s_1 + m_1)E_2}{D} \qquad (A.4.23)$$

where

$$D = (s_1 + m_1)(s_2 + m_2) - m_1 m_2 \qquad (A.4.24)$$

If both marginal propensities to save are nonnegative, D will clearly be positive. Notice also from (A.4.23) that the equilibrium solutions are functions of the levels of autonomous spending in the two countries. The coefficients of these reduced-form equations are the multipliers. Upon differentiating the two equations with respect to E_1, we obtain the effect on the income levels of the respective countries. The results are

$$\frac{dY_1}{dE_1} = \frac{s_2 + m_2}{(s_1 + m_1)(s_2 + m_2) - m_1 m_2}$$

$$\frac{dY_2}{dE_1} = \frac{m_1}{(s_1 + m_1)(s_2 + m_2) - m_1 m_2} \qquad (A.4.25)$$

The second expression is the effect on country 2's income caused by an increase in autonomous spending in country 1. As the term in the numerator makes clear, such an effect occurs because a rise in country 1's income causes it to increase its imports from country 2.

If country 2's marginal propensity to import is zero, the foreign trade multiplier reduces to

$$\frac{dY_1}{dE_1} = \frac{1}{s_1 + m_1} \qquad (A.4.26)$$

which may be recognized as the small-country multiplier derived in the previous section. If country 1's marginal propensity to import is zero as well, the multiplier reduces to the closed-economy multiplier

$$\frac{dY_1}{dE_1} = \frac{1}{s_1} \qquad (A.4.27)$$

Country 1's national income multiplier can be arranged as

$$\frac{dY_1}{dE_1} = \frac{1}{(s_1 + m_1) - m_1 m_2/(s_2 + m_2)}$$

which shows that the denominator is less than $s_1 + m_1$, and it therefore follows that the multiplier can be no smaller than the small-country (exogenous exports) multiplier. Similarly, we can rearrange the expression as

$$\frac{dY_1}{dE_1} = \frac{1}{s_1 + m_1 s_2/(s_2 + m_2)}$$

which shows that the denominator is greater than s_1, so the general multiplier can be no larger than the closed-economy multiplier. In combination, these results imply

$$\frac{1}{s_1 + m_1} \leq \frac{dY_1}{dE_1} \leq \frac{1}{s_1}$$

As shown above, the minimum value of the foreign trade multiplier is the small-country multiplier. Since consumption includes imports, the marginal propensity to import can be no greater than the marginal propensity to consume. In this extreme case the small-country multiplier formula gives a multiplier value of 1. Consequently, we conclude that a $1 increase in aggregate expenditure must raise domestic income by at least $1.

We now consider the combined effect of the change in autonomous expenditures of both economies. Adding together the multipliers, we get

$$\frac{dY_1 + dY_2}{dE_1} = \frac{s_2 + m_2 + m_1}{(s_1 + m_1)(s_2 + m_2) - m_1 m_2}$$

If the marginal propensities to save in the two countries are equal so that $s_1 = s_2 = s$, this expression reduces to

$$\frac{dY_1 + dY_2}{dE_1} = \frac{1}{s}$$

which shows that the total effect on world income equals the ordinary multiplier and that in this case different values of the marginal import propensities do not affect the result.

We next examine the effect of a change in autonomous spending in country 1 on the level of net exports of the respective countries. For country 1 the level of net exports is

$$NX_1 = V_2 - V_1$$

Consequently,

$$\frac{dNX_1}{dE_1} = \frac{dV_2}{dE_1} - \frac{dV_1}{dE_1} \tag{A.4.28}$$

However, from the import function we know that

$$\frac{dV_1}{dE_1} = m_1 \frac{dY_1}{dE_1} \qquad \frac{dV_2}{dE_1} = m_2 \frac{dY_2}{dE_1}$$

so that on using these results together with the multipliers (A.4.23), we obtain the change in country 1's net exports

$$\frac{dNX_1}{dE_1} = \frac{-m_1 s_2}{D} < 0$$

Since this expression is negative, it is evident that country 1's net exports decline while country 2's net exports must increase.

Notice that if country 2's marginal propensity to save is zero, the offset on net exports will be complete. Moreover, as can be seen from inspection of (A.4.28), country 1's multiplier will reduce to the isolated-country multiplier. On the other hand, if country 1's marginal propensity to save is zero, we obtain

$$\frac{dY_1}{dE_1} = \frac{s_2 + m_2}{m_1 s_2}$$

$$\frac{dY_2}{dE_1} = \frac{1}{s_2}$$

$$\frac{dNX_1}{dE_1} = -1$$

Next, let us assume that there is a shift in tastes which raises country 2's autonomous imports and therefore increases 1's autonomous exports. Differentiating (A.4.23) with respect to V_{a2} gives

$$dY_1 = \frac{s_2 + m_2}{D} dV_{a2} + \frac{m_2}{D}(-dV_{a2})$$

$$dY_2 = \frac{m_1}{D} dV_{a2} + \frac{s_1 + m_1}{D}(-dV_{a2})$$

which simplify to

$$\frac{dY_1}{dV_{a2}} = \frac{s_2}{D} \qquad \frac{dY_2}{dV_{a2}} = \frac{-s_1}{D} \qquad\qquad (A.4.29)$$

The shift in tastes has the effect of raising income in country 1 and lowering it in country 2. If the marginal propensities to save are the same, the income gain of country 1 exactly equals country 2's loss, and there will be no change in total world income.

The change in country 1's net exports is given by

$$\frac{dNX_1}{dV_{a2}} = \frac{dV_2}{dV_{a2}} - \frac{dV_1}{dV_{a2}} \qquad\qquad (A.4.30)$$

and from the import functions we have

$$\frac{dV_2}{dV_{a2}} = 1 + m_2 \frac{dY_2}{dV_{a2}} \qquad \frac{dV_1}{dV_{a2}} = m_1 \frac{dY_1}{dV_{a2}}$$

Substituting these results in (A.4.30) and using (A.4.29) gives

$$\frac{dNX_1}{dV_{a2}} = 1 - \frac{m_2 s_1 + m_1 s_2}{D}$$

It is apparent from this result that country 1's net exports increase as a result of the transfer of expenditures and that country 2's net exports decline. However, if either country has a marginal propensity to save of zero, the induced changes completely offset the autonomous shift. If $s_1 = 0$, we get

$$\frac{dY_1}{dV_{a2}} = \frac{1}{m_1} \qquad \frac{dY_2}{dV_{a2}} = 0$$

Hence country 2's income does not change while country 1's income rises exactly enough to increase imports by as much as the initial autonomous increase in exports.

If $s_2 = 0$, we get

$$\frac{dY_1}{dV_{a2}} = 0 \qquad \frac{dY_2}{dV_{a2}} = \frac{-1}{m_2}$$

so that in this case country 1's income fails to change while country 2's income falls exactly enough to reduce imports by the amount of the initial autonomous increase.

A.4.4 A Three-Country Model of Trade and Income Transmission

In this section we consider a three-country case involving countries 1, 2, and 3. Country 1's national income equilibrium condition may be written

$$Y_1 = C_1 + I_1 + G_1 + V_{12} + V_{13} - V_{21} - V_{31} \qquad \text{(A.4.31)}$$

where V_{12} and V_{13} are the exports of country 1 to country's 2 and 3, respectively, and V_{21} and V_{31} are country 1's imports from 2 and 3, respectively. Similar expressions can be written for countries 2 and 3. Consumption in each country depends on its own income level. Therefore write

$$C_i = C_{ai} + b_i Y_i \qquad (i = 1, 2, 3) \qquad \text{(A.4.32)}$$

as the respective consumption functions, where taxes are ignored. Imports in each country depend on their own income levels. Therefore,

$$V_{ji} = V_{aji} + m_{ji} Y_i \qquad \text{(A.4.33)}$$

which states that country i's imports from j equal an autonomous component (V_{aji}) plus an induced component equal to i's marginal propensity to import from j, multiplied by i's income level. For example, country 1's marginal propensity to import from country 2 is m_{21}, its marginal propensity to import from country 3 is m_{31}, and its overall marginal propensity to import is $m_1 = m_{21} + m_{31}$.

For a change in income due to some exogenous expenditure increase, consumption in the respective countries changes by $\Delta C_i = b_i \Delta Y_i$. Similarly, imports arise by $m_i \Delta Y_i$ while exports change by $m_{ij} \Delta Y_j$ plus $m_{ik} \Delta Y_k$. Substituting these changes into (A.4.31) shows that the income changes are

$$\Delta Y_1 = (b_1 - m_1)\Delta Y_1 \quad\quad + m_{12} \Delta Y_2 \quad\quad + m_{13} \Delta Y_3 + \Delta E_1$$

$$\Delta Y_2 = \quad\quad m_{21} \Delta Y_1 + (b_2 - m_2)\Delta Y_2 \quad\quad + m_{23} \Delta Y_3 + \Delta E_2$$

$$\Delta Y_3 = \quad\quad m_{31} \Delta Y_1 \quad\quad + m_{32} \Delta Y_2 + (b_3 - m_3)\Delta Y_3 + \Delta E_3 \quad\quad \text{(A.4.34)}$$

In matrix form this system of three simultaneous linear equations can be written as

$$\mathbf{\Delta Y = A\ \Delta Y + \Delta E} \quad\quad\quad \text{(A.4.35)}$$

where ΔY is the vector of income changes, A is the matrix of coefficients (marginal propensities), and ΔE is the vector of exogenous expenditure changes. The equation can be rearranged as

$$\mathbf{(I - A)\Delta Y = \Delta E} \quad\quad\quad \text{(A.4.36)}$$

It is useful to have a clear picture of what is involved in the $\mathbf{A}$ and $\mathbf{I - A}$ matrices. Accordingly,

$$\mathbf{A} = \begin{bmatrix} b_1 - m_1 & m_{12} & m_{13} \\ m_{21} & b_2 - m_2 & m_{23} \\ m_{31} & m_{32} & b_3 - m_3 \end{bmatrix}$$

and

$$\mathbf{I - A} = \begin{bmatrix} s_1 + m_1 & -m_{12} & -m_{13} \\ -m_{21} & s_2 + m_2 & -m_{23} \\ -m_{31} & -m_{32} & s_3 + m_3 \end{bmatrix}$$

where $\mathbf{I}$ is the identity matrix

$$\mathbf{I} = \begin{bmatrix} 1 & 0 & 0 \\ 0 & 1 & 0 \\ 0 & 0 & 1 \end{bmatrix}$$

Inspection of (A.4.34) suggests that a matrix of all possible multipliers would be given by $\Delta Y / \Delta E$. Such a matrix can be obtained by inverting the $\mathbf{I - A}$ matrix. Note from (A.4.36) that premultiplication by $\mathbf{(I - A)^{-1}}$ yields

$$\mathbf{\Delta Y = (I - A)^{-1} \Delta E} \quad\quad\quad \text{(A.4.37)}$$

Therefore, the multipliers will be the elements of the inverse of $\mathbf{I - A}$.

Computers are good at inverting matrices, so that eases computational labor. However, for analytical purposes it is important to know how to invert a matrix. Indeed, scarcely a subsequent appendix in this book is able to dispense with matrix inversion. Therefore, consider the square matrix

$$\mathbf{B} = \begin{bmatrix} b_{11} & b_{12} \\ b_{21} & b_{22} \end{bmatrix}$$

and take the following steps.

Step 1: Compute the determinant of B. This gives

$$|\mathbf{B}| = \begin{vmatrix} b_{11} & b_{12} \\ b_{21} & b_{22} \end{vmatrix} = b_{11}b_{22} - b_{12}b_{21}$$

Check the result to make sure that $|\mathbf{B}|$ is not zero. If it is, the matrix is said to be *singular* and cannot be inverted.

Step 2: Form a matrix of cofactors of the elements of **B**. A cofactor of an element is the determinant formed by suppressing the other elements in the row and column in which the element appears. Make sure to assign correct signs to the cofactors. If the row plus column index in which the element appears is an even number the cofactor is positive. If the sum of the row-column indexes is odd, the sign of the cofactor is negative. Therefore, the matrix of cofactors of **B** is

$$\begin{bmatrix} b_{22} & -b_{21} \\ -b_{12} & b_{11} \end{bmatrix}$$

Step 3: Interchange the rows and columns of the matrix of cofactors. This is equivalent to turning the matrix on its side, and is called transposition. The transposed matrix of cofactors, called the adjoint of **B,** is

$$\mathbf{B^*} = \begin{bmatrix} b_{22} & -b_{12} \\ -b_{21} & b_{11} \end{bmatrix}$$

Step 4: Form the inverse matrix by dividing each element of the adjoint by the determinant of **B.** Therefore,

$$\mathbf{B^{-1}} = \begin{bmatrix} \dfrac{b_{22}}{|\mathbf{B}|} & \dfrac{-b_{12}}{|\mathbf{B}|} \\ \dfrac{-b_{21}}{|\mathbf{B}|} & \dfrac{b_{11}}{|\mathbf{B}|} \end{bmatrix}$$

Since all elements are divided by $|\mathbf{B}|$, it is obvious that **B** cannot be inverted if $|\mathbf{B}| = 0$.

Step 5: Check the results by premultiplying the inverse by the original B matrix. The result should be the identity matrix. That is,

$$\mathbf{BB^{-1}} = \mathbf{I} = \begin{bmatrix} 1 & 0 \\ 0 & 1 \end{bmatrix}$$

For a matrix such as $I - A$ it is possible to invert the matrix by calculating a power series that involves only matrix multiplication and addition. Define

$$F = I + A + A^2 + A^3 + A^4 + \cdots + A^{n-1}$$

Premultiply both sides by A to get a new series

$$AF = A + A^2 + A^3 + A^4 + \cdots + A^n$$

and then subtract the second series from the first. This gives

$$F - AF = I - A^n$$

If the elements of A^n are very small, this term can be ignored, so

$$(I - A)F = I$$

Premultiply both sides by $(I - A)^{-1}$ to get

$$(I - A)^{-1}(I - A)F = (I - A)^{-1}$$

whence it follows that

$$F = (I - A)^{-1} = I + A + A^2 + A^3 + \cdots + A^{n-1}$$

The general principles having been outlined, we can now return to the three-country foreign trade multiplier example. Suppose an econometrician provides the following parameter estimates for the A matrix:

$$A = \begin{bmatrix} 0.65 & 0.2 & 0.1 \\ 0.15 & 0.6 & 0 \\ 0.05 & 0.1 & 0.7 \end{bmatrix}$$

The first column shows country 1's marginal propensities. The marginal propensity to consume minus its marginal propensity to import is 0.65, its marginal propensity to import from country 2 is 0.15, and its marginal propensity to import from country 3 is 0.05. Its overall marginal propensity to import is 0.2, so its marginal propensity to consume must be 0.85. Columns 2 and 3, respectively, provide the propensities for countries 2 and 3. The elements in the main diagonal are each country's marginal propensity to consume minus its marginal propensity to import.

The $I - A$ matrix is

$$I - A = \begin{bmatrix} 0.35 & -0.2 & -0.1 \\ -0.15 & 0.4 & 0 \\ -0.05 & -0.1 & 0.3 \end{bmatrix}$$

where the elements in the main diagonal equal the sum of the marginal propensity to save and the marginal propensity to import. Country 1's marginal propensity to import is 0.2, its marginal propensity to consume is 0.85, and its marginal propensity to save is 0.15.

The inverse matrix may now be computed in a convenient manner, and the result is

$$(\mathbf{I} - \mathbf{A})^{-1} = \begin{bmatrix} 4.08 & 2.37 & 1.36 \\ 1.53 & 3.39 & 0.51 \\ 1.19 & 1.53 & 3.73 \end{bmatrix}$$

Recalling from (A.4.37) that

$$\Delta \mathbf{Y} = (\mathbf{I} - \mathbf{A})^{-1} \Delta \mathbf{E} \tag{A.4.38}$$

we can write the results as

$$\Delta Y_1 = 4.08 \, \Delta E_1 + 2.37 \, \Delta E_2 + 1.36 \, \Delta E_3$$

$$\Delta Y_2 = 1.53 \, \Delta E_1 + 3.39 \, \Delta E_2 + 0.51 \, \Delta E_3$$

$$\Delta Y_3 = 1.19 \, \Delta E_1 + 1.53 \, \Delta E_2 + 3.73 \, \Delta E_3 \tag{A.4.39}$$

The first column shows that a rise in exogenous expenditure in country 1 of $1 raises its own income by $4.08. It also raises the income of country 2 by $1.53 and country 3's income by $1.19. Notice from the elements in the main diagonal that country 2 has the lowest domestic multiplier (3.39) because it has the highest marginal propensity to save plus its marginal propensity to import (0.6).

APPENDIX TO CHAPTER 5

A.5.1 Comparative Statics of the Closed-Economy IS-LM Model

The equations for the IS and LM curves are

$$F(i) = S(Y, t) - G$$

$$m_s = L(Y, i, W) \tag{A.5.1}$$

where $S = S(Y, t) - G$ denotes that total national saving depends on income, the tax rate, and the level of autonomous government purchases. Differentiating totally while holding wealth W and the tax rate t constant gives

$$S_y \, dY - F_i \, di = dG$$

$$L_y \, dY + L_i \, di = dm_s \tag{A.5.2}$$

or

$$\begin{bmatrix} S_y & -F_i \\ L_y & L_i \end{bmatrix} \begin{bmatrix} dY \\ di \end{bmatrix} = \begin{bmatrix} dG \\ dm_s \end{bmatrix} \tag{A.5.3}$$

Calculation of the inverse of the coefficient matrix gives the solution

$$
\begin{bmatrix} dY \\ \\ di \end{bmatrix} = \begin{bmatrix} \dfrac{L_i}{D} & \dfrac{F_i}{D} \\ \\ \dfrac{-L_y}{D} & \dfrac{S_y}{D} \end{bmatrix} \begin{bmatrix} dG \\ \\ dm_s \end{bmatrix}
\tag{A.5.4}
$$

where D is the determinant of the coefficient matrix, given by

$$
D = S_y L_i + F_i L_y < 0
$$

Since S_y is positive, L_i is negative, F_i is negative, and L_y is positive, the sign of D is negative.

The solution shows that the multipliers in response to a monetary injection are

$$
\frac{dY}{dm} = \frac{F_i}{S_y L_i + F_i L_y} > 0
\tag{A.5.5.1}
$$

$$
\frac{di}{dm} = \frac{S_y}{S_y L_i + F_i L_y} < 0
\tag{A.5.5.2}
$$

It is important to consider the two special cases that involve different assumptions about the nature of the demand for money. The first, sometimes called the classical case, denies the possibility of liquidity preference. In this case $L_i = 0$, so

$$
\frac{dY}{dm} = \frac{1}{L_y}
$$

which suggests that the rise in income is directly proportional to the increase in the money supply. In the extreme Keynesian case there is a "liquidity trap" in which the demand for money is infinitely elastic with respect to the rate of interest. In this case $L_i \rightarrow -\infty$, so

$$
\frac{dY}{dm} = 0 \qquad \frac{di}{dm} = 0
$$

The increase in the money supply fails to lower the rate of interest. It therefore fails to stimulate investment, so national income does not change.

The effects of fiscal policy can be seen from (A.5.4) to be

$$
\frac{dY}{dG} = \frac{L_i}{S_y L_i + F_i L_y} > 0
\tag{A.5.6.1}
$$

$$
\frac{di}{dG} = \frac{-L_y}{S_y L_i + F_i L_y} > 0
\tag{A.5.6.2}
$$

Notice first that, whereas expansionary monetary policy lowers the rate of interest as it raises income, expansionary fiscal policy raises both the rate of interest and the level of income.

In the classical case $L_i = 0$, so

$$\frac{dY}{dG} = 0$$

suggesting that a rise in G fails to raise Y because of complete investment crowd out. The economy cannot expand without an increase in the money supply. In the extreme Keynesian case

$$\frac{dY}{dG} = \frac{1}{S_y + F_i L_y / L_i} = \frac{1}{S_y}$$

because $L_i \to -\infty$. Therefore, the Keynesian case implies the simple multiplier effect without concern for interest rates and investment crowd out. Also, $di/dG = 0$, implying that government borrowing and income expansion can go forward without a rise in interest rates because the expansion can be financed with idle money balances.

Next, we consider the effects of various parameter changes on the multipliers. Begin by raising the marginal propensity to save. Taking the partial derivative of the multipliers with respect to S_y gives

$$\frac{\partial(dY/dG)}{\partial S_y} = \frac{-L_i^2}{D^2} < 0 \qquad \frac{\partial(dY/dm)}{\partial S_y} = \frac{-F_i L_i}{D^2} < 0$$

Therefore, a rise in the marginal propensity to save reduces both the government purchase and the money multiplier.

An increase in the sensitivity of investment to changes in the rate of interest implies a reduction in the value of F_i, the reciprocal of the slope of the investment demand curve. Therefore,

$$\frac{\partial(dY/dG)}{\partial F_i} = \frac{-L_i L_y}{D^2} > 0 \qquad \frac{\partial(dY/dm)}{\partial F_i} = \frac{S_y L_i}{D^2} < 0$$

so the government purchase multiplier falls because there is more investment crowd out, and the money multiplier rises because a given reduction in the rate of interest stimulates more investment.

Finally, an increased sensitivity of the demand for money to changes in the rate of interest implies a reduction in the parameter L_i. Therefore,

$$\frac{\partial(dY/dG)}{\partial L_i} = \frac{F_i L_y}{D^2} < 0 \qquad \frac{\partial(dY/dm)}{\partial L_i} = \frac{-F_i S_y}{D^2} > 0$$

so the government purchase multiplier rises because there is a smaller rise in the rate of interest and therefore less investment crowd out, whereas the money multiplier falls because there is a smaller fall in the rate of interest, thereby stimulating less investment.

A.5.2 An Introduction to Macrodynamics and Stability Analysis

Stability analysis is an essential tool for the macroeconomist. The method of analysis of Part Two is called comparative statics. Equilibrium solutions are calculated by solving for the points of intersection of the functions. A parameter shift then produces a new equilibrium solution. Measuring the changes in the variables that take place between the new and the old equilibrium is called comparative statics. The multipliers calculated or deduced in the text are comparative static results.

Dynamics deals with the economy when it is out of equilibrium, attempting to trace the time-path of adjustment. There is a great deal of implicit dynamics in the verbal discussion of the text, but thus far the dynamics have not been made explicit in the models themselves. However, explicit dynamics are indispensable. For example, forecasting models are necessarily dynamic. In international finance the frequently observed fact that exchange rates tend to overshoot their equilibrium values can only be analyzed with an explicit dynamic model. Similarly, the question of how to pair policy instruments with policy targets, another important issue in global macroeconomics, is answered by stability analysis. Finally, dynamic analysis is an essential supplement to comparative statics because the dynamics verify or refute comparative static results. This appendix addresses itself to showing how to deal with that problem.

To use a simple illustration, we undertake stability analysis for the closed-economy IS-LM model. To make the example a bit more challenging, we add to the investment function the widely accepted hypothesis that investment is an increasing function of the level of income as well as a decreasing function of the rate of interest. Therefore,

$$I = F(Y, i) \qquad F_y > 0 \quad F_i < 0$$

where the parameter F_y is called the *marginal propensity to invest*. The comparative static model now becomes

$$F(Y, i) = S(Y) - G$$

$$m_s = L(Y, i) \tag{A.5.7}$$

where the first equation is the IS curve and the second the LM curve. Note that the tax rate and wealth have been dropped from the saving and liquidity-preference functions since we are not going to change these variables here anyway.

First, consider the slopes of the functions:

$$\left(\frac{di}{dY} \right)_{IS} = \frac{S_y - F_y}{F_i} \gtrless 0$$

$$\left(\frac{di}{dY} \right)_{LM} = \frac{-L_y}{L_i} > 0 \tag{A.5.8}$$

Observe that the slope of the IS curve can now be negative or positive, depending on whether the marginal propensity to save is greater than or less than the marginal propensity to invest. If a rise in income generates more additional investment than saving, saving cannot catch up to investment unless the interest rate rises to slow the growth of investment. That is why the IS curve has a positive slope in such an event.

If we conduct comparative static analysis with this model, we would get as a solution

$$
\begin{bmatrix} dY \\ di \end{bmatrix} = \begin{bmatrix} \dfrac{L_i}{D} & \dfrac{F_i}{D} \\ \dfrac{-L_y}{D} & \dfrac{S_y - F_y}{D} \end{bmatrix} \begin{bmatrix} dG \\ dm \end{bmatrix} \tag{A.5.9}
$$

where D is the determinant of the coefficient matrix, given by

$$
D = L_i(S_y - F_y) + F_iL_y \gtrless 0 \tag{A.5.10}
$$

Notice that the sign of D is now ambiguous, since $S_y - F_y$ could be positive or negative. That was not possible in the analysis of the preceding appendix, where F_y was zero. Since the sign of D is ambiguous, the signs of the multipliers are also ambiguous. For example, the multiplier

$$
\frac{dY}{dm} = \frac{F_i}{L_i(S_y - F_y) + F_iL_y}
$$

could be positive or negative, depending on whether S_y is greater than or less than F_y. Therefore, if the marginal propensity to save is less than the marginal propensity to invest, and the entire denominator is positive, the comparative static model would predict that a rise in the money supply will lower the level of income. That makes little sense, and the dynamics of the case will show why.

To conduct stability analysis, we need to introduce explicit dynamic assumptions about how the variables behave when they are out of equilibrium. Typically, it is assumed that the rate at which income changes is proportional to the difference between investment and national saving. Similarly, we assume that the rate at which the rate of interest changes is proportional to the difference between the demand for money and the supply of money. Therefore, we state the explicit dynamic hypotheses that

$$
\frac{dY}{dt} = k_1[F(Y, i) - S(Y) + G]
$$

$$
\frac{di}{dt} = k_2[L(Y, i) - m_s] \tag{A.5.11}
$$

The derivatives dY/dt and di/dt are, respectively, the time rate of change of income and the rate of interest. Here, t refers to time, not to the tax rate. The coefficients k_1 and k_2 are positive constants, known as *reaction coefficients*, that describe the speed of adjustment.

When we inspect the dynamic differential equations (A.5.11), we see that the functions are in implicit form. The next step is to replace the implicit functions with linear approximations in the neighborhood of equilibrium. The value of saving, for example, is approximated by taking its equilibrium value $\bar{S}$ and adding a correction factor equal to the slope of the saving function multiplied by the difference between the actual value of income and the equilibrium level. Therefore S is approximated by

$$S = \bar{S} + S_y(Y - \bar{Y})$$

which would be a perfect approximation if the saving function were linear. Using this procedure with all the functions in (A.5.11), we get

$$\frac{dY}{dt} = k_1[\bar{I} + F_y(Y - \bar{Y}) + F_i(i - \bar{i}) - \bar{S} - S_y(Y - \bar{Y}) + G]$$

$$\frac{di}{dt} = k_2[\bar{m}_d + L_y(Y - \bar{Y}) + L_i(i - \bar{i}) - m_s]$$

In equilibrium $\bar{I} = \bar{S} - G$, and $\bar{m}_d = m_s$; that is, equilibrium investment equals saving, and the equilibrium demand for money, m_d, equals the supply of money. Consequently, it can be seen that the constant terms drop out of the preceding expressions. They may therefore be written as

$$\frac{dY}{dt} = k_1[-(S_y - F_y)(Y - \bar{Y}) + F_i(i - \bar{i})]$$

$$\frac{di}{dt} = k_2[L_y(Y - \bar{Y}) + L_i(i - \bar{i})] \qquad (A.5.12)$$

In this form the equations are described as *simultaneous, linear, homogeneous differential* equations.

A solution to a differential equation is a formula that satisfies the differential equation and expresses the values of the variables as functions of time alone. Such a solution is of the form

$$Y = \bar{Y} + n_0 e^{qt}$$

$$i = \bar{i} + n_1 e^{qt} \qquad (A.5.13)$$

where e is the exponential (not the exchange rate). The term q is called the characteristic root of the differential equation. We call the system stable if Y approaches $\bar{Y}$, and i approaches $\bar{i}$, with the passage of time. This implies that the root q must be negative. Otherwise, the terms $n_0 e^{qt}$ and $n_1 e^{qt}$ would grow larger as t increases.

Differentiate equations (A.5.13) with respect to time to get

$$\frac{dY}{dt} = q n_0 e^{qt} = q(Y - \bar{Y})$$

$$\frac{di}{dt} = q n_1 e^{qt} = q(i - \bar{i}) \qquad (A.5.14)$$

The right-hand parts of (A.5.14) can now be used to replace the time derivatives in (A.5.12). Making this substitution and rearranging terms, we get

$$\begin{bmatrix} q + k_1(S_y - F_y) & -k_1 F_i \\ -k_2 L_y & q - k_2 L_i \end{bmatrix} \begin{bmatrix} Y - \bar{Y} \\ i - \bar{i} \end{bmatrix} = 0 \qquad (A.5.15)$$

In shorthand form this matrix equation may be written

$$[q\mathbf{I} - \mathbf{KA}][\mathbf{X} - \bar{\mathbf{X}}] = 0$$

where $[q\mathbf{I} - \mathbf{KA}]$ is called the *characteristic matrix* and $[\mathbf{X} - \bar{\mathbf{X}}]$ is called the *characteristic vector*. If it is possible to invert $[q\mathbf{I} - \mathbf{KA}]$, we would be able to write

$$[q\mathbf{I} - \mathbf{KA}]^{-1}[q\mathbf{I} - \mathbf{KA}][\mathbf{X} - \bar{\mathbf{X}}] = 0$$

from which it would follow that $[\mathbf{X} - \bar{\mathbf{X}}] = 0$. This, however, is a trivial result, since it implies that the displacements from equilibrium are zero, whereas what we want is for the equations to hold when the variables are away from equilibrium. From this we infer that $[q\mathbf{I} - \mathbf{KA}]$ cannot have an inverse, and this means that its determinant must equal zero. Therefore, when we write out the *characteristic determinant*, we get

$$\begin{vmatrix} q + k_1(S_y - F_y) & -k_1 F_i \\ -k_2 L_y & q - k_2 L_i \end{vmatrix} = 0 \qquad (A.5.16)$$

When the characteristic determinant is evaluated, the result is the *characteristic equation* (or polynomial)

$$q^2 + [k_1(S_y - F_y) - k_2 L_i]q - k_1 k_2 [L_i(S_y - F_y) + L_y F_i] = 0 \qquad (A.5.17)$$

This is a second-degree polynomial that has two roots, that is, two possible values of q that satisfy the equation. Both roots must be negative if the dynamic system is to be stable. Observe from inspecting (A.5.17) that if all the coefficients in the equation are positive, the equation could not be satisfied by any positive value of q. Consequently, stability of equilibrium requires that the coefficients

$$k_1(S_y - F_y) - k_2 L_i > 0$$

$$-k_1 k_2 [L_i(S_y - F_y) + L_y F_i] = -k_1 k_2 D > 0$$

The first of these inequalities will definitely be satisfied if the marginal propensity to save is greater than the marginal propensity to invest. The same is true of the second inequality. Therefore, a sufficient condition for stability of equilibrium is that the IS curve have a negative slope.

This condition may, however, not be necessary under all conditions. Suppose, for example, that adjustment speed in the money market is such that the rate of interest adjusts so quickly that discrepancies between the demand and supply of money are eliminated instantaneously. Therefore, take the characteristic equation and divide all terms by k_2. This gives

$$\frac{q^2}{k_2} + \left[\frac{k_1}{k_2}(S_y - F_y) - L_i\right]q - k_1 D = 0$$

Then let k_2 become very large; that is, let $k_2 \to \infty$. The equation then reduces to

$$-L_i q = k_1 D$$

so only one root remains, and its value is

$$q = \frac{-k_1 D}{L_i}$$

which must be negative. Therefore, since $L_i < 0$, we require that D be negative. Accordingly,

$$D = L_i(S_y - F_y) + L_y F_i < 0$$

It follows that

$$\frac{S_y - F_y}{F_i} < \frac{-L_y}{L_i}$$

It is evident from (A.5.8) that the left-hand term is the slope of the IS curve, and the right-hand term is the slope of the LM curve. Therefore, stability requires that the slope of the LM curve be greater than the slope of the IS curve. It does not require the IS curve to have a negative slope, provided the money market adjusts substantially more rapidly than the goods market. This assumption, by the way, plays an important role in explanations of exchange rate overshooting.

Finally, if we are willing to assume that the real world is stable in the sense that markets tend to adjust to stable equilibria, we can use the stability condition to rule out comparative static results in unstable cases. To return to the multiplier for a rise in the money supply, we get

$$\frac{dY}{dm} = \frac{F_i}{D} = \frac{F_i}{L_i(S_y - F_y) + F_i L_y}$$

Stability analysis tells us that D must be negative. Therefore, the denominator of the multiplier formula must be negative, so dY/dm is necessarily positive. Stability analysis therefore shows that if an increase in the money supply changes national income at all, the change in income must be positive.

The procedure for conducting stability analysis is complete. However, those who have some knowledge of matrix methods may wish to read the rest of this appendix, which spells out the general case. Consider the simultaneous first-order linear differential equations

$$\mathbf{DX} = \mathbf{K}[\mathbf{AX} + \mathbf{B}] \qquad (A.5.18)$$

where $\mathbf{D}$ is the differential operator, which conveys the instruction to take the first time derivative of $\mathbf{X}$. Therefore, $\mathbf{DX}$ is a column vector of first time derivatives of the variables, $\mathbf{K}$ is a diagonal matrix of reaction coefficients, $\mathbf{A}$ is the coefficient matrix, $\mathbf{X}$ is a column vector of the variables, and $\mathbf{B}$ is a column vector of the autonomous constant terms. If there are n equations and n variables, these vectors and matrices may be written as

$$\mathbf{DX} = \begin{bmatrix} Dx_1 \\ Dx_2 \\ \vdots \\ Dx_n \end{bmatrix} \quad \mathbf{K} = \begin{bmatrix} k_1 & 0 \cdots 0 \\ 0 & k_2 \cdots 0 \\ \vdots & \vdots \\ 0 & 0 \quad k_n \end{bmatrix} \quad \mathbf{A} = \begin{bmatrix} a_{11} & a_{12}\cdots a_{1n} \\ a_{21} & a_{22}\cdots a_{2n} \\ \vdots & \vdots \\ a_{n1} & a_{n2}\cdots a_{nn} \end{bmatrix}$$

$$\mathbf{X} = \begin{bmatrix} x_1 \\ x_2 \\ \vdots \\ x_n \end{bmatrix} \quad \mathbf{B} = \begin{bmatrix} b_1 \\ b_2 \\ \vdots \\ b_n \end{bmatrix}$$

In equilibrium the time derivatives are zero. Let the equilibrium values of the $\mathbf{X}$ vector be $\bar{\mathbf{X}}$. It then follows from (A.5.18) that

$$\mathbf{B} = -\mathbf{A}\bar{\mathbf{X}} \tag{A.5.19}$$

and

$$\bar{\mathbf{X}} = -\mathbf{A}^{-1}\mathbf{B}$$

so the comparative static multipliers are

$$\frac{d\bar{\mathbf{X}}}{d\mathbf{B}} = -\mathbf{A}^{-1}$$

Now use (A.5.19) to replace $\mathbf{B}$ in equation (A.5.18). This gives

$$\mathbf{DX} = \mathbf{K}[\mathbf{AX} - \mathbf{A}\bar{\mathbf{X}}] = \mathbf{KA}[\mathbf{X} - \bar{\mathbf{X}}] \tag{A.5.20}$$

It can be seen that the differential equations are now in homogeneous form, since the constant terms have been eliminated.

Next replace $\mathbf{DX}$ by the trial solutions $q[\mathbf{X} - \bar{\mathbf{X}}]$. Therefore, (A.5.20) becomes

$$q[\mathbf{X} - \bar{\mathbf{X}}] = \mathbf{KA}[\mathbf{X} - \bar{\mathbf{X}}]$$

which is equivalent to

$$[q\mathbf{I} - \mathbf{KA}][\mathbf{X} - \bar{\mathbf{X}}] = 0 \tag{A.5.21}$$

where $[q\mathbf{I} - \mathbf{KA}]$ is the characteristic matrix and $[\mathbf{X} - \bar{\mathbf{X}}]$ is the characteristic vector.

If the matrix equation (A.5.21) is to hold for all values of the displacements $[\mathbf{X} - \bar{\mathbf{X}}]$, it cannot have an inverse. If it did,

$$[q\mathbf{I} - \mathbf{KA}]^{-1}[q\mathbf{I} - \mathbf{KA}][\mathbf{X} - \bar{\mathbf{X}}] = 0$$

and it would follow that $[\mathbf{X} - \bar{\mathbf{X}}] = 0$. Consequently, the characteristic matrix must be singular, and its determinant must equal zero. Therefore,

$$|q\mathbf{I} - \mathbf{KA}| = 0$$

Writing this out in longhand, we have

$$
\begin{vmatrix}
q - k_1 a_{11} & -k_1 a_{12} & \cdots & -k_1 a_{1n} \\
-k_2 a_{21} & q - k_2 a_{22} & \cdots & -k_2 a_{2n} \\
\vdots & & & \vdots \\
-k_n a_{n1} & -k_n a_{n2} & \cdots & q - k_n a_{nn}
\end{vmatrix} = 0
$$

When the determinant is evaluated, we obtain the characteristic equation

$$
q^n + \left[-\sum_{i=1}^{n} k_i a_{ii} \right] q^{n-1} + \left(\sum_{i,j=1}^{n} \begin{vmatrix} -k_i a_{ii} & -k_i a_{ij} \\ -k_j a_{ji} & -k_j a_{jj} \end{vmatrix} \right) q^{n-2}
$$

$$
+ \left(\sum_{i,j,k=1}^{n} \begin{vmatrix} -k_i a_{ii} & -k_i a_{ij} & -k_i a_{ik} \\ -k_j a_{ji} & -k_j a_{jj} & -k_j a_{jk} \\ -k_k a_{ki} & -k_k a_{kj} & -k_k a_{kk} \end{vmatrix} \right) q^{n-3} + \cdots - |\mathbf{KA}| = 0
$$

Inspection of the characteristic equation reveals that the coefficients of the equation are sums of the principal minors of $|\mathbf{KA}|$.[1] The coefficients of q^{n-1} are the sums of the first-order principal minors, the coefficients of q^{n-2} are the sums of the second-order principal minors, the coefficients of q^{n-3} are the sums of the third-order principal minors, and so on, until the constant term is reached, which is the determinant of $\mathbf{KA}$ itself.

APPENDIX TO CHAPTER 6

A.6.1 Comparative Statics of the Flexible Exchange-Rate Model

A simple flexible exchange-rate model with fixed price levels may be stated as

$$F(i) = S(Y) - G + V(Y, e) - X(e) \qquad (A.6.1)$$

---

[1] A principal minor is a determinant (minor) of an element in the main diagonal of a determinant. For example, in the determinant

$$
A = \begin{vmatrix} a_{11} & a_{12} & a_{13} \\ a_{21} & a_{22} & a_{23} \\ a_{31} & a_{32} & a_{33} \end{vmatrix}
$$

the first-order principal minors are a_{11}, a_{22}, and a_{33}. The second-order principal minors are

$$
\begin{vmatrix} a_{11} & a_{12} \\ a_{21} & a_{22} \end{vmatrix}, \quad \begin{vmatrix} a_{22} & a_{23} \\ a_{32} & a_{33} \end{vmatrix}, \quad \begin{vmatrix} a_{11} & a_{13} \\ a_{31} & a_{33} \end{vmatrix}
$$

and the third-order principal minor is the determinant A itself.

$$m_s = L(Y, i) \tag{A.6.2}$$

$$0 = X(e) - V(Y, e) + K(i) \tag{A.6.3}$$

Equation (A.6.1) is the IS curve, (A.6.2) is the LM curve, and (A.6.3) is the foreign balance function. Total differentiation of the equations yields the simultaneous linear equations

$$\begin{bmatrix} S_y + V_y & -F_i & V_e - X_e \\ L_y & L_i & 0 \\ V_y & -K_i & V_e - X_e \end{bmatrix} \begin{bmatrix} dY \\ di \\ de \end{bmatrix} = \begin{bmatrix} dG \\ dm \\ 0 \end{bmatrix}$$

where $0 < S_y + V_y < 1$, $F_i < 0$, $L_y > 0$, $L_i < 0$, $V_e < 0$, and $X_e > 0$.

Inversion of the coefficient matrix gives the solution

$$\begin{bmatrix} dY \\ di \\ de \end{bmatrix} = \begin{bmatrix} \dfrac{L_i(V_e - X_e)}{D} & \dfrac{(F_i - K_i)(V_e - X_e)}{D} & \dfrac{-L_i(V_e - X_e)}{D} \\ \dfrac{-L_y(V_e - X_e)}{D} & \dfrac{S_y(V_e - X_e)}{D} & \dfrac{L_y(V_e - X_e)}{D} \\ \dfrac{-(L_yK_i + L_iV_y)}{D} & \dfrac{K_i(S_y + V_y) - F_iV_y}{D} & \dfrac{-L_i(S_y + V_y) + L_yF_i}{D} \end{bmatrix} \begin{bmatrix} dG \\ dm \\ 0 \end{bmatrix}$$

$$\tag{A.6.4}$$

where D, the determinant of the coefficient matrix, is

$$D = (V_e - X_e)(L_iS_y - L_yK_i + F_iL_y) > 0 \tag{A.6.5}$$

Using (A.6.4) and (A.6.5), we see that the multipliers for a change in the money supply are

$$\frac{dY}{dm} = \frac{F_i - K_i}{L_iS_y - L_yK_i + F_iL_y} > 0 \tag{A.6.6}$$

$$\frac{di}{dm} = \frac{S_y}{L_iS_y - L_yK_i + F_iL_y} < 0 \tag{A.6.7}$$

$$\frac{de}{dm} = \frac{K_i(S_y + V_y) - F_iV_y}{(V_e - X_e)(L_iS_y - L_yK_i + F_iL_y)} > 0 \tag{A.6.8}$$

It is therefore unambiguously clear that expansionary monetary policy raises income, lowers the rate of interest, and raises the price of foreign exchange.

In the absence of capital mobility, $K_i = 0$, and (A.6.6) and (A.6.7) reduce to

$$\frac{dY}{dm} = \frac{F_i}{L_iS_y + F_iL_y} > 0 \tag{A.6.9}$$

$$\frac{di}{dm} = \frac{S_y}{L_iS_y + F_iL_y} < 0 \tag{A.6.10}$$

These are equivalent to the closed-economy multipliers derived in the appendix to Chapter 5. In addition,

$$\frac{de}{dm} = \frac{-F_i V_y}{(V_e - X_e)(L_i S_y + F_i L_y)} > 0 \qquad (A.6.11)$$

which, using (A.6.9), can be seen to equal

$$\frac{de}{dm} = \frac{-V_y}{(V_e - X_e)} \frac{dY}{dm} > 0$$

so the depreciation increases as income change increases.

When capital mobility is perfect, $K_i \to \infty$ and the multipliers become

$$\frac{dY}{dm} = \frac{1}{L_y} > 0 \qquad (A.6.12)$$

$$\frac{di}{dm} = 0 \qquad (A.6.13)$$

$$\frac{de}{dm} = \frac{S_y + V_y}{-(V_e - X_e)L_y} > 0 \qquad (A.6.14)$$

With perfect capital mobility no change in the rate of interest is possible. The income multiplier is the same as the classical closed-economy multiplier with $L_i = 0$.

Using (A.6.6), we can see that an increase in the degree of capital mobility raises the money-income multiplier because

$$\frac{\partial(dY/dm)}{\partial K_i} = \frac{-L_i S_y}{(L_i S_y - L_y K_i + F_i L_y)^2} > 0 \qquad (A.6.15)$$

The multipliers with respect to a change in government purchases are

$$\frac{dY}{dG} = \frac{L_i}{L_i S_y - L_y K_i + F_i L_y} > 0 \qquad (A.6.16)$$

$$\frac{di}{dG} = \frac{-L_y}{L_i S_y - L_y K_i + F_i L_y} > 0 \qquad (A.6.17)$$

so, in general, expansionary fiscal policy raises national income and the rate of interest. However,

$$\frac{de}{dG} = \frac{-(L_y K_i + L_i V_y)}{(V_e - X_e)(L_i S_y - L_y K_i + F_i L_y)} \gtrless 0 \qquad (A.6.18)$$

which may be positive or negative because $L_y K_i$ is positive while $L_i V_y$ is negative. If $L_y K_i + L_i V_y > 0$, it follows that

$$\frac{V_y}{K_i} < \frac{-L_y}{L_i}$$

The term on the left of the inequality is the slope of the FB function; the term on the right is the slope of the LM curve. In this case the slope of the LM curve is greater than the slope of FB. We have called this case relatively mobile capital, in which $de/dG < 0$, so the local currency appreciates because expansionary fiscal policy causes an incipient surplus.

In the absence of capital mobility, $K_i = 0$ and (A.6.16) and (A.6.17) reduce to

$$\frac{dY}{dG} = \frac{L_i}{L_i S_y + F_i L_y} > 0 \qquad (A.6.19)$$

$$\frac{di}{dG} = \frac{-L_y}{L_i S_y + F_i L_y} > 0 \qquad (A.6.20)$$

These equations are identical to the closed-economy results of the appendix to Chapter 5. Also, (A.6.18) implies

$$\frac{de}{dG} = \frac{-L_i V_y}{(V_e - X_e)(L_i S_y + F_i L_y)} > 0 \qquad (A.6.21)$$

so the local currency depreciates since fiscal policy affects only the current account.

With perfect capital mobility $L_i \to \infty$, and (A.6.16), (A.6.17), and (A.6.18) reduce to

$$\frac{dY}{dG} = 0$$

$$\frac{di}{dG} = 0$$

$$\frac{de}{dG} = \frac{1}{V_e - X_e} \le 0$$

so the local currency must appreciate, since the capital-account effect of the fiscal policy is dominant.

A.6.2 Stability of the Flexible Exchange-Rate Model

The dynamic form of the flexible exchange-rate model of Section A.6.1 may be written

$$\frac{dY}{dt} = k_1[F(i) + G + X(e) - S(Y) - V(Y, e)]$$

$$\frac{di}{dt} = k_2[L(Y, i) - m_s]$$

$$\frac{de}{dt} = -k_3[X(e) + K(i) - V(Y, e)] \qquad (A.6.22)$$

The first equation of (A.6.22) states that the speed of income change is proportional to the difference between injections—investment, government purchases, and exports—and leakages—saving, including taxes, and imports. The second equation states that the rate of interest rises if the demand for money exceeds the supply of money at a speed determined by the reaction coefficient k_2. The third equation states that the price of foreign exchange will decline at a rate proportional to the surplus in the balance of payments, as measured by net exports plus the inflow of capital. Admittedly this is a crude formulation, since exports and imports depend on the relative prices and price elasticities of the traded goods in the home country and abroad and this formulation does not get behind the scenes to those issues. However, we do study these problems later in the book, and take note of the problem the omission creates at the end of this appendix.

Linearizing these equations in the manner explained in Section A.6.2 permits them to be written in linear homogeneous form as

$$\frac{dY}{dt} = k_1[-(S_y + V_y)(Y - \bar{Y}) + F_i(i - \bar{i}) - (V_e - X_e)(e - \bar{e})]$$

$$\frac{di}{dt} = k_2[L_y(Y - \bar{Y}) + L_i(i - \bar{i})]$$

$$\frac{de}{dt} = -k_3[-V_y(Y - \bar{Y}) + K_i(i - \bar{i}) - (V_e - X_e)(e - \bar{e})] \qquad \text{(A.6.23)}$$

Replacing dY/dt, di/dt, and de/dt by $q(Y - \bar{Y})$, $q(i - \bar{i})$, and $q(e - \bar{e})$, respectively, gives the matrix equation

$$\begin{bmatrix} q + k_1(S_y + V_y) & -k_1 F_i & k_1(V_e - X_e) \\ -k_2 L_y & q - k_2 L_i & 0 \\ -k_3 V_y & +k_3 K_i & q - k_3(V_e - X_e) \end{bmatrix} \begin{bmatrix} Y - \bar{Y} \\ i - \bar{i} \\ e - \bar{e} \end{bmatrix} = 0$$

Via the argument of Appendix A.5.2, the characteristic matrix cannot have an inverse, and its determinant must therefore equal zero. Evaluation of the characteristic determinant then gives the characteristic equation

$$q^2 + [k_1(S_y + V_y) - k_2 L_i + k_3(V_e - X_e)]q^2$$

$$+ [-k_1 k_2 L_i(S_y + V_y) - k_1 k_3(S_y + V_y)(V_e - X_e) + k_2 k_3 L_i(V_e - X_e)]$$

$$+ k_1 k_2 k_3 (V_e - X_e)(L_i S_y - L_y K_i + F_i L_y) = 0$$

Stability of equilibrium requires all of the coefficients to be positive. Since S_y, V_y, and K_i are positive and L_i and F_i are negative, it is clear that all coefficients will be positive if $V_e - X_e$ is also negative. Although the assumption of the text discussion is that $V_e < 0$ and $X_e > 0$, there may be some doubt about V_e. This will be discussed in detail later, but briefly consider the following problem.

The parameter V_e is the change in imports that accompanies a rise in the price of foreign exchange. Certainly the physical quantity of imports will decline if the price of foreign exchange rises, but what is not clear is whether more or less real income is spent on imports. When the price of foreign exchange rises, domestic consumers see higher import prices, which is so whenever there is a supply restriction. The higher prices cause consumers to purchase fewer units of imported commodities. However, it is not clear whether they will spend less of their income on the commodity because the price and quantity changes move in the opposite direction. If the demand for imports is price-elastic, the proportional rise in price will be less than the proportional decline in quantity. Total expenditures on imports therefore decline, and V_e is negative as normally assumed. But if the demand for imports is price-inelastic, the proportional rise in price will exceed the proportional decline in quantity and more will be spent on imports, despite the decline in the physical quantity of imports. Therefore, V_e could be positive if the price elasticity of demand for imports is less than unity. In this case currency depreciation could have a deflationary effect on the economy, because if consumers increase their outlays on imports, this leaves them with less real income to spend on domestic goods and services.

On the export side, exporters see a rise in demand as a consequence of the rise in the price of foreign exchange, so *both* price and quantity rise in the exporting country. There can, therefore, be no doubt that X_e is positive, so currency depreciation must have a stimulative effect on the economy from the export side.

A.6.3 The Fixed Exchange-Rate Model:
Statics and Dynamics

The fundamental difference between the flexible exchange-rate model and the fixed exchange-rate model is that in the former the exchange rate is an endogenous variable while the money supply is autonomous. In the fixed exchange-rate model the situation is reversed. The money supply becomes the endogenous variable, and the exchange rate becomes autonomous.

To save time and trouble, we simplify at the outset by stating all equations in linear form. Therefore, let

$$I = I_a + F_i i$$

$$S = S_a + S_y Y$$

$$V = V_a + V_y Y$$

$$M = L_a + L_y Y + L_i i$$

$$K = K_a + K_i i$$

where all symbols and their signs are as previously defined. Since the exchange rate is fixed, e is dropped from the equations. Exports therefore become autonomous, and imports depend only on the level of income.

The comparative static model may be written

IS: $(S_y + V_y)Y - F_i i = -S_a - V_a + I_a + G + X = E_1$

LM: $L_y Y + L_i i = m_s - L_a$

FB: $-V_y Y + K_i i = -X + V_a - K_a = E_2$ (A.6.24)

where E_1 and E_2 are sums of the autonomous terms.

To achieve equilibrium with fixed exchange rates, we want the money supply and the level of foreign exchange reserves to adapt so that the LM curve is consistent with the intersection of the IS curve and the FB curve. The equilibrium level of income and the equilibrium rate of interest can be found by solving the IS and FB equations simultaneously. In matrix form these two equations are

$$\begin{bmatrix} (S_y + V_y) & F_i \\ -V_y & K_i \end{bmatrix} \begin{bmatrix} Y \\ i \end{bmatrix} = \begin{bmatrix} E_1 \\ E_2 \end{bmatrix}$$ (A.6.25)

To obtain a solution, we invert the matrix of coefficients and obtain

$$\begin{bmatrix} \bar{Y} \\ \bar{i} \end{bmatrix} = \begin{bmatrix} \dfrac{K_i}{D} & \dfrac{F_i}{D} \\ \dfrac{V_y}{D} & \dfrac{S_y + V_y}{D} \end{bmatrix} \begin{bmatrix} E_1 \\ E_2 \end{bmatrix}$$ (A.6.26)

where

$$D = K_i(S_y + V_y) - F_i V_y > 0$$ (A.6.27)

These results are independent of the money supply.

By using the equilibrium income level $\bar{Y}$ and the equilibrium rate of interest $\bar{i}$ given in (A.6.26) to substitute in the LM curve (A.6.24), we can calculate the equilibrium money supply. The result is

$$\bar{m} = L_0 + \frac{(L_y K_i + L_i V_y)E_1 + [L_y F_i + L_i(S_y + V_y)]E_2}{D}$$ (A.6.28)

Clearly, there is nothing that can be done with monetary policy except to create disequilibrium and alter the level of foreign exchange reserves. However, G is a component of E_1, so from (A.6.26) and (A.6.28) an increase in government purchases can be seen to have the following multipliers:

$$\frac{d\bar{Y}}{dG} = \frac{K_i}{K_i(S_y + V_y) - F_i V_y} > 0$$

$$\frac{d\bar{i}}{dG} = \frac{V_y}{K_i(S_y + V_y) - F_i V_y} > 0$$

$$\frac{d\bar{m}}{dG} = \frac{L_y K_i + L_i V_y}{K_i(S_y + V_y) - F_i V_y} \gtreqless 0$$ (A.6.29)

If capital mobility is perfect, $K_i \rightarrow \infty$ and the multipliers become

$$\frac{d\bar{Y}}{dG} = \frac{1}{S_y + V_y} > 0$$

$$\frac{d\bar{i}}{dG} = 0$$

$$\frac{d\bar{m}}{dG} = \frac{L_y}{S_y + V_y} = L_y \frac{d\bar{Y}}{dG} > 0 \qquad (A.6.30)$$

Therefore, the rise in income equals the simple multiplier as in the extreme Keynesian case (i.e., when $L_i \rightarrow -\infty$) because the money supply automatically adapts by rising in direct proportion to the change in income, with the cash balance ratio L_y being the factor of proportionality.

When capital is completely immobile, $K_i = 0$, and the multipliers become

$$\frac{d\bar{Y}}{dG} = 0$$

$$\frac{d\bar{i}}{dG} = \frac{-1}{F_i} > 0$$

$$\frac{d\bar{m}}{dG} = \frac{-L_i}{F_i} < 0 \qquad (A.6.31)$$

The first two multipliers are equivalent to the classical closed-economy result with $L_i = 0$. The equilibrium money supply drops because the higher rate of interest reduces liquidity preference. Foreign exchange reserves drop an equal amount.

When capital mobility is imperfect, we get the multipliers as written in (A.6.29). Both the equilibrium level of income and the equilibrium rate of interest rise in response to the fiscal stimulus. However, as can be seen by inspecting the money multiplier, the equilibrium money stock may rise or fall, depending on whether $L_y K_i + L_i V_y$ is greater than or less than zero. If

$$L_y K_i + L_i V_y > 0$$

it follows that

$$\frac{-L_y}{L_i} > \frac{V_y}{K_i}$$

which states that the slope of the LM curve is greater than the slope of the FB curve. Capital is therefore relatively mobile, and the equilibrium money stock rises as foreign exchange is accumulated by the monetary authority. However, if $L_y K_i + L_i V_y < 0$, the slope of the LM curve is less than the slope of the FB curve. Capital is therefore relatively immobile, the equilibrium money stock declines, and the monetary authority loses foreign exchange.

To test for stability of equilibrium, write the dynamic version of the model as

$$\frac{dY}{dt} = k_1[-(S_y + V_y)Y + F_i i + E_1]$$

$$\frac{di}{dt} = k_2[L_y Y + K_i i + L_a - m_s]$$

$$\frac{dm}{dt} = -V_y Y + K_i i - E_2 \qquad (A.6.32)$$

The first equation states the familiar hypothesis that the rate of income change is proportional to the excess of injections over leakages. The second equation states that the rate of interest rises at a rate proportional to the excess of the demand for money over the supply of money. The third equation states that the increase in the money supply equals the balance-of-payments surplus.

From previous experience we know that if we replace the variables by their displacements from equilibrium, the constant terms drop out and the equations become homogeneous. Therefore,

$$\frac{dY}{dt} = k_1[-(S_y + V_y)(Y - \bar{Y}) + F_i(i - \bar{i})]$$

$$\frac{di}{dt} = k_2[L_y(Y - \bar{Y}) + L_i(i - \bar{i}) - (m - \bar{m})]$$

$$\frac{dm}{dt} = -V_y(Y - \bar{Y}) + K_i(i - \bar{i}) \qquad (A.6.33)$$

Replacing the respective time derivatives with their trial solutions $q(Y - \bar{Y})$, $q(i - \bar{i})$, and $q(m - \bar{m})$ then permits us to form the matrix equation

$$\begin{bmatrix} q + k_1(S_y + V_y) & -k_1 F_i & 0 \\ -k_2 L_y & q - k_2 L_i & k_2 \\ V_y & -K_i & q \end{bmatrix} \begin{bmatrix} Y - \bar{Y} \\ i - \bar{i} \\ m - \bar{m} \end{bmatrix} = 0 \qquad (A.6.34)$$

It follows that the characteristic determinant is

$$\begin{vmatrix} q - k_1(S_y + V_y) & -k_1 F_i & 0 \\ -k_2 L_y & q - k_2 L_i & k_2 \\ V_y & -K_i & q \end{vmatrix} = 0 \qquad (A.6.35)$$

and that the characteristic equation is

$$q^3 + [k_1(S_y + V_y) - k_2 L_i]q^2 - k_1 k_2 L_i(S_y + V_y)q + k_1 k_2 D = 0 \qquad (A.6.36)$$

where, as before, $D = K_i(S_y + V_y) - F_i V_y > 0$

Stability of equilibrium necessitates negative values for the three roots (q's). The coefficients of the characteristic equation must therefore be positive so that

$$k_1(S_y + V_y) - k_2 L_i > 0$$

$$-k_1 k_2 L_i (S_y + V_y) > 0$$

$$k_1 k_2 D > 0$$

Given the assumed signs of the parameters and the positive reaction coefficients, it is clear that equilibrium is stable, so the comparative static results are valid.

PART THREE

BALANCE OF PAYMENTS AND EXCHANGE RATE ECONOMICS

In Part Three we move to major issues of balance of payments economics. Areas in need of exploration and analysis are the following:

1. Although they were supplemented with stability analysis, the models of Part Two were comparative static models that only hint at such issues as the timing of adjustment of different variables and different markets. They do not explain such dynamic phenomena as exchange rate and current-account overshooting, that is, their tendency to move in the right direction, but often with a long lag; they then tend to go too far beyond equilibrium.
2. There may be ambiguity about the signs of some of the essential parameters. The parameter V_e, the effect on the domestic value of imports of a rise in the exchange rate, gave us some trouble, as noted briefly in Chapter 6. To get a handle on such a problem, we must go behind the macroeconomic curtain to an examination of the characteristics of exports and imports in specific commodity markets.
3. The equilibria of the models of Part Two are *flow* equilibria that, at best, provide an adequate basis for the analysis and interpretation of issues that are short-run in nature. However, over time, flow equilibria will be continuously disrupted as long as *stocks* are not in equilibrium. An important example of this deficiency is in the treatment of capital mobility in response to interest-rate differentials. In Part Two it is implied that a given interest-rate differential will evoke a constant capital flow. The implicit as-

sumption, in other words, is that if an interest-rate differential persists through time, the capital flow is expected to persist at the same level indefinitely. However, this takes no account of portfolio adjustment. A capital inflow implies that foreign wealth holders are accumulating disproportionate amounts of domestic securities. As their portfolios become overstocked with such securities, their willingness to absorb additional amounts of such securities is likely to diminish even if the interest-rate differential persists. Thus it might take ever-widening interest-rate differentials to evoke a constant flow of capital over time.

Similarly, stock equilibrium is not possible as long as a current-account deficit or surplus persists, because a current-account deficit implies accumulation of domestic assets by foreign investors, whereas a current-account surplus implies the opposite. Longer-range equilibrium is therefore not possible unless the current account is in balance.

Specifically, Chapter 8 goes behind the scenes to the markets for exports and imports so as to provide the information needed to characterize correctly the properties of the demand and supply of foreign exchange. The question at issue is, how do the price effects of a devaluation affect the current account? Since devaluation also has aggregate expenditure—so called absorption—effects, Chapter 9 considers these effects and attempts to integrate *expenditure-switching* policy with *expenditure-reducing* policy.

Chapter 10 presents the monetary approach to the balance of payments. This approach provides a quite different way of looking at the balance of payments, and its results seem, at first viewing, to be contradictory to expectation. However, the monetary approach can be integrated into the approach that has been developed in earlier chapters. Moreover, it is most useful for the analysis of longer-range balance-of-payments adjustment and internal price levels, and it helps greatly to explain the strong balance-of-payments behavior of countries such as West Germany and Japan.

Chapter 11 introduces the *asset-market* approach to exchange rate determination. The asset-market theory provides a bridge between the flow equilibria of the short run and the stock equilibria of the long run, as well as a link between essentially Keynesian income-expenditure theory and the monetary theory.

Chapter 12 provides the bridge between theory and policy. This chapter studies elements of the so-called theory of economic policy, in relation to the attainment of external and internal balance. The chapter shows how, for example, internal and external balance can be reconciled. It discusses how policy instruments should be efficiently organized to attain a set of multiple objectives or targets. The avoidance of costly policy errors is discussed, and the problem of how policy can safely proceed when the absence of firm empirical information forces policy to grope in the dark or, as some might say, to wing it.

Chapter 8

The Current Account (I): Price Elasticities and the Trade Balance

8.1 ELASTICITY PESSIMISM

The Bretton Woods negotiations of 1944 produced the post–World War II international monetary system based on a return to fixed exchange rates. During the late 1940s many war-torn countries suffered from a lack of export capacity and from the desperate need for essential imports, especially capital goods, to help rebuild their economies and restore economic growth. Inasmuch as the United States was then the only viable supplier of such essential goods, there was an enormous need for dollars to finance critical imports. The large and persistent dollar deficits gave rise to much theorizing about the nature of the "dollar shortage." This term had a variety of interpretations, but essentially it meant that there appeared to be little that a country could do to avoid trade deficits vis-à-vis the United States.

International capital markets had been all but destroyed by the economic turmoil of the interwar period, and the war added to the disruption. After the war most countries imposed strict controls over the movement of capital. Bank accounts were frequently "blocked," so foreign nationals could not convert their domestic money balances into the precious dollars that were in short supply. Because of these widespread capital controls, financial markets were segmented and capital flows were unresponsive to interest-rate differentials and other normal incentives to move capital.

Under these circumstances economists focused their attention on the current account of the balance of payments while largely ignoring the capital account. Some of those who believed in a chronic dollar shortage based their arguments on the idea that devaluation of the exchange rate might not reduce the excess demand for dollars, because limited export capacity made it impossible to produce more goods for export and because import needs were so critical and essential that they could not be substantially reduced even if the domestic price of imports were to rise sharply. Such analysis of the foreign exchange market necessitated going behind the demand and supply of foreign exchange to an examination of conditions in the specific markets for exports and imports. As will be seen when we describe this analysis in subsequent pages, there appeared to be good reasons for supposing that a devaluation might not reduce the excess demand for foreign exchange, and it could even increase excess demand. Those who subscribed to such a view were characterized as "elasticity pessimists."

The frame of reference for the analysis was fixed exchange rates, and it was asked how a one-time devaluation of the official exchange rate would affect the excess demand for foreign exchange. This question is still highly relevant under the flexible exchange-rate system. If a rise in the price of foreign exchange increases, rather than reduces, excess demand for foreign exchange, the foreign exchange market would be unstable and a flexible exchange-rate system would not be viable. The conditions for improving the balance of trade by devaluation are therefore much the same as the stability conditions. Consequently, the analysis of the first part of this chapter bears importantly on the stability of the flexible exchange-rate system, an issue that was discussed briefly in Chapter 2, more extensively in the appendix to Chapter 6, and briefly in this chapter and the appendix to Chapter 9.

Assume the home country is suffering a trade deficit and undertakes devaluation of its currency vis-à-vis the foreign currency. The first question to be asked is how this devaluation affects the value of exports in terms of foreign currency, that is, the change in foreign exchange earnings. As a result of the devaluation foreign buyers find themselves able to acquire supplies at a smaller cost in foreign exchange. Therefore the importers see the development as an increase in supply, say to S_1 in panel (b) of Figure 8.1. The volume of imports increases to x_1 in panel (b), and the price in the importing country drops to q_1. Meanwhile, exporters in the home country see an increase in market demand, so the demand curve for exports in panel (a) shifts to D_1. The quantity of exports increases from x_0 to x_1, and the home price of exports rises to p_1.

Although the physical volume of exports has increased, the foreign price of exports has declined. Therefore it is not immediately clear whether more or less foreign exchange will be earned from the sale of exports. Prior to the devaluation the rectangle $q_0 x_0$ measured the foreign exchange value of exports. After the devaluation $q_1 x_1$ becomes the foreign exchange

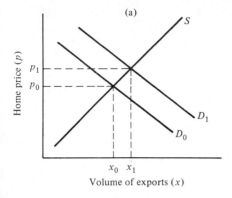

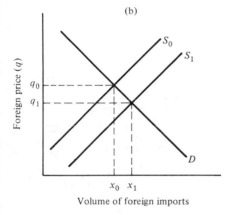

Figure 8.1 Effect of devaluation on export earnings: (a) home country; (b) foreign country.

(ie) amt of XP's ↑ more than Foreign Price ↓, so get net increase in earnings of fonex on export

value of exports. The quantity $q_1 x_1$ will exceed $q_0 x_0$ if the demand for exports is elastic with respect to price. In that case the proportionate rise in the physical quantity of exports exceeds the proportionate decline in the foreign price, so the value of exports increases. But if the demand for exports is price-inelastic, the proportionate rise in exports is less than the proportionate fall in the foreign price, and foreign exchange earnings from export sales decrease.

This reasoning implies that the supply curve of foreign exchange will be positively sloped if the elasticity of demand for exports (n_x) is greater than 1, and negatively sloped if $n_x < 1$. This is shown in Figure 8.2, where it can be seen that the supply of foreign exchange increases when the price of foreign exchange increases, when $n_x > 1$, but declines when $n_x < 1$.

Exports create a supply of foreign exchange. As its mirror image, this supply implies a corresponding demand for dollars by the foreign country. The effect of devaluation on the demand for the home currency can be inferred from panel (a) of Figure 8.1. The devaluation raises both the quantity of exports and the home price of exports, and it therefore

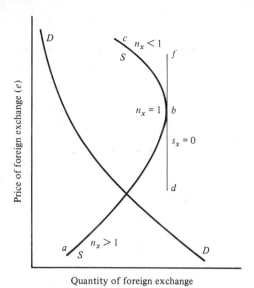

Figure 8.2   The market for foreign exchange.

$\frac{\partial}{\partial o} D^{\#}$ slopes $(-)$

must raise the value of exports denominated in the home currency. In general, therefore, the demand curve for domestic currency is negatively sloping, as seen in Figure 8.3, which shows the effect of devaluation on exports. It is important to note also that the devaluation increases the volume of exports and it therefore has an expansionary effect on the economy, certainly from the export side.

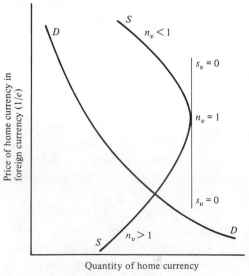

Figure 8.3   The market for home currency.

Next, we consider the effect of devaluation on imports, assuming negatively sloped demand curves and positively sloped supply curves for imports. Figure 8.4 shows the home import market in panel (a) and the market for the same goods as seen in the foreign country. Initially, the devaluation is perceived by importers as a restriction in supply because more units of the home currency are needed to buy the foreign exchange needed to purchase a unit of imports. Therefore, the supply curve shown in panel (a) shifts to the left. As a consequence of the supply restriction, the home price of imports rises from P_0 to P_1, and the physical quantity of imports declines from v_0 to v_1.

Exporters in the foreign country now see the effect of the devaluation as causing a reduction in the demand for their products. Therefore, the demand curve in panel (b) shifts to the left from D_0 to D_1. The physical quantity of goods sold to the home country declines from v_0 to v_1, and the price in the foreign country declines from Q_0 to Q_1.

The change in the amount of foreign exchange expended on imports

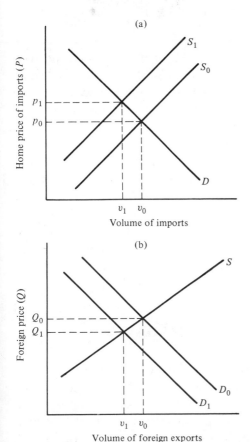

Figure 8.4 Effect of devaluation on import expenditure: (a) home country; (b) foreign country.

is shown in panel (b) of Figure 8.4. The physical quantity of imports has declined, and the foreign price of imports has also declined. Therefore less foreign exchange is spent on imports, since the rectangle $Q_1 v_1$ is necessarily less than $Q_0 v_0$. This means that the demand curve for foreign exchange, shown in Figure 8.2, must be negatively sloping. As the price of foreign exchange rises, the quantity of foreign exchange demanded declines. Therefore, as a general rule, devaluation improves the import side of the trade balance.

The change in the quantity of *home currency* spent on imports can be inferred from panel (a) of Figure 8.4. The physical volume of imports declines, and the home price of imports rises. Originally, $P_0 v_0$ was spent on imports valued in home currency. After the devaluation $P_1 v_1$ was spent on imports. Then $P_1 v_1$ will be less than $P_0 v_0$ if the elasticity of demand for imports, n_v, is greater than 1, that is, if the demand for imports is price-elastic. But $P_1 v_1$ will be greater than $P_0 v_0$ if the demand for imports is inelastic. Therefore, devaluation increases the supply of the home currency if $n_v < 1$ and reduces it if $n_v > 1$. Thus the supply curve of home currency could be backward bending as seen in Figure 8.3.

The possibility that import demand may be inelastic with respect to price raises the important implication that, at least on the import side, devaluation could promote stagflation. The domestic price level rises as the domestic cost of imports rises. But if more local currency is spent on imports after devaluation, consumers will have less real income left to spend on domestic goods and services. Consequently real income and employment may decline. This is an important possibility that carries with it major implications that are explored later on. Meanwhile, recall that it was because we could not tell for certain whether the country would spend more or less of its real income on imports following a change in the exchange rate that we had some difficulty in determining the sign of the parameter V_e in our discussion of the stability of equilibrium in the appendix to Chapter 6. Note, finally, that V_e measures the slope of the supply curve of the home currency of Figure 8.3.

8.2 ELASTICITIES ANALYSIS OF DEVALUATION: A GENERAL APPROACH

We can now comfortably switch to a more general approach that permits us to develop the analysis and its various ramifications more precisely. The approach involves simple algebra. The reader is encouraged to take pencil in hand and to reproduce the various special cases to follow by constructing diagrams such as those of Figures 8.1 and 8.4, as well as the implied demand and supply curves for foreign exchange and the local currency of Figures 8.2 and 8.3, respectively.

Consider first the supply of foreign exchange and the demand for foreign exchange. At issue is the change in the value of net exports denominated in the foreign currency. Therefore, we write

$$NX^* = X^* - V^* \tag{8.1}$$

where the asterisks indicate that net exports, NX^*, are valued in foreign currency. It follows from (8.1) that

$$dNX^* = dX^* - dV^* \tag{8.2}$$

First, consider the value of exports in terms of foreign exchange. Therefore, write $X^* = xq$ and let

$x =$ the physical volume of exports

$q =$ the foreign price of exports

$p =$ the home price of exports

$p = eq$, where e is the exchange rate—the price of foreign exchange

Exports are bought by foreign nationals, so the elasticity of demand for exports must be stated in terms of foreign prices. Therefore, the elasticity of demand for exports is defined as

$$n_x = \frac{-dx/x}{dq/q} \tag{8.3}$$

Exports are supplied by the home country, so the elasticity of supply of exports must be defined in terms of home prices. Therefore, the elasticity of the supply of exports with respect to price is given by

$$s_x = \frac{dx/x}{dp/p} \tag{8.4}$$

Since $p = eq$, it follows that

$$\frac{dp}{p} = \frac{de}{e} + \frac{dq}{q} \tag{8.5}$$

Using this result to replace dp/p in the expression for supply elasticity, we can see that

$$s_x = \frac{dx/x}{dq/q + de/e} \tag{8.6}$$

which expresses the supply elasticity in *foreign* prices and the exchange rate. We see from (8.3) that $dx/x = -n_x(dq/q)$. Substituting this into (8.6) and solving for the change in the foreign price of exports gives

$$\frac{dq}{q} = \frac{-s_x}{n_x + s_x} \frac{de}{e} < 0 \qquad (8.7)$$

if de/e is positive, that is, if the official price of foreign exchange rises. Then, using (8.7) to substitute back into (8.3), we calculate the proportionate change in the quantity of exports as

$$\frac{dx}{x} = \frac{n_x s_s}{n_x + s_x} \frac{de}{e} > 0 \qquad (8.8)$$

Devaluation means that de/e is positive. Equation (8.7) shows that dq/q is negative. The foreign price of exports therefore falls as in Figure 8.1. Adding the proportionate change in foreign price to the proportionate change in quantity gives the proportionate change in the value of exports; that is,

$$\frac{dX^*}{X^*} = \frac{dq}{q} + \frac{dx}{x} \qquad (8.9)$$

which is positive if the proportionate rise in quantity exceeds the proportionate decline in price. Substituting these changes from (8.7) and (8.8) into (8.9) gives

$$\frac{dX^*}{X^*} = \frac{s_x(n_x - 1)}{n_x + s_x} \frac{de}{e} \qquad (8.10)$$

as the proportionate change in the value of exports. Dividing both sides of this expression by de/e gives the elasticity of the supply of foreign exchange with respect to the exchange rate. The elasticity is positive if the demand for exports is elastic. In that event the proportionate rise in the quantity of exports exceeds the proportionate decline in the foreign price of exports, so foreign exchange earnings from export sales rise. But if export demand is inelastic with respect to price, the quantity of foreign exchange earned declines. The proportionate rise in quantity is then less than the proportionate fall in the foreign price, and the elasticity of supply of foreign exchange with respect to the exchange rate is then negative.

We can once again draw the supply of foreign exchange curve of Chapter 2 based on these results. Figure 8.2 depicts the foreign exchange market. The supply curve is positively sloped along the segment *ab,* where it is assumed that the elasticity of demand for exports exceeds unity. As the demand elasticity declines, the slope of the supply curve increases, becoming vertical at point b where $n_x = 1$. Then for $n_x < 1$, the curve takes on a negative slope.

The supply of foreign exchange would be constant throughout if the elasticity of supply is zero. If export capacity cannot be expanded, $s_x = 0$. The domestic price of exports then rises in direct proportion to the devaluation; there is no decline in the foreign price of exports and therefore no increase in the volume of exports. From (8.7) and (8.8), when $s_x = 0$, both dq/q and dx/x are also zero. The competitive advantage gained by devaluation is completely offset by an equiproportionate rise in the home price of exports.

It is important to observe that if the elasticity of demand for exports is high, it would be advantageous to have a high supply elasticity, since that magnifies the increase in foreign exchange earnings. But if the demand for exports is inelastic, it would be better to have a low export supply elasticity to minimize the *reduction* in foreign exchange earnings.[1]

If the elasticity of supply of exports with respect to price is infinite, as might be the case if the economy had excess capacity and unemployed labor at its disposal, the elasticity of supply of foreign exchange with respect to the exchange rate is $n_x - 1$, as can be seen from (8.10). Devaluation increases foreign exchange earnings if $n_x > 1$, but decreases foreign exchange earnings if $n_x < 1$.

The value of imports denominated in foreign currency is

$$V^* = vQ \qquad (8.11)$$

where v is the physical volume of imports and Q is the foreign price of imports. Also let

P = domestic price of imports

$n_v = \dfrac{-dv/v}{dP/P}$ = the elasticity of demand for imports

$s_v = \dfrac{dv/v}{dQ/Q}$ = elasticity of supply of imports

$P = eQ$

---

[1] We can establish this by differentiating (8.10) partially with respect to s_x. This gives

$$\frac{\partial(dX^*/X^*)}{\partial s_x} = \frac{n_x(n_x - 1)}{(n_x + s_x)^2} \frac{de}{e}$$

which is positive if $n_x > 1$. Therefore an increase in the elasticity of supply helps to raise export earnings. But if $n_x < 1$, the partial derivative is negative. Therefore an increase in the elasticity of supply of exports works to further deteriorate export earnings.

It follows from (8.11) that

$$\frac{dV^*}{V^*} = \frac{dv}{v} + \frac{dQ}{Q} \qquad (8.12)$$

and from $P = eQ$ it follows that

$$\frac{dP}{P} = \frac{de}{e} + \frac{dQ}{Q} \qquad (8.13)$$

Using (8.13) and the definition of the elasticities, we see that the elasticities can be expressed in foreign prices as

$$s_v = \frac{dv/v}{dQ/Q} \qquad n_v = \frac{-dv/v}{dQ/Q - de/e}$$

Solving these expressions for dv/v and dQ/Q gives

$$\frac{dv}{v} = \frac{-s_v n_v}{n_v + s_v} \frac{de}{e} < 0 \qquad \frac{dQ}{Q} = \frac{-n_v}{n_v + s_v} \frac{de}{e} < 0 \qquad (8.14)$$

These expressions show that devaluation reduces both the physical volume of imports and the foreign price of imports, so the value of imports must decline. At the time of the devaluation importers discover that they have to give up more local currency to purchase a unit of imports. This implies a leftward shift of the import supply curve. This raises the domestic price of the imports and reduces the quantity of imports purchased. Foreign suppliers therefore see a decline in demand, so the foreign price drops. Since both quantity and the foreign price drop, the devaluation must reduce the quantity of foreign exchange demanded.

Substituting the results in (8.14) into (8.13) gives

$$\frac{dV^*}{V^*} = \frac{-n_v(1 + s_v)}{n_v + s_v} \frac{de}{e} < 0 \qquad (8.15)$$

so the elasticity of the value of imports with respect to the exchange rate is negative. Therefore, devaluation reduces the value of imports and the demand for foreign exchange. The demand curve for foreign exchange is therefore negatively sloped throughout as shown in Figure 8.2.

By using (8.1), (8.10), and (8.15), we obtain the change in the overall balance of trade measured in foreign currency units, namely,

$$dNX^* = \left[X^* \left(\frac{s_x(n_x - 1)}{n_x + s_x} \right) + V^* \left(\frac{n_v(1 + s_v)}{n_v + s_v} \right) \right] \frac{de}{e} \qquad (8.16)$$

A much-discussed case arises when the supply elasticities are both infinite. This could occur if both economies are suffering from excess capacity and unemployed labor. In that event domestic output could be expanded without any significant increase in supply price. The supply elasticities might also be infinite for a small industrialized country. It is a minor purchaser of imports in a large world market, so the world supplies are available in varying quantities at a given world price. Therefore the elasticity of supply of imports, s_v, is infinite. The country sells manufactured output at home and abroad, in competition with foreign manufacturers. A rise in foreign demand for the manufactured goods may not cause the small country's exporters to raise prices for fear of losing out to competition in both domestic and foreign markets. In this event the country supplies additional exports at a fixed price, so the elasticity of supply of exports, s_x, is also infinite.

When s_x and s_v are both infinite, (8.16) implies

$$dNX^* = [X^*(n_x - 1) + V^*n_v]\frac{de}{e} \tag{8.17}$$

Further, if trade is initially balanced so that $X^* = V^*$,

$$dNX^* = X^*(n_x + n_v - 1)\frac{de}{e} \tag{8.18}$$

In this form the condition for improvement in the balance of trade has been called the *Marshall-Lerner* condition, in honor of Alfred Marshall and Abba P. Lerner, who are credited with deriving it. The balance of trade improves in response to devaluation if the sum of the elasticity of demand for exports and the elasticity of demand for imports exceeds unity.

To summarize the Marshall-Lerner case: Devaluation is seen by foreign purchasers as an increase in supply. The foreign price drops, and the quantity of exports increases. But since the elasticity of supply of exports is infinite, there is no increase in the home price of exports despite the rise in demand. The foreign price of exports must therefore drop in proportion equal to the devaluation. Since $dp/p = de/e + dq/q$ and $dp/p = 0$, it follows that $dq/q = -de/e$. The elasticity of the supply of foreign exchange with respect to the exchange rate is therefore exactly the same as the elasticity of demand for exports.

The devaluation is seen by importers as a reduction in supply. The domestic price of imports rises, and the volume of imports declines. But since the elasticity of supply of imports is infinite, the added demand causes no change in the foreign price of imports. Therefore, the domestic price of imports rises by the same proportion as the proportionate rise in the exchange rate. Since $dP/P = de/e + dQ/Q$ and $dQ/Q = 0$, it

Summary

follows that $dP/P = de/e$. The elasticity of demand for foreign exchange then equals the elasticity of demand for imports.

Another relevant small-country case assumes infinitely elastic import supply because the country's demand for imports is too small to affect the world price. On the export side, it sells in a competitive world market, so the amount it sells has no effect on the world price. As far as this country is concerned, the elasticity of demand for exports, n_x, is infinite. The general expression (8.16) then reduces to

$$dNX^* = (X^*s_x + V^*n_v)\frac{de}{e}$$

and if $X^* = V^*$ initially

$$dNX^* = X^*(s_x + n_v)\frac{de}{e} > 0 \tag{8.19}$$

It appears that devaluation is bound to be successful in increasing net foreign exchange earnings. The devaluation expands export sales without reducing the foreign price of exports, and it reduces purchases of imports at a fixed foreign price. Small countries that supply agricultural products to a large world market may be in this position. However, many small agricultural countries individually account for a large fraction of world supplies, and in such cases the condition would not be applicable. Much of the world's cocoa is supplied by Ghana, Tanzania is a large supplier of sisal, and Thailand supplies a large fraction of the world's tapioca. SPECIAL CASE # 1

In the situation regarded as descriptive of war-torn countries after World War II, export capacity cannot be expanded and essential imports cannot be reduced. The demand for imports and the supply of exports are both completely inelastic. In this event the demand curve for imports and the supply curve of exports are both vertical. Setting $n_v = 0$ and $s_x = 0$, we see from (8.16) that $dNX^* = 0$. No improvement in the trade balance is possible, and the trade balance is independent of the exchange rate. From (8.10) we see that when $s_x = 0$, $dX^*/X^* = 0$, so there is no change in export earnings. The rise in the domestic price of exports is exactly the same as the rise in the exchange rate in proportional terms. The supply curve of foreign exchange is therefore vertical throughout. Similarly, (8.15) shows that when $n_v = 0$, $dV^*/V^* = 0$, so there is no change in the demand for foreign exchange. The domestic price of imports rises by the exact same percentage as the rise in the exchange rate. Therefore, the demand curve for foreign exchange is also vertical throughout.

In combination, these assumptions produce indeterminacy in the foreign exchange market. In Figure 8.5 the vertical supply curve implies

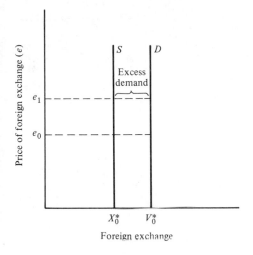

Figure 8.5 The foreign exchange market with inelastic export supply and inelastic import demand.

that the value of exports is X_0^*, and the vertical demand curve implies imports of V_0^*. If the initial exchange rate is e_0, there is excess demand for foreign exchange of $V_0^* - X_0^*$. Devaluation raises the price of foreign exchange to e_1, but this has no effect on excess demand. If the exchange rate were free to fluctuate, it could not find an equilibrium level. Therefore, the assumptions of elasticity pessimism imply an unstable foreign exchange market.   *SPECIA CASE #2*

An alternative set of assumptions is that the demand for foreign exchange remains completely inelastic, as in Figure 8.5 and that, on the export side, supply is elastic while export demand is fairly inelastic. With $0 < n_x < 1$, (8.10) implies that dX^*/X^* is negative, which means the supply curve of foreign exchange is negatively sloped, as shown in Figure 8.6. If the exchange rate initially is e_0, the excess demand for foreign exchange is equal to the distance ab. Devaluation raises the price of foreign exchange to e_1, and the excess demand gap widens to cd. Under flexible exchange rates the equilibrium point, f, is unstable. If the exchange rate is jostled away from $\bar{e}$, a small rise in the exchange rate would create excess demand for foreign exchange, so the exchange rate would keep rising and excess demand would increase. Similarly, a small decline in the exchange rate would create excess supply, so the exchange rate would keep falling and excess supply would increase.

The assumptions of this case imply that an upward *revaluation* of the official exchange rate would actually improve the balance of trade. However, there does not seem to be any case on record where a country with a trade deficit has deliberately set out to reduce its deficit by revaluing its own currency.

Supply is backward bending

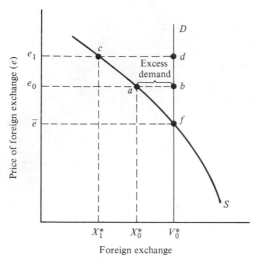

Figure 8.6 The foreign exchange market with a backward-bending supply curve.

Valuing exports and imports in terms of *foreign* prices is important in order to examine the effect of devaluation on net earnings of foreign exchange. However, with respect to its effects on the domestic economy, attention focuses on the effect of devaluation on the value of exports and imports in *domestic* prices.

We can derive the change in net exports valued in domestic prices using previous results by noting that

$$X - V = e(X^* - V^*)$$

so

$$dNX = dX - dV = (X^* - V^*)de + e(dX^* - dV^*) \qquad (8.20)$$

The value of $dX - dV$ can then be calculated directly by using (8.16), which gives $dX^* - dV^*$, and rearranging terms. The result is

$$dNX = dX - dV = \left[X\left(\frac{n_x(1 + s_x)}{n_x + s_x}\right) + V\left(\frac{s_v(n_v - 1)}{n_v + s_v}\right) \right] \frac{de}{e} \qquad (8.21)$$

However, this quick route to a solution skips over a lot of territory. So, to raise understanding, let us put it together piece by piece as before. Following the earlier procedure, we can easily show that

$$\frac{dx}{x} = \frac{n_x s_x}{n_x + s_x} \frac{de}{e} > 0 \qquad \frac{dp}{p} = \frac{n_x}{n_x + s_x} \frac{de}{e} > 0 \qquad (8.22)$$

whence it follows that the proportional change in the value of exports, denominated in local currency, is

$$\frac{dX}{X} = \frac{n_x(1 + s_x)}{n_x + s_x} \frac{de}{e} > 0 \qquad (8.23)$$

The devaluation is seen by foreign importers as an increase in supply. The foreign price drops, and quantity demanded increases. This is seen as an increase in demand by domestic exporters, and the increase in demand raises both the home price and the quantity of exports.

When the supply of exports is infinitely elastic, (8.23) becomes

$$\frac{dX}{X} = n_x \frac{de}{e}$$

so the elasticity of the demand for exports with respect to the exchange rate is the same as the elasticity of demand for exports. Conversely, when the elasticity of supply of exports is zero, $dX/X = -de/e$, so the elasticity of the demand for the local currency with respect to the exchange rate is 1 throughout. The demand for the home currency is clearly a negatively sloped function as shown in Figure 8.3.

The proportionate change in the home currency value of imports is the sum of the proportional change in physical quantity and the proportional change in price. These relative changes are

$$\frac{dv}{v} = \frac{-n_v s_v}{n_v + s_v} \frac{de}{e} < 0 \qquad \frac{dp}{p} = \frac{s_v}{n_v + s_v} \frac{de}{e} > 0 \qquad (8.24)$$

and it follows that

$$\frac{dV}{V} = \frac{-s_v(n_v - 1)}{n_v + s_v} \frac{de}{e} \lessgtr 0 \qquad (8.25)$$

If the demand for imports is price-elastic so that $n_v > 1$, dV/V is negative and the value of imports, denominated in local currency, declines in response to a devaluation. The supply of the home currency therefore also declines. However, if the demand for imports is price-inelastic, $n_v < 1$ and dV/V is positive. In this case devaluation actually increases expenditures on imports, and the supply of the home currency increases. Consequently, the supply curve of the domestic currency would be negatively sloped, as seen in Figure 8.3. As already noted, it is because we could not tell for certain whether the country would spend more or less of its real income on imports following a change in the exchange rate that we had difficulty in determining the sign of the parameter V_e in the discussion of the stability of equilibrium in the appendix to Chapter 6. As explained in the next chapter, this problem arises again when we attempt to determine whether devaluation should be accompanied by absorption-reducing or absorption-increasing policies.

If the supply of imports has a price elasticity of zero, it follows from (8.24) and (8.25) that

$$\frac{dv}{v} = 0 \qquad \frac{dP}{P} = 0 \qquad \frac{dV}{V} = 0 \qquad -\frac{dQ}{Q} = \frac{de}{e}$$

Neither the domestic price nor the quantity of imports changes as the foreign price of imports falls in the same proportion as the rise in the exchange rate. The supply of the home currency would then be constant along the vertical line depicted in Figure 8.3.

If the elasticity of the supply of imports is infinite, the foreign price of imports will not change; hence, $dQ/Q = 0$, and

$$\frac{dv}{v} = -n_v\frac{de}{e} \qquad \frac{dP}{P} = +\frac{de}{e} \qquad \frac{dV}{V} = (1 - n_v)\frac{de}{e}$$

The home price of imports rises in the same proportion as the use in the exchange rate, the elasticity of the physical quantity of imports with respect to the exchange rate equals the elasticity of the demand for imports, and the elasticity of the value of imports with respect to the exchange rate equals $1 - n_v$. If $n_v < 1$, this elasticity is positive, so devaluation raises the domestic currency value of imports and the supply of the home currency. This would put additional downward pressure on the exchange rate, which could make for an unstable foreign exchange market. Whether the market is unstable or not depends on whether the demand for the home currency rises by more than the supply—that is whether the value of net exports increases or decreases.

Looking at equation (8.21), we see that if the supply elasticities are both infinite and the value of exports equals the value of imports, the equation reduces to

$$dX - dV = X(n_x + n_v - 1)\frac{de}{e} \tag{8.26}$$

which again is the Marshall-Lerner condition as in (8.18). In a stable foreign exchange market, devaluation must reduce the excess supply of the home currency, so the value of net exports must rise, and $dX - dV$ must be positive, which again implies that the sum of the demand elasticities must exceed unity.

8.3 ELASTICITY ESTIMATES AND THE *J*-CURVE

A great deal of time and effort has been expended by economists in attempts to measure the supply and demand elasticities for exports and imports. It appears to have been generally established that the demand elasticities are sufficiently large so that the Marshall-Lerner conditions are met. For example, Warner and Kreinin estimated that during the 1970s a 1 percent depreciation of the U.S. dollar was associated with a 1.5 percent increase in the volume of exports.[2]

A major difficulty in assessing the effects of devaluation on net exports is that it takes time for trade flows to adjust to relative price changes, which is another way of saying that elasticities are low in the short run and increase with the amount of time that elapses after the relative price change. Estimates of the time required for relative price changes to produce their full quantitative effects vary a great deal, but seem to average about two years.

When the price of oil was raised by the OPEC cartel in 1973–74, this had little immediate effect on U.S. oil imports, since the short-run demand elasticity for oil was extremely low, having been estimated as roughly −0.2 percent. This meant that a 1 percent rise in the price of oil reduced oil consumption by only two tenths of 1 percent. In the short run, industries using oil had no choice but to pay the higher prices. In the longer run, they switched to alternative energy sources, introduced oil conservation measures, and shifted to technologies that were not as energy intensive. Consumers at first continued to have to use heating oil, their only immediate alternative being to turn down their thermostats and wear warmer clothes. But after a time they adapted by insulating their homes and converting to gas furnaces. Initially, consumers had to pay the higher gasoline prices. But eventually they adapted by joining in car pools, using public transportation, and replacing their gas guzzlers with fuel-efficient autos. Industry responded by greatly increasing the energy efficiency of home appliances and, in response to prodding by the federal government and by the reality of Japanese competition, improved the fuel efficiency of their new automobile fleets.

In the conditions of 1973 the supply of oil was extremely inelastic, with OPEC controlling 85 percent of world oil imports. In the longer run the supply has become elastic. The higher prices spurred exploration and drilling and provided incentives to utilize substitute fuels such as coal,

---

[2] Warner, Dennis, and Mordechai Kreinin, "Determinants of International Trade Flows," *Review of Economics and Statistics,* February 1983.

natural gas, synthetic fuel, and hydroelectric power. New oil producers found it increasingly advantageous to remain outside of OPEC so as not to be subjected to OPEC's production quotas.

In 1972–73 the OPEC cartel had the world economy by the throat because it controlled the bulk of world oil exports and because the demand for oil was inelastic. By 1982 the higher long-run elasticities of both demand and supply had largely destroyed OPEC's monopoly power.

The low short-run elasticities suggest that initially a devaluation may have quite unfavorable effects on both the balance of payments and the domestic economy. If the quantitative response to lower foreign prices is slight in the short run, the proportionate increase in the quantity of exports will be smaller than the proportionate fall in the foreign price, and less foreign exchange will be earned from export sales after the devaluation than before. Excess demand for foreign exchange may therefore persist and even rise in the short run.

In the short run the elasticity of demand for imports may be quite low as in the case of oil. The rise in the domestic price of imports may be substantial without any significant reduction in the volume of imports. Therefore, exporters see little decline in demand, so foreign prices need not decline. Thus the total amount of foreign exchange spent on imports may not decline significantly in the short run.

Eventually the trade-volume response should increase, and the current-account balance will then improve. The time pattern of foreign exchange earnings in response to devaluation may, therefore, follow a *J-curve,* first declining and then improving as the physical volume of exports responds more fully to the decline in their price and as the physical volume of imports responds more fully to the rise in the price of imports.

The problem of sluggish quantity adjustment may be aggravated by the presence of long-term contracts that fix prices and quantities into the future. To assess the effects of this, imagine an extreme example in which all prices and quantities are previously determined in the foreign country's currency. The volume of imports and the foreign currency price paid by importers will then not change at all in response to devaluation, so the demand for foreign exchange remains invariant with respect to exchange rate variations. The foreign currency value of export sales also remains the same. Therefore the supply of foreign exchange is invariant with respect to the exchange rate.[3]

The effects of the sluggishness in the response of trade flows to changes in the exchange rate was clearly illustrated by the U.S. deval-

[3] On the effects of long-term contracts, see Magee, Steven, "Contracting and Spurious Deviations from Purchasing Power Parity," in Johnson, Harry G., and Jacob Frenkel, eds., *The Economics of Exchange Rates,* Addison-Wesley, 1978.

uations of 1971 and 1973. The current-account deficit in 1971 was $1.4 billion. The first devaluation took place in December 1971, but the current-account deficit rose to $5.8 billion in 1972. Previously negotiated contracts appear to have had a lot to do with this. The dollar cost of contracted imports increased while the dollar value of contracted U.S. exports remained the same. The value of imports eventually declined and export volume eventually rose, but it took until 1973 for the current account to swing into surplus. Once the upside of the *J*-curve was reached, the improvement was dramatic, as the current account showed a $7.1 billion surplus in 1973.

More recently, the overvalued dollar began depreciating in early 1985. Despite a sharp depreciation, the trade deficit continued at a record pace throughout 1985 and most of 1986. By October 1986 there were some signs of improvement. Nevertheless studies conducted by the National Bureau of Economic Research (NBER) and the National Association of Manufacturers (NAM) predicted the continuation of a poor trade performance throughout the visible future. The NBER study emphasized that the duration of the trade deficit was, in itself, instrumental in its likely continuation. Foreign competitors seized the opportunity afforded by five years of dollar overvaluation to make irreversible inroads into U.S. markets while U.S. exporters were losing irretrievable ground in foreign markets. It takes time to establish distribution channels, to make advertizing pay off, and to develop consumer product loyalty. A temporary competitive advantage may provide too little time for trade patterns to change substantially. But a long period of such an advantage may produce inroads that are difficult to dislodge. Thus a persistent trade deficit takes on structural elements that may make reversal of the deficit all the more difficult.

The *J*-curve describes the time pattern of the balance of trade following a devaluation. The pattern of the effect of the devaluation on domestic absorption is quite likely to be similar. With a low short-run demand elasticity for imported oil, consumers in industrial countries found themselves spending more real income on imported oil, thereby leaving them with less real income to spend on domestically produced goods and services. However, as the elasticity of demand for oil rises as substitutes are found, expenditures are shifted from imports in the direction of domestically produced fuels and energy-saving appliances and vehicles. Thus the domestic impact of the devaluation also follows a *J*-curve, first tending to reduce absorption and then tending to increase it. Consequently, devaluation could have severe dislocative effects on economies that are heavily dependent on essential imports—first causing recession and then providing expansionary stimulus.

The *J*-curve effect has also given rise to the concept of *vicious* and *virtuous* circles of exchange rate depreciation interacting with changes in the rate of domestic inflation. Countries with strong current accounts and low inflation find their exchange rates appreciating. The most significant initial effect of the appreciation is a decline in the domestic cost of imports. This spreads through the economy, holding inflation in check and further improving the country's competitive position. This country enjoys a virtuous circle—inflation is held down and the current account remains strong, thereby possibly causing further appreciation and further reductions in the domestic inflation rate.

A country suffering substantial inflation finds its exchange rate depreciating. The domestic cost of imports rises. This filters through the economy, raises the inflation rate, and reduces international competitiveness, thus causing further depreciation. This country is caught in a vicious circle of currency depreciation combined with accelerating inflation.[4]

If these *J*-curve phenomena are pronounced, they could imply foreign exchange markets that are unstable in the short run, producing destabilizing changes in exchange rates and inflation rates, but that become stable in the long run as the values of the price elasticities increase. If so, we have ample reason to expect exchange rates to overshoot their long-run equilibrium values under the flexible exchange-rate system.

8.4 EXCHANGE RATE STABILITY AND MACROECONOMIC STABILITY

The obvious weakness of the elasticities approach is its failure to go beyond the foreign exchange market to the economy as a whole. This weakness leads to the discussion of the absorption effects of devaluation of the next chapter. There we will see that *expenditure-switching* policies such as devaluation may have to be combined with *expenditure-reducing* policies that lower domestic demand if devaluation is to have its intended effect in improving the current account. Devaluation affects real national income and the price level. These changes feed back into the foreign exchange market, usually unfavorably, which is why such feedback effects are sometimes called *reversal* factors.

Analysis of these reversal factors and how to deal with them is the subject of the next chapter. Here we close by noting the likelihood that

---

[4] For an analysis of the *J*-curve effect see Blackhurst, Richard, and Jan Tumler, "Trade Relations Under Flexible Exchange Rates," GATT, September 1980.

the entire economy cannot approach a stable equilibrium of prices and output unless the foreign exchange market does so also. The analysis is developed with some care in the appendix to Chapter 9. Here we can give an intuitive explanation with reference to Figure 8.6. The intersection of the demand for foreign exchange and the supply of foreign exchange is at the unstable equilibrium point f. Starting at that point, let a small appreciation take place. This reduces the price of foreign exchange and creates excess supply for foreign exchange rather than excess demand. The price of foreign exchange therefore continues to fall at an ever-faster rate, and the excess supply continues to widen. Since the physical volume of imports increases without limit and the physical quantity of exports declines without limit, it follows that national income must also decline without limit. This suggests that the Marshall-Lerner conditions are a requirement for overall stability as well.

   Is there a limit? Tests for stability are valid only in the neighborhood of equilibrium. They are therefore referred to as *local* stability. Local stability implies *global* stability if the functions are linear, since two straight lines cannot intersect twice. However, the demand and supply of foreign exchange are not likely to be linear functions. In particular, it seems likely that as the volume of exports shrinks as the price of foreign exchange declines, the demand for exports will become more price-elastic, thereby increasing the slope of the supply curve of foreign exchange until it becomes positive. Consequently, the demand and supply curves of foreign exchange could intersect again at a stable equilibrium point, such as point a of Figure 2.3. It is possible, therefore, for a flexible exchange-rate system to settle at a stable equilibrium point, whereas devaluation of a fixed exchange rate may cause foreign exchange earnings to decline if the initial fixed exchange rate is grossly undervalued. However, as suggested earlier, such an unlikely situation implies that the official exchange rate should be revalued rather than devalued.

QUESTIONS FOR REVIEW

1. Analyze the effects of currency devaluation on a country's foreign currency expenditures on imports. What are the effects on its expenditures in terms of domestic currency? What are the implications of your analysis for the demand for foreign exchange and the supply of home currency?

2. Analyze the effect of currency devaluation on a country's foreign exchange earnings from the sale of exports. What are the domestic currency expenditure effects? What are the implications for the supply of foreign exchange and the demand for local currency?

3. Overall, will devaluation improve the balance of trade in terms of foreign currency? What will be the domestic effects of devaluation?

4. Explain the *J*-curve phenomenon. Is there also a *J*-curve operating in terms of the effect of devaluation on the domestic economy?

5. What are the likely effects of devaluation during recession when supply elasticities are high?

6. What are the likely effects of devaluation on a small country that purchases imports in a large world market and sells its exports in such a market?

7. What is the basis for post–World War II "elasticity pessimism"? What are the implications of this for the stability of the foreign exchange market under flexible exchange rates?

SUGGESTIONS FOR FURTHER READING

Blackhurst, Richard, and Jan Tumler, "Trade Relations Under Flexible Exchange Rates," GATT, September 1980.

Johnson, Harry G. and Jacob Frenkel, *The Economics of Exchange Rates,* Addison-Wesley, 1978.

Robinson, Joan, "The Foreign Exchanges," *Essays in the Theory of Employment,* Basil, Blackwell, and Mott, 1974, chap. 5.

Warner, Dennis, and Mordechai Kreinin, "Determinants of International Trade Flows," *Review of Economics and Statistics,* 1983.

Williamson, John, *The Open Economy and the World Economy,* Basic Books, 1983, chap. 8.

Chapter 9

The Current Account (II): Income-Expenditure Effects of Devaluation

9.1 THE ABSORPTIONIST ATTACK ON ELASTICITIES ANALYSIS

Elasticities analysis such as that of Chapter 7 has been widely criticized because it ignored the income-expenditure effects of devaluation. Devaluation tends to increase production in export industries and in import-competing industries. Devaluation therefore tends to raise national income and the price level. As a consequence of the income expansion, the demand for imports will rise. This means that the demand curve for foreign exchange will shift to the right, so excess demand for foreign exchange may persist after the devaluation.

A formal analysis of these effects, coming in the form of a severe attack on the elasticities approach, was launched by S. S. Alexander, then of the IMF staff, in 1952. Alexander began with the proposition that net exports could be expanded only if total production could be raised or if domestic claims against production—what Alexander termed *absorption*—were reduced. To be successful, devaluation would somehow have to bring either or both of these changes about.[1]

National income equals domestic absorption plus net exports; that is,

$$Y = A + (X - V) \tag{9.1}$$

where

$$A = C + I + G \tag{9.2}$$

[1] Alexander, Sidney S., "Effects of a Devaluation on a Trade Balance," *International Monetary Fund, Staff Papers*, 2:263–278, 1952.

Rewriting (9.1), we can see that net exports must equal the difference between national income and absorption; that is,

$$X - V = Y - A \qquad (9.3)$$

Devaluation raises exports and reduces the demand for imports. If the economy has available unemployed labor and underutilized capacity, real national income will expand. The expansion of net exports can then be accomplished by mobilizing hitherto idle resources. It follows from (9.3) that

$$\Delta(X - V) = \Delta Y - \Delta A$$

However, the rise in income raises consumption spending and therefore absorption. The rise in consumption equals the marginal propensity to consume times the change in income. Therefore, if $\Delta A = \Delta C$,

$$\Delta A = b(1 - t)\Delta Y$$

thus,

$$\Delta Y - \Delta A = [1 - b(1 - t)]\Delta Y = s\,\Delta Y$$

It therefore follows that

$$\Delta(X - V) = s\,\Delta Y \qquad (9.4)$$

Expression (9.4) makes clear that the trade balance can improve only to the extent that devaluation raises domestic saving. It does no good to raise production if the resulting increase in income raises consumption by an equal amount. Resources will be released to expand net exports only if the rise in income carries with it a rise in saving. This necessitates a positive marginal propensity to save disposable income and is augmented by a positive income tax rate, provided the government does not increase absorption by spending the higher tax receipts. Although these conditions are likely to be met in industrial countries, it is not at all clear that they will be met in developing countries where private saving is low and tax systems are generally unresponsive to income changes.

The rise in real income that permitted net exports to expand was termed the idle-resource effect by Alexander. However, Alexander suggested that real income might rise a lesser amount because devaluation is likely to cause a deterioration in the terms of trade. Devaluation lowers the foreign price of imports and the foreign price of exports. If the foreign price of exports drops by more than the foreign price of imports, fewer units of imports can be purchased with a given quantity of exports, and the terms of trade are said to deteriorate with an adverse effect on the devaluing country's real income.

We can return to the results of Chapter 8 to examine the effect of devaluation on the terms of trade. Equations (8.7) and (8.4) show that the differences between the proportionate change in the foreign price of exports and the proportionate change in the foreign price of imports is

$$\frac{dq}{q} - \frac{dQ}{Q} = \left[\left(\frac{-s_x}{n_x + s_x}\right) - \left(\frac{-n_v}{n_v + s_v}\right)\right]\frac{de}{e} \qquad (9.5)$$

where, as before, q is the foreign price of exports and Q is the foreign price of imports. A deterioration in the terms of trade implies that the foreign price of exports falls by more than the foreign price of imports. This means that (9.5) must be negative. Consequently,

$$\frac{-s_x}{n_x + s_x} - \frac{-n_v}{n_v + s_v} < 0$$

Multiplying through by -1 and placing the terms over a common denominator gives

$$\frac{s_x(n_v + s_v) - n_v(n_x + s_x)}{(n_x + s_x)(n_v + s_v)} > 0$$

Since the numerator of this expression reduces to $s_x s_v - n_v n_x$, it follows that the terms of trade will deteriorate if

$$s_x s_v > n_v n_x$$

The product of the supply elasticities must therefore exceed the product of the demand elasticities. This condition is satisfied for the several high supply-elasticity cases. Low demand elasticities are unfavorable to the terms of trade. The lower is n_x the greater is the reduction in the foreign price of exports. Similarly, a reduction in the elasticity of demand for imports, n_v, means a smaller fall in the foreign price of imports. A country that is too small to influence the world price of the imports it purchases is bound to suffer a deterioration in the terms of trade when it devalues its currency.

Alexander believed the conditions for deterioration of the terms of trade were likely to be satisfied in most cases. He therefore suggested that devaluation would tend to reduce real income, thereby implying a larger trade deficit for any given level of absorption.

In a subsequent debate with Alexander, Fritz Machlup[2] took the position that real income might rise in response to devaluation even if the economy is at full employment. He pointed out that devaluation

[2] Machlup, Fritz, "Relative Prices and Aggregate Spending in the Analysis of Devaluation," *American Economic Review*, June 1955.

could permit a government to ease controls and trade restrictions. If such easing takes place, the allocation of resources will improve and that will raise real income. This resource allocation effect would then help to improve the balance of trade relative to the level of absorption.

Machlup's point was important at the time of the elasticities-absorption debate, because trade restrictions remained substantial in the early 1950s even though giant strides in multilateral trade liberalization had been made between the end of World War II and the early 1950s.[3] It remains an important consideration in developing countries where a seemingly endless assortment of impediments to external and internal trade is common. It is hardly an accident that the IMF and the World Bank routinely attempt to persuade countries to match the allocative improvements achieved by devaluation with measures designed to improve allocative efficiency throughout the economy.

In the chapter appendix an attempt is made to integrate elasticities with absorption analysis by taking the effect of income change on imports into account. A somewhat simpler version of that analysis can be developed here, provided we are ready to ignore monetary and interest-rate effects. Since we are still concerned, in this section, with an economy at less than full employment, we assume that national price levels are fixed and that the supply elasticities for exports and imports are therefore infinite.

In Chapter 8 we essentially assumed that net exports depend exclusively on the real exchange rate. With fixed prices this means that exports and imports become functions of the nominal exchange rate alone. Therefore the basic Chapter 8 model applicable to our present problem is

$$X - eV = X(e) - eV(e)$$

[3] President Harry S Truman was directly responsible for providing U.S. leadership in postwar trade liberalization. With his support, the Department of State participated in several fruitful rounds of multilateral negotiations at Geneva, Annecy, Torquay, and Havana, where many of the trade restrictions that had been imposed during the interwar period were reduced or eliminated. Tariff rates were sharply slashed, with U.S. tariffs falling to pre-1920s levels. The Geneva meeting produced the General Agreements on Tariffs and Trade (GATT), which set forth rules for the conduct of commercial policy. The overall strategy was to eliminate all trade restrictions except tariffs, and to subject the latter to further negotiation. At the Havana meeting a charter for an International Trade Organization (ITO) was negotiated. This organization would have been responsible for policing member countries' commercial policies in the same way as the IMF is supposed to police their balance-of-payments policies. The ITO was never ratified. By the time it came before the U.S. Congress, the Congress and the State Department had become so demoralized and intimidated by the anticommunist forays of Senator Joseph McCarthy that ratification became impossible. As U.S. support for the ITO was seen to be waning, other countries lost interest in the project, so the ITO was never established. GATT, however, continues to function.

where we now denominate V in foreign currency so that multiplication by e converts this into its domestic currency equivalent.

As in Chapter 8, the change in net exports is

$$d(X - V) = X(n_x + n_v - 1)de$$

if the supply elasticities are infinite, the initial value of the exchange rate is arbitrarily set at $e = 1$ (so that $de/e = de$), and the initial value of exports equals the initial value of imports.

To take direct absorption effects into account, we need to rewrite net exports as

$$X - V = X(e) - eV(e, Y)$$

where the level of national income now appears as an argument in the import function. Under these circumstances, the change in net exports caused by a change in the exchange rate can easily be shown to be

$$d(X - V) = X(n_x + n_v - 1)de - V_y dY \qquad (9.6)$$

where V_y is the marginal propensity to import. Clearly, the effect of income change on the trade balance is adverse if the income change is positive.

From (9.4) we reasoned that the change in net exports must also equal the difference between the change in income and the change in absorption. We saw, moreover, that this implied

$$dY - dA = s\, dY = S_y\, dY \qquad (9.7)$$

where S_y is the national marginal propensity to save.

We can equate (9.6) and (9.7) and solve for the change in income as a function of the change in the exchange rate:

$$dY = \frac{1}{S_y + V_y} X(n_x + n_v - 1)de \qquad (9.8)$$

On inspection of this result we see that the term $1/(S_y + V_y)$ is the small-country multiplier of Chapter 4. We can also see that if the sum of the demand elasticities exceeds unity, devaluation (a rise in e) must raise national income. Since national income changes only because the trade balance changes, the change in net exports must have been positive. We conclude, therefore, that if elasticities analysis predicts a rise in net exports, that prediction will still be valid when the adverse effect of income change on imports is taken into account. Thus, elasticities analysis is qualitatively correct, even if it is likely to overestimate the degree to which devaluation will improve net exports.

9.2 DEVALUATION, THE PRICE LEVEL, AND ABSORPTION

Although devaluation could improve the trade balance if the economy is at less than full employment, the prospects for successful devaluation seem likely to be less favorable when the economy is already at full employment, since total production cannot then be raised. A rise in net exports can then only be achieved by a reduction in absorption. The next question, then, is whether devaluation can reduce absorption when the economy is at full employment.

Devaluation tends to raise the home currency prices of both exports and imports. These price increases feed through the economy and are reflected in a rise in the general price level. Indeed, most of the absorption-changing effects of devaluation are related to the effects, an aggregate expenditure, of a rise in the price level. We met several of these effects in Chapter 7. An expanded list might look as follows:

NOTE ALL ASSUMPTIONS

$\overset{+}{}$ **(1) The Keynes Effect** When the domestic price level rises, the real value of the nation's money supply declines. This decline in the real quantity of money has the effect of shifting the devaluing country's LM curve to the left. It therefore raises the rate of interest and reduces aggregate expenditure by reducing investment and other interest-sensitive expenditures, such as home construction and consumer durable demand. The Keynes effect will work in favor of the devaluation if the monetary authority does not react to the rise in the rate of interest by expanding the nominal money supply. $P\uparrow \Rightarrow \frac{m^s}{P_c}\downarrow \Rightarrow \frac{Dm^s}{Bonds} \Rightarrow S_B\uparrow \Rightarrow P_B\downarrow \Rightarrow i\uparrow \Rightarrow \frac{I}{C_a}\downarrow \Rightarrow \boxed{A\downarrow}$

$\overset{+}{e\uparrow} \Rightarrow$

$\overset{+}{}$ **(2) The Real-Balance Effect** A rise in the price level reduces the real value of the financial wealth that the private sector of the economy holds as claims against the government. The currency held by the private sector is one such claim, and public debt is another. When the real value of these assets declines, it can be expected that the nation's consumption function will shift down, moving the IS curve to the left, thereby reducing absorption. This is the real-balance effect. It presumes that the government will not feel richer as the consequence of the real wealth transfer from the private sector and therefore will not increase government spending. It presumes also that the private sector holds enough financial claims against the government to make the price-level effect on wealth significant enough to reduce consumption. $e\uparrow \Rightarrow P_c\uparrow \Rightarrow \frac{wealth}{P_c}\downarrow \Rightarrow C\downarrow \Rightarrow A\downarrow$

$\overset{+}{}$ **(3) The Money-Illusion Effect** In countries with progressive income taxes based on personal money income, a rise in money income raises the average rate of income tax even if the rise in money income is

$e\uparrow \Rightarrow P_c\uparrow \Rightarrow Y \cdot P_c\uparrow \Rightarrow \overset{Jump \; into \; higher}{tax \; bracket} \Rightarrow Y_d\downarrow \Rightarrow C\downarrow \Rightarrow A\downarrow$

caused entirely by inflation and not by a rise in real income. This reduces real after-tax disposable income and therefore depresses consumption and absorption. This effect is due to *money illusion* in the structure of individual income taxes, that is, by the failure of the tax system to be intelligent enough to distinguish between a rise in nominal income caused by a rise in real income and a rise in nominal income caused by inflation.

Inflation advanced rapidly in the United States in 1974 caused, in large measure, by the quadrupling of oil prices that had been engineered by the OPEC cartel. The economy went downhill rapidly thereafter, as real GNP dropped 4.4 percent between the fourth quarter of 1973 and the fourth quarter of 1974. However, prices as measured by the implicit price deflator for GNP went up 11.4 percent. Consequently, nominal GNP (prices multiplied by quantities) continued to rise (at a rate of 6.5 percent) even though real GNP was declining.

At that time the tax base for the individual income tax in the United States was nominal personal income, which rose 8.7 percent between the end of 1973 and the fourth quarter of 1974. The rising nominal personal income raised the fraction of nominal income taken in taxes from 11.0 to 11.5 percent, causing individual income taxes to jump 13.5 percent at a time when pretax real income was declining. The result was a sharp reduction in consumption expenditure that added to the deflationary forces that were responsible for the severity of the 1974–75 recession.

Money illusion in a tax structure can be beneficial if it helps to contain the rise in absorption during a period of excess demand inflation when real and money income are tending to move in the same direction. In that, even the shifting of taxpayers into higher tax brackets can free resources from consumption in a way that permits net exports to expand. However, when real and money income are moving in opposite directions, as happened during the stagflation of the 1970s, the results can be devastating for output and employment.

Money illusion in tax structures is becoming less widespread, as the experience of the 1970s motivated a number of countries to inflation-index their tax systems. This was usually accomplished by widening tax brackets, exemption, and standard deductions at the rate of inflation. Average tax rates can then rise only if real pretax income increases. Canada was among the first countries to adopt tax indexation, and the United States put such a system into effect in 1985 under legislation passed in 1981 at the urging of President Reagan.[4]

---

[4] The tax reform bill enacted in 1986 suspends the indexing of tax brackets until 1989, but retains indexing of the personal exemption and the standard deduction. The number of tax brackets was reduced to three, and the maximum marginal tax rate was reduced from 50 percent to 33 percent. These changes have removed much of the progressivity of the individual income tax and thereby, also, largely eliminated the need for inflation indexing.

(4) Inflationary Expectations   The Keynes, real-balance, and money-illusion effects tend to be stabilizing in the sense that they tend to contain absorption during an inflationary period. However, working against this is the fact that the rise in the price *level* may raise the expected *rate of inflation.* Devaluation raises the price level; hence if price expectations are elastic, the increase in the price level is interpreted as signaling the onset of an inflationary trend. In fact, if people hold rational expectations and are therefore as smart as economists, the devaluation, or just the anticipation of devaluation, will raise the expected rate of inflation, possibly before any price increases actually take place.[5]

Anticipating higher prices in the future, consumers and other economic agents tend to engage in anticipatory buying, especially of durable goods, in order to beat the expected price increases. If this happens, absorption and import demand will increase. Devaluation normally appears as a supply restriction to importers. The domestic price of imports rises, and the quantity of imports is diminished. However, anticipatory buying in response to the expected inflation may cause the demand curve for imports to shift to the right. This adds to the increase in the price of imports and also increases the physical quantity of imports. If there is no reduction in the physical quantity of imports demanded, foreign suppliers will see no reduction in demand, and the foreign price of imports will not fall. Consequently, since both foreign price and physical quantity may remain unchanged, there will be no reduction in the amount of foreign exchange spent on imports.

The prospect of increased export sales may also be damaged by a rise in the expected rate of inflation. Devaluation tends to raise the domestic price of exports, thereby providing an incentive for exporters and their suppliers to increase production. However, if the devaluation, or the prospect of a devaluation, raises the anticipated rate of inflation, exporters will expect their production costs to rise. Expecting these cost increases to offset the higher export prices, thereby neutralizing the price incentive supplied by devaluation, exporters may take no steps to expand their production.

---

[5] Expectations are said to be inelastic if a price movement is expected to be reversed and price returns to some level considered to be normal. Price expectations are considered elastic if a movement of price in one direction gives rise to the expectation that the price trend will continue. Inelastic expectations are generally regarded as stabilizing, whereas elastic expectations are destabilizing. When price rises and market participants expect the price to return to a lower level, they take the price increase as a signal to enter the market by selling. This then helps to push the price back toward the "normal" or equilibrium level. On the other hand, if the price increase gives rise to the expectation that prices will continue to rise, market participants will take the price increase as a signal to buy and that will then drive the price even higher.

③ Another way in which an increase in the expected rate of inflation raises absorption is through the effect of the rise in the expected rate of inflation on the *real* rate of interest. Although *nominal* interest rates will rise when the expected rate of inflation increases, the rise in the nominal rate of interest will be less than the rise in the expected rate of inflation, so the real rate of interest will fall. To understand this, we need briefly to discuss the relationship between real and nominal interest rates and the expected rate of inflation.

The relationship between the nominal and the real rate of interest is given approximately by[6]

$$i_n = i_r + E\left(\frac{dp}{p}\right) \tag{9.9}$$

where i_n is the nominal rate of interest, i_r is the real rate of interest, and $E(dp/p)$ is the expected rate of inflation.

If money held either in cash or in a bank earns no interest, an annual inflation of 5 percent implies that the purchasing power of the money declines 5 percent. Thus there is an effective negative real rate of interest of 5 percent. If the expected rate of inflation rises, the penalty attached to holding money increases. Wealth holders would then be driven to accept a lower real rate of return on other earning assets to escape the increased real cost of holding money. Therefore, a rise in the expected rate of inflation causes portfolio substitution away from money and toward earning assets. The substitution raises the prices of the earning assets and reduces the real rate of return from those assets. Consequently, the

---

[6] To achieve a real return of i_r, a lender must receive a nominal return greater than i_r sufficient to compensate the lender for the erosion of the purchasing-power value of the loan caused by inflation. That is why a rise in anticipated inflation tends to raise the nominal rate of interest. In a year the nominal value of a loan of $1 is $1 + i_n$. This must equal the real value of the loan with allowance for anticipated inflation. Therefore,

$$1 + i_n = (1 + i_r)\left[1 + E\left(\frac{dp}{p}\right)\right]$$

Multiplying out the right side, we get

$$1 + i_n = 1 + i_r + E\left(\frac{dp}{p}\right) + i_r E\left(\frac{dp}{p}\right)$$

Since the last term on the right side is apt to be quite small, it is generally ignored; thus,

$$i_n = i_r + E\left(\frac{dp}{p}\right)$$

as in (9.9) of the text.

real rate of interest falls as liquidity preference declines, and this, in turn, raises investment and other interest-sensitive expenditure categories, so absorption increases.

Clearly the favorable effects on absorption of a rise in the price level could easily be swamped by the unfavorable effects of a rise in the expected rate of inflation. In that event the prospects for successful devaluation in a fully employed economy are slim. To make devaluation work, the government would have to make a credible guarantee that it intends to prevent rising inflation by accompanying devaluation with absorption-reducing fiscal and/or monetary policies.

(5) The Excise-Tax Effect   Absorption could decline in response to devaluation if the home currency value of imports *rises*. Indeed, Richard Cooper and others[7] have argued that this has happened in some developing countries, especially during the initial phases following devaluation when price elasticities are low. If the country is small and purchases in a world market, a reduction in its demand for imports will not affect the world price. Therefore, the supply of imports is infinitely elastic with respect to price. From (8.24) we can see that under such conditions the change in the home currency value of imports is

$$dV = V(1 - n_v)\frac{de}{e}$$

and $dP/P = de/e$. Therefore the domestic price of imports rises by the same percentage as the percentage devaluation. If the elasticity of demand for imports, n_v, is less than 1, dV will be positive. Therefore, the value of imports denominated in home currency prices rises if the demand for imports is inelastic with respect to price. This effect is magnified when imports, V, are large to begin with. A country that already has a large trade deficit may therefore suffer a large increase in the domestic cost of imports relative to the rise in the value of exports in response to devaluation.[8]

---

[7] Cooper, Richard N., *Currency Devaluation in Developing Countries,* Princeton Essays in International Finance, No. 86 (1971), and P. Krugman and L. Taylor, "Contractionary Effects of Devaluation," *Journal of International Economics,* August 1978.

[8] If the supply elasticities are infinite,

$$d\text{NX} = [-Xn_x - V(n_v - 1)]\frac{de}{e}$$

as seen from (7.25). If the overall balance of trade deteriorates, as measured in domestic currency, $d\text{NX} < 0$, which requires that

$$Xn_x + V(n_v - 1) < 0$$

The effect on the economy is similar to what happened to oil-importing countries when oil prices rose sharply. The price increase had an employment-reducing effect comparable to the effect of a massive increase in excise taxes on essential imports. Because the demand for imports was price-inelastic, the proportionate rise in the domestic price of imports vastly exceeded the proportionate reduction in the quantity imported, so *more* real income was spent on imports. This meant that less real income was available to be spent on other goods, so the demand for domestically produced goods declined. In other words, devaluation may have the effect of *reducing* real domestic absorption from the import side, tending, therefore, to reduce output and employment.

(6) The Terms-of-Trade Effect   A terms-of-trade effect will tend to affect absorption in the opposite direction as the excise-tax effect. This effect was already discussed briefly in the discussion of macroeconomic interdependence in Chapter 6. There we saw that Laursen and Metzler had argued that changes in the terms of trade would have domestic spending effects. In particular, devaluation reduces the economy's real income if the devaluation carries with it an adverse effect on the terms of trade. If the economy's consumption function contains a positive autonomous consumption component (such as the $C_a = 40$ of Chapter 4), a decline in real income will be associated with a rise in the fraction of income consumed and a reduction in the fraction of income saved. This means that real consumption in terms of domestic prices will increase, so domestic absorption rises due to the change in the terms of trade.

To see how this might come about, assume that consumption is a linear function of real income, so the consumption function can be written

$$\frac{C}{\pi} = C_0 + b\left(\frac{Y}{\pi}\right) \qquad (9.10)$$

where C and Y are nominal consumption and income, respectively, and π is the consumer price index. Multiply both sides by π to express consumption in nominal terms:

$$C = \pi C_0 + bY \qquad (9.11)$$

Solving for n_v, we get

$$n_v < 1 - \left(\frac{X}{V}\right) n_x$$

which implies that a higher level of V relative to X increases the allowable value of n_v required for negative dNX. If V is very high relative to X, the condition for deterioration is approximately

$$n_v < 1$$

implying that developments on the export side are overshadowed by the dominant effects on the home currency value of imports.

Next suppose, as we did in Chapter 7, that the index of consumer prices is a weighted average of domestic and import prices such that

$$\pi = p^a(ep^*)^{1-a} \tag{9.12}$$

where p^* is the price of imports in foreign currency, e is the nominal exchange rate, and a is a positive fraction. Finally, and to simplify the example, assume that consumption is the only component of absorption and that net exports are zero. It then follows that $C = Y$, so (9.11) can be written

$$Y = \frac{C_0\pi}{1 - b} \tag{9.13}$$

Using (9.12) to replace π in (9.13) gives nominal income as

$$Y = \frac{C_0}{1 - b} p^a(ep^*)^{1-a} \tag{9.14}$$

Real income in terms of domestic prices is

$$\frac{Y}{p} = \frac{C_0}{1 - b} p^{a-1}(ep^*)^{1-a} \tag{9.15}$$

The effect of a rise in the domestic cost of imports caused by depreciation is then

$$\frac{\partial(Y/p)}{\partial e} = \frac{(1 - a)C_0}{1 - b} p^{a-1} p^{*1-a} e^{-a} > 0 \tag{9.16}$$

which is positive since a is a positive fraction. This means that a rise in the domestic cost of imports raises real consumption in terms of home prices, so domestic absorption increases. Observe that this would not happen if autonomous consumption (C_0) were zero. In that event, the consumption function would intersect the origin, and the percent of income consumed would be constant at all income levels.

9.3 SYNTHESIZING ELASTICITIES AND ABSORPTION ANALYSIS AS A GUIDE TO POLICY

It is obvious that an approach that incorporates both relative price and absorption effects is essential if the effects of devaluation or revaluation are to be adequately assessed. Either form of analysis is not necessarily incorrect. It is, however, incomplete. Recognizing this fact, the late Harry

G. Johnson proposed a "general" theory of the balance of payments, which suggested that, for deficit countries, an *expenditure-switching* policy, such as devaluation, would normally have to be accompanied by *expenditure-reducing* policies, such as lowering monetary growth or reducing government budget deficits. Johnson's approach is "general" in the sense that it attempts to integrate elasticities and absorption analysis; it is not, however, general, inasmuch as it speaks only to the analysis of the current account.[9]

The combination of expenditure switching and expenditure reduction applies to a deficit country that also strains at its available resources and likely suffers considerable inflation. But other conditions of disequilibrium could exist. A country could have a deficit in its current account and at the same time suffer recession. Such a country very probably needs a different set of policies to achieve external and internal balance. Surplus countries, too, have their problems requiring policy adjustment. And finally, there is the issue of coordination of policies between deficit and surplus countries so as to foster orderly adjustment to external and internal balance for countries collectively.

From the discussion it is obvious that there are two major policy variables that must be controlled. The first is the exchange rate, and the second is the level of domestic absorption. Policy that addresses itself to one but not the other could well be ineffective. These considerations suggest a further look at the external-internal balance model introduced in Chapter 2. Therefore, have a glance at Figure 9.1, which reproduces the Swan model described briefly in Chapter 2. The internal (IB) balance curve normally has a negative slope. A rise in absorption is inflationary. But if it is accompanied by appreciation (a fall in the price of foreign exchange), imports will rise and exports will decline; hence, additional resources are made available to the economy, so the excess demand is eliminated. To the right of IB the economy suffers inflation, and to the left it suffers recession. The external balance (EB) curve has a positive slope. A rise in absorption causes a deficit in the current account. To eliminate the deficit, government must raise the price of foreign exchange. To the right of EB the economy has a current-account deficit, and to the left of EB it has a surplus.

How should policy react when the economy finds itself in one of the four zones delimited by the IB and EB functions? Start with point *f* with an economy suffering recession but enjoying a current-account surplus. To eliminate the surplus, one might think it appropriate to appre-

[9] Johnson, Harry G., "Towards a General Theory of the Balance of Payments," *International Trade and Economic Growth: Studies in Pure Theory,* Harvard University Press, 1961.

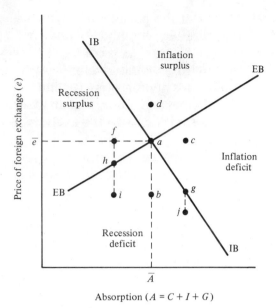

Figure 9.1   Policy adjustment to achieve internal and external balance.

ciate. However, that reduces exports and increases imports, so it worsens
the recession because it moves the economy toward point (*h*) which is
even farther from IB than the starting point. It seems obvious that this
economy would be well advised to reject such a policy and to expand
absorption instead. This moves the economy in the direction of point *a*
and gets the economy closer to both IB and EB. The increase in absorption
raises national income and employment, and the associated rise in the
demand for imports reduces the current-account surplus.

A country suffering a recession and a deficit as at point *b* had better
raise the price of foreign exchange. The devaluation raises exports and
lowers imports, thereby reducing the deficit. Since such policy normally
stimulates the economy, it also moves the economy closer to full employment. If it tried to reach full employment by raising absorption, as
indicated by a move from *b* to *g*, this would worsen the deficit because
imports would rise. If it tried to move toward external balance by lowering
absorption so as to move from *b* to *h*, the resulting aggregate expenditure
reduction would worsen the recession.

A recession combined with a worsening deficit confronted President
Richard M. Nixon in 1971. Realizing that expansionary policies designed
to restore full employment would worsen the deficit, the president drew
the correct conclusion that the dollar was overvalued and that devaluation
was essential. In August 1971 he took the important step of suspending
U.S. gold sales, and he called for negotiations to realign exchange rates.

The dollar was then devalued by the Group of Ten (ten major industrial countries) at the Smithsonian Meeting later that year, and then again in early 1973.

A country suffering inflation and a deficit as at point c needs to get inflation under control by reducing absorption. If it devalues to improve its current account, this stimulates the economy and worsens the inflation. But if it attempts to reduce domestic absorption by restrictive fiscal and monetary policies, this will reduce inflation and, at the same time, reduce import demand, thereby also reducing its external deficit.

The International Monetary Fund (IMF), which makes loans to countries experiencing balance-of-payments difficulties, has frequently required borrowing countries to get their money supplies under control as a condition for IMF assistance. This may be harsh medicine, but often it is the only way to restore balance to economies in the inflation-deficit zone. Most of the IMF's clients are developing countries in Asia, Africa, and Latin America—countries that frequently find themselves suffering from a combination of inflation and balance-of-payments deficit. The IMF is not popular in some of these countries because the deflationary medicine tends to raise unemployment, stunt growth, and cause political unrest. The cure is often considered worse than the disease, so the IMF's austerity programs are not always welcome. However, the logic of the inflation-deficit zone dictates that the first order of business is reduction of domestic inflation.

A country at point d in the inflation-surplus zone should be encouraged to appreciate. West Germany was in this position much of the time in the late 1960s and early 1970s. Ever nervous about inflation, it leaned toward tight budgets and tight money. The result, however, was lower import demand and highly competitive exports, producing a tendency for Germany's current-account surplus to widen. The way to achieve both external and internal balance in an inflation-surplus situation is to appreciate. That, perhaps, is why West Germany was so frequently urged to revalue the deutsche mark by other countries.

As is clear from Figure 8.1, in most cases a combination of exchange rate and absorption policies will be needed. For example, if the economy is at point h, it cannot reach point a without a combination of demand stimulus and devaluation. Demand stimulus alone throws the current account into deficit; devaluation is also needed. At point g external and internal balance cannot both be reached unless devaluation is accompanied by demand restriction. Devaluation by itself causes inflation, which must be offset by a reduction in domestic demand.

The principle that two instruments of policy must normally be adjusted if two targets such as internal and external balance are to be achieved is a well-known rule of the theory of economic policy. The Dutch Nobel laureate Jan Tinbergen is the economist who originated the idea that policy instruments need to be systematically matched with policy targets. In the remainder of this chapter we explore some further elements of the theory of economic policy; Chapter 12 is devoted to it.

Sometimes the appropriate direction in which a policy instrument should change is ambiguous. For example, suppose the economy is at point *i* in the recession-deficit zone. Ultimately, it will have to raise absorption to get to point *a*. But it is hard to know this if available information discloses no more than that the economy is somewhere in the recession-deficit zone. If the country expands absorption, the rise in income raises imports and causes its current-account deficit to increase. If it restricts demand to get rid of its current-account deficit, the recession gets worse. The appropriate direction in which fiscal and monetary policies should move is not clear. The fiscal-monetary instruments may therefore be said to be in a *conflict* or *dilemma* situation. Such policies cannot move the economy closer to one target without moving farther away from the other target. In this particular situation, exchange rate policy has no such problem. At point *i* it is obvious that the currency is overvalued. Depreciation reduces the deficit because net exports rise; at the same time, the rise in net exports stimulates the economy, moving it closer to internal balance.

This illustrates the principle of economic policy that leadership in policy adjustment should be taken by the policy instrument that is *not* in conflict so that adjustment by that instrument carries the economy closer to both targets. Starting at point *i,* the country could devalue its currency to reach point *h* on the EB curve. When *h* is reached, it becomes clear that further devaluation will generate a current-account surplus while the economy remains in recession. The conflict for absorption control policy is now removed, and it becomes apparent that further progress in ridding the economy of recession should be made by expanding absorption.

Point *j* is also a recession-deficit point, so absorption-changing policies are again in a dilemma. Devaluation to *g* eliminates recession before it eliminates the deficit. Therefore, further depreciation will move the economy into the inflation zone. It then becomes clear that the further depreciation must be matched by restrictive monetary-fiscal policies that reduce absorption.

In passing, observe from this last case that it is not necessarily the case that recession invariably calls for expansionary policies that raise absorption. If the economy suffers from a deficit, the devaluation needed to eliminate the deficit might provide sufficient stimulus to get rid of the recession as well. That is the situation implied by point j. It would have been a mistake, under the circumstances, to raise absorption.

Under flexible exchange rates the economy would always be on the IB curve if the exchange rate adjusts automatically to balance the current account. Unfortunately, this frequently does not happen because of large and volatile movements of capital. If the exchange rate did balance the current account, the directive for stabilization policy would be greatly simplified. There would be only two areas of concern, inflation and recession, with which policy needs to concern itself. Fiscal and monetary policy could concentrate on achieving internal balance, and external balance would take care of itself, provided the monetary-fiscal policies do not induce massive capital movements, such as occurred during the first half of the 1980s. Such automatically produced external balance would provide a great potential advantage to the flexible exchange-rate system. But that will happen only if the fiscal and monetary policies are carefully coordinated, in the manner prescribed in Chapter 6, to eliminate major swings in capital movements.

Earlier we noted that the combination of absorption-reducing effects, especially a powerful excise-tax effect, could reduce absorption to an extent that devaluation could throw the economy into recession. In this event the internal balance function would be positively sloped, as shown in Figure 9.2. If the economy is initially at point b enjoying full employment but suffering a balance-of-payments deficit, a devaluation to $\bar{e}$ would put the economy into the recession zone at point c. If the authorities follow the IMF's advice to accompany devaluation with absorption-reducing policy, the economy may end up at point d, which implies a nasty recession involving heavy unemployment. It is hardly surprising, under the circumstances, that developing countries consider the IMF's love affair with austerity programs as inconsistent with their domestic employment and growth objectives. For its part, the IMF will applaud the fact that at point d the country has at long last rid itself of its chronic payments deficit and is entering a welcome period during which it can accumulate foreign exchange.

9.4 INTERNATIONAL COOPERATION TO ACHIEVE EXTERNAL AND INTERNAL BALANCE

It is important to consider how countries may jointly solve their employment and balance-of-payments problems. Is the basis for cooperation present, or will there be conflict or dilemma situations?

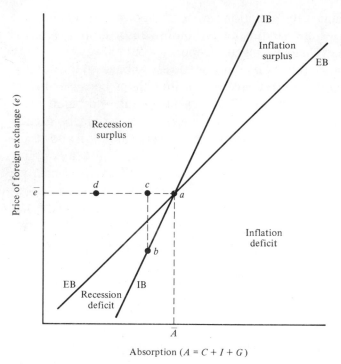

Figure 9.2 External and internal balance when devaluation reduces absorption.

Consider again the economy in recession with a current-account deficit. The deficit means that other countries are running surpluses vis-à-vis the deficit country. If the other countries are also below full employment, so that the recession is international, devaluation by the deficit country will be considered beggar-my-neighbor policy. The devaluation exports domestic unemployment to other countries, worsening the recession in those countries. Other countries will not stand still for what they perceive as a hostile act, so they may also devalue, and the world economy could then suffer competitive depreciation and tariff warfare of the kind that helped to strangle trade and contribute to the Great Depression of the 1930s.

It is obvious that competitive depreciation will not do the job of restoring full employment. Some country has to expand internal demand and assume the role of the "locomotive" that pulls the world economy out of the general recession. If the deficit country does this, its import demand will increase, thereby widening its current-account deficit while increasing the surpluses of the other countries. But if the surplus countries pursue expansionary monetary-fiscal policies, the rise in their income levels increases their imports, so deficits and surpluses shrink all around.

Therefore, the surplus countries should be the locomotives, because an increase in their absorption levels causes *all* countries to move nearer to both external and internal balance.

A constructive arrangement of this sort was agreed upon in principle at the economic summit meeting held in Rambouillet, France, in 1977. At that time all industrial economies were struggling to recover from a major recession and attempting to adjust to the damage done their economies by the 1974 quadrupling of oil prices by the OPEC cartel. In addition, the U.S. dollar was very weak, and there was a substantial current-account deficit. Had the United States played locomotive to the world, this would have widened the deficit and further weakened the dollar. In this situation other major industrial countries agreed to pursue expansionary fiscal and monetary policies in return for which President Jimmy Carter promised, on behalf of the United States, to slow inflation and reduce oil imports through an energy conservation program. A reduction in U.S. oil imports was seen as essential to reduce the demand pressures that helped keep the industrial countries hostage to OPEC.

A situation that may arise when business cycles are not synchronized is that deficit countries will be suffering inflation while surplus countries suffer recession and excessive unemployment. Harmony of interest is clear in this event. The surplus countries should pursue expansionary policy, thereby lowering unemployment and simultaneously reducing the external adjustment problems of deficit countries. The deficit countries, meanwhile, should pursue restrictive policies to contain inflation and further reduce their external deficits. Considerations such as these explain why West Germany, with its strong balance of payments and good anti-inflation record, was frequently urged to adopt more expansionary monetary-fiscal policies.

When there is generalized excessive demand and inflation, the internal balance criterion implies that all countries need to tighten their budgets and their monetary policies. However, if surplus countries take the lead, this will widen their surpluses and move all countries farther away from external balance. Consequently, the burden of initiating appropriate adjustment should be placed on the deficit countries.

All the preceding cases are characterized by an essential harmony of interest between deficit and surplus countries with respect to their internal demand management policies. However, such harmony breaks down when it is the deficit countries that are depressed while the surplus countries suffer from inflation. Expansionary policies by the recession-deficit countries then widen their deficits, and restrictive policies by the inflation-surplus countries widen their surpluses. A glance at Figure 9.1 immediately reveals that in this event there is little choice other than for deficit countries to become more competitive while surplus countries become less competitive; that is, the situation implies that deficit countries must devalue while surplus countries revalue or acquiesce in the devaluations by the deficit countries.

During the fixed exchange-rate era some observers argued that the appropriate way to deal with this dilemma was to abandon the internal balance criterion as it pertained to inflation and to replace it by the external balance criterion. For example, it was suggested by those who valued full employment above other objectives that surplus countries (which are suffering from inflation) should follow expansionary policies that are in violation of the internal balance criterion. The result would be more inflation for surplus countries. But since this eases the balance-of-payments problems of deficit countries, it releases these countries to expand employment in their economies. Put differently, recession-deficit countries could be prevented from achieving full employment because of a balance-of-payments deficit and a shortage of foreign exchange reserves. This constraint, however, could be lifted if the surplus countries were to inflate.

This approach has some appeal for deficit countries, but is likely to be rejected by surplus countries. Such countries are likely to attempt to control inflation rather than inflate even more. If this increased their surpluses, they could normally be expected merely to accumulate reserves or to permit their exchange rates to appreciate, since that would further reduce inflation by lowering the domestic cost of imports.

Finally, note that the conflict case described here was assumed to be the normal situation under the gold standard. Deficit countries were expected actively to pursue deflation to eliminate deficits, and surplus countries were expected to inflate their economies to reduce surpluses. The internal balance criterion was systematically violated by the gold standard rules of the game.

QUESTIONS FOR REVIEW

1. What is the essential message of the absorption approach? Why is the elasticities approach viewed as inadequate?

2. What is the idle-resource effect? Why must a rise in income generate an increase in domestic saving in order to permit the idle-resource effect of devaluation to operate?

3. Discuss the effects of devaluation on domestic absorption with respect to:
   a. the Keynes effect.
   b. the real-balance effect.

   c. the money-illusion effect, especially in tax structures.
   d. inflationary expectations.
   e. the excise-tax effect.

4. Can elasticities and absorption analysis be combined? What is the effect of taking absorption effects into account on the elasticities analysis of devaluation?

5. An integrated "general" approach to the balance of payments requires that external and internal balance be reconciled. This can happen only if policy is able to vary both the exchange rate and the level of absorption. What is the appropriate policy response when
   a. a country suffers from both a deficit and inflation?
   b. a country suffers from a deficit and a recession?
   c. a country has a surplus and a recession?
   d. a country has a surplus and inflation?

6. What is the appropriate approach to adjustment when
   a. all countries suffer from inflation?
   b. all countries suffer from recession?
   c. surplus countries suffer from inflation and deficit countries suffer from recession?
   d. surplus countries suffer from recession and deficit countries suffer from inflation?

SUGGESTIONS FOR FURTHER READING

Alexander, Sidney S., "Effects of a Devaluation on a Trade Balance," International Monetary Fund, *Staff Papers,* 2, 1952.

Cooper, Richard N., *Currency Devaluation in Developing Countries,* Princeton Essays in International Finance, No. 86, 1971.

Harberger, A. C., "Currency Depreciation, Income and the Balance of Trade," *Journal of Political Economy,* 63, 1950.

Johnson, Harry G., "Towards a General Theory of the Balance of Payments," *International Trade and Economic Growth: Studies in Pure Theory,* Harvard, 1961.

Krugman, Paul, and Lionel Tayler, "Contractionary Effects of Devaluation," *Journal of International Economics,* August 1978.

Swan, Trevor, "Longer-Run Problems of the Balance of Payments," In H. W. Arndt and M. W. Corden, eds., *The Australian Economy: A Book of Readings,* Cheshire, 1963.

Tsiang, S. C., "The Role of Money in Trade Balance Stability: A Synthesis of the Elasticity and Absorption Approaches," *American Economic Review,* 51, 1961.

Chapter 10

The Monetary Theory of the Balance of Payments

10.1 INTRODUCTION TO MONETARY AND ASSET-MARKET THEORIES

Between 1960 and 1980 industrial production grew at an average annual rate of 4.1 percent in the United States. Over that same 20-year interval industrial production grew at a rate of 8.6 percent in Japan, more than double the U.S. rate. Inflation was also higher in Japan. Consumer prices rose at an annual rate of 7.5 percent in Japan while consumer prices in the United States were rising at a rate of 5.2 percent.

Given this information, a visitor from outer space unacquainted with the monetary theory of the balance of payments would very likely conclude that Japan's balance of payments during that period must have been far weaker than that of the United States. The visitor would note that more rapid Japanese economic growth would have caused the Japanese demand for imports to grow more rapidly than its exports, and that more rapid inflation would have reduced Japanese international competitiveness. Yet the truth is that it was Japan, and not the United States, that had the stronger balance of payments. Indeed the dollar was under increasing pressure during most of the 1960s, with the result that devaluations were necessary in 1971 and 1973. After that the dollar remained steady until 1978, when it declined sharply again.

Another visitor from a distant planet, trained in the monetarist view, would have no trouble reconciling these seemingly contradictory developments. This visitor would point out that rapid income growth and a high rate of inflation would both increase the demand for money, and if money demand ran steadily ahead of domestically generated money supply, the country would enjoy a balance-of-payments surplus if exchange rates were fixed or appreciation of its currency if exchange rates were free to fluctuate. Consequently, even though the predictions of the monetary theory of the balance of payments appear somewhat counterintuitive at first sight, the theory clearly has much to contribute to an understanding of the balance of payments. This seems especially true from a longer-range perspective.

Unlike elasticities and absorption analysis, which represents improvements in, or modifications to, the analysis of the current account, the monetary theory is an alternative approach that scraps separate analysis of the components of the current and capital accounts and replaces it by a theory of the overall balance of payments. The approach can be introduced by looking at the balance-of-payments equation, namely,

$$X - V + i^*F + K = \Delta R = \Delta M - \Delta D \qquad (10.1)$$

Reading from left to right, we can see that exports, X, minus imports, V, plus net income from foreign investment, i^*F, gives the current-account surplus. When the surplus on capital account, K, is added, the result is the balance-of-payments surplus. Under fixed exchange rates this would equal the increase in foreign exchange reserves, ΔR. However, as seen in Chapter 3, the increase in foreign exchange reserves must equal the increase in the money stock, ΔM, minus the increase in the domestic assets held by the banking system, ΔD.

The approach studied in previous chapters analyzes the determinants of the various components of the current and capital accounts—exports, imports, income from investment, and capital movements. The monetary approach bypasses study of these separate components and looks instead at the right-hand side of the balance-of-payments equation. Therefore, the balance sheet of the domestic banking system, namely,

$$\Delta R + \Delta D = \Delta M \qquad (10.2)$$

becomes the centerpiece of the monetary analysis. Crudely stated, ΔM roughly represents the change in the demand for money. However, money is created by expansion of domestic credit, ΔD, and by a balance-of-payments surplus, ΔR, since a surplus requires the monetary authority to purchase foreign exchange, thereby increasing the money supply. If, then, ΔM is greater than the amount of money created by domestic credit expansion, there must be a balance-of-payments surplus, because otherwise the supply of money cannot be brought into balance with the demand for money.

Suppose we assume a conventional nominal money demand function such as

$$M = L(Y, p, i) \qquad L_y > 0 \quad L_p > 0 \quad L_i < 0 \qquad (10.3)$$

Changes in the demand for nominal money balances must then be

$$\Delta M = L_y\, \Delta Y + L_p\, \Delta p + L_i\, \Delta i \qquad (10.4)$$

Substituting this into (10.2) gives the balance-of-payments outcome

$$\Delta R = L_y\, \Delta Y + L_p\, \Delta p + L_i\, \Delta i - \Delta D \qquad (10.5)$$

which is the fundamental balance-of-payments equation of the monetary approach. A rise in income raises the demand for money, causing a balance-of-payments surplus. The same is true for an increase in the price level. A rise in the rate of interest reduces the demand for money and moves the balance of payments toward deficit. And an increase in the domestic assets of the banking system raises the domestic component of the money stock and moves the balance of payments in the direction of deficit.

The monetary theory may be thought of as a special case of the asset-market theory, which will be examined in Chapter 11. These theories have an advantage over Keynesian theory in that they are theories of stock adjustment. In flow equilibrium a current-account surplus may be offset by a capital-account deficit so that the balance of payments is in equilibrium in the short run. However, this equilibrium cannot be maintained, because a current-account surplus implies that domestic residents are accumulating foreign IOUs, and their portfolios are therefore undergoing continuous changes that will feed back into changes in the balance of payments.

Asset-market theories begin by distinguishing between categories of portfolio (financial) assets. The simplest classification distinguishes between domestic money, M, domestic earning assets, B, and foreign earning assets, F. The nominal value of financial wealth, valued in local currency, may be written

$$W = M + B + eF \qquad (10.6)$$

where e is the nominal exchange rate and W is the nominal value of financial wealth.

Balance of payments and monetary equilibrium occur when wealth holders are satisfied with the relative proportions in which different financial assets are held in their portfolios. Excess supply of money implies excess demand for B and F, with the consequence that both the exchange rate and the rate of interest could be affected. A surplus in the current account implies that domestic residents are accumulating foreign assets, F. If wealth holders regard M, B, and F as imperfect substitutes, the accumulation of F creates excess supply of F and a corresponding excess demand for M and B. The excess supply of F causes the prices of F to drop, so the price of foreign exchange declines. The appreciation of the local currency then gradually eliminates the current-account surplus, causing imports to rise and exports to decline, thereby bringing about longer-run stock equilibrium. Thus, the asset-market theory suggests that in the longer run the balance of payments cannot be in equilibrium unless the current account is also in equilibrium, because, unless that is the case, continuing accumulation and decumulation of foreign financial assets will steadily disrupt portfolio equilibrium and cause exchange rate variations.

The monetary theory of the balance of payments differs from the general asset-market approach in assuming that domestic (B) and foreign bonds (F) are perfect substitutes. The assets are indistinguishable in the minds of investors, who are indifferent with respect to the relative proportions in which they hold the various assets. One asset will be traded for another if there is a temporary price difference caused by interest-rate differentials or changes in exchange rates. Because of this perfect substitutability of financial assets, the monetary theory of the balance of payments considers it sufficient to focus attention only on the determinants of the demand for money and the supply of money. Since an excess demand for money can be supplied by an inflow of reserves, such excess demand implies a balance-of-payments surplus. If there is excess supply of money, this implies a deficit.

Two major strands of the development of monetary theories of the balance of payments should be delineated. One strand, largely the product of practical necessity, may be termed the IMF approach.[1] Although it is a monetary theory, it is essentially a theory of the current account and is generally applied to the analysis of the balance-of-payments problems of developing countries that lack extensive capital markets. The second approach has its origins in domestic monetarism. It takes the view that balance-of-payments equilibrium and monetary equilibrium must go hand in hand. Its historical antecedents are the traditional quantity theory of money and the international price-specie flow mechanism of David Hume. Applied to the balance of payments, it is sometimes called "global" monetarism.

It is important to remind ourselves of the distinction between the financially open and the financially closed economy, as explained in Chapter 6. In the financially closed economy a monetary disturbance initially affects interest rates. This affects aggregate expenditure, which, in turn, affects the demand for imports. The change in the demand for

---

[1] Many of the IMF staff's most important contributions to the monetary literature may be found in a collection of papers edited by Rudolf R. Rhomberg and H. Robert Heller, *The Monetary Approach to the Balance of Payments*, International Monetary Fund, Washington, D.C. 1977.

imports changes the demand for foreign exchange. This interacts with the supply of foreign exchange to determine the balance-of-payments deficit or surplus. In the financially open economy a monetary disturbance shocks asset markets, thereby immediately affecting both interest rates and the exchange rate. If the monetary shock is expansionary, the exchange rate depreciates, causing a subsequent surplus in the current account. Since this implies that foreign assets will be accumulated by domestic residents, this feeds back into the asset and foreign exchange markets, where it is likely to cause subsequent appreciation. The asset-market theory, together with certain dynamic timing assumptions, is therefore most helpful in explaining why a shock that leads to an immediate sharp appreciation or depreciation is then followed by exchange rate movement in the opposite direction.

10.2 MONETARISM

Before proceeding with the monetary theory of the balance of payments, we comment on monetarism and its implications. The keystone of monetarism is its assumption that the nominal demand for money is a "stable" function of nominal expenditures. The classical quantity equation may be written

$$M = kpY \qquad (10.7)$$

where M is the nominal stock of money, k is the cash balance ratio (the average length of time money is held between transactions), p is the price level, and Y is real national income. The real quantity of money is $m = M/p$, and the reciprocal of k is the "velocity," or rate of turnover, of money. The equation, sometimes called the equation of exchange, can be thought of as a truism, since it is a definitional relationship, especially when, as is usually the case, k is calculated by dividing M by nominal national income.

The quantity equation can be made to fit the Keynesian model by making k a function of the rate of interest and specifying that k tends to fall as the rate of interest rises, since a rise in the rate of interest reduces liquidity preference and causes cash balances to be economized so that the period the average dollar is held becomes shorter and money turns over more rapidly.

Orthodox monetarism rejects this hypothesis, arguing instead that k tends, at least in the longer run, to be constant. Few monetarists would try to defend this assumption in strictest terms, since k clearly varies in the short run, but they would tend to deny that these short-run variations are attributable to interest-rate changes. Because the value of k bounces around, the term "stable" is used as an equivocating way of replacing the terms "constant" or "proportional to income." Nevertheless, and despite the disclaimers, many of the arguments of monetarism derive from the assumption of a constant value of k. When that assumption is imposed, a number of major conclusions, many of them contradicting Keynesian analysis, can be inferred.

First, the constant k (or velocity) assumption converts the quantity equation truism into a very powerful theory of the demand for money, since M and pY become proportional to each other.

Second, in monetary equilibrium the demand for money, M_d, equals the supply of money, M_s. Setting the two equal and rearranging the equation, we get

$$pY = \left(\frac{1}{k}\right)M_s$$

which implies that nominal expenditure is directly proportional to the stock of money, the factor of proportionality being velocity $1/k$.

Third, if, as some monetarists assume, the economy tends automatically toward full employment because of the operation of a competitive pricing system, real income çannot be varied. The price level must then be directly proportional to the nominal money stock, so the rate of inflation equals the rate of monetary growth. That is,

$$\frac{dp}{p} = \frac{dM_s}{M_s}$$

since dY/Y and dk/k are both zero. It follows that the control of inflation is merely a matter of controlling the money stock. Milton Friedman, a leading American monetarist, has said that "inflation is everywhere and always a monetary phenomenon." It follows also that if the purchasing-power parity relationship discussed in Chapter 2 holds, the long-run movement of the nominal exchange rate will be equal to the difference between the monetary growth rates in the domestic and foreign economies.

Fourth, viewed in Keynesian terms, the monetarist theory implies that the demand for money is not a function of the rate of interest. The LM curve is therefore vertical, as shown in Figure 10.1. The initial equilibrium is at point a with income of Y_0 and interest rate i_0. The situation implies that fiscal policy cannot raise income. A shift to the right of the IS curve to IS_1 brought about by an expansionary fiscal policy merely raises the rate of interest to i_1, but it does not change the equilibrium level of income. There is one-for-one investment crowd out, with the

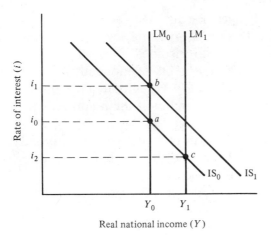

Figure 10.1 Effects of fiscal and monetary policies with monetarist assumptions.

higher government spending merely replacing the investment spending that would otherwise have taken place.

However, a rise in the money stock, which shifts the LM curve so that it intersects IS_0 at point c, raises income in direct proportion to the increase in the money stock. As the central bank purchases government securities in exchange for money balances, security prices rise, interest rates fall, and investment increases. Since wealth holders, in the monetarist interpretation, hold no money in excess of transactions requirements, any excess money is used to purchase bonds. Bond prices therefore continue to rise, and interest rates continue to fall. The process stops when investment has risen to the point where national income rises by enough to eliminate excess supply of money by absorbing the additional money into transactions requirements. Therefore, the theory predicts that Y will rise in direct proportion to the increase in M_s. Of course, if real income cannot be raised, an increase in the nominal quantity of money creates excess demand for goods and services, which raises the price level. As the price level rises, the real quantity of money, $m = M/p$, tends to return to its initial level. From this follows the monetarist proposition that the monetary authority can determine the nominal money supply but has no control over the real quantity of money. In terms of Figure 10.1 the present assumption implies that Y_0 is the full-employment level of income. The shift to LM_1 produces IS-LM intersection at point c. However, real income of Y_1 cannot be attained. There therefore is excess demand for goods and services at point c, which raises the price level and then lowers the real quantity of money, thus moving the LM curve back to LM_0.

Given these assumptions about the demand for money, fiscal policy is seen to be irrelevant, and monetary policy becomes the principal tool of stabilization policy. Because fixed exchange rates make it impossible to control the money supply, it is not difficult to see why monetarists such as Milton Friedman were in the vanguard of those who argued for abandonment of fixed exchange rates. Interestingly enough, global monetarists of a more recent vintage have dispensed with the constant-velocity assumption, and many of them now argue for a return to some sort of fixed exchange-rate standard. Some are even advocating a return to a gold standard.

10.3 THE MONETARY THEORY UNDER FIXED EXCHANGE RATES

The monetary theory of the balance of payments gives many results that appear at variance with those of the Keynesian flow theory described in Part Two. To understand the differences and the special contributions of the monetary approach, we find it useful to compare the approach with the flow theory.

Recall that the balance-of-payments surplus equals the combined surpluses of the current and the capital accounts. Under fixed exchange rates the balance-of-payments surplus equals the increase in foreign exchange reserves, ΔR. Therefore, we can rewrite (10.1) as

$$\Delta M - \Delta D = \Delta R = X - V + i^* F + K \qquad (10.1)$$

Earlier, the current-account surplus was treated separately from the capital account. Specifically, exports were regarded as a function of the real exchange rate, and imports were treated as a function of real income and the real exchange rate. The export function was given by

$$X = X\left(\frac{ep^*}{p}\right)$$

where e is the nominal exchange rate, p is the domestic price level, and p^* is the foreign price level. The assumptions about the signs of the parameters were as follows:

$X_e > 0$, since a rise in the nominal exchange rate makes exports more attractive to foreign consumers;

$X_p < 0$, since a rise in the domestic price level implies a loss of international competitiveness;

$X_{p^*} > 0$, since a rise in the foreign price level implies an increase in international competitiveness.

Similarly, the import function is

$$V = V\left(Y, \frac{ep^*}{p}\right)$$

where

$V_e < 0$, since a rise in the price of foreign exchange makes imports less attractive;

$V_p > 0$, since a rise in the domestic price level makes cheaper foreign goods more attractive;

$V_{p^*} < 0$, since foreign inflation makes foreign goods relatively less attractive.

On combining the export and import functions and adding net investment, i^*F, we write the current-account surplus as

$$CS = X - V + i^*F = X\left(\frac{ep^*}{p}\right) - V\left(Y, \frac{ep^*}{p}\right) + i^*F \qquad (10.8)$$

The condition of the capital account in the flow theory depends on interest-rate differentials and the expected change in the real exchange rate. Although the nominal exchange rate is fixed, the real exchange rate can vary because of differential price-level changes. Therefore, we can write

$$K = K\left[i - i^*, \quad E \Delta\left(\frac{ep^*}{p}\right)\right] \qquad (10.9)$$

as in Chapter 5, to explain the flow of capital. It is normally assumed that a rise in the domestic-foreign interest-rate spread attracts foreign capital. Similarly, expected appreciation of the real exchange rate reduces capital outflows. A rise in expected domestic inflation drives capital abroad to preserve its purchasing-power value, and because a rise in expected domestic inflation may create the expectation that the official exchange rate will be devalued. Similarly, a rise in expected foreign inflation causes capital flight from the foreign country in anticipation of a devaluation and to protect the purchasing-power value of financial assets.

Combining (10.8) and (10.9), we get the equation for the overall balance of payments for the flow model:

$$\Delta R = X\left(\frac{ep^*}{p}\right) - V\left(Y, \frac{ep^*}{p}\right) + i^*F + K\left[i - i^*, E \Delta\left(\frac{ep^*}{p}\right)\right]$$

$$(10.10)$$

The balance-of-payments equation predicts that

1. A rise in national income will reduce the surplus because imports will increase.
2. A rise in the rate of interest will increase the surplus because this attracts foreign capital. A rise in foreign interest rates will do the opposite.
3. A rise in the rate of inflation reduces the surplus because it reduces exports, raises imports, and drives capital abroad.

We can now turn to the monetary theory. As noted earlier, the theory makes no attempt to separate the current from the capital accounts. It ignores the right side of (10.1) and turns its attention instead to the left side. Therefore, the centerpiece of the monetary approach is the monetary survey,

$$\Delta M - \Delta D = \Delta R \qquad (10.2)$$

which states that the increase in reserves, and therefore the balance-of-payments surplus, equals the difference between the increase in the money stock and the rise in domestic credit.

Monetary equilibrium requires the supply of money to equal the demand for money. As noted previously, monetary equilibrium implies

$$\Delta R = L_y \, \Delta Y + L_p \, \Delta p + L_i \, \Delta i - \Delta D \qquad (10.5)$$

which is the fundamental balance-of-payments equation of the monetary approach. Reserves will increase if the price level increases, because a rise in the price level increases the demand for money. Reserves will increase if real income increases, because a rise in income raises the demand for money. A rise in the rate of interest will cause a deficit and a reserve loss because a rise in the rate of interest reduces the demand for money. And an increase in domestic credit causes a deficit and a reserve loss.

These results are startling, to say the least. The monetary theory of the balance of payments appears to predict outcomes that are both counterintuitive and at variance with Keynesian theory. In that theory a rise in income reduced the surplus, a rise in the rate of interest increased it, and a rise in inflation reduced it. Why then do so many respected economists subscribe to the monetary theory, and why does the theory appear to explain some aspects of the behavior of the balance of payments that escape the flow theory?

Monetarists begin by pointing out that changes in the demand for money can be satisfied either through the expansion of domestic credit or through the rise in reserves that accompanies a balance-of-payments surplus. If there is no change in domestic credit, changes in the money supply must come about through balance-of-payments deficits or surpluses. For example, if there is excess demand for money, the excess demand may be satisfied by an inflow of reserves, which translate into an increase in the money supply as the central bank purchases foreign exchange. Consequently, excess demand for money is associated with a surplus in the balance of payments, and excess supply of money is associated with a deficit.

This conclusion is not inconsistent with Keynesian theory. In Keynesian dynamics excess demand for money raises interest rates, which attracts foreign capital and moves the balance of payments into surplus. The higher interest rates may also be expected to lower aggregate expenditure and imports, thereby adding to the tendency toward surplus.

Since the demand for money is a demand for a certain stock of money, a balance-of-payments surplus that raises the supply of money gradually narrows the gap between the demand for money and its supply. Consequently, since the excess demand for money narrows as the surplus persists, the surplus gradually narrows as the demand for money is brought into balance with the supply of money. Therefore, excess demand for money creates only a temporary surplus, whereas excess supply of money creates only a temporary deficit. These results, too, are entirely consistent with Keynesian theory, as explained in Chapters 5 and 6.

If the money supply is increased through the expansion of domestic credit, which would occur if the central bank makes an open-market purchase of domestic securities, this creates excess supply of money and causes a deficit in the balance of payments, as money holders divest themselves of the excessive balances by purchasing foreign goods and financial assets. Since the deficit causes a loss of reserves, the money supply then shrinks as the monetary authority sells foreign exchange. This brings the supply of money back into balance with the demand for money, thereby eliminating the deficit. Keynesian theory predicts the same outcome. The increase in the money supply depresses interest rates, causing a capital outflow, and, since aggregate expenditure may rise, imports will increase, thereby adding to the deficit. Both monetary and Keynesian theories lead to the conclusion that, under fixed exchange rates, it is not possible permanently to expand the money supply by a one-time expansion of domestic credit. The increase in the domestic assets of the banking system is exactly offset by a reduction in reserves, so there is no net change in the money supply. It follows that a permanent deficit in the balance of payments implies continuation of an expansionary domestic monetary policy and that, when this policy is discontinued, the balance of payments will move into equilibrium.

Similarly, a continuing surplus implies that the demand for money grows steadily more rapidly than the domestic component of the money stock. In the monetary theory this could happen due to rapid income growth, which raises the demand for money. Monetarists have argued that the continuing surpluses of West Germany and Japan were attributable to rapid income growth that kept the demand for money in these countries running steadily ahead of their domestically generated money supplies.

Before considering cases where the Keynesian and monetary theories part company, it is important that we discuss some basic assumptions about how interest rates, price levels, and income levels are determined in the monetarist world. The assumptions of "global monetarism" are as follows:

(1) Perfect Capital Mobility   Global monetarists assume that financial assets are perfect substitutes. One implication of this assumption is that domestic open-market operations, which involve the purchase and sale of domestic bonds for money, have effects that are identical to purchases and sales of foreign assets. If the central bank buys bonds, D increases and so does M. If it buys foreign exchange, R increases and so does M. Since it is only the change in M that matters, open-market operations and exchange rate stabilization transactions are essentially identical.

Perfect asset substitution implies perfect capital mobility. If domestic and foreign bonds are perfect substitutes in the minds of investors, changes in the relative supplies of these assets have no effects on asset prices, so there can be no difference between domestic and foreign interest rates if the exchange rate is fixed. Therefore, under fixed exchange rates, the equilibrium domestic interest rate is equal to and determined by the world rate of interest. Under flexible exchange rates uncovered interest parity must hold; that is, the excess of the foreign over the domestic rate of interest must equal the expected rate of appreciation.

(2) Arbitrage and the Law of One Price   The second key assumption of global monetarism is that there is perfect arbitrage in commodity markets that equalizes prices in all markets. To illustrate: Suppose the official exchange rate between domestic and foreign currency is 1, so 1 unit of domestic currency trades for 1 unit of the foreign currency. If a bushel of wheat sells for 5 currency units in the home country and 6 currency units in the rest of the world, it will pay for wheat traders to buy in the domestic market and sell in the world market. This raises the domestic price and tends to lower the world price. The arbitrage continues until prices are equalized in the two markets. If the domestic market is

small relative to the world market, the bulk of the price adjustment occurs in the domestic market. Therefore, domestic prices are largely determined by world prices. The implication of this *law of one price* is that the real exchange rate is constant; that is, ep^*/p cannot be permanently changed. With a fixed official exchange rate, the equilibrium domestic price can change only as the consequence of a change in the world price. Applied to price levels as a whole, the law of one price implies that the domestic price level is determined by the world price level.

(3) Supply-Determined National Income   The third critical assumption of global monetarism is that flexible wages and prices will act to ensure that the economy equilibrates automatically at full employment. Keynesians would agree that this could happen if wages and prices were, in fact, downwardly flexible, but they question the validity of the assumption. Even if there were some wage-price flexibility, Keynesians would still fret that automatic adjustment may take an unconscionable length of time, during which an economy may suffer from heavy and protracted unemployment.

In Chapter 7 we studied aggregate supply and how a closed economy will tend to return to full employment when wages and prices are flexible. To review: High unemployment implies excess supply in labor markets. In competitive labor markets competition among workers for available jobs drives down money wages. Because this reduces the real wage, firms increase employment and output. The additional output generates an equal increase in income. The higher income generates higher consumption, but, since the marginal propensity to consume is less than 1, all of the additional output will not be bought at existing prices. Consequently, excess supply develops in commodity markets. This causes the price level to fall. The lower price level increases the real quantity of money. This depresses interest rates and causes investment to expand. This is the Keynes effect described in Chapter 7. Also, the fall in the price level increases the real value of the financial claims that the private sector holds against the government. This increase in wealth increases consumption, thereby adding to aggregate expenditure. This is the real-balance effect discussed in Chapter 7. Since these mechanisms continue to work to raise income and employment as long as excess supply in labor markets continues, the economy will tend to return automatically to full employment.

Global monetarism adopts the assumption that the economy automatically equilibrates at full employment. Competitive markets combined with the law of one price ensure market clearing, because any excess supply of goods in the domestic market is absorbed in foreign markets. Aggregate expenditure expansion cannot raise the equilibrium level of real income. Such increases can come about only through the expansion of aggregate supply as caused by growth factors such as growing labor force, capital stock, and advances in technical progress that raise the productivity of both labor and capital.

If the three key assumptions are granted, three equations can be added to the monetarist model. Perfect capital mobility implies

$$i = i^*$$

so the domestic rate of interest equals and is determined by the world rate of interest. The law of one price implies a constant real exchange rate, so

$$p = ep^*$$

With a fixed official exchange rate e, the domestic price level p depends on the world price level p^*. The automatic equilibration of the economy at full employment implies that

$$Y = Y_f$$

where Y_f is the full-employment level of real national income.

It is now possible to see exactly why the Keynesian and monetary theories of the balance of payments differ. Consider Figure 10.2, which adapts the IS-LM model to monetarist assumptions. Perfect capital mobility implies that the FB curve is horizontal at the world interest rate i^*. Above i^* there is a surplus, and below it there is a deficit. The level of income is immaterial to the balance-of-payments outcome.

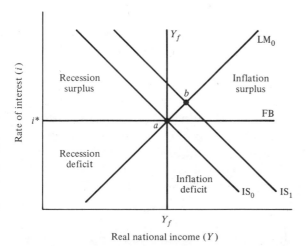

Figure 10.2 Effect of a rise in the world price level in the monetarist model.

The automatic equilibration of national income at full employment implies the vertical line drawn at full employment. Thus $Y = Y_f$ and $i = i^*$. These variables are determined at the outset, and the IS and LM curves must adapt so as to intersect at point a. Let these respective functions be IS_0 and LM_0.

Now suppose that the world price level rises. Commodity arbitrage causes an immediate export surplus as domestic goods are diverted to foreign markets. In the diagram this is reflected in a temporary rise in the real exchange rate rate, which shifts the IS curve to the right (IS_1), where it intersects the LM_0 curve in the surplus zone at point b. As the domestic price level rises, the real quantity of money declines. This tends to shift the LM curve to the left. But this is offset because the monetary authority is accumulating foreign exchange, so the nominal money stock is growing. For convenience, assume the two forces offset exactly so that M/p remains constant and the LM curve remains at LM_0.

As long as the IS and LM curves intersect to the right of Y_f, the price level keeps rising; and as long as the intersection is above i^* the surplus persists and the nominal money supply keeps increasing. The rise in the price level tends to shove the IS curve back toward IS_0 as the real exchange rate declines and the trade surplus dwindles. Equilibrium is reestablished at point a. All equilibrium real variables return to their original value. The only change is a higher domestic price level, which once again equals the foreign price level multiplied by the nominal exchange rate.

The results are as predicted by global monetarism. The upward change in the price level has been associated with a temporary balance-of-payments surplus. Once the price *level* reaches its new equilibrium, the surplus is eliminated.

Next suppose the world interest rate i^* rises. This is illustrated in Figure 10.3. Initially the economy is in equilibrium at point a. The rise in the world interest rate to i_1^* shifts the FB curve up to FB_1. Point a now implies a deficit, because the world interest rate is temporarily above the domestic interest rate i_0^*. The deficit causes the money supply to shrink, moving the LM curve to the left. But the intersection with the IS_0 curve is at point c, where the deficit is combined with an income level below full employment. The resulting deflationary forces reduce wages and prices, thereby expanding employment and output as international arbitrage raises exports and reduces imports, thereby also eliminating the deficit. Therefore, the IS curve shifts up to IS_1, and general equilibrium is established at point b.

It can be seen that the domestic interest rate has risen and that this has been accompanied by a temporary balance-of-payments deficit, exactly as predicted by global monetarism.

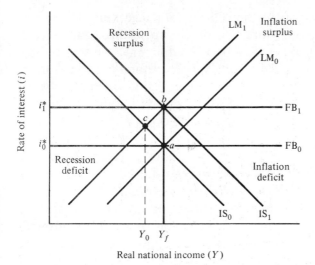

Figure 10.3 Effect of a rise in the world rate of interest in the monetarist model.

Next, suppose economic growth increases potential (full employment) national income. In Figure 10.4 this is shown as a shift to the right of Y_f from Y_{f0} to Y_{f1}. Point a, the initial equilibrium, now implies unemployment. Therefore, wages and prices tend to fall, and international commodity arbitrage produces a trade surplus that shifts the IS curve to the right. The surplus also increases the money supply, thereby shifting the LM curve to the right. Equilibrium is established at point b. The global monetarism proposition that a one-time rise in real income generates a temporary balance-of-payments surplus follows immediately.

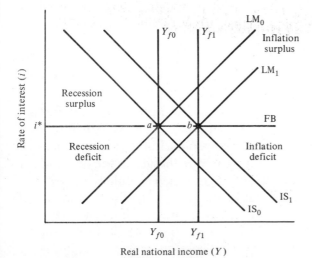

Figure 10.4 Effect of a rise in potential output.

Where does devaluation of the official exchange rate fit into this picture? If we have done our work attentively up to this point we can easily see that the analysis of devaluation is no different than the analysis of the effects of a rise in the world price level. Therefore, return to Figure 10.2 and let the official price of foreign exchange be increased. This raises the competitiveness of domestic goods, thereby shifting the IS curve to the right, where it intersects the LM_0 curve at point b. However, since point b is to the right of Y_f, wages and prices rise, which tend to move the IS curve back toward IS_0. Meanwhile, the higher prices reduce the real quantity of money, shifting the LM curve to the left, but the surplus raises the nominal quantity of money, tending to move LM in the opposite direction. Equilibrium is then reestablished at point a. The net effect of the devaluation is to cause a temporary balance-of-payments surplus with an ultimate proportionate increase in the price level that matches the proportionate devaluation and returns the real exchange rate to its original value. Global monetarist logic therefore shows devaluation to be a waste of time. In fully employed economies and with perfect capital mobility causing the capital account to dominate the balance-of-payments outcome, that is certainly apt to be the case.

We now quickly compare the monetarist and Keynesian results by way of summary. In Keynesian theory a rise in the equilibrium price level usually comes about through the expansion of domestic demand. This raises the domestic price level above the international price level, thereby reducing international competitiveness. In the global monetary theory the domestic price level is pulled along by international prices and rises only if foreign price levels are rising. If the rise in the domestic price level lags behind the rise in the world price level, the country's competitive position would actually improve, thereby making a higher price level consistent with a balance-of-payments surplus. Therefore, the difference between the Keynesian and monetarist results can be reconciled by the fact that in Keynesian theory the equilibrium price level is internally (endogenously) determined, whereas in global monetarism it is externally, or autonomously, determined.

In Keynesian theory a rise in the rate of interest attracts foreign capital and reduces aggregate expenditure and imports. This implies a tendency toward a balance-of-payments surplus. In the global monetarist model a rise in the rate of interest implies a reduction in the demand for money and a deficit in the balance of payments. The difference between the two theories lies in the fact that in the monetarist theory the rate of interest is determined by external factors. If foreign interest rates rise, this will cause a capital outflow, which reduces the domestic money supply and pulls up the domestic interest rate. Therefore a rise in the domestic interest rate is consistent with a capital outflow, provided the outflow is initiated by rising foreign interest rates.

In Keynesian theory income expansion increases the demand for imports, tending to move the balance of payments into deficit. In the monetary theory a rise in income raises the demand for money and moves the balance of payments into surplus. In Keynesian theory it is normally assumed that national income expands as the result of domestic aggregate expenditure expansion. In global monetarism it is assumed that the economy tends automatically to equilibrate at full employment. Demand expansion cannot therefore raise the equilibrium level of income. Increases in real income come about through the expansion of aggregate supply due to growth of available factor inputs and improvements in the productivity of the factors. With a fixed nominal money stock such growth implies downward pressure on the price level. If the growth is accompanied by growth in labor productivity, unit labor costs will decline, and this too will tend to slow domestic inflation. Consequently, international competitiveness tends to improve, and rapid economic growth causes the balance of payments to generate a surplus.

It can be seen that in all these cases the difference between Keynesian and monetarist results come about from different assumptions with respect to how income, prices, and interest rates are determined. In the Keynesian model these variables are endogenously determined, depending in large measure on aggregate demand. In the monetarist model they are, for all practical purposes, autonomous, depending on external forces as well as aggregate supply.

We have seen that devaluation is viewed by global monetarism as producing no more than a temporary balance-of-payments surplus, since price-level movements offset the effect on the real exchange rate of a decline in the nominal exchange rate. It is noteworthy that some global monetarists believe that a return to fixed exchange rates would be appropriate. This is something of a paradox, since leadership in the original intellectual thrust for flexible exchange rates was provided by monetarist economists, largely on the grounds that economies would recapture control of their money supplies under flexible exchange rates. The new view is particularly strongly held by those global monetarists who believe that price levels move more readily in the upward direction than they do in the downward direction. An extreme form of the argument might claim that in industrial countries up-ratcheting floors exist that permit only wage-price increases. In this case any movement of the exchange rate is inflationary. Price levels rise in countries with depreciating currencies but remain fixed in countries with appreciating currencies. The net effect of the exchange rate movement therefore is to raise the average world price level. Meanwhile, the rigidity of wages and prices in the appreciating country causes the deflationary impact to be reflected in lower output and employment. Then, if this is combatted by expansionary monetary-fiscal policy, the net effect of the exchange rate movement is a further rise in world inflation.[2]

The extent to which the monetary theory of the balance of payments is valid depends, in large measure, on the adequacy of its essential assumptions. How valid are these assumptions? With respect to perfect commodity arbitrage and the law of one price, John Williamson comments that

> ... it is only the prices of homogeneous primary commodities that are equated internationally by arbitrage, while the prices of manufactures deviate quite widely depending on the source of supply. Exchange rate changes influence relative prices, certainly in the short run and even persisting in the medium run. The hypothesis that arbitrage quickly equates goods prices internationally has probably been rejected more decisively by empirical evidence than any other hypothesis in the history of economics.[3]

Although extensive capital mobility is a major factor in the balance of payments of most industrial countries, there is little empirical support for the proposition that capital is perfectly mobile. Econometric evidence suggests that in most cases capital is relatively immobile in the sense of Chapters 5 and 6; that is, the FB function tends to be more steeply sloped than the LM curve. The United States economy seems to be the only exception. In the Federal Reserve's multicountry model, the United States is the only country in which expansionary fiscal policy tends to produce a balance-of-payments surplus. Apparently the improvement in the balance of payments caused by the higher interest rates exceeds the deterioration caused by the effect of income expansion on the current account. But this is not true for most other countries, where current-account effects tend to predominate.

Can real income be considered exogenous as assumed by global monetarism? It probably can in some less developed economies where agricultural and extractive enterprises produce as much as possible to sell in world markets. But in the industrialized world, characterized by severe and protracted periodic recessions, the assumption is at variance with

[2] See Goldstein, Morris, "Downward Price Flexibility, Ratchet Effects, and the Inflationary Impact of Import Price Changes," International Monetary Fund, *Staff Papers*, 24, 1977. Goldstein's survey of the evidence suggests that there is not an enormous amount of empirical support for the ratchet hypothesis.

[3] Williamson, John, *The Open Economy and the World Economy,* Basic Books, New York, 1983. p. 201.

experience. The most famous systematic and intellectually satisfying attack on the theory that the economy regulates itself automatically was launched by John Maynard Keynes in 1936.[4] Keynes argued that workers would resist money-wage reductions even when there is excess supply of labor. He went on to argue that even if wages could be made to fall, there was no guarantee that the accompanying fall in the price level would raise employment, since the rise in the real quantity of money caused by the lower price level might simply be absorbed by liquidity preference. In that case interest rates would not fall and investment would not be stimulated. On a practical level he pointed out that investment was not likely to be responsive to interest-rate changes when there was ample excess capacity, and that an increase in the real quantity of money could be brought about far less painfully and effectively by increasing the nominal money supply than by waiting around for this to happen because of falling prices. Finally, he suggested that even if the automatic forces were to work, their operation would be so slow and sluggish that massive and continuing unemployment would probably invite revolution prior to any return to high employment. "In the long-run we are all dead," was Keynes's response to those who insisted on applying long-run theoretical results to immediate emergencies.

More recently there has been a revival of the classical automatically adjusting view by economists variously described as "new classical macroeconomists" or "rational expectationists." Their notion is that deviations from full employment are random, that their causes are unanticipated shocks, and that economic stabilization cannot be adequately dealt with by monetary-fiscal actions. The reason is that people, anticipating the effects of the policies, will take steps to guard themselves against any adverse anticipated consequences of the action. For example, if people learn from experience that a tax cut will raise the price level, the prospect of a tax reduction will immediately cause money-wages to be forced up to prevent real wages from declining. Since this raises unit labor costs, it raises prices; thus, when the tax cut increases nominal disposable income, the increase in real disposable income is neutralized by the price increases. The tax cut therefore fails to stimulate the economy, and it has no other effect than to raise the price level. The only way the tax cut could help is if it were unanticipated and takes people by surprise. Unfortunately, economic policy cannot be systematically conducted by trying to fool people all the time.

Lengthy debates over the relevance of rational expectations have raged for the past 15 years. We cannot summarize all that here. However,

[4] Keynes, John Maynard, *The General Theory of Employment, Interest, and Money,* Harcourt Brace, London, 1936.

we can note that rational expectations predicts that deviations from full employment will be random. In practice, however, statistical analysis discloses that these deviations are highly correlated with each other. Second, if we subscribe to rational expectations, we would have to assume that policy had nothing to do with the depression of the 1930s or with the major recession of 1982. Rational expectations had considerable vogue during the 1970s when expansionary policies did little more than produce inflation, as predicted. However, it lost much of its appeal when the world economy skidded into the recession of 1982. In light of that experience, as outlined in Chapter 1, it would take a very brave man to maintain that the economy is effectively self-regulating and that government policies had little to do with causing the trouble.

If the monetary theory can be understood as the product of special assumptions applied to the Keynesian model, it would have to be regarded as little more than a throwback to obsolete premises. The claim that it properly emphasizes monetary equilibrium as a condition of balance-of-payments equilibrium is hardly startling, since any Keynesian would make the same assertion, as is obvious from the IS-LM model. Are there, then special contributions of the monetary theory?

To answer this question, we examine attempts to integrate the monetary theory of the overall balance of payments with the flow theory of the current account. The approach of Kouri and Porter[5] is particularly helpful in this respect. They take the monetary equation for the overall balance of payments and subtract from it the current-account equation of the flow model. This subtraction leaves the capital-account surplus as a residual.

To explore this approach, begin with the monetary survey and subtract the current-account surplus, CS, from both sides. This gives

$$\Delta R - CS = \Delta M - \Delta D - CS$$

where $\Delta M - \Delta D$ is the overall surplus. When CS is subtracted, the result is the surplus in the capital account. Therefore,

$$K = \Delta R - CS = (\Delta M - \Delta D) - CS$$

The term ΔM measures the change in the demand for money, ΔD measures the increase in the money supply caused by domestic credit expansion, and CS measures the increase in the money supply caused by a

[5] Kouri, Penti, and M. G. Porter, "International Capital Flows and Portfolio Equilibrium," *Journal of Political Economy,* May 1974. See also Frenkel, J. A., T. Gylferson, and J. F. Helliwell, "A Synthesis of Monetary and Keynesian Approaches to Short-Run Balance of Payments Theory," *Economic Journal,* September 1980.

current-account surplus. Therefore, K, the capital inflow, measures that part of the change in the demand for money that is not satisfied by domestic credit expansion or the current-account surplus.

When we use (10.5) to replace ΔR and (10.8) to replace CS, we obtain

$$K = (L_p \, \Delta p + L_y \, \Delta Y + L_i \, \Delta i - \Delta D)$$

$$- \left[X\left(\frac{ep^*}{p}\right) - V\left(Y, \frac{ep^*}{p}\right) + i^* F \right] \qquad (10.11)$$

Thus, the change in the demand for money depends on *changes* in p, Y, and i, whereas the change in the money supply depends on the change in domestic credit and the *levels* of p and Y. The combined approaches yield the following implications:

1. In the very short run, and with fixed exchange rates, p, p^*, and Y may all be taken as given. This means the current-account surplus remains fixed while the rate of interest is the only variable available to equate the demand for money with the supply of money. If there is excess demand for money, there will be a capital-account surplus until the rate of interest rises by enough to eliminate the excess demand.

    This result implies that in the very short run the capital inflow and the rate of interest are closely linked. This is also what (10.9) of the flow theory says, namely,

$$K = K\left[i - i^*, \ E \, \Delta\left(\frac{ep^*}{p}\right) \right] \qquad (10.9)$$

so there appears to be little conflict between the two approaches in terms of short-run analysis. However, there are, two important differences. First, (10.9) predicts that a given interest-rate differential provokes a uniform flow of capital through time. The flow of capital depends on the *level* of the interest rate. The monetary theory points out that the capital inflow, by raising the money supply, reduces excess demand for money, thereby rendering the capital inflow temporary. This implies that the capital inflow depends on the *change* in the rate of interest, as seen in (10.11). The second difference is that if we take (10.9) to predict the change in the capital flow caused by a change in the rate of interest, we get

$$dK = K_i \, di$$

But if capital mobility is perfect, K_i is infinite, so the equation is useless for predicting the magnitude of the change in the capital inflow. Therefore, for purposes of short-run balance-of-payments forecasting, an equation of the type proposed by Kouri and Porter, which amalgamates the monetary and flow approaches, is essential when the degree of capital mobility is so high as to be virtually perfect.

2. At the opposite extreme, suppose that capital is immobile and that the flow of capital is zero. If K is zero, the balance-of-payments equation becomes

$$L_y \, \Delta Y + L_p \, \Delta p + L_i \, \Delta i = \Delta D + X\left(\frac{ep^*}{p}\right) - V\left(Y, \frac{ep^*}{p}\right) + i^*F$$

The left-hand terms add up to the changes in the demand for money. The right-hand terms are the changes in the supply of money. The change in reserves in this case is the current-account surplus. Therefore, without capital mobility, and for a given change in domestic credit, changes in the money supply require adjustments in the current account of the balance of payments. If the demand for money does not change because p, Y, and i are fixed or exogenously determined,

$$\Delta D = -\left[X\left(\frac{ep^*}{p}\right) - V\left(Y, \frac{ep^*}{p}\right) + i^*F \right]$$

and the creation of domestic credit implies a current-account deficit. This is what happens in the IMF model, which we will study in the next section.

3. In long-run equilibrium the demand for money equals the supply of money, and p, Y, and i are at their equilibrium values. With no change in domestic credit, the demand for money equals the supply of money only if the current account is balanced. The balance-of-payments equation becomes

$$0 = X\left(\frac{ep^*}{p}\right) - V\left(Y, \frac{ep^*}{p}\right) + i^*F$$

With income at its full-employment equilibrium value, it is clear that adjustment with fixed exchange rates necessitates price-level adjustments. Avoidance of long-term balance-of-payments problems requires countries to hold domestic inflation to the world average.

10.4 THE MONETARY APPROACH: IMF VARIETY

One of the most important functions of the IMF is its role as a lender to countries experiencing short-run balance-of-payments deficits. Inasmuch as the IMF will not extend credit indefinitely, it requires assurances that the borrowing country's deficit will be temporary, and this generally requires that the borrowing country take policy steps designed to halt or reverse the deficit. The IMF monitors compliance with its "conditionality" during the period of the loan. It is in this context that a simple model of the balance of payments of borrowing countries is essential to the IMF's work.

The approach utilized by the IMF is a monetary approach that was initially formalized by J. J. Polak, long-time director of the IMF's research department and economic counselor to the executive directors.[6] It begins with the standard monetarist assumption that the cash balance ratio is constant. Therefore,

$$Y_t = \left(\frac{1}{k}\right)M_t \tag{10.12}$$

where Y_t and M_t are, respectively, nominal national income and the nominal money stock at time t. The second major behavioral assumption is that imports, V_t, are directly proportional to the preceding period's nominal national income level. Therefore,

$$V_t = vY_{t-1} \tag{10.13}$$

where v is the marginal propensity to import with respect to money income. With these behavioral relations, plus the additional assumptions of fixed exchange rates, zero capital mobility, and exogenously determined exports, it follows that the condition of the balance of payments can be changed only by changing the level of imports, which depends, in turn, on the stock of money. Combining (10.12) and (10.13), we see that

$$V_t = \left(\frac{v}{k}\right)M_{t-1} \tag{10.14}$$

[6] Polak, J. J., "Monetary Analysis of Income Formation and Payments Problems," International Monetary Fund, *Staff Papers*, November 1957. Reprinted in International Monetary Fund, *The Monetary Approach to the Balance of Payments*, R. R. Rhomberg and H. R. Heller, eds., Washington, D.C., 1977.

Hence, imports are proportional to the money stock of the preceding period. When combined with the level of autonomous exports, X_a, this import function gives the net export level as

$$\text{NX}_t = X_a - V_t = X_a - \left(\frac{v}{k}\right)M_{t-1} \tag{10.15}$$

From this expression it is clear that a balance-of-payments deficit implies an excessively large money supply, whereas a surplus implies the opposite. Needed in this oversimplified world is tighter control of the money supply if the balance of payments is to be moved from deficit to surplus.

Now recall the monetary survey of the country. As noted previously, the balance sheet identity requires that

$$\Delta M = \Delta D + \Delta R \tag{10.2}$$

which calls attention to the fact that a change in the money stock can come about either through the expansion of domestic credit, ΔD, or a balance-of-payments deficit or surplus as measured by ΔR. Presumably the change in domestic credit can be controlled by the monetary authority and may therefore be considered an autonomous variable. The change in foreign exchange reserves depends on the balance of payments; that is,

$$\Delta R_t = \text{NX}_t = X_a - V_t = X_a - \left(\frac{v}{k}\right)M_{t-1}$$

This means that the change in the money stock is

$$\Delta M_t = \Delta D_t + \Delta R_t = \Delta D_t + X_a - \left(\frac{v}{k}\right)M_{t-1} \tag{10.16}$$

so the change in the money stock depends on autonomous exports, the growth of domestic credit, and the preceding period's money stock. Since $\Delta M_t = M_t - M_{t-1}$, (10.16) can be written as

$$M_t = \left(1 - \frac{v}{k}\right)M_{t-1} + X_a + \Delta D_t \tag{10.17}$$

Hence, the level of the money stock is determined by the preceding value of the money stock, the level of exports, and the growth of domestic credit.

When the money supply is in equilibrium, $M_t = M_{t-1} = \bar{M}$, where $\bar{M}$ is the equilibrium money stock. Replacing M_t and M_{t-1} by $\bar{M}$ in (10.17) gives the equilibrium money stock as

$$\bar{M} = \frac{X_a}{v/k} + \frac{\Delta D_t}{v/k}$$

But when the money supply is constant, $\Delta M = 0$, and it must then follow from the monetary survey that

$$\Delta R_t = -\Delta D_t \tag{10.18}$$

Therefore a balance-of-payments deficit can then exist only if there is positive domestic credit creation. The solution to a deficit in the balance of payments lies in reducing the growth of domestic credit. If policy reduces ΔD to zero, the ongoing balance-of-payments deficit will require the monetary authority to sell foreign exchange. Since that reduces the money stock, the demand for imports declines and the balance of payments is then brought into equilibrium. It follows that, after a disturbance, balance-of-payments deficits and surpluses will be temporary, if domestic credit is not permitted to grow.

Although this model seems naive and oversimplified in the extreme, it appears to have had rather profound effects on IMF policies toward deficit countries. When such a country applies to the IMF for a balance-of-payments loan, the IMF responds by sending a staff "standby" mission to the country to negotiate a loan agreement. If the IMF agrees to make the loan, it imposes terms on the borrowing country that must be met. Usually, such "conditionality" is in the form of a commitment to reduce the growth of domestic credit, as is indicated to be necessary by the model. The IMF then provides foreign exchange or SDRs (special drawing rights) to the borrowing country on a continuing basis; that is, it makes only a fraction of the assistance available during a given period of time. If the conditionality is violated, the agreement is abrogated, and IMF assistance is automatically terminated.

The structure of the IMF model implies that the control of domestic credit is crucial and that balance-of-payments improvement can be bought only by reducing imports. It is mute on the subject of exchange rate variation, and it makes no attempt to distinguish between real and nominal magnitudes. Since a reduction in imports necessitates reduction in nominal income, either inflation must decline or real output must decline, and in the model it does not matter which one does the declining. But if real output declines, the prescription to restrict domestic credit is disastrous, especially to a developing economy, and if inflation declines, then surely the assumption of exogenously determined exports is untenable. The assumption is that export prices are established in world markets. If that is the case, a reduction in domestic inflation reduces production costs relative to world prices, and this provides an incentive to increase production for export.

The IMF's approach was initially born of necessity. Most developing countries lacked the facilities to generate adequate data that permit the structure of their economies to be reliably described. However, financial data are generally available from the central bank, and trade statistics are generated by customs offices. An approach that requires only these modest data sources quite naturally commends itself. This is, to be sure, a bit like the drunk who looks for the wallet he has lost under a street lamp where the light is best rather than where he thinks he might have lost it. But such groping is inevitable when data and statistical resources are meager. It is a lot easier for the Fund to determine when conditionality is violated by establishing a domestic credit criterion than to base it on some other likely candidate, such as the government's budget deficit. The magnitude of short-run changes in budget deficits can only be guessed at in many countries.

The Fund's staff has itself suggested a number of reasons why the monetary approach is so attractive. For one thing, the framework is very simple. Rhomberg and Heller write as follows:

> . . . the Nature of the Fund's work on balance of payments problems of member countries made it desirable to have available a framework for quantitative analysis that was sufficiently manageable to be serviceable during staff missions to foreign capitals.[7]

They also argue that

> Less developed countries typically have a simpler financial structure than do more developed countries. In the absence of well-developed asset markets and financial instruments, there are relatively few alternatives to either holding funds in monetary form or spending them on domestic or foreign goods and services. . . .[8]

Finally, these authors note that

> . . . a monetary framework for analyzing the balance of payments effects of economic policy was particularly appropriate for many developing countries, particularly Latin America, in which control over domestic credit was in fact relied on as a major instrument . . . of demand management and balance of payments control.[9]

Exclusive emphasis on domestic credit control seems like a narrow approach to policy. However, restriction of domestic credit growth is

---

[7] IMF, *The Monetary Approach to the Balance of Payments,* op. cit., p. 6.

[8] Ibid., p. 7.

[9] Ibid., p. 7.

more than merely a monetary policy directive, especially in the case of developing countries that lack extensive capital markets. When the government runs a budget deficit, it must borrow. If it borrows from the private sector of the economy, the private sector accepts bonds, B, and the government receives money, which it then spends. Therefore, the money stock remains unchanged because the government puts back what it took out, but the bond holdings and financial wealth of the private sector increase. The alternative way of domestically financing the deficit is to borrow from the central bank. The central bank accepts the government's IOUs as an asset and creates a line of credit for the government. When the government spends the balances in its central bank account, the money holdings of the private sector of the economy increase.

Quite generally, this implies that we can write

$$\Delta B + \Delta M = p(G - T) \tag{10.19}$$

This expression is known as the government's budget restraint. It states that the nominal budget deficit must equal the increase in government bonds plus money holdings of the private sector of the economy. This requirement has powerful implications for the relationship between fiscal and monetary policies in all countries. Our concern here, however, is with the developing countries that are the IMF's principal clients. In such countries private saving may be negligible and a capital market virtually nonexistent. Therefore, the government does not have the option of selling its bonds to the private sector in the way that finance ministries in industrial countries can. The best they can do is sell government IOUs to the central bank. In terms of the budget restraint this implies that ΔB is zero, so

$$\Delta M = p(G - T)$$

which shows that the growth in the domestic component of the money stock exactly equals the nominal budget deficit of the government. Put differently, even if there is no domestic credit extended to the private sector, domestic credit grows by the amount of the government's borrowings from the central bank. We can therefore see that the condition to reduce the growth of domestic credit will very likely require the government to take steps to reduce its budget deficit.

According to the principle of Occam's razor, simple models are better than complicated models, provided both yield equally satisfactory results. As a workaday tool there is much to commend the IMF's approach. Unfortunately, it is sometimes misleading, and its directives to reduce domestic credit may generate unemployment and retard economic growth. However, a similar criticism could be applied to many other approaches to the balance-of-payments problems of developing nations. For example, as we saw in Chapter 8, devaluation could be deflationary if the demand for imports is inelastic with respect to price. The conventional devaluation-deflation combination of policy implied by the external-internal balance approach could therefore also be harmful.

10.5 FLEXIBLE EXCHANGE RATES AND THE MONETARY APPROACH

Under fixed exchange rates the balance-of-payments equation predicts the balance-of-payments deficit or surplus and therefore the change in foreign exchange reserves. Under a pure flexible exchange-rate system there is no intervention by the monetary authority, and the balance-of-payments equation is then designed to predict movements in the exchange rate. The money supply, in turn, becomes an autonomous variable that can be determined by monetary policy.

The key assumptions needed to construct a monetarist flexible exchange-rate model are as follows:

1. Portfolios adjust instantaneously to disequilibrium. Domestic and foreign financial assets are perfect substitutes, so there is no distinction between domestic and foreign bonds. If we wish, we can imagine that there is only one bond in the world. This assumption implies uncovered interest parity; that is,

$$i - i^* = E\left(\frac{\Delta e}{e}\right) \tag{10.20}$$

which states that the expected rate of depreciation of the local currency must equal the difference between the domestic and the foreign rate of interest.

2. Domestic and foreign goods are seen as perfect substitutes by consumers, and prices are flexible and determined in competitive markets. This implies that there is effectively only one good. The law of one price must hold. Therefore, the equilibrium real exchange rate is fixed, and

$$p = ep^* \tag{10.21}$$

so the equilibrium domestic price level p equals the nominal exchange rate e multiplied by the foreign price level p^*. If a bushel of wheat costs $10 in the United States and £5 in the United Kingdom, the exchange rate must be 2, that is, £1 costs $2.

Now suppose the demand for money is of the explicit form

$$\frac{M}{p} = Y^{\alpha} e^{-\beta i} \tag{10.22}$$

where **e** is the exponential. Taking natural logarithms of this expression gives

$$\ln M = \ln p + \alpha \ln Y - \beta i \tag{10.23}$$

For convenience, rewrite this as

$$m = p + \alpha y - \beta i \tag{10.24}$$

where $m = \ln M$, the natural logarithm of the nominal money stock
          $p = \ln p$, the natural logarithm of the price level
          $y = \ln Y$, the natural logarithm of real income
          $\alpha =$ the income elasticity of the demand for money, $(\Delta M/M)/(\Delta Y/Y)$
          $\beta =$ the interest *semi*elasticity of the demand for money with respect to the rate of interest, $(\Delta M/M)/\Delta i$

Next assume an identical demand for money function for the rest of the world. Therefore, let

$$m^* = p^* + \alpha y^* - \beta i^* \tag{10.25}$$

Then subtract m^* from m:

$$m - m^* = (p - p^*) + \alpha(y - y^*) - \beta(i - i^*) \tag{10.26}$$

and rearrange this equation with $p - p^*$ as the dependent variable. Therefore,

$$p - p^* = (m - m^*) - \alpha(y - y^*) + \beta(i - i^*) \tag{10.27}$$

From (10.21) we can see that on taking natural logarithms, we get

$$\ln e = p - p^*$$

Using this to replace the price-level differentials in (10.27) gives the fundamental monetary equation of the exchange rate:

$$\ln e = (m - m^*) - \alpha(y - y^*) + \beta(i - i^*) \tag{10.28}$$

The equation states that the price of foreign exchange will rise if the domestic money supply rises more rapidly than the foreign money supply, that the price of foreign exchange will fall if domestic income grows more rapidly than foreign income, and that the price of foreign exchange will rise if the domestic-foreign interest-rate differential widens.

Much more can be done with the basic equation (10.28) by introducing additional assumptions. First, recall that the condition for un-covered interest-rate parity is

$$i - i^* = E(\Delta \ln e)$$

because the change in the natural log equals the percentage change. Using this in (10.28) eliminates the interest-rate differential from the equation and permits it to be expressed as

$$\ln e = (m - m^*) - \alpha(y - y^*) + \beta E(\Delta \ln e) \qquad (10.29)$$

and it follows that a rise in the expected price of foreign exchange will raise the current price of foreign exchange.

If the expected rise in the price of foreign exchange equals the dif-ference between the expected domestic and foreign inflation rates, we can write

$$E(\Delta \ln e) = E(\Delta \rho) - E(\Delta \rho^*)$$

which may be used to further change (10.29) to

$$\ln e = (m - m^*) - \alpha(y - y^*) + \beta[E(\Delta \rho) - E(\Delta \rho^*)] \quad (10.30)$$

The equation states that a relative increase in the domestic money supply raises the price of foreign exchange, and a rise in the relative expected rate of inflation also raises the price of foreign exchange.

Another assumption frequently made in monetarist models of the exchange rate is that income levels are at their full-employment values, determined exogenously by factors outside the model, such as capital stock, labor force size, and growth of productivity. Equation (10.30) then becomes

$$\ln e = (m - m^*) - \alpha(y_f - y_f^*) + \beta[E(\Delta \rho) - E(\Delta \rho^*)] \qquad (10.31)$$

which implies that the country with the highest real growth rate will experience appreciation; that is, the price of foreign exchange will decline.

When expectations are "rational," differential inflation rates equal expected differences in monetary growth rates. Therefore,

$$E(\Delta \rho) - E(\Delta \rho^*) = E(\Delta m - \Delta m^*)$$

Moreover, the expected growth of money supplies is often assumed to follow a random walk. This means the best prediction of the future mon-etary growth rate is today's monetary growth rate. If this is the case, (10.31) reduces to the very simple statement

$$\ln e = (m - m^*) - \alpha(y_f - y_f^*) + \beta(\Delta m - \Delta m^*) \qquad (10.32)$$

For a given full-employment income differential, the exchange rate depends entirely on differential money stocks and their rates of growth.

The countries with least rapid monetary growth rates will experience appreciation, whereas countries with rapid monetary growth rates will experience depreciation.

The flexible exchange-rate period that began in 1973 has been characterized by the tendency for exchange rates to overshoot; that is, the exchange rate appears to go too far in the right direction and then reverses itself. Monetarist theorists, as well as others, have attempted to deal with this problem by replacing the strict purchasing-power-parity assumption with the more realistic assumption that commodity prices are sticky, requiring time to adjust to market changes. Asset prices are assumed to adjust instantaneously to asset-market shocks, but commodity prices respond more slowly because of the existence of long-term contracts, imperfect information, and sluggishness in the response of consumers to price changes.

Perhaps the most well-known of the monetarist overshooting models is the model of Rudiger Dornbusch of MIT.[10] In his model, purchasing-power parity holds, but only in the long run. An increase in the money supply eventually causes a proportionate depreciation. However, during the transition the initial depreciation exceeds the long-run depreciation and is then followed by a period of appreciation toward the long-run equilibrium exchange rate. Because prices are sticky, monetary expansion initially raises the real quantity of money. This reduces the domestic rate of interest, causing an incipient deficit in the capital account, which then causes a sharp depreciation. The magnitude of the short-run depreciation is such that the rationally expected future appreciation cancels out the domestic-foreign interest-rate differential—that is, so that uncovered interest-rate parity holds. Since this short-run asset-market equilibrium is associated with a subsequent decline in the real quantity of money as well as expected appreciation, the exchange rate then appreciates to its long-run equilibrium.

Formally, assume that income levels are at full employment and determined exogenously. Expectations are rational, and money supply generation follows a random walk. The expected rate of monetary growth therefore equals the current rate of monetary growth, which, in turn, equals the expected rate of inflation. This implies that in the long run the equilibrium exchange rate is as given by (10.32); that is, by

$$\ln \bar{e} = (m - m^*) - \alpha(y_f - y_f^*) + \beta(\Delta m - \Delta m^*) \qquad (10.32)$$

where the bar over the exchange rate indicates the long-run equilibrium value of the exchange rate.

[10] Dornbusch, Rudiger, "Expectations and Exchange Rate Dynamics," *Journal of Political Economy*, December 1976.

In the short run, when the exchange rate differs from its long-run equilibrium value, it is expected to move toward its equilibrium value at a rate proportional to the difference in the two exchange rates. Therefore, that part of the change in the exchange rate due to the discrepancy may be written

$$-k(\ln e - \ln \bar{e})$$

Since the long-run, rationally expected, exchange rate change is the difference between the monetary growth rates $\Delta m - \Delta m^*$, the overall expected change is

$$E(\Delta \ln e) = -k(\ln e - \ln \bar{e}) + \Delta m - \Delta m^* \qquad (10.33)$$

Uncovered interest parity holds, so $E(\Delta \ln e) = i - i^*$. Using this in (10.33) and solving for the difference between the actual and the equilibrium exchange rates gives

$$\ln e - \ln \bar{e} = -\frac{1}{k}[(i - \Delta m) - (i^* - \Delta m^*)] \qquad (10.34)$$

This is a very interesting result. Since the expected inflation rates equal the monetary growth rates, $i - \Delta m$ and $i^* - \Delta m^*$ are, respectively, the domestic and foreign real interest rates. Therefore, the difference between the log of the spot rate ($\ln e$) and the log of the equilibrium exchange rate ($\ln \bar{e}$) is proportional to the real interest-rate differential. As the real interest-rate differential narrows, the gap between the actual and the equilibrium exchange rates diminishes. When an expansionary monetary shock causes the domestic real interest rate to decline temporarily—because prices adjust sluggishly—capital outflows raise the price of foreign exchange above its equilibrium value.

Equation (10.34) predicts the overshooting effect. To get the value of the exchange rate, we substitute (10.33) into (10.34) to replace $\ln \bar{e}$ and thereby obtain

$$\ln e = (m - m^*) - \alpha(y_f - y_f^*) + \beta(\Delta m - \Delta m^*)$$

$$-\frac{1}{k}[(i - \Delta m) - (i^* - \Delta m^*)] \qquad (10.35)$$

The modern flexible exchange-rate period began in 1973. By 1978 enough experience had been accumulated to provide the data needed to conduct empirical testing of various hypotheses. Between 1973 and 1978 empirical tests were generally favorable to the monetary hypothesis. Exchange rates appreciated in response to increases in relative income growth and depreciated in response to increases in relative monetary growth rates. However, the experience of 1978, during which the dollar depreciated sharply against the deutsche mark despite more rapid monetary growth in Germany than in the United States, ran counter to monetarist expectations. The traditional notion that the dollar depreciated because rapid U.S. income growth raised the demand for imports seemed to provide a better explanation. Similarly, the sharp appreciation of the dollar in 1980 fits the traditional notion that interest-rate differentials were primarily responsible. Unfortunately, when different hypotheses are tested against the data, they often fit their data periods quite well, but then go astray when the equations are asked to forecast exchange rates. To interpret the behavior of the dollar during the 1980s, we must go beyond simple Keynesian and monetarist models and examine the modern asset-market theory of exchange rate determination. That is the job of the next chapter.

QUESTIONS FOR REVIEW

1. Explain the monetary approach to the balance of payments. What are its advantages over other approaches such as elasticities, absorption, and income expenditure?
2. What is "global monetarism"? What are the assumptions of global monetarism? What are the implications of these assumptions for the analysis of the effects of
   a. a rise in the price level?
   b. a rise in real income?
   c. a rise in the rate of interest?
3. Contrast these results with Keynesian results. Can they be reconciled?
4. Interpret the strength of the Japanese and West German balance of payments using the monetary theory.
5. Why are global monetarists unenthusiastic about the effectiveness of devaluation in eliminating a balance-of-payments deficit? How should the deficit be eliminated?
6. Describe the IMF brand of monetary model? Is it a model of the overall balance of payments or a model of the current account? What is IMF conditionality? When the IMF requires a reduction in the growth of domestic credit, does this also have implications for government fiscal policy?
7. What are the determinants of the exchange rate in the monetary model of flexible exchange rates? What are the shortcomings of the model? Can they be repaired?

SUGGESTIONS FOR FURTHER READING

Dornbusch, Rudiger, "Expectations and Exchange Rate Dynamics," *Journal of Political Economy,* December 1976.

Frenkel, J. A., T. Gylferson, and J. F. Helliwel, "A Synthesis of Monetary and Keynesian Approaches to Short-Run Balance of Payments Theory," *Economic Journal,* September 1980.

Frenkel, J. A., and Harry G. Johnson, *The Monetary Approach to the Balance of Payments,* Allyn and Unwin, 1976.

Goldstein, Morris, "Downward Price Flexibility, Ratchet Effects, and the Inflationary Impact of Import Price Changes," International Monetary Fund, *Staff Papers,* 1977.

Kouri, Penti, and M. G. Porter, "International Capital Flows and Portfolio Equilibrium," *Journal of Political Economy,* May 1974.

Rhomberg, Rudolph R., and H. Robert Heller, *The Monetary Approach to the Balance of Payments,* International Monetary Fund, 1977.

Chapter 11

Asset Markets and Flexible Exchange Rates

11.1 INTRODUCTION

The asset-market approach to exchange rate determination shares with other contemporary theories of the financially open economy the view that the behavior of markets for financial assets is central to the condition of the balance of payments in the short run. It parts company with the monetary theory in rejecting the assumption that financial assets are perfect substitutes. It differs from Keynesian theory in that it is a theory of stock adjustment rather than flow equilibrium. Its dynamic assumptions are that asset markets clear rapidly, whereas commodity markets clear slowly because of sticky prices and sluggish adjustment of commodity flows to price changes. Such timing assumptions can easily be incorporated into Keynesian and monetarist models.

The most important assumption of the asset-market theory is that financial assets are imperfect substitutes in the minds of investors. Even if domestic and foreign financial assets are similar in most respects, investors may perceive differences in risk caused by differences in the ease of sale (liquidity), tax treatment, default risk, political risk, and exchange risk. There may be differences arising from differences in political climates and the stability or instability of governments and their economic policies. Differences in risk may arise from intercountry economic structures. Rates of return are very likely to bounce around more sharply if a country specializes in the production of commodities that exhibit large price swings, as opposed to commodities that enjoy stable prices. There is also exchange risk involved in the purchase and sale of foreign assets, since exchange rates vary unexpectedly. A very important fact that causes investors to view domestic and foreign bonds as imperfect substitutes is the circumstance that international business cycles and national economic policies are not perfectly synchronized or harmonized with respect to time. When the yield is expected to rise on one type of domestic asset, chances are that yields on all domestic assets are also expected to rise. Consequently, investors cannot hedge against capital loss by diversifying their portfolios into domestic assets. But since interest rates on foreign assets may be expected to remain the same, or even fall, because of different foreign economic policies, or simply because foreign countries are in a different phase of the business cycle, diversifying into foreign portfolios can reduce the risk perceived by investors.

In this chapter we begin with some essential principles of portfolio management that go beyond the perfunctory notes of Chapter 5. We then consider the asset-market theory in the short run, and then we integrate that analysis with the long-run development of the balance of payments. Throughout this discussion we assume that exchange rates are free to fluctuate and that the domestic money supply is controlled by the central bank.

11.2 PORTFOLIO CHOICE AND FOREIGN INVESTMENT

The modern theory of portfolio choice stems from seminal work by Harry P. Markowitz and James Tobin.[1] Tobin's objective was to place the Keynesian theory of liquidity preference on a firmer footing than it had been placed by Keynes. Pre-Keynesian economists could not imagine that anyone would be so irrational as to hold money, which earns little or no interest, when that money could be converted into earning assets. The demand for money was therefore seen as exclusively a transactions demand. People hold an average idle balance because money receipts and disbursements are not perfectly synchronized with respect to time. Keynes then attempted to explain the presence of sizable idle-money balances by introducing a "liquidity preference" motive based on interest-rate expectations. Since interest rates are low during depression, the expectation that they will return to a higher normal level leads wealth holders

---

[1] Markowitz, H. P., "Portfolio Selection," *Journal of Finance,* May 1952; and James Tobin, "Liquidity Preference as Behavior Towards Risk," *Review of Economic Studies,* February 1958. Application of Tobin-Markowitz portfolio choice theory to the study of international capital movements is provided by W. H. Branson, *Financial Capital Flows in the United States Balance of Payments,* North-Holland, Amsterdam, 1968.

to prefer cash to bonds to avoid the anticipated capital losses on bonds when the expected rise in interest rates takes place.

Keynes' theory has been much criticized. Perhaps the most telling criticism is the assumption of inelastic interest-rate expectations, that is, that interest rates will return to a normal higher level. If such expectations were generalized to other variables, the economy could not remain depressed for long. Low wages and prices would be considered abnormal, so this would spur hiring in anticipation of higher future wages and raise production in anticipation of higher prices. If capital goods prices were abnormally low, firms would be likely to expand investment outlays to take advantage of the temporarily lower cost of capital. Consequently, such expectations would spur recovery and render untenable Keynes' concept of underemployment equilibrium.

Tobin liberated liquidity preference from dependence on interest-rate expectations by showing that even if there is no expectation that interest rates would rise, wealth holders would nevertheless diversify their portfolios—holding both bonds and cash—because of the greater riskiness of bonds. Riskiness in this context means that if capital gains or losses could be sustained with equal likelihood, the asset characterized by the largest variability in gains and losses is the riskiest.

Figure 11.1(a) shows the possible outcomes for an earning asset. The horizontal axis measures the capital gain or loss, and the vertical axis shows the probabilities of the outcomes. If the rate of interest is expected to remain constant, the most likely outcome is a capital gain, g, of zero. However, other outcomes are possible. A large capital gain of $2\sigma_g$ is possible, but the probability is low. With a bell-shaped normal curve describing the probabilities, a distance of $1\sigma_g$ in either direction from zero exhausts roughly 67 percent of the possible outcomes. Put differently, 67 percent of the time the capital gain or loss will lie within one standard deviation of the mean of zero. Two standard deviations (i.e., $2\sigma_g$) in either direction of the mean exhausts about 96 percent of the possible outcomes. Therefore, there is only a 4 percent chance that a capital gain or loss in excess of two standard deviations can occur.

The standard deviation of the capital gain provides a measure of the riskiness of an earning asset. With a fairly riskless asset, as illustrated in Figure 11.1(b), the probable outcomes cluster near zero. Hence the standard deviation is low. For a risky asset, the distribution of outcomes is more widely spread. A large capital gain is more likely, but so too is the probability of a large capital loss. This is a risky asset, and it has a large standard deviation. Consequently, the standard deviation may be used as a measure of the riskiness of an asset: the larger the standard deviation, the greater the risk.

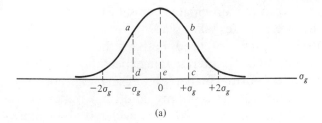

(a)

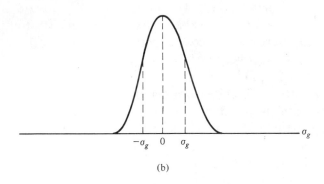

(b)

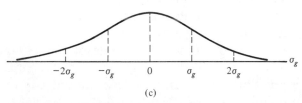

(c)

Figure 11.1 (a) Probability of capital gain or loss from bondholding: (b) a low-risk asset; (c) a high-risk asset.

To push the analysis further, we must understand the concept of mathematical expectation. The ideas are simple, and a summary of the rules is provided in the chapter appendix. The expected value of a random variable, written, $E(g)$ is the most likely long-run outcome. It is therefore the average value or the mean. For the asset in Figure 11.1(c), $E(g) = 0$; that is, the most likely outcome is that there will be neither a capital gain nor loss.

The variance of g, written σ_g^2 is obtained by subtracting the expected value of g from g, squaring this result, and taking the expected value:

$$\text{variance of } g = \sigma_g^2 = E[g - E(g)]^2$$

But since $E(g) = 0$ under present assumptions, we have

$$\sigma_g^2 = E(g)^2$$

The standard deviation is simply the square root of the variance.

Next consider Figure 11.2. The return on a portfolio is measured on the vertical axis and the risk, σ_r is measured horizontally. The line OC_0 is the opportunity locus. It shows the terms on which the investor perceives the way the market converts risk into return. At point O the investor has a riskless portfolio but earns nothing on it. If OB represents total assets, point C_0 shows that the investor believes a maximum return of BC_0 is possible, but at the price of maximum riskiness.

If the investor is a risk averter for whom risk and return are imperfect substitutes, there will be a set of preferences that can be represented by indifference curves such as I_1, I_2, and I_3. At point a the investor reaches indifference curve I_1. But this is not an optimal portfolio. The indifference curve shows that the investor would be willing to accept ac additional risk for cd additional return. However, the investor believes the market would reward a greater additional return equal to cb. Therefore, the investor is clearly better off at b than at a. In fact, the investor will continue to be better off by accepting more risk for greater return until point b, where the opportunity locus is tangent to the highest possible indifference curve. The investor would like to reach I_3 or an even higher indifference curve but cannot get there given the opportunity locus and the constraint of total wealth. Consequently, the investor settles for point b, receiving a return from the portfolio of r_0 and accepting risk of σ_{r0}.

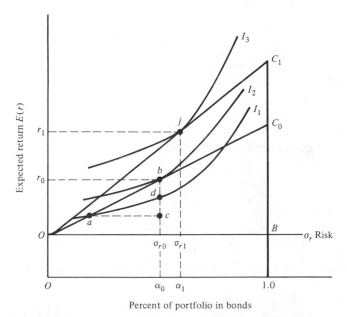

Figure 11.2 Optimal distribution of portfolio assets.

Now suppose there are only two available assets: money, a riskless asset that provides no return, and bonds, which yield a return of i percent. Let α be the percent of an investor's portfolio in bonds. At equilibrium the portfolio consists of α_0 percent bonds and $1 - \alpha_0$ money. The return on \$1 invested in bonds is $g + i$, where g is the rate of capital gain. If α percent of the portfolio is invested in bonds, the return on the portfolios is

$$r = \alpha(g + i)$$

The expected value of the return on the portfolio is

$$E(r) = \alpha E(g) + \alpha i$$

But since $E(g) = 0$,

$$E(r) = \alpha i \qquad (11.1)$$

so the expected value of the return depends on the rate of interest and the percent of the portfolio invested in bonds. The variance of r is given by

$$\sigma_r^2 = E[r - E(r)]^2$$

Since

$$r - E(r) = \alpha(g + i) - \alpha i = \alpha g$$
$$[r - E(r)]^2 = \alpha^2 g^2$$

so

$$\sigma_r^2 = E[r - E(r)]^2 = \alpha^2 E(g)^2 = \alpha^2 \sigma_g^2$$

Taking the square root, we see that

$$\sigma_r = \alpha \sigma_g \qquad (11.2)$$

Therefore the riskiness of the entire portfolio depends on the percent of the portfolio invested in bonds and the standard deviation (riskiness) of the capital gain on bonds.

Figure 11.2 shows that r_0 divided by σ_{r0} gives the slope of the opportunity locus. Therefore, from (11.1) and (11.2)

$$\frac{E(r)}{\sigma_r} = \frac{\alpha i}{\alpha \sigma_g} = \frac{i}{\sigma_g}$$

so the slope of the opportunity locus is the ratio of the rate of interest to the standard deviation (riskiness) of bonds.

We can now see that a rise in the rate of interest rotates the opportunity locus in a counterclockwise manner. If the new opportunity locus is OC_1, tangency with I_3 is at point j, implying a higher fraction of the portfolio invested in bonds. Because the market offers greater return, the wealth holder is willing to assume additional risk, and he or she therefore converts some money into extra bonds. Therefore, a rise in the rate of interest reduces liquidity preference, whereas a decline in the rate of interest increases liquidity preference. It follows that the portfolio demand for money is a decreasing function of the rate of interest. It also follows that the basis for a portfolio demand for money need not be Keynes's expectation of rising future interest rates.[2]

An important implication of Tobin's analysis of portfolio choice is that the diversifying investor will use an increase in wealth so as to adjust his or her portfolio to include more of *all* the assets in the portfolio. Therefore, an increase in wealth in the form of additional bonds will cause the investor to convert some of the bonds into money. If given more money, the investor will use part of it to buy more bonds. Conse-

---

[2] Tobin's investor is a risk averter for whom risk and return are imperfect substitutes. Such investors are portfolio diversifiers. They will hold a combination of assets rather than put all their eggs in one basket. If risk and return were perfect substitutes, their indifference curves would be straight lines and they would then be "plungers." They hold one or the other of the assets but not both. Figure 11.3 illustrates the case of a plunger. At point a he is willing to give up ab return for a risk reduction of bc. But the market tells him he can reduce his risk by the greater amount bd. Therefore, he sells bonds until he has none left, because the reduction in return reduces his risk by amounts that make him feel better off. The investor reaches his highest indifference curve at point O, where he holds only money. But if the interest rate rises so that the opportunity locus has a greater slope than the indifference curve, he suddenly takes the plunge, moving his entire portfolio into bonds, since each bond he buys now increases his risk by less than he is willing to sacrifice for the additional return. He therefore moves to point C' on indifference curve I_3.

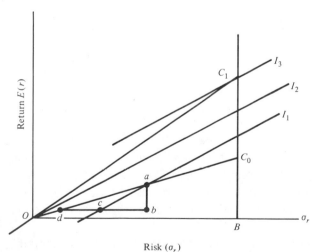

Figure 11.3 Portfolio choice of a plunger.

quently, an increase in wealth raises the demand for all assets—bonds, money, and, by inference, foreign assets. Thus, an essential addition to the theory of the demand for money is that the demand for money is an increasing function of the level of wealth, in addition to being a function of the level of income and the rate of interest, as explained earlier.

We can now introduce foreign investment into the discussion. Suppose there are two financial assets, domestic and foreign bonds, respectively. The domestic interest rate is i, and the foreign interest rate is i^*. The respective percentage capital gains are g and g^*. Let α percent of the portfolio be invested in foreign bonds and $1 - \alpha$ in domestic bonds. The return on the portfolio is

$$r = (1 - \alpha)(i + g) + \alpha(i^* + g^*)$$

If $E(g)$ and $E(g^*)$ are both zero, the expected value of the return on the portfolio is

$$E(r) = (1 - \alpha)i + \alpha i^*$$

To calculate the variance of r, proceed as before; that is, first take $E(r)$ from r to get

$$r - E(r) = (1 - \alpha)(i + g) + \alpha(i^* + g^*) - (1 - \alpha)i - \alpha i^*$$

which implies that

$$r - E(r) = (1 - \alpha)g + \alpha g^*$$

Squaring the result gives

$$[r - E(r)]^2 = (1 - \alpha)^2 g^2 + 2\alpha(1 - \alpha)gg^* + \alpha^2 g^{*2}$$

The variance of r is the expected value of this result. Therefore,

$$\sigma_r^2 = (1 - \alpha)^2 E(g)^2 + 2\alpha(1 - \alpha)E(gg^*) + \alpha^2 E(g^*)^2 \qquad (11.3)$$

where $E(g)^2$ is the variance of capital gains on domestic bonds, $E(g^*)^2$ is the variance of the capital gain on foreign bonds, and $E(gg^*)$ is called the covariance of the gain between domestic and foreign bonds.

Inspection of (11.3) shows that the riskiness of the portfolio depends on the riskiness of domestic and foreign assets independently, as well as the extent to which capital gains and losses in the two countries are correlated. A positive covariance implies that capital gains and losses on one asset are correlated with similar gains and losses on other assets. However, if the covariance is negative, a capital loss on one asset tends to be offset by a gain on the other assets. When this is the case, the riskiness of the portfolio is reduced.

This is an important fact that helps to explain portfolio diversification into foreign assets. Empirical research discloses that the covariances between domestic and foreign assets are generally lower than the co-variances between different classes of domestic assets. The lower covari-ances between domestic and foreign assets means that changes in rates of return on different domestic assets are more highly correlated than changes in the rates of return between domestic and foreign assets. This means that it is more difficult to hedge against risk by portfolio diversi-fication into domestic assets alone, and that riskiness can be reduced by diversifying into foreign assets. Business cycles are not perfectly synchro-nized internationally, government economic policies differ, and the structure of economies may be significantly different. All of these factors contribute to a lower covariance between returns on domestic and foreign assets than between different categories of domestic assets.

Notice from (11.3) that if the variances of g and g^* are the same, so that domestic and foreign assets are independently equally risky, the variance of r will be less than the variance of g if the covariance between domestic and foreign assets is negative. Thus portfolio diversification into foreign assets may make sense even if interest rates are the same in both countries, and the independent riskiness of the individual assets is the same.

We can now summarize the main results:

1. Portfolio diversification is a rational response to risk for investors for whom risk and return are imperfect substitution. Most inves-tors probably fit into this category.
2. A rise in the rate of interest leads to greater risk taking by investors who rebalance portfolios in the direction of greater risk and re-turn. A rise in the rate of interest is therefore associated with a decline in liquidity preference, that is, a lower portfolio demand for money.
3. Portfolio diversifying investors will attempt to spread increases in wealth over all portfolio assets. Therefore an increase in wealth raises both the demand for money and the demand for bonds, domestic and foreign.
4. Portfolio diversification into foreign assets makes sense even when foreign assets bear identical risks and returns as domestic assets if the covariance of risk between domestic and foreign assets is negative.
5. If the spread between domestic and foreign interest rates changes, this provokes a one-time readjustment of portfolios. This means that the short-run capital movements induced by the changing interest-rate spread will be temporary. Therefore, the flow of short-term capital depends on *changes* in the interest-rate spread

rather than on the magnitude of the spread. It follows that the financing of a constant current-account deficit through time would require a steadily increasing rise in the spread between domestic and foreign interest rates.

6. Suppose investors in the country customarily put 10 percent of their portfolios into country A bonds and 20 percent into country B bonds. An increase in wealth causes investors to distribute the wealth in such a way that the existing percentages of the various assets are roughly maintained. Therefore, a rise in wealth will induce a capital inflow from country B that is likely to be about double the inflow from country A. This portfolio growth effect implies that if investors are accustomed to holding the IOUs of a given country, that country will find it easier to make additional borrowings in the future.

11.3 SHORT-RUN ASSET-MARKET EQUILIBRIUM[3]

The important variables that influence the balance of payments are real income levels, price levels, interest rates, and exchange rates. In addition, the portfolio choice theory suggests that financial wealth may also be an important determinant. The asset-market theory of exchange rate determination begins by assuming that in the very short run prices and income levels are constant or exogenously determined. This leaves only the rate of interest, the exchange rate, and the level of financial wealth available to equilibrate markets for financial assets. Therefore, a good starting point for the discussion of the asset-market theory is to study the relationship between wealth, the rate of interest, and the exchange rate in determining equilibrium in the market for domestic and foreign financial assets.

To simplify the discussion, we ignore foreign developments and study the asset markets of a single country. We assume that there are only three financial assets that investors view as imperfect substitutes. The assets are money, M, domestic bonds, B, and foreign bonds, F. All variables are in nominal terms. For a given stock of M, B, and F there is a total stock of financial wealth, given by

$$W = M + B + eF \qquad (11.4)$$

where B is denominated in domestic currency and F is denominated in foreign currency.

---

[3] The discussion of this section relies heavily on William H. Branson's paper, "Asset Markets and Relative Prices in Exchange Rate Determination," *Socialwissenschaftliche Annalen,* 1977.

In the short run, investors can acquire more F only by giving up some M and/or B. An open-market operation by the central bank that raises M must reduce B. As explained in Chapter 10, a government budget deficit increases B and W by the amount of the deficit if the government bonds are sold to the private sector. If the bonds are sold to the central bank, both M and W rise by the amount of the deficit while B remains constant. The current account enters the asset-market picture because a current-account surplus implies an increase in F, that is, an increase in net foreign IOUs held by domestic residents.

The portfolio choice theory of liquidity preference implies a money demand function in which the demand for money diminishes as the rate of interest rises, and increases as wealth increases. With income and prices fixed in the short run, monetary equilibrium implies

$$M = L(i, W) \qquad L_i < 0 \quad L_w > 0 \qquad (11.5)$$

where L_i is the reduction in liquidity preference caused by a rise in the rate of interest.

Equilibrium in the market for domestic bonds depends on the same two variables. When the rate of interest rises, the quantity of bonds demanded increases, and when financial wealth increases, wealth holders add bonds to their portfolios. Therefore,

$$B = B(i, W) \qquad B_i > 0 \quad B_w > 0 \qquad (11.6)$$

Foreign financial assets are also included in investor portfolios. When wealth increases, portfolio balance implies an increase in the quantity of foreign assets that wealth holders wish to hold. A rise in the rate of interest reduces the attractiveness of both money and foreign assets, so wealth holders substitute B into their portfolios in place of M and F. Therefore, equilibrium in the market for foreign assets is given by

$$eF = F(i, W) \qquad F_i < 0 \quad F_w > 0 \qquad (11.7)$$

Furthermore, since the asset substitution in the direction of bonds must result in an equivalent reduction in the holding of M and F, it must follow that the parameters L_i, B_i, and F_i are linked in such a way as to cause them to sum to zero. This means that

$$B_i = -(L_i + F_i)$$

Since B_i is positive and L_i and F_i are both negative, B_i must exceed the absolute value of L_i and F_i individually. This is an important property of the asset-market theory. It implies that a rise in the rate of interest will cause substitution toward domestic bonds away from *both* money and foreign assets.

The exchange rate enters the demand for money, bonds, and foreign assets indirectly through its effect on wealth. It is important to understand that a change in the exchange rate does not provide a relative price effect that leads to portfolio substitution. To see why this is true, imagine that the exchange rate equals 1; thus, $1000 equals £1000. Assume also that the foreign rate of interest is 10 percent, so a foreign asset worth £1000 yields earnings of £100. Then let the dollar rise so that $1000 can now be converted into £2000 worth of foreign bonds. The interest on this is £200, but when this is converted back into dollars at the current exchange rate, the earnings once again equal $100. We therefore see that the appreciation of the dollar permits a greater value of foreign securities to be bought, but the dollar value of the interest and the principal are unaffected. Thus a change in the exchange rate does not cause a relative price change that leads to a substitution between domestic and foreign bonds. The change in the exchange rate does, however, carry with it a wealth effect since the domestic currency value of foreign assets held by domestic residents changes when the exchange rate changes.

The model consists of four equations in three variables. One equation is therefore redundant and can be eliminated. For example, once the demand for B and F is known, the demand for money, M, is automatically determined by the difference between the wealth constraint, W, and B and F. In other words, we could write the model as

$$B = B(i, W) \qquad B_i > 0 \quad B_w > 0 \tag{11.6}$$

$$eF = F(i, W) \qquad F_i < 0 \quad F_w > 0 \tag{11.7}$$

$$M = W - B(i, W) - F(i, W) \tag{11.8}$$

where the last equation defines monetary equilibrium. There are now three endogenous variables (i, W, and e), and the exogenous variables are the nominal money supply M, the nominal value of the stock of domestic bonds B, and the foreign currency value of the stock of domestically held foreign assets F.

The comparative statics of the model are worked out in the appendix to the chapter. For the purposes of the text discussion, it is instructive to consider a simple diagramatic representation. Therefore, consider Figure 11.4 and suppose equilibrium in the markets for M, B, and F prevails at point a. If the exchange rate rises, the home currency value of foreign assets held by domestic residents rises. This raises the wealth of investors, who respond by attempting to spread the incremental wealth to rebalance their portfolios. This creates excess demand for money, which forces up the rate of interest. Therefore, monetary equilibrium implies a positive association between the price of foreign exchange and the rate of interest. This is shown as the positively sloped MM curve of Figure 11.4.

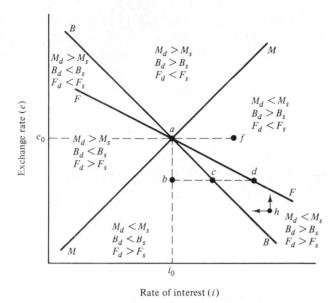

Figure 11.4 Short-run asset-market equilibrium.

If the exchange rate is fixed at e_0 and the rate of interest is above i_0, the demand for money would be lower than at i_0. Such a situation implies the presence of excess money supply. Therefore, to the right of MM there is excess supply of money $(M_d < M_s)$, whereas to the left of MM there is excess demand $(M_d > M_s)$.

Similarly, the diversification of the wealth increase caused by the rise in the price of foreign exchange raises the demand for B. This raises bond prices and lowers interest rates. Therefore, the BB curve, which specifies bond market equilibrium, must be negatively sloped. At point f the rate of interest exceeds i_0, indicating a greater demand for bonds. Therefore, to the right of BB there is excess demand for bonds $(B_d > B_s)$, and to the left of BB there is excess supply of bonds $(B_d < B_s)$.

If the rate of interest rises, the demand for foreign assets declines, as domestic assets are substituted for foreign assets. This reduces the demand for foreign exchange, lowers the price of foreign exchange, and therefore reduces the exchange rate. This implies an inverse association between the rate of interest and the exchange rate in the market for foreign assets, shown as the FF curve. At point b the exchange rate is too low with interest rate i_0. Therefore, there is excess demand for foreign assets, so points below and to the left of FF imply excess demand for F, whereas points above and to the right of FF imply excess supply.

One asset market cannot be in equilibrium if the others are not also in equilibrium. Therefore, the three functions must intersect at a common point. This is point a in Figure 11.4, which implies that short-run asset-market equilibrium is attained at exchange rate e_0 and interest rate i_0. Changes in the equilibrium values of e and i can be analyzed by studying how monetary and fiscal policies, as well as foreign interest-rate changes and the supply of F, shift the various functions. But since the values of the three assets sum to total wealth, a change in i and e that restores equilibrium in two of the markets must automatically also do so for the third market. Therefore, it is sufficient to conduct the analysis of the effects of shocks to the asset markets by using any two of the three curves.

An excess demand for bonds implies that bond prices are too low, so bond prices will rise and interest rates will fall. Similarly, an excess demand for F implies that the price of foreign exchange is too low, so the exchange rate must rise to raise the price of foreign assets. Given these dynamic assumptions, it is essential that the slope of BB be steeper than the slope of FF. If it were not, the asset markets would be dynamically unstable. A stable case is illustrated in Figure 11.4. Assume that i and e are at point h, where the rate of interest is higher than the rate required to put the bond market into equilibrium. Bond prices are therefore lower than their equilibrium values, so point h implies excess demand for bonds. Similarly, at h the exchange rate is below the exchange rate that would put the market for F into equilibrium. Foreign asset prices are therefore below their equilibrium values, implying excess demand for F. The excess demand for B raises bond prices and lowers the rate of interest, and the excess demand for F raises the price of foreign assets, thereby raising the exchange rate. Therefore, the movements of i and e are in the direction of equilibrium, as indicated by the arrows drawn at point h.

Figure 11.5 shows an unstable case. The slope of the FF curve is now assumed to be steeper than the slope of BB. Consequently, point h now implies excess supply in both markets. The excess supply of bonds drives down bond prices and raises interest rates, and the excess supply of foreign assets drives down the price of foreign exchange. The direction of movement of the variables is now such that the disequilibrium widens, as indicated by the arrows drawn at point h.

The stability of the asset markets rests on the requirement that the slope of BB be greater than the slope of FF. This is very likely to occur because the rate of interest is likely to have a relatively more powerful effect in restoring domestic bond market equilibrium, whereas the exchange rate has a relatively more powerful effect in restoring equilibrium in the market for foreign assets. That circumstance—that is, the comparative advantage of the two variables in equilibrating the respective markets—is implied by the slopes of BB and FF. In Figure 11.4 we see that a decline in the exchange rate from point a to b requires a rise in the rate of interest of only bc to restore domestic bond market equilibrium,

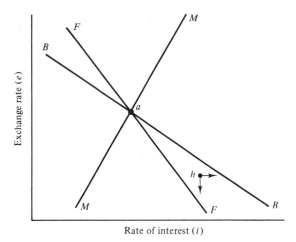

Figure 11.5 Unstable equilibrium in the asset markets.

but a larger rise of *bd* to restore equilibrium in the market for foreign assets.

We can now study the effects of changes in various asset supplies on the equilibrium values of the interest rate and the exchange rate. If the supply of one asset increases while the others are held constant, wealth increases. As asset holders rebalance their portfolios, relative asset prices change. Like the income and substitution effects of the theory of consumer choice, such a rise in wealth will have both wealth and substitution effects, due to relative price changes. When one asset is swapped for another, as when the monetary authority increases *M* by buying *B*, there is no change in wealth. The effects on *i* and *e* are then pure substitution effects. The same goes for an exchange rate stabilization operation when the government buys or sells *F* in exchange for *M*.

Suppose we begin with the effect of expansionary fiscal policy. As explained in the last chapter, if the government finances the deficit by borrowing from the central bank, both *M* and *W* increase by the amount of the deficit. The rise in wealth increases the demand for both *B* and *F*, as wealth holders try to rebalance their portfolios. Excess demand for both *B* and *F* develops. The effects are shown in Figure 11.6. At the existing exchange rate e_0, there is excess demand for foreign assets. A higher exchange rate would be needed to eliminate the excess demand. Therefore the *FF* curve must have shifted up and to the right to FF_1. At the existing rate of interest there is excess demand for domestic bonds. Bond prices would have to be higher and the interest rate lower to eliminate the excess demand. Therefore the *BB* curve must have shifted to the left. The intersection of the BB_1 and FF_1 curves is at point *b* with

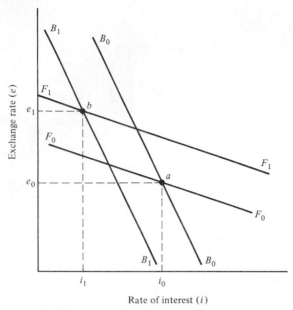

Figure 11.6 Effect of a money-financed government budget deficit ($\Delta M = \Delta W$).

interest rate i_1 and exchange rate e_1. Therefore, a budget deficit financed by money creation lowers the rate of interest and raises the price of foreign exchange.

If the deficit is financed by the sale of bonds to the private sector, B and W increase by the amount of the deficit. The effects are shown in Figure 11.7. The increase in wealth raises the demand for F. Therefore, at the existing exchange rate e_0, there is excess demand for F. Thus higher F prices would be needed to eliminate the excess demand. The FF curve must therefore have shifted upward and to the right. The increase in the supply of B creates excess supply in the market for domestic bonds. Lower bond prices and higher interest rates would be needed to eliminate the excess supply. Therefore, the BB curve must have shifted to the right. The new intersection is at point b, where the rate of interest is higher, but the effect on the exchange rate is ambiguous. The interest rate must rise, since the increase in the supply of B overcomes the increase in the demand for B caused by the positive wealth effect. On the other hand, the increase in wealth tends to raise the demand for F, tending to raise the price of foreign exchange, but the higher rate of interest implies substitution away from F toward B, tending to lower the price of foreign exchange.

Without further information it is not possible to say which of the effects will be dominant, so the effect of the expansionary fiscal policy

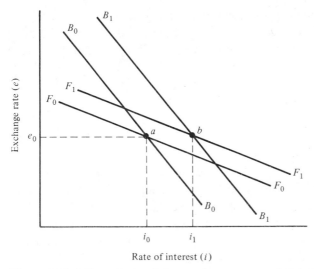

Figure 11.7   Effect of a bond-financed government deficit ($\Delta B = \Delta W$).

on the exchange rate is ambiguous. If domestic and foreign assets are close substitutes, any rise in interest rates will produce a sharp substitution from F to B. In this case the substitution effect will dominate over the wealth effect, and the price of foreign exchange will decline. This is what happened in response to the expansionary fiscal policies of the United States in the 1981–85 period. The dollar appreciated as the price of foreign exchange fell.

Notice that this result is very similar to the results of the Keynesian approach discussed in Chapter 6. An increase in government expenditures that shifted the IS curve to the right tended to improve the capital account because of a higher rate of interest, but the policy caused the current account to deteriorate because of higher income and import demand. When capital was relatively mobile, implying an FB curve flatter than the LM curve, the capital-account effect is dominant, so the incipient surplus appreciated the home currency. Those FB and LM slopes implied that F and B were closer substitutes than B and M, and that is when the asset-market theory also predicts appreciation.

Next let there be a current-account surplus. This disturbs the asset markets by increasing F as foreign IOUs are accumulated. The added F creates excess supply for foreign assets, and since the rise in F initially raises wealth, the wealth increase translates into excess demand for bonds and money. To rebalance portfolios, wealth holders attempt to convert part of their F holdings into B and M. The excess supply of F tends to drive down the price of foreign exchange, so the local currency appreciates. The excess demand for money drives up the rate of interest, and the excess demand for bonds does the opposite. Consequently, an increase in interest rates that would move the money market closer to equilibrium would increase the excess demand for bonds. Therefore, interest-rate changes cannot operate to equilibrate the bond and money markets. However, as long as there is excess demand for bonds and money, there must be excess supply of foreign assets, so the price of foreign exchange continues to decline until the excess supply is eliminated. This occurs when the proportionate appreciation of the currency equals the proportionate increase in F; that is, when $-de/e = dF/F$. At that point the appreciation cancels the wealth effect, and the bond and money markets return to equilibrium at the preexisting rate of interest. We conclude that the accumulation of F implied by a current-account surplus has no effect on the equilibrium rate of interest, and that the local currency appreciates at a rate equal to the proportionate change in F. The result appeals to common sense, since it would be remarkable if a current-account surplus affected the equilibrium interest rate.

When the central bank increases the money supply in the usual manner of purchasing domestic assets, M increases, B declines, and W remains the same. At the existing rate of interest there is excess supply of money and excess demand for bonds. As wealth holders buy bonds, they push up bond prices and lower the rate of interest. This increases the demand for foreign assets and raises the price of foreign exchange. Therefore, an open-market purchase of domestic assets unambiguously lowers the rate of interest and depreciates the local currency. This is shown in Figure 11.8. Since the open-market purchase involves a swap of M for B, the market equilibrium FF curve is unchanged. But the interest rate must be lower to equilibrate the bond and money markets, which implies that the MM and BB curves must have shifted to the left. The new equilibrium is at point b with a lower rate of interest and a higher price of foreign exchange. Expansionary monetary policy therefore causes depreciation of the home currency.

Suppose, instead, that the monetary authority purchases foreign assets from domestic holders to depreciate the local currency. This creates excess supply of M and excess demand for F. Therefore, the rate of interest falls, and the local currency depreciates. In this case BB stays in place, but MM and FF both shift up, as Figure 11.8 also shows.

Comparison of point b in Figure 11.8 with point c shows that for a given shift in MM, the domestic open-market purchase lowers the rate of interest by more, and depreciates the local currency by less, than the open-market purchase of foreign assets. It therefore appears that when domestic and foreign financial assets are imperfect substitutes, the monetary authority can affect the exchange rate without changing the money

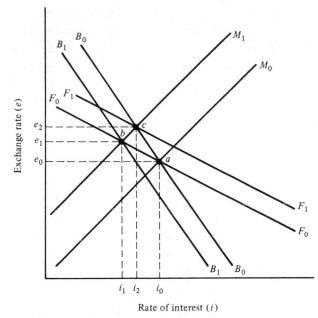

Figure 11.8 Effects of expansionary monetary policy.

supply by a policy of "sterilized intervention," which amounts to a shift in the composition of the central bank's portfolio between domestic and foreign assets that leaves the money supply unchanged.

The results are summarized in Table 11.1, which shows the direction of change of the rate of interest and the exchange rate. Expansionary monetary policy lowers the rate of interest and raises the price of foreign exchange. The interest rate will fall by more in a domestic open-market operation, and the price of foreign exchange will rise by less than it would for an equal change in the money stock brought about by central bank

**TABLE 11.1   EFFECTS OF SHOCKS TO
                         ASSET MARKETS**

	Δi	Δe
Open-market purchases		
Domestic assets ($\Delta M = -\Delta B$)	−	+
Foreign assets ($\Delta M = -e \, \Delta F$)	−	+
Expansionary fiscal policy		
Bond-financed ($\Delta B = \Delta W$)	+	+ or −
Money-financed ($\Delta M = \Delta W$)	−	+
Current-account surplus		
($\Delta W = e \, \Delta F$)	0	−

purchases of foreign assets. Expansionary fiscal policy raises the rate of interest if the deficit is financed by bond sales to the private sector, but the effect on the exchange rate is ambiguous. The higher interest rate lowers the demand for F, but the increase in wealth raises it. If the budget deficit is financed by borrowing from the central bank, the money supply increases and the interest rate declines while the price of foreign exchange rises. A current-account surplus implies a decline in the price of foreign exchange with no change in the rate of interest.

11.4 THE CURRENT ACCOUNT AND LONG-RUN EXCHANGE RATE ADJUSTMENT

Under flexible exchange rates the exchange rate must adjust so that the overall balance of payments is in equilibrium. However, short-run asset-market equilibrium may imply either a deficit or a surplus in the current account balanced by a corresponding surplus or deficit in the capital account. A current-account surplus affects asset markets because it increases the supply of foreign assets held by domestic residents. A current-account deficit does the opposite. Since portfolio balance implies that the stocks of M, B, and F must grow at the same rate, long-run equilibrium necessitates adjustment of the exchange rate so as to eliminate a current-account deficit. Only then will the stock of net foreign assets held by domestic residents remain unchanged, so the exchange rate settles at its long-run equilibrium level.

Suppose the economy enjoys continuing full employment, so the real variables of the economy remain unchanged. Also suppose that at the existing price level and stocks of M, B, and F the short-run equilibrium exchange rate e_0 is below its long-run equilibrium value. The result is a current-account surplus. Foreign assets held by domestic residents accumulate at a rate equal to the current-account surplus. Therefore, we may write the current surplus as

$$\Delta F = X\left(\frac{ep^*}{p}\right) - V\left(Y_f, \frac{ep^*}{p}\right) + i^*F$$

where i^*F is net income from foreign investment.

If the exchange rate is to approach a stable long-run equilibrium value, ΔF must diminish through time. The increase in F causes wealth holders to respond by selling foreign assets, so the local currency tends to appreciate. This reduces exports and raises imports, thereby reducing net exports and the rate of accumulation of F. But as F increases, investment income i^*F increases, and this tends to widen the surplus increasing ΔF. Approach to a stable long-run equilibrium necessitates that the trade effects of appreciation overcome the investment income effect of continued F accumulation. If investment income rises faster than the reduction in net exports, the current-account surplus widens and the rate of appreciation will accelerate.

In the final equilibrium we must have

$$\Delta F = 0 = X\left(\frac{ep^*}{p}\right) - V\left(Y_f, \frac{ep^*}{p}\right) + i^*F$$

With a large amount of income from foreign investment, the country can enjoy a permanent trade deficit, the excess of imports over exports being offset by investment income. The country will also enjoy an improvement in its terms of trade, since the real value of its currency will be higher the greater its income from foreign investment. Finally, the amount of investment income i^*F will increase as the long-run equilibrium exchange rate to be reached increases. Consequently, as noted by William Branson,

> ... the long-run equilibrium value of the exchange rate is partially determined by the adjustment process itself; as F changes, so does investment income. The final value for e is the one that yields a trade balance that just offsets the final value of investment income.[4]

It can be seen, then, that a country with a large amount of net investment income from foreign assets will enjoy a higher standard of living because its net exports will be lower and because this allows it to be less competitive than countries with less (or negative) investment income. Its real price of foreign exchange will be lower, and it therefore enjoys favorable terms of trade. These facts are a major reason why the U.S. current-account deficits of 1981–86 have given rise to so much concern. As the United States moves from a net creditor to a net debtor nation, net investment income declines, implying that the dollar must ultimately depreciate to a level that imposes less favorable terms of trade than it enjoyed prior to the appreciation, which began in 1980. As the United States becomes a major debtor nation, it will ultimately have to export more than it imports, and it will have to do this with unfavorable terms of trade.

The adjustment process implied by the asset-market theory may be depicted as follows. A disturbance to asset markets such as might be brought about by expansionary domestic open-market policy has an immediate pronounced effect on the rate of interest and the exchange rate.

[4] Branson, W. H., "Asset Markets and Relative Prices in Exchange Rate Determination," *Socialwissentschaftliche Annalen,* 1977, p. 82.

This, together with investment income i^*F, determines the current-account surplus. The surplus equals the rate of accumulation of foreign assets, ΔF, which then feeds back into the asset markets, having the effect of appreciating the local currency if ΔF is positive:

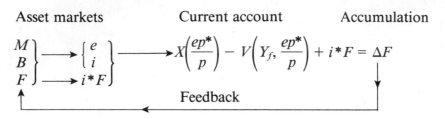

$$\text{Asset markets} \qquad\qquad \text{Current account} \qquad\qquad \text{Accumulation}$$

$$\left.\begin{array}{l} M \\ B \\ F \end{array}\right\} \longrightarrow \left.\begin{array}{l} e \\ i \end{array}\right\} \longrightarrow X\!\left(\frac{ep^*}{p}\right) - V\!\left(Y_f, \frac{ep^*}{p}\right) + i^*F = \Delta F$$

$$\uparrow \qquad\qquad\qquad\qquad\qquad\qquad \text{Feedback}$$

As a final step, it is important to relinquish the assumption that the price level is constant. However, to isolate the effect of price-level adjustment, we assume that Y is at its full-employment value Y_f and that i^* and p^* remain unchanged. The latter imply a small-country assumption. It is also helpful to assume that in the initial situation investment income is zero and that net exports also equal zero, so the current account is in balance. Assume that the monetary authority expands the money stock by purchasing domestic assets. The monetary policy has the immediate effect of lowering the rate of interest and causing a sharp increase in the price of foreign exchange. Consider Figure 11.9 and assume that initially $p_0 = e_0 = 1$. Then let an expansionary monetary shock raise the price of foreign exchange to e_1 at t_1.

In the long run the increase in the money supply raises the price level in proportion to the increase in the money stock. Let this rise in the price level be to p_1 in Figure 11.9. If net exports are to return to their

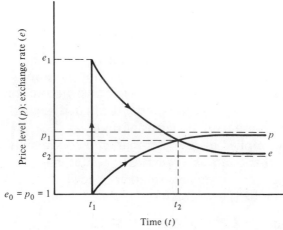

Figure 11.9 Long-run adjustment of the price level and exchange rate.

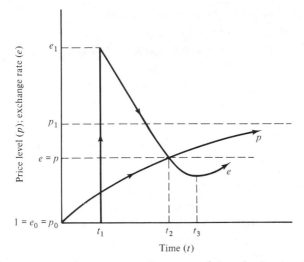

Figure 11.10 Long-run adjustment of the price level and exchange rate with slow price-level adjustment.

initial value of zero, the nominal price of foreign exchange must rise in proportion to the rise in the price level. Therefore, the first approximation of the long-run behavior of the exchange rate is that it will follow the price level, so $\Delta e/e = \Delta p/p$.

However, this outcome ignores the effect of investment income. The initial depreciation causes an export surplus, so F accumulates and investment income rises. If the currency depreciates in exact proportion to the rise in the price level, net exports would return to zero. But due to the intervening export surplus, investment income is higher; hence there would be a current-account surplus when net exports return to zero. Consequently, accumulation of foreign assets continues, and the local currency continues to appreciate. Thus the nominal price of foreign exchange must fall by more than the proportionate rise in the price level to restore current-account equilibrium. Let this final exchange rate be e_2 in Figure 11.9. When the path of the declining price of foreign exchange crosses the rising price level path (at t_2), p will equal e, so $e/p = 1$, as in the initial situation. Net exports will therefore be at their original level. However, positive investment income implies a current-account surplus, so the price of foreign exchange continues to decline. Therefore, the path of the nominal exchange rate crosses the price-level path, yielding a long-run equilibrium characterized by a lower *real* exchange rate. The real price of foreign exchange is therefore permanently reduced.

If the price level adjusts slowly local currency appreciation will eliminate the current-account surplus at a time when the price level is still rising. Because of the continuing rise in the price level, net exports then decline, so the current account swings into deficit and the local currency then depreciates. In Figure 11.10 the intersection of p with e is at time t_2. Thereafter, the local currency continues to appreciate because of the continuing current-account surplus due to investment income. At t_3 the current account is balanced. But since the price level is still rising, the country's competitive position continues to deteriorate, so the current account moves into deficit. Therefore, after t_3 the local currency once again depreciates.

Once again we see that it is the sluggish price-level responses, relative to the speed of asset-market responses, that are responsible for exchange rate overshooting. Initially the currency depreciates sharply as the result of the monetary shock. It then appreciates in response to the current-account surplus, and it then depreciates once more as the consequence of the ongoing increase in the price level.

QUESTIONS FOR REVIEW

1. What are the implications of the modern theory of portfolio choice for the demand for money? How does this theory provide the basis for an asset-market theory of exchange rate determination? Why are domestic and foreign assets imperfect substitutes? Why are bonds and money imperfect substitutes? What is the effect of a rise in wealth on the demand for various financial assets?

2. If the demand for money, domestic bonds, and foreign bonds are functions of the exchange rate and the rate of interest, what happens to
   a. the rate of interest that maintains money market equilibrium following a rise in the exchange rate? (Why is MM positively sloped?)
   b. the rate of interest that maintains bond market equilibrium following a rise in the exchange rate? (Why is BB negatively sloped?)
   c. the exchange rate that maintains equilibrium in the market for foreign assets following a rise in the rate of interest? (Why is FF negatively sloped?)

3. Why must the BB curve be more steeply sloped than the FF curve? What is the common-sense explanation for this?

4. What is the effect of a current-account surplus on the exchange rate and the rate of interest? Why is it not possible for a change in the rate of interest to produce equilibrium in the bond and money markets?

5. What is the effect of an open-market purchase by the monetary authority on the exchange rate and the rate of interest?

6. What is the effect of an open-market purchase of foreign assets on the exchange rate and the rate of interest? In what ways are the effects similar, and in what ways do they differ from those in Question 5?

7. If the government finances an increase in spending by selling bonds to the private sector, what happens to the rate of interest and the exchange rate? Why is the effect on the exchange rate ambiguous?

8. Taking both short- and longer-range effects into account, what is the time-path of the exchange rate apt to look like following an expansionary monetary shock? Will the real exchange rate be different at the new equilibrium? Will the exchange rate reach a new equilibrium?

9. What will happen to the real exchange rate in the long run? In what ways do countries benefit from asset accumulation?

SUGGESTIONS FOR FURTHER READING

Branson, William, H., "Asset Markets and Relative Prices in Exchange-Rate Determination," *Socialwissenshaftliche Annalen,* 1977.

Branson, William H., *Financial Capital Flows in the United States Balance of Payments,* North-Holland, 1968.

Johnson, H. G., and Jacob Frenkel, *The Economics of Exchange Rates,* Addison-Wesley, 1978.

Markowitz, Harry P., "Portfolio Selection," *Journal of Finance,* May 1952.

Tobin, James, "Liquidity Preference as Behavior Towards Risk," *Review of Economic Studies,* February 1958.

Chapter 12

External and Internal Balance and the Theory of Economic Policy

12.1 THE STATIC THEORY OF ECONOMIC POLICY

In Part Four we turn to the appraisal of institutional and policy issues in relation to the international monetary system. Before we turn to those issues, it is important to take one more step; we need to adapt our theoretical apparatus to the systematic organization of economic policies. Such systematic organization is often called the theory of economic policy. The Dutch Nobel laureate Jan Tinbergen is credited with introducing the approach. Many other economists have contributed to its development, and the Canadian economist Robert A. Mundell has been most instrumental in providing fertile applications to international macroeconomic issues.[1]

The theory of economic policy represents a *normative* approach to macroeconomics, as opposed to a *positive* approach. A question of positive macroeconomics would be to ask how much a $50 billion tax increase will lower employment and prices, and how the policy will affect the exchange rate. These are issues of cause, effect, and measurement. The approach does not ask if the resulting changes are desirable or undesirable. The normative theory of economic policy turns the question around. It begins by establishing normative *target* values for employment, prices, and the exchange rate, and it then asks what kind of policy changes are needed if the targets are to be achieved.

---

[1] Tinbergen, Jan, *Economic Policy: Principles and Design,* North-Holland Amsterdam, 1956. Many of Mundell's papers on international macroeconomic issues are collected in his volume *International Economics,* Macmillan, 1968. See especially chaps. 11, 14, 15, and 19–21.

The static theory of economic policy suggests that if there are two targets of policy, there must be at least two independently effective *instruments* of policy available if the targets are to be achieved. This idea, that there must be at least as many policy instruments as there are targets, is *Tinbergen's rule*. A two-target case illustrates the rule. Suppose internal and external balance depend on government purchases, G, and the money supply, m_s, in linear relationships, so

$$Y^* = a_{11}G + a_{12}m_s$$

$$B^* = a_{21}G + a_{22}m_s \qquad (12.1)$$

where Y^* and B^* are the target income and balance-of-payments outcomes, respectively. The a_{ij} coefficients are the multipliers. Two targets imply two equations, and a solution necessitates two instruments of policy.

If we have only one instrument, we might have

$$Y^* = a_{11}G$$

$$B^* = a_{21}G$$

We could achieve Y^* or B^* by varying G, but we cannot achieve both targets simultaneously except by accident. Thus a second instrument is needed. Adding a second instrument may not, however, be sufficient unless the second instrument is *independently effective*. If we raise m_s and simultaneously lower G to offset the inflationary effect of the rise in m_s, and if these changes, in conjunction, have no effect on the balance of payments, the two instruments are interchangeable and nothing is gained by adding the second instrument. Put differently, the instruments are not independently effective if the rate at which government purchases must be substituted to compensate for the employment loss caused by a reduction in the money supply is the same as the rate of substitution of G for m_s needed to maintain external balance. In (12.1) this situation implies that the ratio of multipliers a_{11}/a_{12} equals a_{21}/a_{22}. When this is the case, the equations cannot be solved simultaneously for G and m_s.[2]

As a general rule, it is desirable to deal with problems at their source. If aggregate expenditure is deficient or excessive, policy should attempt

---

[2] Recall the discussion of matrix inversion in the appendix to Chapter 4. If the coefficient matrix is

$$\begin{bmatrix} a_{11} & a_{12} \\ a_{21} & a_{22} \end{bmatrix}$$

its determinant equals $a_{11}a_{22} - a_{12}a_{21}$. But if $a_{11}/a_{12} = a_{21}/a_{22}$, it follows that $a_{11}a_{22} = a_{12}a_{21}$; thus the determinant is zero, and the matrix is singular. This means it cannot be inverted, and the simultaneous equations cannot be solved.

to offset the deficiency or the excess with a demand-management response. If a shock to the economy comes from the supply side, effective policy indicates the need for an offsetting supply response. When oil prices were raised in 1974, it acted as a massive restriction in aggregate supply. As a consequence of the higher oil prices, general price levels rose sharply in industrial countries. The purchasing-power drain caused by the higher-priced oil and by unindexed personal income-tax structures contributed to aggregate expenditure reduction. The net effect was stagflation, that is, a situation in which both inflation and unemployment were rising simultaneously. In the United States the initial policy response was to attempt to contain inflation as the Federal Reserve tightened monetary policy, and President Gerald Ford's administration held back government spending and permitted the structural budget surplus to increase.[3] The policy response added to the restrictive forces that were already pushing the economy into a severe recession. In attempting to stabilize prices through demand restriction, the policy worsened the employment problem.

A constructive approach would have recognized that the oil shock was supply side in origin. Restrictive aggregate demand policy could not deal effectively with the problem because a restrictive response designed to slow inflation worsened recession, whereas an expansionary policy designed to raise employment would have worsened inflation. Regrettably, no effective short-run supply-side remedy seemed available at the time. With hindsight it can be said that prior establishment of a stockpile of oil for use in such emergencies would have eased the shock, as would the prior existence of a variable oil tariff that could have been reduced in order to offset partially the higher price of oil. Professor Morris Adelman of MIT suggested the United States fight fire with fire by organizing oil importers into a monopsony that would agree to purchase oil only through sealed bids. That would provide individual OPEC countries with an incentive to undercut the cartel price, thereby helping to defang OPEC. However, President Nixon was so absorbed with his Watergate travails that no effective response to OPEC was attempted.

Extreme care must be exercised in the selection of policy targets. The scarcity of effective instruments renders economy in the selection of targets essential. Care must be exercised not to treat a potential instrument as a target. Converting an instrument into a target spells a double loss because it expands the number of targets and simultaneously reduces the number of instruments. Worse, the choice of a particular economic mag-

---

[3] President Ford advertised his anti-inflation priorities by wearing a "Whip Inflation Now" (WIN) button on his lapel. When turned upside down the button was said to stand for "No Immediate Miracles." Some of the president's detractors said it stood for "Nothing In Mind."

nitude as a target may create instability and be inconsistent with the attainment of other primary targets.

Presumably the relevant targets for macroeconomic policy are external and internal balance. External balance means balance in the current account with allowance for long-term capital movements. Internal balance means reasonable full employment without excessive inflation. The word "reasonable" is important. For example, the goal of zero unemployment is unrealistic. Unemployment rates below 3 percent of the labor force have only been achieved in the United States during periods of national emergency. When the unemployment rate is pushed too low, wage rates begin to rise more rapidly than productivity growth, unit labor costs increase, and price inflation ensues. During the early 1960s President John F. Kennedy's Council of Economic Advisers (CEA) established a 4 percent unemployment rate as an "interim" target. Subsequent experience suggested that 4 percent unemployment would be incompatible with price stability, so the target or benchmark unemployment rate has gradually been raised. Today the Congressional Budget Office takes a 6 percent unemployment rate as the basis for its structural budget calculations, and the CEA in its February 1984 *Economic Report* suggested that the benchmark unemployment rate may be as high as 6.5 percent.[4]

Similarly it is widely believed that to rid an economy of inflation entirely would require that the economy be restrained to such low levels of employment and capital utilization as to be socially unacceptable. It has been shown that in the United States a price crawl of 2 to 3 percent is likely to occur simply because of the difficulty of appropriately allowing for increases in productivity and product quality in the computation of the price indexes used to measure inflation.

Irrelevant targets are harmful because they interfere with the attainment of the primary external-internal balance targets. For example, there is evidence that the Federal Reserve has had a historical preference for stable interest rates. But targeting interest rates for their own sake is destabilizing. Suppose there is a negative shift in consumer sentiment that lowers consumption and therefore raises unemployment. Since the demand for money and credit declines, interest rates tend to fall. If the Federal Reserve is committed to preventing such a decline in interest rates, it must sell government securities, thereby pursuing a restrictive monetary policy when instead it should attempt to prevent the decline in the economy with an expansionary policy. Designation of an interest-rate target is inconsistent with the use of money supply growth as a policy instrument with which to deal with, say, inflation, because the money

[4] Congressional Budget Office, *The Economic Outlook,* February 1984, *Economic Report of the President,* February 1984.

supply growth rate appropriate to curb inflation may not maintain the desired level of interest rates. Furthermore, and as explained in Chapter 6, interest-rate targeting is likely to be incompatible with a macroeconomic policy program that attempts to change national income without transmitting major shocks to other economies.

Recent years have witnessed the growth of support for proposals designed to constrain the federal budget in the United States. Proposals have been introduced that would limit taxes and spending to a maximum percentage of GNP, to require annual budgetary balance, or to move toward budgetary balance within a specified time. The latter policy was adopted by Congress in the form of the Gramm-Rudman deficit reduction act that requires budgetary balance to be achieved by fiscal year 1991. Although there are good reasons for wishing to get the budget under better control, most economists are nevertheless nervous about mechanical budget rules, because such rules are generally incompatible with the use of fiscal policy as an instrument of stabilization policy. For example, it is known that a slump in the economy automatically creates a budget deficit because tax receipts decline while transfer outlays, especially on unemployment compensation, increase. These so-called "automatic" or "built-in" stabilizers help to cushion the decline in the economy. However, if the budget deficit is not permitted to increase, the additional deficit caused by recession would have to be offset by tax increases and/or expenditure reductions that further extinguish purchasing power and worsen the recession. Thus, targeting the budget deficit comes at the price of the destabilization of income and employment, and it is therefore incompatible with the internal balance target.

From the perspective of the theory of economic policy, the fixed exchange-rate system carried with it the severe liability that, by targeting the exchange rate, the system robbed countries of the use of monetary policy as an instrument available for use in securing internal balance. Deficits implied shrinking money supplies with deflationary effects, and surpluses implied growing money supplies with inflationary effects. The problem was particularly acute for countries that suffered from both recession and a balance-of-payments deficit simultaneously. To prevent its currency from depreciating, the monetary authority was obliged to sell foreign exchange, thereby causing its own money supply to shrink and worsening the recession.

Sometimes a fairly innocent and reasonable proposal is seen to be harmful and destabilizating when subjected to analytical scrutiny. For example, many countries have treated their foreign exchange reserves as policy targets. The IMF implicitly supports such targeting in its dealings with potential borrowers, and the United States supported such targeting during the international monetary reform negotiations of 1972–74. Suppose a country has been suffering a balance-of-payments deficit and that its reserves are depleted. Suppose, also, that policy has brought about the elimination of the deficit by the use of restrictive monetary-fiscal policies that have slowed the economy. If the restoration of balance-of-payments equilibrium finds the country with depleted reserves, a reserve target forces additional contraction in the economy; thus, the balance of payments can swing into surplus, and reserves can be accumulated. Then, once reserves are restored to their target level, policy turns expansionary, thereby once again inflating the economy and again overshooting balance-of-payments equilibrium, since reserves accumulate as long as the surplus lasts. It can be seen therefore that targeting of policy toward the attainment of a foreign exchange target has dangerous implications for the overall stability of an economy.[5]

Regrettably this sort of thing goes on much of the time. Debtor countries that must meet large annual interest obligations are forced to target their reserves. It is hardly surprising that the goal of internal balance is severely compromised in the process.

In the sections that follow we examine the dynamic issues raised by the quest for an efficient adjustment path in response to changes in policy instrument values. Among the questions that might be asked are the following:

1. How should policy instruments proceed when some of them are in conflict or dilemma states? That is, what is an orderly policy response when the movement of a particular policy instrument in the direction of attaining one target causes the economy to move farther away from another target? We have already discussed this question in Chapter 9, but more needs to be added.
2. Should all policy instruments aim for all targets simultaneously, or should certain instruments of policy be *assigned* to certain specific targets? If so, what is *correct assignment?* What are the consequences of incorrect assignment?
3. What is the most efficient adjustment path toward the policy targets? Should policy attempt to reach its targets quickly by one-time adjustment of instrument variables, or does this risk overshooting with the consequent need for reversal and the unflattering characterization of policy as stop-and-go.

[5] Mundell, Robert A., "The Monetary Dynamics of International Adjustment Under Fixed and Flexible Exchange Rates," *Quarterly Journal of Economics,* May 1960. Reprinted in Mundell, *International Economics.*

4. Should policy attempt more or less *continuous* adjustments, or should policy adjustment be taken in *discrete* steps? If fiscal policy can only be taken in discrete steps, does this create a bias in favor of monetary policy that can be adjusted continuously? Does this favor flexible exchange rates that vary continuously, as opposed to adjustable fixed exchange rates that are only changed occasionally in discrete jumps?

12.2 MUNDELL'S ANALYSIS OF FIXED EXCHANGE RATES AND THE MONETARY-FISCAL MIX

The United States economy entered the 1960s mired in recession and an eight-year history of subpar economic growth. It also entered the decade with a balance of payments that was in deficit thanks primarily to persistently large capital outflows, as U.S. industry invested in foreign subsidiaries and U.S. investors bought foreign earning assets.

In 1962 Robert A. Mundell, then of the staff of the IMF, published a short but ingenious and influential paper that pointed the way to a resolution of the problem facing the United States.[6] Mundell's resolution rested on the important fact that expansionary fiscal policies tend to raise interest rates, whereas expansionary monetary policies lower them. As a result, the monetary and fiscal instruments were seen to be *independently effective* with respect to their influence on employment and the balance of payments.

We can easily guess at the outcome after having studied Chapter 6. There we saw that monetary policy has a tough time changing the level of income under fixed exchange rates. Therefore, with a certain degree of hindsight, we can guess that the solution to the deficit-recession problem will amount to a change in the monetary-fiscal mix that combines expansionary fiscal policy to raise employment with restrictive monetary policy to improve the balance of payments. Mundell's approach is from the perspective of the theory of economic policy, which is our concern in this chapter, and the analysis raises the issue of changes in the policy *mix,* so it is well worth considering in some detail.

When the money supply is increased and the budget deficit is increased, macroeconomic policy is said to be expansionary. When the

---

[6] Mundell, Robert A., "The Appropriate Use of Monetary and Fiscal Policy Under Fixed Exchange Rates," International Monetary Fund, *Staff Papers,* March 1962. Reprinted in Mundell, *International Economics.*

opposite happens, it is restrictive. But when the change in fiscal policy tends to raise national income, whereas the change in monetary policy tends to lower it, we call that a change in the policy mix. Such changes are usually viewed with suspicion by the uninitiated, since it seems as if the policies are merely working at cross-purposes. It is therefore very important to understand the various ways in which changes in the policy mix can be beneficial. The potential for such benefits arises when instruments are independently effective. If they are not, mix changes produce little except confusion.

Consider Figure 12.1. The fiscal instrument is government purchases, G, measured on the vertical axis. The monetary instrument is the money supply, m_s, measured horizontally. In Mundell's paper the two instrument variables were the budget deficit and the rate of interest, respectively, but G and m_s will do just as well—in fact, better because the interest rate and the budget deficit are not really autonomous instrument variables, since both are endogenous, varying with the level of income.

Let the economy be at point a in Figure 12.1, where point a provides full employment. Then let m_s be reduced to reach point b. The deflationary effect of this reduction in the money supply on national income can be offset by a rise in G so as to reach point c. Point c is therefore another point of internal balance. It follows that the internal balance

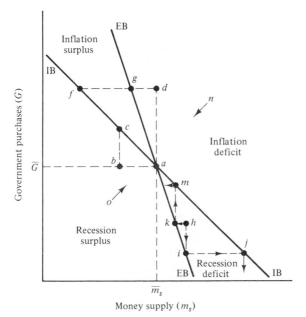

Figure 12.1 Mundell's analysis of monetary and fiscal policy assignment under fixed exchange rates.

curve is a negatively sloped function, such as IB in Figure 12.1. A lower money supply can be offset by a higher level of government purchases, and vice versa. At points below and to the left of IB, the money supply and government purchases are both too low to prevent recession; above and to the right they are too high to prevent inflation.

Now go back to point a to study external balance, where external balance now means equilibrium in the *overall* balance of payments, including both the current and the capital accounts. Assume that the balance of payments is in equilibrium at point a. Then let government purchases rise to reach point d. The rise in G raises income and causes deterioration of the current account by raising imports. However, the rise in G also raises the rate of interest and improves the capital account. Point d could imply a surplus in the balance of payments if capital is relatively mobile in the sense of Chapters 5 and 6. However, Mundell assumed a relatively immobile case, so, following his assumption, we stipulate that the negative current-account effect dominates the positive capital-account effect and that point d therefore implies a deficit in the balance of payments.

To eliminate the deficit, monetary policy becomes restrictive. Suppose the restriction carries the economy to point f on the IB curve. At point f national income is the same as at a. Consequently, the level of imports is the same, and therefore so is the current account. But at point f the money supply is lower, and government purchases are higher than at a. Both of these changes raise the rate of interest. Therefore, there must be a larger capital inflow at point f than there was at point a. If at point a the overall balance of payments was in equilibrium, it must be in surplus at f because of the greater capital inflow. It follows that some *lesser* reduction in the money supply, perhaps to point g, would have been sufficient to restore balance-of-payments equilibrium. Consequently, the EB curve is the more steeply sloped curve that passes through points a and g.

The EB curve specifies the combinations of G and m_s that keep the balance of payments in equilibrium. A high level of G and a low level of m_s, such as at point g, implies a capital-account surplus matched by a current-account deficit. At point i, on the other hand, the low level of G and high level of m_s imply a low rate of interest. Therefore, there is a capital-account deficit matched by a current-account surplus. To the left of the EB curve G and m_s, in combination, are too low to prevent a balance-of-payments surplus, and to the right of the EB curve they are, in combination, too high to prevent a deficit.

Now assume that the economy suffers from a deficit and a recession, as at point h. If fiscal policy makes the mistake of attempting to eliminate the deficit by moving to point i, the recession gets worse. If monetary policy responds by expanding the money supply to reach point j on IB, the recession is eliminated but the deficit is worse than before. These responses are destabilizing as each round of policy adjustment carries the economy southeastward with an ever-expanding money supply, an ever-declining level of government purchases, and a worsening of both the deficit and the recession.

The difficulty lies in the fact that the respective policy instruments have aimed for the wrong target. This is said to be a *misassignment* of instruments to targets. Correct assignment requires monetary policy to respond to the balance of payments and fiscal policy to the needs of the domestic economy. Monetary policy would reduce the money supply to reach point k, which eliminates the deficit but worsens the recession. Fiscal policy then responds by raising G to reach point m, which eliminates the recession but edges the balance of payments back into deficit, but this new deficit is now less than before. Clearly, if this sequence of steps is continued, point a will be approached where both internal and external balance are attained.

Correct assignment is implied by the slopes of the target functions. These slopes are the ratios of the multipliers of (12.1). For a given reduction in m_s, the increase in G that offsets the deflationary effects of the reduction in m_s is less than the change that would be required to offset the balance-of-payments effect. Therefore monetary policy enjoys a comparative advantage in coping with the balance of payments, whereas fiscal policy enjoys a comparative advantage in coping with the domestic economy. This conclusion is much the same as the conclusion reached in Chapter 6.

If the economy suffers from both inflation and a deficit, as at point n, it is appropriate for both fiscal and monetary policy to become more restrictive, as indicated by the arrow at n. If the economy suffers from recession but enjoys a surplus, both policies should become more expansionary, as indicated by the arrow at o. But if there is a recession combined with a deficit, a mix change is called for implying an expansionary fiscal policy combined with a restrictive monetary policy. Finally, if the economy suffers inflation but enjoys a balance-of-payments surplus, it should change the mix by lowering G to slow inflation and increasing m_s to eliminate the surplus.

Point a in Figure 12.1 is the only really satisfactory outcome. There is only one combination of G and m_s that achieves both the internal and the external balance targets. Consequently, it can be seen that fiscal and monetary policies may not be used interchangeably to suit convenience or ideological preference. Fiscal policy, for example, is often criticized for being cumbersome and difficult to time correctly, whereas monetary policy can be changed easily. And traditionally, conservatives have shunned fiscal policy because it invites budget deficits and "irresponsible" government spending. However, if there is more than one target for stabilization policy, the luxury of avoiding fiscal changes cannot be afforded. The solution, perhaps, is to improve the flexibility and timing of fiscal policy rather than to discard the instrument.

It is regrettable that many American economists have put so much energy into a dreary and seemingly endless debate that pits fiscal policy against monetary policy. The theory of economic policy teaches that these instruments should be viewed as complementary arms of macroeconomic policy rather than as mutually exclusive competitors. That is also the message of Chapter 6, which showed that destabilizing capital movements could be avoided if fiscal and monetary policies were properly coordinated.

The question, however, remains whether the easy fiscal–tight money mix of policy is a solution for a country suffering recession and a balance-of-payments deficit. If capital is highly mobile, it may be impossible, except temporarily, to change the money supply and manipulate interest rates. Even when possible, raising interest rates to attract a capital inflow is likely to be harmful to the country's growth prospects, since higher interest rates tend to crowd out investment. Certainly the tight money–easy fiscal mix that characterized U.S. policy in the 1980–84 period has been roundly criticized for just that reason. Among the critics are Martin Feldstein and Alan Greenspan, both former Chairmen of the Council of Economic Advisers under Republican Presidents, Paul Volcker, former Chairman of the Federal Reserve Board, and James Tobin, a Nobel laureate and a member of the Council of Economic Advisers under President John F. Kennedy. Tobin has long argued that slow productivity growth in the United States relative to productivity growth in such countries as Germany and Japan reflects a tendency for the U.S. economy to save and invest an inadequate fraction of national product. The capital stock is viewed as too small and not sufficiently modern. Therefore Tobin favors a policy mix of more restrictive fiscal policy combined with a more generous monetary policy, which, in combination, would lower interest rates and promote a higher level of investment spending.[7]

Promoting a capital inflow by raising interest rates is at best a short-run expedient. As we learned from the asset-market analysis of the foreign exchange market, a one-time rise in domestic interest rates will attract a capital inflow that, however, diminishes with time as portfolios are ad-

---

[7] Tobin, James, "Stabilization Policy Ten Years After," *Brookings Papers on Economic Activity,* 11, 1980.

justed. After a while a country may have higher interest rates without any capital inflow. It will then be worse off than before, having a deficit in its balance of payments combined with the liability of higher interest rates.

In Chapter 6 it was suggested that monetary policy should be combined with fiscal policy in a manner that prevents major changes in short-run capital movements rather than in a manner that deliberately induces such movements. If monetary-fiscal policy is coordinated in the manner proposed in Chapter 6, and the country suffers a balance-of-payments deficit, then the message of the theory of economic policy is clear. Another policy instrument is needed, which, in this case, is quite obviously adjustment of the exchange rate.

Finally, manipulation of interest rates to attract short-run capital is not exactly a neighborly thing to do. A country that eliminates a deficit by inducing a capital inflow merely transfers the deficit to those who suffer a capital outflow. Other countries, whose current accounts may be quite strong, nevertheless suffer all of the disadvantages that go with a deficit in the balance of payments. These countries can be expected to retaliate in kind. If, then, all countries ease their budgets and tighten up their monetary policies, the end result will be a worldwide escalation of interest rates and a slowing of world economic growth. The country, or countries, that initiated the escalation by using policy to manipulate the capital account will then find their payments deficits continuing. All things considered, therefore, it hardly seems as if it pays to play this game.

12.3 DISCRETE POLICY ADJUSTMENT AND THE PROBLEM OF OVERSHOOTING

Policy adjustment is rarely smooth or continuous. Monetary policy is capable of being continuously adjusted, but a smooth road to equilibrium is not always possible because the effects of monetary policy are not entirely predictable, due to changes in velocity and variable lags in the impact of monetary policy. Fiscal policies, such as tax changes, tend to bite with a one-time impact, and it is difficult and embarrassing to reverse a fiscal decision on short notice. In the United States income taxes were reduced in early 1964. By the middle of 1965 the escalation of the Vietnam War had created the need for a tax increase. However, President Lyndon Johnson resisted the advice to raise taxes, in part because taxes had been lowered only recently. Under the adjustable peg Bretton Woods system, exchange rate adjustments often occurred long after the need for such adjustment was necessary, and, when the devaluations occurred, the changes in official currency prices were sometimes needlessly large.

Policy changes are therefore frequently stepwise or discrete rather than continuous. Such discrete adjustments carry with them the danger that the policy change will be inadequate to the task, or that it will be too powerful and cause the target variables to overshoot the mark, or that it risks dynamic instability, whereas continuous adjustment does not. Critics will denounce discrete policies as "stop-and-go," and the opposition party will gather ammunition for use against the incumbent government at the next election.

This section briefly considers some additional issues raised by discrete, or discontinuous, adjustment. Systematic analysis of such policy adjustment introduces a new mathematical topic in the form of *difference* equations, which are explained in the first chapter appendix. The second appendix derives the stability conditions, and therefore the correct assignment, for the analysis of this section.

To illustrate the problems raised by discrete or stepwise adjustment, we return to the external-internal balance model introduced in Chapters 2 and 9. Figure 12.2 shows the EB and IB curves with the economy at point *a* suffering recession with its current account in balance. The assignment of absorption to internal balance produces an absorption policy change that lands the economy at point *b*. This eliminates the recession but causes a deficit. Therefore, the exchange rate is devalued, so the economy moves to point *c*. This eliminates the deficit but now puts the economy in the inflation zone; hence, it now becomes necessary to reduce absorption to point *d*. The adjustment is stable, producing progressively smaller necessary policy changes, but it is costly and inefficient because

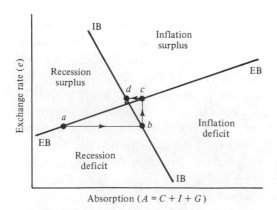

Figure 12.2 Discrete adjustment: stable.

it implies overshooting and the need for policy reversal, even though the individual policy changes hit their respective targets accurately.

The situation is worse in Figure 12.3. It differs from Figure 12.2 in that the EB curve now is steeper than the IB curve. With continuous adjustment, this change in the slopes would create no problems and the adjustment would be stable, as noted in the next section. But with discrete adjustment, the assignment becomes unstable. Starting again at point *a*, absorption is raised to reach *b*. This eliminates recession but causes a deficit. Therefore, the price of foreign exchange is raised to reach point *c*, which rids the economy of the deficit but creates inflation. The inflation can then be eliminated by a reduction in absorption to point *d*, which creates a surplus, so the price of foreign exchange must be lowered to point *f*. This puts the economy roughly where it started (at *a*) but with a recession that is worse than the initial recession. If the sequence is continued, policies will oscillate back and forth and the economy will suffer ever-wider swings of recession and inflation, and deficits and surpluses. The assignment has become incorrect because of the flattening of the IB curve relative to the EB curve, since this change in the slopes of the functions implies that absorption has a relatively more powerful effect on external balance, whereas exchange rate policy is more powerful in offsetting internal balance. If the *absolute value* of the slope of IB is greater than the absolute value of the slope of EB, correct assignment requires absorption to target IB and exchange rate policy to target EB. But if EB has a larger slope than IB in terms of absolute value, the assignment must be switched.

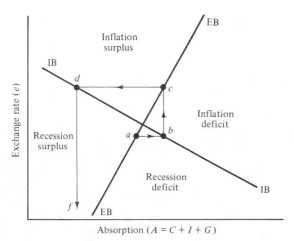

Figure 12.3 Discrete adjustment: unstable.

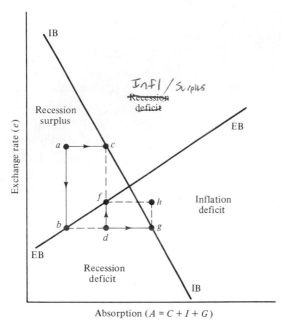

Figure 12.4   Simultaneous discrete adjustment: stable.

Correct assignment is not sufficient to produce a satisfactory adjustment path. Figure 12.4 is the same as Figure 12.2, except that the beginning point, *a,* is in the recession-surplus zone. The price of foreign exchange is lowered to aim for *b* on the EB curve while absorption is raised in an effort to reach point *c* on the IB curve. In combination, the two policy changes miss both targets because the economy lands at point *d* with a recession and a deficit. This leads to a rise in absorption to reach point *g* and a devaluation to reach point *f*. Subsequently, the combined policies put the economy at point *h* in the inflation-deficit zone. If these policy sequences keep up, all four of the zones will be entered in a counterclockwise manner and the economy will be back in the recession-surplus zone after four rounds of policy adjustment. The adjustments are stable because IB is steeper than EB, so equilibrium is approached. But it is a costly way to conduct policy.

Figure 12.5 shows the IB curve with a positive slope. This could occur if Y_e is positive; that is, a rise in price of foreign exchange reduces absorption and national income. Here assignment of absorption to IB and the exchange rate to EB is correct, provided the IB curve is more steeply sloped than the EB curve. From point *a* absorption is raised to eliminate recession at point *b*. This causes a deficit, which can be eliminated by devaluing to point *c*. This is deflationary, but the recession is

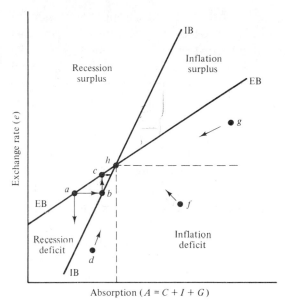

Figure 12.5 Sequential adjustment: stable.

now less severe than it was at *a*. Incorrect assignment would have called for a fall in the price of foreign exchange from point *a* to attempt to reach IB, as shown by the downward arrow drawn at *a*.

The difficulties caused by discrete adjustment aimed directly at individual targets arise from the side effects of the policy actions. When absorption is raised to reach internal balance and the price of foreign exchange is raised to reach external balance, the second policy change may add to absorption, thereby causing the total increase in absorption to be excessive. Reaching both internal and external balance without overshooting or other policy mistakes necessitates that each policymaker understand the side effects of his or her own actions as well as the side effects of other policy instruments. This clearly necessitates a knowledge of where all targets lie so that the location of overall equilibrium can be identified. Correct assignment in a larger sense must mean that there is a common national economic plan to which all instruments aspire, even though each instrument directs its policy actions only to the target implied by correct assignment, that is, the target over which its relative influence is the greatest.

But what if sufficient information is absent, as is often the case, especially in developing countries that lack the data to identify the functional relationships that describe the structure of their economies? Consider Figure 12.5 again, where the IB curve is negatively sloped, which could occur with price-inelastic import demand. Suppose it is known that the country suffers from inflation and a deficit. That much is obvious to all, including foreign advisers or IMF staff missions called in to assist with the country's problems. However, inflation and a deficit could imply a point such as *d* or *f* or *g* all in the same zone. Appropriate policy responses differ at the different points. At *f*, a conventional response of devaluation combined with a reduction in absorption is appropriate. But at *d*, getting to equilibrium implies that the deflationary effect of the indicated devaluation will be so strong that getting to overall equilibrium at *h* will require expansion of absorption despite initial inflation. Similarly, at point *g* it appears that the required reduction in absorption will so improve the balance of payments that getting to *h* necessitates some appreciation.

Notice from Figure 12.5 that the solution to this problem lies in identifying the *quadrants* with *h* as the origin, in which the respective points lie. How can these quadrants be distinguished if information, beyond that the economy suffers inflation and a deficit, is absent? An imaginative economic adviser might proceed as follows. She asks the exchange rate authority if he believes that devaluation will more readily eliminate the deficit than the recession. She asks the absorption authority the same question with respect to the likely effect of a change in absorption. If the absorption authority answers that it will require less of a quantitative response to eliminate inflation than to eliminate the deficit, and if the exchange rate authority agrees (that is, less of a devaluation is needed to eliminate inflation than to eliminate the deficit), these two answers create a presumption that the economy must be at a point such as *d*, which is closer to IB than to EB for both policy instruments. A sharp devaluation combined with some small increase in absorption may then be safely prescribed.

If the authorities agree that external balance can be more easily achieved by use of their respective instruments, this creates a presumption for a point such as *g*, which is closer to EB than to IB for both instruments. A major reduction in absorption combined with a moderate appreciation may then be proposed.

Finally, if the authorities disagree about the quantitative response needed for their respective instruments to reach IB and EB, this creates a presumption that the economy is at a point in the quadrant containing point *f*. Absorption requires a smaller response to reach IB than to reach EB, whereas exchange rate policy requires a smaller devaluation to reach EB than IB. Since point *f* is implied by these answers, policy to reduce absorption and to devalue is then indicated.

12.4 CONTINUOUS ADJUSTMENT, STABILITY, AND EXCLUSIVE ASSIGNMENT

Continuous policy adjustment is preferable to stepwise adjustment because it minimizes the risk of incorrect assignment and reduces the probability of overshooting and oscillation. Figure 12.6 shows the EB and IB curves, with the IB curve having a positive slope, which implies that devaluation has an expansionary effect on the economy. Since IB is more steeply sloped than EB, the indicated assignment is for absorption to aim for internal balance and exchange rate policy to aim for external balance.

Begin at point *a* with the economy in recession combined with balance-of-payments equilibrium. Absorption is raised to eliminate recession, and as this pulls the balance of payments into deficit, the exchange rate is continuously raised to prevent a deficit. Therefore there is a direct path to equilibrium from *a* to *b* along the EB curve.

The arrows at point *a* indicate the appropriate direction of change for the policy instruments. This would be the same regardless of the assignment. If the assignment were reversed, the exchange rate would be raised in response to the recession. Since this would put the balance of payments into surplus, absorption would be raised as the exchange rate is raised. The path of motion is again from *a* to *b* along EB. Therefore, we can see that correct assignment is unimportant if adjustment is con-

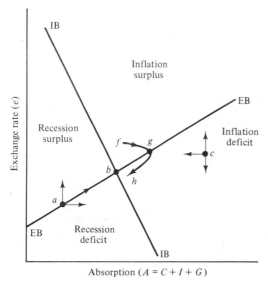

Figure 12.6 Continuous policy adjustment.

tinuous, if the indicated direction of movement of the instruments is independent of the assignment, and if the starting point is on one of the target functions.

At point c there is inflation and a deficit. Absorption clearly needs to be reduced. Exchange rate policy is in a dilemma and could go up or down, depending on the target it selects. Here it is best to ignore assignment and take a wait-and-see attitude, delaying adjustment until absorption policy causes the economy to reach one of the target functions. At that time the conflict is removed, and the appropriate direction of movement of the exchange rate becomes clear.

Under the worst of circumstances an instrument in a dilemma state might ignore the conflict as well as correct assignment and move aggressively toward the wrong target. At point f there is inflation and a surplus. Suppose absorption is raised aggressively to eliminate the surplus while the exchange rate is lowered slowly to eliminate inflation. This would pull the economy to a point such as g, where EB is reached, so there is no further increase in absorption. However, because inflation persists, the exchange rate continues to be lowered, pulling the economy into the inflation-deficit zone. When that happens, absorption must be reduced to eliminate the deficit, so the policy arrow curves around to point h and then to equilibrium at b. Overshooting occurs because one policy has attacked a target too aggressively relative to the other policy. Nevertheless, and despite the incorrect assignment, the ultimate movement is toward equilibrium. Thus we conclude that continuous policy is likely to be far less destabilizing than stepwise policy.

When the demand for imports is inelastic with respect to price so that devaluation reduces absorption, the IB curve becomes negatively sloped. If it is steeper than the EB curve, the increase in absorption needed to offset the internal effect of devaluation is less than the increase in absorption needed to offset the external effect. Therefore, correct assignment implies absorption to internal balance and exchange rate policy to external balance. At point a of Figure 12.7 absorption must be raised to reach internal balance, and since this pulls the economy into deficit, the exchange rate must be raised. Reversal of the assignment produces a path such as from a to c, therefore leading to continuously wider divergence from the targets. Correct assignment is therefore essential, because individual policies cannot move closer to one target without moving the economy farther away from the other target. Needed at point a is a change in the policy mix. When that occurs, correct assignment is essential.

At point d in the inflation-deficit zone there is no apparent dilemma—absorption must be reduced and the exchange rate must be raised. This could produce an adjustment path from d to f. When f is

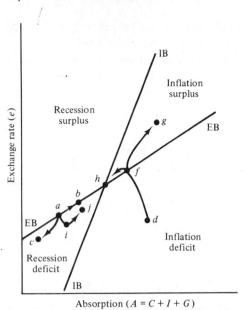

Figure 12.7 Continuous policy adjustment.

reached, the deficit is eliminated. But since the inflation continues, further depreciation to slow inflation creates a surplus, which then invites expansion of absorption. The adjustment bends to the northeast from f to g in a destabilizing manner because the assignment is incorrect. Had absorption been reduced to stem inflation when point f is reached, the adjustment path would have bent to the southwest (from f to h) on the way to equilibrium. Even though a policy mix change was not initially indicated at point d, adjustment sooner or later creates the need for a mix change once one of the targets is reached.

The examples thus far have assumed that assignment is exclusive. That is, correct or incorrect, it has been assumed that each instrument of policy picks one and only one target at which to aim. However, even if the basic assignment is correct, policies may not be able to resist the temptation to assist in the attainment of other targets. For example, if the economy is at full employment, absorption policy may attempt to foster balance of payments adjustment. Or, if the balance of payments is in equilibrium, the exchange rate authority may vary the exchange rate to export unemployment or inflation, as the case may be. Such policy responses, though tempting, are likely to prove inadvisable.

Consider Figure 12.7 again. Starting at point a, absorption must be raised to combat recession. If exchange rate policy tries to export unemployment by appreciation, this is equivalent to ignoring the fact that the rise in absorption will cause a deficit. The adjustment path may then go form *a* to *i*, signaling that exchange rate policy is destabilizing and needs to be reversed to move the economy toward equilibrium. In general, therefore, policy assignment should be exclusive. Pick the correct target and stick to it. Otherwise policy reversals and costly side effects are likely to occur.

12.5 CORRECT ASSIGNMENT: A SIMULATION FOR THE U.S. ECONOMY

What is the correct assignment of policy instruments to economic targets for the U.S. economy? An attempt to answer this question was made by utilizing the quarterly econometric forecasting model of Data Resources Incorporated (DRI) to calculate various policy multiplier impacts.[8] The targets selected were the civilian unemployment rate, the implicit price deflator for GNP, the ratio of nonresidential fixed investment to GNP, and the exchange rate, defined as the value of the dollar against a weighted average of foreign currencies. The unemployment rate is a major indicator of the level of real economic activity, the GNP deflator measures inflation, the ratio of investment to GNP measures additions to capital stock and therefore to the growth of potential output, and the exchange rate determines the competitiveness of the economy in international transactions.

The policy changes analyzed were a reduction in the rate of the payroll tax, a rise in the rate of the investment tax credit (ITC), an increase in federal purchases of goods and services, and increases in nonborrowed reserves that translate into increases in the money supply.[9]

Table 12.1 shows the policy multipliers. The entries in the table are percentage changes in the target variables measured nine quarters after the change in the instruments. For ease of comparison, the policy changes are scaled so that each change has the same effect on the unemployment rate. Thus row 1 of the table shows that each policy change achieves a

[8] The author is indebted to Dr. Craig Elwell, Analyst in Econometrics, Economics Division, Congressional Research Service of the Library of Congress, for supplying the results discussed in this section.

[9] Reduction in the rates of the individual and corporate income tax were also simulated, but the effects of these are not reported in Table 12.1. A reduction in the individual income tax has similar effects on the several targets to those of a rise in government purchases. The only conspicuous difference is in the effects of the policies on the exchange rate. Whereas a reduction in taxes lowers the dollar, the rise in government purchases raises it by a small amount. The reason appears to be that tax reductions raise consumption, which has a larger import content than government purchases. Government purchases raise the value of the dollar because the resulting higher interest rates attract foreign capital.

TABLE 12.1 INSTRUMENT-TARGET RELATIVE MULTIPLIERS
IMPLIED BY THE DATA RESOURCES MODEL

Instrument target	(1) Payroll tax	(2) Investment tax credit	(3) Federal purchases	(4) Money supply	
Unemployment rate	−10.0	−10.0	−10.0	−10.0	(1)
Ratio of investment to GNP	0.3	8.1	1.1	1.9	(2)
Rate of inflation	6.9	9.1	13.2	13.2	(3)
Exchange rate	−1.5	−1.0	0.9	−6.3	(4)

10 percent reduction in the unemployment rate. For example, this could signify a decline of 0.8 percentage points from 8 percent to 7.2 percent.

The table has been arranged to pair targets and instruments in a way that reflects correct assignment. As can be seen, the assignment implied by the DRI model is to use payroll taxes to influence the unemployment rate, the ITC for the ratio of investment to GNP, federal purchases to manage inflation, and the money supply for the exchange rate. These results are quite in line with what one would expect from a priori considerations.

The assignment of payroll taxes to the unemployment rate stems from the fact that a payroll tax reduction has a substantially less powerful effect on inflation than it does on unemployment. A reduction in the rate of the payroll tax stimulates the economy and lowers unemployment, but at the same time it reduces labor costs as perceived by employers. Consequently, the expansionary demand effect of the tax reduction on the price level is moderated by the favorable cost-decreasing effect. Indeed, the DRI simulation showed that the rate of inflation actually declined for four quarters following the tax reduction. Thereafter, the effect of demand expansion causes the price level to rise, but the increase remains well below the inflation increases of the other policies for an equal reduction in unemployment.

Row 2 of the table indicates that of the instruments considered investment incentives can best be provided by an increase in the rate of the investment tax credit. This credit permitted investing firms to deduct a fraction of the cost of new machinery and equipment from their corporate tax liability. Of the simulated policy changes none comes close to having as powerful an effect, although monetary policy does better than the other fiscal measures because the expansionary monetary policy tends to lower interest rates, whereas the expansionary fiscal policies tend to raise them. A change in the statutory rate of the corporate income tax has effects that are quite similar to a rise in the ITC, although the budget cost for equal investment effects is less for changes in the ITC that influence investment directly.

According to the simulations, changes in federal purchases have a relative advantage in the control of inflation. As shown by row 3 of the table, this is immediately evident in comparison with payroll taxes and the ITC. Monetary policy has virtually the identical effect on unemployment and inflation as changes in government purchases. However, since monetary policy has an overridingly powerful effect on the exchange rate (column 4, row 4), it is necessary to assign monetary policy to exchange rate control and federal purchases to inflation, provided the exchange rate is a policy target.

The powerful effect of monetary policy on the exchange rate stems from the fact that monetary policy is the only instrument that affects the current and the capital accounts of the balance of payments in the same direction. To review, an expansionary monetary policy tends to lower interest rates and raise national income. The fall in the rate of interest causes investors to switch to higher-yield foreign assets, and the resulting capital outflow depreciates the currency. The rise in national income increases the demand for imports, and that too tends to depreciate the currency. Therefore, both the current and the capital accounts of the balance of payments change in a direction to depreciate the currency. This is not true for any of the fiscal-policy options. Expansionary fiscal policy raises national income and interest rates. The rise in national income increases the demand for imports, thereby tending to depreciate the currency, but the rise in the rate of interest causes an inflow of capital that tends to appreciate the currency.

12.6 SUMMARY

Considerable territory has been traversed in this chapter. A summary of results and principles of economic policy seems essential. We will want to keep these principles in mind as we analyze the policy issues raised in the remainder of this book.

1. There must be at least as many independently effective instruments of policy as there are targets.
2. Economic problems can best be dealt with at their source. A monetary disturbance suggests the need for a monetary response. A demand-side disturbance should be neutralized by an offsetting

demand response. A supply-side disturbance can be dealt with most effectively if the supply problems are faced directly.

3. Targets must be chosen carefully, and irrelevant targets should be avoided. Conversion of instruments such as the budget into targets is doubly costly, since instruments are lost as targets multiply. Although the economist is entitled to no more influence in the selection of targets than is any other citizen, the economist can play the useful role of pointing out the dangers and consequences of selecting various targets.

4. When a policy instrument is in a conflict or dilemma state, implying that movement in the direction of one target carries the economy farther away from the other target, sound policy suggests a wait-and-see posture for the conflict instrument while policy is conducted by the instrument that is not in conflict.

5. If both instruments are in conflict, the problem can usually be resolved by a change in the policy mix.

6. The appropriate change in the policy mix is dictated by correct assignment. Each instrument should aim for the target over which it has the greatest relative influence.

7. Assignment should be exclusive. Policy instruments should resist the temptation to help other instruments to achieve their targets, since such well-intentioned assistance often destabilizes the instrument's own assigned target, generally necessitating a reversal of the direction of the policy.

8. Discrete or stepwise policy adjustment runs a greater risk of overshooting, oscillation, and instability than continuous adjustment of policy. The development of more flexible policy instruments should be a continuing subject for investigation by the policy-oriented economist.

Finally, the reader is urged to study the three appendixes to this chapter. The first appendix introduces the subject of difference equations. The second appendix derives the stability conditions for the external-internal balance model when policy adjustment is discrete. The final appendix considers the continuous case and lays out the general principles of deriving correct assignment from stability conditions.

QUESTIONS FOR REVIEW

1. Explain the logic of Tinbergen's rule for the necessity of applying at least as many policy instruments as there are targets. Why must the instruments be independently effective? What is meant by independent effectiveness?

2. Targets must be consistent. Why might the following goals be inconsistent?
   a. full employment and a balanced government budget
   b. full employment and stable interest rates
   c. stable interest rates and stable exchange rates
   d. a target rate of GNP growth and a target rate of improvement in the current account of the balance of payments
   e. balance-of-payments equilibrium and a foreign exchange reserve target

3. What is meant by correct assignment of policy instruments to targets? What is the importance of correct assignment?

4. What is the basis for Mundell's assignment rule with respect to monetary-fiscal policy and external-internal balance?

5. What are the consequences of incorrect assignment? Is correct assignment a stability condition? Can you think of actual cases of incorrect assignment and their consequences?

6. What are the advantages of a policy instrument that is capable of continuous adjustment, as opposed to an instrument that can only be changed in periodic discrete steps?

7. Suppose there are two instruments and two targets. How should policy proceed if
   a. neither instrument is in a dilemma?
   b. one instrument is in a dilemma?
   c. both instruments are in a dilemma?

8. If you have studied the appendix to this chapter, you are ready for this question. Assume there are two policy reaction functions, $A^* = A(x, y)$ and $B^* = B(x, y)$, where A^* and B^* are the targets and x and y are the instruments.
   a. Calculate the slopes of the target functions? When are the instruments independently effective?
   b. Assuming that policy adjustment is continuous, construct a dynamic policy-adjustment model involving two simultaneous nonlinear differential equations.
   c. Convert the equations into linear homogeneous equations and then derive the characteristic matrix and characteristic vector.
   d. Explain why the characteristic matrix cannot have an inverse. Then form the characteristic determinant and derive the characteristic equation.
   d. Use the stability condition to ascertain correct assignment.
   e. Should assignment be exclusive?

SUGGESTIONS FOR FURTHER READING

Cooper, Richard, *Economic Policy in an Interdependent World,* MIT Press, 1980. Especially chaps. 7, 9, and 11.

Dornbusch, Rudiger, *Dollars, Debts and Deficits,* MIT Press, 1986, chap. 3.

Johansan, Leif, *Public Economics,* North-Holland, 1965. Especially chap. 2.

Mundell, Robert A., *International Economics,* Macmillan, 1968. Especially chaps. 11, 14, 15, and 19–21.

Tinbergen, Jan, *Economic Policy: Principles and Design,* North-Holland 1956.

Tobin, James, "Stabilization Policy Ten Years After," *Brookings Papers on Economic Activity,* 11, 1980.

Appendixes to Part Three

APPENDIX TO CHAPTER 9

A.9 Price and Income Effects in the Flexible Exchange-Rate Model

This appendix elaborates the integration of absorption with elasticities analysis discussed in the text. Since the issue there was the effect of one-time devaluation, the theme here is varied by looking at the flexible exchange-rate model. We might also recall from Chapters 6 and 7 that the supply curve of the home currency could be backward-bending. This means that the sign of the parameter, V_e, the effect of an increase in the exchange rate on the value of imports denominated in the home currency, is ambiguous. Consequently, stability analysis must be broadened beyond that of Chapter 6.

Let the flexible exchange-rate model be

$$Y = C(Y) + F(i) + G + X(e) - eV(Y, e)$$
$$m_s = L(Y, i)$$
$$0 = X(e) - eV(Y, e) + K(i) \qquad \text{(A.9.1)}$$

The first equation states that equilibrium national income equals the sum of consumption, investment, government purchases, and net exports. The second equation defines monetary equilibrium. The third equation specifies equilibrium in the balance of payments as occurring when net exports plus the net inflow of capital equal zero. Imports, V, are here denominated in foreign currency. It is therefore necessary to multiply the foreign exchange value of imports by the price of foreign exchange, e, to convert the imports into a domestic currency equivalent.

The comparative statics are accomplished by differentiating the equations totally. This gives

$$(S_y + eV_y)dY - F_i\, di - H\, de = dG$$

$$L_y\, dY + L_i\, di \qquad\quad = dm_S$$

$$eV_y\, dY - K_i\, di - H\, de = 0 \qquad\qquad \text{(A.9.2)}$$

where $S_y = 1 - C_y$ and

$$H = X_e - V(Y, e) - eV_e$$

We assume that initially all prices and the exchange rate equal 1. Therefore, H becomes

$$H = X_e - V(Y, e) - V_e \qquad\qquad \text{(A.9.3)}$$

and (A.9.2) becomes

$$(S_y + V_y)dY - F_i\, di - H\, de = dG$$

$$L_y\, dY + L_i\, di \qquad\quad = dm_s$$

$$V_y\, dY - K_i\, di - H\, de = 0 \qquad\qquad \text{(A.9.4)}$$

Inversion of the coefficient matrix gives the solution

$$
\begin{bmatrix} dY \\[1ex] di \\[1ex] de \end{bmatrix} =
\begin{bmatrix}
\dfrac{HL_i} & \dfrac{-H(F_i - K_i)}{D} & \dfrac{HL_i}{D} \\
\end{bmatrix}
$$

$$
\begin{bmatrix} dY \\[2ex] di \\[2ex] de \end{bmatrix} =
\begin{bmatrix}
\dfrac{HL_i}{D} & \dfrac{-H(F_i - K_i)}{D} & \dfrac{HL_i}{D} \\[2ex]
\dfrac{HL_y}{D} & \dfrac{-HS_y}{D} & \dfrac{-HL_y}{D} \\[2ex]
\dfrac{-(L_yK_i + L_iV_y)}{D} & \dfrac{K_i(S_y + V_y) - F_iV_y}{D} & \dfrac{-L_i(S_y + V_y) + L_yF_i}{D}
\end{bmatrix}
$$

$$
\times \begin{bmatrix} dG \\[1ex] dm_s \\[1ex] 0 \end{bmatrix} \qquad\qquad \text{(A.9.5)}
$$

where

$$D = -H(L_iS_y - L_yK_i + L_yF_i)$$

Note that the multipliers for the changes in income and the rate of interest with respect to G and m_s are exactly the same as they were in the model of the appendix to Chapter 6. However, the change in the exchange rate is now given by

$$\frac{de}{dG} = \frac{-(L_yK_i + L_iV_y)}{D} = \frac{-(L_yK_i + L_iV_y)}{-H(L_iS_y - L_yK_i + F_iL_y)}$$

$$\frac{de}{dm} = \frac{K_i(S_y + V_y) - F_iV_y}{D} = \frac{K_i(S_y + V_y) - F_iV_y}{-H(L_iS_y - L_yK_i + F_iL_y)} \qquad \text{(A.9.6)}$$

Inspecting these results, we see that the signs of de/dG and de/dm_s depend on the sign of H. For the comparative static results to make sense the increase in the money supply must raise the price of foreign exchange, which means that H must be positive. Let us now have a closer look at this term.

As given in (A.9.3) the value of H is

$$H = X_e - V(Y, e) - V_e$$

where $V(Y, e)$ is the value of imports, X_e is the partial derivative of exports with respect to the exchange rate—that is, $X_e = \partial X/\partial e$—and V_e is the partial derivative of the value of imports with respect to the exchange rate—that is, $V_e = \partial V/\partial e$. These partial derivatives can be written as follows:

$$X_e = \left(\frac{e}{X}\frac{\partial X}{\partial e}\right)\frac{X}{e} = \left(\frac{\partial X/X}{\partial e/e}\right)\frac{X}{e} \qquad V_e = \left(\frac{e}{V}\frac{\partial V}{\partial e}\right)\frac{V}{e} = \left(\frac{\partial V/V}{\partial e/e}\right)\frac{V}{e} \qquad \text{(A.9.7)}$$

Inspection of these expressions shows that the terms in parentheses are the respective elasticities of the supply of foreign exchange and the demand for foreign exchange with respect to the exchange rate. When the price elasticities of the supplies of exports and imports are infinite, the home price of exports and the foreign price of imports are independent of the exchange rate. The proportionate decline in the foreign price of exports then equals the proportionate increase in the exchange rate, and the home price of imports rises by an equal proportionate rise as the price of foreign exchange. This means that the price elasticity of the demand for imports is the negative of the elasticity of import demand with respect to the exchange rate, and the elasticity of demand for exports is the same as the elasticity of export demand with respect to the exchange rate.

The foregoing assumptions about supply elasticities therefore imply that

$$X_e = n_x \frac{X}{e} \qquad V_e = -n_v \frac{V}{e}$$

and since $e = 1$ initially, it follows that

$$X_e = n_x X \qquad V_e = -n_v V$$

Substituting these results into the expression for H gives

$$H = X(n_x + n_v - 1)$$

which is the familiar Marshall-Lerner condition. Since H must be positive, it follows that the sum of the demand elasticities for exports and imports must exceed unity.

When the model is tested for stability of equilibrium using the conventional assumptions as in the appendix to Chapter 6, the characteristic equation is

$$q^3 + [k_1(S_y + V_y) - k_2 L_i + k_3 H]q^2$$
$$+ [-k_1 k_2(S_y + V_y) + k_1 k_3(S_y + V_y)H - k_2 k_3 HL_i]q$$
$$- k_1 k_2 k_3 H(L_i S_y - L_y K_i + F_i L_y) = 0$$

For all of these coefficients to be positive, as necessitated by stability of equilibrium, H must be positive. Therefore, the Marshall-Lerner conditions must be met. In other words, the entire economic system cannot be stable unless the foreign exchange market is also stable. If the foreign exchange market is unstable, as at point f in Figure 8.4 a small rise in the price of foreign exchange creates excess demand for foreign exchange rather than excess supply. The price of foreign exchange therefore continues to rise at an ever-faster rate and the excess demand widens. Since the physical quantity of imports declines as long as the price of foreign exchange is rising, and the physical quantity of exports rises as long as the price of foreign exchange is rising, it must follow that national income must rise without limit.

APPENDIX TO CHAPTER 11

A.11.1 Analytics of the Short-Run Asset-Market Model

A.11.1.1 Properties of the Model The equations of the asset-market model as defined in the text are

$$M = L(i, W) \qquad L_i < 0 \quad L_w > 0 \qquad \text{(A.11.1a)}$$

$$B = B(i, W) \qquad B_i > 0 \quad B_w > 0 \qquad \text{(A.11.1b)}$$

$$eF = F(i, W) \qquad F_i < 0 \quad F_w > 0 \qquad \text{(A.11.1c)}$$

$$W = M + B + eF \qquad \text{(A.11.2)}$$

It is important to understand the relationships between the parameters of the model. Substituting (A.11.1) into the wealth constraint (A.11.2) gives

$$W = L(i, W) + B(i, W) + F(i, W) \qquad \text{(A.11.3)}$$

and differentiating with respect to i, holding W constant, gives

$$0 = (L_i + B_i + F_i)di$$

It follows that these parameters must sum to zero. Furthermore, since

$$B_i = -(L_i + F_i)$$

and assuming that F_i is nonzero, it must be that $B_i > -L_i$. Consequently, the model incorporates the important assumption that a rise in the rate of interest causes portfolio substitution toward bonds away from *both* money and foreign assets.

Next differentiate (A.11.3) with respect to W. This gives

$$(1 - L_w - B_w - F_w)dW = 0$$

and it can therefore be seen that the wealth parameters must sum to unity. Since each of these parameters is positive, each one must be a positive fraction.

Next consider the slopes of the MM, BB, and FF functions. Differentiate (A.11.1) with respect to i, W, and e to get

$$0 = L_i \, di + L_w \, dW$$

$$0 = B_i \, di + B_w \, dW$$

$$F \, de = F_i \, di + F_w \, dW \qquad (A.11.4)$$

From (A.11.2) it can be seen that the change in wealth that accompanies a change in the exchange rate is

$$dW = F \, de$$

Using this result in (A.11.4) gives

$$0 = L_i \, di - L_w F \, de$$

$$0 = B_i \, di - B_w F \, de$$

$$F \, de = F_i \, di - F_w F \, de$$

Rearranging these expressions gives the slopes of the respective functions:

$$\left(\frac{de}{di}\right)_M = \frac{-L_i}{FL_w} > 0$$

$$\left(\frac{de}{di}\right)_B = \frac{-B_i}{FB_w} < 0$$

$$\left(\frac{de}{di}\right)_F = \frac{F_i}{F(1 - F_w)} < 0 \qquad (A.11.5)$$

so we can see that the slope of MM is positive while the slopes of BB and FF are both negative.

A.11.1.2 Stability of Equilibrium   To test for the stability of equilibrium, we make the dynamic assumptions that the rate of interest falls in response to excess demand in the bond market, and that the price of foreign exchange rises in response to excess demand in the market for foreign assets. Accordingly, we write

$$\frac{di}{dt} = -k_1[B(i, W) - B]$$

$$\frac{de}{dt} = k_2[F(i, W) - eF]$$

As in previous tests for stability of equilibrium, we begin by linearizing the equations. We then replace the left-hand time derivatives by their trial values and rearrange to form the characteristic matrix and characteristic vector. We then set the characteristic determinant equal to zero, and this gives the characteristic equation

$$q^2 + [k_1 B_i + k_2 F(1 - F_w)]q + k_1 k_2 F[B_i(1 - F_w) + B_w F_i] = 0$$

The second coefficient of the characteristic equation is definitely positive. The characteristic roots will be negative and the equilibrium will be stable if the third coefficient is positive as well. Therefore stability of equilibrium requires that

$$B_i(1 - F_w) + B_w F_i > 0$$

Rearranging the expression, we get

$$- \frac{B_i}{B_w} < \frac{F_i}{1 - F_w}$$

so it is clear that stability of equilibrium requires the slope of BB to be steeper than the slope of FF.

A.11.1.3 Comparative Statics: Effects of Accumulation and Policy Changes

Once the parameter values are restricted as above, any of the equations can be eliminated from the model. Accordingly, to conduct comparative static analysis, we eliminate the monetary equilibrium equation and use (A.11.1b) and (A.11.1c), namely,

$$B = B(i, W) \qquad eF = F(i, W) \tag{A.11.6}$$

We then obtain the needed third equation by substituting the equilibrium values of B and F into the wealth constraint. This gives the demand for money as a residual and monetary equilibrium as

$$M = W - B(i, W) - F(i, W) \tag{A.11.7}$$

Differentiating these three equations totally with respect to i, W, and e gives

$$\begin{bmatrix} B_i & B_w & 0 \\ F_i & F_w & -F \\ L_i & L_w & 0 \end{bmatrix} \begin{bmatrix} di \\ dW \\ de \end{bmatrix} = \begin{bmatrix} dB \\ e \, dF \\ dM \end{bmatrix}$$

We obtain the coefficients of the third row of the coefficient matrix by differentiating (A.11.7):

$$-(B_i + F_i)di + (1 - B_w - F_w)dW = dM$$

But since $L_i = -(B_i + F_i)$ and $L_w = 1 - B_w - F_w$, the equation can be written

$$L_i \, de + L_w \, dW = dM$$

which is identical to the derivative of $M = L(i, W)$.

The determinant of the coefficient matrix is

$$D = F(B_i L_w - B_w L_i) > 0 \tag{A.11.8}$$

which is positive. When the coefficient matrix is inverted, we obtain the solution

$$\begin{bmatrix} di \\ dW \\ de \end{bmatrix} = \frac{1}{D} \begin{bmatrix} FL_w & 0 & -FB_w \\ -FL_i & 0 & FB_i \\ F_iL_w - F_wL_i & B_wL_i - B_iL_w & B_iF_w - B_wF_i \end{bmatrix} \begin{bmatrix} dB \\ e\,dF \\ dM \end{bmatrix}$$

(A.11.9)

We can now proceed to an examination of the effects of various changes in the right-hand vectors, which show the exogenous changes.

The Effect of a Current Surplus   A current surplus raises F, so the right-hand vector becomes

$$\begin{bmatrix} dB = 0 \\ e\,dF = e\,dF \\ dM = 0 \end{bmatrix}$$

Now, di and dW are both zero, so there is no change in the rate of interest or wealth. The change in the exchange rate is

$$de = \frac{(B_wL_i - B_iL_w)e\,dF}{F(B_iL_w - B_wL_i)} < 0$$

It follows that

$$\frac{de}{e} = \frac{-dF}{F}$$

so the price of foreign exchange falls at the rate of accumulation of foreign assets.

Expansionary Fiscal Policy: Bond Financed   In this case the right-hand vector is

$$\begin{bmatrix} dB = dB \\ e\,dF = 0 \\ dM = 0 \end{bmatrix}$$

so the results are

$$di = \frac{L_w(dB)}{B_iL_w - B_wL_i} > 0$$

$$dW = \frac{-L_i(dB)}{B_iL_w - B_wL_i} > 0$$

$$de = \frac{(F_iL_w - F_wL_i)(dB)}{D} \gtrless 0$$

These results show that expansionary fiscal policy financed by bond sales raise wealth and the rate of interest, but the effect on the exchange rate is ambiguous. Appreciation of the home currency occurs if

$$F_iL_w - F_wL_i < 0$$

which implies

$$\frac{F_i}{F_w} < \frac{L_i}{L_w}$$

This condition is likely to be satisfied if the rise in the rate of interest leads to a large substitution of bonds in favor of foreign assets combined with a low degree of substitution from money to bonds. As noted in Chapter 6, this condition appears to be satisfied in the United States but not in other countries.

Expansionary Fiscal Policy: Money Financed If the bonds are sold to the central bank, the money stock increases. Therefore, the right-hand vector becomes

$$\begin{bmatrix} dB = 0 \\ e\,dF = 0 \\ dM = dB \end{bmatrix}$$

This implies

$$di = \frac{-B_w(dB)}{B_iL_w - B_wL_i} < 0$$

$$dW = \frac{B_i(dB)}{B_iL_W - B_wL_i} > 0$$

$$de = \frac{(B_iF_w - B_wF_i)(dB)}{D} > 0$$

In this case wealth again rises, but the rate of interest falls and the price of foreign exchange rises. Money-financed budget deficits therefore tend to depreciate the local currency.

Expansionary Monetary Policy: Purchase of Domestic Bonds A central bank purchase of domestic securities raises M and lowers B. Therefore,

$$\begin{bmatrix} dB = -dM \\ e\,dF = 0 \\ dM = dM \end{bmatrix}$$

which implies

$$di = \frac{-(L_w + B_w)(dM)}{B_iL_w - B_wL_i} > 0$$

$$dW = \frac{(L_i + B_i)(dM)}{B_iL_w - B_wL_i} = \frac{-F_i(dM)}{B_iL_w - B_wL_i} > 0$$

$$de = \frac{[-F_i(L_w + B_w) + F_w(L_i + B_i)](dM)}{D} = \frac{-F_i(dM)}{D} > 0$$

As expected, the expansionary monetary policy lowers the rate of interest, depreciates the local currency, and, because of the depreciation, raises wealth. These results can be stated categorically, since $B_i > -L_i$ and $F_i < 0$.

Expansionary Monetary Policy: Purchase of Foreign Assets

If the monetary authority purchases F, the right-hand vector becomes

$$\begin{bmatrix} dB = 0 \\ e\, dF = -dM \\ dM = dM \end{bmatrix}$$

This implies the following results:

$$di = \frac{-B_w(dM)}{B_i L_w - B_w L_i} < 0$$

$$dW = \frac{B_i(dM)}{B_i L_w - B_w L_i} > 0$$

$$de = \frac{[B_i(L_w + F_w) - B_w(L_i + F_i)](dM)}{D} = \frac{B_i(dM)}{D} > 0$$

As with the domestic open-market purchase, the rate of interest falls, the exchange rate depreciates, and wealth rises. However, because $L_w + B_w$ exceeds B_w, the rate of interest falls by less, and because B_i exceeds $-F_i$, the depreciation is greater. Because of the greater depreciation, there is a larger wealth effect.

Sterilized Intervention to Depreciate the Exchange Rate

Sterilized intervention operates to depreciate the local currency by reducing the supply of foreign assets while increasing the supply of domestic assets. Therefore, the right-hand vector is

$$\begin{bmatrix} dB = dB \\ e\, dF = -dB \\ dM = 0 \end{bmatrix}$$

and this implies

$$di = \frac{L_w(dB)}{B_i L_w - B_w L_i} > 0$$

$$dW = \frac{L_i(dB)}{B_i L_w - B_w L_i} > 0$$

$$de = \frac{[L_w(F_i + B_i) - L_i(F_w + B_w)](dB)}{D} = \frac{-L_i(dB)}{D} > 0$$

The sale of bonds drives up the rate of interest, and the depreciation of the local currency causes a positive wealth effect. From the last expression it appears that sterilized intervention works best when domestic and foreign bonds are poor substitutes, implying a highly interest-sensitive demand for money.

A.11.2 Mathematical Expectation

A random variable is sometimes said to be a variable whose values are determined by a chance device. This does not mean the variable is unpredictable. It may vary systematically in response to changes in other variables. However, the outcome is not always exactly as predicted because it may involve errors or *residuals*. For example, an econometrician may estimate a consumption income relationship as

$$\hat{C}_i = a + bY_i$$

where Y_i is the value of income for the ith observed sample value, and $\hat{C}_i$ is the predicted level of consumption. However, the actual value and the predicted value may be different by the amount of an error term, or residual, of u_i. Consequently, $u_i = C_i - \hat{C}_i$. This implies that the previous equation could be written

$$C_i = a + bY_i + u_i$$

which is the way such equations are normally represented.

Under the circumstances we say that C_i and u_i are random variables. The variable C can be predicted by Y, but the prediction is subject to error. If the prediction is to be unbiased, then, on the average and in the long run, C_i must equal its predicted value so that in the long run the errors must average to zero. Therefore it is customary to write

$$E(u_i) = 0$$

where $E(u_i)$ is the *expected value* of the error, that is, the average error in the long run.

The rules for working with expected values are fairly simple. Among the more important are the following:

1. The expected value of a constant equals the constant. Therefore if a is a constant, $E(a) = a$.
2. The expected value of a random variable is the long-run outcome. It is therefore the average, or mean value, of the variable. Therefore,

$$E(X) = \bar{X}$$

where $\bar{X}$ is the mean of the X's. A fair game is defined as one in which the long-run outcome is zero. Therefore, if $E(X) = 0$, the game is considered fair.
3. The expected value of a constant term times a random variable equals the constant term times the expected value of the random variable. Therefore,

$$E(aX) = aE(X) = a\bar{X}$$

4. The variance of the random variable X is defined as

$$\sigma_X^2 = E[X - E(X)]^2 = E(X - \bar{X})^2$$

and the standard deviation of the random variable is the square root of the variance.

5. The variance of aX is $a^2\sigma_X^2$. Since

$$E[aX - E(aX)]^2 = E[aX - aE(X)]^2 = a^2E[X - E(X)]^2$$

it follows that the standard deviation of aX is $\sigma_{aX} = a\sigma_X$.

6. The covariance between two random variables X and Y is defined as

$$E(X - E(X))(Y - E(Y)) = \sigma_X\sigma_Y$$

APPENDIX TO CHAPTER 12

A.12.1 An Introduction to Difference Equations

The mathematics of continuous motion with respect to time is called *differential* equations. In such a continuous model the value of a variable is represented as a function of its own time derivatives. For example,

$$a\frac{d^2y}{dt^2} + b\frac{dy}{dt} + cy = d$$

is a linear, second-order, nonhomogeneous differential equation. It is a second-order equation because of the second time derivative, and it is nonhomogeneous because of the presence of the constant term d.

Many economic processes, however, are discontinuous, or discrete. Most policy changes are of that nature; the change in one variable in the current period may represent a lagged response to a change of another variable in a previous period, and economic data gathering and processing divides time into arbitrary discrete intervals such as years, quarters, and months. Because of the nature of the data, all econometric forecasting models are specified in terms of *difference* equations. In such equations variables do not change continuously; they are assumed constant throughout a period of time, and they jump or fall abruptly to another value at the beginning of the next period.

A difference equation such as

$$y_t = by_{t-1}$$

is a linear, first-order, homogeneous equation. If a constant term or a term that grows autonomously is added, the equation becomes nonhomogeneous, as in

$$y_t = by_{t-1} + c$$

or

$$y_t = by_{t-1} + ck^t$$

If the difference equation spans two time periods as in

$$y_t = ay_{t-1} + by_{t-2} + c$$

it is a second-order difference equation.

Compound interest may be represented by the difference equation

$$p_t = (1 + i)p_{t-1} \qquad \text{(A.12.1)}$$

If we know the value of the beginning loan at time $t = 0$, we can multiply it by $1 + i$ (i is the rate of interest) to get the value of the loan at time $t = 1$. Therefore,

$$p_1 = (1 + i)p_0 \qquad \text{(A.12.2)}$$

Knowing p_1, we can calculate p_2 by again using the difference equation. This gives

$$p_2 = (1 + i)p_1$$

But since $p_1 = (1 + i)p_0$, it follows that

$$p_2 = (1 + i)^2 p_0 \qquad \text{(A.12.3)}$$

We can readily see that if we continue this process, the value of p_t can be stated as a function of time and the initial value of the loan. That is,

$$p_t = (1 + i)^t p_0 \qquad \text{(A.12.4)}$$

which is a formula that satisfies the difference equation and the initial condition p_0. Such a formula is called the *solution* to the difference equation. Notice that the solution is of the form

$$p_t = \lambda^t K \qquad \text{(A.12.5)}$$

that is, a constant, λ, raised to the power t, multiplied by another constant that depends on the initial condition. The constant λ is called the *characteristic root* of the difference equation, just as q was the root of the differential equations of previous appendixes. Inspection of (A.12.5) shows that the value of the root determines the time-path of p_t. If $\lambda > 1$, p_t grows steadily; if $-1 < \lambda < +1$, p_t diminishes; and if $\lambda < 0$, p_t oscillates back and forth, since a negative number raised to an even power is positive and when raised to an odd power it is negative.

As another simple economic example, consider the multiplier process. Let national income at time t be

$$Y_t = C_t + I \qquad \text{(A.12.6)}$$

where I is autonomous. Suppose that consumption responds to changes in income with a one-period lag so that

$$C_t = bY_{t-1} + C_a \qquad \text{(A.12.7)}$$

Substituting the consumption function into (A.12.6), we get

$$Y_t = bY_{t-1} + C_a + I \qquad \text{(A.12.8)}$$

which is a first-order, linear, nonhomogeneous difference equation.

To obtain a solution, we normally proceed by splitting Y_t into its equilibrium value $\bar{Y}$ plus a displacement from equilibrium u_t. Therefore, let

$$Y_t = u_t + \bar{Y} \qquad (A.12.9)$$

Substituting this into (A.12.8) gives

$$u_t + \bar{Y} = b(u_{t-1} + \bar{Y}) + C_a + I \qquad (A.12.10)$$

In equilibrium the displacements equal zero. Therefore, setting u_t and u_{t-1} equal to zero and solving for $\bar{Y}$ gives

$$\bar{Y} = \frac{C_a + I}{1 - b} \qquad (A.12.11)$$

and it hardly comes as a great surprise that equilibrium income equals autonomous expenditure times the multiplier.

Next, notice that since $C_a + I = \bar{Y}(1 - b)$, we can write (A.12.10) as

$$u_t + \bar{Y} = bu_{t-1} + b\bar{Y} + \bar{Y}(1 - b)$$

where it is evident that the constant terms cancel out so that we are left with the linear, homogeneous difference equation

$$u_t = bu_{t-1} \qquad (A.12.12)$$

To move quickly to a solution, we try a formula such as (A.12.5) as a *trial solution*. Therefore we try

$$u_t = \lambda^t K \qquad (A.12.13)$$

Since $u_{t-1} = \lambda^{t-1} K$, we substitute the trial values into (A.12.12) to get

$$\lambda^t K = b\lambda^{t-1} K$$

and since all terms are divisible by $\lambda^{t-1} K$, it follows that the root λ is

$$\lambda = b \qquad (A.12.14)$$

Substituting the now-known value of λ into (A.12.13) gives

$$u_t = b^t K \qquad (A.12.15)$$

Using this in (A.12.9), we get

$$Y_t = b^t K + \bar{Y} \qquad (A.12.16)$$

The final step is to solve for K. This necessitates knowledge of Y_t at some point in the past, that is, an initial condition. Therefore let $Y_t = Y_0$ at $t = 0$. Equation (A.12.16) then becomes

$$Y_0 = b^0 K + \bar{Y}$$

and it follows that

$$K = Y_0 - \bar{Y} \qquad (A.12.17)$$

Using this result in (A.12.16) gives the complete solution

$$Y_t = b^t(Y_0 - \bar{Y}) + \bar{Y} \qquad (A.12.18)$$

The behavior of the model can now be examined. Stability of equilibrium requires that Y_t approach $\bar{Y}$ as t grows larger. Therefore the *transient* term $b^t(Y_0 - \bar{Y})$ must become smaller. This happens if $-1 < b < 1$. Since the marginal propensity to consume is a positive fraction, $0 < b < 1$; thus, stability is ensured, and Y_t returns steadily toward $\bar{Y}$, following a disturbance that causes Y_0 to differ from $\bar{Y}$.

If $b < 0$, then $b^t(Y_0 - \bar{Y})$ alternates between positive and negative values. Therefore a negative root implies period-by-period oscillation of Y_t. The oscillations are *damped* and the system is stable if b lies between -1 and 0, but if $b < -1$ the oscillations grow larger and the system is said to be *antidamped* or unstable.

If we have the second-order, homogeneous difference equation

$$au_t + bu_{t-1} + cu_{t-2} = 0 \qquad (A.12.19)$$

we proceed as before, by using the trial solution

$$u_t = \lambda^t K$$

Therefore,

$$a\lambda^t K + b\lambda^{t-1} K + c\lambda^{t-2} K = 0$$

Dividing all terms by $\lambda^{t-2} K$ gives

$$a\lambda^2 + b\lambda + c = 0 \qquad (A.12.20)$$

This is the *characteristic equation*. Since this is a second-degree polynomial, there are two possible values of λ that satisfy the equation. These *characteristic roots* can be derived by using the quadratic formula

$$(\lambda_1, \lambda_2) = \frac{-b \pm \sqrt{b^2 - 4ac}}{2a} \qquad (A.12.21)$$

If $b^2 - 4ac > 0$, the square root can be taken and the roots are said to be *real*. If $b^2 - 4ac < 0$, the square root cannot be taken and we then have *complex* roots.

For the moment we assume the roots are real and known, as the result of our using (A.12.21). The complete solution is of the form

$$u_t = K_1(\lambda_1)^t + K_2(\lambda_2)^t \qquad (A.12.22)$$

where the K's are constants that depend on two required initial conditions. If $Y_t = Y_0$ at $t = 0$, and $Y_t = Y_1$ at $t = 1$, we can easily solve for the K's to get the complete solution.

Stability requires that $u_t \to 0$ as $t \to \infty$. Therefore *both* of the roots must lie between -1 and $+1$ in a stable system. If one or both of the roots exceeds $+1$ and the K's are positive, u_t will grow in ever-larger steps. If one or both of the roots is negative, u_t will exhibit period-by-period oscillation. As t continues to grow, the behavior of u_t becomes increasingly determined by the root with the largest absolute value, that is, by the *dominant root*.

With this introduction behind us, we can move to the next appendix, which specifies the internal-external balance model as a set of simultaneous difference equations. Although we have skipped discussion of complex roots here, we will encounter them in the next appendix.

A.12.2 External and Internal Balance with Discrete Adjustment

The mathematical analysis of the discussion of Section 12.3 begins with the comparative static internal-external balance model introduced in Chapter 2. Let internal balance be given by the functions

$$Y^* = Y(A, e) \qquad Y_a > 0 \quad Y_e \gtrless 0 \qquad (A.12.23)$$

Now, $Y_a > 0$ because national income rises when absorption rises, but the sign of Y_e is ambiguous. Normally, it may be assumed to be positive because a rise in the price of foreign exchange usually raises national income, but the opposite could be true if the demand for imports is inelastic with respect to price. That is a relevant possibility in the short run.

The target current-account surplus function may be written

$$B^* = B(A, e) \qquad B_a < 0 \quad B_e > 0 \qquad (A.12.24)$$

A rise in absorption reduces the current-account surplus, whereas a rise in the price of foreign exchange increases it. Therefore B_a is negative, and B_e is positive.

To calculate the slopes of the functions, we differentiate both functions totally while holding Y^* and B^* constant. Therefore,

$$0 = Y_a dA + Y_e de$$

$$0 = B_a dA + B_e de$$

from which it follows that

$$\left(\frac{de}{dA}\right)_y = -\frac{Y_a}{Y_e} \gtrless 0$$

$$\left(\frac{de}{dA}\right)_b = -\frac{B_a}{B_e} > 0 \qquad (A.12.25)$$

The slope of the internal balance function measures the rate at which the exchange rate must be changed to offset the effects of a change in absorption on internal balance. If $Y_e > 0$, as normally assumed, the slope of the internal balance curve is negative, as in Chapter 2. Depreciation is then required to offset the internal effect of a decline in absorption. But if $Y_e < 0$, which could happen if the elasticity of demand for imports is low, depreciation may be deflationary and must then be accompanied by a rise in absorption to prevent income from declining. The internal balance curve in this case is positively sloped.

The slope of the external balance curve is definitely positive. It measures the rate at which depreciation must be substituted for changes in absorption to keep the balance of payments in equilibrium. A rise in absorption raises the demand for imports, so depreciation is needed to maintain external balance.

We can now turn to the dynamics of policy adjustment. Let the policy instruments adjust to discrepancies between their actual and their target values, namely,

$$\Delta A_t = k_1(A_t^* - A_t)$$

$$\Delta e_t = k_2(e_t^* - e_t) \tag{A.12.26}$$

where it is assumed at the outset that correct assignment requires absorption to target internal balance and exchange rate policy to target external balance. Each instrument adjusts in proportion to the difference between its target value and its actual value. The target functions are IB and EB. They may be expressed in linear form as

$$\text{IB:} \quad A_t^* = a + be_t$$

$$\text{EB:} \quad e_t^* = c + dA_t \tag{A.12.27}$$

from which it can be seen that the target levels of A^* and e^* at any moment of time depend on the actual value of the other policy variable. The parameter b is the reciprocal of the slope of the IB curve. Therefore,

$$\frac{1}{b} = -\frac{Y_a}{Y_e} \gtrless 0 \tag{A.12.28}$$

which is negative if Y_e is positive and positive if Y_e is negative. Similarly, d is the slope of the EB curve. Consequently,

$$d = -\frac{B_a}{B_e} > 0$$

which is positive because B_a is negative and B_e is positive.

The change in absorption and the exchange rate may be written, respectively, as

$$\Delta A_t = A_{t+1} - A_t$$

$$\Delta e_t = e_{t+1} - e_t \tag{A.12.29}$$

Using (A.12.29) and (A.12.27) to make substitutions in (A.12.26) gives

$$A_{t+1} - A_t = k_1(a + be_t - A_t)$$

$$e_{t+1} - e_t = k_2(c + dA_t - e_t) \tag{A.12.30}$$

which is a set of simultaneous, linear, nonhomogeneous difference equations.

If policy attempts to reach its target in one jump, the k's have a value of 1, so (A.12.30) simplify to

$$A_{t+1} = a + be_t$$

$$e_{t+1} = c + dA_t \qquad (A.12.31)$$

The second equation may be substituted into the first to eliminate e_t and to express the equation entirely in terms of A and its lagged values. Alternatively, the first equation can be used to eliminate A_t from the second equation. The results are

$$A_{t+1} = a + bc + bdA_{t-1}$$

$$e_{t+1} = c + da + bde_{t-1} \qquad (A.12.32)$$

These equations are linear, second-order, nonhomogeneous difference equations. Since the coefficient of A_{t-1} and e_{t-1} is the same bd in both equations, it is evident that they will have the same characteristic equation and identical roots. Consequently, we see that simultaneous difference equations (as well as simultaneous differential equations) have a single characteristic equation and that, in most cases, one variable cannot be stable unless the other is stable.

To eliminate the constant terms and make the equations homogeneous, we define

$$A_t = u_t + \bar{A}$$

$$e_t = v_t + \bar{e} \qquad (A.12.33)$$

and substitute these expressions into (A.12.32) to obtain

$$u_{t+1} + \bar{A} = a + bc + bd(u_{t-1} + \bar{A})$$

$$v_{t+1} + \bar{e} = c + da + bd(v_{t-1} + \bar{e}) \qquad (A.12.34)$$

In equilibrium u_t and v_t both equal zero, so the equilibrium solutions are

$$\bar{A} = \frac{a + bc}{1 - bd} \qquad \bar{e} = \frac{c + da}{1 - bd} \qquad (A.12.35)$$

When these equilibrium values are substituted into (A.12.34), the constant terms drop out, so the equations become the linear homogeneous equations

$$u_{t+1} = bdu_{t-1}$$

$$v_{t+1} = bdy_{t-1} \qquad (A.12.36)$$

The next step is to utilize a trial solution of the form

$$u_t = K\lambda^t \qquad v_t = L\lambda^t$$

and substitute these into (A.12.36). Thus,

$$K\lambda^{t+1} = bdK\lambda^{t-1} \qquad L\lambda^{t+1} = bdL\lambda^{t-1}$$

which implies that the characteristic equation is

$$\lambda^2 - bd = 0$$

Clearly there are two characteristic roots:

$$\lambda_1 = \sqrt{bd} \qquad \lambda_2 = -\sqrt{bd}$$

which are equal but of opposite sign.

The complete solution may now be written as

$$A_t = \bar{A} + K_1(\sqrt{bd})^t + K_2(-\sqrt{bd})^t$$

$$e_t = \bar{e} + L_1(\sqrt{bd})^t + L_2(-\sqrt{bd})^t \qquad (A.12.37)$$

There are two important cases to be analyzed in determining the behavior of the policy variables, depending on the value of Y_e. First, assume that $Y_e > 0$ so that appreciation stimulates the economy. In this case $bd > 0$ and $\sqrt{bd}$ can be taken. The roots are then real. The sign of $K_1(\sqrt{bd})^t$ is positive, indicating monotonic policy steps, but the sign of $K_2(-\sqrt{bd})^t$ alternates between positive and negative values, indicating period-by-period oscillation. Neither root is dominant; therefore the system could oscillate, depending, in this case, on the starting point (the initial conditions that determine the values of the K's and L's).

Stability of equilibrium requires the roots to lie between -1 and $+1$. Therefore $|\sqrt{bd}| < 1$. Accordingly, $|bd| < 1$, so stability implies

$$|d| < \left|\frac{1}{b}\right|$$

Since $|d|$ is the absolute value of the slope of the external balance curve and $|1/b|$ is the absolute value of the slope of the internal balance function, the IB curve must be steeper than the EB curve. If not, the assignment of policies to targets is incorrect, and destabilizing and must be reversed.

In the more usual case in which b is negative because Y_e is positive, the IB curve has a negative slope. In this event $bd < 0$ and $\sqrt{bd}$ cannot be taken. In such a case the roots are said to be *complex conjugate* and are written as

$$\lambda_1 = \alpha + \beta i = 0 + \sqrt{-bd}\sqrt{-1}$$

$$\lambda_2 = \alpha - \beta i = 0 - \sqrt{-bd}\sqrt{-1} \qquad (A.12.38)$$

where $i = \sqrt{-1}$, α is the *real* part of the complex roots, and βi is the *imaginary* part. Notice that if i is raised to successively higher powers,

$$i^0 = 1$$

$$i^1 = \sqrt{-1}$$

$$i^2 = (\sqrt{-1})^2 = -1$$

$$i^3 = (\sqrt{-1})^3 = -\sqrt{-1}$$
$$i^4 = (\sqrt{-1})^4 = 1$$
$$i^5 = i^1 = (\sqrt{-1})^5 = \sqrt{-1}$$

and so on. Thus, as t increases, i^t repeats itself every four periods; that is, $i^t = i^{t-4}$. Consequently, we should not be surprised to find that the difference equations imply oscillating behavior when the roots are complex.

The solutions of (A.12.37) become

$$A_t = \bar{A} + K_1(\alpha + \beta i)^t + K_2(\alpha - \beta i)^t$$

$$e_t = \bar{e} + L_1(\alpha + \beta i)^t + L_2(\alpha - \beta i)^t \qquad (A.12.39)$$

but this is not helpful because of the presence of the complex roots. To deal with this difficulty, plot the complex roots as in Figure A.12.1. The horizontal axis measures the real part, the vertical axis the imaginary part. The line OZ is the hypotenuse of the right triangle formed with angle θ at the origin. Its distance is

$$M = \sqrt{\alpha^2 + \beta^2}$$

and is termed the *modulus* of the complex roots. Evidently,

$$\alpha = M \cos \theta \qquad (A.12.40a)$$

and

$$\beta = M \sin \theta \qquad (A.12.40b)$$

Substituting these values for α and β into (A.12.33) gives

$$A_t = \bar{A} + K_1(M \cos \theta + Mi \sin \theta)^t + K_2(M \cos \theta - Mi \sin \theta)^t$$

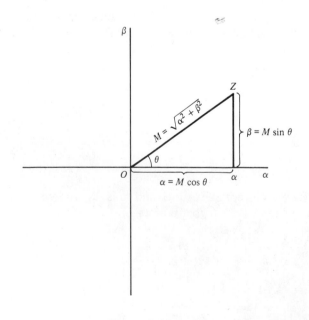

We may factor M^t from the terms in parentheses, and we can further make use of a proof known as De Moivre's theorem, which states that

$$(\cos \theta + i \sin \theta)^t = \cos \theta t + i \sin \theta t$$

to rearrange the preceding equation:

$$A_t = \bar{A} + M^t(N_1 \cos \theta t + N_2 \sin \theta t) \qquad (A.12.41)$$

The term in parentheses is an oscillating wave with constant amplitude. If, for example, θ is 45°, it would take eight periods to complete a cycle. Since this term is repetitive with constant amplitude, the growth or diminution of the cycles depends on M^t. But M is the modulus, so

$$M^t = \sqrt{\alpha^2 + \beta^2}^t$$

and it follows that stability depends on whether the modulus is greater than or less than 1. Stability of a difference equation model is therefore said to require the modulus of the complex roots to lie within the *unit circle* of the *complex plane.*

If the modulus exceeds +1, M^t grows as t increases, the amplitude of fluctuations in A_t increases, and the system is unstable. Therefore, the stability condition in the example of this chapter is

$$1 > \alpha^2 + \beta^2 = -bd$$

This implies

$$d < \left| \frac{1}{b} \right|$$

Consequently, stability of equilibrium requires the the IB curve to be steeper than the EB curve.

Observe, finally, that the real parts of the complex roots in this example are zero. Since $\alpha = 0$, $\cos \theta = 0$, so θ must be 90°. Consequently, a cycle is completed in four periods. Therefore, if we start in the deficit-recession zone, policy adjustment puts the economy in successive steps through all three of the other zones and reenters the deficit-recession zone after four periods of adjustment.

A.12.3 Continuous Policy Adjustment: Ascertaining Correct Assignment

In this appendix we use the Mundell model of Section 12.2 to study continuous policy adjustment and the determination of correct assignment. In the preceding appendix we assumed that correct assignment was known. In this appendix we make no such assumption but rather permit the analysis itself to disclose appropriate assignment.

Mundell's internal and external balance functions may be written,

$$X^* = X(G, M) \qquad X_g > 0, \quad X_m > 0$$

$$F^* = F(G, M) \qquad F_g < 0, \quad F_m < 0 \qquad \text{(A.12.22)}$$

where X^* is the target level of national income and F^* is the target balance of payments surplus. Increases in G and M both raise aggregate expenditure and reduce the balance of payments surplus.

The slope of the respective functions is given by,

$$\left(\frac{dG}{dM}\right)_x = -\frac{X_m}{X_g} < 0$$

$$\left(\frac{dG}{dM}\right)_f = -\frac{F_m}{X_g} < 0 \qquad \text{(A.12.23)}$$

and both slopes can therefore be seen to be negative, as assumed by Mundell.

The policy adjustment model can now be written,

$$k_{11}DG + k_{12}DM = X^* - X(G, M)$$

$$k_{21}DG + k_{22}DM = -[F^* - F(G, M)] \qquad \text{(A.12.24)}$$

In this formulation D is the differential operator, so that DG is equivalent to dG/dt. The k_{ij} are policy adjustment coefficients that measure the strength with which an instrument responds to discrepancies between the actual values of X and F and their target values. The analysis is greatly facilitated if the dynamic model is so set up that all of the k's are positive. Thus, the model as written states that G and M will be raised when national income is below X^*, and that both policy variables are lowered if the actual balance of payments surplus is below its target value, that is when there is a deficit in the balance of payments.

Taking linear approximations in the neighborhood of equilibrium gives the homogeneous equations,

$$k_{11}DG + k_{12}DM = -X_g(G - G^*) - X_m(M - M^*)$$

$$k_{21}DG + k_{22}DM = \quad F_g(G - G^*) + F_m(M - M^*) \qquad \text{(A.12.25)}$$

To note the similarity between the policy-adjustment model and other examples of stability analysis, we write these equations in matrix form. Therefore, write

$$\mathbf{KDP} = \mathbf{A[P - P^*]} \qquad \text{(A.12.26)}$$

and note the similarity between this and Equation (A.5.19), namely,

$$\mathbf{DX} = \mathbf{KA[X - X^*]} \qquad \text{(A.5.19)}$$

Observe that the main difference between these matrix equations is that the $\mathbf{K}$ matrix appears on the left-hand side of (A.12.26) and on the right-hand side of (A.5.19). Therefore, the policy adjustment coefficients that measure policy responses and the reaction coefficients that measure adjustment speeds are similar.

Formally, one matrix can be regarded as simply the inverse of the other. Note that if we premultiply (A.12.26) by $\mathbf{K}^{-1}$ we get,

$$\mathbf{DP} = \mathbf{K}^{-1}\mathbf{A}[\mathbf{P} - \mathbf{P}^*]$$

which is an equation identical in all respects to (A.5.19).

The next step is to replace the DP's by their trial values. If we assume trial values such as

$$DG = G^* + e^{qt} \qquad DM = M^* + e^{qt}$$

it follows that

$$DG = q(G - G^*) \qquad DM = q(M - M^*)$$

so that,

$$\mathbf{DP} = q[\mathbf{P} - \mathbf{P}^*]. \qquad (A.12.27)$$

Upon substituting this result in the left-hand side of (A.12.26), we get,

$$\mathbf{K}q[\mathbf{P} - \mathbf{P}^*] = \mathbf{A}[\mathbf{P} - \mathbf{P}^*]$$

and that

$$[\mathbf{K}q - \mathbf{A}][\mathbf{P} - \mathbf{P}^*] = 0 \qquad (A.12.28)$$

where $[\mathbf{K}q - \mathbf{A}]$ is the characteristic matrix and $[\mathbf{P} - \mathbf{P}^*]$ is the characteristic vector. Here $\mathbf{K}$ is the matrix of policy adjustment coefficients given by,

$$\mathbf{K} = \begin{bmatrix} k_{11} & k_{12} \\ k_{21} & k_{22} \end{bmatrix}$$

and its determinant is

$$|\mathbf{K}| = k_{11}k_{22} - k_{12}k_{21} \qquad (A.12.29)$$

which may be positive or negative depending on the strength of policy adjustment towards the respective targets.

The characteristic determinant is

$$|\mathbf{K}q - \mathbf{A}| = \begin{vmatrix} k_{11}q + X_g & k_{12}q + X_m \\ k_{21}q - F_g & k_{22}q - F_m \end{vmatrix}$$

and since the value of the determinant must equal zero, the characteristic polynomial is

$$|\mathbf{K}|q^2 + [k_{22}X_g - k_{11}F_m - k_{21}X_m + k_{12}F_g]q - |\mathbf{A}| = 0 \qquad (A.12.30)$$

Stability of equilibrium requires all of the coefficients to have the same sign. Policy has no control over the sign of $|\mathbf{A}|$ since $|\mathbf{A}|$ depends on the values of the structural parameters of the model. Therefore, we begin by examining $|\mathbf{A}|$ and that will tell us how $\mathbf{K}$ should be arranged, that is, how the policies should conduct themselves. The determinant of $\mathbf{A}$ is given by

$$|\mathbf{A}| = \begin{vmatrix} -X_g & -X_m \\ F_g & F_m \end{vmatrix} = -X_g F_m + F_g X_m$$

which is negative if

$$-X_g F_m < -F_g X_m$$

This implies that

$$-X_g/X_m > -F_g/F_m$$

which, as shown by (A.12.23), implies that the slope of the internal (X) balance function is greater than the external (F) balance function. Since both functions have negative slopes, this implies that the F curve is steeper than the X curve.

Inasmuch as economic theory suggested that the F curve would be the steeper of the two curves, we conclude that $|A|$ must be negative so that $-|A|$ is positive. The characteristic equation then implies that $|K|$ must also be positive if policy is to be stabilizing. Recalling that the determinant of K is

$$|K| = k_{11}k_{22} - k_{12}k_{21}$$

and that the model has been arranged so that all the adjustment coefficients are positive, we can see that stability would be assured if k_{21} and k_{12} were set equal to zero. That means that fiscal policy should not concern itself at all with external balance and that monetary policy should not concern itself at all with internal balance. Therefore, assignment should be exclusive. If $|A|$ is negative, fiscal policy should aim its efforts at internal balance exclusively while monetary policy aims exclusively at external balance. One policy instrument should not make the mistake of assisting the other policy to achieve its target since this risks the destabilization of its own target.

This presumption is confirmed by inspecting the second coefficient of the characteristic equation. The terms $k_{22}X_g$ and $-k_{11}F_m$ are both positive. But the terms $-k_{21}X_m$ and $k_{12}F_g$ are both negative unless the adjustment coefficients are set at values of zero.

Of course if it turns out that $|A|$ is positive, the assignment should then be reversed. $|K|$ should then be organized so as to make it negative which can best be done by setting k_{11} and k_{22} equal to zero. Fiscal policy then aims for external balance while monetary policy aims for internal balance.

PART FOUR

THE INTERNATIONAL MONETARY SYSTEM

Having digested the analytical materials of previous chapters, we can now proceed with ease to the interpretation of past events and contemporary problems. In Chapter 13 we describe the evolving characteristics of the international monetary system from the nineteenth-century gold standard to the demise of the Bretton Woods system in 1973. Attention focuses on the anatomy of successes and failures in the hope that historical experience will serve as a useful guide to the understanding of contemporary problems. After examining the pre–World War I gold standard, the narrative moves to the unsuccessful attempt to reestablish the gold standard after the war and the subsequent chaotic conditions of the 1930s. The post–World War II Bretton Woods system is then described, and the causes of its eventual breakdown are traced. The chapter concludes with a description of reform efforts designed to salvage the floundering system.

Chapter 14 discusses major aspects of the international monetary system during the flexible exchange-rate era that began in 1973. The causes and consequences of unexpectedly large fluctuations in real exchange rates are analyzed. The optimistic promises of flexible exchange-rate advocates are contrasted with the sobering realizations. And, finally, the mounting global debt problem is reviewed. What caused the explosive rise in global debt? What are its likely consequences for the world economy? And how can the problem be dealt with?

Chapter 15 concludes the book with a survey of suggestions for international monetary reform. One section reviews suggestions for reducing countries' vulnerability to external shocks resulting from large and unstable capital movements. A second section deals with suggested guidelines for government exchange market intervention. Included are such proposals as wider bands, crawling and gliding pegs, the reference-rate proposal, and the proposal to target countries' reserve levels. A third section discusses the concept of the optimum currency area, that is, a group of regions or countries with the characteristic that it is desirable to maintain fixed exchange rates or have a uniform currency inside the area, and the further characteristic that it is desirable to have exchange rate flexibility between the entire area and other optimum currency areas. This leads, quite naturally, to the international monetary system as it might productively evolve by the year 2010.

Chapter 13

The International Monetary System to 1973

13.1 THE NINETEENTH-CENTURY GOLD STANDARD

In Chapter 1 we noted that an international monetary system has four requirements: (1) It must provide a procedure for determining exchange rates. (2) It must provide a generally acceptable reserve asset to be used in the settlement of deficits and surpluses. (3) It must provide adjustment mechanisms that ensure that deficits and surpluses even out in the long run. (4) It must provide for the growth of reserves in order to finance economic growth and the expansion of international trade.

With the emphasis on the word system, it is fair to say that the nineteenth-century gold standard was the first really well-organized international monetary system. However, countries certainly pursued conscious international economic policies prior to that time. Perhaps the most well-known policy was the attempt, by eighteenth-century France, to enhance national power by gold accumulation. This policy, known as mercantilism, attempted to maximize exports, minimize imports, and thereby maximize the accumulation of gold.

Equating gold with national power seems quaint to modern minds, even though some still adhere to such notions. But it did make a certain amount of sense during the nationalistic and warlike environment of King Louis XIV. Military adventurism was high on the list of national activities, and that could best go forward if the monarch had available to him a substantial war chest of gold with which arms and provisions could be easily acquired on foreign soil. Thus gold did, in fact, provide national power.

The term "neomercantilism" is still widely used today to characterize a foreign economic policy perspective that is autarchic, inward-looking, and nationalistic. Such policy considers national autonomy and economic self-sufficiency as its primary goals, and it is quite ready to achieve such objectives as high domestic employment and favorable terms of trade at the expense of other countries. Neomercantilism was widespread during the 1930s when country after country imposed trade restrictions, devalued its currency, and imposed exchange controls in an effort to raise domestic employment at the expense of other countries.

In contrast, there is the liberal approach, which emphasizes the gains from the free and open movement of goods and services, supports the concept of a collective approach to monetary and exchange rate issues, and regards the enhancement of national power as an unsuitable use of economic policy. The intellectual thrust for the liberal economic order came primarily from the English classical economists of the late eighteenth and early nineteenth centuries. Adam Smith's *Wealth of Nations,* published in 1776, argued that economic progress comes from the "division of labor," by which Smith meant specialization, and that the division of labor was limited only by the size of the market. David Ricardo contributed the law of comparative advantage, which showed that countries could enjoy higher output levels with the same quantity of factor inputs, provided they specialized in their areas of greatest relative efficiency and traded freely with each other. In the monetary sphere, David Hume ridiculed the mercantilist preoccupation with gold accumulation by suggesting that the gains from a gold inflow were illusory because such an inflow would lead to a rise in the price level, thereby diminishing the real value of the gold. Similarly, a country suffering a gold loss would undergo price deflation, thereby raising the purchasing-power value of its remaining gold. It also followed from Hume's theory of specie flow that an export surplus procured by various restrictive devices would not be permanent, since the inflow of gold would increase the price level, thereby reducing the country's competitive advantage, so the hard-earned surplus would dwindle and possibly become a deficit.

While British economists were providing the intellectual basis for the liberal international economic order, the success of British industry appeared to demonstrate that free markets and free trade were the most promising road to rapid industrialization, capital accumulation, and rising living standards. Since industrialization was accomplished earlier in Britain than elsewhere, the second half of the nineteenth century found Britain with a surplus of savings over domestic investment that became the principal source of capital for the financing of economic development in other lands. These countries found it important to maintain the parity of their own currencies with the pound sterling, and to ensure that their currencies would be convertible into British pounds. Others, therefore, tended to march in step with British policy toward gold, and they looked to London for leadership in financial affairs. Thus the gold standard evolved without benefit of an international conference or the signing of any formal treaties. The so-called heyday of the system was the period between the Franco-Prussian War of 1870 and the beginning of World War I in 1914.

Gold ruled as king during that period. Until 1870 silver had competed with gold as an international reserve currency. In the United States agitation to adopt a bimetallic standard continued until the late 1890s as populists, representing agrarian and debtor interests, demanded expansion of the nation's money supply to stem the price deflation that characterized the post 1870 period. Unfortunately, bimetallic standards tend not to work very well. The market prices at which gold and silver exchange are almost certain to depart from the official price at which the two metals can be exchanged at the national treasury. When that happens, there is a run on the treasury. For example, if silver mining output increases due to a mineral discovery and if the market price of silver declines because of the increase in supply, owners of silver can exchange their silver for gold at the treasury at the higher official price. This soon exhausts the gold reserves of the treasury and turns the bimetallic standard into a silver standard with silver as the remaining reserve currency. "Bad" money therefore drives out "good" money, a phenomenom known as Gresham's law.

Gresham's law is extremely important. It tends to operate whenever there are competing reserve assets. The substitution of one reserve asset for another can cause monetary shrinkage, exchange rate instability, and other disruptions. The gold exchange standard of the 1920s was extremely unstable. Under the post–World War II Bretton Woods system there was a constant scramble to prevent the bad currency (the dollar) from driving out the good money (gold). And, as we will see in Chapter 15, there is good reason to believe that the multicurrency reserve system that has recently evolved contains similar potential for instability.

To join other countries on the gold standard, a country simply had to define the value of its own currency in terms of gold, to permit unlimited gold exports and imports, and to agree to buy and sell gold unconditionally in exchange for its own currency at a fixed price. When each country defined its currency in terms of gold, the effect was to peg currency values to each other, thereby creating a system of fixed exchange rates. During the 1880–1914 period the official value of the British pound sterling was fixed at $4.866. If the market price of the pound sterling were

$5.00, an American importer would have had to pay $5.00 for each pound needed to pay for imports if he bought pounds directly. But if he spent $4.866 to purchase gold at the U.S. Treasury, he could convert that into £1 at the British Treasury at a saving of $0.134 ($5.00 − $4.866). Consequently, when the pound tended to rise, gold tended to flow to Great Britain. When the pound tended to decline against the dollar, the opposite tended to happen. Speedy arbitrage would tend to ensure that the market price and the official price would never deviate very much.

In practice, the dollar-pound exchange rate fluctuated within a narrow range because of the presence of transportation costs. A pound sterling's worth of gold cost about $0.026 to ship from New York to London. Consequently, the pound would have had to rise above $4.866 + $0.026 = $4.892 before gold would have been transferred to London, and it would have to have fallen below $4.866 − $0.026 = $4.840 before gold would have been transferred from London to New York. These outer limits were called the gold import and export points for Great Britain.

Countries on the gold standard were expected to abide by two unwritten laws. The first was that the convertibility of a country's currency into gold be unconditional and that it would not, under any circumstance, consider a change in the official price of gold. Exchange rates were therefore to be frozen as well as fixed. The rationale can be seen by comparing the likely behavior of speculators under rigidly fixed exchange rates as opposed to their behavior under an adjustable peg system. For example, under the adjustable peg system, such as the post–World War II Bretton Woods system, a deficit in the U.S. balance of payments would be reflected in reserve losses and in the fact that the pound would always be at the upper gold point of $4.892. This information signals to speculators that the dollar is overvalued and, since the monetary authority is losing reserves, that the government will soon be forced to devalue the dollar. Anticipating a rise in the official dollar price of the pound, speculators would sell dollars to acquire pounds with the intention of buying the dollars back more cheaply after the devaluation. Such action would be reflected in accelerating capital outflows that widen the deficit, accelerate the loss of reserves, and therefore force a devaluation that might otherwise have been avoided. To avert such destabilizing speculation, authorities considered it necessary to stick to the previously established official price at all costs. Convinced that the official price will never change, speculators would regard that as the normal equilibrium price. Therefore if the pound were to rise, speculators would regard the higher price as abnormal. They would then sell pounds, rather than buy them, thereby moving the market price back toward the official price.

These considerations make it easy to see why advocates of a return to a gold or other fixed exchange-rate system often argue that an adjustable peg system tends to fail precisely because it is not a genuine fixed exchange-rate system. They claim that the game is lost once countries show a willingness to devalue or revalue their currencies, because speculation then will tend to become destabilizing when the market judges a currency to be seriously over- or undervalued.

In order to make the fixed gold price commitment stick, government must moderate reserve losses, and this means it must prevent large and persistent deficits. This accounts for the second unwritten law of the gold standard—that a country suffering a balance-of-payments deficit would be expected to pursue a restrictive monetary policy to slow or reverse gold outflows and bring the balance of payments into equilibrium. Symmetrical commitments were expected on the parts of surplus countries. This meant that monetary policies were to be directed exclusively to external balance requirements. Such monetary policies would be consistent with internal balance if a deficit coincides with domestic inflation and a surplus coincides with domestic recession. But if a surplus country suffers inflation and a deficit country suffers recession, the monetary policy requirements would be such that monetary policy would worsen both inflation and recession in the respective countries. Nevertheless, countries were expected to follow such monetary policies in the interest of protecting their gold reserves and maintaining the fixed exchange-rate commitment.

Under the gold standard it was expected that balance-of-payments adjustment would be facilitated by flexible price levels. If the demand for British goods rose in the United States, this would increase the demand for pounds, thereby tending to raise the dollar price of pounds. Gold would then flow from the U.S. Treasury to the Bank of England. As the Treasury sells gold, it buys back dollars, and as the Bank of England buys gold, it sells pounds. Consequently, the money supply declines automatically in the United States and rises automatically in Great Britain. This has a restrictive effect on the economy in the United States and an expansionary effect on the British economy. The decline in aggregate expenditure in the United States tends to reduce wages and prices while the opposite happens in Great Britain. As a result there is a change in the real exchange rate that makes U.S. goods more attractive and British goods less attractive, so the deficit in the U.S. balance of payments tends to dwindle and move into surplus while the opposite happens to the British balance of payments. In addition, since the money supply changes would cause interest rates to rise in the United States and to decline in Great Britain, the U.S. current-account deficit would, in part, be financed and offset by a capital inflow into the United States.

To summarize provisionally: gold was the reserve currency; the exchange rate regime was one of rigidly fixed exchange rates; and the adjustment mechanism operated through the influence of changing money supplies on price levels and interest rates. The logic of the system greatly appealed to those who believed in natural harmony and who distrusted government interference in economic affairs. Fixed exchange rates and a commitment to gold convertibility would enforce a discipline that would prevent countries from inflating their currencies. Abiding by the rules of the game meant that price levels would fall in deficit countries and rise in surplus countries, thereby ensuring overall price stability. The rules of the game also implied that the burden of balance-of-payments adjustment would fall equitably among deficit and surplus countries.

There is a fourth requirement for an international monetary system—it must provide reserve growth in a manner sufficient to accommodate the growth of trade but not so rapidly as to be inflationary. It appeared that an obvious weakness of the gold standard, true of any metallic standard, is that the growth of reserves depends haphazardly on fortuitous gold discoveries. Moreover, since the level of gold reserves also determined the size of a nation's money supply, there seemed to be no orderly way to generate appropriate rates of monetary growth.

Defendants of the gold standard had a ready reply to this criticism. They argued that if real income tended to grow more rapidly than the world's money stock, this would reduce price levels. This meant that the cost of mining gold would decline relative to the official price of gold, and this would encourage gold production. Similarly, if gold reserves and money supplies were growing more rapidly than justified by growth of potential output, the resulting inflation would raise the cost of gold production relative to the official price of gold, so gold production would be discouraged. The natural order would prevail to ensure adequate world monetary growth without government intervention.

Like many other notions about the gold standard, this idea was far-fetched—fine in theory, but irrelevant in practice. Throughout history, additions to the world's gold stock appear to have been the result of fortuitous discoveries of gold and to improvements in mining technology that permitted easier recovery and refining. This was no less true during the nineteenth century. Gold production increased in response to the gold discoveries in California in 1848 and again in response to discoveries in the Klondike and in South Africa in the 1890s. Mining technology also advanced during the century. From 1870 to 1895 price deflation proceeded unmercifully in the United States as the consequence of inadequate money supply growth. There is no evidence that this stimulated gold production. It did stimulate agitation to expand the money supply, which finally subsided in response to the gold discoveries of the 1890s.

It has been estimated that the world's money supply grew fairly steadily at an annual rate of about $3\frac{1}{2}$ percent between 1870 and 1913. The gold stock grew at a far slower rate, and the rate of growth was not steady. Money supply growth was achieved by the rapid growth of financial institutions and by financial innovations that generated bank deposits as additions to the stock of currency. According to Robert Triffin, about 90 percent of the world's monetary expansion over the period was in the form of deposit credit; thus, by 1913 deposit credit and paper currency accounted for almost 90 percent of the total world money supply. The shortage of gold, rather than bringing about a rise in the supply of gold, created an incentive to find substitutes.

The world economy grew rapidly during the era of the gold standard. World merchandise exports tripled between 1880 and 1914, and large amounts of capital flowed from the mature British economy to other lands, where it enabled economic development to move forward at a rapid pace. The pains of major inflations and deflations were avoided, and wage and price trends in different countries were similar, so severe maladjustments and dislocations were averted. The period was favored by an abundance of scientific discoveries and technological advances that provided ample investment opportunities, by a favorable international investment climate promoted by the absence of major wars and international tensions, and by the rapid development and availability of abundant raw material supplies. Adjustment in such an environment of growth is far easier and less painful than in a stationary or stagnant one. For example, with productivity and real wages growing rapidly, adjustment to a payments deficit could be achieved by a barely noticeable slowdown in the rate of wage increase rather than by the need to lower the absolute wage level, which would be required in the absence of growth in labor productivity.

As a consequence of the appearance of success, there developed a mystique about the gold standard that proved destructive, since it prompted countries to seek a return to the gold standard after World War I when conditions were such that gold standard arrangements were no longer workable. Countries discovered to their sorrow that wages and prices were no longer flexible, so balance-of-payments adjustments were bought at the cost of fluctuations in output and employment rather than in wages and prices. The general inflation caused by World War I had been so severe that the gold stock was grossly inadequate as a reserve asset at prewar parities. And the different inflation rates that had been suffered by different countries during and after the war produced a situation in which exchange rates, at the prewar parities, were chronically at variance with purchasing-power parity, thereby implying large balance-of-payments deficits and surpluses.

Only as the result of subsequent research and reappraisal of the gold standard has it become apparent that the mystique of the gold standard had been largely an idealized fiction. The adjustment mechanism had not operated in the manner prescribed by the theory. The incidence of adjustment had not been fairly distributed between deficit and surplus nations. And, generally, the benefits of the system had not been nearly as great as they had been cracked up to be. The system did work fairly well as seen from the perspective of a central country such as Great Britain, but countries on the periphery, especially those that supplied agricultural products and raw materials, suffered considerable instability and hardship. In fact, the pain of adjustment was so great in some cases that countries occasionally altered their official exchange rates or let their currencies float to mitigate the harsh discipline of the gold standard.

The theory of current-account adjustment under the gold standard predicted that a balance-of-payments deficit (surplus) leads to an outflow (inflow) of gold. This reduces (increases) the country's money supply and leads to a decline (rise) in the price level. This improves (worsens) its international competitive position, thereby reversing the current account. In practice, however, the theory hardly received a fair test, because very little gold actually flowed from one country to another. In addition, later research showed that current accounts adjusted much more rapidly than could be explained by differential movements in price levels. As suggested in Chapter 4, this speedier adjustment undoubtedly came about because of fluctuations in real income levels. When a country's export demand falls, a deficit develops in its current account. But since the decline in exports reduces national income, it also reduces the demand for imports, thereby tending to offset a major part of the deficit. Had countries had available adequate national income and employment data, as well as the benefits of Keynesian multiplier theory, they would have discovered the fact that adjustment had actually been bought, in part, by painful fluctuations in income and employment rather than in relatively harmless changes in wages and prices. As it was, the income effect was not considered in gold standard theorizing, which caused the picture to be painted in brighter tones than circumstances warranted.

The absence of substantial gold flows seems to have been largely due to the prompt response of short-term capital movements to current-account deficits. Even without money supply changes caused by gold flows, adherence to the rules of the game prompted countries' central banks to undertake restrictive actions, in response to a current-account deficit, that raised interest rates and attracted the short-term capital that financed the current account. The principal means for doing this was to vary the central bank's discount rate, that is, the rate at which the central bank lends to commercial banks. When the Bank of England raised its "bank rate," other interest rates followed, and capital was attracted. This prevented the exchange rate from moving outside the gold points, thereby preventing gold losses. It was even possible, in this manner, to attract gold while simultaneously having a current-account deficit.

Robert Triffin's study of adjustment under the gold standard suggests that the adjustment burden fell, to a heavily disproportionate degree, on exporters of agricultural products and raw materials.[1] When the Bank of England raised its bank rate, the slowdown in the British economy reduced the demand for imported raw materials. Because the supply of such commodities is inelastic with respect to price, this caused a sharp decline in their prices. In addition, since inventories of these materials were largely financed by borrowing in London, a rise in British interest rates induced stock reductions that added to supplies, thereby further depressing their prices. The income losses suffered by the supplier countries would then cause a reduction in their demand for British manufactured goods, so the prices of these goods would also fall. However, since the supply elasticity for manufactured goods was (and is) greater than the supply elasticity of agricultural commodities, the decline in British export prices was less than the decline in import prices. Britain's terms of trade therefore improved at the expense of the materials-exporting countries and at exactly the time that gold standard theory would have predicted the opposite. The price declines caused sharp income losses in materials-exporting countries. Such countries sometimes found it necessary to depreciate their currencies against gold and the pound, and to suspend their commitment to gold convertibility, in efforts to restore their export markets. The adjustment process was anything but symmetrical.

Finally, long-term investment played an important role during the gold standard era, and that, too, influenced the adjustment process. Britain was the principal supplier of long-term capital, although some other European countries also became capital exporters prior to World War I. It has been estimated that foreign investment equaled 4 percent of British national income in 1880, 7 percent in 1905, and 9 percent in 1913. This 9 percent accounted for fully one half of total British saving in 1913. For the recipient countries, this was the source of capital that enabled them to develop their economies. A steady flow of long-term capital also meant that current-account deficits could be run for an extended period of time without the need for adjustment. Unfortunately the flow of capital was uneven, and this unevenness was sometimes a source of income shrinkage

[1] Triffin, Robert, "The Evolution of the International Monetary System," *Princeton Studies in International Finance*, No. 12, 1964.

and instability. Professor James Ingram of the University of North Carolina explains the reasons for this as follows:

> When the British economy was booming, its demand for raw-material imports would be rising and British capital would flow abroad to develop additional sources of supply. In the peripheral countries, these capital inflows would increase their capacity to import, already swollen by favorable prices for their exports of raw materials. But when Britain's boom gave way to recession, the capital flows would dry up and, at the same time, prices of raw material exports would fall. Thus the peripheral countries would face a sharp reduction in their capacity to import goods and services from the outside world. In this way, the system tended to exaggerate economic instability in the peripheral countries. This instability was evidently too severe to be accomodated through internal price and wage adjustments, and the peripheral countries responded by allowing their currencies to fluctuate against gold.[2]

In conclusion, any system of fixed exchange rates is likely to encounter difficulties. Conflicts between the goals of external and internal balance are inevitable. When currency prices are pegged, changes in the real exchange rate can come about only through changes in price levels. And if price levels are rigid, balance-of-payments adjustment will necessitate fluctuations in real income and employment. These problems are compounded by the fact that the automatic intervention required to maintain official parities causes changes in money supplies, so monetary policy is no longer usable for the purpose of achieving internal balance. The adjustment problem can be eased if official parities are occasionally changed to reflect market conditions, but this raises a new problem in that an adjustable peg system invites destabilizing speculation. A gold or other form of metallic standard carries with it the additional difficulty that reserve growth tends to be haphazard and unrelated to the needs of the international economy. This problem can be addressed by developing a supplementary reserve asset, such as the dollar or other national currency. However, such a "gold exchange" standard brings Gresham's law into play. If the market values gold more highly than the official gold-dollar parity, dollars will be exchanged for gold at national treasuries, the gold moves into private hoards, and is then no longer a reserve asset. The gold exchange standard automatically becomes a dollar standard giving rise to additional problems, as we will see later in this chapter.

Although there are some who favor a return to the gold standard, they are in the minority and there is little enthusiasm for reversing the

---

[2] Ingram, James C., *International Economics,* 2nd ed., 1986. Wiley, p. 135.

process by which gold has come to play a diminishing role in the international monetary system. In addition to the economic issues already noted, a return to gold would necessitate a large increase in official gold prices. That would cause a huge redistribution of wealth in favor of individuals and countries that have hoarded gold, and it would greatly increase the incomes of gold producers. Few people today wish to raise the prices of South African gold stocks or throw a major windfall gain in the direction of the Soviet Union or the world's "gold bugs" and speculators.

13.2 BETWEEN THE WORLD WARS: 1918–40

Anarchy and chaos are the words that most readily come to mind when one contemplates an attempt to characterize international monetary relations during the so-called interwar period. Much of the economic integration that had occurred prior to World War I was destroyed by the war. As a consequence of the war, the Austro-Hungarian Empire was dismantled, communism took over in Russia, and Germany was saddled with huge reparations payments that were to greatly complicate international monetary relations. Many countries suffered wartime destruction of productive capacity while others found the war an opportunity to develop their own industries. Creditor countries had liquidated their assets to pay for the war, and some erstwhile debtor countries, most notably the United States, became creditor countries. Prices doubled in the United States during the war, but that was less than the increases of 150 and 250 percent in Britain and France, respectively.

The outbreak of the war caused most countries to suspend their gold convertibility commitment. After the war came a quest for "normalcy" that included efforts to restore the gold standard. However, the wartime differential inflation rates made a return to prewar parities impractical, so countries delayed returning to the gold standard and many currencies fluctuated during the 1919–26 period. It seems to have been widely assumed that restoration of the gold standard was desirable. The question was not whether, but when, and at what official parities. Although some advocated a return to the prewar parities, others felt it necessary to take account of the vastly different inflation rates experienced by countries during the war, and such opinion counseled the fixing of exchange rates at more realistic parities. It was at this time that economists revived the purchasing-power-parity theory, which generally operated on the shaky assumption that the prewar real exchange rates were appropriate. This implied that nominal exchange rates should be set so as to offset the effects of differential price-level changes on the real exchange rate. The Swedish economist Gustav Cassel suggested that the prewar pound price of $4.866 should be multiplied by the ratio of postwar U.S. prices to British prices to find the appropriate dollar-pound exchange rate.[3] With 1914 as the base year (=100), this implied a dollar price for the pound of $4.866(202/246) = $4.00. Similar calculations suggested that the French franc should be fixed at about 55 percent of its prewar parity in terms of the dollar. The United States forced the issue prematurely by announcing its intention to resume gold sales at the prewar price of $20.67 an ounce. Many other countries quickly realized that to join the United States in this project was to saddle themselves with huge deficits and immediate gold losses. Consequently, they postponed a decision to peg their currencies, and they permitted their currencies to float, at least temporarily. This was true even for Great Britain, the mother and shepherdess of the gold standard, despite her determination ultimately to restore prewar parities. Returning to the gold standard was one thing; returning at prewar parities under the conditions prevailing in 1920 was something quite different.

Countries responded to the postwar environment in different ways. By early 1920 the British pound had fallen to about $3.40 in foreign exchange markets. Policymakers were determined to restore the prewar parity of $4.86; consequently, British financial policies became harshly restrictive. However, wages and prices were downwardly inflexible, so the deflation resulted in severe unemployment and labor strife. The rigidity of the price level meant that imports continued to be attractive and exports continued to be uncompetitive. British exports also encountered heavy weather abroad because the war had given other countries opportunities to make inroads into traditionally British markets. Nevertheless, the pound gradually recovered so that by 1924 the goal of the prewar parity seemed within reach. Since there was a general expectation that convertibility of the pound into gold would soon become a reality, foreign capital moved in to purchase pounds, and this added temporary strength to the exchange value of the pound.

The restoration of convertibility came in 1925 when the Chancellor of the Exchequer, Winston Churchill, announced that gold would again be sold at the prewar price. This step proved disastrous. The capital inflows that had anticipated convertibility dried up, pressure on the British gold stock resumed, and the deflationary policies therefore had to be continued. Apparently obsessed with the desire to maintain its status as the world's banker, Britain's policymakers inflicted a degree of deflationary pressure

[3] Cassel, Gustav, *Money and Foreign Exchange After 1914,* Macmillan, 1923.

on the economy that caused high unemployment and severe hardships throughout the 1920s and denied Britain a share of the prosperity that most countries enjoyed during the decade. Predictably, the government's policies evoked sharp outcries on the parts of labor leaders as well as some economists. John Maynard Keynes published two polemics, one entitled *The Economic Consequences of Mr. Churchill,* in which he castigated "outworn dogmas," denounced the deflationary policies, and ridiculed the gold standard as a "barbarous relic."[4]

Britain's problems were not rendered any easier by the policies of other countries. The United States enjoyed a balance-of-payments surplus and gold inflows during the early 1920s. However, the Federal Reserve decided not to play according to the gold standard rules. Rather than permitting the money supply to increase in response to the gold inflows, the Fed attempted to dampen the inflationary effects of the inflows by offsetting the money supply increases with open-market sales of domestic assets. This gold sterilization represented an important watershed, marking a conscious effort on the part of American economic policy makers to place the goal of internal balance ahead of external balance. However, it also introduced the problem that when surplus countries refuse to permit inflation, the entire burden of adjustment then falls on deficit countries, with the consequence that an overall deflationary bias is inflicted on the world economy.

While the British were taking the path of deflation and what they regarded as moral rectitude, the French were doing the opposite. The French economy had been severely damaged by the war, and reconstruction required large-scale government expenditures. These expenditures were not matched by tax increases in part because of political instability and in part because it was optimistically assumed that reparations payments from Germany would help balance the budget. The government issued large volumes of short-term debt to finance its expenditures. Not wishing to slow reconstruction because of higher interest rates, the Bank of France bought large amounts of this debt, thus increasing the money supply rapidly. Thus, in sharp contrast to Britain, France adopted highly expansionary fiscal and monetary policies.

The prewar value of the franc had been slightly over $0.19. By early 1920 the franc had depreciated to less than $0.08. It stabilized for the next two years, but after early 1922 it went into a period of steady decline, falling below $0.03 in mid-1926. French governments came and went as if through a revolving door, so it became clear that the expansionary

---

[4] Keynes, John Maynard, *A Tract on Monetary Reform,* Macmillan, 1924, and *The Economic Consequences of Mr. Churchill,* Macmillan, 1925.

policies would probably continue. Consequently, there developed a nearly universal expectation that the franc was likely to continue to fall. Speculators then ensured that this would happen. Importers accelerated purchases from abroad while exporters held on to their foreign exchange earnings. Holders of francs liquidated them to purchase foreign assets. The franc continued to decline.

This process was interrupted briefly when the conservative Raymond Poincare formed a new government in late 1923. He borrowed $100 million from J. P. Morgan and Co. and used this to purchase francs, thereby lending strength to the franc and giving speculators a slap on the wrist. However, the government fell at the general election of May 1924, so the restrictive policies that had been proposed by Poincare were shelved.

By July 1926 the franc had fallen to a low of $0.02. Poincare again formed a government, and this time his fiscal and monetary program was adopted. The franc then rebounded to $0.04 in December at which time the Bank of France announced its intention to stabilize the franc. The floating exchange-rate period was now over, and France was, for practical purposes, back on the gold standard. With confidence in the franc restored, capital began to return, and the franc then appeared to be clearly undervalued. But rather than permit the franc to appreciate further, the Bank of France accumulated foreign exchange, which it then converted into gold. Since a large part of this gold accumulation came at the expense of the British gold stock, French policy operated, as a companion to American monetary policy, to force continuation of British deflationary policies.

The 1920–25 period was important for the future, since it fostered widespread antipathy to flexible exchange rates, which, in turn, colored the post–World War II negotiations that established the Bretton Woods system of fixed exchange rates. However, subsequent reevaluation of the period suggested that Britain's problems were self-inflicted and could not be attributed to a floating pound, and French fiscal and monetary policies would very quickly have undermined any attempt by the government to return to gold. The claim that the discipline of the gold standard would have forced France to change its monetary and fiscal policies appears unrealistic in the extreme. One fact that makes flexible exchange-rate experiences seem so chaotic is that surrounding conditions are so adverse that fixed exchange rates are not feasible, and governments then float their currencies out of sheer desperation. More recently, when flexible exchange rates came into being in 1973, the world economy very quickly had to deal with the energy crisis, exceedingly adverse world food production conditions, and the shock of transition from a fixed exchange-rate system in which exchange rates had gotten badly out of line. Flexible exchange rates did not cause these problems. It is safe to say that a fixed exchange-rate system would never have been able to absorb and withstand such major shocks as wars or severe supply restrictions, such as those that occurred during the 1970s. One can say without fear of much contradition that the fixed exchange-rate system is a fair-weather system. Comparison of the 1880–1914 period with a period such as the years from 1919 to 1925 cannot possibly produce a fair or relevant comparison.

The fair-weather nature of the gold standard became painfully apparent during the years following Britain's return to gold in 1925. In 1922 only ten countries were on the gold standard. By 1927 there were 38, indicating that failure was not for lack of desire. But the system had no staying power. It collapsed in 1931, and by 1936 there were hardly any countries left that retained a commitment to sell gold at a fixed price. Keynes had long ago pronounced the system "dead as mutton."

The system, during the interwar period, faced many severe obstacles that it had not previously had to contend with. The first problem was that there simply wasn't enough gold to go around. War inflation meant that the existing stock of gold was inadequate when valued at prewar prices. This shortage could have been alleviated by increasing the price of gold to take inflation into account. However, this path was blocked by the determination of both the United States and Great Britain to honor dollar and sterling claims with the same amount of gold as previously. The old theory that high commodity prices relative to the official price of gold would discourage gold production seemed also to be working, and very little gold was produced. A world economic conference held in Genoa, Italy, in 1922 suggested dealing with this problem by having countries withdraw gold from circulation and by encouraging countries, other than the main financial centers, to hold convertible currencies, rather than gold, as their reserves. Many countries did, in fact, withdraw gold coins from circulation, and a gold cum-convertible currency system was established when Britain resumed convertibility in 1925. This system came to be called the gold exchange standard.

Regrettably, similar international cooperation was not in evidence with respect to such matters as determining appropriate and consistent currency parities, or cooperating in the adjustment process, or figuring out a way for Germany to perform the miracle of maintaining reparations payments without permitting her to earn the gold needed to make these payments through an export surplus. One of the phenomena that writers about the period usually emphasize is growing nationalism together with increasing erosion of the liberal outlook and its replacement by a narrower mercantilist attitude. When push came to shove, countries went it alone. We have already seen that the United States sterilized its gold inflows and refused to permit the economy to suffer inflation as a consequence of her surplus. We also saw that France fixed its exchange rate so as to undervalue the franc, and she then used this position to accumulate gold, thereby first compounding the problems of other countries and finally acting to undermine the gold exchange standard. Most countries followed suit. Hardly anyone was prepared to play the gold standard game in view of their concern with domestic employment and their lack of confidence in the cooperation of others. By 1931 even the British had had enough. Looking back on the period, one marvels at the weirdly inconsistent policies pursued. Germany was expected to pay reparations in gold. But the only way to earn gold is to run an export surplus or to borrow. However, running a surplus is not possible if other countries are busy erecting tariff walls to keep out German goods. For a time Germany kept up reparations payments by foreign borrowing, mostly in New York. But when the stock market crashed in 1929, this source of credit vanished, Germany could not pay her bills, those in other countries that were dependent on a flow of German funds could not maintain their commitments, either, so the entire global credit structure came tumbling down, as the crash in New York reverberated throughout the world.

There was no cooperative effort designed to establish appropriate exchange rates, with the consequence that currency parities, once determined, were such that large and continuous deficits and surpluses were implied. Countries simply went back on the gold standard at some rate preferred by the country. The pound became greatly overvalued, and the dollar and the franc were undervalued, thus ensuring that Britain and other countries with overvalued currencies would suffer deficits and deflationary pressures. Even if a country attempted to find an appropriate exchange rate, it could not do so because it had no way of knowing what rates would be adopted by countries that had not yet returned to the gold standard. International capital was also highly mobile, but unlike the prewar period when capital movements tended to be stabilizing, short-term capital flitted around the world in response to rumors, political crises, and the like. There were frequent speculative runs of "hot money" that were disruptive and that helped to harden governments' determination to insulate their economies from external shocks.

In an insightful summary of the essence of the problem, James Ingram notes that

> Nations were no longer willing to let their domestic economic conditions be determined by the dictates of external influences. It is significant that in the pre-1914 period gold movements were small and adjustment surprisingly quick and effective, while in the postwar period gold movements

were large but adjustment slow and ineffective. The reason for this change is that nations deliberately blocked the adjustment mechanism called for by gold-standard theory.[5]

France began pegging her exchange rate in late 1926. The official return to the gold standard came two years later, in combination with a new law that prohibited the Bank of France from issuing currency not backed by gold. Consequently, the Bank of France immediately converted foreign exchange earnings into gold, thereby violating the rules of the gold exchange standard under which she was expected to hold foreign exchange. With both France and the United States accumulating gold, the already inadequate gold stock came to be concentrated in these two countries.

Meanwhile, the countries that were losing gold were subjected to more serious deflationary pressures. They had to rely to an increasing degree on reserves of foreign exchange as a means of settlement in an environment of diminishing confidence that the foreign exchange would be accepted in lieu of gold.

To make matters worse, the gold exchange standard contained a technical flaw that virtually ensured unstable money supplies. Most countries, including the United States, had laws that required currency issues to be backed by gold. Thus, when gold was lost, central banks automatically had to repatriate currency issues by open-market sales. Under the circumstances, if one central bank decided to convert its pounds into gold, this would simply change the composition of that central bank's reserves. But the gold reserves of the Bank of England would be reduced, and this would force monetary contraction in Great Britain without bringing about a symmetrical increase in the money supply of the country receiving gold. Loss of gold usually meant monetary contraction, but increases in a country's gold reserves could be sterilized.

As the world economy entered the 1930s, it was already heading into a major economic cataclysm. Deflationary pressures were widespread, and many countries were sliding into depression. The Wall Street crash of 1929 had wiped out much financial wealth in the United States and had forced the suspension of German reparations payments. The political situation was deteriorating as Nazism was threatening to take control in Germany. Raw materials prices were depressed, and supplying countries could not meet their obligations, forcing Australia and five Latin American countries to abandon the gold standard. Owners of financial wealth found it difficult to guard the value of their holdings. Their extreme

[5] Ingram, op. cit., p. 156.

uneasiness readied them to abandon a currency at the slightest sign of weakness.

The first major run came in May 1931 when rumors of insolvency led to a wholesale withdrawal of deposits from the Credit Anstalt, Austria's largest bank. This was followed by capital flight from Germany. In the summer foreign depositors began removing funds from British banks, and the drain of British gold reserves accelerated to flood levels. Although the Bank of England received hastily negotiated loans from the Federal Reserve and the Bank of France, the flight from the pound could not be stopped. The British, faced with the choice of further deflation of an already depressed economy or the suspension of gold sales, finally opted for the latter. Many other countries soon followed, and that put an end to the futile attempt to resurrect the prewar gold standard.

Following the demise of gold, international monetary relations degenerated into a destructive free-for-all in which countries scrambled to protect themselves from foreign shocks and simultaneously sent deflationary shocks to others. Not knowing how to deal effectively with unemployment, countries tried to ship their unemployment abroad. Steep tariff barriers were erected, import quotas were imposed, currencies were depreciated competitively, and exchange controls designed to reduce or eliminate the flow of international capital were imposed. Since it is not possible for all countries simultaneously to export their unemployment, these measures, taken as a whole, were futile. The volume of international trade shrank dramatically, in part because of shrinking income levels and in part because of the panoply of trade barriers. Countries kept out imports and simultaneously discovered that they could not sell their exports because others were playing the same desperate game. Inefficient domestic production tended to replace efficient foreign production on a worldwide scale. These efficiency losses added to the general depression of real incomes.

Most countries were unwilling to permit their currencies to fluctuate freely. Many established so called exchange-stabilization funds that participated in foreign exchange markets. Often such participation involved deliberate attempts to depreciate the currency in order to export unemployment. Currency blocs were formed. The Sterling Area was established, comprising the countries of the former British Empire. The pound was the reserve currency, and exchange rates were fixed among the participant countries. A "dollar bloc" also evolved among countries that held reserves in dollars and found it convenient to maintain a fixed parity between their currencies and the dollar.

The international capital market was virtually destroyed by the proliferation of exchange controls that prevented individuals from exchanging national currencies. For example, in order to stem a capital outflow in 1931, the German government froze the deposits of foreigners in German banks. The owners of these deposits were prohibited from withdrawing them until given permission to do so by the government. The purpose was to stem the capital outflow and reduce the supply of the blocked currency in foreign exchange markets, thereby reducing pressure on the exchange rate.

The policies pursued by the United States were more noteworthy for their colorful inventiveness than for their effectiveness or rationality. It was, after all, important to *Do something!* By 1933 prices had fallen some 30 percent below their 1929 level. Real gross national product had also fallen 30 percent. One fourth of the nation's labor force had been idled, some 12 million persons in all. Industry, trade, and agriculture were flat on their backs. The new administration of Franklin D. Roosevelt came into this situation armed with the attitude that just about any form of economic activism would be preferable to the inertia of the Hoover administration with its remote promises that "prosperity is just around the corner."

Among the deep thinkers of President Roosevelt's "brain trust" was Professor George Warren, who reasoned that, since real output and prices had both dropped 30 percent since 1929, it stood to reason that if prices could be jacked up ("reflated"), then output and employment would recover. Looking for a radical solution, President Roosevelt embraced this crackbrained notion. Thus the theory of a monetary crank became the rationale for New Deal economic policies. It found expression in the bizarre attempt artificially to inflate farm prices by destroying crops and slaughtering animals, and by the National Industrial Recovery Act (NIRA), which suspended the antitrust laws and encouraged business firms to form trade associations so that they could collude and charge monopoly prices. How consumers were expected to buy the higher-priced output was never made clear.[6]

In the international sphere the president began by imposing an embargo on gold exports and obtaining legislation making it illegal for private citizens to hold gold. Then, in early 1934, Congress passed the Gold Standard Reserve Act, which raised the official U.S. price of gold from

[6] Any student of Economics 101 should be able to explain that the reluctance of wages and prices to fall is an obstacle to economic recovery. Yet Warren's theory argued the opposite. The most charitable interpretation one can give for a policy of putting a floor to prices is that this will break deflationary expectations. Such expectations tend to cause economic activity to be postponed as firms wait for wages to decline before raising production and employment, and as consumers and business firms postpone purchases on the assumption that prices of consumer goods and capital goods will fall further. In the shell-shocked condition of the economy of 1933, such an interpretation makes a certain amount of sense.

$20.67 to $35.00 per ounce. This represented an increase in the gold price of 69.3 percent, and Professor Warren predicted that prices would quickly show a similar increase.

It is hardly surprising that the prediction was wrong. However, by attracting and purchasing gold, the Treasury increased the money supply, so at least the policy was expansionary, although in a drastically beggar-my-neighbor manner. The rise in the price of gold attracted most of the world's monetary gold to the United States, so by 1940 the United States owned the bulk of the world's gold reserves. Since U.S. gold purchases were made by the Treasury with dollars paid to foreigners, the dollars found their way to the foreign exchange market where they acted to depreciate the dollar relative to other currencies. Thus U.S. policy depreciated the dollar sharply, despite the fact that the United States had plenty of gold and was not suffering a balance-of-payments deficit. Needless to say, foreign countries viewed the action as an exceedingly hostile act. Although the British had tried to dissuade President Roosevelt from going ahead with his gold policy, their overtures were in vain. As Lord Robbins said, ". . . it had been easier to bamboozle the President than to unbamboozle him."[7]

The policy actions and reactions of countries during the 1930s amounted to a negative sum game in which the world economy came out the clear loser. The countries that showed the best economic performance were those that had been most aggressive in pursuing policies that damaged other countries. As countries went about the job of planning their post–World War II economic policies, they agreed on one fundamental point. Economic nationalism and international monetary anarchy had been disastrous. It was important to avoid the pitfalls of the interwar period and to devise an international monetary system based on mutual cooperation so as to reconcile the domestic employment objectives of all countries with the benefits of a liberal trading and a favorable foreign investment climate. The incentive to seek domestic gains at the expense of other countries had to be destroyed.

13.3 BRETTON WOODS: 1944–73

The United States entered World War II immediately after the bombing of Pearl Harbor on December 7, 1941. Economic planning for the post-

[7] Robbins, Lionel, *The Great Depression,* Macmillan, 1934, p. 124. British economists have never been hesitant to share their expertise with politicians. Their success with President Roosevelt was not noteworthy, however. On one occasion Keynes had an interview with Roosevelt, at which time Keynes attempted to explain his theory of the multiplier. After the meeting Roosevelt confided to an associate that it was an interesting theory, but that he "didn't believe in it."

war period began fairly soon thereafter. American and British treasury officials met as early as 1942 to begin the outlines for a new liberal international economic order. Their deliberations produced the inputs for the plans that were hammered out in final form at an international conference of 44 nations held in Bretton Woods, New Hampshire, in 1944. The conference established the rules for the post–World War II international monetary system; it created the International Monetary Fund (IMF) to police the system and provide short-term credit to countries experiencing balance-of-payments problems; and it created the International Bank for Reconstruction and Development (now known as the World Bank) to provide financing for postwar reconstruction and economic development.

The backdrop for the negotiations was the monetary chaos and economic nationalism of the interwar period. This experience led to several considerations that strongly influenced the negotiations.

1. The experience with freely fluctuating exchange rates had left a bad taste in everyone's mouth. It was therefore assumed without question that the postwar system should be one of fixed exchange rates.
2. The Great Depression and war inflation had sensitized all countries to the importance of internal balance considerations such as high employment and inflation control. Since fixed exchange rates would be likely to get out of line, it was agreed that exchange rates would have to be modified from time to time in order to prevent the resulting deficits and surpluses from imposing inflationary and deflationary pressures and to prevent countries from resorting to restrictions on trade and payments, which occurred during the 1930s. An adjustable peg system of exchange rates was therefore envisioned.
3. To avert destructive competitive depreciation, the conference accepted that exchange rates were subjects for negotiations between countries and that realignment of exchange rates would only be undertaken in consultation and with IMF approval.
4. Since it was recognized that an adjustable peg system could easily promote destabilizing speculation, there was agreement that countries could impose exchange controls in order to quell or prevent such speculation.

Unfortunately, there was sharp disagreement on two fundamental and closely related issues. The failure to resolve these problems in a satisfactory manner led to patchwork solutions that were to haunt and eventually undermine the system. These issues were (1) the choice of a suitable reserve asset and (2) provision for the growth of international reserves.

The leader of the British delegation was John Maynard Keynes himself. Keynes presented an ingenious plan that would have placed the IMF in the role of a world superbank that would act as a clearing house for the settlement of payments deficits and surpluses. National currencies were not to be used as reserves. Instead there would be a new monetary unit that Keynes called the bancor. Each country would receive a quota of bancors. Subsequently it could acquire more bancors by depositing gold or by earning them from other countries. Deficits and surpluses would be settled by entering credits and debits in countries' bancor accounts with the IMF. For example, if the United States ran a deficit with Great Britain, the United States would lose bancors while Great Britain would gain them. Countries with continuing deficits could utilize an overdraft facility provided by the IMF. To encourage deficit countries to reduce their deficits, the IMF would charge interest on these loans. To encourage surplus countries to participate in the adjustment process, the IMF would penalize such countries' excessive bancor accounts by attaching an interest penalty. The Keynes plan also anticipated the need for additional reserves as the world economy grew, and this could be accomplished by the simple device of increasing countries' bancor quotas as the need arose. Thus, under the Keynes plan the IMF would have become a super world central bank that would have had powers very similar to a country's central bank.

In proposing a mechanism for the systematic growth of world reserves, Keynes attempted to correct the problem of inadequate gold reserves and the sporadic nature in which the supply of newly mined gold tended to vary. By eliminating national currencies as a reserve asset, the plan eliminated the difficulties associated with a multicurrency reserve system, such as the gold exchange standard. As usual, Keynes was ahead of his time. He was also British and therefore more acutely sensitive to the problem of reserve shortages. Britain had spent much of the previous quarter of a century feeling the pinch of inadequate reserves, but the United States had not. And what, after all, was the United States going to do with all that gold it had worked so hard to acquire and bury in Fort Knox? The United States rejected the idea in 1944, only to resurrect it some 12 to 13 years later.

In proposing a new reserve asset, Keynes addressed the so-called nth country problem, which later came to be extremely damaging to the Bretton Woods system. The problem arises as follows. If there are two countries in the world, there is only one exchange rate. To peg the exchange rate, it is sufficient for one country's central bank to intervene in the foreign exchange market. The monetary authorities of both countries can intervene simultaneously, but that works only if they have agreed on the exchange rate. Similarly, if there are n countries, each country confronts only $n - 1$ exchange rates. If $n - 1$ pick their exchange rates vis-à-vis country n, then the exchange rate of the nth country is automatically determined with respect to the other $n - 1$ countries. Consequently, a consistent set of exchange rates requires that one country must play a passive role. Its exchange rate is determined by the decisions of the other countries.

For the nth country, its passive role is both an advantage and a disadvantage. The disadvantage is that it has to accept the exchange rates that are presented to it, and, as the United States discovered in the early 1970s, it can only get exchange rates changed with considerable difficulty, since it will have to obtain agreement from the other countries. The advantage, on the other hand, is that the other $n - 1$ countries have to do the exchange market intervention, thereby sacrificing control of their money supplies, whereas the nth country is free to pursue the monetary policy of its own choosing in accordance with its concept of internal balance.

The problem for the world economy posed by the freedom of the nth country is that the monetary policies of all countries tend to be dictated by the nth country's monetary policies, and that inflationary or deflationary pressures are therefore also likely to be determined by the nth country's taste for high employment as opposed to low inflation. If the nth country pursues a deflationary monetary policy, this will be reflected in a surplus in its balance of payments and a tendency for its currency to appreciate. To prevent the appreciation, other countries will have to sell from their reserves of the nth country currency. In so doing they reduce their money supplies, so the conservative monetary policy of the nth country forces generalized monetary contraction. Conversely, if the nth country pursues an expansionary monetary policy, this leads to a deficit in its balance of payments and a tendency for its currency to depreciate. To prevent the depreciation, the other countries must buy the currency of the nth country and, in so doing, expand their domestic money supplies. The inflationary monetary policy of the nth country is therefore generalized to all countries. Thus the system as a whole is likely to develop a deflationary or an inflationary bias, depending upon the behavior of country n.

By creating the bancor, the Keynes plan would have added currency $n + 1$ to the system. It is not quite like other currencies, since it could not be bought and sold in private markets. Nevertheless, the nth country then has to be concerned with the level of its bancor reserves with the

IMF, since it is these reserves that it needs to settle its balance of payments. Consequently, it has to conduct its monetary policies with an eye to its bancor reserves, just as the other $n - 1$ countries are obliged to do.

It is very important to bear this nth country problem in mind when we discuss the Bretton Woods system. In its early phases, when the dollar was scarce and many other countries ran deficits, the system appeared to have a deflationary bias. Later, when the United States ran deficits and the dollar was plentiful, the exact opposite happened.

For the U.S. negotiators the biggest sticking point of the Keynes plan was the overdraft facility, that is, the large amount of bancors that deficit countries would have been entitled to borrow under the plan. It was obvious that other countries would have to run large deficits with the United States after the war. Their capital stocks had been damaged, and their export capacity was low. Since the United States was the only viable source of capital goods, imports from the United States would necessarily have to be large. Keenly aware of these circumstances, the U.S. delegation suspected that the generous overdraft facility was a thinly veiled attempt to gain unlimited credit from the United States.[8]

The plan that was finally adopted and implemented was an American plan drafted by Harry Dexter White, an official of the U.S. Treasury. Under the White plan the United States was to retain its gold price of $35 an ounce. Other countries were to define their currency values in terms of gold as well, but it was understood that the dollar was to be the intervention currency that countries would buy and sell in order to peg their exchange rates. The practical effect of this was to designate the United States as the nth country. Other countries fixed their currency prices in terms of the dollar, and the U.S. was responsible for maintaining the gold-dollar parity.

Countries were to hold their reserves in the form of gold and foreign currency. The foreign currency most frequently held was the dollar. Exchange rates could vary slightly because a small band of 1 percent on either side of parity was established. Intervention by central banks was not required as long as currency prices remained inside this band.

To provide the IMF with resources with which to assist countries desiring to borrow, the White plan established quotas for individual countries based on their economic importance. The country then contributed funds to the IMF equaling its quota. One fourth of this was to be in gold, and the remainder in the country's own national currency.

---

[8] Commentators about U.S. opposition to the Keynes plan are fond of pointing to the "irony" that in rejecting the Keynes plan and later providing assistance under the Marshall Plan, the U.S. gave away in the form of grants what it might otherwise have provided through repayable loans.

Countries would be permitted to borrow from IMF resources. The first one fourth of the quota—called the first tranche, or slice—could be borrowed automatically. Additional borrowings necessitated IMF approval. The IMF was to charge interest on its loans to encourage borrowing countries to reduce their deficits, and to finance the IMF's operations.

The White plan was a very conservative one. It rejected the concept of a super reserve asset whose supply could be regulated systematically, just as countries manage their domestic money supplies. Instead, it returned gold to a prominent position, and it made no provision for the growth of international reserves. Its meager acknowledgment of the nth country problem came in the form of the notion that the United States, in being responsible for maintaining the dollar price of gold, would be forced to share the adjustment burden with other countries.[9] The implicit bargain of the Bretton Woods arrangement was that other countries would stabilize the dollar and agree to hold dollars as reserves, whereas the policies of the United States were to be directed to the stabilization of the U.S., and therefore also other, economies. Such a system could function well only as long as U.S. monetary-fiscal policies were well behaved in the eyes of other countries.

The IMF's charter was extremely vague about how countries were to adjust their balance of payments. A deficit country was expected to use its own reserves as a first line of defense. If it needed additional reserves, it was expected to borrow from the IMF. If the deficit proved to be temporary, no further steps were needed; thus, the IMF's lending facility acted as a buffer by supplementing countries' reserves and thereby helping them to avoid restrictive or deflationary measures. If the deficit proved to be deep rooted and the country refused to permit deflationary reductions in its money supply, it would then be considered to be in "fundamental disequilibrium" and would be expected to devalue its currency after consultation with the IMF. Capital outflows in anticipation of devaluation could be prevented by introducing temporary exchange controls. The term "fundamental disequilibirum" was never carefully defined, and subsequent events would find exchange rates tending to remain frozen even in the face of persistent deficits and surpluses. When changes in official parities did take place, devaluations greatly outnumbered revaluations, indicating that the adjustment burden once again was to fall heavily on deficit countries.

---

[9] Another "irony" that commentators enjoy clucking over developed when it was later disclosed that Harry Dexter White had at one time been a member of the Communist Party, yet White supplied a plan that was anything but revolutionary. Meanwhile Keynes, despised by radicals as a capitalist running dog of the worst kind for his efforts to patch up the hated profits system, supplied the more visionary and innovative plan.

The IMF charter did contain a "scarce-currency" clause designed to force surplus countries to share in the burden of adjustment. This clause provided that if the IMF's holdings of a particular country's currency were being exhausted, the IMF could declare the currency scarce and other countries could then impose discriminatory trade restrictions against the country's exports. It was hoped that, in order to avoid such discriminatory treatment, surplus countries would take steps to reduce their surpluses.

The scarce-currency clause was never invoked and was later abolished. Indeed, the adjustment problem under Bretton Woods was never managed in a satisfactory way. It became more serious as time passed. Along with two other fundamental problems called the "confidence" and the "liquidity" problems, described later, these problems caused the system to fail.

The IMF was formally established in 1946. Its role was sharply limited during the first ten years of its existence for a number of reasons. The resources available to the IMF were far too meager to make any impact on the major problem of that time, namely, financing the huge deficits that war-torn countries had to run with the United States in order to reconstruct their economies. The United States addressed this problem with the Marshall Plan, which supplied some $20 billion to European countries damaged by the war. Countries receiving Marshall aid were not also permitted to borrow from the IMF, and that further diminished the IMF's role. As a policeman of the international monetary system, there was nothing to police, because most European countries waited until 1958 to make their currencies convertible, thereby establishing the Bretton Woods system in practice as well as on paper. Balance-of-payments adjustment during that ten-year period was facilitated by the policy of the United States to reduce greatly its import tariffs from prewar levels. This enabled European countries to earn additional dollars and helped to end the dollar shortage.

By 1955 the U.S. balance of payments had turned around, and subsequent deficits converted, what had been a dollar shortage, into a dollar glut. Reconstruction had proceeded rapidly, European export capacity had been restored, and sharp devaluations by Britain and others in 1948 had placed these countries in a strong competitive position. Rapid growth abroad, moreover, had produced an investment climate that attracted large sums of American capital. American companies built overseas subsidiaries and acquired foreign productive assets that often ended up producing goods that might otherwise have been produced at home and exported. All of these factors contributed to a sharp turnaround in the U.S. balance of payments. After 1955 the United States was almost continually in deficit.

Initially the balance-of-payments turnaround had a beneficial effect inasmuch as it permitted European countries to accumulate reserves that enabled them to restore convertibility in 1958. But very soon thereafter the U.S. deficit became a continuing problem. Adjustment was rendered difficult by the clear intention to avoid deflationary policies. Although the Eisenhower administration had pursued conservative fiscal and monetary policies during the 1950s, the deficit had not responded, and when President John F. Kennedy announced his intention to get the country "moving again," and Congress eventually responded by lowering taxes in early 1964, it was clear that the United States had no plans for sacrificing rapid growth and high employment in order to get its balance of payments in better shape.

The United States responded to its deficit in various ways. To stem the gold outflow, the United States encouraged foreign central banks to hold their dollar earnings instead of converting them into gold at the U.S. Treasury. To make this more palatable, the United States enabled central banks to earn interest on their dollar holdings by supplying them with special interest-bearing Treasury bonds. To stem the capital outflow, the government undertook a campaign to discourage U.S. firms from investing abroad.

For a time these makeshift arrangements worked fairly well. The dollars that were being supplied by the U.S. deficit were welcomed because they added to perceived needs for additional reserves to accommodate economic growth and the growth of trade. But the system that was evolving was dangerously unstable. This was clearly spelled out as early as 1960 by Professor Robert Triffin of Yale.[10] Since there was no provision in the Bretton Woods system for the creation of international reserves, the deficit in the U.S. balance of payments was essential, since that was what enabled reserves to grow, which, in turn, made world economic expansion and the growth of international trade possible. The difficulty with this, noted Triffin, is that as this process continues, the dollars held throughout the world will grow in relation to the gold stock of the United States, thereby steadily eroding confidence in America's ability to redeem its obligations in gold. Thus, said Triffin, the Bretton Woods system was heading for a "confidence crisis." When central banks become nervous enough, they will begin converting their dollars into gold, and when others see this happening, they will all come clamoring for gold, just as had happened to Britain in 1931.

To avoid such a development, the United States would have to eliminate its balance-of-payments deficit. But if that happened, there would be insufficient reserves and the world economy would suffer a

[10] Triffin, Robert, *Gold and the Dollar Crisis,* Yale, 1960.

deflationary "liquidity crisis." Thus the "Triffin dilemma" implied that the world economy was caught between a rock and a hard place. If the U.S. deficit were to be eliminated, there would be a liquidity crisis, and if the U.S. deficit were not eliminated there would be a confidence crisis. It was hardly surprising that Triffin suggested restoration of elements of the Keynes plan. Currencies would be convertible into a reserve asset created by the IMF rather than into dollars, and the new IMF asset could be increased by increasing countries' quotas periodically. Thus, both the liquidity and confidence problems would be eliminated at a single stroke.

Along with these problems, the Bretton Woods system suffered from increasing rigidity that prevented balance-of-payments adjustment. During the days of the acute dollar shortage, the United States eased the deficit problems of other countries by import liberalization policies, including major tariff reductions. Later, when other countries enjoyed surpluses, they too eased their import restrictions. But by 1960 this convenient and constructive method of adjustment had been largely exhausted. Commitment to full employment and price stability were primary concerns in all countries, and permitting these important domestic goals to be sacrificed to the balance of payments was unthinkable. Moreover, exchange rates had tended to become frozen. The idea of an adjustable peg system as provided in the IMF charter was never implemented, as countries became determined to hang onto existing parities if at all possible. In fact there had not been a single major currency realignment during the five years that preceded the British devaluation of 1967. In most countries politicians viewed devaluation as a major political liability, indicative of national weakness and a failure of the government to control inflation. It was not possible to discuss devaluation plans openly because that would have caused speculative runs from the currency. Governments therefore swore up and down that they would never devalue, and since they did not wish to be seen as liars, they avoided devaluation if at all possible.

The first major crisis of the Bretton Woods system occurred in 1967 when Great Britain devalued the pound after denying, often and adamantly, that such a step was being contemplated. This shook confidence in the system and accelerated the gold drain from the U.S. Treasury. In the face of this crisis, countries agreed to the creation of a two-tier gold market. The market price could fluctuate, while the official price at which governments exchanged gold among themselves would remain in place. This could work only if governments refrained from selling gold to private individuals. It was, therefore, agreed that governments would not buy or sell gold except to each other. This had the effect of freezing official gold reserves. The amount of monetary gold could neither be increased nor decreased, so it became obvious that any further expansion of world liquidity would have to be in the form of dollars. Moreover, the United States discouraged other central banks from buying U.S. gold; thus, gold's function as a reserve asset was effectively eliminated. Gresham's law had done its work; the Bretton Woods system became a de facto dollar standard.

The deficit in the U.S. balance of payments continued to get worse. The Vietnam War produced an acceleration of inflation beginning in 1968, so the dollar became increasingly overvalued. The current-account surplus dwindled steadily after 1964, recovered slightly during the 1970 recession year, and then turned sharply negative in the following two years. As the deficit widened, the outflow of dollars accelerated. Countries now found themselves importing inflation from the United States; to prevent the dollar from falling relative to their own currencies, their monetary authorities had to purchase the surplus dollars. In doing so, they paid with their own currencies, thereby expanding their money supplies at highly inflationary rates.

Speculative crises increased in frequency after 1967. In 1968–69 there were runs from the French and Belgian francs, the British pound, and the Canadian dollar. In 1969 Germany was so overwhelmed by an inflow of capital that her money supply jumped 25 percent in a single week. Canada became the first country to break with the system by permitting the Canadian dollar to float in 1970. In early 1971, yielding to pressure from President Nixon, the Federal Reserve switched to an expansionary monetary policy designed to promote recovery from the 1970 recession in time, cynics said, to ensure the president's reelection in 1972. This was enough to touch off the long-awaited flight from the dollar. Responding to the crisis, President Nixon announced, in August 1971, that the United States was closing its gold window and would no longer sell gold. He also called for negotiations to bring about currency realignment. To prod countries into cooperating, the president imposed a temporary surcharge on U.S. imports. At that point other countries felt that they had no choice but to float their currencies.

It seemed as if the sick Bretton Woods patient had drawn his last breath. There were, however, a few flickers of life. The countries that had permitted their currencies to fluctuate were not happy with this outcome and wished, instead, to establish a new, more suitable, set of fixed exchange rates. However, realignment of official parities was not easy to accomplish, especially with the United States as the nth country. Cutting the dollar loose from gold did nothing to lower the dollar vis-à-vis other countries. It was the other countries who, by their purchases and sales of dollars, determined the price of the dollar. Even countries running large surpluses with the United States were reluctant to revalue against the dollar unless other countries did so, because unilateral revaluation of a country's currency would appreciate the currency vis-à-vis all currencies, not just the dollar. This meant that a revaluing country could lose its competitive edge, even with respect to countries with which its currency parity was appropriate. Ever desirous of protecting export industries, countries generally were reluctant to revalue their currencies unilaterally.

Accordingly, it was clear that official currency prices would have to be changed within the context of multilateral negotiations. Such negotiations were held at the Smithsonian in Washington in December 1971. The negotiations were extremely arduous and proved to be unsatisfactory. The United States raised the official price of gold by a modest 8 percent, and some of the stronger currencies were revalued by small amounts. It took only seven months for the agreement to come unglued. A run on the pound caused the British to resume their currency float. The U.S. balance of payments continued to deteriorate, as recovery of the economy from recession increased the demand for imports. In early 1973, further negotiations produced more revaluations, but when this failed to stem the tide, the countries of the European Economic Community (EEC) cut their ties to the dollar. The flexible exchange-rate system installed itself by default.

In the end, countries were driven to float their currencies to get their money supplies under control. Dollar reserves had risen 60 percent in 1970–71, as compared with about 20 percent during all of the 1960s. The huge outpouring of dollars had forced countries to buy dollars in exchange for their own currencies, and the enormous money supply increases that this entailed fueled a highly inflationary world boom in 1973. As Robert Triffin noted,

> The adoption of floating rates was a desperate attempt by each surplus country acting independently to stem this inflationary flood.[11]

13.4 POSTMORTEM: THE SDR AND THE REFORM DEBATE

The deficiencies of the Bretton Woods system inspired a huge outpouring of imaginative suggestions by academics, which began with Triffin's 1960 analysis. Official negotiations on international monetary reform began

---

[11] Triffin, Robert, "Jamaica: Major Revision or Fiasco?", in E. M. Bernstein, *Reflections on Jamaica,* Essays in International Finance, Princeton, 1976, p. 46.

in 1965 with meetings of the so-called Group of Ten major industrial countries. These meetings led to the subsequent creation of the Special Drawing Right (SDR) at the 1967 IMF meetings held in Rio de Janiero. The SDR was similar to Keynes's bancor. It represented a credit supplied by the IMF that could be used as a reserve asset by countries in settlement of their balance-of-payments deficits. Countries could use the SDR credits to purchase foreign exchange from the IMF, which they could then use for the purpose of intervening in the foreign exchange market. The first allocation of SDRs occurred at the beginning of 1970, even though it was hard to make the case that there was much of a liquidity shortage at the time.

The initial allocations were in direct proportion to countries' IMF quotas. The question of how future SDR creations would be distributed caused a great deal of controversy. The developing countries represented at the meetings wanted these additional allocations for themselves. They attempted to establish the principle of the "link," which would combine SDR creation with development assistance.

The developing countries argued that the link would actually assist the international monetary system inasmuch as all the industrial countries appeared to be trying to run balance-of-payments surpluses most of the time. Consequently, said the developing countries, we will be happy to purchase your surplus output provided that financing can be arranged. Therefore, give us the new SDRs. Although there was something to the theory of too many industrial countries chasing surpluses, the industrial countries were leery of the proposal, preferring to keep development assistance moving through normal channels, such as the World Bank. The United States took the negotiating position that the link would burden the SDR in its initial phases.

Initially, the SDR was valued at $1. Later, when currencies began to fluctuate, this had to be changed and the value of the SDR was determined as a weighted average of currency prices. This was an important step because it meant that, by converting its currency reserves into SDRs, a country could hedge against exchange risk. If one currency depreciates, some other currency must appreciate, so the value of the SDR remains largely unaffected. This would make the SDR a desirable reserve asset and encourage countries to reduce their reliance on national currencies as reserve assets.

The creation of the SDR amounted to the adoption of the Triffin plan. The key idea was that the SDR would be used to supply liquidity. The United States could then reduce its deficit without creating a liquidity crisis. That would, at the same time, avert a confidence crisis, especially since countries could buy SDRs with their reserve accumulations. The idea appealed to economists and officials of the Kennedy-Johnson administrations of the 1960s, as well as to many foreign economists and public officials. Foreigners were especially pleased with the idea that, since the dollar was no longer needed to supply liquidity, the United States could no longer use the liquidity argument as an excuse for dodging its responsibility to reduce its balance-of-payments deficit.

During the 1960s most economists and nearly all government officials were intent on retaining some form of fixed exchange-rate system. The strictest form advocated was a return to an unvarnished gold standard. This was the view of President de Gaulle of France and his economic guru, Jacques Rueff. The French, accordingly, were the most adament opponents of the SDR. At the other extreme, there was a somewhat relaxed group that, seeing the Bretton Woods system evolve into a de facto dollar standard, suggested that the world should simply relax and enjoy that condition. It is true that the dollar was overvalued, but that was part of the original bargain that had cast the United States in the role of the nth country. Without such overvaluation the system could not have received the dollars it needed as reserves, and some countries would not have been able to enjoy the export-led growth that had contributed greatly to their prosperity. Therefore, solve the confidence problem by eliminating gold as a reserve asset. Let the dollar be the reserve and intervention currency, and let the United States, as the nth country of the system, practice benign neglect, although not to the point where it is exporting inflation. This position gained a certain amount of strength from the circumstance that, until 1971, the United States actually ran a current-account surplus. Exports exceeded imports, so it was not as if the United States were stealing goods and services from abroad. The deficit came about from U.S. capital outflows, and, it was argued, that was an appropriate role for a rich industrial country like the United States. The intensity with which the relaxed view was offered quite understandably diminished as the current-account surplus dwindled. It became increasingly difficult to characterize U.S. neglect of its balance of payments as benign.

In the meantime, academic economists, many from the Chicago school of monetary economists, revived the issue of flexible exchange rates as a suitable subject for discussion, and they succeeded in building a very strong case for flexible exchange rates, as we will see in the next chapter. However, there was little support for flexible exchange rates among President Johnson's advisers. But, with the arrival of the Nixon administration in 1969, the official U.S. attitude changed. Although official statements suggested that the United States was prepared to cooperate in the reform of the Bretton Woods system, the suspicion was growing that the United States was ready to scuttle the system and replace it by flexible exchange rates.

After the first SDR allocation in 1970, the Bretton Woods system began to unravel in earnest. In an effort to salvage the system, the IMF organized the so-called Committee of Twenty (C-20) to recommend steps that might nurse the system back to health. At its initial meetings in 1972 there was a general presumption that the Bretton Woods system could be resurrected if some of its more chronic deficiencies could be corrected. There was agreement on the following three important points. First, it was widely felt that exchange rates had to show far greater flexibility. Second, it was accepted that countries should be treated symmetrically with respect to adjustment and the settlement of deficits and surpluses. Third, it was agreed that the SDR should replace the dollar as the principal reserve asset.

There were, however, sharp disagreements between the United States, the other industrial countries, and the developing countries. The other industrial countries initially insisted that it was essential to restore the gold convertibility of the dollar. It was not clear how this could be accomplished, given the small size of the U.S. gold stock relative to outstanding dollar reserves, except by raising the official price of gold sharply, a step that the United States was not willing to take. Although willing to discuss convertibility, the U.S. position was that it had been the absence of adequate incentives to reduce surpluses on the part of other countries that had forced the United States into deficit. America therefore proposed that countries be given the option to float their currences and to change the par value of their currencies by modest amounts without prior IMF approval. The developing countries, finally, were concerned primarily with ensuring a large and dependable flow of reserves to their countries. These countries generally favored a system of fixed exchange rates with ample provision for the creation of reserves.

There were four major areas for potential reform that were considered. First, it was agreed that balance-of-payments adjustment mechanisms needed to be improved. Second, rules should be established governing the settlement of deficits and surpluses. Third, rules and guidelines needed to be established to govern the magnitude and composition of international reserves. Fourth, and in deference to developing countries, an attempt, would be made to link SDR creation with development assistance.

During the early stages of debate most of the participants wanted exchange rates to be based on par values with currencies convertible into reserves. The United States indicated willingness to accept this, if there were some adjustment mechanism that would place adjustment pressure on surplus countries. In order to accomplish this, the United States proposed the concept of reserve indicators. The idea was that excessive accumulation of reserves would indicate that the country's currency was undervalued, and the country would then have to take steps to eliminate its surplus. Robert Solomon explains the intricacies of this as follows:

> A structure of "reserve indicators" would be established with a "norm" or base level for each country such that the sum of all "norms" was equal to the total of world reserves. If countries' reserves increased or decreased disproportionately and reached various reserve indicator points, signals of the need for adjustment would be emitted and countries would be expected to adopt policy measures aimed at correcting their surpluses or deficits. Ultimately, if countries failed to take adequate actions to reverse the movement in reserves, "sanctions" or "graduated pressures" . . . would be applied by the IMF.[12]

To provide additional incentive for surplus countries to adjust, the United States also proposed to make one of the reserve indicator points a "convertibility point," so any excess of reserve accumulation over this level would not be eligible for conversion into gold or other primary reserve asset. In combination, it was hoped, these two proposals would produce symmetrical adjustment pressure on surplus and deficit countries.

In focusing on reserve levels as indicators of disequilibrium, the U.S. proposal had the advantage that it could bypass the difficult question of determining equilibrium exchange rates. Regrettably, the nature of the adjustment steps that surplus countries would have to take was never made clear. Some guidelines might usefully have been offered. For example, if a surplus country is already at full employment and concerned with inflation, it would be inconsistent with the goal of internal balance to propose additional demand expansion to slow reserve accumulation. Therefore, appreciation would be a preferred alternative since that has an anti-inflationary effect. Conversely, if the surplus country suffers from recession, appreciation would add to the deflationary forces; hence, in such a case stimulation of internal demand is called for as a means of moving toward both external and internal balance. Par-value adjustments are not, therefore, always the appropriate response to balance-of-payments disequilibrium.

As noted in Chapter 12, a reserve indicator system has built into it a technical flaw that makes for instability. The reason, as explained earlier, is that adjustment measures designed to achieve particular reserve levels tend to overshoot the adjustments required to restore equality of receipts

[12] Solomon, Robert, *The International Monetary System,* Harper and Row, 1982, p. 241.

and payments. Consequently, the targeting of policy toward the attainment of a foreign exchange reserve target tends to bring about oscillating behavior in the exchange rate and other important variables.

The desire of an overwhelming majority of C-20s members to restore convertibility of the dollar created a heavy preoccupation with this problem. Because the value of the U.S. gold stock had fallen considerably below the potential outstanding dollar claims against it, restoration of convertibility would have necessitated a large increase in the official price of gold or the substitution of an alternative asset to replace gold.

The United States was firmly opposed to an increase in the official price of gold. It was argued that revaluation of gold would cause gold to gain in importance as a reserve asset, whereas it was desirable to reduce the role of gold and increase the role of the SDR. Gold was said to be an inferior reserve asset because its supply could not be controlled, whereas the supply of SDRs could. Gold was a speculative asset, whereas the SDR was not.

To foster the replacement of gold and restore convertibility, it was proposed to establish a "substitution account." Such an account, maintained at the IMF, would permit surplus countries to convert their accumulations of dollars and other national currencies into SDRs rather than gold. A far-reaching proposal by the Italian delegation visualized official settlements on a multilateral basis through the IMF rather than on a bilateral basis between central banks as in the past. The United States would pay to or receive from the IMF an amount of SDRs equal to its deficit or surplus. Other surplus countries could then turn in dollar balances to the IMF in exchange for the SDRs. Deficit countries, presumably, would be losing SDRs either to the United States or to other surplus countries. Thus, the SDR would become the vehicle for payments settlement and currency convertibility.

Momentum to implement the substitution account dwindled as the C-20 negotiations continued, because the dollar overhang problem rapidly faded away with the arrival of the oil crisis in 1973. Everyone was going to need lots of dollars in order to purchase the suddenly much more expensive oil from the OPEC oil producers. Indeed, the whirlwind pace at which the international economic climate changed during the 1972–74 period precluded the attainment of substantial progress by C-20. C-20 very quickly appeared to be attempting to reform a system that was already damaged beyond repair.

After initial hostility to flexible exchange rates, C-20 issued a draft outline of reform in March 1973, the date of the EEC's decision to float, that finally conceded the need for occasional exchange rate floating. The grudging concession stated that

> Members of the Committee recognized that exchange rates must be a matter for international concern and consultation and that in the reformed system the exchange rate regime should remain based on stable but adjustable par values.

So far, nothing but the old story. But then

> It was also recognized that floating rates could provide a useful technique in particular situations. There was also general agreement on the need for exchange market stability and on the importance of Fund surveillance of exchange rate policies.[13]

Late in 1973 the Arab-Israeli war broke out, leading in mid-October to the oil embargo and an initial oil price increase of more than 50 percent. In December OPEC raised the price of oil again to four times its initial level. Inasmuch as OPEC oil was invoiced in dollars, this caused a sharp strengthening of the dollar as well as enormous uncertainties surrounding the balance-of-payments prospects of oil-importing countries.

> One consequence of the uncertainty was general agreement—sometimes tacit, sometimes overt—that the regime of floating exchange rates would go on for some time. No country was ready to commit itself to a par value or central rate in the face of the unknowns in its future balance of payments.[14]

Thus, the oil shock proved to be the final blow undercutting the effort at systematic and comprehensive reform of the international monetary system. By January 1974, at the next C-20 meeting, the deficit in the U.S. balance of payments had disappeared, and the uncertainties created by the oil crisis made action on long-term reform seem impractical. Consequently, C-20 shifted to what was called an "evolutionary" approach. This apparently meant that C-20 would consider urgent matters requiring immediate attention, but would defer major reform issues for later consideration. Among the immediate matters were the value of the SDR, which was to be based on the average value of a "basket" of currencies, the establishing of a continuing body in the IMF at the ministerial level to study reform, and conditions for the conduct of exchange rate floating. Beyond some minor changes, nothing came of the reform effort of 1972–74. With a floating dollar the question of a return to par values

---

[13] Communique of the Committee of the Board of Governors on International Monetary Reform and Related Issues, March 27, 1973. Reprinted in IMF Survey, April 9, 1973, p. 100.

[14] Solomon, op. cit., pp. 258–259.

was academic. Even France—the staunchest advocate of a return to par values—was itself floating its currency in mid-1974.

QUESTIONS FOR REVIEW

1. What are the essential requirements for the successful operation of an international monetary system? What is the importance of each characteristic?
2. Appraise the nineteenth-century gold standard against the criteria specified in Question 1. What were the strengths and weaknesses of the gold-standard?
3. Why did the attempt to restore the gold standard during the 1920s fail? How did the international monetary system contribute to the depression of the 1930s?
4. Contrast the Keynes plan with the White plan. What were the advantages and disadvantages of each?
5. Describe the nth-country problem. What are the advantages and disadvantages for the nth country? for other countries?
6. Why does an adjustable peg system tend to encourage destabilizing speculation?
7. The problems of the Bretton Woods system have been characterized as adjustment, liquidity, and confidence. What was the nature of these problems, and how did they interact?
8. What was the rationale for the creation of the SDR? Could the SDR serve a useful purpose under the present international monetary system? Why would the establishment of a substitution account be desirable?
9. Describe and criticize the reserve indicator proposal considered by the Committee of Twenty.
10. Was the Bretton Woods system characterized by a deflationary bias or an inflationary bias? Explain carefully.

SUGGESTIONS FOR FURTHER READING

Bernstein, Edward M., *Reflections on Jamaica,* Princeton Essays in International Finance, 1976. See especially the papers by Robert Triffin and John Williamson.

Ingram, James C., *International Economics,* 2nd ed., Wiley, 1986, chaps. 8, 9.

Keynes, John Maynard, *A Tract on Monetary Reform,* Macmillan, 1924.

Keynes, John Maynard, *The Economic Consequences of Mr. Churchill,* Macmillan, 1925.

Kindleberger, Charles P., *The World in Depression, 1929–39,* University of California Press, 1986.

Robbins, Lionel, *The Great Depression,* Macmillan, 1934.

Solomon, Robert, *The International Monetary System,* Harper and Row, 1982.

Triffin, Robert, *Gold and the Dollar Crisis,* Yale, 1960.

Triffin, Robert, "The Evolution of the International Monetary System," *Princeton Studies in International Finance,* No. 112, 1984.

Chapter 14

The Flexible Exchange-Rate System and the Global Debt Problem

14.1 INTERNATIONAL MONETARY ARRANGEMENTS IN THE POST–BRETTON WOODS PERIOD

When the Bretton Woods system fell apart in early 1973, countries were left to manage their balance-of-payments problems without the benefit of guidance from an international agreement. It took until 1976 before it was agreed to amend the IMF's charter to sanction fluctuating exchange rates and to deal with other payments issues. To succeed C-20, which disolved in 1974, the IMF established an Interim Committee at the ministerial level to consider amendments to its charter. The major issues with which the committee concerned itself in its early years were (1) the nature of the exchange rate regime, (2) the role of gold, (3) new financing facilities, and (4) the substitution account that had been initially proposed during the C-20 deliberations.

Agreement with respect to exchange rates was not possible until the United States, committed to the legalization of floating, and France, committed to restoration of par values, were able to compromise their differences. The French position was modified rapidly in response to violent economic upheavals, which, by 1975, included a major recession. Consequently, at the Rambouillet Summit of November 1975, it finally became possible to agree on a new Article IV of the IMF's charter dealing with exchange rates. The new Article IV stated that each member should follow policies compatible with its commitment to

1. Endeavor to direct its economic and financial policies toward the objective of fostering orderly economic growth with reasonable price stability, with due regard to its circumstances.

409

2. Seek to promote stability by fostering orderly underlying economic and financial conditions and a monetary system that does not tend to produce erratic disruptions.

3. Avoid manipulating exchange rates or the international monetary system in order to prevent effective balance-of-payments adjustment or to gain an unfair competitive advantage over other members.

The article went on to state that countries may adopt exchange rate arrangements that include (1) the maintenance of a value for currencies in terms of the SDR or some other denominator other than gold, (2) cooperative arrangements by which they maintain the value of their currencies in relation to the value of the currency or currencies of other members, or (3) other exchange rate arrangements of a member's choice. The article also provided for the possible restoration of a fixed exchange-rate system provided that 85 percent of the voting power in the IMF favored such a change. That could easily be prevented by the United States or by the countries of the EEC acting in unison.

C-20 had sanctioned temporary floating during periods of emergency. The new Article IV recognized the status quo. It permitted countries to pursue the exchange rate policies of their choice, provided they do not manipulate exchange rates in a way that might be harmful to other countries.

Finally, the new Article IV directed the IMF to exercise "firm surveillance over the exchange rate policies of members, and, . . . adopt specific principles for the guidance of all members with respect to those policies." The members, in turn, were expected to cooperate with the IMF in the provision of information and were obliged to consult with the Fund on their exchange rate policies when requested to do so.

These changes were ratified at the meeting of the Interim Committee in Jamaica in 1976 and formally incorporated into the IMF charter in 1978. They superseded C-20's 1974 guidelines, which had endorsed the reserve indicator approach.

The effort to continue to reduce the importance of gold as an international reserve asset continued. At its fourth meeting, in August 1975, the Interim Committee agreed to abolition of an official price of gold, elimination of the obligation to use gold in transactions with the IMF and the IMF's authority to accept gold, the sale of one sixth of the gold holdings of the IMF for the benefit of poor countries, and the sale of an equal amount to members at 35 SDRs an ounce. The abolition of the official gold price put a formal end to the postwar gold standard, and the disposition of the IMF's gold stock was a major step in eliminating gold as a reserve asset. There was, however, some concern that a provision that permitted monetary authorities to engage in voluntary gold purchases and sales might be a step in the opposite direction. Indeed it was curious that countries still held onto gold reserves despite the fact that the new IMF rules prohibited countries from tying their currencies to gold, so gold had completely lost its place as a usable reserve asset.

The IMF issued SDRs of $4 billion in 1979, and again in 1980 and 1981. It also attempted to make the SDR a more attractive reserve asset by raising the yield on SDRs from 60 percent to 100 percent of a weighted average of short-term money market rates in the five countries with the largest IMF quotas—France, Germany, Japan, the United Kingdom, and the United States. It expanded the possible use of the SDR by altering the currency basket for valuation of the SDR, reducing it to those same five currencies. However, extensive use of the SDR as a reserve asset necessitated the establishment of a substitution account that would have required countries to deposit their foreign exchange reserves at the IMF in exchange for SDRs. Although the IMF pursued the effort to establish a substitution account, these efforts failed to reach fruition.

The SDR has proven to be of only limited importance in the international monetary system. In its initial years, the flexible exchange-rate system reduced the need for reserves and brought about currency realignment. Even though reserves grew rapidly between 1972 and 1980, SDRs were only a small fraction of the total. Countries still preferred dollars as a reserve currency. The dollar could be used as an intervention currency, whereas the SDR, lacking private markets for the asset, could not. Dollar holdings could be converted into short-term U.S. securities to earn interest. Although interest is earned on SDRs, only that part of SDR holdings in excess of a country's allocation earns interest, whereas amounts below allocation require interest payments from the country. Dollars also were popular, since an increasing fraction of trade, most notably OPEC oil, was invoiced in dollars. Finally, SDR creation was opposed by those who feared the inflationary effects of additional liquidity creation. Since pressure for additional SDR allocations came mainly from developing countries, it was feared that new allocations were a veiled form of development assistance that might better be made through the lending activities of the World Bank and other development institutions. In a postmortem on the SDR, E. M. Bernstein, a former research director of the IMF, noted in 1976 that

> The truth is that SDRs have not yet acquired the degree of international acceptance where countries would prefer to hold them instead of gold or even instead of currencies.[1]

[1] Bernstein, E. M., "Reflections on Jamaica," Princeton *Essays in International Finance,* No. 115, 1976, p. 5.

Countries adopted a wide variety of exchange rate policies. The countries of the EEC developed a system in which their currencies were essentially fixed with respect to each other, with all the EEC currencies floating jointly against currencies outside the union. The currencies of Canada, Japan, the United Kingdom, and the United States were permitted to fluctuate, which meant that over one half of world trade went on between countries with flexible exchange rates. Most developing countries attached their currencies to the currency of a major industrial country. Roughly 50 currencies are pegged to the dollar. Other countries pegged their currencies to the currencies of former colonial powers, such as France and the United Kingdom. Still others pegged their currencies to the SDR or to a market basket of currencies variously defined, and a few practiced a crawling peg.

The evolution of the European Monetary System (EMS) was a particularly interesting and important development. An agreement to prevent major fluctuations between their currency prices developed even before the suspension of dollar purchases in March of 1973. In 1972, the countries of the EEC agreed to intervene so as to prevent rates inside the EEC (cross rates) from fluctuating as much as was possible, given their intervention points against the dollar. This was dubbed the "snake in the tunnel" because the currencies snaked back and forth together inside the tunnel of the U.S. intervention points. The Benelux countries (Belgium, the Netherlands, and Luxembourg) maintained even tighter cross rates, thereby earning the appelation, the "worm in the snake."

In March 1973, when the EEC countries suspended dollar purchases, the tunnel was blown up, but the snake survived and added Norway and Sweden. Membership fell off during the succeeding years, but the severe currency turmoil of 1978 powered a new movement to stabilize cross rates inside the EEC. This movement culminated in the creation of the EMS, which was intended to be a step in the direction of complete currency union. That would mean a common currency and a uniform monetary policy. The EMS created its own reserve asset, the European Monetary Unit (EMU) to be used, as the SDR, to settle surpluses and deficits inside the EMS. However, even among the countries of the EMS there have been vastly different inflation rates that have caused the need for frequent realignment of parities. The EMS still lacks a uniform currency and a uniform monetary policy, and it has not developed an integrated reserve pool. Nevertheless, the EMS is of great interest and importance since its progress seems likely to influence the nature of future developments along regional lines.

Countries have also managed their reserves in the manner they consider best suited for themselves. Despite flexible exchange rates, the 1970s witnessed a virtual explosion of reserve growth. By 1980, total reserves, not counting gold, had risen from $56 billion in 1970 to $322 billion. Dollars accounted for much of this increase, with dollar reserves rising from $35 billion to $173 billion over the same period. Other currencies, such as the Japanese yen, the pound sterling, the Swiss franc, the French franc, and the Dutch guilder, have also been added to countries' reserves. Economists fear that this multicurrency reserve system is potentially unstable, since action by a monetary authority to alter the composition of its reserve portfolio could set off destabilizing runs against currencies that show signs of weakening. It has been argued that the weakness of the dollar in 1978 was in part caused by fears that monetary authorities would sell off their surplus dollars. Such a run had occurred in 1976 when an overhang of sterling balances had caused destabilizing speculation against the pound.

The new Article IV strongly emphasized the need for countries to conduct their domestic stabilization and their exchange rate policies in a manner that would not injure other countries. Thus far there is little evidence that countries have paid attention to the article. However, the perception is growing that countries cannot affect their domestic interest rates without causing disruptive changes in exchange rates and without sending severe macroeconomic shocks abroad. It has also become painfully clear that the industrial countries need to arrive at a coherent economic growth policy so that the debt problems of the developing countries can be relieved. But thus far, and despite considerable lip service to such catchy words as "harmonization," "cooperation," and "coordination," very little of a positive nature has been accomplished. Recently, Secretary Baker proposed the adoption of "indicators" to serve as guideposts to policy. These indicators seem to be targets for GNP growth, current-account changes, and the like. The idea is the sensible one of developing yardsticks that permit performance to be compared with targets so that appropriate corrective action is then indicated. Almost immediately after proposing this plan, the GNP target was faulted, because GNP can be made to grow more rapidly by increasing exports, thereby possibly increasing current-account imbalances. Clearly, the growth of domestic absorption is a more appropriate indicator of economic performance. Targets must be chosen with care, as discussed in Chapter 12.

The concept of IMF surveillance of countries exchange rate policy has evoked little more than a few yawns. The IMF is in a position to flex its muscle only over countries that need its resources. This excludes nearly all of the industrial countries that float their currencies, as well as other countries, such as OPEC members, that maintain fixed exchange rates but usually enjoy strong balance-of-payments positions. The IMF can hardly be expected to be an effective police officer, since it has no weapon or authority with which to enforce the law. Indeed, with the passage of the Bretton Woods system in 1973, the IMF's role as manager of the international monetary system has been all but eliminated, and most of its subsequent work has been in assisting developing countries. Thus the IMF has, in effect, evolved into a development institution alongside the World Bank. It differs from the World Bank in that its concerns are primarily with short-run emergencies, whereas the World Bank is expected to assist in longer-term development. However, even this distinction is becoming blurred. During the 1970s the IMF established a "special facility" to assist countries with "chronically weak balances of payments," meaning international basket cases that could never repay their balance-of-payments loans on time. IMF lending to these countries is for longer periods, permitting countries enough time to introduce the reforms needed to improve their balance of payments and overall economic performance. This facility evolved into what is now known as the "structural adjustment facility."

At the 1987 IMF meetings the IMF's new managing director, Michel Camdessus of France, indicated the IMF's intention to extend surveillance to monitoring countries' performance relative to the indicators. Since this implies interference with countries' internal economic policy, it can be expected to evoke little more than the usual polite lip service from countries that do not need the IMF's assistance.

In 1973, the first year of the floating-rate system, the world economy found itself in the throes of an inflationary boom. Consumer prices rose 11 percent in Canada and the United States, 13 percent in the EEC countries, and almost 25 percent in Japan. Money supplies had risen sharply in 1972 as countries bought dollars, and in the U.S. expansion was propelled by the depreciation of the dollar, which raised net exports. On the supply side there was a worldwide shortage of agricultural products and raw materials caused, in part, by adverse world food production conditions. The import demands for these products rose sharply in the industrial countries, only to be met by declining and inelastic supply. World grain production declined 3 percent in 1973 due to drought and other natural factors. In the United States, farm prices rose 50 percent, and grain prices increased 70 percent.

In the fall of 1973 another Arab-Israeli war flared up, and this led to the imposition of an oil embargo by the OPEC countries against the noncommunist industrial countries. By the time the embargo was lifted in March 1974, the cost of imported crude oil had risen from a preembargo level of about $3 per barrel to $12 per barrel. For the industrial countries the quadrupling of oil prices caused a condition of virulent stagflation. On the supply side, the higher cost of imported oil shifted countries' aggregate supply curves to the left, as higher production costs implied that previous output levels could only be produced with much higher price levels. On the demand side, the rise in oil prices acted as if it were a heavy excise tax. Since the short-run demand for oil is inelastic with respect to price, a rise in its price increases expenditures on oil, sucking purchasing power from consumers, thereby reducing domestic absorption. The result was the severe inflationary recession of 1975, as industrial production fell 8.8 percent in the United States, 6.7 percent in the EEC, and 10.6 percent in Japan. These declining output levels were accompanied by a renewal of inflation as consumer prices rose 9.1 percent in the U.S., 13.1 percent in the EEC countries, and 11.9 percent in Japan.

For the developing countries, the rise in the price of oil was an unmitigated disaster. The cost of their oil imports quadrupled, their export markets dwindled as the industrial countries went into recession, and the cost of their imports from industrial countries skyrocketed because of inflation. The first oil crisis marked the first stage in the explosion of global debt that raised the debt of the non-oil-developing countries more than fivefold by 1983.

For the industrial countries the recession of 1975 was the worst since the Great Depression of the 1930s. Recovery proved to be a slow and arduous process because countries were reluctant to undertake expansionary measures at a time of severe inflation. European officials began saying, at this time, that expansionary policies would be useless because of real wage rigidity, despite unemployment rates in the 10 percent zone. The United States managed a somewhat more rapid recovery, but that caused a deterioration in the current account and a depreciation of the dollar that gathered speculative momentum in 1978. In response, the United States was forced, for the first time, to intervene in the foreign exchange market in support of the dollar.

In 1979 the revolution in Iran caused a shortage of oil that enabled OPEC to raise its prices again, this time to about $30 per barrel. This caused a new stagflationary shock that once again slowed down the industrial economies. The non-oil-developing countries/suffered the same problems as in 1974–75, but this time there was the added problem of sharp increases in interest rates caused by rising price levels running up against more slowly growing money stocks, thereby reducing real money stocks.

In late 1979 the Federal Reserve launched its anti-inflationary monetary policy that reversed the downtrend of the dollar and led, in conjunction with subsequent expansionary fiscal policies, to a further sharp interest-rate escalation and a steady and sharp appreciation of the dollar.

Attempting to stem the depreciation of their currencies and the imported inflation that went with it, other countries reacted by joining the Fed in the practice of monetary restriction. The result was excessive world monetary shrinkage and the recession of 1982–83, which exceeded even the recession of 1975 in severity.

The recession did have the effect of calming the inflation that had gotten worse throughout the 1970s. However, recovery was again slow, and world economic growth, during the 1980s, has been disappointing. The continued outpouring of U.S. federal debt sustained the upward pressure on interest rates, and key countries such as West Germany and Japan were reluctant to stimulate their economies. The non-oil-developing countries underwent a third round of escalating debt, as the recession curtailed their export markets and the appreciation of the dollar increased the cost of their imports.

An overview of developments suggests that world economic performance during the 1970s and 1980s was much poorer than during the Bretton Woods era of the 1950s and 1960s. The recessions of 1974–75 and 1982–83 were far worse than any of the recessions of the 1950s and 1960s. On the average there was more unemployment, more inflation, and far slower growth. In many countries economic development was stalled, and per capita incomes decreased in less fortunate areas of the world. The mountains of debt that were accumulated were indicative of enormous redistributions of the world's wealth.

14.2 THE BEHAVIOR OF REAL
EXCHANGE RATES

Figure 14.1 shows the behavior of the Japanese yen, the British pound, the West German deutsche mark, and the U.S. dollar. The solid lines show the nominal exchange rates, and the hatched lines show the real exchange rates. The dollar gathered strength in 1976 largely because OPEC sold its oil in exchange for dollars. There then followed a period of steady weakening, with a sharp fall in 1978. It then embarked on an uptrend that lasted until 1985. The deutsche mark and the yen exhibited fairly consistent strength during the 1970s. Both showed large appreciations between 1973 and 1978. Until 1977, the pound was weak when the opening of Britain's North Sea oil fields contributed to its upsurge.

The most important phenomenon shown by these charts is the sharp movement of real exchange rates. According to the theory of purchasing-power parity, real exchange rates ought not to have changed

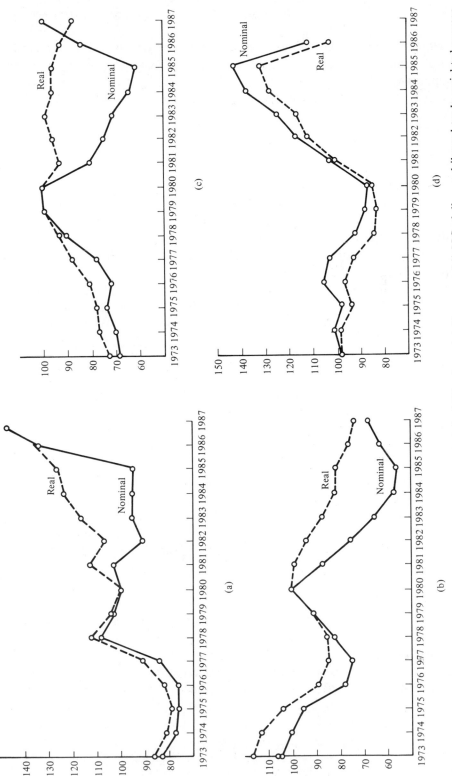

Figure 14.1 Real and nominal exchange rates: (a) Japan; (b) United Kingdom; (c) Germany; (d) U.S. dollar multilateral-trade weighted average value, March 1973 = 100. (*Source: Economic Report of the President,* January 1987.)

at all. But that was clearly not the case. The first order of business is to inquire into the causes and consequences of these swings in real exchange rates.

Large swings in exchange rates produce costly economic effects. The instability of the foreign trade sector is probably the most important cost. The 1979–83 appreciation of the dollar has been associated with sharp contractions in production for export and intensified competition from imports. Over a sustained period of currency overvaluation industrial capacity may shrink and employment may shift elsewhere with all of the economic costs and social travail associated with decline. If the currency depreciates in the future, and the competitive position of the affected industries is restored, they may find it difficult to expand adequately due to shortages of capacity and the atrophy of labor skills. The inflation that accompanies the effect of depreciation on import prices would be accentuated by the capacity shortages.

The problem of instability in the foreign trade sector, although serious, is less severe for the United States than for small countries that are relatively more trade dependent. For small countries, the net export expansion induced by depreciation is immediately reflected in sharp increases in national expenditures and often in the price level. It has been estimated by the IMF that a 10 percent depreciation of the dollar results in a 1.5 percent increase in consumer prices in the United States. In contrast, in Belgium, where imports equal 60 percent of GNP and wages are indexed to consumer prices, a 10 percent depreciation would mean an estimated 7.5 percent rise in prices.[2] Accordingly, it is not surprising that smaller countries have developed arrangements to fix their exchange rates with respect to their major trading partners.

Capital gains and losses, particularly on long-term assets, are another problem of fluctuating exchange rates. As long as the real exchange rate is roughly constant, borrowers can compare implicit real costs of borrowing in different countries with confidence that they are considering correct relative prices. When real exchange rates change abruptly in an unpredictable manner, however, international borrowers can face huge losses through a depreciation of their home currencies, since more of such currencies are then needed to repay a loan denominated in foreign currency.

Losses associated with depreciation of a major reserve currency such as the dollar may add to the costs of a flexible exchange-rate system. Artus and Young explain that

---

[2] Artus, Jacques, and Ann K. McGuirk, "A Revised Version of the Multilateral Exchange Rate Model," International Monetary Fund, *Staff Papers,* 1981, 275–309.

... developments with respect to the U.S. dollar in 1978 had major repercussions throughout the system, as virtually every country found some
of its important bilateral rates changing significantly ... with the bulk of
official reserves held in U.S. dollars, this meant major changes in the value
of international reserves, and put pressure on reserve holders to consider
diversifying their portfolios.[3]

The pressure to diversify reserve holdings may, in turn, be a source of
exchange rate instability, because any major action to change the composition of official reserves could cause major exchange rate movements.
The same authors note that

The overhang of official sterling balances seems to have played a destabilizing role through 1976. More recently, there have been signs that actual
or potential diversification out of U.S. dollar reserve balances was a factor
in the weak behavior of the dollar in 1978.[4]

Changes in real exchange rates also affect the distribution of income
and create regional booms and busts. If the dollar depreciates in real
terms, the prices of tradable goods rise relative to other prices and income
is redistributed toward trade-related industries. If these industries are re-
gionally concentrated, there will be a regional boom as the result of the
depreciation and, conversely, a slump at times of appreciation. If the
exchange rate followed overall prices—that is, purchasing-power parity—
there would be no change in real exchange rates and these effects would
not occur.

Although it might be expected that sharp and erratic fluctuations
in exchange rates will tend to reduce trade in favor of domestic economic
activity, this has not appeared to happen. World trade grew rapidly during
the 1970s. United States exports grew from 7.8 percent of real GNP in
1973 to 10.8 percent in 1980. It is also noteworthy that econometric
models fail to disclose significant trade impacts stemming from the switch
to flexible exchange rates in 1973.

Why do exchange rates fluctuate so much? Advocates of flexible
exchange rates predicted that exchange rates would move so as to offset
differential inflation rates and to maintain approximate purchasing-power
parity. Real exchange rate movements would occur slowly as a consequence of the uneven pattern of development in different countries, that
is, developments consisting of resource discoveries, technological break-

[3] Artus and Young, op. cit., p. 683.

[4] Ibid., p. 680.

throughs, and other forces that affect productivity growth, causing changes in international competitiveness.

In practice, however, real exchange rates have deviated sharply from purchasing-power parity. The most important reason, which we have emphasized continually, is that the demand and supply of foreign exchange are influenced to a larger extent by the conditions of financial markets than by the longer-range changes in trade flows and international competitiveness. This view is certainly consistent with what we observe from experience.

Differences in perceived real interest rates, brought about by changes in nominal interest rates and/or inflationary expectations, are an important source of capital movements and exchange rate variation. Robert Dunn describes the behavior of the pound sterling in recent years as follows:

> . . . sterling appreciated sharply in 1979–80 when the arrival of a new Conservative administration led many market participants to expect a prompt deceleration of U.K. inflation. Since nominal interest rates remained very high, expected real yields increased sharply, making British assets seem very attractive. Increasing North Sea oil production combined with increases in oil prices, added to the upward pressure on sterling. When the inflation failed to decline promptly and oil prices stopped rising sterling depreciated sharply.[5]

Dunn then switches to the behavior of the dollar and writes:

> The dollar declined sharply in 1977–78 because of a weaker current account and widespread doubts about the macroeconomic policies of the incoming administration. It then appreciated sharply in 1981–82, when extraordinarily high nominal yields combined with an expectation of decelerating inflation to create very high expected real yields on dollar assets.[6]

The magnitude of exchange rate fluctuations also depends in part on the speed with which flows of trade adjust to changes in exchange rates. If the appreciation caused by a capital inflow quickly reduces exports and raises imports, then a large swing in the exchange rate will be forestalled, so deviations from purchasing-power parity need not be great. It appears, however, that trade flows respond sluggishly to changes in exchange rates. Therefore, financial factors, such as changes in relative asset supplies that cause interest-rate differentials and capital movements, tend

---

[5] Dunn, Robert, "The Many Dissapointments of Flexible Exchange Rates," *Princeton Essays in International Finance,* No 154, 1983, p. 9.

[6] Ibid., p. 9.

to cause large exchange rate shifts unmitigated by offsetting responses in trade.

As an example, depreciation should eliminate an excess demand for foreign currencies by expanding export earnings and reducing payments for imports inasmuch as prices of exports denominated in foreign currency fall, whereas the prices of imports denominated in domestic currency increase. However, if the quantitative response to lower foreign prices is slight in the short run, the proportionate increase in the quantity of exports will be smaller than the proportionate fall in price, and less foreign exchange will be earned from export sales after the depreciation than before. The excess demand for foreign currency may therefore persist and even widen in the short run, thereby producing additional depreciation.

As we noted in Chapter 9, the problem of sluggish quantity adjustment may be aggravated by the presence of long-term contracts that fix both prices and quantities into the future. As an extreme example, imagine that all prices and quantities are previously determined in the foreign country's currency. The volume of imports and the foreign currency price paid by importers will then not change at all in response to depreciation, so the demand for foreign exchange is invariant with respect to exchange rate variations. Though the example is extreme, there does seem to be evidence that flexible exchange rates, by increasing exchange rate uncertainty, have promoted the wider use of long-term contracts and weakened the incentive of traders to respond to the cost and price differentials that result from short-run exchange rate changes.[7] Discussing the problem of sluggish current-account adjustment, Artus and Young note that

> ... the adjustment process in the goods market has not worked well. The Federal Republic of Germany, Japan, and Switzerland have maintained strong current account positions despite the appreciation of their currencies both before and after the establishment of flexible exchange rates. The total current-account surplus of these three countries increased from about $8 billion in 1972 to $31 billion in 1978. ... the United States has continued to experience recurring current account deficits despite the marked effective depreciation of the U.S. dollar that took place during that period.[8]

Another important reason for the failure of exchange rate movements to bring current accounts into balance appears to have been the

[7] Magee, Steven, "Contracting and Spurious Deviations from Purchasing Power Parity," in Johnson, H. G., and Jacob Frenkel, eds., *The Economics of Exchange Rates,* Addison-Wesley, 1978.

[8] Artus and Young, op. cit, p. 666.

absence of macroeconomic policies designed to facilitate adjustment. National income equals absorption plus net exports. Consequently, net exports can be increased only if absorption declines relative to national income. Exchange rate depreciation may improve competitiveness, but, since the resulting increase in net exports also stimulates the economy, depreciation raises absorption, increases the demand for imports, and tends to raise the price level. If these expenditure-increasing effects are not neutralized by restraining monetary and fiscal policies, depreciation of the currency may not achieve significant increases in net exports. Artus and Young summarize their discussion by noting that

> ... flexible rates can play a useful role only if ... (1) there is a supporting demand-management policy, (2) changes in the relative prices between domestic goods and foreign goods are sustained, and (3) a shift in relative prices leads to a switch in domestic and foreign demand between foreign goods and domestic goods.[9]

The same authors, emphasizing the importance of harmonizing internal demand policies with the conditions for external equilibrium, point out that

> All the major econometric models of world trade ... show conclusively that year-to-year changes in the volume of imports and exports are dominated by variations in real aggregate demand. During the first one or two years, offsetting effects that may result from exchange rate induced variations in relative prices are generally only a small fraction of the effects of demand changes.[10]

In summary: Exchange rates have varied widely since 1973. They have frequently overshot the values thought to be consistent with current-account equilibrium. They have appreciated despite deteriorating current accounts, and depreciated despite strong international competitiveness on the part of an economy. The instability of expectations, leading to bandwagon effects and speculative bubbles in exchange markets, the frequent failure of capital movements to flow in a stabilizing manner, and the effect of income changes in determining the demand for imports have all played important roles.

This situation is clearly unsatisfactory. Because of the severity of international shock transmission, countries' control over conditions in their domestic economies has been greatly reduced. Frustration over this

[9] Ibid, p. 662.

[10] Ibid., p. 669.

fact could once again lead to efforts to install shock-proofing by resort to mercantilist policies that obstruct trade and prevent the movement of capital. Such a turn of events would be exceedingly costly and should be avoided. But to do so will require some major cooperative efforts at reform. The first step along this path would be to ask why the flexible exchange-rate system has worked so differently than had been envisioned by its proponents.

14.3 THE FLEXIBLE EXCHANGE-RATE SYSTEM: PROMISES VERSUS REALITIES

Critics of flexible exchange rates blame much of the deterioration in world economic performance that has marked the flexible exchange-rate period on the failure to restore a par-value system. Supporters of flexible exchange rates point out that flexible exchange rates did not create the oil crises and other sources of misfortune. They would add that a fixed exchange-rate system could probably not withstand the shocks to which it would have been subjected in the 1970s. Not the least of these shocks was the transition from a par-value system in which exchange rates had become chronically misaligned. Nor could flexible exchange rates be blamed for the poor management of governments' monetary-fiscal tools and their stubborn resistance to the obvious necessity for a multilateral approach that attempts to harmonize interest rate policies and develop a consistent plan for reaching economic goals.

The flexible exchange-rate system certainly has not functioned the way its more enthusiastic supporters had predicted. Strong advocates tend to make exaggerated claims that come back to haunt them, so it is easy to say "I told you so." Nevertheless contrasting performance against promises is a useful exercise that permits us to see where the promises went wrong and what might be done to improve the system. That is the task of this part of the chapter. In doing this, we will also be providing a summary that reviews much of the turf that has been covered in previous sections. We begin by listing the claims, and we then take them up for discussion.

1. Exchange rates between countries are largely determined by the relative income and price levels of the countries. Since these variables move slowly, exchange rates will also move slowly. Real exchange rates will tend to remain fixed, whereas nominal exchange rates should comply with purchasing-power parity.

2. Speculation under a flexible exchange-rate system will be stabilizing, thereby reducing the amplitude of exchange-rate fluctuations.

3. Flexible exchange rates enable countries to recapture control of their monetary policies. Freed from the obligation to buy and sell foreign exchange, countries will be able to establish and maintain internal targets for monetary growth rates appropriate to their particular economies and economic objectives.

4. Since exchange rates will tend to move so as to bring current accounts into balance, each country's domestic income level will equal its level of absorption. The effects of countries' monetary and fiscal policies will therefore be contained inside the country, and there will be no spillover effects. Shock transmission is thereby eliminated. As a corollary, countries are free to pick their unemployment and price-level targets independently of the choices of other countries.

5. Flexible exchange rates will tend to promote free trade because protectionism will no longer be a useful device for raising employment.

6. The deflationary bias of the fixed exchange-rate system will be eliminated. The burden of adjustment will be shared equally by all countries.

Now let us compare the performance against the claims. We begin with the assumption of purchasing-power parity and stabilizing speculation. We have already discussed several aspects of the purchasing-power-parity issue in the previous section, so this review can go quickly. Long-run trends in the movement of exchange rates were expected to reflect differential inflation rates. If the United States has a 5 percent inflation rate while inflation in the rest of the world proceeds at an 8 percent rate, this would be expected to result in a 3 percent appreciation of the dollar. The slower domestic rate of inflation would give U.S. exports a competitive advantage and cause domestic products to be substituted for foreign-produced goods and services. The result would be an incipient surplus, which was to be eliminated by an appreciation that restored preexisting competitive relationships.

When this assumption of purchasing-power parity was combined with the additional assumption that speculators will correctly forecast the long-range "fundamentals" that explain inflation trends, and when it was perceived that it is less painful and costly to allow exchange rates to adjust to different inflation rates than to compel price levels to adjust with fixed exchange rates, the case for flexible exchange rates became very strong.

Another glance at Figure 14.1 shows that the assumption that exchange rates will follow purchasing-power parity has been erroneous. If the exchange rates were ruled by purchasing-power parity, the real exchange rates would have remained roughly constant as nominal exchange rates move to offset differences in inflation rates. Purchasing-power parity is likely to be approximated when the only shocks that affect the balance of payments are different rates of inflation, or if trade flows are so highly responsive to changes in exchange rates that major fluctuations in exchange rates would not be needed to reequilibrate trade following a disturbance.

Such conditions have not been fulfilled in practice. The earlier advocates of flexible exchange rates were not fully appreciative of the fact that the exchange rate is an asset price and that the behavior of the exchange rate is dominated by capital flows rather than by changes in current accounts. In the purchasing-power-parity world the expectation was that since income and price levels change slowly, exchange rates would do so also. But they have bounced around quite sharply, but not more sharply than stock prices and other asset prices. Consequently, there really is nothing terribly unusual about the large fluctuations in exchange rates that have been experienced, especially since governments have done such a poor job of stabilizing asset prices. To put it differently, the optimistic purchasing-power-parity view comes from the perspective of the financially closed economy as defined by Ronald McKinnon. The relevant perspective, however, is that of the financially open economy.

The asset-market theory of exchange rate determination provides a more appropriate view of the likely behavior of exchange rates. For example, in the old view an expansionary monetary policy would be expected to raise the price level and depreciate the exchange rate over time. In the asset-market theory the long-run effect may be the same. But in the short run, income and price levels do not adjust, and the impact of the monetary policy is felt largely in financial markets where the exchange rate is altered by the reactions of portfolio readjustment. Thus the expansionary monetary policy causes an initial sharp depreciation, as the reduced supply of domestic bonds causes portfolio substitution in the direction of foreign bonds. This improves the competitive position of the economy and gradually raises exports and lowers imports, causing a surplus in the current account. The surplus causes wealth holders to accumulate foreign assets, and this then causes a period of currency appreciation that gradually eliminates the current-account surplus. But if the price level responds slowly to the expansionary effects of the monetary policy, it will still be rising when the current account reaches balance; therefore, subsequently, the rising price level causes a current-account deficit that once again depreciates the currency.

The asset-market theory is one way in which the tendency for exchange rates and current accounts to overshoot can be explained. They tend to move in the right direction to correct disequilibrium, but they tend to go too far, thereby creating the need for reversal. It is the phenomenon of capital mobility, combined with sluggish quantity and price-level adjustments, that appears to cause the problem. It means that adjustments have been sloppy, and in this there is a cost, since export and import industries have suffered from instability. It does not necessarily mean that the situation would be improved by a par-value system. Indeed, John Williamson has written that

> . . . capital mobility has rendered the continued use of the adjustable peg impractical. The reason is fundamental; under capital mobility, exchange markets can be in equilibrium only if all existing stocks of the several currencies are willingly held, which requires either that the stocks themselves be adjusted according to the gold standard "rules of the game" or that the expected yields of different currencies be adjusted in order to satisfy the conditions of asset-market equilibrium [11]

Unfortunately, the fact that purchasing-power parity has not been approximated in practice means that market exchange rates fail to reflect conditions of international competitiveness. They therefore do not provide optimal signals to guide the international allocation of productive resources. When the local currency is low, export capacity tends to be expanded, and when the currency appreciates, the expansion proves to have been excessive. Hence, excess capacity and the need to transfer labor to other sectors arise.

Critics of flexible exchange rates have long argued that speculative flights of funds cause excessive swings in exchange rates. This was certainly true during the 1920s and 1930s, and these critics see no reason to suppose that a return to flexible exchange rates would produce different results. In their view intervention by monetary authorities is essential in order to offset the disruptive effects of destabilizing speculation.

Advocates, however, argued that flexible exchange rates would necessarily force speculators to behave in a manner that fosters stability, because speculators who cannot forecast basic market trends, the so-

---

[11] Williamson, John, "The Benefits and Costs of an International Monetary Nonsystem," in Bernstein, E. M., ed., *Reflections on Jamaica,* p. 55.

called fundamentals, will not survive. If the currency appreciates above its long-run equilibrium level, intelligent speculators will consider the current price abnormally high and will therefore sell the currency. In doing so, they bring about a stabilizing correction in the price. On the other hand, speculators who incorrectly think that the long-run equilibrium price is higher take the rise in the currency as indicating the beginning of an upward trend. They therefore buy the currency, only to discover later that they have made a costly mistake. Such speculators tend to buy when the currency is high and sell when it is low, and in the process they bankrupt themselves. Surviving speculators must, therefore, be those whose market activity tends to have a stabilizing effect.

It severely taxes credulity to believe that speculators normally behave in such a helpful manner. When incompetent speculators are driven from a market, there are often twice as many ready to replace them. Thus, at any one time, there are apt to be a significant number of inept speculators whose operations are such that they destabilize markets. With the trade deficit and the dollar both rising during the 1980–84 period, there was the general belief that the dollar was getting overvalued and would have to come down. Many speculators who knew that the dollar would have to fall had the confidence that they could get out of dollars in time. They therefore continued to buy dollars, thus creating a "speculative bubble" that sustained the dollar's appreciation beyond expectation as well as beyond a reasonable level.

There seems even to be some justification in the theory that if there is anything wrong with speculation, it is that there isn't enough of it. The word "speculation" has a negative connotation, and speculators are regarded as sinister manipulators, no better than thieves. Some speculators even invent euphemistic names for themselves, as when Ivan Boesky calls himself an "arbitrager," Robert Vesco is a "financier," and Robert Brennan is a "venture capitalist." So as not to be tainted by association with such characters of dubious repute, banks and multinational corporations deliberately refrain from any activity that could be construed as speculative buying and selling, as a result of which they rob the market of activity that would help to stabilize it. James Ingram makes this point as follows:

> Commercial banks often simply act as intermediaries, bringing sellers and buyers of foreign exchange together but taking no net position in a currency. Multinational corporations are at pains to emphasize that their business is production and sales of goods and services, not currency speculation. Individuals face obstacles in the market, notably from the foreign exchange departments of commercial banks, which want to be assured that proposed

transactions are not mere speculation. The result is that the scope for a broad, resilient speculative response is greatly reduced. When a sudden shock causes a currency to fall, the speculative demand that could sustain it is unable to function.[12]

The third ace in the hole for the early flexible exchange-rate advocate was the proposition that flexible exchange rates would make it possible for countries to control their domestic money supplies. We have already discussed this at length in Chapter 6, so the present review can go quickly. We know that money supplies fluctuate in response to the balance of payments under fixed exchange rates. A surplus causes the money supply to increase, as the monetary authority purchases excess supplies of foreign exchange at the official exchange rate by paying out domestic currency, whereas a deficit causes the money supply to decrease. It is difficult, therefore, to use monetary policy as an effective tool to achieve the internal balance goals of high employment and price stability.

Under flexible exchange rates, this problem is eliminated. Since central banks no longer need to purchase and sell their own currency in exchange for foreign exchange, they can conduct domestic open-market operations and control their money supplies. Unfortunately, however, capital mobility, which the early advocates did not take into account, renders this simple proposition a great deal more complicated. In the absence of capital mobility an expansionary monetary policy would raise national income. This would raise the demand for imports and depreciate the currency. The depreciation would stimulate exports, and slow the rise in imports in such a way as to maintain equality between exports and imports. Thus national income rises by the amount of the increase in domestic absorption, and there are no spillover effects on other economies.

However, when the degree of capital mobility is high, the currency depreciates and net exports rise. This raises national income, but since net exports in other countries decline, the increase in income and employment that is generated comes at the expense of income and employment in foreign countries. To prevent the appreciation of their currencies, foreign monetary authorities may feel they have no choice other than to imitate the initiating country's expansionary monetary policy. They therefore expand their money supplies, and thus neutralize the restrictive shock. Thus the monetary action of one country has forced the other country to adopt similar monetary policies. As Robert Dunn has said,

[12] Ingram, James, *International Economics*, p. 221.

Domestic monetary policy again faces an international payments constraint: it must approximate the monetary policy being pursued abroad in order to avoid large exchange rate movements.[13]

The notion that flexible exchange rates ensure monetary policy independence, though correct in a technical sense, is apparently only a superficial gain. Under Bretton Woods, the United States, in its role as the nth country, dictated the monetary policies of other countries. Rapid monetary expansion in the United States led to a rise in the U.S. balance-of-payments deficit, which required other countries to increase their dollar purchases, thereby causing their money supplies to increase more rapidly. There is reason to suppose that this situation has not changed significantly. The dollar is still the world's "key" currency, and the United States, by engaging in less intervention in foreign exchange markets than others, has continued in its role as the nth country. Because so much trade is invoiced in dollars, it is important for other countries to maintain exchange rate stability between their currencies and the dollar. Thus, when the dollar depreciates, as it did in the early 1970s and in 1977–78, countries bought dollars to stem the appreciation of their currencies, thereby increasing their money supplies. After 1979, when the dollar appreciated, countries' monetary authorities sold dollars to stem the depreciation of their currencies, thereby reducing their money supplies. Foreign monetary policies therefore imitated U.S. monetary policy when the changes in the value of the dollar were initiated by U.S. monetary policies. Commenting on the foreign response to the U.S. tight money policies of the 1979–82 period, Robert Dunn noted that

> ... Europeans made it clear that they did not believe their economies required the degree of monetary tightness maintained in the United States. Yet they felt compelled by their exchange rate goals to maintain interest-rate yields approaching those in New York. If the European central banks had instead pursued a monetary policy based purely on domestic considerations, the resulting interest-rate differentials would have produced large capital outflows and sharp depreciations of the European currencies. . . . European governments and central banks were reduced to asking the United States to ease its monetary policy so that they could ease theirs.[14]

Ronald McKinnon has taken the argument one step further.[15] He argues that the United States directs its monetary policy toward a money

[13] Dunn, Robert, op. cit., p. 11.

[14] Dunn, op. cit., p. 12.

[15] McKinnon, Ronald I., "An International Standard for Monetary Stabilization," Institute for International Economics, *Policy Analyses in International Economics,* vol. 8, 1984.

growth target, whereas other countries use their monetary policies to stabilize their dollar exchange rates. This means that when the dollar appreciates, foreign monetary authorities sell dollars, reducing their own money supplies. Meanwhile, the Federal Reserve neutralizes the increase in the U.S. money supply caused by foreign intervention activity by engaging in open-market sales. Therefore, the total world money supply declines, as it did after 1979, tending to cause world deflation. Depreciation of the dollar causes the world money supply to swing in the opposite, inflationary, direction. Foreign monetary authorities buy dollars, increasing their own money supplies and reducing the U.S. money supply. But the Federal Reserve then offsets the decline in the U.S. money supply by engaging in open-market purchases. Consequently, when the dollar depreciates, the world money supply increases, which causes inflation, as in the early 1970s and again in 1977–78. McKinnon's solution to this problem is to get major countries to agree to a target rate for world money growth and to ask each country to direct its monetary policy to the attainment of that rate. We will examine this idea in the next chapter, which studies reform proposals.

Meanwhile, let us consider the fourth claim, that exchange rates will bring current accounts into equilibrium, causing each country's income to equal its absorption, thereby preventing macroeconomic shock transmission to other countries. It is clear that fixed exchange rates cause expansionary and restrictive shocks in one country to be transmitted to others. A rise in national income in the United States raises import demand. Since the net exports of trading partners therefore rise, an expansionary impulse is felt in these countries. If their trade surpluses also require exchange market intervention to maintain fixed exchange rates, foreign money supplies will rise and the expansionary impact is augmented.

Early advocates of flexible exchange rates argued that a rise in import demand due to economic expanion would not change net exports. An increase in the demand for imports caused by a rise in income would create an incipient deficit that would cause the dollar to depreciate and foreign currencies to appreciate. This currency depreciation would slow the rise in imports and increase exports and thus would drive the trade balance back into equilibrium. Since net exports would therefore not change, national income in each country would equal its level of domestic absorption. Therefore, the entire income gain is felt in the initiating country while the other countries are insulated against the macroeconomic shock.

This argument again is rendered incorrect by capital mobility. Expansionary monetary policy causes a capital outflow that depreciates the currency and raises net exports. Foreign net exports decline by the same amount. Domestic national income rises because of the increase in net exports, and foreign national income falls for the same reason. If capital mobility is perfect, interest rates will remain largely unchanged, so the income gain in the initiating country is almost entirely due to its theft of income and employment from abroad. Similarly, whereas monetary policy raises employment by stealing employment from abroad, expansionary fiscal policy becomes ineffective because the stimulus from the fiscal policy is exported. The fiscal policy raises interest rates, attracts foreign capital, and appreciates the currency. This reduces net exports, and the impact of the fiscal policy is transferred to foreign countries.

The corollary proposition, that countries would be free to pick their unemployment and price-level targets independently of the choices of other countries, also perishes under the barrage of foreign shocks. There are, however, additional reasons that should be elaborated. The proposition focuses attention on countries' "Phillips curves."

A country's Phillips curve can be plotted by measuring its unemployment rate on the horizontal axis and its corresponding inflation rate on the vertical axis. When a line of best fit is drawn through the points, the result is the Phillips curve. The Phillips curve for the United States during the 1950s and 1960s is shown in Figure 14.2. There appears to

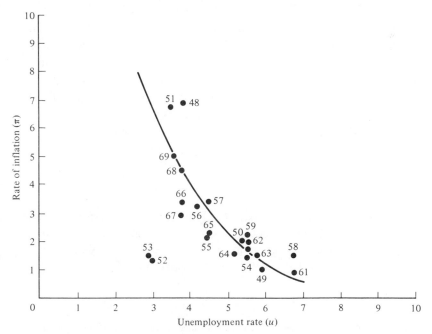

Figure 14.2 Phillips curve, 1948–69: $\pi = -4.2 + 32.5(1/u)$.

be an inverse relationship between unemployment and inflation—the higher the unemployment rate, the lower the rate of inflation. This discovery hardly adds anything to the understanding of inflation, since the inverse relationship could occur either through demand-side considerations, or cost-push-type arguments. A low unemployment rate implies a high level of employment and personal income that boosts consumer spending, thereby tending to raise prices. With a high unemployment rate, consumers' incomes would be depressed and so would their demand for goods and services. Prices would therefore rise more slowly. That is the demand side of the coin. The supply-side interpretation is that a low unemployment rate implies shortages of labor, especially skilled labor. Employers attempt to attract skilled workers by offering higher wages. This raises costs and tends to push up prices.

The Phillips curve called attention to the fact that there is a potential trade-off between unemployment and inflation. A country committed to low unemployment could achieve that only at the cost of rapid inflation. A country committed to price stability could have that only at the cost of higher unemployment.

The early advocates of flexible exchange rates argued that such a choice between unemployment and inflation was not available to countries under fixed exchange rates. A country opting for low unemployment would have a higher inflation rate than countries with less ambitious employment targets, and it would therefore suffer a balance-of-payments deficit that would eventually exhaust its foreign exchange reserves and force it to abandon its high employment target. However, under flexible exchange rates, a country with an ambitious employment target and a high inflation rate would merely experience depreciation of its currency at a rate equal to the difference between its rate of inflation and foreign inflation rates. The country would not lose reserves, its money supply would not be reduced by a balance of payments deficit, and it could therefore sustain its policy. The late Harry G. Johnson, one of the most forceful and articulate of the early flexible exchange-rate advocates, argued that

> Flexible rates would allow each country to pursue the mixture of unemployment and price trend objectives it prefers, consistent with international equilibrium being secured by appreciation of the currencies of "price stability" countries relative to the currencies of the "full employment" countries.[16]

---

[16] Johnson, Harry G., "The Case for Flexible Exchange Rates," Federal Reserve Bank of St. Louis, *Review*, 51, 1969, p. 18.

The trouble with countries' Phillips curves is that they have proven quite unstable. During the 1970s, Phillips curves shifted steadily to the right as unemployment and inflation increased over the decade. These shifts were so dominant relative to movements along Phillips curves that the notion of a trade-off between unemployment and inflation was all but destroyed.

The unemployment rates and associated inflation rates for the United States for 1969–82 are shown in Figure 14.3. The result contrasts sharply with the apparently stable relationship of the 1950s and 1960s. When the year-to-year points are connected, the pattern that emerges is a spiraling upward and to the right. Although standard Phillips curves might be discerned for 1970–72, 1976–79, and 1981–82 each successive curve is farther to the right. On balance, therefore, inflation increased as unemployment rose, rather than the opposite. Much of this deterioration was undoubtedly caused by the supply shocks of the 1970s. These shocks caused aggregate supply curves to shift to the left, thereby causing both lower output and higher prices. But, in addition, there is a substantial body of analysis that predicts that Phillips curves will shift to the right, and the unemployment-inflation trade-off will deteriorate, because of expansionary monetary policies that attempted to push unemployment below sustainable levels.

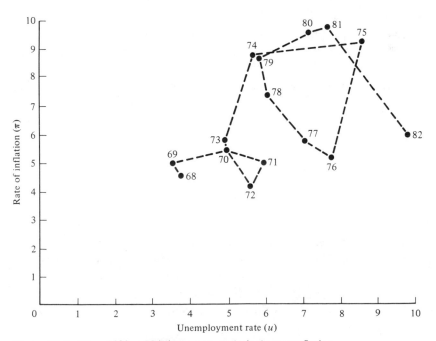

Figure 14.3 The shifting Phillips curve and virulent stagflation.

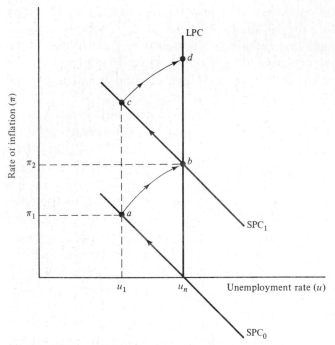

Figure 14.4 Short- and long-run Phillips curves.

An argument of this sort was first made by Professor Milton Friedman of the University of Chicago in his 1968 presidential address before the American Economic Association.[17] Friedman called the unemployment rate that is consistent with the intersection of the labor market demand and supply curves the "natural" rate of unemployment. In Figure 14.4, suppose this is the unemployment rate u_n, and assume that the Phillips curve SPC_0 intersects u_n at a zero rate of inflation. If the government attempts to lower the unemployment rate to u_1, the economy moves to point a along the SPC_0 curve. This expansionary policy raises the rate of inflation to π_1. Since employers will hire more workers if real wages fall, this policy action could have reduced unemployment only because prices rose without a corresponding increase in money-wages. Workers will not tolerate this reduction in their real wages for long, so when labor contracts are renegotiated money-wages will rise, thereby raising real wages. But this raises unemployment. Consequently, the inflation-unemployment path abandons SPC_0 and moves upward and to the right toward point b, producing a period of stagflation—a situation in which both unemployment and inflation are getting worse.

[17] Friedman, M., "The Role of Monetary Policy," *American Economic Review,* 1968.

At point b unemployment is back at u_n, but both wages and prices are now rising at a rate of π_2. If the government still wants unemployment to be u_1, it will have to reenforce the expansionary policies by raising the rate of monetary growth again. This would move inflation and unemployment upward and to the left along a new short-run Phillips curve, SPC_1 toward point c. But when wages catch up again, the path of π and u turns toward the northeast in the direction of point d.

The implication of Friedman's analysis is that governments cannot lower unemployment permanently below the natural rate of unemployment. Attempts to do so merely result in accelerating inflation. In the long-run, a government that follows an overly ambitious employment target will cause a movement upward at u_n along the vertical line LPC. This is the long-run Phillips curve. There is, therefore, no unemployment-inflation trade-off possible in the long run.

An equation for SPC_0 might be

$$\pi = a(u_n - u)$$

where u is the actual unemployment rate and π is the rate of inflation. Once the short-run Phillips curve becomes SPC_1, an additional term needs to be added to reflect the upward shift. Therefore,

$$\pi = a(u_n - u) + x$$

This is called the "expectations-augmented" Phillips curve, where x is the expected rate of inflation. At point b the rate of inflation is π_2, which equals x. If wages are set on the assumption that the inflation rate will continue at that rate, the economy will remain in long-run equilibrium at that point on the long-run PC curve. Therefore, x must represent the expected rate of inflation.

A glance at the expectations-augmented Phillips curve suggests that a situation of stagflation could easily be caused by government activities, or by foreign developments, that raise the expected rate of inflation. Obviously, it is crucial for countries to keep inflationary expectations under control. But that is difficult to do if the government is committed to the use of its monetary-fiscal tools to maintain a low level of unemployment. Such policy generates inflation and depreciates the currency. The depreciation also signals to citizens that the inflation rate is likely to be on the rise.

After surveying the evidence, Jacques Artus and John Young of the IMF staff concluded that

> There would thus be few today who would argue for flexible exchange rates on the grounds that they give countries a significant amount of freedom

over the long run to choose a higher level of employment at the expense of more rapid price increases.[18]

The fifth item on the list of claims made for flexible exchange rates is that they would serve the cause of trade liberalization. Under the fixed exchange-rate system the use of tariffs, quotas, and other import restrictions often commended itself as a substitute for devaluation, since the balance of payments and macroeconomic effects of such restrictive policies were similar. By reducing imports, a tariff or a quota improved the balance of payments, helping to defend the exchange rate, and by causing domestic products to be substituted for traded goods, it also raised domestic employment. The employment, however, was bought at the expense of employment abroad rather than being generated at home. This method of raising employment was, therefore, viewed as a beggar-thy-neighbor policy of a highly destructive sort. It invited retaliation and headed countries in the direction of economic autarchy.

Early advocates of flexible exchange rates, mindful of the disastrous consequences of mercantilism in the 1930s, argued that tariff protection under flexible exchange rates would no longer be successful in raising employment. If this were the case, the employment-generating argument could no longer be used as a pretext for protection. Protection for certain industries would cause an initial decline in imports. This decline would produce an incipient trade surplus that appreciates the currency. Net exports are then again brought into equilibrium as the appreciation lowers exports and increases imports. Thus, the tariff is accompanied by what amounts to a tax on exports and on the unprotected import-competing industries. No domestic employment is created in the process. Seen from this point of view, the net effect of the protection is misallocation of resources that remain in high-cost, protected industries.

It seems extremely doubtful that flexible exchange rates have caused protectionism to wane. Protectionism is no longer blatantly advocated on the strength of its impact on overall aggregate demand since such demand management has come to be regarded the proper province of monetary and fiscal policy in most countries. But protectionism continues to be advanced as a means of maintaining employment in specific import-competing industries. The argument is occasionally heard that if auto workers are protected, this will adversely affect workers in exporting and other import-competing industries, but most people do not seem to understand the connection or believe that it exists. An IMF study issued in 1978 found that protectionism had increased substantially during the

[18] Artus, Jacques R., and John H. Young, "Fixed and Flexible Exchange Rates: A Renewal of the Debate," op. cit., p. 659

early years of the flexible exchange-rate period.[19] Some writers have even gone to the length of blaming the volatility of exchange rates for increased protection.[20] Appreciation of the currency increases import competition, whereas depreciation reduces it. But these effects do not neutralize each other, because protection, once in place, tends to remain entrenched. Thus, it is claimed that currency overvaluation leads firms to seek protection from intensified foreign competition, and the protection then remains in place even after the currency depreciates and restores the industries' original competitive position.

There is no question that the dollar appreciation of the early 1980s and the resultant trade deficit have greatly increased protectionist sentiment and pressure in the United States. To his credit, President Ronald Reagan has stood firm against most of these pressures. Nevertheless, protectionism was recently granted to specialty steel products and to the lone remaining U.S. manufacturer of motorcycles. Meanwhile, other workers and firms were asking for, and in some cases receiving, trigger prices and import quotas to save jobs in the steel industry, marketing agreements and domestic content legislation for autos, and quotas for textiles, sugar, copper, and shoes. Democratic politicians have made the trade deficit a campaign issue and, in 1988, Congress passed a trade bill that would oblige the president to take retaliatory measures against countries that discriminate against U.S. exports.

It probably is not wise to conclude that flexible exchange rates have encouraged protectionism. However, wide swings in exchange rates appear to have this effect. These wide swings seem to be more of a reflection of the failure of countries to manage their monetary-fiscal tools in a responsible and stabilizing manner than to any inherent instability in the flexible exchange-rate system itself.

Finally, advocates of flexible exchange rates have argued that the asymmetrical adjustment pressures of the fixed exchange-rate system would be eliminated. This asymmetry occurred largely because surplus countries were unwilling to permit their money supplies to expand as a result of their surpluses. These sterilization policies prevented inflation and placed the entire burden of adjustment on the deficit countries. These countries were therefore required to suffer additional deflation and unemployment. Therefore, the world's average level of unemployment was higher than it should have been. The system, therefore, came with a built-in deflationary bias.

[19] International Monetary Fund, IMF pamphlet series, *The Rise in Protectionism*, No. 24, 1978.

[20] McCullock, Rachel, "Unexpected Real Consequences of Floating Exchange Rates," Princeton, *Essays in International Finance*, No. 153, 1983.

The foregoing seems descriptive of the 1920s, when the gold sterilization activities of surplus countries imposed deflationary pressures on the world economy. However, fixed exchange rates need not always work that way. During the later years of the Bretton Woods system, an inflationary bias engulfed the system, as U.S. deficits led to worldwide excessive monetary expansion.

These various asymmetries were eliminated by the adoption of flexible exchange rates. In fact, opponents of flexible exchange rates argued that the deflationary bias allegedly associated with the fixed exchange-rate system would be replaced by a new bias toward too much inflation. Freed from the monetary "discipline" of being forced to peg their exchange rates, countries would embark on ambitious employment and development programs that would inflate their economies.

In Chapter 9 we met another version of this argument. This argument suggested the existence of a "ratchet effect" caused by the tendency for wages and prices to be downwardly sticky in industrial countries. Depreciation increases the prices of traded goods and transmits an inflationary impulse to the economy of the depreciating country. Meanwhile, in the appreciating countries, downward inflexibility of wages and prices prevents a symmetrical price-level decline. These changes alone would raise the average price level in the world when exchange rates vary. In addition, the rigidity of wages and prices in the appreciating countries causes unemployment. If the governments of these countries pursue expansionary policies to return their economies to full employment, these policies will further raise the world's price level. It is fortunate, indeed, that empirical evidence fails to lend much support to this ratchet hypothesis.[21]

To conclude: It appears that the performance of the flexible exchange-rate system has fallen far short of expectation, but that does not mean an alternative system would have done much better. It seems likely that market-determined exchange rates are here to stay, if for no other reason than that foreign exchange markets are now so vast that the amount of intervention governments would need to undertake to influence exchange rates is so enormous that their money supplies would fly wildly out of control.

14.4 THE GLOBAL DEBT PROBLEM

Imports are the lifeblood of economic development. Developing countries especially need the capital goods produced in industrial countries that

---

[21] Goldstein, Morris, "Downward Price Flexibility, Ratchet Effects, and the Inflationary Impact of Import Price Changes," International Monetary Fund, *Staff Papers*, 1977.

embody new technology. Imports can be financed by the sale of exports, by borrowing from abroad, and by receiving foreign aid. If a country is to avoid future trouble when it borrows, it must ensure that the borrowing finances new investment that yields a rate of return in excess of the interest and amortization charges on the borrowing. In that case the borrowing pays off in higher real income for the borrowing country without forcing future belt-tightening to repay the loans and keep up interest payments.

Much of the international borrowing that has occurred since 1973 has been to finance current consumption rather than investment. Since this creates no tangible income-generating asset that defrays interest and amortization charges, it means that future consumption has to be sacrificed to meet interest and amortization costs. To avoid belt-tightening, countries can, for a time, resort to additional borrowing. This postpones the problem, but since the cost of credit will rise and lines of credit will eventually shrink, the country will ultimately be forced to export more than it imports, since it must use part of its export receipts to defray interest and amortization charges that were contracted in the past. Under such circumstances its standard of living declines as resources are transferred abroad. Because the country will probably be forced to restrict imports, its economic growth prospects will also deteriorate.

The foreign debt incurred by developing countries exploded into a fivefold increase after 1973. The enormous overhang of global debt that now exists has become an enormous bone in the throat of the world economy, threatening to choke off economic growth not only in the debtor countries but in the entire world economy as well. A debt-driven worldwide recession of major proportions may not be avoidable unless aggressive steps to head off such a calamity are taken.

After living beyond their means for over a decade, many countries now find it increasingly difficult to borrow, and an excruciating period of retrenchment has set in. Some debtor countries' obligations are so great that they must pay so much in annual interest and debt amortization charges that these service charges, when subtracted from export earnings, leave little foreign exchange available to purchase essential imports. The problem is especially acute in Latin America, where past extravagance by Argentina, Brazil, and Mexico has undermined economic growth and reduced living standards. Import restrictions necessitate a combination of devaluation, which produces adverse terms of trade, deflation, which produces unemployment, and exchange and trade restrictions, which produce resource misallocations that further reduce real income levels. When import restrictions also reduce the availibility of capital goods, capital formation and employment expansion cannot go forward.

Developing country debt also creates major problems for industrial countries. Their export markets shrink when debtor countries restrict imports. Since much of the debt is owed to large commercial banks in industrial countries, the stability of their banking systems is endangered. It is the latter that appears to be causing the most attention in the financial press and public debates, yet it would appear that the threat to export markets is of greater fundamental concern. Without healthy export markets many industrial countries seem incapable of maintaining high employment, since, for reasons to be detailed later, they find it difficult to generate sufficient domestic absorption.

A default by any of the major debtor countries could cause a severe banking crisis. However, it is not at all clear that the economy at large would be greatly harmed. Bankers, of course, propagate the notion that the economy cannot be healthy unless their banks are healthy in order to ensure the government's willingness to bail them out. But as long as depositors are protected by deposit insurance, major runs on banks are not likely. Even if there is a severe deposit drain at some individual banks, central banks can easily maintain the liquidity of the economy by open-market purchases and/or by direct loans to banks through their discount windows. Bank stockholders would, to be sure, suffer losses. But it is not clear why either sympathy or taxpayers' money should be wasted to protect stockholders that should have known better than to invest in banks that are in the habit of making uncollectible loans.

Although there have been suspensions of interest payments, major defaults have thus far been avoided. All parties have a huge stake in preventing default, and the IMF has made rescue packages more palatable to borrowers and lenders by intervening as a supplementary lender. Though tempting as default may seem to a debtor country, the country knows that if it defaults this will eliminate any prospect for obtaining future credit, and that even the short-term credits that are routinely supplied to finance imports would quickly vanish. A defaulting country has to confront the prospect of becoming an international pariah unable to acquire imports except by bartering for them with specific exports. Since the resumption of economic growth will necessitate fresh capital to finance imports, a default would be lethal to a debtor country's prospects. A defaulting country will also be in the doghouse with respect to other debtor countries because the others also wish to keep lines of credit open.

Table 14.1 shows the growth of the debt of the non-oil-developing countries. The debt grew from $130 billion in 1973 to $686 billion in 1983. The huge jump between 1973 and 1978 coincided with the first OPEC oil price increase. The further doubling of oil prices in 1979 added the second debt explosion. The third big increase came during the worldwide recession of 1982–83.

When the OPEC cartel quadrupled oil prices in 1974, this added directly to the cost of oil imports. The rise in oil prices was a primary

TABLE 14.1 NON-OIL-DEVELOPING COUNTRIES
External Debt

Item	1973		1978	1980	1982	1983
Total Debt (billion $)	$130		343	485	650	686
Of Asian countries	30		80	116	154	168
Of Latin American countries	44		133	193	288	299
Ratio of Debt to Exports of Goods and Services (%)						
All non-oil-developing countries	115		131	113	148	154
Asian countries	93		76	68	81	83
Latin American countries	176		218	188	283	300
Ratio of Debt Service to Exports of Goods and Services (%)						
All non-oil-developing countries	16	16	20	18	25	22
Asian countries	7		10	8	11	10
Latin American countries	30		42	36	55	48

Source: International Monetary Fund, *World Economic Outlook,* April 1984 and September 1984.

factor in the major inflationary recession suffered by the industrial countries in the mid-1970s. Because of the recession, the import demands of
the industrial countries declined, and because of the inflation the cost of
industrial products purchased by developing countries increased. All
of these factors contributed to huge current-account deficits among the
non-oil-developing countries. Faced with these deficits, countries either
had to curtail their imports, thereby killing off economic development,
or they had to borrow. Many of them borrowed heavily. They were encouraged to do so by low interest rates and by the commercial banks in
industrial countries who were awash in petrodollars that had been deposited by the OPEC countries. An informal recycling triangle was established. First, OPEC acquired its surpluses by the sale of high-cost oil
to non-oil countries. The surpluses were then deposited in commercial
banks in industrial countries. The commercial banks then lent the petrodollars back to their countries of origin. The redistribution of the world's
financial wealth that took place in this manner was enormous.

It was obvious from the start that this was a very dangerous recycling
mechanism. The bank loans were largely made to finance current consumption rather than investment, which meant they probably could not
be repaid. If you are a banker and you know that the loan you are making
cannot be repaid, you are either very stupid or you are a thief, counting
on a government bailout at the expense of the taxpayer. The banks did,
to be sure, require that the loans be guaranteed by the governments of
the borrowing countries, thereby ensuring that the debt problem would

be a public issue. Having guaranteed the loans, governments of the borrowing countries became responsible for maintaining the viability of the debt.

The circumstances clearly warranted some imaginative planning on the parts of governments. The IMF did its part by establishing an "oil facility" under its able new managing director, Johaness Witteveen of the Netherlands. Witteveen borrowed funds from OPEC and then lent them to oil-importing countries at a nominal charge. Hollis Chenery, vice-president of the World Bank, proposed a plan that would provide OPEC with an incentive to lend petrodollars to the governments of the industrial countries rather than to commercial banks. The governments of these countries would then relend the funds to the developing countries on favorable terms. The interest-rate differential between these loans and the rates that would be needed to lure OPEC into cooperation would then be absorbed by the industrial countries as their contribution to economic development. Most constructive proposals fell on deaf ears. The commercial banks were praised for doing a good job of recycling petrodollars, and the industrial countries felt that they had enough problems what with inflation and recession plaguing them simultaneously.

The second wave of debt expansion came in 1979 when OPEC again raised the price of oil. The industrial economies went into another period of stagnation, causing reductions in the export earnings of debtor countries. Furthermore, a new problem appeared in the form of a drastic rise in world interest rates. Much of the debt had been negotiated on the basis of floating interest rates. The usual rate that was used as a reference point was the London Interbank Rate (LIBOR), and 2 percent was customarily added. LIBOR rose from $6\frac{1}{2}$ percent in 1977 to 19 percent in 1980–81, thereby greatly increasing the interest cost of debt service. Countries now found themselves having to borrow additional funds to pay the interest on existing debt. It was becoming ever more painfully obvious that there were not tangible assets behind the loans that would render repayment possible. Nevertheless, the commercial banks continued to lend, figuring that returns in excess of 20 percent were too tempting to resist. Besides, what were they going to do with the new flood of petrodollars that OPEC had deposited with them?

Another $200 billion was added to the debt as a direct consequence of the 1982–83 recession. High interest rates continued, thanks to the monetary policies of the industrial countries. The recession in these countries was so severe that debtor countries' exports again stagnated. The period also witnessed the sharp appreciation of the dollar. Since oil, and many other imports of the developing countries, are denominated in dollars, the cost of imports was driven up. More recently, there has been a small amount of relief thanks to breaks in interest rates and international oil prices, and to the depreciation of the dollar.

A useful way to assess the burden of debt is to compare the level of the debt with countries' exports, and the debt-service obligations to exports. These measures are shown in Table 14.1. Between 1973 and 1983 the ratio of debt to exports increased from 115 percent to 154 percent, and the ratio of debt-service charges to exports increased from 16 percent to 22 percent. For some individual countries the picture is much worse. By 1982 Argentina's debt-service obligations actually exceeded the value of its exports, and debt service gobbled up 87 percent and 56 percent of export earnings in Mexico and Brazil, respectively.

It would be misleading and one-sided to attribute the debt problem entirely to OPEC, high interest rates, and sluggish growth in industrial countries. Some countries weathered these storms quite nicely without major debt increases. The debt-export ratio for Asian countries actually declined between 1973 and 1983 (Table 14.1). The bulk of the debt explosion took place in Latin American countries, where the debt-export ratio rose from 176 percent in 1973 to 300 percent in 1983. It should also not be forgotten that the United States has become the world's largest debtor nation as a consequence of its cumulative current-account deficits. The common characteristics shared by the U.S. and the Latin countries were the maintenance of overvalued exchange rates for an extended period of time and the use of international credit to finance consumption rather than investment.

The striking difference between the performance of the Asian countries and the Latin American countries was due to a variety of factors. Four of these factors especially stand out.

(1) Growth Strategy   Import substitution versus export promotion have vied with each other as competing economic development strategies. Import substitution attempts to develop domestic industries that produce goods that displace imports, thereby reducing reliance on imports and exposure to foreign shocks. Normally the strategy requires government protection of the "infant industries" in the form of tariffs, quotas, and subsidies. The industries tend to be inefficient even when well managed. They generally cannot compete in international markets, and their market size is thus, limited to the domestic market, which is likely to be too small to enable the industry to enjoy economies of scale.

Had Adam Smith been alive today, he would have argued that import substitution is an inferior strategy that would tend to fail if tried. Smith would have considered export promotion far more promising. Success in invading foreign markets requires efficient production, progressive management, and a favorable relative price situation. This is likely to mean that a country following this strategy will take pains to maintain an undervalued currency to assist in export promotion. The undervaluation also means that its import demands will be low. The country will therefore be able to finance its imports from export proceeds, and it will not need to run up huge foreign debt obligations. Even when it does borrow, the expansion of its exports will hold the debt-export ratio to manageable levels. Since the export industries compete in world markets, they can enjoy economies of scale that will bring with them large gains in labor productivity. Finally, a country following this strategy will enjoy a more stable economic environment, since its reliance on such unstable traditional sources of foreign exchange as agriculture and mining will be reduced. Adam Smith would have reminded countries that the success of such countries as Japan, South Korea, and Taiwan attests to the potential benefits of heeding his dictum that the division of labor is limited only by the size of the market.

Export promotion reduces the reliance of a country on primary products for its export revenues. Between 1969 and 1980 the Philippines were able to reduce their ratio of primary commodity exports to total exports from 96 percent to 63 percent. The reduction for Singapore was 76 percent to 46 percent; for South Korea it was 86 percent to 10 percent. Although the Latin countries also reduced their reliance on primary commodity exports, the reductions were smaller than in Asia. Argentina went from 96 percent to 77 percent, Brazil from 97 percent to 61 percent, and Mexico from 88 percent to 61 percent.

(2) Exchange Rate Policy An export promotion strategy cannot succeed if the country's currency is overvalued. However, as measured against purchasing-power-parity criteria, the real exchange rates of most Latin American countries became increasingly overvalued during the 1970s and early 1980s. This meant it was difficult to export, that imports were encouraged, and current-account deficits were large. To finance the deficits, the Latin countries resorted to borrowing.

An overvalued currency has very pleasant short-run consequences. It reduces domestic inflation and permits consumers to enjoy foreign goods that are inexpensive in terms of domestic currency. The United States was able to finance its consumption binge of 1980–85 by maintaining high interest rates that automatically attracted foreign capital, which enabled the current-account deficit to be financed. Not having that option, the Latin countries financed their current-account deficits by borrowing from commercial banks. Since the ability to enjoy quality consumer goods was primarily of benefit to the wealthier classes, these upper-income groups developed a vested interest in currency overvaluation that made the cessation of borrowing and the elimination of current-account deficits all the more difficult. The situation was not improved by the bad habit of Latin politicians of representing themselves as defenders of a strong currency. Better death than devaluation seems to have been the watchword.

The Latin countries enjoyed a period of astonishingly rapid growth between 1960 and 1981. The economies tripled their size in terms of gross domestic product (GDP), as real GDP rose at an average annual rate of about 6 percent. However, imports grew even more rapidly than GDP while exports grew less rapidly, so current-account deficits mounted. Some of the slow export growth was caused by less rapid growth in the industrial economies. But part of the difficulty was due to the overvaluation of the currency.

Although many countries ran into trouble because of the higher cost of oil imports, the Mexican case illustrates that possession of oil reserves is not an unmixed blessing that exempts a country from debt troubles. With the development of its oil fields, Mexico believed that the promised land had arrived. Giddy from being awash in oil, the Mexican government embarked on a set of ambitious and costly social and development programs. Its oil exports enabled Mexico to maintain a high value of the peso, which encouraged imports and made it difficult for its other export industries to compete in foreign markets. When world oil prices broke, the revenues from oil exports declined sharply and its other export industries were unable to overcome the erosion that had set in during the high peso era. Unwilling or unable to take corrective action, Mexico resorted to heavy borrowing and became the second-largest Latin American debtor, as its debt rose from $8.6 billion in 1973 to $82.0 billion in 1982.

(3) Exchange Controls   Another important difference between Asian and Latin countries was that the Asian countries maintained exchange control systems that enabled governments to conserve foreign exchange and to hold down nonessential imports. Lacking such controls, the Latin countries spent much of their foreign exchange earnings on consumer goods, thereby bloating their current-account deficits. Inflation, political instability, and fear of devaluation also produced incentives for citizens to transfer their wealth abroad. Funds borrowed in New York flowed back to the same place in the form of deposits by jittery Latin citizens. In a country such as Jamaica the drain of capital was accompanied by a brain drain, as a large fraction of the country's better-educated citizens pulled up stakes because of a hostile political climate. Argentina,

Mexico, and Venezuela all suffered massive capital flights, thereby greatly increasing their debt problems. Some effort to introduce workable exchange controls was surely justified by the circumstances.

(4) Supply of Capital   Real interest rates were abnormally low in the industrial countries during much of the 1970s. Nominal interest rates hardly exceeded inflation rates, so real rates were minimal. This encouraged countries to borrow heavily. In some cases Latin countries actually borrowed more than they needed to finance their current-account deficits, using the surplus to build up foreign exchange reserves. But the Latin loans were with commercial banks who insisted on variable interest rates. Thus, when interest rates rose in 1979, Latin debtor countries found that their excessive borrowing had suddenly imposed an enormous and unanticipated interest burden.

Economic growth all but ceased in the Latin countries after 1980. Without the ability to expand purchases of imports, these countries could not grow. The economic and social problems created by the cessation of growth are frightening. Writing in 1984, Thomas Enders and Richard Mattione noted that

> To take advantage of the jobs that expansion created, armies of people moved from the countryside to the city. When economic growth stopped, unemployment, always a problem with a labor force still growing at the high fertility rates of the 1960s became severe. Hunger threatens to reach large segments of the population. Given the protests in Sao Paulo, Rio de Janeiro, Santiago, and Lima, Latin American leaders wonder whether the political system will hold.[22]

It is worth sorting out the ingredients of a debt problem in a somewhat formal manner that focuses attention on the essential steps that must be taken to mitigate the problem. Roughly, the change in debt equals the current-account deficit. As before, we separate the investment-income component from the other current-account items, and we can therefore write

$$\Delta D_t = i^* D_{t-1} + V_t - X_t \qquad (14.1)$$

where D_t is the nominal value of foreign debt, i^* is the nominal foreign rate of interest, and imports V_t and exports X_t are measured in nominal terms. Since $\Delta D_t = D_t - D_{t-1}$, we can write (14.1) as

$$D_t = (1 + i^*) D_{t-1} + V_t - X_t$$

[22] Enders, Thomas O., and Richard P. Mattione, *Latin America: The Crisis of Debt and Growth*, Brookings, 1984, p. 2.

Dividing both sides by X_t, we get the debt-export ratio

$$\frac{D_t}{X_t} = (1 + i^*)\frac{D_{t-1}}{X_t} + \frac{V_t}{X_t} - 1 \qquad (14.2)$$

Nominal export growth depends on the growth of nominal GNP in the industrial countries. Therefore, let

$$X_t = (1 + g^*)(1 + P^*)X_{t-1} \qquad (14.3)$$

where g^* is the growth rate of real GNP and P^* is the rate of inflation of the industrial countries. Using (14.3) in (14.2) gives

$$d_t = \frac{1 + i^*}{(1 + g^*)(1 + P^*)} d_{t-1} + v_t - 1 \qquad (14.4)$$

where d_t is the ratio of debt to exports and v_t is the ratio of imports to exports.

This expression shows the very important fact that the interest component of the debt-export ratio depends critically on the rate of interest relative to the rate of growth of nominal GNP in the industrial countries. When interest rates are high, as between 1979 and 1983, while industrial countries' growth rates stagnate, the interest component of the debt-export ratio jumps sharply. For example, nominal GNP in the United States grew at a rate of 8 percent a year between 1978 and 1983. With an interest rate of 15 percent, this would imply an annual increase in the interest component of the debt export ratio of 6.5 percent per year for as long as such conditions prevail. This means that as long as the interest rate exceeds the growth rate of nominal GNP in industrial countries, the debt-export ratio will rise without limit even if there is no increase in the ratio of imports to exports. Clearly, if there is to be relief from the debt problem, it is essential to reduce interest rates and to speed up the growth of exports. The latter depends on the growth of export markets and therefore, to a large extent, on the growth rates of the industrial countries.

The ratio of imports to exports, v_t, is also of obvious importance. When import growth exceeds export growth, the debt-export ratio rises, and when imports grow less rapidly than exports, the debt-export ratio falls, provided the interest component does not increase. We know that imports depend on domestic real income and the real exchange rate and that exports depend on foreign income and the real exchange rate. Thus the ratio of imports to exports depends on these same arguments. That is,

$$v_t = v\left(Y, Y^*, \frac{ep^*}{p}\right)$$

This implies that the change in the import-export ratio will vary roughly, as indicated by an expression such as

$$\Delta v_t = a(g - g^*) + b\left(P - P^* - \frac{\Delta e}{e}\right) \tag{14.5}$$

where a and b are positive constants. It can be seen that the import-export ratio rises if domestic real income growth exceeds foreign real income growth; and the purchasing-power-parity term shows that v_t rises if the domestic rate of inflation exceeds the foreign rate of inflation, and/ or if the currency appreciates in nominal terms or fails to depreciated enough to maintain purchasing-power parity.

Announcement by a debtor country that it is unable to meet its obligations sets in motion a negotiating machinery that has become painfully familiar. Since most of the debt is government guaranteed, the governments of the debtor countries are heavily involved. Other parties to the negotiations are the commercial banks that hold the questionable loans, the IMF, and central bank and treasury officials of the industrial countries. The incentive to avoid default, or even suspension of interest payments, is enormous.

The rescue packages that emerge from these negotiations require concessions on the parts of both debtors and creditors. The debtor country must take steps to improve its ability to service debt. This usually means the country must find ways to reduce imports and increase exports. Normally that implies cuts in government spending and reductions in money growth rates to slow inflation. In some cases the IMF has insisted on currency devaluation and has intruded into such sensitive areas as the government's wage and welfare policies.

Although debtor countries are not thrilled by the IMF's invasion into their internal affairs and by the harshness of its austerity programs, they realize that they need the IMF's help. They therefore resist the impulse to denounce the IMF publicly as the handmaiden of the banking interests. The IMF's demands are not one-sided; the banks must also make major concessions. The IMF usually insists that the banks reschedule their loans, which means they must stretch out the time over which the loans must be repaid. Interest charges must be pared down, and the banks must come up with fresh money to lend to the debtor countries. Finally, the IMF attempts to ensure that the bailout burden is equitably shared by insisting that all the banks that have lent to a particular country participate in the agreement. The IMF obtains its muscle by contributing its own resources to the rescue package. If the banks did not cooperate, the IMF would not put up its share. Since agreement would be far less likely without the IMF's contribution, the IMF usually gets its way.

Making new loans so that the interest on past debt can be paid amounts to solving a problem by making it worse. But in the curious world of banking and finance, it is possible to maintain the fiction that all is well as long as current obligations are being met even if to do so requires throwing good money after bad. But that is what the rescue packages do. Although the IMF's austerity programs are designed to lower debt-export ratios, there is little assurance that continuation of bailout negotiations of this sort will cause the problem to be diminished significantly.

The piling up of debt in Latin America has created a "growth crisis" because these economies were unable to sustain their growth once their credit lines began to dry up and it became necessary to reduce imports. To right the balance after many years of current-account deficits, countries have had to devalue currencies, tighten budgets, reduce subsidies, and curtail monetary growth. As a consequence, living standards have fallen, social unrest has been on the rise, and the fragile democratic political institutions that have been forged are at risk.

There is a further danger in that the Latin growth malaise will become generalized into a world growth crisis because the debt overhang represents a major deflationary force. It would not do violence to reality to sort the countries of the world economy into three major categories. The first category is the group of countries that cannot grow and raise living standards without importing more than they export. The second group of countries consists of countries that cannot apparently maintain growth and prosperity without exporting more than they import. Thus the first group tends to suffer from supply shortages, and the second group suffers from deficient absorption. The third group of countries includes the economies that are flexible enough so that they need not rely on current-account deficits to provide either additional demand or additional goods. These countries are less affected by the debt crisis than the others, although some, such as the United States, are deeply involved because of their role in financing the debt.

Many non-OPEC developing countries fit into the first category. Some are so poor that domestic savings are too meager to provide sufficient resources to sustain a reasonable rate of capital formation. Others, such as the Latin debtors, are not poor relative to other developing countries. But their political institutions, their primitive tax systems, and the expectations of their people are such that it is difficult or impossible for their governments to pursue policies that reduce consumption in order to make room for the expansion of investment and economic growth. Adequate investment and capital formation are therefore critically dependent on a large volume of imports.

West Germany and Japan are conspicuous cases of the second category. Both have benefited for so long from export-led growth that their economies are structurally attuned to export surpluses. Without such surpluses, national income would shrink sharply and unemployment would rise. The people of both countries tend to save unusually large fractions of their income. In Germany "sparsamkeit" (frugality) is a virtue second only to "tüchtigkeit" (industriousness). Since the government is expected to set a good example and also live within its means, there is no domestic offset for the surplus savings so that export surpluses must be run to keep national income from shrinking. In addition, as noted in Chapter 7, the Germans seem to believe in the curious asymmetry that demand stimulus received from abroad in the form of higher export orders is beneficial, raising production and employment, whereas internal absorption-raising stimulus merely generates inflation. And, as also suggested in Chapter 7, there could be something to this theory if there is a floor to real wages. In that case, internally generated demand could be inflationary. A rise in absorption raises import demand. This depreciates the currency, raises consumer prices, and provokes an upward money-wage adjustment that prevents real wages from falling so that output and employment cannot increase. Rising export demand, on the other hand, appreciates the currency. This lowers consumer prices and permits the product real wage to fall, thereby allowing output and employment to rise. This belief, in combination with a historic fear of inflation, makes it easy to see why West Germany is so resistant to pressures to assume locomotive responsibilities and why it needs an export surplus to prosper.

The most severe shortage suffered by the Japanese is a shortage of land. Space limitations prevent the average Japanese family from purchasing the spacious and lavish homes, costly home furnishings, and automobiles that represent a large fraction of personal consumpion in other countries. One consequence of this is that Japanese workers save a large fraction of their income with an eye to future purchase of a tiny parcel of real estate that will be exceedingly expensive. Another is that the Japanese could not possibly use the vast outpouring of goods and services that their factories are capable of producing. To be efficient, these industries must operate on a large scale, and since the domestic market is severely limited, productivity cannot be expanded without export growth. The government could ease the problem by eliminating protection for domestic rice production against imports. This would provide extra land for housing, it would enable Japanese consumers to purchase imported rice at one fourth the cost of domestic production, and it would reduce Japan's mammoth trade surplus. But the government knows that it would be playing with fire if it pursued a policy that destroyed traditional agriculture and developed dependency on food imports. Thus Japan, with constricted potential for adding to domestic consumption, is another economy with surplus savings that must be offset by a trade surplus if a high level of economic activity is to be sustained.

Prosperity in a world economy characterized by groups of "natural" deficit and "natural" surplus countries can be maintained, but only if the current-account deficits and surpluses can be sustained indefinitely. That, however, implies ever larger foreign debts owed by the deficit countries to the surplus countries, and as interest costs are added to the debt, the debt-export ratio can easily become explosive. When creditors become nervous and refuse additional financing—they do not even have to ask for repayment—the honeymoon comes to an abrupt halt. The debtor countries must then reduce their imports, thereby throwing their economies into low gear, and the creditor countries lose the export demand that sustains economic activity in their countries. The end result is worldwide growth cessation and the strong possibility of severe and protracted recession or even a major depression.

A constructive partnership in dealing with this dilemma would require industrial countries to reduce interest rates, raise the growth of their economies by internal demand stimulation, and eliminate trade restrictions against imports. The debtor countries, in turn, could ease the problem if they reduced their inflation rates, adopted realistic exchange rates, and pursued policies that stimulate domestic investment rather than consumption. The first step toward a solution might constructively be a change in the mix of U.S. monetary-fiscal policy toward a combination of tighter budget and easier money. That would lower interest rates and stimulate growth in the industrial countries. It would further depreciate the dollar, thereby also reducing the cost of imports to debtor countries. Natural creditor countries such as Germany and Japan, which have the greatest stake in maintaining strong export markets, must be willing to participate more heavily in the financing of international debt by increasing their contributions to the capital of the IMF and the World Bank. They must eliminate import restrictions, and they must reduce the dependence of their economies on externally generated aggregate demand. Failing such steps, the world economy will be in for a rough slide down a deflationary chute.

QUESTIONS FOR REVIEW

1. Despite flexible exchange rates, international reserves grew enormously during the 1970s. To what do you attribute such enormous reserve growth? What are the dangers of a multicurrency reserve system?

2. The flexible exchange-rate period has been characterized by sharp fluctuations in real exchange rates. Why did exchange rates stray so far from purchasing-power parity? What are the economic consequences of fluctuations in real exchange rates?

3. Early advocates of flexible exchange rates argued that currency speculation would necessarily be stabilizing under flexible exchange rates. What was the rationale for this view? Is it possible for there to be too little speculation?

4. Early advocates of flexible exchange rates argued that countries would recapture control of domestic monetary policy. To what extent has this been true?

5. Early advocates of flexible exchange rates argued that exchange rates would vary so as to bring current accounts into balance. Each country's income would equal its absorption and there would be no spillover effects on other countries when one country raises or lowers its income level. Why has this proven to be incorrect?

6. Do flexible exchange rates permit a country to pick its own unemployment-inflation trade-off targets?

7. Early advocates of flexible exchange rates believed that flexible exchange rates would promote free trade. Why has this not been so? In what way could flexible exchange rates lead to growing trade restriction?

8. What are the determinants of a country's debt-export ratio? What steps must be taken if debt-export ratios are to decline?

9. The huge growth of global debt appears to be having a deflationary effect on the world economy. Analyze why this is the case. Unemployment rates are very high in both debtor and creditor countries. Is there a connection? What must be done to avert world deflation?

10. What accounts for the fact that debt-export ratios in Asian countries did not rise despite two major oil shocks and two major recessions in the industrial countries. What was the difference between Asian and Latin countries?

11. What are the dangers of maintaining an overvalued currency? What are the advantages and disadvantages of an undervalued currency?

SUGGESTIONS FOR FURTHER READING

Artus, Jacques, and John H. Young, "Fixed and Flexible Exchange Rates: A Renewal of the Debate," International Monetary Fund, *Staff Papers,* 1979.

Artus, Jacques, and Ann K. McGuirk, "A Revised Version of the Multilateral Exchange Rate Model," International Monetary Fund, *Staff Papers,* 1981.

Dornbusch, Rudiger, *Dollars, Debts and Deficits,* MIT Press, 1986, part II.

Dunn, Robert, "The Many Disappointments of Flexible Exchange Rates," *Princeton Essays in International Finance,* No. 154, 1983.

Enders, Thomas O., and Richard P. Mattione, *Latin America: The Crisis of Debt and Growth,* Brookings, 1984.

Friedman, Milton, "The Role of Monetary Policy," *American Economic Review,* 1968.

Johnson, Harry G., "The Case for Flexible Exchange Rates," Federal Reserve Bank of St. Louis, *Review,* 51, 1969.

Magee, Steven, "Contracting and Spurious Deviations from Purchasing Power Parity," in Johnson, H. G. and Jacob Frenkel, eds., *The Economics of Exchange Rates,* Addison-Wesley, 1978.

McCulloch, Rachel, "Unexpected Real Consequences of Floating Exchange Rates," *Princeton Essays in International Finance,* No. 153, 1983.

McKinnon, Ronald I., "An International Standard for Monetary Stabilization," Institute for International Economics, vol. 8, 1984.

Chapter 15

Improving the International Monetary System

15.1 STABILIZING THE FLOW OF CAPITAL

In this final chapter we consider proposals to improve the operation of the international monetary system. As discussed in the last chapter, the principal problem stems from the unexpectedly large fluctuations in real exchange rates. This has caused instability in countries' foreign trade sector, transmitted severe macroeconomic shocks to entire economies, tended to increase protectionism, and rendered the task of maintaining stable economic conditions within countries much more difficult. Much of the instability seems to be due to the massiveness of shifts in the movement of capital. With financial transactions dominating the behavior of exchange rates, current accounts have not equilibrated, and countries' monetary and fiscal policies have not affected domestic economies as intended while transmitting severe shocks to other economies.

The quest for better control over capital movements is hardly new. Capital flight has been a recurrent problem for the international monetary system. In assessing different schemes for controlling capital flows, we must remember that capital movements are essential to the maximization of world output and income. Without capital movements flexible exchange rates would equilibrate current accounts. This means that resource transfers between countries would not be possible, so the surplus savings of capital-rich countries would not be available to ease saving shortages in capital-poor countries. Rates of return on new investment would not be equalized, so the world's capital stock would be inefficiently allocated and world real income would be below its potential. Consequently, programs designed to stabilize capital movements should be careful not to stifle capital movements. A constructive program might attempt to counter short-run speculative runs to minimize macroeconomic shocks while encouraging productive international investment.

15.1.1 Capital Controls

Direct controls over international capital movements have, historically, been the most frequent approach to stemming capital outflows. Countries simply make it illegal to transfer capital from one country to another. Countries that are hard pressed for foreign exchange reserves have rationed their reserves by forcing importers to obtain licenses and giving importers of essential commodities more favorable terms on which to purchase foreign exchange than they give for imports that are deemed to be nonessential or luxury items. Exporters are prohibited from holding foreign exchange and are required to deposit their foreign exchange earnings with a government agency such as the central bank. Foreign exchange for the purpose of making foreign investments is denied. Bank accounts are sometimes blocked. Sometimes the accounts may be used to make domestic transactions, but they cannot be transferred abroad.

Controls over capital flows are notoriously difficult to enforce. Money can be transmitted and exchanged in innumerable inconspicuous ways. To the extent that controls are successful, they very often curtail not only short-term speculative capital movements but also those that funnel resources into their most productive uses. A resource discovery or an innovation that can best be exploited in a particular location raises the return on capital in that country. Capital therefore tends to flow there, generating demand for the country's currency and appreciating the currency. The appreciation reduces exports, increases imports, and, through the resulting trade deficit, causes real resources to flow to the country where the rate of return on new investment is higher. Thus foreign savings supplement domestic savings in financing the new activity. Effective capital controls obstruct this process, limiting countries to investing only what is saved locally and producing less efficient employment of the world's capital with losses in global income.

The difficulty of enforcing capital controls increases with the duration of controls as exporters, importers, and potential investors learn how to circumvent the law. Robert Dunn notes that

> Ingenious investors can devise ways to move capital through almost any control system, false invoicing being the best known route. The primary

impact of capital controls often seems to be loss of respect for the law, as many developing countries have discovered to their sorrow.[1]

Studies of capital controls show that limitations imposed on capital transactions may produce offsetting increases in other payments items. If importers are prohibited from investing abroad, they can sometimes induce a foreign national or bank to do it on their behalf, provided they pay a higher price for the goods they import or accept fewer units of merchandise than they are pretending to receive.[2] As a result, balance-of-payments statistics will record a rise in imports rather than a capital outflow. Exporters can arrange similar circumventions of the law. For example, those who service tourism in countries attempting to conserve foreign exchange often prefer credit card charges rather than cash dollar receipts. Dollar earnings would have to be sold to the central bank at an unfavorable exchange rate. However, a U.S. credit card company could deposit credit card charges in a U.S. bank on behalf of the foreign merchant or hotel keeper. This causes the value of exports to be understated. In addition, having lost foreign exchange, the government may then deny foreign exchange to importers. In all such ways capital flows sneak out via the current account. Clearly a government that tries to enforce capital controls and punish offenders will have its hands full, especially since the offenders are likely to be influential citizens.

A form of capital control that has been frequently used is the so-called multiple exchange rate, which fixes, and attempts to enforce, different exchange rates for different types of international transactions. One such plan fixes a rate for current-account transactions and permits the rate for capital transactions to float. One aim of this procedure is to insulate the current account from shocks emanating from the capital account. Another purpose is to attain artificially favorable terms of trade for trade in goods and services. Such a scheme might seem appealing as a means of easing the difficulties caused for trade-impacted industries by exchange rates that appear misaligned because of large-scale capital movements. However, a clean float for the capital account requires the account to be in balance. The exchange rate must reach a level at which private-sector capital inflows (currency purchases) are matched by outflows (currency sales). This means that no net transfers of capital are possible and that world capital resources will be inefficiently allocated. Had such a system been tried during the 1980–85 period, the U.S. dollar

[1] Dunn, Robert, "The Many Disappointments of Flexible Exchange Rates," *Essays in International Finance,* Princeton University, December 1954.

[2] Argy, Victor, "Exchange Rate Management in Theory and Practice," *Princeton Studies in International Finance,* International Finance Section, Princeton University, 1982.

would have risen to much higher levels, and foreign capital would not have been available to help finance U.S. investments or budget deficits.

15.1.2 Taxing Exchange Transactions: The Tobin Proposal

Professor James Tobin of Yale, a Nobel laureate and member of President Kennedy's Council of Economic Advisers, has proposed reducing the volume and variability of capital movements by imposition of a worldwide tax of 1 percent on the value of any spot conversion of one currency into another. The tax

> ... would be an internationally agreed uniform tax, administered by each government over its own jurisdiction. Britain, for example, would be responsible for taxing all inter-currency transactions in Eurocurrency banks and brokers located in London, even when sterling was not involved.[3]

The purpose of the tax is to obstruct short-term capital movements, not to inhibit trade. For administrative reasons, however, transactions undertaken to finance trade could not be exempted. Thus the tax would amount to a uniform 1 percent ad valorem tariff on all trade. Although it might somewhat reduce the volume of trade and misallocate resources, this would, in Tobin's words, be preferable to

> the burdens of much more damaging protectionist and autarkic measures designed to protect economies . . . from the consequences of international financial shocks.[4]

Although the proposal is for a uniform tax on all exchange transactions, it poses a greater obstacle to some types of transactions than to others. The purchase of foreign exchange to finance imports is a one-way transaction involving a 1 percent tax. However, the purchase of foreign exchange to invest usually implies a subsequent sale, because the proceeds ultimately will be reconverted into the original currency. Financial transactions therefore imply a round-trip tax of 2 percent. An interest-rate differential in excess of 2 percent for at least a year would be necessary to make the transaction worthwhile. By contrast, a 90-day investment also involves a 2 percent round-trip cost, but since interest is earned for only one fourth of a year the differential between foreign and domestic

---

[3] Tobin, James, "A Proposal for International Monetary Reform," *Eastern Economic Journal,* 4, July/Oct. 1978, pp. 158–159.

[4] Tobin, op. cit., p. 159.

interest rates would have to be in excess of 8 percent. Thus, as desired, the proposal would penalize short-term capital movements heavily while levying only a small penalty on trade and long-term investments.

For any given tax as a percent of the funds exchanged, the duration of the commitment necessary to make the investment advantageous would vary inversely with the difference in rates of return. With a 2 percent round-trip tax, a difference of 2 percent would require an investment of more than one year to recoup the tax and gain a profit. A span of only 1 percent would necessitate an investment of more than two years. A 4 percent gap (roughly the maximum that existed from 1979–85) would permit an advantage on investments of as little as six months. Thus, a tax expressed as a percent of funds exchanged would permit more funds to move into the high-return country as the differential widens. Whether the responsiveness of capital flows to *changes* in the differential would be less than without the tax is an empirical question that cannot be answered without study. The tax would mitigate the overall role of capital flows in exchange markets, but may or may not add to exchange rate variability.

To eliminate the influence of changing differential returns on the length of profitable exchanges, Tobin's proposal might be amended by varying the rate of the tax automatically in proportion to the short-term interest-rate differential prevailing between the currencies involved in the conversion. For example, if the rate of the tax automatically rises from 1 percent to 2 percent as the interest-rate differential widens from 2 percent to 4 percent, the widening differential would not trigger as sharp a capital movement as with a tax fixed as a percentage of the amount converted. The mimimum break-even period for the round trip would remain at one year. Capital movements therefore would be stabilized as well as reduced in magnitude.

This amendment would have the desired objective of permitting interest-rate differentials between countries that are consistent with individual countries' domestic policy objectives, without interference from capital flows. It moves farther in the direction of the financial segmentation desired by Tobin, providing greater national independence in carrying out monetary and fiscal policies.

By suppressing some capital flows, the tax may reduce the responsiveness of the demand for and supply of foreign exchange to changes in the exchange rate. These demand and supply functions would be more heavily influenced by current-account forces, as seems desirable. Since the price elasticities of exports and imports tend to be low in the short run, the variability of exchange rates could increase. However, such short-run variability appears to be less of a problem than chronic and persistent exchange rate misaligment. Because of the recent and growing dominance of prevailing securities market conditions, exchange rates persist that do not reflect competitive conditions in international trade and produce extremely large current-account imbalances for long periods. A reform that makes exchange rates more sensitive to current-account conditions should reduce excessive and persistent misalignment, yielding less instability in the trade sectors and a better allocation of resources, even if it is purchased at the price of more short-term "jumpiness" of exchange rates.

This proposal, first made more than ten years ago to address an increasingly critical problem, has received remarkably little attention. Despite certain limitations, the plan appears to warrant serious study, especially the version that varies the tax rate as interest-rate differentials change. An attractive by-product of the scheme is that it could raise many billions of dollars of government revenue given the massive size of foreign exchange transactions.

15.1.3 Multilateral Coordination of Monetary Policy: The McKinnon Plan

Professor Ronald McKinnon of Stanford University makes an excellent case for the proposition that it has largely been the uncoordinated conduct of monetary policies that has been responsible, first, for the breakdown of the Bretton Woods system and, subsequently, for the economic and exchange rate instability of the flexible exchange rate period. McKinnon argues that, since 1970,

> ... fluctuations in American money growth were magnified by monetary fluctuations in the rest of the world. This greater instability in world money growth is related to the breakdown of the fixed exchange rate regime.[5]

After World War II the world economy moved increasingly in the direction of a "dollar standard." Trade in goods, services, and financial assets came to be conducted more and more heavily in dollars, and the dollar also became the principal form in which countries held their international reserves. Because of this increasing importance of the dollar, there developed a strong incentive for foreign monetary authorities to stabilize their exchange rates vis-à-vis the dollar, with the consequence that foreign monetary policies were frequently directed to stabilizing the

---

[5] McKinnon, Ronald I., "An International Standard for Monetary Stabilization," *Institute for International Economics*, 8, March 1984, p. 47.

dollar values of their currencies rather than to some internal objective. As the nth country of the system, the United States was able to direct its monetary policy toward internal objectives. The consequence of the different monetary policy objectives was an asymmetry in the conduct of policies that has inadvertently caused a great deal of global macroeconomic instability because of fluctuations in world monetary growth.

As explained in Chapter 14, the asymmetry operates as follows. A fall in the exchange value of the dollar leads foreign central banks to intervene to dampen the appreciation of their currencies. Dollars are bought by foreign monetary authorities, so foreign money supplies increase. Meanwhile, the U.S. Federal Reserve offsets the decline in the U.S. money supply by engaging in open-market purchases of domestic securities. This sterilization operation by the Fed, in combination with foreign central bank purchases of dollars, has the effect of raising the world money stock. The effect of the fall in the dollar, therefore, is an inflationary one on the world economy.

The opposite happens when the dollar appreciates. To stem depreciation of their currencies, foreign monetary authorities sell dollars in return for their own currencies. The Fed then, in pursuit of a monetary growth target, eliminates the increase in the U.S. money supply by engaging in open-market sales of domestic securities. The combined actions of the monetary authorities causes the world money supply to shrink. Consequently, appreciation of the dollar has been associated with a deflationary effect on the world economy.

It can be seen that the asymmetry noted by McKinnon stems from different objectives of monetary policy. Foreign monetary authorities attempt to stabilize their exchange rates with respect to the dollar while the U.S. monetary authority aims for a target rate of monetary growth for the U.S. economy. These different policy targets result in a rise in the world money stock when the dollar depreciates, causing world inflation, and a decline in the world money stock when the dollar appreciates, causing world recession.

The record seems to confirm McKinnon's hypothesis. Foreign money supplies were increased sharply from 1971 to 1973 because of dollar purchases by foreign central banks who were attempting to prevent depreciation of the dollar. Meanwhile, the United States continued to expand its money supply rapidly.

In 1977–78 Treasury Secretary Michael Blumenthal was believed to be "talking down the dollar," and it was feared that the departure of Arthur Burns as Federal Reserve chairman would create a more inflation-tolerant Federal Reserve Board. These factors were instrumental in causing investors to shift out of dollar-denominated assets. The dollar depreciated 35 percent against the yen and the D-mark over two years. Foreign money supplies grew rapidly, as foreign monetary authorities tried to stem the depreciation of the dollar. Their behavior probably added to the severe world inflation of the late 1970s.

The opposite situation developed in the early 1980s. In late 1979 the Federal Reserve shifted to a restrictive monetary policy, provoking a sharp increase in nominal interest rates. The subsequent election of a conservative president strengthened the expectation that the antiinflationary monetary policy would continue and helped to translate the rise in nominal interest rates into a rise in real interest rates. Rates received a further boost from the expansionary fiscal policies that began in 1981. Abroad there were fears excited by the possibility of Soviet intervention in Poland, the election of a socialist government in France, and the removal of exchange controls in Japan. All of these factors increased the demand for dollars, launching the dollar on an extraordinary appreciation that continued for nearly five years. To moderate the appreciation, foreign central banks intervened from time to time with dollar sales in exchange for their own currencies, thereby reducing supplies of the latter. Therefore, according to McKinnon,

> What began as disinflation in the United States turned into the worldwide economic slump of 1981–82. In effect, there had been a big increase in the derived demand for US base money which—being on a monetarist rule—the Fed did not accommodate.[6]

McKinnon's solution to the problems created by intercountry differences in monetary policy objectives is to multilateralize monetary policy by having countries agree to a common world money growth objective. Hopefully this would provide stable world money growth for a highly integrated world economy in a way that permits individual countries to deviate from the world standard so as to stabilize exchange rates. McKinnon proposes that the United States, Germany, and Japan project desired money growth targets for their respective countries and that a joint rate of world money growth be determined as a weighted average of these rates. The rate that emerges from such a computation would serve as the international norm for money growth.

The next step in McKinnon's program is a directive designed to stabilize exchange rates. If the dollar's exchange value is rising relative to the yen, the U.S. should raise its money supply growth above the norm, thereby depressing the dollar, while the Japanese monetary authority would simultaneously reduce the rate of monetary growth so as

---

[6] McKinnon, op. cit., p. 49.

to push up the yen. Together the policies would be calibrated so that the world's money growth would continue at the target rate. The rule for the short run therefore is to

> ... increase the money supply above its long-run norm when the exchange rate appreciates and reduce the domestic money supply when depreciation threatens.[7]

The intention of this blueprint for monetary cooperation is to eliminate the policy asymmetry identified by McKinnon while taking into account countries' preoccupations with their dollar exchange rate. Since exchange rates would be stabilized, there would be fewer disturbances to export- and import-competing industries and therefore less protectionism and a reduction in the transmission of inflationary and deflationary shocks.

This proposal directs monetary policy toward the attainment of external balance. It is important to ask whether the conduct of monetary policy in the proposed way is consistent with internal balance. Put differently, since changes in national monetary growth are activated by changes in the exchange rate, is that an appropriate signal for monetary action to maintain internal balance?

McKinnon's second rule amounts to asking monetary authorities to lean against the exchange-rate wind in the same way as the Federal Reserve, in the past, has often leaned against the wind of interest-rate changes. Monetary policies that attempt to lean against the interest-rate wind are today almost universally condemned as potentially destabilizing. Interest rates could rise because of a tax cut or because of an increase in liquidity preference. The tax cut is an expansionary real shock, whereas the increase in liquidity preference is a restrictive monetary shock. Yet a monetary policy directed towards moderating fluctuations in interest rates would have to respond to both types of shock with monetary expansion. As a general rule, monetary policy that stabilizes interest rates in response to a monetary shock will be stabilizing, since the monetary policy then offsets the effect of the monetary shock. But if the disturbance that causes interest rates to change is a *real* disturbance, such as a tax cut, a change in investment demand, an autonomous change in exports, or a change in government expenditure, then the monetary response designed to stabilize interest rates will add to the destabilizing force of the real shock.

---

[7] McKinnon, op. cit., p. 22.

These same criticisms apply to leaning against the exchange-rate wind. The same monetary shock that reduces interest rates tends also to depreciate the currency. A reduction in liquidity preference will reduce the rate of interest, tend to raise domestic spending, and depreciate the currency. In such an event it is appropriate to follow McKinnon's second rule to reduce the rate of money growth.

However, McKinnon's rules could well produce destabilizing policy responses to real shocks. An inflationary real shock such as an autonomous increase in domestic consumption tends to cause the current account to deteriorate, but because it raises the rate of interest, the capital account tends to improve. If the current account effect is dominant, the currency depreciates, so following McKinnon's second rule would tend to offset the inflationary effect of the real shock. On the other hand, if the capital account effect is dominant, the currency appreciates, so an expansionary monetary policy, as called for by McKinnon, would add further inflationary pressure. Thus in the present case McKinnon's second rule works correctly, but only when the current account effect of the shock dominates the capital account effect.

However, even this much cannot be safely said if the real shock arrives from abroad. Suppose an attractive new commodity developed in country 1 increases country 1's exports to country 2. Country 1 therefore receives an expansionary real shock, while country 2 suffers a deflationary real shock. Country 1's currency must appreciate since its net exports rise and economic expansion raises its interest rates. The opposite must be true in country 2. McKinnon's second rule would then require country 1 to raise its monetary growth rate in response to the appreciation, while country 2 would be required to do the opposite. The result is to worsen inflation in country 1 and to worsen country 2's unemployment problem.

There are a number of cases in which McKinnon's rule would be likely to work well. For example, the anticipated election of a radical government is likely to raise inflationary expectations and nominal interest rates. A capital outflow may develop despite the rise in nominal interest rates, so the currency depreciates. Real interest rates fall, however, when the expected rate of inflation rises. Since this would be inflationary, it calls for reduction in the money supply, as would occur under McKinnon's rule. Similarly, when Britain became an oil exporter, the rise in the world price of oil in 1979 prompted a capital inflow on the expectation that the pound would rise. The inflow appreciated the pound, causing a deterioration of net exports and an unexpectedly sharp recession in 1980–81. The decline in economic activity might have been moderated had the monetary authority responded to the rise in the value of sterling by following McKinnon's directive to accelerate money growth.

An example of how McKinnon's second rule would produce perverse policy responses is provided by the dilemma that monetary policy would have encountered in response to the U.S. fiscal policies of the early 1980s. These fiscal policies drove up interest rates, attracted a capital inflow, and appreciated the dollar. According to McKinnon, this

> . . . clearly signaled that the Federal Reserve should have expanded the US money supply to prevent the dollar from appreciating so sharply; the depression of 1982 in the United States would then have been mitigated.[8]

McKinnon is correct. But such monetary policy would have added monetary expansion to a highly expansionary fiscal policy, causing inflation to accelerate at a time when it was the clear intention of the Federal Reserve to slow inflation. Such a response may or may not have been preferable. But in proposing the inflationary option, McKinnon violates his own belief that the appropriate role for monetary policy is to "stabilize the purchasing-power value of the national money." Note also that the rule would have required other countries to slow their monetary growth rates in response to the appreciation of the dollar. Whether or not they proceeded at McKinnon's behest, many countries did try to prevent the depreciation of their exchange rates by reducing monetary growth rates, with disastrously depressing consequences.

Finally, had the U.S. fiscal stimulus been even larger, the McKinnon rule would have required a commensurately greater dose of monetary stimulus. Therefore, inflation generated by fiscal policy would be accentuated by monetary policy. Conversely, the rule implies that recessions caused by fiscal policy would be deepened by monetary restriction. These considerations, however, do less to discredit McKinnon's proposal than to call attention to the fact that bad fiscal policies are going to create problems that will make an entire policy package perform poorly.

The most fundamental difficulty with McKinnon's rules is that they are incomplete. As the perversity of McKinnon's monetary responses to real shocks suggests, it is not possible to accomplish everything with monetary policy alone. From the theory of economic policy we know that if countries wish to target both external and internal balance, they will have to adjust at least two policy instruments to attain their goals. Normally, a monetary shock should be offset by a monetary response and a real shock should be offset by a real-side response. That is another way of saying that fiscal policy must also be an essential ingredient in an overall

[8] McKinnon, op. cit., p. 29.

economic stabilization program. The next section addresses this issue. It is shown that McKinnon's monetary proposals can be easily adapted to an integrated program of world economic stability.

15.1.4 Good Neighbor Macroeconomics

An optimal approach to containing capital mobility should be consistent with the attainment of external and internal balance, it should minimize major macroeconomic shocks to foreign countries, and it should foster trade liberalization and promote the flow of capital to its most productive uses. None of the approaches yet discussed in this chapter accomplishes all of these aims. From the analysis of Chapter 6 it would appear that the best hope for an orderly flow of international capital lies in the pursuit of coordinated domestic macroeconomic policies and in the international harmonization of interest rates. It is useful to remind ourselves of how this can be accomplished.

Under flexible exchange rates and high capital mobility, expansionary monetary policy lowers domestic interest rates and causes a capital outflow and a depreciation of the currency, which raises exports and reduces imports. The policy thus raises income and employment, but does so largely at the expense of employment in other countries where trade balances deteriorate. It can be expected that foreign countries will respond to the deflationary impulse with expansionary monetary policies of their own. This could neutralize the capital flows, return exchange rates to their original levels, and restore the preexisting net export position. In such an event, the joint monetary policies will be expansionary only through their effects on world interest rates.

When the degree of capital mobility is high, expansionary fiscal policy, by raising interest rates, attracts sufficient foreign capital to appreciate the currency. The appreciation reduces exports, raises imports, and thereby transmits an expansionary impulse to foreign countries. Part of the intended stimulus is lost to the domestic economy and sent abroad, where it may be unwelcome.

Expansionary monetary policy can be prevented from stealing employment from abroad, while expansionary fiscal policy can be prevented from exporting much of its stimulus, if the two policies are pursued jointly in a coordinated manner. Expansionary fiscal policies raise interest rates, whereas expansionary monetary policies lower them. Therefore, a joint monetary-fiscal expansion could be implemented in such a way as to prevent major interest-rate changes. This prevents capital movements, stabilizes exchange rates, and prevents major disruptions to trade balances and foreign economies. Restrictive policies designed to contain inflation could be conducted in a similarly coordinated manner.

Coordinated policy, as outlined here and in Chapter 6, appears to be the most promising route to exchange rate stabilization that does not stifle trade or desirable capital movements. It necessitates no international agreement, but it does require commitment on the parts of the monetary and fiscal authorities within and among major countries to work in harmony. That is easier said than done. Internal coordination seems potentially easier in Europe and Japan with their more integrated government economic authorities than in the United States with its separation of fiscal and monetary authority, the frequently doctrinaire approach to policy adopted by different administrations, and the tendency of American economists to view fiscal and monetary policies as rivals rather than as potential cooperating arms of policy.

If there is a single theme that runs throughout much of the international monetary reform literature, it is that no reform of the international monetary system is likely substantially to improve the operation of the system in the absence of appropriately coordinated stabilization policies. Conversely, should such policies be put in place, little in the way of reform of the system might be needed. J. Carter Murphy, writing for the conservative American Enterprise Institute, states that

> No doubt the greatest contribution governments can make to exchange rate stability and to the efficiency of private speculation in the exchange markets lies in what they can do to coordinate and stabilize monetary and fiscal policies within and between nations.[9]

In discussing the role of the monetary-fiscal policy mix within countries, Murphy echoes the claim that

> The mix in the use of instruments of monetary and fiscal policies is vital to the outcome of the measures taken. And until governments give closer attention to the implications of their policy mixes for relative credit conditions among countries, their efforts at policy making risk substantial failure even when the governments agree on demand management goals.[10]

There is a school of thought that argues that macroeconomic policy coordination would work better if the international "rules of the game" were tightened. Such tightening often seems to mean fixed exchange rates.

---

[9] Murphy, J. Carter, *The International Monetary System,* American Enterprise Institute, Washington, D.C., 1979, p. 75.

[10] Murphy, op. cit. p. 254.

In addressing the question of whether fixed exchange rates would impose monetary-fiscal discipline, Jeffrey Sachs argues that

> Under floating exchange rates policymakers might try to manipulate the exchange rate to their national advantage: under fixed rates, they might instead try to manipulate the rate of reserve accumulation or some other policy variable. Nor do tighter rules of the game necessarily overcome the inflationary bias of national policymakers. If national policy makers lean towards overly inflationary policies, global policy coordination by these same policy makers might make the inflationary bias even worse.[11]

It is unfortunate that coordination sometimes appears as a code word for the restoration of fixed exchange rates. Monetary-fiscal coordination would certainly not be any less necessary following a return to fixed exchange rates. It is well known that domestic monetary policy has to be sacrificed if fixed exchange rates are adopted. However, the asset-market theory of exchange rate determination suggests that fixed exchange rates will require the sacrifice of fiscal policy as well. The reason is that both forms of policy affect relative asset supplies and therefore the demand for foreign exchange. It is true, as noted earlier, that coordinated use of these policy tools permits internal stabilization policy to go forward without setting off capital movements. However, if the exchange rate must first be fixed, coordinated policy implies that fiscal policy must adapt itself to monetary policy rather than monetary policy adapting itself to fiscal policy. Since fiscal policy is a less flexible tool than monetary policy, managing such a policy is likely to be difficult.

It is important to emphasize that the coordination of domestic monetary-fiscal policies to achieve domestic targets without creating international interest-rate differentials and disruptive capital flows does not represent exchange rate pegging in any relevant sense. It is true that if monetary-fiscal expansion is conducted so as to minimize international shock transmission, the effect of the policies will be to stabilize the exchange rate. But this does not mean that policy is directed toward fixing the exchange rate in response to economic changes. For example, if the country's competitive position improves because of rapid productivity growth, this will create an incipient surplus and currency appreciation that the policy authorities should expect and welcome.

Internal coordination of policy designed to achieve an employment target without disruptive international effects implies that interest rates cannot be used as instruments for achieving solely domestic objectives,

---

[11] Sachs, Jeffrey, "The Uneasy Case for Greater Exchange Rate Coordination," American Economic Association, *Papers and Proceedings,* May 1986, p. 339.

such as stimulating investment or faster growth, since coordination implies that domestic interest rates must be harmonized with the rates prevailing elsewhere. Thus, a country cannot also unilaterally lower the level of domestic interest rates. To get interest rates down, the country must obtain foreign cooperation. During the 1985–87 period world economic growth was sluggish, so all-around lowering of interest rates seemed desirable. Since world inflation had greatly abated while unemployment remained high, the appropriate coordinated approach in such a climate is expansionary monetary policy on the part of *all* major industrial countries. Jointly restrictive fiscal policies would also lower world interest rates, but since such fiscal policies would reduce world aggregate expenditure, such joint policies are less desirable in an environment of excessive unemployment and inadequate utilization of productive capacity.

The years 1985–86 witnessed a sharp revival of interest in international macroeconomic coordination as the Reagan administration, under the leadership of Treasury Secretary James Baker, retreated from its free-market philosophy in favor of a more pragmatic approach. Meetings of the Group of Five (G-5) finance ministers produced the promise of coordinated actions to lower world interest rates and to bring down the dollar. The U.S. position in these discussions has been confusing, because it was not clear whether it was our objective to bring down world interest rates to stimulate economic growth, or whether the objective was to narrow U.S.-foreign interest-rate differentials to depreciate the dollar and reduce the U.S. trade deficit. To achieve the latter, the United States could unilaterally pursue a more restrictive fiscal policy. Since that is politically difficult, the United States has taken to asking other countries to pursue expansionary fiscal policies that would raise foreign interest rates, thereby narrowing interest-rate differentials, reducing the inflow of capital, and depreciating the dollar. Jeffrey Sachs notes that

> . . . following the (G-5) accord the United States has been prodding Germany and Japan to increase their interest rates, through tight money and larger budget deficits. This aspect of policy coordination would be self-destructive as well as short sighted.[12]

And further,

> For the United States to be urging a reversal of the fiscal discipline at a time when it has itself recognized the urgency of fiscal restraint is irresponsible . . . ,[13]

[12] Sachs, Jeffrey, op. cit., p. 339.

[13] Sachs, op. cit., p. 339.

especially when many countries had made politically painful adjustments to get their budgets under control. The effort to force others to imitate dreadful U.S. fiscal policies as a substitute for straightening out fiscal policy in the United States hardly qualifies as macroeconomic policy coordination.

Finally, it is useful to examine how McKinnon's rules for monetary stability might be adapted to the requirements of good neighbor macroeconomics. In other words, is it possible to combine monetary cooperation à la McKinnon with domestic monetary–fiscal coordination as outlined above? Adoption of McKinnon's first rule should, in itself, help to eliminate major fluctuations in countries' income and employment levels, not only by eliminating fluctuations caused by systematically inconsistent monetary policies, but also by creating a stable and predictable monetary environment. It is scarcely necessary to be an intransigent monetarist to appreciate the advantages of such a reform in the conduct of world monetary policy.

Should recession nevertheless arrive in country A, the authorities would be expected to stimulate the economy with expansionary fiscal policies. The appropriate monetary response will depend on the effect of the fiscal policy on the exchange rate. For the present we continue to assume that the degree of capital mobility is so high that currencies will appreciate in response to the fiscal policy. In this event, McKinnon's second rule is entirely compatible with the good neighbor approach. The country should simply follow McKinnon rule 2 and raise its monetary growth rate. If the depreciation of other countries' currencies is not completely offset by country A's coordinated policies, rule 2 would require them to reduce their monetary growth rates, and that would be appropriate because the depreciation of their currencies provides expansionary stimulus to their economies.

If inflation is the primary problem for country A, it would be appropriate for the country to tighten its budget. That would lower interest rates in the country. If capital is highly mobile, the resulting capital outflow would depreciate the currency. McKinnon rule 2 then implies a slowing of country A's monetary growth rate, as is appropriate. Meanwhile, if the currencies of other countries appreciate despite the coordinated policies of country A, that will have a restrictive effect on their economies, making it appropriate for them to follow rule 2 by raising monetary growth.

If the recession is worldwide, it would be incumbent on all countries to utilize expansionary fiscal policies. World monetary growth could also be temporarily raised above target. But this should be undertaken through the coordinated effort of the monetary authorities of the major countries.

A symmetrical argument applies to a condition of worldwide inflation. It would, of course, be appropriate to consider the appropriate mix between world monetary and world fiscal expansion. If, for example, world interest rates are judged to be too high to promote sufficiently rapid economic growth, then the bulk of the stimulus should come from joint monetary expansion.

McKinnon's rules would be inappropriate when capital mobility is relatively low. In that event expansionary fiscal policy could depreciate rather than appreciate the currency of country A. To see how monetary policy should respond to this situation, assume again that a recession develops in country A. If expansionary fiscal policy of country A depreciates its currency, McKinnon rule 2 would require reduction in its rate of monetary growth. But that would be inappropriate because the country is already suffering unemployment. Thus rule 2 would need to be suspended *if a country's currency depreciates when the country's unemployment rate is above an acceptable target level.* Since other countries' currencies would be appreciating, the deflationary effect of the appreciation would warrant observance of McKinnon rule 2, that is, expand the money supply more rapidly in response to currency appreciation.

If country A suffers from excessive inflation and tightens its budget in response, and if, as a consequence, its currency appreciates, it should not be asked to raise its monetary growth rate. Other currencies will be appreciating and the deflationary effects of this should then be offset by raising monetary growth in the other countries in keeping with McKinnon's second rule.

What is being suggested here is an orderly policy response to monetary and real shocks. A *monetary* shock such as a reduction in liquidity preference will reduce the rate of interest, tend to raise national income, and depreciate the currency. In such an event it is appropriate to follow McKinnon's second rule to reduce the rate of money growth. On the other hand, if there is an expansionary *real* shock such as an autonomous rise in consumption, this will tend to raise national income, raise the rate of interest and, in the high capital mobility case, appreciate the currency. Raising the rate of monetary growth, as prescribed by rule 2, would be further inflationary and therefore inappropriate. Therefore, once again the previous directive, that no country should be asked to raise its monetary growth rate under inflationary conditions, should be invoked. The appropriate response by the country sustaining the expansionary real shock is fiscal restraint. In that manner it can offset the real shock while simultaneously cooperating in the effort to stabilize world monetary conditions, and also living within the rules of good neighbor macroeconomics.

If the real shock is in the form of an expenditure shift that raises country A's export demand matched by a corresponding rise in country B's import demand, country A receives an expansionary real shock while country B suffers a restrictive real shock. Country A's currency will appreciate while country B's will depreciate. Neither country should then respond to the change in its exchange rates with a monetary response, following rather the rule that country A should not raise monetary growth in an inflationary environment, while country B should not lower monetary growth in response to declining aggregate demand. For a country to follow McKinnon rule 2 in this case would be extremely unwise, not only in terms of its destabilizing effect on its own economy, but also in terms of its effect on the other economy. Expansionary monetary policy by country A would send a second deflationary shock to country B, whereas restrictive monetary policy by country B would send a second expansionary shock to country A.

These remarks suggest that there is nothing incompatible with McKinnon's overall monetary-policy strategy and the need for each country to practice good neighbor macroeconomics by coordinating its domestic fiscal and monetary policies in a manner that reduces international shock transmission, *provided no country is asked to reduce its rate of monetary growth during a period of excessive unemployment or to raise its rate of monetary growth during a period of excessive inflation.* There is nothing extraordinary about such a commonsense rule of thumb. Following it means that the world economy will have a somewhat larger money stock than prescribed by the target rate during recession, and a somewhat smaller stock during a period of excessive inflation, as is appropriate.

To implement this program, when countries negotiate an appropriate target rate of world monetary growth, each country should also be asked to define its realistically attainable target rates of unemployment and inflation. Policy action can then proceed within a stable and predictable environment in which the policy actions of each country will be understood and approved of by other countries, as consistent with their mutual interest in attaining global macroeconomic stability. Destructive episodes such as the excessive inflation of the 1970s and the descent into the world depression of the early 1980s would then be largely avoided.

Regrettably, the tendency in much recent discussion of macroeconomic stabilization policy has been to discount the importance of fiscal policy. Yet the theory of economic policy teaches that if there is more than one objective of stabilization policy, then more than one independently effective instrument of stabilization policy will be needed to achieve the multiple targets of policy. Indeed, as we have seen, the weakness of McKinnon's prescription is precisely that it attempts to use a single policy instrument to achieve both a stable monetary environment and stable exchange rates. As experience with fixed exchange rates has amply proved, this simply cannot be done. Nor can good neighbor macroeconomics be successfully conducted without combining monetary policy with fiscal policy. As has been suggested here, however, McKinnon's rules make a great deal of sense once appropriately conducted fiscal policy is included in the approach to policy, and provided monetary policy is redirected away from targeting the exchange rate, as under McKinnon, towards more relevant income and employment targets. If the program as outlined here is followed, exchange rates will tend to be far more stable. But this is a by-product of the program, not a primary target.

To summarize the proposed rules for good neighbor macroeconomics within an environment of stable monetary growth, the major trading countries of the world should negotiate an agreement that provides for the following:

1. Countries would agree to target a uniform world rate of monetary growth as the goal for their own monetary policies.
2. If one country enters a period of less than full employment, that country should be responsible for taking expansionary fiscal measures. The opposite would be true for any country whose economy is characterized by excessive demand and inflationary pressures.
3. Countries should raise their rates of monetary growth when their currencies appreciate, provided conditions in their economies are not inflationary. Countries should lower their rates of monetary growth when their currencies depreciate, provided unemployment in the country is not excessive.

15.2. GOVERNMENT INTERVENTION AS A SOURCE OF EXCHANGE RATE INSTABILITY

Governments themselves have been guilty of contributing to capital movements that cause exchange rate instability. Sometimes the temptation to manipulate exchange rates to serve domestic macroeconomic ends has not been resisted, and governments have not been content to eliminate foreign exchange reserves, even under flexible exchange rates, or to manage their foreign exchange portfolios in a stabilizing manner.

The term "clean float" is used to signify the absence of direct government interference in foreign exchange markets. Government influence over exchange rates would be extensive nonetheless because of the effects of monetary and fiscal policies on asset markets. If clean floating were practiced, however, monetary authorities would not accumulate or decumulate foreign exchange reserves.

Flexible exchange rates have not eliminated the desire of monetary authorities to hold reserves. Between 1972 and 1980 the reserves of the OECD countries, excluding the United States, more than doubled. After 1980, reserves of those same countries declined significantly, as foreign central banks sold dollars, presumably to slow its meteoric rise. These changes have been interpreted as suggesting that countries were trying to change the dollar's value for domestic economic purposes. Depreciation of the dollar reduces the competitiveness of foreign export industries in competition with U.S. industries and reduces employment in foreign countries. Dollar appreciation tends to add to inflation abroad by raising the domestic cost of imports, including oil. The large foreign reserve accumulations of the 1970s have been interpreted by some economists as evidence that countries were trying to prop up the dollar's sagging value to maintain the competitiveness of their export industries.[14] The reversal of reserve accumulation after 1980 likewise has been interpreted as an attempt to hold the dollar down once inflation had taken over as the macroeconomic problem of overriding importance. Although it has practiced a stricter nonintervention policy than most countries, the United States intervened heavily in 1978, when the "dollar rescue operation" lent support to the dollar so as to reduce the impact of rising import prices on inflation. Then, after a strict nonintervention period, the U.S. agreed, in principle, to seek more orderly exchange rates at the Tokyo Economic Summit of 1986.

If the flexible exchange-rate system has been influenced by governments in pursuit of economic objectives, one country's gain as the result of such manipulation is very likely to be another country's loss. Such use of exchange rates is essentially competitive in nature and likely to provoke countermeasures that could degenerate into trade and macroeconomic warfare. Practicing good manners in monetary-fiscal policy is prescribed in Article IV of the IMF charter. Beyond this, however, the fact that governments may be a source of instability is regarded by some

---

[14] The evidence seems fairly clear that between 1974 and 1977 the Japanese government was actively attempting to depress the exchange value of the yen relative to the dollar as part of an export promotion program. See Argy, Victor, "Exchange Rate Management in Theory and Practice," Princeton Studies in International Finance, International Finance Section, No. 50 October 1982.

as a problem that could be so severe that several proposals have been offered to help the international economy guard against it.

The Reserve Indicator Proposal Heavy reserve accumulation by a monetary authority is evidence that the accumulating country's currency is undervalued, because the authority has been selling its own currency in exchange for reserves. As seen in Chapter 13, this was the position taken by the United States during the C-20 negotiations of 1972–74. The United States proposed a "reserve indicator" rule under which excessive accumulation signals the need for exchange rate revaluation or other adjustment measures by the accumulating country. Under one proposal excessive accumulations would have been deposited with the IMF and subjected to penalties in the form of negative interest payments.

A reserve indicator system would require countries to agree on upper and lower bounds for reserve stocks. Countries that accumulate reserves greater than the agreed level would be obliged to sell foreign exchange to appreciate their currencies. Countries losing reserves would undertake to buy reserves to depreciate their currencies.

Reserve indicators have been considered attractive because they appear to bypass the difficult problem of estimating equilibrium exchange rates. This problem, however, cannot be avoided by focusing on reserve levels. As noted earlier, there is danger that reserve targeting would cause oscillating exchange rate movements if the reserve targets chosen are inconsistent with exchange rates that yield balance-of-payments equilibrium. If a return to balance-of-payments equilibrium finds a country with excessive reserves, selling reserves to reach the target level may force additional appreciation so that a balance-of-payments deficit is generated that then permits reserves to decumulate. Once reserves are restored to their target level, continuation of an overvalued exchange rate and a payments deficit causes reserves to fall below their target level. Purchases of reserves (sales of domestic currency) then brings about depreciation, a subsequent balance-of-payments surplus, and reserve accumulation. However, the process again overshoots equilibrium because reserve accumulation continues as long as the surplus lasts.

The theoretical argument that a reserve-targeting policy causes exchange rates systematically to overshoot their equilibrium levels is confirmed by a simulation study by Peter Kenen.[15] Kenen modeled the effects of an automatic intervention rule based on reserve levels. Exchange rate

[15] Kenen, Peter B., "Floats, Glides, and Indicators: A Comparison of Methods for Changing Exchange Rates," *Journal of International Economics,* 5, May 1975, 107–182. For the theoretical development see Mundell, Robert A., "The Monetary Dynamics of International Adjustment Under Fixed and Flexible Exchange Rates," *Quarterly Journal of Economics,* 74, May 1960.

adjustments were limited to 5 percent per year, triggered by reserve-level changes that deviated by plus or minus 15 percent from a base-period level. Very poor results characterized such policy. The simulated exchange rate oscillated sharply and took more than ten years to settle near its stationary equilibrium level.

Reserve accumulation does not necessarily mean that exchange rates need to be adjusted. If a country is accumulating reserves while suffering from recession, appreciation of its currency raises imports and reduces exports, worsening the recession. Similarly, a country losing reserves and also suffering from inflation can reduce its payments deficit by depreciation, but that adds to inflation. Consequently, a mechanical reserve indicator has major drawbacks. The appropriate form of adjustment depends on specific economic conditions. And, unless the reserve indicator were combined with measures designed to stabilize private capital flows, it is doubtful that limits on official reserves would have much impact on the course of exchange rates or trade.

The Reference-Rate Proposal   The reference-rate proposal is designed to prevent governments from undertaking destabilizing intervention. The authors of the plan, Wilfred Ethier and Arthur I. Bloomfield, suggest the adoption of the plan even if it is the intention to maintain flexible exchange rates.[16]

The proposal retains the fixed parities of the fixed exchange rates but reverses the role of intervention. Instead of prescribing conditions under which intervention is required, it prescribes rules under which intervention is prohibited. Under Bretton Woods, countries were required to intervene to keep exchange rates from moving away from official parities. Under the reference-rate proposal government sales of domestic currency are prohibited when the local currency is below parity, and purchases are prohibited when it is above parity. Intervention to move exchange rates towards the reference parity or zone would be permitted but not required.

Acceptance of this proposal would prevent monetary authorities from acting to push down the exchange value of a currency that is already weak and from lending additional support to a currency that is already strong. Intervention to manipulate exchange rates for domestic purposes would be impeded. The proposal could also reduce destabilizing speculation, because intervention, when it occurs, will always be in the direction of the reference rate.

[16] Ethier, Wilfred, and Arthur I. Bloomfield, "Managing the Managed Float," *Essays in International Finance,* Princeton University, No. 112, 1975.

The reference-rate plan requires a forecast of equilibrium exchange rates if it is to provide a realistic basis for intervention. If the reference rate is frequently adjusted, it loses its value as a point of reference. If it is infrequently adjusted, it loses touch with economic conditions. Whereas the reserve indicator approach implicitly assumes that failure of exchange rates to adjust to equilibrium levels is aggravated by government intervention, the reference-rate proposal makes the opposite assumption that market exchange rates will frequently diverge from equilibrium rates because of destabilizing speculation.

The reference-rate proposal assumes that government officials are better forecasters than market participants. Although progress has been made in understanding the dynamics of exchange markets, forecasting efforts have not yielded good results, and further work is needed before such a system could be effectively established.

Multiple-Currency Reserves and the Substitution Account   Although the dollar is by far the most important reserve currency in the world, other currencies, such as the D-mark and the yen, have been growing in importance as reserve currencies held by monetary authorities. The system that has been evolving is called a multicurrency reserve system. There is danger that such a system may add to exchange rate instability if monetary authorities copy private speculators by engaging in currency speculation on their own behalf. For example, if a foreign monetary authority expects the dollar to decline, it may sell its dollars in exchange for yen in order to protect the value of its reserves. Since this depresses the dollar, it adds to the other forces making for a weak dollar and could touch off a wave of speculative selling that causes a far greater decline in the dollar than indicated by economic conditions.

The substitution account, which would be provided by the IMF, is the device that has most frequently been suggested to ensure the international monetary system against instability from this source. Such an account would permit countries to deposit their foreign exchange holdings at the IMF in exchange for SDRs. The existence of such a facility would provide monetary authorities with an automatic hedge against exchange risk. Since the value of the SDR is determined as a weighted average of the values of the major currencies, the appreciation of one currency would be matched by depreciation of others, leaving the value of the SDR largely unaffected. With reserves held in the form of SDRs, the temptation to sell potentially weak currencies, adding to destabilizing speculative forces, would be avoided.

A proposed substitution account first figured prominently in the C-20 negotiations of 1972–74. It was then believed that such an account would substitute dollar-to-SDR convertibility for the no-longer-credible dollar-to-gold convertibility commitment. The SDR would thereby gain in importance as a reserve asset, and the Bretton Woods system could be revived by reestablishing a credible system of convertibility.

Under flexible exchange rates the substitution account becomes important as a device for insuring monetary authorities against exchange risk. In the short-run purchases of other currencies with dollars would, as explained by Robert Solomon,

> . . . either push up the exchange rate of the currencies being acquired or, if the countries on the receiving end intervened in the market to stabilize their exchange rates, undermine monetary policies.[17]

In the longer run the outcome could be a multicurrency reserve system that is dangerously unstable, since it would be vulnerable to shifts of reserve holdings from one reserve currency to another in response to exchange and interest-rate expectations as well as to political developments. Solomon goes on to explain that

> The main purpose of the proposed substitution account is to restrain the development of such a system. At the same time the account would facilitate the phasing out of the dollar as a reserve currency and the emergence of the SDR as the principle reserve asset. . . .[18]

With these considerations apparently in mind, IMF managing director Johannes Witteveen proposed in 1978 that a new SDR allocation be combined with the deposit of reserve currencies in a substitution account in exchange for further SDRs. In its annual report for 1979 the IMF stated that

> . . . a substitution account would permit a change in the composition of members' reserves unaccompanied by potentially disturbing transactions in foreign exchange markets.[19]

15.3 CRITERIA FOR GOVERNMENT EXCHANGE MARKET INTERVENTION

Many proposals to reform the international monetary system represent suggested guidelines for government intervention in foreign exchange markets. This is not surprising because the difference between one ex-

---

[17] Solomon, Robert, *The International Monetary System, 1945–1981,* Harper & Row, 1982, p. 283.

[18] Solomon, op. cit., p. 288.

[19] IMF, Annual Report, 1979, p. 56.

change rate system and another lies primarily in differences in official intervention policy.

Under fixed exchange rates intervention is persistent and automatic. The commitment to par values forces monetary authorities to exchange foreign currency for domestic money at prices constrained within a narrow range of permissible variation. Asset markets are continuously disturbed as the money supplies of deficit countries shrink while the money supplies of surplus countries increase.

The opposite extreme is the clean float, under which money supplies are sheltered from balance-of-payments developments. However, exchange rates continue to be affected by other macroeconomic policies. Fiscal measures that increase the budget deficit add to the supply of domestic securities, raising interest rates; monetary expansion substitutes money in place of domestic earning assets, lowering interest rates.

A number of proposals have in common the fact that they are halfway measures that attempt to avoid the rigidities of the fixed exchange-rate system and the drastic exchange rate fluctuations that have characterized the floating-rate system. We begin with a discussion of conditions under which intervention is justified as a supplement to a flexible exchange-rate system. Because it is sometimes considered desirable to intervene without affecting money supplies, the technique of "sterilized" intervention is explained. We then examine proposals to prevent extreme and erratic exchange rate fluctuations. Then we consider the concept of an optimum currency area within which exchange rates are fixed and between which they fluctuate. These various strands then provide the input into some notes on a possible international monetary system of the future.

15.3.1 Criteria for Intervention Under Flexible Exchange Rates

Even under a clean float intervention is widely considered to be desirable to counter "disorderly markets." Disorderly markets are difficult to define, but may be characterized as day-to-day ups and downs that do not reflect underlying trends. Such bumps are usually referred to as exchange rate "volatility." Intervention to counter volatility is required of members of the IMF under its "Principles for the Guidance of Members Exchange-Rate Policies," adopted in 1977. The second of the three principles states

> A member should intervene in the exchange market if necessary to counter disorderly conditions which may be characterized inter alia by disruptive short-term movements in the exchange value of its currency.[20]

[20] IMF Survey, May 2, 1977, p. 132.

The presumption is that suppression of volatility will not change the average value of the currency over an extended period. Intervention that goes beyond countering volatility is usually termed intervention to stem "variability."

From the advent of floating in 1973 until 1981, the United States sometimes intervened actively in exchange markets. In 1981, however, Beryl W. Sprinkel, undersecretary of the Treasury for monetary affairs, proclaimed the Reagan administration's intention to pursue a clean float. Testifying before the Joint Economic Committee of Congress Sprinkel said

> Significant and frequent intervention by governments assumes that a relatively few officials know better where exchange rates should be than a large number of decision makers in the market, and that public funds should be put at risk on the basis of that assumption.[21]

As Sprinkel's statement shows, opponents of intervention believe that there is no presumption that official intervention will be better informed than other market participants. Indeed, opponents of intervention often go much further by claiming that much of the instability that has characterized the floating-rate system is in fact due to ill-advised official intervention. The trouble, in other words, is that the float has not been permitted to be clean. Such critics disparagingly speak of dirty and filthy floats that hardly qualify as candidates for inclusion among floating currencies. Michael Mussa, a member of President Reagan's Council of Economic Advisers, reflects this view when he states that

> . . . official agencies have intervened extensively in foreign exchange markets, and the behavior of exchange rates has presumably been affected by the direct and indirect effects of this official intervention. For this reason, we cannot conclude that observed peculiarities in the behavior of exchange rates necessarily reflect defects in the operation of the market mechanism.[22]

After the election of 1984 the Reagan administration's position underwent a significant change. James Baker succeeded Donald Regan as Treasury secretary and Beryl Sprinkel moved from the Treasury to the Council of Economic Advisers, where his rigidly doctrinaire views could more easily be ignored. The force of events embodied in the persistent and growing trade deficit, massive job losses in manufacturing caused by import competition, the inability of farmers and others to compete in

---

[21] Sprinkel, Beryl W., Statement Before the Joint Economic Committee, May 4, 1981.

[22] Mussa, Michael, "The Role of Official Intervention," *Occasional Papers,* No. 6., Group of Thirty, New York, 1981, p. 14.

foreign markets, and growing protectionist pressures in Congress all combined to force the administration to rethink its priorities and attitudes. The result has been an attempt by Secretary Baker to cooperate with other countries in efforts to lower the dollar, a willingness expressed at the Tokyo Summit to intervene in foreign exchange markets, and a major reversal of Federal Reserve policy. In late 1984 the Fed lowered the discount rate, an action that was followed by four additional reductions by mid-1986, and there was a sharp increase in the rate of growth of the basic (M_1) money supply.

Supporters of intervention point to the costs of exchange rate variability claiming that many of these costs are avoidable through judicious intervention. As noted by Robert Solomon,

> There appears to be a cobweb-like pattern to the interaction of exchange rates and current-account positions, as both tend to overshoot. If this is a valid proposition, it follows that reversible shifts in resources are taking place, and this presumably involves social costs.[23]

To review some of the costs quickly, unstable current accounts imply instability in export- and import-competing industries, causing alternating bouts of overcapacity and unemployment with undercapacity and labor scarcity, and with severe secondary (multiplier) effects throughout the economy. The inflationary pressures that accompany depreciation's effect on import prices would be accentuated by shortages, and the deflationary effects of appreciation would be accompanied by domestic surpluses. Excessive exchange rate variation also inflicts capital losses, affects the distribution of income, and provides monetary authorities with an incentive to diversify their reserve portfolios, leading to a potentially unstable multiple-currency reserve currency system. Protectionism has grown during the flexible exchange-rate era, and this too has been in large measure provoked by the instability of export- and import-competing industries.

J. Carter Murphy has outlined some conditions under which intervention in foreign exchange markets is appropriate if the principal objective is to preserve a flexible exchange-rate system.

1. Intervention is appropriate if expectations are "elastic" so that a movement in one direction of the exchange rate causes market participants to expect continued movement in the same direction. Acting on this expectation, speculators engage in market behavior

---

[23] Solomon, Robert, "Official Intervention in Foreign Exchange Markets: A Survey," The Brookings Institution, December 1982, p. 4.

that causes the expectation to be realized. This situation is most likely to occur during periods when there is little consensus as to the equilibrium exchange rate. Murphy notes that

The government, as intervenor in the exchange markets, can by the scale of its operations break such a self-fulfilling chain when smaller and necessarily profit-motivated market participants would still hesitate to move against it.[24]

2. Intervention in the foreign exchange market may be useful when uncertainty is so great that stabilizing private speculative activity is inadequate. Murphy suggests that

Stability in the exchange rates may . . . contribute to government policy goals such as price stability and stable aggregate output and employment. In such circumstances, limited government speculation aimed at giving depth to the market in the absence of private speculation may be justified.[25]

3. Intervention in foreign exchange markets may be justified when government officials have knowledge of future policies and other events not known to the public. There is the danger that officials may manipulate exchange rates to put their pet policies in a better light, so such intervention should be permitted for only very short periods.

If these guidelines are followed, along with the IMF's requirement to reduce exchange rate volatility, the result could be the reduction of excessive exchange rate variability caused by inadequate knowledge on the part of private market participants. They could reduce destabilizing speculation and provide a substitute when stabilizing speculation is inadequate. Such intervention would not interfere with fundamental market forces either in the short run or in the long run.

15.3.2 Sterilized Versus Nonsterilized Intervention

Nonsterilized intervention in foreign exchange markets occurs when the monetary authority either buys or sells its own currency in exchange for other currencies. This affects the money supplies of the countries whose

---

[24] Murphy, J. Carter, *The International Monetary System,* American Enterprise Institute, Washington, D.C. 1979, p. 74.

[25] Murphy, op. cit., p. 74.

currencies are involved in the transaction and may seriously interfere with the monetary policy objectives of the respective countries.

To shelter money supplies from the effects of intervention, economists have suggested that monetary authorities engage in sterilized intervention. For example, if the Federal Reserve wishes to raise the dollar relative to the D-mark without changing money supplies, it may sell D-mark-denominated earning assets in return for D-marks. The D-marks are then used to purchase dollars in the foreign exchange market. To prevent the dollar purchases from reducing the U.S. money supply, the Fed simultaneously purchases U.S. government securities. The net effect of these operations is to leave the two money supplies unchanged. The Fed's asset portfolio, however, now shows a reduction in its stock of D-mark securities and an increase in its stock of U.S. securities. Private portfolios show the opposite. Since the supply of D-mark securities in private markets increases while the supply of U.S. securities declines, it can be expected that D-mark securities will fall in price while dollar-denominated securities rise in price. The result, as predicted by the asset-market theory, is a decline in the price of foreign exchange. Thus the dollar is made to appreciate without this necessitating a reduction in the U.S. money supply.

The private sector must be induced to accept this rearranging of portfolios through incentives provided by shifts in relative asset prices, or the assets must be perfect substitutes. If the assets are imperfect substitutes, the value of D-mark-denominated securities must fall relative to the value of the replaced U.S. securities. However, if the assets are perfect substitutes, the changes in the composition of private portfolios between assets denominated in different currencies will not affect interest rates and the exchange rate. If wealth holders are indifferent to the currency of denomination of the securities, their relative prices will not change, and sterilized intervention would then have no effect on interest rates, capital movements, or exchange rate.

We should qualify this conclusion by noting that when the central bank intervenes, it sends a signal to the market indicating the direction it wishes the exchange rate to move. This may produce speculative activity that alters the exchange rate in the desired direction even when the assets are perfect substitutes.

Studies of the effectiveness of sterilized intervention suggest that this is not a promising form of intervention. The magnitude of the changes in the relative supplies of financial assets needed to have a substantial impact on exchange rates is very large. Effective intervention is therefore likely to require nonsterilized intervention that alters money supplies.[26]

[26] See Obstfeld, Maurice, "Can We Sterilize? Theory and Evidence," *American Economic Review*, 72, May 1982, 45–50.

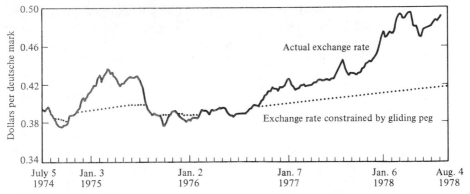

Figure 15.1 Actual exchange rate and exchange rate constrained by gliding peg, July 5, 1974, to August 4, 1978.

15.3.3 Alternative Criteria for Exchange Market Intervention

In this section we consider alternative criteria designed to reduce exchange rate variability. Earlier we met two such criteria—the reserve indicator approach and the reference-rate proposal—which were designed to prevent governments from manipulating exchange rates in an undesirable manner. The topic of this section, however, is the issue of using the government's intervention capability constructively to reduce exchange rate variability.

The Gliding Peg The gliding peg proposal calls for mandatory exchange market intervention when the actual exchange rate deviates from a value obtained from a moving average of past exchange rates.[27] The advantage of the gliding peg is that it offers stability of exchange rates and yet gradually adjusts the exchange rate in response to market forces. The disadvantage is that the adjustment misses turning points and tends to lag far behind the market when there is steady upward or downward pressure on the exchange rate over an extended time. This can be seen in Figure 15.1, which compares the actual dollar–D-mark rate with the exchange rate constrained by a gliding peg. As the figure makes clear, some of the swings of the dollar–D-mark rate would have been reduced in amplitude, but in the presence of the strong upward pressure in the value of the D-mark the formula generates a very sizable lag in adjustment. Intervention would have to have been virtually continuous beginning in late 1977.

[27] Gliding pegs were first proposed in the 1960s by a number of economists. See Murphy, J. Carter, "Moderate Exchange Rate Variability," *National Banking Review,* 3, 1965, 151–161, and Black, J. "A Proposal for the Reform of Exchange Rates," *Economic Journal,* 76, June 1966, 288–295.

This means that it would have been impossible to conduct a monetary policy that was independent of the need to stabilize the exchange rate. Therefore it is not at all clear that a gliding peg would provide much improvement over a fixed exchange-rate system or over a clean float.

The Crawling Peg A proposal that has attracted much attention and has in fact been implemented by some Latin American countries is the crawling peg. This differs from the gliding peg in that intervention by the monetary authority is discretionary, whereas gliding pegs are automatic, being based on past actual exchange rates.[28] Under the crawling peg proposal, the government attempts to determine an appropriate exchange rate and intervenes in a manner that causes that exchange rate to be approached slowly and smoothly rather than quickly. This proposal is also intended to reduce exchange rate variability and overshooting while permitting market forces to determine the path of exchange rates.

A major problem with the crawl is that the monetary authority must correctly assess the direction in which market forces are tending to move the exchange rate over the period of the crawl. Once in place, the crawl policy is based on forecasts and analyses made in the past. Thus the question arises as to how often the plan needs to be reviewed and the crawl objective revised. If it is revised continuously, the policy loses any semblance of a crawl; if it is not revised for long periods, the exchange rate may get further and further out of line with market forces. Crawling in the wrong direction is a possibility.

Announcement of impending depreciation at a specific rate will set off speculative activity that may defeat the intention of the crawl. Suppose the decision is to lower the dollar vis-à-vis the D-mark by 5 percent over the coming year. If speculators know the dollar will be worth 5 percent less in a year, they will sell dollars with the intention of buying them back more cheaply later. The effect of such activity would be an immediate sharp depreciation of the dollar, which defeats the intention of the policy.

It has been pointed out that such speculation could be prevented if the 5 percent gain from the speculation is wiped out by a 5 percent rise in interest rates on dollar-denominated assets. That may be true, but such policy forces monetary policy to adopt an interest-rate target that may be destabilizing and inconsistent with internal balance. And it certainly will not avoid speculation, since market participants who reason that a 5 percent crawl will be accompanied by a rise in interest rates will quickly unload dollar-denominated earning assets in anticipation of capital losses.

---

[28] See Williamson, John, "The Crawling Peg," *Essays in International Finance,* Princeton University, December 1965.

In the absence of any clear notion where the equilibrium exchange rate lies, it has been suggested that the rate of the crawl should equal differences in inflation rates—that is, purchasing-power parity. Therefore if inflation in Germany is 2 percent and inflation in the U.S. is 5 percent, the dollar should be depreciated 3 percent against the D-mark over the same time period. However, if this were done the only real gain over rigid exchange rates would be the prevention of over- or undervaluation due to different rates of inflation. All other sources of disequilibrium would be ignored. Therefore, as noted by Robert Dunn,

> . . . control over the nominal money supply would again be lost or at least greatly compromised. Balance-of-payments considerations would again become vital in determining macroeconomic policies, even when they conflict with domestic goals.[29]

Purchasing-power-parity criteria implicitly take current-account balance as the condition for equilibrium. But if the exchange rate is not permitted to vary in response to a rise in the profitability of investment in a particular country, the flow of resources needed to exploit this greater profitability will not take place. A higher rate of return attracts capital, appreciates the currency, and makes imports cheaper and exports more expensive; hence, the current account shows a deficit represented by a net inflow of resources that enables the more profitable opportunity to be exploited. If the exchange rate is not permitted to move in this manner, the process of allocating the world's stock of capital efficiently will be thwarted.

These harsh criticisms not withstanding, the purchasing-power-parity criterion is useful when inflation is the overriding force making for misaligned exchange rates. With inflation rates often exceeding 100 percent annually, Latin American countries have found their inflation rates to be a useful guide to the appropriate rate of depreciation, and some of them have pursued exchange market intervention in a manner that resembles the crawling peg.

The Target Zone The target zone or "wider-bands" proposal has figured prominently in recent discussions of international monetary reform. In 1974 the IMF issued a set of guidelines for countries to follow in their intervention policies. One such guideline was the suggestion that a member move its exchange rate toward a target zone to be determined in consultation with the IMF and projected as a three- to four-year equilibrium value for the currency. If the market exchange rate remains inside

[29] Dunn, op. cit., p. 26.

the band, no intervention is called for. If the market rate tends to move above (or below) the upper (or lower) limit, intervention then takes place to push the exchange rate back inside the band. Although this guideline was superseded by the second amendment to the IMF charter, considerable support for such a method of intervention continues.[30]

The principal objective of the target zone proposal is to contain drastic swings in exchange rates while permitting exchange rates to adjust to market forces by supplying a band for nonintervention substantially in excess of the plus and minus 1 percent from parity of the Bretton Woods system. Since the band would be subject to review every three years, it could be adjusted in the light of economic trends. It is therefore a modified par-value system designed to overcome the tendency of the Bretton Woods system for par values to become frozen and out of line with market forces.

A major disadvantage of the proposal is that intervention activity forces monetary policy to be diverted to exchange market stabilization. Intervention activity is likely to be heaviest during periods of major disequilibrium in national economies. At such times control of monetary policy for internal balance purposes is especially important. However, exchange market intervention at such times makes it impossible to conduct stabilizing monetary policy effectively.

The destabilizing speculative activity that plagued the Bretton Woods system after 1966 would return. If the currency tends regularly to the lower part of the band, speculators will infer that it is overvalued and that the next review with the IMF will produce a devaluation of the band. Therefore, expecting the currency to depreciate, speculators will sell the currency, thereby putting added pressure on the exchange rate. It seems likely that market exchange rates will tend either to the bottom or to the top of the band, thereby inviting continuous destabilizing speculation and forcing continuous intervention by the monetary authority. Monetary policy would once again be hamstrung.

Establishing an appropriate target zone for the next three years requires forecasting accuracy. But forecasts of exchange rates and current accounts have shown large errors even for projections of only a year's duration. Forecasts that project current accounts and exchange rates for three or four years are likely to produce even larger errors. The discrepancies cast doubt on the ability of governments to forecast equilibrium exchange rates with any degree of accuracy or confidence. Although empirical test of different exchange rate determination theories often support

---

[30] See Williamson, John, *The Exchange Rate System,* Institute for International Economics. Washington, D.C., September 1983, chap. 4.

the theories, the resulting equations have not generally produced accurate exchange rate forecasts. Therefore, as argued by Thomas Willett,

> If the target zones were broad enough to take into account the difficulties of estimating correct exchange rates—especially with a time horizon of several years . . .—they would become much too loose to be linked to current account positions. They . . . rest on undue faith in econometric models . . . and in the ability of international experts to forecast international financial developments and to estimate correct or appropriate exchange rates accurately enough to make such an approach realistic.[31]

Despite this unenthusiastic assessment, note that the European Monetary System (EMS) is a variant of a wide-band scheme in operation. Central rates are established but are periodically reviewed to prevent them from becoming outmoded. Since 1979 there have been numerous changes in central rates. However, the changes appear to have been sufficiently small, so market exchange rates were not drastically affected.

15.4 GEOGRAPHIC INTERVENTION: THE OPTIMUM CURRENCY AREA

The presence of the dollar as a monetary unit that serves as a means of payment in New York as well as California seems indispensable to the U.S. economy. A situation in which each of the 50 states had its own currency unit that fluctuated freely with respect to every other state's currency unit conjures up such an image of chaos and uncertainty that it is virtually unthinkable. If each state had its own currency and a fluctuating exchange rate, there would surely be less interstate trade, less interstate investment, and less interstate mobility of factors. The cost in lost real income would very likely be enormous. The advantages of a uniform currency in promoting greater economic efficiency are undeniably great.

The efficiency argument is the single most persuasive argument in favor of fixed exchange rates. Although different countries have different national currencies and different monetary policies, proponents of the efficiency argument believe that the effects of a uniform world currency can be approximated by a fixed exchange-rate system that permits currencies to be traded at previously established fixed prices.

---

[31] Willett, T. R., *Floating Exchange Rates and International Monetary Reform,* American Enterprise Institute, 1977, pp. 121–122.

There is, however, a major difference between a single currency and fixed exchange rates. Robert Mundell explains that

> A single currency implies a single central bank and therefore a potentially elastic supply of interregional means of payment. But in a currency area comprising more than one currency ... no central bank can expand its own liabilities much faster than other central banks without losing reserves and impairing convertibility. This means ... there will be a difference between inter-regional adjustment and international adjustment even though exchange rates in the latter case are fixed.[32]

Imagine two countries, A and B, that initially enjoy full employment, price stability, and balance-of-payments equilibrium. Then assume that the equilibrium is disturbed by a shift in demand from the goods of country B to those of country A. The effect is a surplus in country A's balance of payments matched by an equal deficit in B's balance of payments. If prices are flexible, equilibrium in the balance of payments will be restored by changes in relative prices. Since the demand for A's goods increases, prices rise in A, and since the demand for B's goods declines, prices fall in country B. The restoration of equilibrium finds the terms of trade more favorable to A and less favorable to B. Therefore, the effect of the shift in demand is to raise real income in A and to lower it in B.

However, if prices are downwardly rigid, the decline in the demand for B's goods causes unemployment in B. The final outcome then depends on the responses of the monetary authorities in the respective countries. This response is likely to differ, depending on whether A and B have a common monetary unit or whether they each have their own monetary units and independent monetary policies.

If each country has its own monetary authority and fixed exchange rates are maintained, A's monetary authority is very likely to attempt to prevent inflation. This action worsens unemployment in B. Meanwhile, B's monetary authority cannot combat the unemployment without worsening the deficit, thereby causing reserves to dwindle. Therefore, Mundell concludes that

> The policy of surplus countries in restraining prices imparts a recessive tendency to the world economy on fixed exchange rates. . . .[33]

On the other hand, if regions A and B share a common currency and a common monetary policy directed toward full employment,

[32] Mundell, Robert A., "A Theory of Optimum Currency Areas," *International Economics,* Macmillan, 1968, p. 178.

[33] Mundell, op. cit., pp. 178–179.

unemployment in B leads to expansionary monetary policy that accentuates the inflation in region A. Mundell therefore reasons that

> Full employment . . . imparts an inflationary bias to . . . a currency area with a common currency.[34]

At this juncture the advocate of flexible exchange rates enters the discussion to claim that neither unemployment nor inflation need be tolerated if the exchange rate between A and B is permitted to fluctuate. Depreciation of B's currency (and appreciation of A's) means that trade between the regions can remain balanced, that A's monetary authority can act to prevent inflation, and that B's monetary authority can act to combat unemployment. The terms of trade move in favor of A in exactly the same way as they would have moved had internal prices been flexible.

It can be seen that internal price flexibility and flexible exchange rates are close substitutes. In either case country B's terms of trade deteriorate, and it suffers a loss in real income. The presence of wage-price rigidity can be interpreted to mean that country B is unwilling to accept real income losses brought about by declining wages and prices, but that it will accept the real income loss through depreciation of its currency. Thus, the case for flexible exchange rates is sometimes seen as based on money illusion—that is, it makes a difference how the real income loss is brought about. Mundell notes that

> The thesis of those who favor flexible exchange rates is that the community in question is not willing to accept variations in real income through adjustments in its money wage rate or price level, but that it is willing to accept virtually the same changes in its real income through variations in the rate of exchange.[35]

As noted, the advantage of fixed exchange rates is greater efficiency. A uniform currency creates an environment of greater certainty than one in which exchange rates fluctuate, and the degree of uncertainty is compounded as the number of fluctuating currencies multiplies. Conversely, the case for flexible exchange rates is primarily an employment argument. If so, the question arises as to whether it is possible to gain the best of both worlds, that is, efficiently conducted trade as well as high and stable employment. The search for such a solution has led economists Robert Mundell and Ronald McKinnon, among others, to explore the notion of an "optimum currency area." Such an area would comprise a number

[34] Mundell, op. cit., p. 179.

[35] Mundell, op. cit., p. 184.

of countries, or regions, within which fixed exchange rates, or better yet a uniform currency with a single monetary policy, are maintained. The currency of this area would then be free to fluctuate with respect to other currency areas. The EMS represents such a currency area in practice. Countries inside the EMS peg their currencies to each other, and the currencies then float in unison with respect to currencies outside the EMS. Intervention by the monetary authorities of the countries inside the currency area is selective, being based on geography, with the central banks buying and selling the currencies of countries inside the union (but not outside the union) at a fixed price.

What then is an optimum currency area? First, the optimum currency area may not coincide with national boundaries. Mundell explains the point in the following extended citation:

> Suppose that the world consists of two countries, Canada and the United States, each of which has separate currencies. Also assume that the continent is divided into two regions that do not correspond to national boundaries— the East, which produces goods such as cars, and the West, which produces goods such as lumber products. To test the flexible-exchange-rate argument . . . assume that the U.S. dollar fluctuates relative to the Canadian dollar, and that an increase in productivity in the automobile industry causes an excess demand for lumber products and an excess supply of cars.
>
> The immediate impact . . . is to cause unemployment in the East and inflationary pressure in the West, and a flow of bank reserves from the East to the West because of the former's regional balance-of-payments deficit. To relieve unemployment in the East the central banks in both countries would have to expand the national money supplies or, to prevent inflation in the West, contract the national money supplies. (Meanwhile the Canada-U.S. exchange rate would move to preserve equilibrium in the national balances). Thus unemployment can be prevented in both countries but only at the expense of inflation; or, inflation can be restrained in both countries but at the expense of unemployment; or, finally, the burden of adjustment can be shared between East and West with some unemployment in the East and some inflation in the West. But both unemployment and inflation cannot be escaped. The flexible exchange rate system does not serve to correct the balance-of-payments situation between the two regions (which is the essential problem), although it will do so between the two countries; it is therefore not necessarily preferable to a common currency or national currencies connected by fixed exchange rates.[36]

Mundell then notes that

> The preceding example does not destroy the argument for flexible exchange rates, but it might severely impair the relevance of the argument if it is

---

[36] Mundell, op. cit., p. 180.

applied to national currencies. The logic of the argument can in fact be rescued if national currencies are abandoned in favor of regional currencies.[37]

Second, it seems reasonably clear that the optimum currency area must be fairly large and that it should be as economically self-sufficient as possible. Small countries tend to have high import propensities and to be more dependent on essential imports than are large countries. If 60 percent of a country's GNP is involved in international trade, fluctuations in the country's exchange rate will be directly transmitted into comparably large fluctuations in GNP. If the currency depreciates, the domestic cost of imports rises. If these are imports, such as food, that figure importantly in consumer expenditures, the resulting rise in the price level reduces real wages, so the real wages of workers decline, much as would have occurred had the exchange rate been fixed and wages been flexible. The money illusion, on which the argument for flexible exchange rates is based, is not sustainable if imports figure heavily in the cost of living. Moreover, if workers demand upward wage adjustments to offset the higher prices, the country loses the competitive edge gained from the depreciation, which then sets the stage for a further cycle of depreciation.

Third, it is essential for the effective operation of a currency region that it be characterized by substantial mobility of productive factors within the region. If there is a shift in demand from B to A, both of which lie inside the region, there will tend to be unemployment in B and inflation in A. That, however, could be avoided if workers and capital respond to higher earning opportunities and move to region A. In the United States, the Houston, Texas, area enjoyed a boom in the wake of the oil price increases of the 1970s. Meanwhile, higher energy costs contributed to a slump in other parts of the country. In response, many workers in various parts of the country pulled up stakes and headed for Houston's booming economy, thereby alleviating labor surpluses in the depressed areas and labor shortages in the Southwest. Then, during the 1980s, as world oil prices fell sharply, it was the Houston economy that suffered depression. But the pain would be eased if Houston's surplus labor force is rapidly absorbed in other parts of the country.

Mundell underscores the importance of intraregional factor mobility as follows:

> If the world can be divided into regions within each of which there is factor mobility and between which there is factor immobility, then each of these regions should have a separate currency which fluctuates relative to all

[37] Ibid., p. 180.

other currencies. This carries the argument for flexible exchange rates to its logical conclusion.[38]

He continues:

> ... a region is an economic unit, whereas a currency domain is partially an expression of national sovereignty. ... The validity of the argument for flexible exchange rates therefore hinges on the closeness with which nations correspond to regions. The argument works best if each nation (and currency) has internal factor mobility and external factor immobility.[39]

Finally, the countries that organize themselves into a currency area must be prepared to pursue a common monetary policy. Such a policy will be far easier to conduct if substantial intracurrency-area factor mobility is present. If it is not, the earlier difficulties associated with a shift in demand from B to A recur. Unemployment in B can be averted only at the price of inflation in A, or inflation in A can be averted only at the price of unemployment in B. If B's monetary authority decides to go it alone by pursuing an expansionary monetary policy to alleviate unemployment, it will lose reserves to A's central bank and eventually be unable to sustain the intraregional fixed exchange-rate commitment. The efficiency advantage of the fixed exchange rate would then be lost.

15.5 AN INTERNATIONAL MONETARY SYSTEM FOR THE FUTURE?

To commemorate the fortieth anniversary of the Bretton Woods conference, economists and monetary officials convened in Bretton Woods, New Hampshire, in 1984. The conference offered both a retrospective and a prospective on the international monetary system. One of the participants, Professor Richard Cooper of Harvard University, a former assistant secretary of state for economic affairs under President Jimmy Carter, offered his vision of the international monetary system in the year 2010. Cooper echoed the common complaint that

> ... flexible exchange rates, while they offer some degree of greater national autonomy, do not effectively insulate national economies from external influences, and indeed in some instances may even exacerbate the impact of external influences on national economic developments.[40]

[38] Ibid., pp. 184–185.

[39] Ibid., p. 185.

[40] Cooper, Richard, "A Monetary System for the Future," *Foreign Affairs,* Fall 1984, vol. 63, No. 1, p. 176.

Another serious problem with the current system is that it lacks an appropriate reserve asset and that reserve creation is haphazard. Cooper notes that

> ... the principal reserve medium today is a national currency, the U.S. dollar, dependent in large part for its supply on the policies of the United States. This has been accepted, more or less grudgingly, because it has worked reasonably well and there is no clear feasible alternative. But it leaves a deep sense of uneasiness around the world, even when the United States in the judgement of others is relatively well behaved; and the uneasiness grows dramatically when in such periods as 1970–71 and 1978 and 1981–82 the rest of the world, or parts of it, believe the United States is not well behaved.[41]

Cooper believes that this situation will become increasingly intolerable, in part because the relative economic importance of the United States seems likely to decline. In this connection he notes that

> ... as the United States shrinks in relation to the rest of the world, as it is bound to do, the intrinsic weaknesses of reliance on the U.S. dollar will become more apparent, especially in the United States, where the possible reaction of foreign dollar-holders will become an even greater constraint on U.S. monetary policy. ... The natural growth in the labor force and the rate of capital accumulation are both higher in many parts of the world than they are in the United States.[42]

These defects of the system are bound to cause pressures for change. One route would be the autarchic-mercantilist route:

> One possibility is that the frustrations arising from the sense of loss of national control will lead to significant attempts to reassert national control by sharply reducing the openness and permeability of national economies to external influence. ... It would probably involve a reversion to extensive use of restrictions over capital movements. And since capital transactions cannot be effectively separated from current transactions, there would be a tendency to extend restrictions to current transactions as well.[43]

A more constructive approach would attempt to combine a stable macroeconomic environment with the benefits of unrestricted movements of goods, capital, and factors of production. Such an environment, in Cooper's view, requires fixed exchange rates, because current and future

[41] Ibid., p. 175.

[42] Ibid., p. 175.

[43] Ibid., p. 176.

trends in the world economy are such that the optimum currency area will grow in a way that encompasses nearly the entire globe. In the years to come,

> . . . financial factors will still dominate the determination of exchange rates in the short run. In view of the greater sensitivity of production to changes in real exchange rates, governments must reduce arbitrary movements in real exchange rates in order to maintain an open trading system.[44]

Better still,

> . . . we will need a system of credibly fixed exchange rates . . . if we are to preserve an open trading and financial system. Exchange rates can be most credibly fixed if they are eliminated altogether.[45]

Eliminating exchange rates means eliminating national currencies and reserve assets such as gold. That means complete monetary integration with a single currency unit. The SDR would either have to be replaced or become the world currency. The supply of the monetary asset would be controlled by a world central bank. The entire world need not agree to the plan, but it is essential that all the major industrial powers do so. Thus, in effect, the world economy will become the optimum currency area. It has already moved in this direction in the realm of financial services, and will continue to do so even more as the relative importance of manufacturing declines and the importance of services, including financial services, increases. Also,

> Real incomes per capita will be over 50 percent higher than they are today. The world will be very electronic . . . not only will large-scale financial transactions take place virtually instantaneously to any part of the world . . . but even retail transactions in financial services and in goods can take place electronically . . . householders will be able to purchase information regarding taxation, investments, retirement possibilities, or education by consulting electronic catalogues and information sources in their own homes. Even goods will be able to be purchased by inspecting them on a television screen, placing the order electronically, and having them delivered in a relatively short time. English will become even more widespread as the language of commerce.[46]

With higher real incomes and lower relative prices for long distance transportation, much more travel will take place than occurs today. Reliable,

[44] Ibid., p. 177.

[45] Ibid., p. 177.

[46] Ibid., p. 177.

high speed and low cost communications over the globe will permit management control of production locations in many places. Lower transportation costs will encourage trade. These factors taken together are likely to
result in greater possibilities for substitution of geographic locations, not
only in manufacturing production but also in many services. Thus, real
movements in exchange rates will be highly disruptive of profits, production
and employment in any particular location.[47]

To paraphrase by way of a summary interpretation: The importance
of distance and geographic location are diminishing. Already these di-
mensions play hardly any role in financial transactions. With further
developments in low-cost transportation and the diffusion of production
throughout the world, distance and geography will become even less important in trade as well as in services. All this means the optimum currency
area is growing and that fluctuations in real exchange rates are bound to
become increasingly disruptive.

The world central bank will operate pretty much as any central
bank in the world operates today. It can provide domestic credit by open-
market purchases of government securities and by making loans to commercial banks. Its governing board would be made up of representatives
from the member countries in much the same way as the executive boards
of the World Bank and the IMF are constituted today. As is also true for
these institutions, the voting power of each country would be in proportion to its economic importance. To create a stable macroeconomic environment, the Bank's board would probably wish to provide liquidity
at a rate that accommodates the growth of global GNP. If a particular
region in the world needs stimulus, the Bank could favor that region by
purchasing securities from that country's government, thereby providing
credit to the afflicted region.

Individual countries could continue to conduct their own fiscal policies. However, governments could no longer finance their spending by
printing and spending currency or by borrowing from their central banks.
Thus, inflationary government spending would be eliminated, as governments are forced to finance their deficits in the world capital market.
Government expenditures and receipts would be made in the common
currency. Each country could set its own fiscal policy, but any country
that engaged in excessive borrowing would find it increasingly costly and
difficult to continue to finance deficits, as would be true for any business
enterprise.

It seems likely that fiscal policies will be far more stabilizing than
at present. Forced to pay attention to world capital market conditions,
governments will have an incentive to increase their borrowing during

[47] Ibid., p. 177.

periods of low interest rates and decrease borrowing when interest rates are high. Since interest rates would follow the world business cycle if the world central bank follows a monetarist money growth rule, deficit financing by the governments would be heaviest during periods of world recession and would tend to decline as the world economy revives.

Balance-of-payments adjustment

> . . . would be as easy, or as difficult, as it is between regions of the United States or any other large country today. The adjustments would be automatic except insofar as it was cushioned by capital inflows induced by fiscal actions. Automatic balance of payments adjustment sometimes leads to unemployment, as following a shift in demand away from the products of a particular region or country. Fiscal policy in its various forms could be used to cushion such unemployment. In addition . . . there would be considerable net immigration into the present industrial democracies by early in the next century, and the distribution of that flow of migrants would provide considerable flexibility to the labor force in the region as a whole.[48]

Cooper envisions collaboration among the "industrial democracies" to put the plan into effect. Where would this leave the developing countries? Probably wherever they wish to be. Most developing countries already fix their exchange rates and are more accustomed to the arduous problems associated with borrowing in international capital markets than the governments of industrial countries. Presumably, many, if not most, such countries would find it advantageous to scrap their own currencies and place themselves in the protective environment of the supercurrency area. Institutions such as the World Bank would continue to provide long-term development assistance, and the IMF could continue its growing evolution into a development institution dealing with shorter-range problems such as temporary financial assistance for oil purchases and the assistance it renders in Third World debt negotiations.

In this system for the future, open economies would cease to exist as we know them. The economics of the closed economy—now the global economy—would once again become relevant.

QUESTIONS FOR REVIEW

1. What is the rationale for exchange controls? Why are exchange controls difficult to enforce? What are their economic disadvantages?
2. Give a critique of the Tobin plan to reduce capital movements by imposing

---

[48] Ibid., p. 181.

a 1 percent tax on each currency conversion in the foreign exchange market? Would it make sense to vary the rate of the tax in proportion to domestic-foreign interest-rate differentials?

3. McKinnon argues that appreciation of the dollar causes monetary contraction throughout the world, whereas a fall in the dollar has the opposite effect. What is the basis for this view? Is it similar to the nth country problem of the Bretton Woods system?

4. Would the world economy benefit from a target rate of monetary growth independent of conditions in individual countries?

5. Would it be beneficial to accelerate monetary growth when the currency appreciates and to decelerate monetary growth when the currency depreciates? What are the advantages and disadvantages of such a policy?

6. How can governments, pursuing their own interests, become a source of instability in foreign exchange markets? What should be done about this problem?

7. Suppose the Federal Reserve wishes to depreciate the dollar without increasing the U.S. money supply. How should it proceed? Will such sterilized intervention be effective?

8. What is the rationale for a crawling peg? How should the rate of appreciation or depreciation be determined? What are the disadvantages of a crawling peg? When might it be particularly useful?

9. What is the advantage of widening the band for exchange market intervention? Is this an improvement over an adjustable peg? Does it again restrict monetary policy?

10. What is an optimum currency area? What characteristics must be present if an optimum currency area is to function effectively?

11. What is the case for world monetary integration? Could countries still use fiscal policies? How would fiscal policy be constrained?

SUGGESTIONS FOR FURTHER READING

Argy, Victor, "Exchange Rate Management in Theory and Practice," *Princeton Studies in International Finance,* International Finance Section, Princeton University, 1982.

Cooper, Richard, "A Monetary System for the Future," *Foreign Affairs,* 63, Fall 1984.

Ethier, Wilfred and Arthur I. Bloomfield, "Managing the Managed Float," *Princeton Essays in International Finance,* No. 112, 1975.

Kenen, Peter B., "Floats, Glides, and Indicators: A Comparison of Methods for Changing Exchange Rates," *Journal of International Economics,* 5, 1975.

McKinnon, Ronald I., "An International Standard for Monetary Stabilization," Institute for International Economics, 8, 1984.

Mundell, Robert A., *International Economics,* Macmillan, 1968, chaps. 11, 12.

Murphy, J. Carter, *The International Monetary System,* American Enterprise Institute, 1979.

Murphy, J. Carter, "Moderate Exchange Rate Variability," *National Banking Review,* 3, 1965.

Mussa, Michael, "The Role of Official Intervention," *Occasional Papers,* No. 6, Group of Thirty, 1981.

Sachs, Jeffrey, "The Uneasy Case for Greater Exchange Rate Coordination," American Economic Association, *Papers and Proceedings,* 1986.

Solomon, Robert, *The International Monetary System,* Harper & Row, 1982.

Tobin, James, "A Proposal for International Monetary Reform," *Eastern Economic Journal,* 4, 1978.

Williamson, John, "The Crawling Peg," *Princeton Essays in International Finance,* 1965.

Williamson, John, "The Exchange Rate System," Institute for International Economics, 1983.

Index

Note: *Italicized* page numbers indicate material in figures. Page numbers followed by *n* indicate material in notes.

Absolute advantage, 22–23
Absorption, 40–42, 57–59, 62, 332–336
  domestic, 127, 251
Absorption analysis, 239–255, 346–349
Adelman, Morris, 322
Adjustable peg system, 20, 45, 374, 380, 391. *See also* Bretton Woods system; Fixed exchange rates
Aggregate demand, 151–157, 173. *See also* IS-LM model
Aggregate expenditure, 57, 155–157
  devaluation and, 239–255, 346–349
Aggregate expenditure function, 68–71, 151, 183, 185
Aggregate income, 95, 98, 184–185, 272–275, 278–280
Aggregate production function, 157–160
Aggregate supply, 151
  and international adjustment, 177–181
  and wage levels, 157–165, 175–177
Aggregate supply function, 151–154, 160, *161, 174*

Alexander, Sidney S., 239–241
Appreciation, 29
  of dollar, 293, 437
Arbitrage, 42–43, 271–274, 278, 374
Argentina, 439, 443–445
Argy, Victor, 456*n*, 473*n*
Arndt, H. W., 40*n*
Artus, Jacques, 418–419, 421, 422, 435–436
Asset-market equilibrium, 62, 262–263, 295–318, 349–355, 425–426, 467. *See also* Monetary policy
Auto industry, 7, 24–25
Autonomous exports, 79–81, 84–86, 184–186, 190

Baker, James, 468, 479–480
Balance of payments (BOP), 16, 18–21, 51–56, 250–258
  absorption approach to, 57–59, 62
  adjustments, 177–181, 403–404
    under fixed exchange rates, 104–105, 112–117, 178–181
    under flexible exchange rates, 117–120

and asset-market equilibrium, 62, 295–318, 349–355
and Bretton Woods system, 396–400
equation for, 49–51, 62–63
equilibrium level of, 105–110, 112–120, 125–126
external-internal balance model, 39–42, 323, 332–336
and gold standard, 375–381
and IS-LM model, 104–112
monetary approach to, 51–56, *57,* 62, 113–117, 260–264, 267–293
and monetary policy-fiscal policy mix, 143–147
monetary theory of, 260–264, 267–293
United States, 59–62
Balance of payments (BOP) deficit, 37, 38
Balance of payments (BOP) function, 105–106, 261–262, 268–269, 282
Balance of payments (BOP) surplus, 37, 55–56
Balance of trade, 29–30. *See also* Net exports

Balance of trade
 (*Continued*)
 with autonomous
  exports, 80–81
 and devaluation, 218–
  232, 240–258
 internal, 40–42, 323–324
Balances, real, 155–156,
 176, 244, 272
Bancor, 392–394, 398, 401
Banking system, 440–442.
 See also Central banks;
 Federal Reserve
 System
 monetary survey, 51–56,
 57, 269
Bank of England, 16, 19,
 25, 375, 379, 387, 388
Bank of France, 383–384,
 387, 388
Basic balance, 39
Beggar-thy-neighbor policy,
 25, 390, 436
Belgium, 418
Benelux countries, 412
Bernstein, E. M., 114*n*, 411
Bilateral exchange rate, 29
Bimetallism, 15, 373
Black, J., 483*n*
Blackhurst, Richard, 236*n*
Bloomfield, Arthur I., 475–
 476
Blumenthal, Michael, 460
Boesky, Ivan, 427
Bonds, 96–99, 263, 266,
 271, 287, 352–354, 425
 and asset-market
 equilibrium, 304–314
 and portfolio choice,
 296–304
Branson, William H., 304*n*,
 315
Brazil, 439, 443, 444
Brennan, Robert, 427
Bretton Woods system, 15,
 17, 20, 25–26, 29, 36–
 38, 62, 104–105, 113–
 114, 217, 331–332,
 373, 374, 384, 390–
 400, 403, 414, 429
Budget deficits, 3, 9, 53–55,
 309–310
 policy adjustment and,
 331–340, 360–366
 relationship to trade
 deficits, 10–13, 58–59
Budget restraint, 287
Budgets. *See* Budget
 deficits; Fiscal policy;
 Real-balance effect
Burns, Arthur, 460

Camdessus, Michel, 414
Canada, 5, 6, *88,* 89, 245,
 399, 412, 414
Capital
 in aggregate production
 function, 157–160
 marginal product of,
 158–160, 171–173
 rental price of, 171, 172
Capital account, 24, 50–51,
 61, 104, 108–109
Capital controls, 217–218,
 455–457
Capital factor ratio, 170–
 173
Capital inflows, 35, 50, 63,
 104, 107
Capital mobility, 5–7, 23–
 26, 45–46, 255, 267–
 269, 281–282, 426,
 428–431, 445–446,
 491–492
 in Bretton Woods system,
 397
 controls on, 217–218,
 455–457
 in global monetarism,
 271, 273, 278
 inflows, 35, 50, 63, 104,
 107
 and interest rates, 3, 7,
 11–13, 107–110
 in interwar period, 386–
 389
 in monetary policy-fiscal
 policy mix, 143–147,
 465–472
 outflows, 50, 104
 policies to stabilize, 454–
 472
 in closed economy,
 122–130
 in open economy, 123,
 130–142
 and tax on foreign
 exchange, 457–459
Capital outflows, 50, 104
Capital stock, 170–173
Carter, Jimmy, 3, 257, 492
Cash balance ratio, 96
Cassel, Gustav, 382
Central banks, 5, 19–21,
 37–38, 95, 378–379,
 440. *See also* Federal
 Reserve System
 Bank of England, 16, 19,
 25, 375, 379, 387, 388
 Bank of France, 383–384,
 387–388
 convertibility
 commitment of, 15–16

World Bank, 242, 401,
 411, 414, 496
Chenery, Hollis, 442
Chipman, J. S., 87*n*
Churchill, Winston, 382
Classical theory, 372
 absolute advantage in,
 22–23
 of balance of payments,
 115–117
 comparative advantage
 in, 22–23, 372
 wage determination in,
 164–165
Clean float, 473, 478, 479
Closed economy, 11, 67–
 75, 183–184, 187, 188,
 263–264
 income determination,
 68–75, 92–104, 164–
 165
 multipliers for, 73–74,
 84, 127, 142, 184
 in recession, 172–174
 stabilization policy, 122–
 130, 134
Committee of Twenty
 (C-20), 403, 405, 406,
 409, 410, 474, 476–477
Comparative advantage,
 22–23, 372
Comparative static analysis,
 103–104, 194–198
 of asset-market
 equilibrium, 306–309,
 351–355
 economic policy, 320–
 326
 of fixed exchange rates,
 208–210
 of flexible exchange rates,
 203–206
Consumer price index
 (CPI), 3, 8, 168, 169,
 250. *See also*
 Deflation; Inflation;
 Prices
Consumption expenditures,
 4, 74
Consumption function, 69–
 70, 81–82, 155–156,
 183, 184, 186, 249–250
Convertibility, 6, 15–16
Convertibility point, 404
Cooper, Richard N., 248,
 492–496
Corden, M. W., 40*n*
Covered interest-rate parity,
 290–292
Covered positions, 44

Crawling peg system, 20, 484–485
Credit controls, 284–288
Credit expansion, 53
Cross rates, 42–43, 412
Crowd-out effect, 164
Current account, 24, 39–40, 49–51, 60–62, 104, 108–109, 421–422
deficits, 444–445
flow theory of, 280–282
and gold standard, 378–379
income-expenditure effects of devaluation, 239–255, 346–349
and long-term exchange rate adjustment, 314–318
price elasticities and trade balance, 217–237
Current account surplus, 352

Data Resources Incorporated (DRI), 340–342
Debt-export ratio, 447–449
Defense expenditures, 9, 13
Deficits. *See also* Budget deficits
balance of payments, 37, 38
current account, 444–445
incipient, 117–118
trade, 4, 10–13, 58–59
Deficit zone, 108–109
Deflation, 389n, 437. *See also* Consumer price index; Inflation; Prices
and dollar standard, 460–465
in interwar period, 382–383, 387–388
Deflationary gap, 73
De Gaulle, Charles, 402
Demand. *See also* Money demand
aggregate, 151–157, 173
foreign exchange, 39–42
Deposit credit, 377
Depreciation, 256–257
and behavior of real exchange rates, 418–423
of dollar, 29, 235, 293, 390, 418–419, 430–431
and inflation, 236
Depression, Great, 147, 256, 387–390, 415. *See also* Recessions

Dernburg, T. F., 68n, 92n, 104n
Devaluation, 16–19, 26, 38, 147, 218–237, 277–278
aggregate expenditure effects of, 239–255, 346–349
in Bretton Woods system, 395
British, 398–399
defined, 29
elasticities analysis of, 222–236, 241–243
and gold standard, 374
in monetarism, 276
policy adjustment and, 331–340, 360–366
Developing countries, 240, 242, 248, 253, 255, 287–288, 401, 403, 414, 415, 438–451, 496. *See also specific countries*
Development assistance, 411
Difference equations, 332, 356–360
Diminishing marginal productivity, 158
Dirty float, 20, 479
Discount rates, 19
Disorderly markets, 478
Disposable income, 183
Diversification, 297–304, 307
Dollar
appreciation of, 293, 437
depreciation of, 29, 235, 293, 390, 418–419, 430–431
devaluation of, 252–253
Dollar bloc, 388
Dollar shortage, 217–218
Dollar standard, 459–465
Domestic absorption of resources, 127, 251
Domestic credit, 52
Dornbusch, Rudiger, 291
Dunn, Robert, 420, 428–429, 455–456, 485

Economic Consequences of Mr. Churchill, The (Keynes), 383
Economic growth
and global debt problem, 439–451
and national income equilibrium, 275
Economic policy, 3–5, 7–13. *See also* Fiscal

policy; Monetary policy; Monetary policy-fiscal policy mix; Stabilization policy
adjustment of, 331–340, 360–368
and balance of payments, 39–42, 250–258
correct assignment of instruments in, 340–342
static theory of, 320–326
Economies of scale, 443, 444
Eisenhower, Dwight D., 397
Elastic expectations, 45, 297
Elasticities analysis
absorption analysis versus, 239–255, 346–349
of devaluation, 222–232, 241–243
policy based on, 250–258
time considerations in, 233–236
Elwell, Craig, 340n
Employment
and balance of payments, 114–117
equilibrium level of, 164–165
expansion of, 160
and wage policy, 165–177
Enders, Thomas, 446
Endogenous exports, 77, 81–86, 186–190
Endogenous imports, 186–190
Epstein, Gerald, 10, 13
Equation of exchange, 264
Equilibrium
balance of payments, 105–110, 112–120, 125–126
and employment, 164–165
foreign exchange, 30–35
in IS-LM model, 101–104, 112–120
monetary, 95–98, 165, 269, 305, 306
national income, 274, 275
short-run asset-market, 307–308, 349–355
Equilibrium level of income, 95, 98, 184–185, 272–275, 278–280

Equilibrium rate of interest, 98

Ethier, Wilfred, 475–476

European Economic Community (EEC), 6, 62, 114, 166, 400, 405, 412, 414, 415

European Monetary System (EMS), 412, 487, 490

European Monetary Unit (EMU), 412

Eurosclerosis, 169

Exchange control systems, 445–446

Exchange rate protection, 25

Exchange rates, 14–21, 472–487. *See also* Bretton Woods system; Devaluation; Fixed exchange rates; Flexible exchange rates; Foreign exchange; Gold standard
  asset-market approach to, 62, 262–263, 295–318, 349–355, 425–426, 467
  clean float, 473, 478, 479
  cross, 42–43, 412
  defined, 6, 29
  dirty float, 20, 479
  monetary equation of, 289–293
  multiple, 29, 456
  in the 1980s, 7–9
  nominal, 18, 30–31, 106
  official, 29
  real, 17–18, 30, 106, 107, 381–382, 416–423
  revaluation, 29, 38, 229, 400

Exchange risk, 401

Exchange-stabilization funds, 388

Excise taxes, 248–249, 415

Expansionary fiscal policy, 144, 147–149, 431
  and asset-market equilibrium, 309–311, 352–353
  effects of, 100–101, 152, 156, 157, 162–164, 168, 195, 265–266, 326–327
  with expansionary monetary policy, 146
  in financially closed economy, 124–126, 128–130, 134

in financially open economy, 132–134, 137–139
  and flexible exchange rates, 128–130, 133–134, 140–142, 168–169

Expansionary monetary policy, 147
  and asset-market equilibrium, 312–318, 353–354
  effects of, 99–100, 152, 156, 157, 164, 168–169, 173, 195, 326–327, 342, 425–426, 428–430
  with expansionary fiscal policy, 146
  in financially closed economy, 123–124, 126–128
  in financially open economy, 131–137
  and flexible exchange rates, 126–128, 133, 139–140, 142, 168–169
  as tool of monetarism, 266–267

Expectations. *See also* Rational expectations theory
  deflationary, 389*n*
  elasticity in, 44–45, 297
  inflationary, 246–248
  and Phillips curve, 435
  and tax cuts, 279

Expenditure-reducing policy, 251

Expenditures
  aggregate, 57, 68–71, 151, 155–157, 183, 185, 239–255, 346–349
  consumption, 4
  defense, 9, 13
  income-expenditure equilibrium, 71–72, 81–82, 110

Expenditure-switching policy, 251

Export function, 106, 267

Export-led growth, 25

Export promotion, 443–444

Exports. *See also* Balance of trade
  autonomous, 79–81, 84–86, 184–186, 190
  debt-export ratio, 447–449
  effect of devaluation on, 218–220

endogenous, 77, 81–86, 186–190
  import-export ratio, 447–448
  net, 59, 83–85, 177, 185, 188, 189

External-internal balance model, 39–42, 251–255, 323, 332–336, 360–366

Factor mix, 170–173

Factor mobility, 491–492

FB function, 109

Federal Reserve System, 19–21, 95, 388, 460. *See also* Central banks; Monetary policy
  in interwar period, 383
  monetary policies of 1980s, 3–5, 7–9, 10
  Multi-Country Model (MCM), 147–149, 278
  open-market policy of, 52–53, 113–114, 136, 428–430

Feldstein, Martin, 330

Fiscal policy. *See also* Expansionary fiscal policy; Monetary policy; Monetary policy–fiscal policy mix
  balance of payments and, 57–59, 62
  and money supply, 124–126, 128–130, 132–134, 137–142
  1980s, 9–13
  in stabilization, 132–134, 137–142

Fixed exchange rates, 6–7, 16–19, 21, 36–38, 62, 218, 258, 373–374. *See also* Bretton Woods system; Gold standard
  balance of payments adjustments, 104–105, 112–117, 178–181
  comparative statics of, 208–210
  and expansionary fiscal policy, 124–126, 132–133, 137–139, 142
  and expansionary monetary policy, 123–124, 131–132, 134–137, 142
  future need for, 493–496

and government
intervention, 478
and monetary policy,
267–288, 324
and monetary policy-
fiscal policy mix, 326–
331, 466–467
stability analysis of, 211–
212
and uniform world
currency, 487–492
Fixed factor proportions,
170
Fleming, J. Marcus, 131
Flexible exchange rates, 7,
15–16, 19–21, 24, 39–
42, 114, 402–403, 405–
406
adoption of, 409–416
arguments favoring, 127–
128
asset-market approach to,
295–318, 349–355
balance of payments
adjustments, 117–120
and behavior of real
exchange rates, 416–
423
comparative statics of,
203–206
criteria for government
intervention under,
478–481
and devaluation, 218–
237
and expansionary fiscal
policy, 128–130, 133–
134, 140–142, 168–169
and expansionary
monetary policy, 126–
128, 133, 139–140,
142, 168–169
and interwar period,
381–385
monetary theory under,
288–293
and Multi-Country
Model, 147–149, 278
and multilateral
coordination of
monetary policy, 459–
465
price and income effects,
346–349
promises versus realities
of, 423–438
and reference-rate
proposal, 475–476
and reserve indicator
proposal, 403, 474–475

stability analysis, 206–
208
and substitution account,
405, 476–477
Ford, Gerald, 322
Foreign exchange, 5–6, 28–
36. See also Bretton
Woods system;
Exchange rates; Fixed
exchange rates;
Flexible exchange
rates; Gold standard
arbitrage, 42–43, 271–
274, 278, 374
defined, 28–29
demand and supply of,
39–42
equilibrium in, 30–35
expansionary policy and,
129–130
external-internal balance
of, 251–255, 331–340,
360–366
forward exchange, 29,
43–44
government intervention
in markets for, 472–
487
reserves, 14–15, 25–26,
269–270, 324–325,
474–477
speculation, 44–45, 424–
428
taxes on transactions,
457–459
Foreign trade effect, 156,
176
Foreign trade matrix, 86–
89, 190–194
Forward exchange, 29, 43–
44
Forward rate, 29
France, 5, 371, 402, 407,
409, 411, 412
Bank of France, 383–384,
387, 388
in interwar period, 381,
383–384, 386–388
Frenkel, Jacob A., 234n,
280n
Friedman, Milton, 127,
265, 267, 434–435
Full employment level of
income, 175–177
Fundamental
disequilibrium, 395

General Agreement on
Tariffs and Trade
(GATT), 24, 242n

General Theory of
Employment, Interest,
and Money, The
(Keynes), 67–68
Germany, 4, 25, 88, 89,
166, 253, 257, 381,
383, 385–389, 399,
411, 416, 450, 461
Gliding peg, 483–484
Global monetarism, 237,
263, 271–273, 278
GNP deflator, 340
Gold exchange standard,
15, 380, 385–387, 392
Gold standard, 6, 15, 17–
19, 29, 36, 104–105,
178, 258, 371–390, 410
Gold Standard Reserve Act,
(1934), 389–390
Goldstein, Morris, 278n,
438n
Good Neighbor
macroeconomics, 465–
472
Government purchases, 4,
9, 13, 177, 342
effects of, 100–101
multipliers for, 73–74,
184, 196, 205
Graham, Frank D., 45n
Gramm-Rudman deficit
reduction act, 324
Great Britain, 17, 179–181,
372–373, 463
Bank of England, 16, 19,
25, 375, 379, 387, 388
and Bretton Woods
system, 392–394, 396,
398–399
and gold standard, 373–
375, 378–380
in interwar period, 381–
383, 385–386, 388
Great Depression, 147, 256,
387–390, 415
Greenspan, Alan, 330
Gresham's law, 373, 380,
399
Gross domestic product
(GDP), 445
Gross national product
(GNP), 9, 58–59, 413
nominal, 245, 447
real, 4
Group of Five (G-5), 468
Group of Ten, 253, 401
Growth. See Economic
growth
Gylferson, T., 280n

Hedging, 43–44
Heller, H. Robert, 263*n*, 283*n*, 286
Helliwell, J. F., 280*n*
High-powered money, 155
Home currency, 222
Hume, David, 67, 263, 372

Idle-resource effect, 240
Import-export ratio, 447–448
Import function, 76, 78, 81–82, 106, 185, 186, 188, 268
Imports
  effect of devaluation on, 221–222
  endogenous, 186–190
Import substitution, 443–444
Incipient deficit, 117–118
Incipient surplus, 117–118
Income. *See also* National income
  disposable, 183
  equilibrium level of, 95, 98, 184–185, 272–275, 278–280
  and flexible exchange rates, 346–349
  levels of, in transactions demand for money, 95–96
  real, 96, 173
Income determination
  in closed economy, 68–75, 92–104, 164–165
  IS-LM model in, 105–112
  model of, 164–165
  in open economy, 75–89, 184–194
Income effect, 378
Income-expenditure equilibrium, 71–72, 81–82, 110
Income taxes, 9, 331, 340*n*, 341–342
  indexing of, 245, 245*n*–246*n*
  progressive, 244–245
Indexing
  of income taxes, 245, 245*n*–246*n*
  wage, 167–169, 175
Indexing of income taxes, 245, 245*n*–246*n*
Induced multiplier, 89
Industrialization, 372

Inelastic expectations, 44–45
Infant industries, 24, 443
Inflation, 3, 430, 485. *See also* Consumer price index; Deflation; Prices; Stagflation
  and aggregate demand, 153–154
  and balance of payments, 114–117
  dollar standard and, 460–465
  and exchange rate depreciation, 236
  and flexible exchange rates, 438
  and gold standard, 375, 377–380
  international occurrence of, 116–117
  in interwar period, 381–383
  and money illusion, 244–245
  and money supply, 265
  1970s, 414–416
  policy adjustment and, 331–340, 360–366
  policy to control, 253, 257–258
  and unemployment, 4, 431–436
Inflationary expectations, 246–248
Ingram, James, 380, 386–387, 427–428, 428*n*
Injections, 71, 83–84
Interest-rate parity, 290–292
Interest rates, 276–277
  and asset-market equilibrium, 304–314
  and capital mobility, 3, 7, 11–13, 107–110
  and gold standard, 379
  and inflationary expectations, 247–248
  and investment, 92–95, 99–100, 107–110, 247–248, 279
  in liquidity preference demand for money, 95–100, 296–297, 305
  and national income equilibrium, 274, *275*
  nominal, 420, 446
  and portfolio choice, 296–304

  real, 23–24, 420, 446
  in stabilization policy, 131–142, 462
  as target, 323–324
  and tax on foreign exchange, 457–459
  in transactions demand for money, 96–98, 101, 195–196
Internal balance of trade, 40–42, 323–324
International adjustment, 177–181
International Bank for Reconstruction and Development (World Bank), 242, 391, 401, 411, 414, 496
International liquidity, 15–17, 28–29
International Monetary Fund (IMF), 14, 24, 28, 242, 253, 255, 263, 283–288, 324, 391–398, 401, 406, 409–411, 413–414, 418, 436–437, 440, 442, 448–449, 496
  and substitution account, 405, 476–477
  and target zones, 485–486
International monetary system, 13–21. *See also* Bretton Woods system; Fixed exchange rates; Flexible exchange rates; Gold standard
  adjustment mechanism, 14, 16, 18–21
  essential elements of, 14–15
  future possibilities for, 492–496
  and global debt problem, 438–451
  and government intervention in exchange rates, 472–487
  growth of reserves, 15–17, 413
  and optimum currency area, 487–492, 494–495
  reform suggestions, 304–307, 454–496

reserves in, 14–17, 25–
26, 269–270, 324–325,
413, 474–477
Special Drawing Rights
in, 400–403, 405, 410–
412, 476–477, 494
stabilization of capital
flows in, 454–472
between World Wars,
381–390
International Trade
Organization (ITO),
242n
Investment, 4
and asset-market
equilibrium, 304–314
and gold standard, 377–
380
and interest rates, 92–95,
99–100, 107–110, 247–
248, 279
international, 23–24
portfolio choice and,
296–304
and tax on foreign
exchange, 457–459
Investment crowd-out
effect, 164
Investment function, 93
Investment tax credit
(ITC), 340–342
Involuntary
unemployment, 161–
162, 167
Iran, 415
IS curve, 94–95
IS-LM model, 173–175
and aggregate demand,
154–157
in balance of payments
function, 104–120
comparative statics of,
103–104, 194–196, 198
construction of, 94–99
equilibrium adjustments
in, 101–104, 112–120
fiscal versus monetary
policy in, 99–101
and interest rates, 92–102
liquidity preference
demand for money in,
95–100
stability analysis, 103–
104, 197–203, 206–208
in stabilization policy,
122–147
transactions demand in,
95–96, 101
Italy, 5

Jamaica, 445
Japan, 4, 6, 25, *88,* 89, 146,
166, 260, 411, 412,
414–416, 444, 450–
451, 461, 473n
J-curve, 234–236
Johnson, Harry G., 128,
234n, 250–251, 432
Johnson, Lyndon B., 331,
402

Kenen, Peter, 474–475
Kennedy, John F., 323,
330, 397, 402
Keynes, John Maynard,
67–68, 162, 279, 383,
385, 392–394, 398, 401
Keynes effect, 155, 176,
244, 272
Keynesian theory
of capital flow, 267–269
income determination,
165
income expansion in, 277
interest rates in, 276–277
liquidity preference in,
296–297
money wage in, 279
price increases in, 276
Kouri, Penti, 280, 282
Kreinin, Mordechai, 233

Labor, 491–492
in aggregate production
function, 157–160
and capital stock, 170–
173
marginal product of,
158–160, 171
Latin America, 439, 443–
446, 449, 485
Laursen, Sven, 130, 249
Law of comparative
advantage, 22–23, 372
Law of diminishing
marginal productivity,
158
Law of one price, 271–273,
278
Leakages, 71, 83–84, 185
Lerner, Abba P., 227
Levi, Maurice, 42n
Liberalism, 372
Life-cycle theory of
consumption, 155
Liquidity, international,
15–17, 28–29
Liquidity crisis, 398

Liquidity preference
demand for money,
95–100, 296–297, 305
Liquidity trap, 100, 132,
142, 195
LM curve, 98–100. *See also*
IS-LM model
Local stability, 237
Locomotive theory, 89
London Interbank Rate
(LIBOR), 442

McCarthy, Joseph, 242n
McCullock, Rachel, 437n
McGuirk, Ann K., 418n
Machlup, Fritz, 68, 241–
242
McKinnon, Roland I., 122,
425, 429–439, 459–
465, 469–472, 489
Macroeconomic
independence, 128–
130
Magee, Steven, 234n
Managed float, 20, 479
Marginal product of capital,
158–160, 171–173
Marginal product of labor,
158–160, 171
Marginal propensity to
consume, 74
Marginal propensity to
import, 78, 106, 186
Marginal propensity to
invest, 102–103, 197
Marginal propensity to
save, 78, 102–103, 110,
186, 189
Markowitz, Harry P., 296–
304
Marshall, Alfred, 227
Marshall-Lerner condition,
227, 232, 237, 348–349
Marshall Plan, 394n, 396
Mathematical expectation,
279–280, 298–304,
355–356
Mattione, Richard, 446
Mercantilism, 371, 423,
436, 493
Metzler, Lloyd A., 68, 87n,
130, 249
Mexico, 439, 443–446
Minimum wages, 162, 175–
177
Monetarism
assumptions of, 264–267,
271–273, 278–280

Monetarism (*Continued*)
under fixed exchange
rates, 267–288, 324
under flexible exchange
rates, 288–293
International Monetary
Fund approach to, 263,
283–288
Monetary equilibrium, 95–
98, 165, 269, 305, 306
Monetary policy. *See also*
Expansionary
monetary policy;
Federal Reserve
System; Fiscal policy;
Monetary policy-fiscal
policy mix
and balance of payments,
51–56, *57,* 62, 113–
117, 260–264, 267–293
effects of, 342
and money supply, 51–
56, *57,* 123–124, 126–
128, 131–133, 136–
137, 139–140
multilateral coordination
of, 459–465
in 1980s, 3–5, 7, 9, 10
in stabilization, 131–137,
139–140, 142
types of restrictive, 144
Monetary policy-fiscal
policy mix
and balance of payments,
143–147
and fixed exchange rates,
326–331, 466–467
multilateral coordination
of, 465–472
Monetary shocks, 470
Monetary survey, 51–56,
57, 269
Money demand
liquidity preference, 95–
100, 296–297, 305
and money supply, 97–
99, 195–196, 261–263,
265–267, 269–271, 282
transactions, 96–98, 101,
195–196
Money illusion, 162, 244–
245, 489, 491
Money stock, 284–285
Money supply, 177, 204–
205. *See also* Federal
Reserve System
and balance of trade
adjustment, 179–181
decreases in, 112–113

and fiscal policy, 124–
126, 128–130, 132–
134, 137–142
and flexible exchange
rates, 428–430
and gold standard, 375–
381
increases in, 99–100,
111–112
and monetarism, 264–
267
and monetary policy, 51–
56, *57,* 123–124, 126–
128, 131–133, 136–
137, 139–140
and money demand, 97–
99, 195–196, 261–263,
265–267, 269–271, 282
Money wage, 160–162, 166,
167, 175, 179, 279,
434–435
Monopsony, 322
Multi-Country Model
(MCM), 147–149, 278
Multilateral exchange rate,
29, 456
Multiple-currency reserve
system, 476–477
Multipliers
for change in money
supply, 204–205
in closed economy, 73–
74, 84, 127, 142, 184
foreign trade, 87–89, 187,
188
government purchase,
73–74, 184, 196, 205
induced, 89
investment, 73–74, 184
money, 99, 196
money-income, 205
in open economy, 78–83,
86–87, 185–187
policy, 340–341
Mundell, Robert A., 131,
320, 325*n,* 326–331,
474*n,* 488–492
Murphy, J. Carter, 466,
480–481, 483*n*
Mussa, Michael, 479

National Association of
Manufacturers
(NAM), 235
National Bureau of
Economic Research
(NBER), 235
National income (NI), 151,
187–188

and balance of payments,
112–120
and devaluation, 239–
243
supply-determined, 272–
275, 278–280
National Industrial
Recovery Act (NIRA),
389
Nationalism, 385–390, 493
National saving function,
184
Neoclassical theory, 170
Neomercantilism, 372
Net exports, 59, 83–85,
177, 185, 188, 189. *See
also* Balance of trade
New Deal, 389
Nixon, Richard M., 252–
253, 322, 399, 402
Nominal exchange rates,
18, 30–31, 106, 381–
382, 416–423
Nominal GNP, 245, 447
Nominal interest rates, 420,
446
Nominal national income,
151
Nonintervention, 20
Nonsterilized intervention,
481–482
Normative approach, 320
Norway, 412
*N*th country problem, 392–
395, 460

Official exchange rates, 29
Official reserves, 28–29, 50
Oil, 12, 146, 154, 166, 233–
234, 245, 249, 257,
322, 405–406, 411,
414–416, 440–443,
445, 463
Open economy, 5–7, 11,
264
income determination in,
75–89, 184–194
multipliers, 78–83, 86–
87, 185–187
stabilization policy, 123,
130–142
Open-market operations,
52–53, 113–114, 136,
428–430
Optimum currency area,
487–492, 494–495
Organization for Economic
Cooperation and

Development
(OECD), 24, *88*
Organization of Petroleum
Exporting Countries
(OPEC), 146, 154,
233–234, 245, 257,
322, 405–406, 411,
414–416, 440–443
Oudiz, Gilles, 147*n*
Overshooting, 333–336, 338

Payroll taxes, 341
Perfect capital mobility, 46
Philippines, 444
Phillips curve, 4, 431–436
Poincare, Raymond, 384
Polak, J. J., 283
Policy. *See* Economic
Policy
Policy mix. *See* Monetary
policy-fiscal policy mix
Porter, M. G., 280, 282
Portfolio choice, 296–304,
307
Portfolio demand for
money, 95–100
Portfolio risk, 97
Positive approach, 320
Prices. *See also* Deflation;
Inflation
and balance of payment
adjustment, 177–181
changes in, 106–107,
109, 163–164, 276
consumer price index, 3,
8, 168, 169, 250
effect of devaluation on,
218–237, 244–250
and flexible exchange
rates, 346–349
and gold standard, 375–
380
in interwar period, 381–
383
and law of one price,
271–273, 278
and national income
equilibrium, 274
Price-specie flow theory, 67
Private saving function, 184
Production function, 157–
160, 170, 172–173
Profit maximization, 159–
160
Progressive income taxes,
244–245
Protectionism, 24–26,
242*n*, 388, 436–437,
443, 480

Purchasing-power-parity,
30–31, 179, 291, 377,
381–382, 419, 420,
423–426, 485

Quotas, 24–26, 388, 436–
437, 443

Random walk, 290, 291
Ratchet effect, 438
Rational expectations
theory, 279–280, 298–
304, 355–356
Reaction coefficients, 198
Reagan, Ronald, 9, 10, 13,
245, 437, 468, 479
Real-balance effect, 155–
156, 176, 244, 272
Real exchange rates, 17–18,
30, 106, 107, 381–382,
416–423
Real gross national product,
4
Real income, 96, 173
Real rate of interest, 23–24,
420, 446
Real shock, 470–471
Real terms of trade, 30
Real wage, 159–164, 166–
169, 171–173, 175,
179, 434–435
Recessions. *See also* Great
Depression
competitive depreciation
in, 256–257
economic policy as cause
of, 253, 255
elasticity and absorption
analysis for, 251–255
factor mix and, 172–174
international occurrence
of, 116–117
in 1970s, 166, 245, 399,
415, 440–441
in 1980s, 3–4, 8–13, 146–
147, 416, 442–443
policy adjustment and,
331–340, 360–366
Reference-rate proposal,
475–476
Regan, Donald, 479
Rental price of capital, 171,
172
Reserve indicator proposal,
403, 474–475
Reserves
foreign exchange, 14–15,

25–26, 269–270, 324–
325, 413, 474–477
and gold standard, 373,
376
growth of, 15–17, 413
international, 397
official, 28–29, 50
supplementary, 380
Residuals, 355
Restrictive fiscal policy, 149
Restrictive monetary policy,
144
Revaluation, 38, 229, 400
defined, 29
Reversal factors, 236–237
Rhomberg, Rudolf R.,
263*n*, 283*n*, 286
Ricardo, David, 22, 372
Risk
exchange, 401
portfolio, 97, 297–304,
307
Robbins, Lionel, 390
Robinson, Joan, 68
Roosevelt, Franklin D.,
389–390
Rueff, Jacques, 402

Sachs, Jeffrey, 147*n*, 168,
467, 468
Saving function, 72, 75, 93–
95, 184
marginal propensity to
save, 78, 102–103, 110,
186, 189
Shocks, *313*
demand, 153
foreign economy, 7, 9
monetary, 470
real, 470–471
supply, 433
Silver, 373
Singapore, 444
Smith, Adam, 372, 443,
444
Smithsonian agreement,
400
Snake in the tunnel, 412
Solomon, Robert, 404, 477,
480
South Korea, 444
Special Drawing Rights
(SDRs), 14, 285, 400–
403, 405, 410–412,
476–477, 494
Specialization, 372
Speculation, in currency,
44–45, 424–428

Spending. *See* Expenditure and *entries beginning with* Expenditure
Spot rate, 29, 43–44
Sprinkel, Beryl W., 39, 479
Stability analysis, 34–35, 103–104, 197–212
Stability condition, 103–104
Stabilization agreements, 162
Stabilization policy, 122–149
  coordinating monetary-fiscal policy in, 143–147, 461–472
  elasticity and absorption analysis in, 250–255
  evidence on effects of, 147–149
  in financially closed economy, 122–130, 134
  in financially open economy, 123, 130–142
  and government intervention, 472–487
Stable equilibrium, 34
Stagflation, 10, 153–154, 175, 222, 322, 415, 435
Steel industry, 24–25, 437
Sterilized intervention, 113–114, 313, 354–355, 383, 387, 437–438, 460, 478, 481–482
Sterling Area, 388
Steven, Magee, 421n
Stock
  capital, 170–173
  money, 284–285
Structural adjustment facility, 414
Subsidies, 443
Substitution account, 405, 476–477
Supply, 153. *See also* Aggregate supply; Aggregate supply function; Money supply
Supply shocks, 433
Surpluses
  balance of payments, 37, 55–56
  current account, 352
  incipient, 117–118
Swan, Trevor, 40n, 46

Swan model, 251
Swap arrangements, 105
Sweden, 412

Taiwan, 444
Target zone, 485–487
Tariffs, 24–26, 242n, 388, 436–437, 443
Tastes, 189
Taussig, Frank, 67
Taxes
  cuts in, 279
  on foreign exchange transactions, 457–459
  indexing of, 245, 245n–246n
  and saving function, 94–95
  types of
    excise, 248–249, 415
    income, 9, 244–245, 331, 340n, 341–342
    payroll, 341
    progressive, 244–245
Tax function, 70, 183
Technology
  and labor versus capital stock, 170–173
Terms-of-trade effect, 30, 249–250
Third World debt, 10, 12–13
Tinbergen, Jan, 254, 320–321
Tinbergen's rule, 321
Tobin, James, 96–97, 143, 296–304, 330, 457–459
Trade balances. *See* Balance of trade; Net exports
Trade barriers, 24–26, 242n, 388, 436–437, 443, 480
Trade deficits, 4
  relationship to budget deficits, 10–13, 58–59
Trade restrictions, 24–26, 242n, 388, 436–437, 443, 480
Transactions demand for money, 95–98, 101, 195–196
Triangular arbitrage, 43
Triffin, Robert, 114, 377, 379, 397–398, 400
Truman, Harry S, 242n
Tumler, Jan, 236n

Uncovered interest parity, 46

Unemployment, 19, 388, 438
  and inflation, 4, 431–436
  involuntary, 161–162, 167
  target rates of, 323
Unions, 162
United Kingdom, 5, 411, 412
United States, 36, *88*, 89, 144, 147–149, 166, 169, 217, 245, 257, 260, 278, 411, 412, 414, 415, 437, 443
  assignment of policy instruments and, 340–342
  balance of payments, 59–62, 403–404
  and behavior of real exchange rates, 416–423
  and bimetallism, 15, 373
  and Bretton Woods system, 113–114, 390–400, 429
  budget constraints in, 324
  and coordination of monetary policy–fiscal policy mix, 468–469
  economic policy in 1980s, 3–5, 7–13
  and flexible exchange rates, 409
  and foreign exchange reserve policy, 324–325
  and gold standard, 375–376
  intervention in exchange markets, 479–480
  in interwar period, 381–383, 385–386, 388–390
  and minimum wage, 175
  and nth country problem, 392–395, 460
  oil shock and, 322
  Phillips curves, 433
  Special Drawing Rights and, 401–403
Unstable equilibrium, 34–35

Value of marginal product, 159–160
Venezuela, 446
Vesco, Robert, 427
Vietnam War, 399
Volcker, Paul, 3, 330

Wage-price flexibility, 19–
   20, 178–179
Wages
   and aggregate supply,
      157–165, 175–177
   indexed, 167–169, 175
   minimum, 162, 175–177
   money, 160–162, 166,
      167, 175, 179, 279,
      434–435
   policy for, and
      employment, 165–177
   real, 159–164, 166–169,
      171–173, 175, 179,
      434–435

value of marginal
   product and, 159–160
Warner, Dennis, 233
Warren, George, 389–390
Wealth, 244
   and asset-market
      equilibrium, 304–314
   in consumption function,
      155–156
   increases in, 301–303
   in portfolio demand for
      money, 97–98
Wealth of Nations (Smith),
   372

West Germany. *See*
   Germany
White, Harry Dexter, 394–
   395
Willett, T. R., 487
Williamson, John, 278,
   426, 484*n*,
   486*n*
Witteveen, Johannes, 442,
   477
World Bank, 242, 391, 401,
   411, 414, 496

Young, John, 418–419,
   421, 422, 435–436